PUBLICATIONS OF THE NEW CHAUCER SOCIETY

THE NEW CHAUCER SOCIETY

Studies in the Age of Chaucer, the yearbook of The New Chaucer Society, is published annually. Each issue contains substantial articles on all aspects of Chaucer and his age, book reviews, and an annotated Chaucer bibliography. Manuscripts should follow the *Chicago Manual of Style*, 15th edition. Unsolicited reviews are not accepted. Authors receive free twenty offprints of articles and ten of reviews. All correspondence regarding manuscript submissions should be directed to the Editor, David Matthews, School of Arts, Histories and Cultures, University of Manchester, Oxford Road, Manchester, M13 9PL, United Kingdom. Subscriptions to The New Chaucer Society and information about the Society's activities should be directed to David Lawton, Department of English, Washington University, CB 1122, One Brookings Drive, St. Louis, MO 63130. Back issues of the journal may be ordered from The University of Notre Dame Press, Chicago Distribution Center, 11030 South Langley Avenue, Chicago, IL 60628; phone: 800-621-2736; fax: 800-621-8476, from outside the United States: phone: 773-702-7000; fax: 773-702-7212.

Studies in the Age of Chaucer

Studies in the Age of Chaucer

Volume 31
2009

EDITOR

DAVID MATTHEWS

PUBLISHED ANNUALLY BY THE NEW CHAUCER SOCIETY

WASHINGTON UNIVERSITY IN ST. LOUIS

The frontispiece design, showing the Pilgrims at the Tabard Inn, is adapted from the woodcut in Caxton's second edition of *The Canterbury Tales*.

ISBN-0-933784-33-3
ISSN 0190-2407

CONTENTS

REVIEWS

AN ANNOTATED CHAUCER BIBLIOGRAPHY, 2007

Mark Allen, Bege K. Bowers

CONTENTS

Studies in the Age of Chaucer

THE PRESIDENTIAL ADDRESS
The New Chaucer Society
Sixteenth International Congress
July 17–22, 2008
Swansea University

The Presidential Address

Cosmopolitan Chaucer, or, The Uses of Local Culture

John M. Ganim
University of California, Riverside

Eᴠᴇɴ ɪꜰ ᴡᴇ ᴡᴇʀᴇ ɴᴏᴛ ʜᴏʟᴅɪɴɢ our Sixteenth Biennial Congress in Wales, I would have begun with the ending of *Culhwch and Olwen*, when Ysbaddaden finally concedes to Culhwch but reminds him that he would not have succeeded without the help of many others. If I named everyone to whom I owe a debt for my term of office, I would end up reciting a list only slightly shorter than those in *Culhwch and Olwen*.[1] Since the founding of the New Chaucer Society, the Presidential Address has migrated in form and location: in some of the early congresses, something of an after-dinner speech; in some others, an example of the influential scholarship of our past presidents. More recently, in addresses by David Wallace and Paul Strohm, the address has become something like a keynote, pointing us toward emerging new formations. In some others, such as that of Mary Carruthers, the address has warned us about impending institutional issues concerning our place in the humanities.[2] Since the early 1990s, the last panel has traditionally re-

[1] I owe a special debt to some people who could not attend the Congress, most of all past president Alfred David, with whom I first studied Chaucer, and to Linda David. Thanks also to past president Paul Strohm, with whom I studied in graduate school. For constant advice and encouragement, thanks to David Lawton, executive director of the Chaucer Society and to the Trustees, and to my immediate predecessor, David Wallace. Stephanie Trigg and Tom Prendergast patiently listened to a draft of this address and Geraldine Heng kindly read a version. The subject of this address was inspired by conversation at a memorable dinner party with Martha Nussbaum hosted by Stephanie Hammer. I didn't quite get it, Bea did, so thanks again to Bea Ganim, as usual, for everything.

[2] Mary Carruthers, " 'Micrological Aggregates': Is the New Chaucer Society Speaking in Tongues?" *SAC* 21 (1999): 3–26; Paul Strohm, "The Presidential Address: Rememorative Reconstruction," *SAC* 23 (2001): 3–16; David Wallace, "New Chaucerian Topographies," *SAC* 29 (2007): 1–19.

sponded to the Congress and its papers as a summary session. Fortune has placed my own address at the very end of the Congress, offering an opportunity to do a few of these things myself, but I have modified the format by asking some of the newer voices among us to respond to what I will say, and to offer a few words from their perspective about the challenges we might face and the dialogues we might enter over the next few years.[3]

For the past fifteen years or so, debates on political and social policy have revolved around concepts of cosmopolitanism.[4] Can one be a citizen of the world, and, if so, how does one discharge or enact such a position? Initially, the cosmopolitan was presented as an alternative to a rising tide of communitarianism, but it soon grew in many contradictory directions, as did the communitarianism it sought to replace, the latter with its freight of nostalgia, patriotism, and isolationism. Cosmopolitanism has its own contradictions, including an uncertainty about interdiction and intervention, a conflict between relativism and universalism and a dawning recognition that cosmopolitanism for many populations is not so much a choice as a condition brought about by trauma and dislocation. A few years ago, amid debates on issues involving citizenship and immigration, Derek Pearsall spoke about the brutal xenophobia of Chaucer's London and the apparent acquiescence of the poet in

[3] Participants in the panel discussion in Swansea were Bettina Bildhauer, Marion Turner, Cord Whitaker, and George Edmondson. My thanks again for their thoughtful and articulate responses.

[4] The literature on cosmopolitanism has grown immensely in the past decade. Some of the most widely discussed or widely consulted volumes are Martha C. Nussbaum, *For Love of Country: Debating the Limits of Patriotism*, ed. Joshua Cohen (Boston: Beacon Press, 1996); Kwame Anthony Appiah, *Cosmopolitanism: Ethics in a World of Strangers* (New York: W. W. Norton, 2006); Jacques Derrida, *On Cosmopolitanism and Forgiveness*, trans. Mark Dooley and Michael Hughes (New York: Routledge, 2001); Ulrich Beck, *The Cosmopolitan Vision*, trans. Ciaran Cronin (Cambridge: Polity, 2006). Several of my colleagues at Riverside have published important related studies: Susan Ossman, ed., *Places We Share: Migration, Subjectivity, and Global Mobility* (Lanham, Md.: Lexington Books, 2007); Toby Miller, *Cultural Citizenship: Cosmopolitanism, Consumerism, and Television in a Neoliberal Age* (Philadelphia: Temple University Press, 2007); Adriana Craciun, "Citizens of the World: Emigrés, Romantic Cosmopolitanism, and Charlotte Smith," *Nineteenth-Century Contexts* 29 (2007): 169–85; and John Christian Laursen, "Publicity and Cosmopolitanism in Late Eighteenth-Century Germany," *History of European Ideas* 16 (1993): 117–22. A pioneering essay on the cosmopolitan and medieval literature is Robert E. Edwards, "The Metropol and the Mayster-Toun: Cosmopolitanism and Late-Medieval Literary Culture." *Cosmopolitan Geographies*, ed. Vinay Dharwadker (New York: Routledge, 2001), 33–62. See also Marla Segol, "Medieval Cosmopolitanism and the Saracen-Christian Ethos." *CLCWeb: Comparative Literature and Culture* 6.2 (2004); http://docs.lib.purdue.edu/clcweb/vol6/iss2/4.

that xenophobia, resulting in one of the factors that allowed the "nationalization" of Chaucer's poetry as a symbol of Englishness by British criticism.[5] He contrasted that with how Chaucer was understood by nineteenth-century readers in the United States, who ignored the possibility of a closed community based on English tradition and emphasized a sense of identity in the *General Prologue* that reflected Walt Whitman's invitation for everyone to share democratic, and hence, American values. At present, American, and perhaps also British readers, might have reason to be more pessimistic in their readings. The cosmopolitan ideals of universal human rights have been invoked as a rationale for chaotic and selective military interventions, while the exercise of those ideals at home has been increasingly narrowed.[6]

The ideological origins of cosmopolitanism lie with Kant, and the revival of interest in Kantian ideas in 1980s Paris almost certainly resulted from the exhaustion of the Cold War and its politics, as French intellectuals moved back to basics. The roots of cosmopolitan theory have also been traced back to the Middle Ages, to Marsilius of Padua and to Dante's *De Monarchia*, to the Peace of God, and perhaps even to the inclusion of non-Latin intellectuals in the governance of the late Roman Empire. Whatever the validity of these medieval sources, I want to argue that it would help us and help the many thinkers worrying about these issues to bring them to bear on what we do. My theme for today is the tension between local and cosmopolitan cultures in Chaucer, how this tension has been reflected in Chaucer studies, and how we can use it to advance our teaching and writing about Chaucer. Part of the appeal of cosmopolitan studies is that it is one of the few developments that has been exported from the humanities to other disciplines such as political science, sociology, and economics. As such, it resembles the situation twenty years ago, when historians, anthropologists, and sociologists advocated the close-reading techniques of a New Criticism that was just then being called into question by literary scholars, though later we imitated those very techniques when we found them in a Nata-

---

[5] Derek Pearsall, "Chaucer and Englishness," The Sir Israel Gollancz Memorial Lecture, *PBA* 101 (1999): 77–99, and "Strangers in Late-Fourteenth-Century London," *The Stranger in Medieval Society*, ed. F. R. P. Akehurst and Stephanie Cain Van D'Elden, Medieval Cultures 12 (Minneapolis: University of Minnesota Press, 1997), 46–62.

[6] Bruce Holsinger, *Neomedievalism, Neoconservatism, and the War on Terror* (Chicago: Prickly Paradigm Press, 2007), offers an eloquent and concise account of the contradictory medievalism of current policy debates.

lie Zemon Davis or a Clifford Geertz.[7] I am not going to mention the names of the many philosophers and theorists who could be invoked to justify cosmopolitan theory, because I think it is more interesting to see how it emerges from literary readings. I want to start with a once-influential statement about Chaucer:

Nowhere else during the Middle Ages are profound and varied social currents described with so much concrete truth, so much sympathy and humor as in fourteenth century England. I am thinking of course of Chaucer's Canterbury Tales. . . . Chaucer's narrators are pilgrims from all walks of life . . . they are sharply characterized and the relations between them are vividly set forth. Thus the [frame] supplies a lively picture of the social scene in England. Chaucer . . . does not hesitate to employ as narrators persons such as Boccaccio uses only as characters in his stories. In thus representing much lower classes as endowed with awareness and judgment, Chaucer communicates a much sharper and more political picture of the country. The style, indeed, is less homogeneous and sure and there is hardly a sign of humanism.[8]

In *Literary Language and Its Public in Late Antiquity and the Middle Ages*, this is one of the few observations that Erich Auerbach made about English literature, though at the end of *Mimesis* he arrestingly turns to Virginia Woolf as a model of a universal realism.[9] Auerbach's case for Chaucer's importance, however, lies in how local his writing is, with "hardly a sign of humanism."

Auerbach's observations are noteworthy because by insisting on the local genius of Chaucer's work, he carries on a nineteenth-century valuation of Chaucer on the basis of content rather than on the basis of style, form, or narration, all of which are the technical bases for Chaucer's modernist or New Critical reputation. But Auerbach's remarks are also noteworthy because of the way we have come to think about Auerbach himself. I am referring of course to the eloquent and impassioned essays

---

[7] See John M. Ganim, "The Literary Uses of the New History," in *The Idea of Medieval Literature: New Essays on Chaucer and Medieval Culture in Honor of Donald R. Howard*, ed. James M. Dean (Newark: University of Delaware Press, 1992), 209–26.

[8] Erich Auerbach, *Literary Language and Its Public in Late Latin Antiquity and in the Middle Ages*, trans. Ralph Manheim (Princeton: Princeton University Press, 1993), 325–26.

[9] Erich Auerbach, *Mimesis: The Representation of Reality in Western Literature*, trans. Willard R. Trask (Princeton: Princeton University Press, 1953).

by Edward Said at the beginning of his career and at the end of his life.[10] Auerbach becomes for Said a model of the intellectual in exile, pursuing a transnational humanism. "I may also mention," writes Auerbach in *Mimesis,* "that the book was written during the war and at Istanbul."[11] From this, Said deduced, "the book owed its existence to the very fact of the Oriental, the non-occidental, exile and homelessness."[12] But there are exiles and there are exiles. In the summer of 1933, Nazi students had denounced Leo Spitzer and other Jewish academics to the administration of the University of Cologne. Spitzer left Germany for Istanbul; one of his potential replacements at the University of Cologne was reputed to be Ernst Robert Curtius. Was Istanbul really that foreign? By the time Auerbach arrived in Turkey, Spitzer had already instituted a pan-European literature program that moved toward a concept of a world literature, much as he had placed the Middle Ages as a center rather than a lacuna between the ancient and modern worlds.[13]

I began writing about Middle English literature in emulation of Erich Auerbach's *Mimesis,* which I read young enough not to be appropriately intimidated by it. Auerbach wrote infrequently about Middle English literature, leaving that to his colleague Spitzer, and even when he wrote on Shakespeare, he was uncharacteristically awkward and far from the core of the work. In recent years, I have been much more influenced by Edward Said, and like many of us medievalists who have tried to come to terms with the capaciousness of *Orientalism,* felt that he was more or less orientalizing the Middle Ages itself, a trope I would eventually trace and disaggregate. For Said, what was important about Auerbach was a transcultural humanism that expressed itself when he was talking most insistently about the West.

Cosmopolitanism might be thought of as a political analogue to such a humanism, and it is that theme I want to align with Chaucer studies. Bruce Holsinger has alerted us to the occult medievalism of much cur-

---

[10] Edward W. Said, "Erich Auerbach, Critic of the Earthly World," *Boundary 2* 31 (2004): 11–34. See also Emily Apter, "Saidian Humanism," *Boundary 2* 31 (2004): 35–53.

[11] Auerbach, *Mimesis,* 557.

[12] Edward W. Said, *The World, the Text, and the Critic* (Cambridge, Mass.: Harvard University Press, 1983), 8.

[13] See Hans Ulrich Gumbrecht, " 'Pathos of the Earthly Progress': Erich Auerbach's Everydays," in Seth Lerer, ed., *Literary History and the Challenge of Philology: The Legacy of Erich Auerbach* (Stanford: Stanford University Press, 1996), 13–35; Emily Apter, "Global *Translatio*: The 'Invention' of Comparative Literature, Istanbul, 1933," *Critical Inquiry* 29 (2003): 253–81.

rent theory, from Bataille to Lacan.[14] We might ask how someone like Said, who paid little attention to Chaucer and who virtually dismissed Dante in *Orientalism*, reveals any such association. Given the short shrift offered by Said to the medieval (despite his awareness of Auerbach's interactions with his fellow global medievalists such as Spitzer and Curtius), and given the suspicion of postcolonial criticisms of canonical medieval authors, one wonders about how deeply such an inquiry could advance.[15] Chaucer, from such a point of view, becomes the archetype of the colonial itself, an emblem of an irreducible Englishness. And part of the answer is the respect Said showed toward the work of the great romance philologists—Auerbach, but also Spitzer and Curtius—who branched out from but always returned to the Middle Ages as a home ground. Auerbach's sympathy for Dante dates from his early career, but it develops profoundly in his later writings, notably in *Mimesis*, as he subliminally identified with Dante's position as exile. Lovingly if erringly re-creating in their imagination the Florence of their earthly life, the denizens of the *Inferno* paralleled, as Auerbach understood, the homelessness of Dante himself, who is warned in the *Paradiso:* "Tu proverai sì come di sale / lo pane altrui, e come è duro calle / lo scendere e 'l salir per l'altrui scale" ["You shall come to know how salt is the taste of another's bread, and how hard the path to descend and mount by another's stair"].[16] Auerbach's comments on Chaucer, by contrast, reveal some resentment at a poet who seemed to be comfortably ensconced in his homeland, and who therefore reflects it immediately and without the mediation of exile and remembrance. Behind these comments is a sense that the poet has not risen above these details, above providing a window into a particular time and place. But in this regard Dante is easier to place than Chaucer.

Chaucer is the most communitarian of poets. The *General Prologue* draws a portrait of a society subsuming its differences, or trying to sub-

[14] Bruce W. Holsinger, *The Premodern Condition: Medievalism and the Making of Theory* (Chicago: University of Chicago Press, 2005).

[15] I am thinking of course of Gayatri Spivak's questioning of the possibility of applying postcolonial theory to Chaucer; see Spivak, "The Making of Americans, the Teaching of English, and the Future of Cultural Studies," *NLH* 21 (1990): 781–98 (785). The most elaborate answer to Spivak's question, which is really more of an aside dealing with the curriculum, is in the essays in Jeffrey Jerome Cohen, ed., *The Postcolonial Middle Ages* (New York: St. Martin's Press, 2000).

[16] *The Divine Comedy: Paradiso*, trans. Charles S. Singleton, 2 vols., Bollingen Series 80 (Princeton: Princeton University Press, 1975), Canto XVII, lines 58–60, p. 191.

sume its differences. Works such as *The Parliament of Fowls* urge the virtue of compromise and delayed gratification as part of the ideal plan of nature. If *The Second Nun's Tale*, for instance, offers a version of community that is finally more cultic than public, it does so through the sublimation necessary to communitarianism.

Chaucer is also the most cosmopolitan of writers. He is the "grant translateur," explaining cultures to one another.[17] He is part of the explicitly international circle of Richard II's court. Petrarch, the model of the cosmopolitan, citizen of all times as well as of all places, is eulogized by the Clerk. The world of Chaucer's poetry is global both in time and place, from Ancient Greece and Troy and Rome, to Asia, to the shores of the Mediterranean, with images that take us from a desert in Libya to India.

Yet what renders these polarities particularly Chaucerian is the way in which local cultures and cosmopolitan ideals engage each other. The Parson is identified as associated with a place, but it is a nameless parish, in contrast to the array of place-names elsewhere in the *General Prologue*: "Wyd was his parisshe, and houses fer asonder."[18] Such a geographic image could be a reference to the decimation of the countryside by the waves of plague in the fourteenth century and the consequent abandonment of local parishes by prelates who "ran to Londoun" (I.509). It could also be an allegorical or figural statement, generalizing the Parson as the priest of the world, in an almost Langlandian sense. But its poetic effect is to portray the landscape of home as an alien place, desentimentalized, isolated and hard, the first of many de-romanticized landscapes of the islands that culminate in the great plays of the Celtic literary revival and the novels of Thomas Hardy. In the Parson's portrait, it is the people who make the land and not the land that makes the people. A number of papers at the Congress have addressed the strangely foreign landscape of Chaucer's England. As Joseph Taylor observed in his paper (Section 26), " 'Fer in the North, I cannot tell where': Collapsing Spaces in the Extimate North in Chaucer's *Reeve's Tale*," the geographic North of England is often imagined as primitive and underdeveloped.

---

[17] In Deschamps' famous phrase; *Oeuvres complètes*, ed. Henri Auguste Edouard, Marquis de Queux de Saint-Hilaire, and Gaston Raynaud, Société des Anciens Textes Français, 11 vols. (Paris: Firmin Didot, 1878–1904; repr. New York: Johnson, 1965): 2:285 (138–40).

[18] *Canterbury Tales*, I.491; citations of Chaucer are from *The Riverside Chaucer*, gen. ed. Larry D. Benson (Boston: Houghton Mifflin, 1987).

The Parson's portrait is of course immediately preceded by that of the Wife of Bath, whose description is a virtual gazetteer of places and place-names: Bath, Ypres, Ghent, Jerusalem, Rome, Boulogne, Galicia, Cologne, which she has visited with her spurs upon her feet, as the Parson has visited his parish homes "Upon his feet" (I.495). Christian Zacher long ago identified the *General Prologue* as part of a discourse of curiosity about the world that links it with such works as *Mandeville's Travels*.[19] But it is also a precursor to unwilling dislocations that disenchant the romance of travel. I need not repeat the dystopic readings of the Knight's portrait that derive from demythologizing arguments, from Terry Jones onward, except to say that it is finally impossible to recover the sense of a triumphant and heroic headline from the past that E. T. Donaldson famously heard in the echoes of battles that would have resounded like news of El Alamein and Iwo Jima.[20] It is a long way from Donaldson's analogy to Andrew James Johnston's description in his paper, "A Crusade Not Told: Knight, Squire, and the Family Drama of the Exotic" (Session 20) of the Knight as a "hysterical crusader" scurrying from battle to battle, unaffected by the cultures he meets. Similarly, Victoria Weiss's "Tale of Two Diplomats: Chaucer and Ibn Khaldun at the Court of Pedro the Cruel of Castile in the 1360s" (Session 3) notes the relative uninterest of either traveler in the practices of the other. In "Crusader 'Femenye': or, Why Does the Knight Tell 'The Knight's Tale'?" (Session 20), Jennifer Summit's account of crossdressing tournaments by crusaders in the Holy Land describes an internalized performance of defeat as gendered.

It is perhaps therefore of some significance that *The Knight's Tale* begins with the unwilling relocation of the Amazon brides, who are paraded from the land of "femenye" to the land of patriarchy. A few lines later, the women of Thebes appear, having been waiting as refugees in the sanctuary of the "Goddesse Clemence." "We han ben waitynge al this fourtenyght" (I.929), they say, expressing the temporal uncertainty of the dispossessed. Needless to say, the male protagonists, Palamon and Arcite, undergo defeat, imprisonment, exile, and homelessness, including, in Arcite's case, the classic migrant experience of willed invisibility.

[19] Christian K. Zacher, *Curiosity and Pilgrimage: The Literature of Discovery in Fourteenth-Century England* (Baltimore: Johns Hopkins University Press, 1976).

[20] Terry Jones, *Chaucer's Knight: The Portrait of a Medieval Mercenary* (New York: Methuen, 1985); Geoffrey Chaucer, *Chaucer's Poetry: An Anthology for the Modern Reader*, selected and ed. E. T. Donaldson (New York: Ronald Press, 1975), 1042.

Yet their suffering, as exquisitely accounted as it is, finally is represented as an expression of a sort of agency denied to the tale's female characters.

The *General Prologue* negotiates in an almost dizzying manner between the cosmopolitan and the local, most famously in the opening lines, where we move from a universal perspective to a positioned address. It replicates this negotiation in its diction, from the universal Latinate rhetoric of its opening to the vernacular of its portraits, though throughout the consistency of register can be illusory. As Ardis Butterfield informed us in the Biennial Chaucer Lecture, there is more than one "Chaucerian Vernacular." Elsewhere, notably in *Troilus and Criseyde*, Chaucer directly engages with the possibility of literary cosmopolitanism. "Go, litel bok, go," he writes at the end of Book 5, "And kis the steppes were as thow seest pace / Virgil, Ovide, Omer, Lucan, and Stace" (V.1786, 1791). Chaucer here speaks across languages and centuries to likeminded authors in a gesture (or series of translatable nonverbal gestures such as kissing, kneeling, and bidding farewell) that invokes the Petrarchan ideal of a conversation among greats, even as it recalls Dante's invitation to pose with his idols in Limbo. We need not rehearse the question of the multiplication of narrators that once preoccupied criticism of the ending of the *Troilus* except to note that the possibility of a cosmopolitan translation and representation is dismissed in the condemnation of "payens corsed olde rites" (V.1849) a few lines later. We might ascribe this to a different voice, but we might also think of Chaucer as confronting irreconcilable differences. Rejecting "the forme of olde clerkis speche / In poetrie" (V.1854–55) rejects the cosmopolitan potential of poetry. In some sense, the ending exposes what the poem has been about, presenting Trojan life in Books 2 and 3 as civilized, sophisticated, and cosmopolitan in its almost decorative sense, while the war that awaits outside the city walls reminds us of the xenophobia that drives the conflict. "I am of Grekes so fered that I deye" (II.124), says Criseyde, whose own exchange as a prisoner represents a degraded translation.

Once one recognizes this pattern, it seems to be everywhere, from Constance's journeys in *The Man of Law's Tale* to Griselda's resigned exile from her humble cottage in *The Clerk's Tale* to her husband's cosmopolitan palace, to Criseyde's situation in no-man's land, to the many abandonments and exiles of *The Legend of Good Women*. The dialectic of the cosmopolitan and the local in Chaucer thus seems to me framed in the language of necessity rather than freedom. Neither location nor mobility is necessarily imbued with an essential virtue. At the same time, the local is rarely as celebrated in Chaucer as we would assume it to be or as we would want it to be, at least as expressed in the desire for the local Chaucer that Auerbach, the exile, almost jealously described. Chaucerian communities are often cultic at best, expressions of populist provincialism at worst. And if the final result is what Peggy Knapp aptly called the social contest, it is not because of the expressed ideals of the *Canterbury Tales*.[21] Even in *The Parliament of Fowls*, the communitarian ending is something of an improvised negotiation, allowing each interest group to pursue its own agenda. A very strong case can be made, as it has been in books by Kathy Lavezzo and Thorlac Turville-Petre, that Middle English literature demonstrates a sense of national identity, against the influential argument of Benedict Anderson in *Imagined Communities* that national identity does not in fact develop until the early modern period and the rise of print culture.[22] Yet it must be admitted that what is interesting about Chaucer's sense of a nation is his openness to expressions of multiple, competing, and overlapping identities, of which national identity is by no means preeminent. In a way, we have defined something of the sort already, with our focus on minority cultures, on Jews, on Lollards, on heretics, and on people like Margery Kempe, a stranger in her own land.

Margaret C. Jacob, in *Strangers Nowhere at Home*, traces the cosmopolitan ideal back before its articulation in such eighteenth-century thinkers as Kant and Voltaire.[23] Cosmopolitan exchange had long been a norm in certain professions and associations at least from the sixteenth century on, she argues, and she singles out alchemists and merchants as groups that forged international and cross-cultural links. Yet Chaucer's alchemist, the Canon, is constantly on the run, excluded from any coherent solidarity. The merchant in *The Shipman's Tale* is not notably broad in his perspective, and while mercantile mobility may underlie *The Man of Law's Tale*, it proposes other shared values as ethically superior. Chaucer's own Merchant in the *General Prologue* espouses what seems

---

[21] Peggy Knapp, *Chaucer and the Social Contest* (New York: Routledge, 1990).

[22] Benedict Anderson, *Imagined Communities: Reflections on the Origin and Spread of Nationalism* (London: Verso, 1983); Kathy Lavezzo, ed., *Imagining a Medieval English Nation* (Minneapolis: University of Minnesota Press, 2004); Thorlac Turville-Petre, *England the Nation: Language, Literature, and National Identity, 1290–1340* (Oxford and New York: Clarendon Press, 1996).

[23] Margaret C. Jacob, *Strangers Nowhere in the World: The Rise of Cosmopolitanism in Early Modern Europe* (Philadelphia: University of Pennsylvania Press, 2006).

to be a national policy to allow his activities to prosper. Boccaccio's merchants travel the world and absorb its languages and cultures, but Chaucer's merchants are comparatively limited. Chaucer's narrators, even when they gesture toward the cosmopolitan, are always deeply embedded in the local. Significantly, *The Knight's Tale* makes the broadest claim for a translation of values across time, and *The Squire's Tale* one of the broadest claims for the translation of values across geographies. Both claims are undergirded by the transnational (if one-sided) values of chivalry. Chaucer's cosmopolitanism is finally more dialectical and self-critical than that of some of his contemporaries. Gower's *Confessio Amantis* (though not necessarily Gower's other works) works toward a universal cultural and theological system of values, and Boccaccio's *Decameron* draws portraits of cosmopolitanism in its more limited sense of manners and sophisticated adaptation. Elliot Kendall's paper, "Communities Without Buildings in Medieval Romance" (Session 54), came close to defining the cosmopolitan as a form of mobile communitarianism.

A prominent critique of cosmopolitanism is of its one-sided philosophical universalism. Chaucer's universalism was once one of the reasons for his canonical status. There is always a danger of reinscribing an older cosmopolitanism and humanism, the theme of Chaucer criticism from Dryden to Leigh Hunt, with its notion that Chaucer is for all time, understandable despite his language, because of his delineation of a human essence. But in fact what Chaucer does is to collocate universal principles with concrete, and sometimes deconstructing, situationalization. Medieval cosmopolitanism itself could be circular or self-serving. In Raymond Llull, for instance: "Ah, what great good fortune it would be if . . . all people could unite and become one people." For Llull, this meant "one religion and one belief" in the *Book of the Gentile and The Three Wise Men*, and that religion was Christianity.[24] As Cord Whitaker reminded us in "Mixed Blood: Understanding Baptism by Blood in 'The Man of Law's Tale'" (Session 20), conversion in medieval narratives is often described by means of the languages of race and of violence. Indeed, one of the most compelling debates in recent scholarship has been our own extensive writings as Chaucerians attempting to come to terms with *The Prioress's Tale*. Our arguments about the ethics and politics of

[24] Ramon Llull, *Selected Works of Ramon Llull*, ed. and trans. Anthony Bonner (Princeton: Princeton University Press, 1985).

reading the tale after the twentieth century deserve to be brought to a wider audience than ourselves as Chaucer scholars and our students. As Sessions 44 and 58 both demonstrated, perhaps nowhere else in Chaucer studies are the conflicts between local explication and transhistorical ethics so urgently addressed.

These thematic links between our own historical moment and that of the literature we study have not ended with the twentieth century and its horrors. As border literature has demonstrated, exile can be experienced locally. Cosmopolitanism is not so much a desire as an existence mandated by history. The idea of the border, which can cover border studies as well as actual and virtual demarcations, began over twenty years ago as a strategic intervention in thinking about national identity, immigration and movements of population, and the hybrid state of culture in the late twentieth century, especially in advanced industrial and postindustrial states. Border Studies, that is, was the obverse or inverse of postcolonial studies, pointing to how fragile the self-conception of imperial powers really could be, and deliberately provocative in relation to that self-conception. Chaucer rarely uses the word "border," and when he does it is usually an abstract, geometrical, or technical term; most usages occur in the *Astrolabe*. Still, the most affecting moments in Chaucer's works are meditations on borders. Troilus looks from the ramparts of Troy to see if Criseyde is returning from the enemy camp. Dorigen stares at the rocks that mark the seas that her husband must traverse to return home. For Alycone in *The Book of the Duchess*, dreams cross the border between the living and the dead. Borders, newly underlined on our maps and across fields and deserts, as they have been in the part of the United States I now live in, complicate our own sense of what local experience and cosmopolitan ideals mean to us. We might turn to a local example.

In 1960, Raymond Williams published his novel *Border Country*, about coming of age and exile, and being Welsh and British.[25] Like Said, Williams had little to say about medieval literature, perhaps because it was the bulwark of an English studies he sought to remake, not least of all by a shift to British studies, with the tension between the local and the general (or the imperial) that may not be transparent to non-British readers. But there was an interesting turn toward the end of his life.

---

[25] Raymond Williams, *Border Country: A Novel* (1960; New York: Horizon Press, 1962).

Less well known outside Britain is a narrative cycle in the form of a historical novel called *People of the Black Mountains*.[26] Published in two volumes, it tells the story of everyone who has lived in a single place in Wales over archaeological and historical times, narrated as a series of flashbacks. The narrator is Glyn, a man who has returned from his successful life in England to accompany his mother to their family home. He grows worried about his grandfather, who has not returned from a long walk, but his musings as he searches for him turn into a series of visions about whom else might have walked here, beginning with the Stone Age, proceeding through Celtic, Roman, Anglo-Saxon, Viking, and Norman times. King Arthur, as Artorius, takes haven here, but he is more or less a threat to local culture, and it is not even clear to the people living at the time whether he is a real figure or a legend. Attempting to extort some neighboring peoples, he has forgotten good Brythonic grammar and uses the wrong grammatical gender, inadvertently giving them permission to release livestock he had commandeered. Harold Godwinson manages to evict the Normans for a time and rides through the valley. The Normans return in another story. Local resistance is a window into Owain Glyndwr's rebellion. In one of the last chapters we have, Sir John Oldcastle appears as a character seeking sanctuary. The novel is a wonderful vision of history with Wales as the center of the world, making the local itself cosmopolitan. The outside world will come to you, whether you like it or not.

Before his death, Williams spoke about writing the novel:

The defeats have occurred over and over again and what my novel is then trying to explore is simply the condition of anything surviving at all. It's not a matter of the simple patriotic answer: we're Welsh, and still here. It's the infinite resilience, even deviousness, with which people have managed to persist in profoundly unfavourable conditions, and the striking diversity of beliefs in which they've expressed their autonomy.[27]

In the novel itself, the protagonist, Glyn, meditates on how place can create a common culture out of even violently opposed experiences. Like

---

[26] Raymond Williams, *People of the Black Mountains. 1, The Beginning* (London: Chatto & Windus, 1989); Raymond Williams, *People of the Black Mountains. 2, The Eggs of the Eagle* (London: Paladin, 1992).

[27] Raymond Williams, *Resources of Hope: Culture, Democracy, Socialism* (London and New York: Verso, 1989), 321–22.

Williams, and like the protagonist of the earlier novel, *Border Country*, he is an intellectual returning to his roots:

At his books and maps in the library, or in the house in the valley, there was a common history which could be translated anywhere, in a community of evidence and rational inquiry. Yet he had only to move on the mountains for a different kind of mind to assert itself: stubbornly native and local, yet reaching beyond to a wider common flow, where touch and breadth replaced record and analysis; not history as narrative but stories as lives.[28]

Williams is clearly setting forth his own aesthetic here, which combines both the books and maps; indeed, *People of the Black Mountains* often reads like a docudrama. But he is also reversing the categories of the local and the cosmopolitan that Said saw in Auerbach. Said admired Williams greatly, though he complained that Williams mistakenly thought that English literature was about England. Strikingly, Said ends *Culture and Imperialism*, a more broadly used if less broadly read book, with a medieval reference. "I find myself returning again and again to a hauntingly beautiful passage," he writes, "by Hugo of St. Victor, a twelfth-century monk from Saxony." The passage is from Hugh of Saint Victor's *Didascalicon*: "The person who finds his homeland sweet is still a tender beginner; he to whom every soil is as his native one is already very strong; but he is perfect to whom the entire world is a foreign place."[29] Said cites Jerome Taylor's translation, but he is reading the passage with reference to Auerbach's advice that it is a model for anyone wishing to transcend imperial, national, or provincial limits.[30] It is a very Auerbachian reading offered by Said, for rather than stressing the mystic transcendence of the world implied in Hugh's last clause, Said emphasizes the requirement of "working through attachments, not by rejecting them."[31] Readers of *Mimesis* will recognize Auerbach's emphasis on the earthly world as echoing his famous but controversial reading of the *Inferno*, in which he argues for the primacy of the earthly world and the Florence that Dante has left behind.[32] Williams at the end of

---

[28] Williams, *People of the Black Mountains*, 1:10–12.

[29] Edward W. Said, *Culture and Imperialism* (New York: Vintage Books, 1994), 335.

[30] Hugh of Saint Victor, *Didascalicon: A Medieval Guide to the Arts*, trans. Jerome Taylor (New York: Columbia University Press, 1961).

[31] Said, *Culture and Imperialism*, 336.

[32] Auerbach, *Mimesis*, 202; significantly, Edward Said wrote the introduction to the fiftieth anniversary edition of the English translation of *Mimesis*, much of which is con-

his life also turns to the Middle Ages, and what he does is more or less reverse the procedure of the *Canterbury Tales* by replacing pilgrimage with place, by replacing a structured social order with the requirements of the natural world and men and women who live in accord or in conflict with it. Interestingly, *People of the Black Mountains* corrects a view of medieval literature and culture that he had taken earlier. Williams had earlier referred to Langland in *The Country and the City* in the context of a discussion of a certain kind of pastoral utopianism, which is not how any of us nowadays reads *Piers Plowman*.[33] It was Auerbach, who, a few lines after the quotation about Chaucer that I began with, understood Langland the way we do now, as someone who grasped the understanding of lived life as an ethical and profoundly political activity, and who preached the possibility of a universal justice. In some sense, these different twentieth-century relocations of the local and the cosmopolitan are needed to help us think about Chaucer in the twenty-first century. Conversely, the cosmopolitan and the local are restlessly in tension in Chaucer (and Chaucer studies), and the questioning of their relative positions is an example of what Chaucer can teach us about the claims of cosmopolitanism, or, for that matter, the claims of indigeneity.

In the remainder of my talk, I would like to address the dangers and pleasures of our own provincialism and our potential cosmopolitanism. And so, Part 2, my suggestions to the Society as an outgoing president, some of which are already being implemented.

First, we need to begin to speak again to our colleagues in other periods. I was struck by the hypermedieval schedule of this summer: the Leeds International Medieval Congress, the enormously successful Gower meetings in London, the International Arthurian Society in Rennes, the *Brut* conference and so on. We literally could go the entire summer without meeting or speaking to anyone who is not a medievalist. This is a sign of great things: Chaucer studies, or Medieval Studies in general, have never been so rich, multiple, and wide ranging. And yet few Chaucer books over the past few decades have been widely dis-

---

cerned with meditations on the significance of the earthly, the secular, and the worldly. See Erich Auerbach, *Mimesis: The Representation of Reality in Western Literature*, trans. Willard R. Trask, with a new introduction by Edward W. Said (Princeton: Princeton University Press, 2003).

[33] Raymond Williams, *The Country and the City* (New York: Oxford University Press, 1973), 11, 44. Williams is, however, critiquing the notion of a rural golden age in this context. By cycling through the list of possible paradises lost, he more or less predicts the plot of *People of the Black Mountains*.

cussed or had significant impact outside the field. In her plenary lecture, "The Poverty of Historicism," Catherine Belsey opined that we as medievalists had addressed some thorny theoretical problems related to the New Historicism in ways that her colleagues working on later periods should be aware of, and yet one has the sense that our conclusions and evidence are not being translated into the studies of other historical moments. There have been a few exceptions, such as the work of Carolyn Dinshaw because of the way she imports and changes feminist and queer paradigms, and the work of Geraldine Heng because of the way she imports and changes postcolonial paradigms; and both scholars have been engaged in significant transhistorical projects.[34] One of the germs of this talk was reading one of Said's last books, on humanism, and finding a reference to David Wallace's work on Boccaccio and Petrarch.[35] As we move into microhistories (and I include my recent papers here), we find ourselves in the quandary of mining intense local interests at the risk of losing our cosmopolitan identities. Where this pattern has not been the rule, it has been in the realm of transhistorical cultural theory, as in Aranye Fradenburg's psychoanalytically informed essays or Jeffrey Cohen's work on the monstrous.[36] In my own work, *Chaucerian Theatricality* has had some life in performance studies, and *Medievalism and Orientalism* crosses several centuries so doesn't actually count.[37] It may be that I am repeating what Lee Patterson urged us to do a decade ago, which is to attend conferences in other fields or to publish in volumes or journals that cross periods.[38] At the same time, I question whether a straining for interdisciplinarity or transhistoricity by themselves is a solution. But we need to get out more. We need to become more cosmopolitan.

[34] Geraldine Heng, *Empire of Magic: Medieval Romance and the Politics of Cultural Fantasy* (New York: Columbia University Press, 2003); Carolyn Dinshaw, *Getting Medieval: Sexualities and Communities, Pre- and Postmodern* (Durham: Duke University Press, 1999).

[35] Edward W. Said, *Humanism and Democratic Criticism* (New York: Columbia University Press, 2004), 46.

[36] L. O. Aranye Fradenburg, *Sacrifice Your Love: Psychoanalysis, Historicism, Chaucer*, Medieval Cultures 31 (Minneapolis: University of Minnesota Press, 2002), and Louise Fradenburg and Carla Freccero, *Premodern Sexualities* (New York: Routledge, 1995); Jeffrey Jerome Cohen, *Of Giants: Sex, Monsters, and the Middle Ages* (Minneapolis: University of Minnesota Press, 1999), and Cohen, ed., *The Postcolonial Middle Ages*.

[37] John M. Ganim, *Chaucerian Theatricality* (Princeton: Princeton University Press, 1990); *Medievalism and Orientalism: Three Essays on Literature, Architecture, and Cultural Identity* (New York: Palgrave Macmillan, 2005).

[38] Lee Patterson, "On the Margin: Postmodernism, Ironic History, and Medieval Studies," *Speculum* 65 (1990): 87–108, esp. 104.

Second, we need to be sure that we are abreast of new technologies and not swept away by them. Medievalists have always been at the forefront of academic computing, driven by the need to make rare texts accessible and to make available the visual worlds of medieval cultures. One of our achievements over the past two years has been our efforts, thanks to David Lawton, Frank Grady, and David Matthews, to publish *SAC* in electronic form. This is essential for our future because of library budgeting priorities and increased access for scholars and students worldwide. Two decades ago, the publication format of choice in our field became the collection of essays, often emerging from conferences, and reflecting the rapidly changing nature of the humanities as well as our newly collaborative models for scholarship. But it also reflected the realities of budgets for libraries large and small, which were more likely to purchase a volume in a series than a new or emerging journal. Now, online access and the almost violent shift in budgeting priorities toward electronic formats have reversed that advantage. Impact factors and numbers of citations will now be driven by electronic availability. At the same time, our vigilance will be required. Even as research universities begin to acknowledge the value of online publication, hierarchical rating systems threaten to dilute their status. Dual-publication formats tend to result in the elimination of print copies from collections. While delayed electronic access is built into most contracts, the business model rather resembles that of print journalism, which at present is in a protracted crisis. I have no easy answers, but as medievalists and as humanists, we must take a role in guiding the collection agendas of our institutions. Since I have been teaching Lord Byron lately, I share with him an admiration for Luddites, but we really need to position ourselves as agents of change, not as subjects or victims of change. We have done a good job thus far.

The richness of scholarship and scholarly projects that have resulted from the Society's sponsorship is beyond question. Where we have struggled as a Society is in addressing our pedagogical responsibilities, despite the many excellent roundtables and panels at our congresses and elsewhere, and despite the work of so many individual members of the Society in relation to local and national educational practice. In response, the Trustees have established a standing committee of the Chaucer Society to encourage the teaching of Chaucer at all levels, but especially in secondary schools and community colleges, and I hope all of us will support its efforts. Doing so will also mean that those of us at research universities should be defending the scholarly efforts of those employed at institutions devoted largely to teaching. We should be working with TEAMS and other bodies to develop materials and protocols for the reanimation of Chaucer and medieval literature in the curriculum in institutions where it has been neglected or minimized. I refer you to past president Mary Carruthers's Presidential Address for a complete intellectual rationale. Why should such an effort be necessary? A personal example. Last year I was invited back to my high school in Weehawken, in a small town across the Hudson River from Manhattan, to be inducted into the Academic Hall of Fame, which was something I was very pleased to learn actually existed. On the block I grew up on, between 22nd and 24th Streets, one-tenth of a mile, the following languages were spoken: Italian, Czech, Polish, Greek, Serbian, Armenian, Arabic, German, Swiss-German, and probably some others I did not know about. The ceremony took place in Scheutzen Park, founded by the American Plattdeutsch Society, where, the month before, Miss German America had been crowned. Such a conglomeration was not unusual in the large East Coast cities of my youth, and in fact now can be found in previously insular countries in Europe. As Colin McCabe noted in his plenary lecture, "Dating English as a National Language," modern London is even more diverse, calling into question whether indeed English remains a national language. In my speech, I recited some lines from *Beowulf* and some lines from the *Canterbury Tales* and said that when people asked me where I learned this, I said I was from New Jersey, since most people cannot tell the difference between Anglo-Saxon and a Jersey accent. The very good and dedicated teacher who had organized the event wrote to me afterward and said that the students had lobbied her and asked her why they weren't learning this. She gracefully exited by saying that linguistics was not her favorite subject in college. I certainly did not learn to recite in high school, but I took it as a literally teachable moment, and referred them to Daniel Kline's excellent Web page as well as the NCS links site.[39] If I am petitioning for a more public way of doing our work, it can be argued that our classrooms are our closest access to a public. Here again a contradiction: our syllabi have never been more creative, adventurous, or experimental. And we have a steady influx of motivated students, however anxious

[39] Daniel T. Kline, *Geoffrey Chaucer Online: The Electronic Canterbury Tales,* http://www.kankedort.net/.

some of us may be about the source of that motivation in computer and video games, films, popular culture, and fantasy literature with medieval coloring. Yet the place of Chaucer and medieval literature in the curriculum has never been more uncertain. Hiring in colleges and universities in the field has improved somewhat, but that is because departments went for as long as a decade without a dedicated position in the field, and one slot now replaces what would have been two slots at the beginning of my career and four or five before it began. And in any case, early periods are being merged in job descriptions with alarming rapidity, as if the past all looked the same. By creating a constituency for ourselves, in addition to the capture-and-conversion model we depend on to a great extent, we will find ourselves in a much stronger position.

The Society might also explore a more literal mode of cosmopolitanism. We should explore ways of supporting faculty exchanges among our membership. Many Medieval Studies Centers in the United States have informal or formal arrangements for such visits, as do many colleges within the United Kingdom. While the daunting list of conferences I have mentioned above means that we spend lots of time with one another, more extended time for dynamic visiting faculty members to interact with postgraduate students, and with colleagues in other fields, would be a way for us to break out of disciplinary cages. It would also help us develop stronger connections between anglophone and non-anglophone centers of research and teaching, the importance of which will be abundantly evident when we meet, in two years, in Siena.

THE BIENNIAL CHAUCER LECTURE
The New Chaucer Society
Sixteenth International Congress
July 17–22, 2008
Swansea University

The Biennial Chaucer Lecture

Chaucerian Vernaculars

Ardis Butterfield
University College London

Bilingual Chaucer

I F ONLY, WE JOKE TO OUR STUDENTS, we could hear Chaucer speak. Yes, his poetry is full of speech, but what of his daily, domestic, historical voice? James Russell Lowell in 1849 may have heard "a delighted gurgle" when he read Chaucer, but for most of us it seems irrecoverable, in the same way that we are resigned to the absence in all those Life Records of any reference to his poetry or his life as a poet.[1] But one of those records does contain his authentic voice. It is in French. The scene is a court chamber on October 15, 1386, where Chaucer, called as a witness to the "dispute between Sir Richard Scrope and Sir Robert Grosvenor as to the right to bear certain arms," is describing how he noticed these arms hung outside an inn as he was walking down Friday Street. This scene has itself been beautifully described by Paul Strohm in an essay on London itineraries, and shown to be rich in sym-

I would like to record my thanks to Brian Cummings for his unstinting support in the preparation of this lecture. The text has not been altered from the form in which it was delivered at the Congress, although one or two cuts have been reinstated and footnotes supplied.

[1] James Russell Lowell, "Chaucer," *Conversations on Some of the Old Poets* (London, 1845), 25, cited in Helen Phillips, "Chaucer and the Nineteenth-Century City," in *Chaucer and the City*, ed. Ardis Butterfield (Cambridge: D. S. Brewer, 2006), 193–210 (199); *Chaucer Life-Records*, ed. Martin M. Crow and Clair C. Olson (Oxford: Clarendon Press, 1966).

bolic and spatial meaning.[2] However, there is perhaps yet more to glean from it in terms of its language. Chaucer's account begins, in fact, not only in French but in France:

Demandez si lez armeez dazure ove un bende dor apparteignent ou deyvent apparteigner au dit Monsieur Richard du droit et de heritage dist qe oil qar il lez ad veu estre armeez en Fraunce devaunt la ville de Retters et Monsieur Henry Lescrop armez en mesmes les armeez ove un label blanc et a baner et le dit Monsieur Richard armeez en lez entiers armez dazure ove un bende dor et issint il lez vist armer par tout le dit viage tanqe le dit Geffrey estoit pris.

Asked if the arms of azure with a *bende dor* belonged or ought to have belonged to the aforesaid Monsieur Richard by right and heritage. He said yes, for he had seen them bearing arms in France in front of the town of Retters [Rethel] and Monsieur Henry Lescrop bearing the same arms, his arms having a white label[3] and banner[4] and the aforesaid Monsieur Richard armed in the full arms of azure with a *bende dor* and having proceeded forth he saw them in arms during the whole campaign until the aforesaid Geffrey was captured.[5]

The whole deposition gives us a brief glimpse of two Chaucers, one walking down a London street, ever alert—as one is—to the possibility of a quick drink in a new establishment, and the other journeying along a northern French road in the midst of war.[6] These two Chaucers, one a Londoner, the other a frequent traveler to the Continent, form the bilingual and bicultural heart of this lecture.[7] It comes naturally to Chaucer

---

[2] Paul Strohm, *Theory and the Premodern Text* (Minneapolis: University of Minnesota Press, 2000), 3–19 (5–7).

[3] *OED*: Her. "A mark of cadency distinguishing the eldest son of a family and consisting in a band drawn across the upper part of the shield having (usually three) dependent points (label of three points)."

[4] *OED*: "Heraldically, a banner means a square or quadrangular flag, displaying the arms of the person in whose honour it is borne, and varying in size from that of an emperor, six feet square, to that of a knight banneret, three feet square. In this sense we still commonly speak of the banners of the Knights of the Garter, in St. George's Chapel, Windsor." See also *Anglo-Norman Dictionary* (*AND*), at http://www.anglo-norman.net/, *baner²*.

[5] Crow and Olson, *Life-Records*, 370–71 (my translation); they mistakenly give "Rethel" as "Réthel."

[6] It is not clear precisely where Chaucer was taken prisoner. Edward's army began the siege of Rheims in December 1359, but was forced to withdraw on January 11, 1360. Chaucer's ransom was paid on March 1, 1360; a truce followed on March 10, soon after his release, and he was back in England by the end of May.

[7] I use the term "bilingual" here more loosely than a linguist would allow, but in order to raise wider issues about the often rather loose, yet intricate, relationships between vernaculars in the Middle Ages.

both to speak French and to discuss this heraldic dispute with easy reference to his own experience back and forth across the Channel. It may
seem disingenuous of me to claim that this piece of legal French is a
genuine echo of Chaucer's own voice, but it reads very informally, and
contains not only Chaucer's own query about the new *herbergerie* but
also the voice of an unnamed individual who replies conversationally:
"Nenyl sieur . . ." There is some reason to suppose in view of court
practices of the time that Chaucer did speak this French (recorded as it
is in the third person) and every reason to recall that spoken as well as
written French was utterly familiar to him.[8]

As my slightly perplexing title indicates, I hope, this lecture is about
the fact that Chaucer had more than one vernacular. That our only
record of Chaucer's speech should be in French is a significant accident.
Jill Mann once asked me what language I thought Philippa of Hainault
spoke. It is a deceptively simple question, as she well knew. One would
have to reply that it might depend at least partly on where Philippa was
at any one time. In the Low Countries, where she stayed with Edward
III for long periods in the 1330s and 1340s, and where two of her sons
were born (Lionel in Antwerp and John in Ghent), she is likely to have
used her Picard-inflected Valenciennes French in court. In England,
Anglo-French was the language of the court; her own French would
naturally have been understood, and perhaps she had learned English as
well, but there may have been no need. If, as seems likely, Chaucer's
wife were indeed the Philippa who was daughter of Sir Paon de Roet, a
Valenciennes knight, then her linguistic background would have been

---

[8] I am grateful to Paul Brand for consultation on this point. The question of when
French ceased to be spoken for the purposes of legal argument among lawyers and
justices in the main common-law courts remains a matter of debate. See W. M. Ormrod,
"The Use of English: Language, Law, and Political Culture in Fourteenth-Century England," *Speculum* 78 (2003): 750–87, for up-to-date references. The learning exercises
edited and discussed in Samuel E. Thorne and John Baker, ed., *Readings and Moots at
the Inns of Court in the Fifteenth Century, Vol. II: Moots and Readers' Cases* (London: Selden
Society, 1990), show how French was taught in the reciting of pleadings and arguing of
cases until the 1670s. Baker thinks they are unlikely to have been "a fifteenth-century
innovation" (xxxiii). A description of 1539 recounts how "young learners . . . pleaded
and declared in homely law-French" before the older benchers, received responses and
arguments also in law-French from two more "utter barristers," and then in English
from the benchers (lx). None of this proves that Chaucer spoke his lay testimony in
French in this Court of Chivalry, but it does indicate that there was an active culture of
spoken French in the courts over a long period. One might also remark that the deposition does not read like "translationese": nor are there any untranslated words in English
(other than the street name, "Frydaystrete").

similar to the queen's. It could be that Chaucer's pillow talk was conducted in Picard.[9]

Some of this is idle speculation, some not. Speaking in Swansea helps us to understand why these questions matter. Swansea is part of a linguistic borderland that has undergone rapid change in recent years. An organization such as Menter Iaith Abertawe, in partnership with the Welsh Tourist Board, "promotes and encourages the use of the Welsh language" and supplies grants to businesses to help them to function bilingually.[10] Welsh has been reclaimed as a language of bureaucracy, and a new Welsh medium secondary school has just opened. This resurgence of Welsh against the dominance of English has odd links with my own linguistic background. If you will forgive the personal reference, I was brought up in Pakistan, and then India, with a Swiss-German mother and Anglo-Indian father, Anglo-Indian in the sense that he was the second generation of his English family to be born on what was the Indian Subcontinent. I was the third. My grandfather, after partition, had brought the family to live first in Suffolk and then in Swansea, of all places, so my father, having been brought up on the beautiful Gower coast, took his own family back to Pakistan from Wales. Swiss-German was not the obvious language of choice in the foothills of the Himalayas, so I happily picked up Urdu as well as English, and later, smatterings of Hindi, Tamil, and Marathi.

I always used to think this linguistic and cultural mishmash had a weirdness that was best kept quiet, but one gradually realizes, especially living in London, that stories of complex linguistic layering are rife. It is good to be reminded that contemporary society has a rampant multilingualism that is far removed from the strict monolingualism of modern academic prose. Often, I suspect, we function in more than one language or have done so as children, and yet, unless this linguistic knowledge is as it were official, we keep it fiercely removed from our academic discourse. But these complex interrelations, privacies, and tensions between kinds of linguistic knowledge, between what is official and unofficial, oral and written, academic and social, and of course racial and ethnic, are central not only to our own sensitivities about language

[9] For discussion of the vernacular mottos ascribed to Philippa see Ardis Butterfield, *The Familiar Enemy: Chaucer, Language and Nation in the Hundred Years War* (Oxford: Oxford University Press, 2009), chap. 4.

[10] http://www.swansea.gov.uk/index.cfm?articleid; eq 24747; accessed July 15, 2008, and February 13, 2009.

but to those of the past as well. Coming out about our linguistic incompetences as well as competences may have important consequences for our work as medievalists.

To point out that Chaucer had two primary vernaculars and not just one is immediately to engage in some difficult issues of linguistic status. That French was important to Chaucer is perhaps the oldest chestnut in Chaucer criticism. But we are oddly ambivalent about its importance and even silent about it. The two great beacons of twentieth-century scholarship on Chaucer and France, Charles Muscatine and James Wimsatt, remain on our reading lists for their superlative scholarship, but also, I fear, because their legacy has been surprisingly static.[11] The ways in which Chaucerians talk currently about "the French tradition" are not only still heavily in debt to Muscatine and Wimsatt, but perhaps even trapped in a debt cycle. For although "the French tradition" gains much lip service in our work, there is also a certain insouciance. We take it for granted; we ignore it; we often claim that Chaucer moved on from it. In the meantime, much has changed since 1957, especially in two fields that are crucial to any discussion of Chaucer and his knowledge of French: vernacularity and translation. I want to argue that these two venerable topics need to be set afresh against and within Chaucer's relationship to French and to France. I do so partly in conscious and grateful homage to several previous biennial lecturers: David Wallace, who drew attention to the importance of Flanders as a third element (outside English and French) in Chaucerian discourse; Carolyn Dinshaw's linking of India to modern English constructions of the past; Alastair Minnis, who urged us to collocate vernacularity and secularity; and Susan Crane, most recently, on the strange language of birds.[12]

My subject is the cultural traffic and translation between France and England in the Middle Ages in a time of war. To explain this subject, I want to introduce the peculiar and ambiguous figure of the envoy. I

---

[11] Charles Muscatine, *Chaucer and the French Tradition: A Study in Style and Meaning* (Berkeley and Los Angeles: University of California Press, 1957); James I. Wimsatt, *Chaucer and the French Love Poets: The Literary Background of "The Book of the Duchess"* (Chapel Hill: University of North Carolina Press, 1968) and *Chaucer and His French Contemporaries: Natural Music in the Fourteenth Century* (Toronto: University of Toronto Press, 1992).

[12] David Wallace, " 'In Flaundres,' " *SAC* 19 (1997): 63–91; Carolyn Dinshaw, "Pale Faces: Race, Religion, and Affect in Chaucer's Texts and Their Readers," *SAC* 23 (2001): 19–41; Alistair Minnis, " 'I speke of folk in seculer estaat': Vernacularity and Secularity in the Age of Chaucer," *SAC* 27 (2005): 25–58; Susan Crane, "For the Birds," *SAC* 29 (2007): 23–41.

mean this in the literal sense, in that Chaucer works as an envoy between two cultures. But I also mean it figuratively, in the way that the act of translation between languages is always a kind of embassy, a tense process of diplomacy, truce, and counterfeit. I mean it, finally, formally, as the idiosyncratic literary device Chaucer uses throughout his works in letters and lyrics and to bring narrative to closure. By way of example, I will work my way from *Boece* through the Boethian lyrics to *Troilus and Criseyde*, finishing with *The Manciple's Tale*.

To take vernacularity first: thus far it has largely been about the relationship between Latin and English, and, as Alastair Minnis implied, the theological glamour of this story of English has recently tended to drown out secular concerns. In this story, as Sarah Stanbury rather wickedly put it, English is sometimes given a "heroic agency," cast as "a powerfully oppositional voice" to the claims of the clerical exclusivity of Latin as if employing English were "an ethical good," as if "English was conscious of itself" (98).[13] French, if it appears at all in this theological narrative, is one of the repressors, or, at best, mediators, a means, but little more, toward the larger process of Englishing.[14]

Translation studies have indeed involved French far more thoroughly, especially in the word-for-word model that remains a basic tool of source study, but the most original and far-reaching thinking, notably by Rita Copeland and also Ruth Evans, has emphasized that it is important for modern readers of medieval texts to see translation as more than a matter of style or local verbal transfer, but of a shaping ideology.[15] Further perspectives on the colonial or postcolonial sides of translation are continuing to develop.[16]

[13] Sarah Stanbury, "Vernacular Nostalgia and *The Cambridge History of Medieval English Literature*," *TSLL* 44 (2002): 92–107.

[14] Nicholas Watson and Fiona Somerset are examples of scholars who have commented on the need to "reassess the roles of Latin and Anglo-Norman" in studies of the vernacular; see "Preface: On 'Vernacular,'" *The Vulgar Tongue: Medieval and Postmedieval Vernacularity*, ed. Fiona Somerset and Nicholas Watson (University Park: Pennsylvania State University Press, 2003), xi.

[15] Rita Copeland, *Rhetoric, Hermeneutics, and Translation in the Middle Ages: Academic Traditions and Vernacular Texts* (Cambridge: Cambridge University Press, 1991); Ruth Evans, "Translating Past Cultures?" in *The Medieval Translator*, ed. Roger Ellis and Ruth Evans (Exeter: University of Exeter Press, 1994), 20–45.

[16] See, for instance, Jeffrey Jerome Cohen, ed., *The Postcolonial Middle Ages* (Basingstoke: Macmillan, 2000); Patricia Clare Ingham and Michelle R. Warren, eds., *Postcolonial Moves: Medieval Through Modern* (New York: Palgrave Macmillan, 2003); Ananya Jahanara Kabir and Deanne Williams, eds., *Postcolonial Approaches to the European Middle Ages: Translating Cultures* (Cambridge: Cambridge University Press, 2005); Sharon Kinoshita, *Medieval Boundaries: Rethinking Difference in Old French Literature* (Philadelphia:

My argument, then, building on recent work that sees vernacularity and translation as two sides of the same coin, is that the relationship between English and French, far from being a topic that has lost its way, is poised to transform our approach to both areas. I emphasize that what I offer here is in some sense speculative and involves making suggestions about new directions for research. It was tempting to provide something rather different: long, close readings of the French poetry that seems to have most informed Chaucer's ways of writing not merely for the sake of understanding Chaucer better, but in order to appreciate what was causing vernacular literature across Europe to transform itself. This work needs doing and I urge us all to do it: although the *Roman de la Rose*, Machaut, Froissart, and occasionally Deschamps are standard reference points in modern writing on the dream poetry, in particular, their poetry is less well known in detail than we might expect and, in any case, deserves new and vibrant cross-channel readings. But I wanted also to go more deeply into questions about how Chaucer may have responded to French writing that are perhaps more directly methodological and ideological. The first is what difference it makes to our sense of vernacularity to think of it in England as involving two vernaculars and not just one. The second: How does Chaucer's bilingualism (I leave aside for the present his knowledge of other languages, such as Genoese, Tuscan, Flemish, and Latin) affect our understanding of his work as a writer? Do we, to put it bluntly, need to think in further, different ways about translation?

French and Anglo-French

Things are moving fast in linguistic research on the status of French in the fourteenth century. But it is an area that is fraught with sometimes competing interests and perspectives, both cultural and disciplinary, and the issues need to be disentangled carefully. Many of the old pieties about the use of French in England are being questioned and indeed overturned, particularly through the work of such scholars as David Trotter, Serge Lusignan, and Richard Ingham. But a few remain, and, as they would all be the first to insist, the rich potential of this and future research is only just emerging. The issues are entangled because

University of Pennsylvania Press), 2006; Sylvia Huot, *Postcolonial Fictions in the Roman de Perceforest: Cultural Identities and Hybridities* (Cambridge: D. S. Brewer, 2007).

they involve a triangular relationship between English, Anglo-Norman, and continental French. This relationship looks different from each of the three sides, and I am now going to offend everybody by attempting to describe how.[17]

Starting with English (given the context of this lecture), I think it is fair to say that for those interested in the later fourteenth century, Anglo-Norman has tended to be seen as a language and literature that is on its way out. Whatever importance it is recognized to have had with Latin in the trilingual world of the earlier medieval period, many scholars insist that by the late fourteenth century English is taking over. The starting point for the most recent major history is the "newly artic-ulate vernacularity" evident from about 1350, this "powerful move to use English for literary writing."[18] Where French is given center stage, especially in Chaucerian circles, it is continental French. A major linguis-tic consequence of this is that Chaucer's French borrowings are largely assumed to be from continental French. William Rothwell (as I shortly discuss in more detail) has conducted a long and eloquent crusade against this assumption, pouring out example upon example of the extent to which the French in Chaucer's English is largely Anglo-Norman.[19]

---

[17] New work on insular French includes the comprehensive and still ongoing revision by David Trotter of the *Anglo-Norman Dictionary*, directed initially by William Rothwell, Louise W. Stone, and T. B. W. Reid; the monumental specialist editions of the Anglo-Norman Text Society, particularly by Tony Hunt; important translations and contextual work, especially of twelfth- and thirteenth-century female devotional texts (Jocelyn Wogan-Browne, *Saints' Lives and the Literary Culture of Women, c. 1150–c. 1300: Virginity and Its Authorizations* [Oxford: Oxford University Press, 2001]); and the pioneering studies by Serge Lusignan on linguistic practices in royal administration in France and England in *Parler vulgairement: Les Intellectuels et la langue française aux XIIIe et XIVe siècles* (Paris: Vrin; Montreal: Les Presses de l'Université de Montréal, 1986) and *La langue des rois au Moyen âge: Le français en France et en Angleterre* (Paris: Presses Universitaires de France, 2004). For particular instances of revisionary linguistic research, see David Trot-ter, ed., *Multilingualism in Later Medieval Britain* (Cambridge: D. S. Brewer, 2000), and "Language Contact, Multilingualism, and the Evidence Problem," in *The Beginnings of Standardization: Language and Culture in Fourteenth-Century England*, ed. Ursula Schaefer (Frankfurt: Peter Lang, 2006), 73–90; and Richard Ingham, "Syntactic Change in Anglo-Norman and Continental French Chronicles: Was There a 'Middle' Anglo-Nor-man?" *French Language Studies* 16 (2006): 25–49.

[18] James Simpson, *The Oxford English Literary History, Vol. 2, 1350–1547: Reform and Cultural Revolution* (Oxford: Oxford University Press, 2002), 6.

[19] See, among others, "The Missing Link in English Etymology: Anglo-French," *MÆ* 60 (1991): 171–96; "The Legacy of Anglo-French: *Faux amis* in French and English," *Zeitschrift für romanische Philologie* 109 (1993): 16–46; "The Trilingual England of Geof-frey Chaucer," *SAC* 16 (1994): 45–67; and "Henry of Lancaster and Geoffrey Chaucer: Anglo-French and Middle English in Fourteenth-Century England," *MLR* 99 (2004): 313–27.

From the point of view of Anglo-Norman studies, its distinguished tradition has largely been preoccupied with the twelfth and thirteenth centuries, considered to be the height of Anglo-Norman literary production. Regarded as the poor relation of both English and continental French, however, its promoters have been—historically—relatively few. Their prodigious textual scholarship—Tony Hunt immediately springs to mind—has nonetheless shown the way toward the huge amount of material still waiting to be edited, read, and critically assimilated, a task being conducted with corresponding energy by Jocelyn Wogan-Browne and Thelma Fenster and others. A remaining challenge, among so much else, is to take up Rothwell's gauntlet for the fourteenth century. It may be that the figure of Gower is the best catalyst for this: many here have just spent some intensive days pondering the new multilingual directions that Gower studies are taking. We feel an enlivened sense that Gower's French and Latin writings deserve to be treated as more than merely his "non-English" works.[20]

From continental French, finally, it is hard to see very much interest in either Middle English or Anglo-Norman (I obviously exclude here the important work of l'Association des Médiévistes Anglicistes de l'Enseignement Supérieur). If, for the English, Anglo-Norman is the losing vernacular, then for the French it is a kind of bastard vernacular. Though again the winds are changing. A *colloque* on "Anglo-Normande" was recently held at the Palais de l'Institut de France in which the Anglo-Norman Text Society was formally presented to the Académie des Inscriptions et Belles-Lettres.[21] I am very hopeful that the *courtoisie* of this event may prove to have been a milestone in the history of cross-channel French, which hitherto, on the French side, has consisted partly in polite indifference or even amusement.[22]

---

[20] I refer to the First International Congress of the John Gower Society, "1408–2008: The Age of Gower," July 12–16, 2008, held immediately before the Sixteenth International New Chaucer Society Congress in Swansea.

[21] Journée d'études anglo-normandes, L'Institut de France (Académie des Inscriptions et Belles-Lettres), June 20, 2008. The proceedings of this *colloque* are forthcoming in *Comptes Rendus de l'Académie des Inscriptions et Belles-Lettres* 9 (2009).

[22] Anglo-Norman fabliaux, for example, have in the past received faint praise from continental scholars. See Nico van den Boogaard, "Le Fabliau anglo-normand," in *Nico H.J. Boogaard autour du XIIIe siècle—études de philologie et de littérature médiévale*, ed. Sorin Alexandrescu, Fernand Trijkoningen, and Willhem Noomen (Amsterdam: Rodopi, 1985), 179–89, and the introduction to *Eighteen Anglo-Norman Fabliaux*, ed. Ian Short and Roy Pearcy, Anglo-Norman Text Society 14 (London: Anglo-Norman Text Society, 2000), 1–5.

The argument here, continuing the one put forward in Paris, is that triangulation is the key. We do not have a single relationship between two languages, English and French, but a set of relationships between several language boundaries that are played out within England as much as they are across the channel. The dialogue between English and continental French is indeed vital, but it cannot be studied in isolation from that between English and French within the islands (here including Ireland as well as Wales and Scotland), and between insular French and continental French across the channel. I would like to urge not only that more of us walk through the open door between English and Anglo-Norman, but also that we collectively renegotiate the channel as a free route of exchange between continental and insular French. As part of this, as I have argued elsewhere, a consensus is growing that the term Anglo-French is preferable to Anglo-Norman. One reason is that like the term Anglo-Indian or Anglo-Irish, it has a central core of ambiguities: from the point of view of language, we might be talking of the French used by the English in England, or the French used by the French in England, or even the French used by the English in France. Each of these situations represents a quite different hierarchical relationship between the two languages.[23]

New Etymologies

There are many ways of illustrating these comments. Perhaps the most obvious is lexical. A favorite example in my own research—and really far too rich a case for these purposes—is the word *fraunchise*. This and countless other examples have explosive implications for the etymologies currently enshrined in the major English dictionaries. For the *Middle English Dictionary* misleadingly lists both *frank* and *fraunchise* as Old French when the words have a long history in Anglo-French.[24] This is more than mere etymology, but as Howard Bloch long ago argued, a matter of cultural assumptions that run very deep.[25] *Franc* goes back in

[23] See Ardis Butterfield, "Guerre et paix: l'anglais, le français et 'l'anglo-français,'" *Comptes Rendus de l'Académie des Inscriptions et Belles-Lettres* 9 (2009): 7–23. In my view, the phrase "French of England," while it draws necessary attention to the importance of insular French for a wider understanding of the literatures of England, unfortunately perpetuates an insular perspective on this French, rather than an awareness that insular French and continental French need to be studied together.

[24] See *AND, franc¹, franc²* and *franc³,* and *franchise.*

[25] R. Howard Bloch, *Etymologies and Genealogies: A Literary Anthropology of the French Middle Ages* (Chicago: University of Chicago Press, 1983).

continental terms to Francia and so functions as a powerful but conflicted metonym for both French and German. In Anglo-French as well as continental French its tentacles of influence reach out into many spheres of social and legal organization with a vast range of meanings involving freedom. From here it is a short step to ethical definition and the linking of personal and social freedom to a free act of generosity or bravery, which is where we meet it in Chaucer's Franklin and his *Tale*. By the time of that piece of writing, *franc* has seeped semantically into the very bedrock of English legal usage where *estre franc* is to be freely accessible to all and a *franc compaignoun* is a full member of a guild. At the same time, in a parallel development, *franc* also capitalizes on its status as a personal substantive, a free man or *franc/Franche home*. Without a much fuller investigation, it is not possible to delve into the possibility of friction in any of these usages between what one might call a "French" and an "English" meaning: for the most part, there seems to have been a silent or sleeping pun between English notions of freedom and French identity.

Fraunchise is an example of simple lexis: another, equally explosive direction of current research concerns multilingual word formations.[26] Textual evidence is increasingly being brought to light of the patterns and habits of linguistic layering: co-formations of Latin, French, and English in a wide range of administrative and financial documents. This research, along with work on syntax, idioms, and phrase formation, is all revealing how older philological and dialectal boundaries require fundamental revision. It reminds us of the obvious but usually ignored truth that before the existence of dictionaries, there may have been a very different sense of linguistic identity and categorization, especially in the usage of vernaculars, but in Latin as well.

But where for Rothwell, as a founder of the *Anglo-Norman Dictionary*, these discoveries serve to promote the importance and relevance of Anglo-Norman, it is equally important, from the perspective of Middle English, to think through some other factors and implications. For ironically, it seems to me that he underplays the great influx of continental French in the fourteenth century into Anglo-French as well as English. As a result of war, a burgeoning diplomatic and military administration,

---

[26] For example, Laura Wright, *Sources of London English: Medieval Thames Vocabulary* (Oxford: Clarendon Press, 1996) and "The Records of Hanseatic Merchants: Ignorant, Sleepy, or Degenerate?" *Multilingua* 16 (1997): 339–50. See also "Multilingualism in the Middle Ages," a collaborative project in the Worldwide Universities Network.

the presence of long-term prisoners on English soil, and the frequent traffic of personnel back and forth across the channel and on the Continent, the context of language use in England was far from insular. Moreover, cross-channel linguistic exchange was not only practiced among the educated and socially elevated, but was also perpetrated by roaming mercenary companies and, of course, merchants.

It leads me to argue that we need to be alive to the moments when a continental French word becomes Anglo-French and then gains a newer continental French resonance, and all this happening in an "English" context. *Fraunchise*, for example, acquires an extra allegorical literary layer, articulated in the *Rose* and widely promulgated by Machaut and his contemporaries.[27] What is confusing here is that of course this produces a double cultural layering in English usage. These words perform their dual custom in a subtle process of cultural reference, inward to an English, that is Anglo-French, construction of social personhood and outward to a fictional French personification of "free" behavior. Chaucer seems to use the word three times in the *Romaunt of the Rose* and in a handful of other contexts: here I suggest we find a genuine moment of French shaking off its Anglo-French meanings in becoming English. But the crucial point is that the same word is used to effect the translation.[28]

Many issues are at stake here. The notion of vernacularity is both more capacious and uncertainly inclusive than we may have thought. Perhaps the most important argument first of all is that "vernacular" in England does not mean only "English." It has become an almost completely shared practice in current scholarship to use the word "vernacular" to mean only English. But just as we have learned that we must

---

[27] See the references cited in the *Dictionnaire du Moyen Français* (ATILF / Nancy Université—CNRS), http://www.atilf.fr/dmf (hereafter *DMF*). A representative instance may be found in the following passage from Machaut's *Le Jugement dou Roy de Behaingne* (c. 1340), lines 1990–95:

Si vint Franchise, Honneur et Courtoisie,
Biauté, Desir, Leësse l'envoisie,
Et Hardiesse,
Prouesse, Amour, Loiauté et Largesse,
Voloir, Penser, Richesse avec Juenesse,
Et puis Raison qui de tous fu maistresse.

Compare also Deschamps' *Lai de Franchise* (given this rubric in the manuscript).

[28] See *MkT* (*CT*, VII.2664); *MerT* (IV.1987); *FranT* (V.1524); *ParsT* (X.450–55); *Ven*, line 59; there are twelve uses in *Rom*; in Fragment A (generally attributed to Chaucer): lines 955, 1211, 1238; Fragment B: 2007, 3003, 3501, 3507, 3575, 3592, 3608, 4906; Fragment C: 5865.

disengage ourselves from too easy an equation between Chaucer and the rise of English, so now perhaps we are ready to see how powerfully the retrospective image of Chaucer as "English" has repressed any desire to recognize that he was not working only with English but with a second vernacular that was both his and the enemy's, both used within the English court and to articulate the Anglo-French war that was a constant feature throughout his lifetime (and before and beyond).

But to call this vernacular "French" is also perhaps too easy. Allowing due status to Anglo-French in our inquiries helps us to realize that French is a plural category, with boundaries that shift and reposition themselves the longer we study them. French and Latin, in England, are not "non-English," any more than English is straightforwardly non-French. That instinct to separate, in a sense a casualty of modern lexicographical practice, must be resisted and questioned at every opportunity.[29] We need a new etymology, a new approach to etymology that allows for permeability between linguistic histories. It is important to add that this argument applies equally to continental French. There is no norm or standard of Parisian French until the use of French in the *chancellerie royale* began to increase dramatically in the fourteenth century,[30] and the influence of French was so wide, from what is now the Netherlands and Belgium down to the Languedoc and Italy and east into the Mediterranean and beyond, that many kinds of French were in use. Italian, likewise, as Dante implicitly reveals in his *De vulgari eloquentia*, had no common spoken form until reunification in the late nineteenth century.

Forein English in Chaucer's *Boece*

In the rest of this lecture, I want to think further about what this "new etymology" may mean for our understanding of translation, and especially of Chaucer's practices as a translator. My approach will not be conventionally lexical, despite the fact that lexis still has so much to tell us about Chaucer's English. Study of Chaucer's relationship to French has been rather bedeviled by word counts and word formation, as if one could prove how "French" Chaucer was being by how many French-

[29] A model for this kind of approach may be found in the remarkable study by J. N. Adams, *Bilingualism and the Latin Language* (Cambridge: Cambridge University Press, 2003).

[30] Lusignan, *La langue des rois*, 95–153 (esp. 119–22).

derived words he employed, or conversely, how "English" by the number of English words.[31] As I have just sought to demonstrate, these very definitions are often rather suspect, and often depend on predefining English as Germanic or even Norse. Such statistics tell us more about historiography than language and give us very few answers to other kinds of question, such as what Chaucer thought *about* English or French, what kind of linguistic identity he wished or was even able to ascribe to English (or French). The deep structure of Anglo-French in Chaucer's English makes it harder to know when he felt he was using a "French" word. To put it another way, can we find a way of recognizing when Chaucer's French struck *him* as foreign? We may leap to assume that he is translating when in fact he is drawing on a word well known to him in Anglo-French. Even more complicated, it may be a word that he knew bilingually as readily from continental French. So I propose to think more laterally, and see if it is possible to uncover a sense of Chaucer's own reactions to the words he uses through two routes, one historicist, the other more theoretical. One involves the richly ambiguous trope of the envoy/*envoi*, at once historical agent and literary form. The other, which will allude in passing to some work by Dipesh Chakrabarty and Gayatri Spivak, concerns processes of cultural translation.

My starting point in introducing these lines of inquiry is Chaucer's *Boece*. *Boece* is of interest here for a variety of reasons: it happens to be the only work of Chaucer's that employs the adjective "forein," doing so eighteen times.[32] That it occurs in a work that Chaucer is producing out of Latin, a French translation and a Latin commentary (or two) provides the opportunity to observe him close up working with all three languages as he endeavors to make sense of Philosophy's exposition. My argument is that his uses of "forein" are indices of an education in linguistic and philosophical strangeness that Chaucer develops elsewhere in his writings.

Chaucer's engagement with the "forein" begins early in the translation in Book 1, metrum 2, where Boethius builds up a powerful picture

---

[31] The classic representative of this approach is Joseph Mersand, *Chaucer's Romance Vocabulary* (New York: Cornet, 1939).

[32] I discount here *LGW* 1962, where it means privy. The references are: *Bo,* Book I, metrum 2, line 4; *Bo* I.pr.4.113; *Bo* II.pr.2.25; *Bo* II.pr.5.73; *Bo* II.pr.5.96; *Bo* II.pr.5.126; *Bo* III.pr.3.70; *Bo* III.pr.3.80; *Bo* III.pr.6.37; *Bo* III.pr.6.45; *Bo* III.pr.9.29; *Bo* III.pr.9.71; *Bo* III.metrum.9.7; *Bo* III.pr.12.191; *Bo* IV.pr.3.25; *Bo* IV.pr.3.105; *Bo* IV.pr.4.199; *Bo* V.pr.4.216.

of mental darkness. Chaucer's text is here quoted alongside Boethius's original and Jean de Meun's French translation:[33]

"Allas! How the thowht of man, dreynt in overthrowynge depnesse, dulleth and forletith his proper cleernesse, myntynge to goon into foreyne dyrknesses as ofte as his anoyos bysynesse wexeth withowte mesure, that is dryven to and fro with wordely wyndes!"

(lines 1–4)

"Ha lasse! comme la pensee de cestui, plungiee en trebuichable parfondece, rebouche et, sa propre clarté delaissiee, [tendant] a aler en foraines tenebres et sa nuisable cure, par quantes foiz [est elle] demenee par les vens terriens, craist elle sens fin."

"Heu quam precipiti mersa profundo
Mens ebet et propria luce relicta
Tendit in externas ire tenebras,
Terrenis quociens flatibus aucta
Cressit in immensum noxia cura."

Chaucer's own rendering of the French seems to respond to Jean de Meun's own heightened response to the Latin. Jean uses the word "trebuichable"[34]—a precise but also vividly metaphoric realization of the Latin idea of falling—which Chaucer gives as "overthrowynge" and this sets up the severe disorientation to come of "foreyne dyrknesses" [foraines tenebres]. In both the French and then the English, "forein" comes as a sharpened version of "externas": it adds a notion of incomprehension to that of distance, which seems to increase its horrors. From here on, in Books 2 and 3, "forein" becomes part of an increasingly political discussion of worldly power. Latin "externa" is rendered as "forein" and now also "[e]strange": it is not just that one must cast away worldly goods, but they must come to seem strange. Their very nature must be "maked foreyne fro the," that is, recognized to have characteristics that owe nothing to you and hence do not in any way belong to you.

[33] *Chaucer's Boece: A Critical Edition Based on Cambridge University Library, MS Ii.3.21, ff. 9r–180v*, ed. Tim William Machan (Heidelberg: Winter, 2008), 5; Latin original and Jean de Meun's translation are quoted from *Sources of the Boece*, ed. Machan (Athens and London: University of Georgia Press, 2005), 28–29.
[34] See *Altfranzösisches Wörterbuch*, ed. Adolf Tobler and Erhard Lommatzsch, 10 vols. (Berlin, 1925–76): *trebuchable*: "Qui fait trébucher, périlleux"[causes one to stumble, dangerous].

Although this might seem to be simply a strong way of expressing a form of detachment, the *Consolatio* goes on to show that human disengagement takes complex forms. There is time to comment on just one instance. It strikes home at Boethius's own situation of being a trusted adviser, or as Chaucer puts it a "familier," who finds himself in prison. Philosophy, with piercing frankness, exposes this relationship, supposedly of trust and confident personal knowledge, as fragile. Having held the two terms "familiar" and "tyrant" apart throughout the passage, she suddenly drives them devastatingly into collision:

And what pestylence is moore myhty for to anoye a wyht than a famylier enemy?

(*Boece* 3.pr.5.68–70)

Et quelle pestilance est plus puissant a nuire que familiers anemis?

(105)

Que vero pestis efficacior ad nocendum quam familiaris inimicus?

(102)

This comes at the heart of a long and difficult lesson in how to harden oneself away from familiarity into foreignness. Chaucer learns it twofold, ethically and linguistically. For the words "forein" and "strange" become strange to him as he translates. They are well known to him, part of his Anglo-French linguistic heritage. But here, in the act of translating the bitterly painful history of a man whose sense of integrity was traduced, who found familiarity turn incomprehensibly into hostility, Chaucer himself learns to use "forein" and "strange" as foreign words, as words that he translates into English in their own guise, unchanged, yet alienated. Like *fraunchise*, but more troublingly in this case, translation takes place across a semantic gap that opens up within a word rather than between one word and its chosen linguistic other.[35]

---

[35] *Forein* is attested in the *AND* under the following spellings: *forein, foreyn, forain, forayn, foran, foren, foreint, forien; forrein; foreyin, foreigne; furain, furein; ferein, f. foreynne (farein)*. Its meanings include, as an adjective: 1. "extraneous, alien," (law): situated outside the jurisdiction of a town etc, not local; 2. outer, exterior; outer, secular 3. Foreign, distant, geographically distant, remote in blood 4. (of time) distant, and as a noun: 1. Foreigner, alien; (of guild) non-member 2. Outskirts, area outside city walls 3. (law): Forinsec (that is, foreign) service. In Middle English, spellings attested are: *forein* (adj.) Also *foren, foran, forren, furren, ferren* (and as noun: *forin*). The meanings are closely similar, though with more emphasis on a *forein* as "one born in another country or belonging to a different nation," a stranger, a traveler. As an adjective, *forein* has additional meanings including 3. *forein womman* meaning prostitute, also alien to one's nature, contrary, inimical and 4. Public, and also inferior. In Middle French (*DMF aforain, forein*) is only attested once in Machaut, meaning external; otherwise the more

This conjunction impressed upon Chaucer in the *Boece* between the estranged prisoner's intellectual history, the forcing on him via Jean de Meun of the word "forein," and the hard activity of translating took deep root in his writings, indeed in his own philosophy. We have had many subtle readings connecting these with his domestic political context: here I want to emphasize the broader international context of war, a conflict that was happening linguistically as much as politically or militarily. It seems to me that the war constitutes the undiscussed epicenter of the relationship between English and French in this period. Anglo-French conflict was not only a constant fact or threat throughout Chaucer's lifetime, but it shaped the period, and indeed is a way in which the medieval era has uniquely influenced the political constructs of the modern Western world. No modern version of nationhood is complete without an understanding of how these two nations each discovered a distinct existence through sharing the most extended continuous historical agon of any two Western nations. The English monarchs continued to call themselves "king" or "queen" of France until the 1802 Treaty of Amiens, and documents recently discovered (to mutual amusement) in the British National Archives show that the French government proposed that the queen become sovereign of France in 1956.

The strains on language are complex because of the doubleness of French for Chaucer. As Anglo-French, it is a homely language for him, but even continental French is not straightforwardly "forein" to him since it is a language that he engages in domestically and professionally as well as through literature. On top of this, we must not forget that continental French was not a stable, unchanging backcloth, but a language that was itself going through a huge expansion, stimulated from the 1370s by Charles V's ambitious program of translation from Latin.[36] More than one thousand French words (including *comedie, tragedie, comique,* and *tragique*) are first found in the writings of Nicole Oresme,

---

common attestation is *aforain* (Picardie, Wallonie), meaning 1. a stranger, someone who lives outside the jurisdiction of a lordship, kingdom, or the franchise of a town and 2. Exterior, not relevant. For *estrange*, the *AND* also lists *estraunge; estrangne, estraigne; estraunger; strange, straunge, straunger.* The meanings overlap considerably with *forein*, although they also include 4. Outside one's experience, with meanings ranging from wondrous, marvellous, unusual to hostile, harsh, dreadful. In the *MED straunge* is listed with *straung, strang(e, straunche, straunce, strounge, strong(e, (?gen.) stranges & (error) storge; pl. stra(u)nges, stranghis, (?gen.) straungene,* and again the overlap of meanings is high. There are more attested applications to dress, food, astronomy, and language.

[36]Lusignan, *La langue des rois,* 124; Lynn Staley, *Languages of Power in the Age of Richard II* (University Park: Pennsylvania State University Press, 2005), 78–93.

whose glosses in Aristotle's *Politiques* include an appended glossary on Aristotle's *notables* terms.[37] Moreover, French writers—Philippe de Vitry, Jean de le Mote, Machaut, and Deschamps—were increasingly conscious of the threat of English as a "familier enemye," if not fully yet as a language, then certainly as a military power.

Envoys and *envois*

We can observe the pressure of war on Chaucer's investigation of strangeness with particular clarity in his use of the *envoi*. This apparently minor poetic device has much to teach us about the characteristics of Anglo-French linguistic exchange in a time of complex diplomatic tensions. Let me introduce this briefly through some heavily Boethian works, the five so-called Boethian lyrics and *Troilus and Criseyde*. All are marked by the insistent theme of tested and threatened friendship. All document great strains on language. In the first *ballade* of the three-*ballade* structure of *Fortune,* the "pleintif," through the "whirling" wheel of Fortune, has lost the capacity to know "frend fro fo." Here and also in *Lak of Stedfastnesse*, words are set in opposition to each other, apposed in the same line:

> as wele /or wo / now poeere & now honour
> (*Fortune*, line 2)[38]

That this is more than a simple point about reversal is suggested by the second *ballade* of Fortune. Here, arguing back against the plaintiff's accusations, she tries to reassure him in her refrain that he still has his best friend:

> & ek thow hast thy beste frende alyue
> (*Fortune*, 32, 40, 48)

But the poignancy of the Boethian context contributes to a feeling of ironic anxiety about this assertion, and indeed the plaintiff bites back

[37] Maistre Nicole Oresme, *Le Livre de Politiques d'Aristote, published from the text of the Avranches Manuscript 223*, by Albert Douglas Menut, Transactions of the American Philosophical Society, n.s. 60, part 6 (Philadelphia: The American Philosophical Society, 1970).

[38] *Geoffrey Chaucer: The Minor Poems*, ed. George B. Pace and Alfred David (Norman: University of Oklahoma Press, 1982), 110. Citations of these Boethian lyrics are all from this edition.

that he well knows the friends that pay allegiance to her. Various attempts have been made to identify this "best" friend with Richard II and his "textual environment": my concern is less to do with seeking a specific historicization of the *ballade* and more to argue for a link between the treachery of friendship and the turning of words.[39]

Further commentary on Chaucer's practices in these five lyrics may be found in *The Former Age*. Occurring in just two manuscripts, one of which is the copy of *Boece* in CUL MS Ii.3.21 that also has *Fortune* interpolated directly beneath it after Book 2, metrum 5, this formally anomalous poem in seven stanzas plus an *envoi* not only draws on the golden-age material from the *Consolatio*, probably supplemented by the versions in Ovid, the *Rose*, Deschamps,[40] Virgil, and perhaps Tibullus, but amplifies it in two directions, those of war and linguistic confusion. Both these threads are drawn out in the *envoi*, which refers to Nimrod—tyrant, warmonger, builder of fortifications, and builder of the tower of Babel—in the same breath as the weeping and crying of our present days, filled with:

> Dowblenesse & tresoun & enuye
> poyson & manslawhtre & mordre in sondry wyse
> (*The Former Age*, 63–64, p. 101)

Four out of five of the Boethian lyrics have *envois*, and seven out of ten of his *ballades* in total. The context for Chaucer's use of the *envoi* remains relatively unexplored.[41] This is not the place to give a detailed account,

---

[39] *Fortune* occurs in ten manuscripts. Aage Brusendorff, *The Chaucer Tradition* (Oxford: Clarendon Press, 1925), argued that it has a source in two of Deschamps' *ballades*: see *Oeuvres Complètes de Eustache Deschamps*, ed. le Marquis Queux de Saint-Hilaire and Gaston Raynaud, Société des Anciens Textes Français, 11 vols. (Paris: Firmin Didot, 1878–1903), 2:140–42, nos. 286–87, repr. in Brusendorff, *Chaucer Tradition*, 242–44; Wimsatt thinks that Machaut's *ballade* no. 96 is a further source ("Chaucer, Fortune, and Machaut's 'Il m'est avis,'" in *Chaucerian Problems and Perspectives: Essays Presented to Paul E. Beichner C.S.C.*, ed. Edward Vasta and Zacharias P. Thundy [Notre Dame, Ind.: University of Notre Dame Press, 1979], 119–31 [74]), but the resemblances are all rather general. The Deschamps ballades are copied, in the unique collected manuscript of his works, BNF fr. 840, straight after his poem addressed to Chaucer; because of this, it has been assumed that they were sent to Chaucer along with it. See Pace and David, ed., *The Minor Poems*, 104, and Wimsatt, *Chaucer and His French Contemporaries*, 255.

[40] Ballade No.1317, *Oeuvres Complètes*, ed. Queux de Saint-Hilaire and Raynaud, 7:79–80.

[41] Seth Lerer's *Chaucer and His Readers* (Princeton: Princeton University Press, 2003) provides a fine and far-reaching discussion of the afterlife of Chaucer's *envois*: their "prelife," however, has not been so fully sketched. Among those who have written on Chau-

but some brief comments may be appropriate.[42] It is important to note, first, that a remarkable coincidence occurs in the fourteenth century between the political and literary circumstances of negotiation. For just as the machinery of diplomatic communication grew more complicated and the person of the envoy was relied upon more extensively, the poetic *envoi*, in the shape of an addition to the strophic pattern of a chant royal or *ballade*, reappeared and became a dominant feature of lyric composition. We all know that Chaucer himself had an important, though somewhat mysterious, role as envoy. Outside the highest level of diplomatic missions, including secret missions, the person sent would be an ordinary knight or clerk from the king's household, a *familiaris*. Chaucer had precisely this role in several journeys between 1376 and 1381. The first, on December 23, 1376, was on the king's secret business ("in secretis negociis domini regis") in the company of Sir John de Burley, the brother of Sir Simon Burley, who was a close associate of Chaucer, especially in the 1380s, and became tutor to Richard II.[43] In the records that survive of subsequent journeys that Chaucer made on Anglo-French diplomatic business, the formula "in secretis negociis domini regis" occurs repeatedly, on trips to Flanders, Paris, and Montreuil (1377), "parts of France" (1381), and Calais (1387).[44] Chaucer was not alone in this among contemporary writers and promoters of lyric and other courtly poetry: Guichard d'Angle (who was imprisoned in Spain with Oton de Graunson), Richard Stury, and Chaucer are all listed by Froissart as English envoys to Montreuil in the spring of 1377.[45] Deschamps was another; Machaut had a flourishing career as notary and royal secretary, and the so-called Lollard or Chamber knights closely associated with Chaucer (of whom Stury was one, and Sir John Clanvowe) were nearly all seasoned military campaigners and diplomats with strong connections in France.[46]

---

cer's *envois*, Craig Bertolet, in his "Chaucer's Envoys and the Poet-Diplomat," *ChauR* 33 (1998): 66–89, is the closest to my topic, but takes a rather different approach that looks at Chaucer's political indirection.

[42] For a more extended discussion, see Butterfield, *The Familiar Enemy*, chap. 5.

[43] Michael Hanly, "Courtiers and Poets: An International Network of Literary Exchange in Late Fourteenth-Century Italy, France, and England," *Viator* 28 (1997): 305–32.

[44] As many biographers have commented, the specific nature of many of these trips remains vague. I leave aside here the trips to Lombardy.

[45] André Crépin, "Chaucer et Deschamps," in *Autour d'Eustache Deschamps: Actes du colloque . . . Amiens, 5–8 Novembre 1998,* ed. Danielle Buschinger (Amiens: Presses du Centre d'études médiévales, Université de Picardie-Jules Verne, 1999), 39–40 and n. 4.

[46] See K. B. McFarlane, *Lancastrian Kings and Lollard Knights* (Oxford: Clarendon Press, 1972), 177–81.

It is not easy to pinpoint the very first revival of the poetic *envoi* in the fourteenth century. The device is known first in troubadour song, where it often has the term *tornada*, and then becomes more common in the trouvères, where it is an important element in thirteenth-century *jeux-partis* as well as *chansons d'amour*.[47] *Envois* are messages, and draw on the language of letters, of sending (*envoyer*) and commissioning (*mander*). Their status is often only uncertainly authorial: it is not possible to be sure from the manuscript transmission whether an *envoi* has been added by a scribe or whether multiple *envois* indicate separate performance traditions. In the complex and still not fully understood history of the *formes fixes*, the formerly lower-style genres originally associated with dance, such as the *rondet de carole* and the *ballette,* were taken up as higher-style genres, principally the *ballade* and *rondeau*; and the formerly higher-style *grand chant courtois* dropped out of fashion and was replaced by the *chant royal* and—though the social context was different—the *ballade*.[48] The use of *envois* thus passed from the *grand chant* to the *chant royal*: and then, in a further leap, to the genre that dominated fourteenth-century lyric composition.

The *chant royal* was characteristic, like the *jeu-parti*, of the town-centered puy productions of Arras, Lille, and Valenciennes.[49] These start to appear in the early decades of the fourteenth century. They consistently have five strophes and an envoy, usually addressed to "Prince," the Prince of the puy: one of the earliest may be the five-strophe *chanson* cited by Nicole de Margival in his *Dit de la Panthère d'amours* (c. 1290–1328).[50] Parallel to their composition, the *ballade* genre started to settle into the formal three-strophe + refrain pattern that Machaut was to establish emphatically in midcentury.[51] But although his eight surviving

[47] Roger Dragonetti, *La Technique poétique des trouvères dans la chanson courtoise* (1960; Geneva: Slatkine Reprints, 1979), 304–70.

[48] Deschamps signals this in *L'Art de dictier*, ed. and trans. Deborah M. Sinnreich-Levi (East Lansing, Mich.: Colleagues Press, 1994). But note the confusion in BNF fr. 840 between *chant royal* and *ballade*: the section rubric is "chansons royaulx," but each poem is given the heading "balade."

[49] As Deschamps explains, *L'Art de dictier*, 64–65.

[50] Bernard Ribémont, ed., *Nicole de Margival, Le Dit de la Panthère*, CFMA 136 (Paris: Champion, 2000), lines 2556–600.

[51] The so-called origin of the *formes fixes* is a traditionally contentious topic among modern scholars. Since Lawrence Earp's pioneering article, "Lyrics for Reading and Lyrics for Singing in Late Medieval France: The Development of the Dance Lyric from Adam de la Halle to Guillaume de Machaut," in *The Union of Words and Music*, ed. Rebecca A. Baltzer, Thomas Cable, and James I. Wimsatt (Austin: University of Texas Press, 1991), 101–31, newer research, especially on the ballettes of Oxford Douce 308

chants royaux all had *envois*, it was not Machaut who introduced the *envoi* to the *ballade*: none of his 246 *ballades* has one.[52] The story is very different for Deschamps: nearly a third in total.[53]

Deschamps is thus often assumed to be the first to add *envois* to the *ballade*. But Chaucer also composed *ballades* with *envois* consistently and perhaps began (dating is always conjectural) at an early date. Wimsatt is keen to argue that Deschamps' *envois* were not a direct model for Chaucer's: rhyme schemes and numbers of lines seem independently explored by each author.[54] Evidently both authors on either side of the channel found it equally natural to pick up and work with a device that articulated poetically a major aspect of their professional lives. Chaucer's work with *envois*, like Deschamps', is distinctive and exploratory, indeed many of them, such as the Envoy to *The Clerk's Tale*, are among the most awkward, ruptured, and idiosyncratic moments in his oeuvre. Chaucer's group of philosophical and political lyrics makes full use of *envois* and other debate structures (such as the *responsio* alternations of *Fortune*) and are full of links to Deschamps.[55] References to letters ("this lytel writ . . . I sende yow," *Bukton*, lines 25–26), to prison (*Bukton*, line 14), a French song refrain (or perhaps incipit) (*Fortune*, line 7), a bille (*The Complaint unto Pity*), to "Brutes Albyon" (*Purse*, line 22) and, as we have seen, divided loyalties among friends (*Fortune*), and the wretchedness and dishonesty of present times (*The Former Age, Truth*) set these poems firmly within the lyric discourse of the Hundred Years War. They also, perhaps most explicitly, in the *envoi* to the so-called *Complaint of Venus*, translated from five *ballades* by Graunson, turn out to be places that

---

and the works of Adam de la Halle, is sketching out a much more detailed picture than before of the nature and fact of change at the turn of the century and the decades following: *The Chansonnier of Oxford Bodleian MS Douce 308: Essays and Complete Edition of Texts*, ed. Mary Atchison (Aldershot: Ashgate, 2005); *The Old French Ballette: Oxford Bodleian Library, MS Douce 308*, ed. Eglal Doss-Quinby and Samuel N. Rosenberg, with Elizabeth Aubrey (Geneva: Droz, 2006). See Ardis Butterfield, *Poetry and Music in Medieval France from Jean Renart to Guillaume de Machaut* (Cambridge: Cambridge University Press, 2002), chap. 16; M. Everist, "Motets, French Tenors, and the Polyphonic Chanson ca. 1300," *The Journal of Musicology* 24 (2007): 365–406.

[52] The figure is Lawrence Earp's, *Guillaume de Machaut: A Guide to Research* (New York: Garland, 1995), 241. See James Laidlaw, "L'Innovation métrique chez Deschamps," in *Autour d'Eustache Deschamps*, ed. Buschinger, 127–40.

[53] Laidlaw reports 274 out of 916 isometric ballades and 10 out of 92 heterometric ones, in "L"Innovation métrique."

[54] Wimsatt, *Chaucer and His French Contemporaries*, 259.

[55] V. J. Scattergood, "The Short Poems," in *Oxford Guides to Chaucer: The Shorter Poems*, A. J. Minnis, V. J. Scattergood, and J. J. Smith (Oxford: Oxford University Press, 1995), 483–503 lists these links.

hold some of his most enigmatic references to translation, to English, and Englishing.

The "Scandal" of Translation: Subaltern English

In the last part of this lecture, I want to consider two final examples, Criseyde's second letter and, as a brief coda, *The Manciple's Tale*. Both seem to me to tell us a great deal about Chaucerian vernaculars and translation. *Troilus* is of course another and vastly more extended poem of, about, and immersed in war. I do not have time here to talk about Pandarus as envoy, though the language of diplomacy has enormous relevance to the work as a whole and to my larger subject of war, nation, and language.[56] This final letter is perhaps for me the most painful moment of the poem: the extraordinary emotional intensity that has built up during Book 5 peaks in this letter, where Criseyde lays herself bare as the "transfuge" [the turncoat], the "beste frend" who goes over to the other side. I want to pause over the following lines:

> Come I wole; but yet in swich disjoynte
> I stonde as now that what yer or what day
> That this shal be, that kan I naught apoynte.[57]

Chaucer exacerbates the pain by allowing these lines to contain so much bewilderment. The rhyme puts together two words that—so far as we can possibly tell—are first used in English by Chaucer. And for once, although each word exists separately in Anglo-French, it is hard to find a precedent for the two together. The context for *desjoindre* is much more rich in continental French: a favorite of Machaut and Christine de Pizan, it finds its place in a context of female disarray, a sense that is also picked up and reused frequently in Lydgate.[58] In Anglo-French history, the context is more narrowly legal and involves the verb *aturner*: "aturner en disjointe."[59] The word *aturner* in Anglo-French but not in

---

[56] See Butterfield, *The Familiar Enemy*.

[57] *Troilus and Criseyde,* V.1618–20, quoted from Larry D. Benson, gen. ed. *The Riverside Chaucer* (Oxford: Oxford University Press, 1988).

[58] See *desjoindre* in the *DMF*. The entry gives twenty references to Machaut and twenty to Christine de Pizan; for Lydgate, see *MED*, disjoint(e (a), *Siege of Thebes*, line 3273; *Resoun and Sensualite*, line 4312 and *Troy Book*, 4.3656.

[59] See *AND*, *disjointe*, and the citation given from *Britton* (a thirteenth-century legal compilation, perhaps attributable to Bracton): "coment qe deus ou plusours soint fetz attournez en disjointe, tut eit chescun le poer soen seignur . . ."; *AND*, *aturner*, v.a.7: (law) to transfer someone's allegiance v.n.2: (law) to transfer one's allegiance to a new lord.

continental French includes the meaning of transferring allegiance. Tentatively, then, it seems as if Chaucer may have taken into English a Middle French usage that, in so powerful a scene of female dilemma, became a locus classicus in English thereafter.[60] But it is tempting also to wonder whether Chaucer also had in mind that residual Anglo-French sense of betrayal.

In trying to think through what Chaucer is conveying here, one of the key aspects of these lines, and indeed of the whole letter, perhaps of Criseyde *tout court,* is that blankness of exchange that Jacques Derrida has so eloquently described in writing of the envoy. In the first chapter of *La Carte postale,* entitled "Envois," Derrida explores, with comically incessant wordplay, how letters both assume and forestall comprehension in their transport of meaning between writer and recipient.[61] It is characteristic of the correspondence between Criseyde and Troilus in Book 5 that their letters precisely do not answer one another. Troilus never receives a reply to his own assertions and questions; Criseyde's responses seem, weirdly and agonizingly, to be addressed to someone else. But in these lines, above all, the failure is most acute. For she seems to be talking not merely of emotional disorientation, but of time being out of joint. Her ability to control events through the power of her own will is so at sea that although she "wole come" she cannot tell "what yer or what day/ That this shal be."

I want to suggest that this is a subaltern temporal fracture: "What I have called subaltern pasts may be thought of as intimations we receive—while engaged in the specific activity of historicizing—of a shared, unhistoricizable, and ontological now. This now is, as I have tried to suggest, what fundamentally rends the seriality of historical time and makes any particular moment of the historical present out of joint with itself."[62]

Chakrabarty and Spivak, both Bengali intellectuals, use the term "subaltern" to think through two problems of cultural translation, in Spivak's case of the other-languaged female whose "texts must be made to speak English" and in Chakrabarty's of the modern Indian peasant

---

[60] The wife in *The Shipman's Tale* also stands "in . . . disjoynte" (VII.411); the tale's dating is not secure enough to draw conclusions about chronological priority.

[61] *La Carte postale: De Socrate à Freud et au-delà* (Paris: Flammarion, 1980); *The Post Card from Socrates to Freud and Beyond,* trans. Alan Bass (Chicago: University of Chicago Press, 1987).

[62] Dipesh Chakrabarty, *Provincializing Europe: Postcolonial Thought and Historical Difference* (Princeton: Princeton University Press, 2000), 113.

(his term) and how his or her voice might speak in a Western model of historical narrative.[63] They both talk of the "scandal" of translation: of the way in which the discipline of modern Western secular academic history cannot deal, for instance, with a peasant who claims that his prayers to the gods provoked him into rebellion. The peasant's prayers are untranslatable as a form of history: in their own terms, the prayers tear that history apart since they destroy its explanatory coherence and its ability to tell an event sequentially.[64] So they are translated into quite different terms: economic, social, or psychological. Any attempt to allow the peasant's explanation its own force would not make academic sense. For that kind of translation to happen, we need a new system of exchange, and one that recognizes the impossibility of the old.

We are more used than Chakrabarty, as medievalists, to the ways in which religious narratives are bound to a different sense of time and history from that which modern historians now possess. Perhaps also, unlike modernist intellectuals, we can more easily recover a time when English as a language did not yet have cultural power, but was even culturally subordinate to French. But I nonetheless think Chakrabarty's sense of the extraordinary fissures between one set of cultural expectations and another is powerfully applicable to Criseyde's utterance. This is because, with Spivak's help, he recognizes that the notion of scandal that they are both attaching to translation goes hand in hand with another notion, that of intimacy: "There remains something of a 'scandal'—of the shocking—in every translation, and it is only through a relationship of intimacy to both languages that we are aware of the degree of this scandal."[65]

I have not got time to unravel this as far as I would wish, but it may be enough to say that being a bilingual translator helps one simultaneously to understand the barrier between the two languages and to find it invisible. Something like this may have been the case for Chaucer: for on the one hand, he was able to write English easily, whatever the dependence on French or Latin or any other language, yet at other times he seems to stutter, to find the experience of writing a subaltern lan-

---

[63] Gayatri Chakravorty Spivak, "The Politics of Translation," *Outside in the Teaching Machine* (New York: Routledge, 1993), 179–200 (182).

[64] "The archives thus help bring to view the disjointed nature of any particular 'now' one may inhabit; that is the function of subaltern pasts" (Chakrabarty, *Provincializing Europe*, 108).

[65] Ibid., 89.

guage overwhelming. This is such a moment: Criseyde finds herself scandalously untranslatable, an impossible element of exchange that reveals how English needs continental French and yet has its own dark layer of Anglo-French meaning below. It comes as no surprise that Troilus should think this letter "al straunge," nor to find Chaucer inserting here his second reference to Lollius (V.1653), that strange source of fake linguistic authority.

In turning finally to *The Manciple's Tale*, it is worth noting how Chaucer, in this quasi-*envoi*, the final piece of verse in his vast idiosyncratic prosimetrum of the *Canterbury Tales*, should stutter again. Threads from *Troilus and Criseyde* and the *Envoy to Scogan* as well as the *Complaint to Venus* tighten into another dark commentary on speech. The moral of this tale-telling crow—"keep your tongue"—is uttered twenty-two times in the last fifty lines, and the atmosphere is heavy with treachery, violence, and linguistic confusion. Criseyde half-decided to risk "janglerie," but the story of the crow shows that using someone else's language (the crow sings "Cokkow! Cokkow! Cokkow!"—another bird's language) may lead to deadly miscomprehension and the curse of perpetual inarticulacy. Throwing a Flemish proverb into the mix ("litel jangling causeth muchel reste," IX.350), Chaucer may be alluding to the murderous consequences of racial hatred, when the Flemings were killed during the Rising for their mispronunciation of English "bread and cheese."[66] But perhaps more tellingly, one of the analogues for the tale, the Englished version of the *Seven Sages of Rome*, has the bird (here a magpie) speaking French:

> The burgeis hadde a pie in his halle,
> That couthe telle tales alle
> Apertlich, in freinch langage
> (2201–3)[67]

French is a language in which to speak "apertlich" but the threat of violent disorder is not far away.

In answer to the question of where we go after Muscatine and Wimsatt, we do more than write about style or check sources. We attempt

---

[66] *Chronicles of London*, ed. C. L. Kingsford (Oxford: Clarendon Press, 1905), 15.

[67] *The Seven Sages of Rome*, ed. Karl Brunner, EETS o.s. 191 (London: Oxford University Press, 1933), 100–104, repr. in *Sources and Analogues of the Canterbury Tales*, 2 vols., ed. Correale and Hamel (Cambridge: D. S. Brewer, 2005), 2:771.

to be genuinely cross-cultural and put behind us the desire to see French and French literature as a "background" to Chaucer but rather a very insistent and conflicted presence, and one that was not to seem less vivid until the losses of Henry VI's reign. Taking account of Chaucer's bilingual vernacularity suggests that we need to think again first about Englishness and second about his view of international culture. We cannot understand Englishness without seeking to understand what was then its superior cultural other of Frenchness. Source study often has the unfortunate consequence of seeming to imply that these texts in other languages and cultures are somehow marginal to the center that was English. But it was English that was marginal and not fully identified or identifiable as an international discourse for much longer yet into the future, and the notion of English as central is surely not there until the nineteenth century and imperialism. Fourteenth-century English had a subaltern status, and like modern Welsh, Irish, Cornish, and Hebridean was full of local energy. But it was not yet on the cusp of national let alone international triumph, and certainly it did not perceive itself in those terms. Anglo-French and French, through the prosecution of war, defined English concerns for longer than we think. Chaucer's labors with language showed him to be deeply aware of the strains caused by war on those who were "familiar enemies," who even shared the same tongue, and were only gradually, often unwillingly, discovering their mutual estrangement.

Little Nothings:

The Squire's Tale and the Ambition of Gadgets

Patricia Clare Ingham
Indiana University

“T HE WORLD OF THE ROMANCES,” writes Richard Kieck-
hefer, “seems at times a vast toy shop stocked with magical delights.”[1]
Kieckhefer's popular history of magic in the Middle Ages thus casts the
enchanting pull of romances as a fantasy associated with childhood. The
toy-shop metaphor may seem odd for the medieval context, however.
Following the work of Philippe Ariès, social historians have long sur-
mised that childhood did not properly exist during the Middle Ages, a
hard-scrabble time (apparently) little able to afford the trifles of childhood play.[2]

This assumption has come under important revision in recent years,
a move corroborated by the discovery of large numbers of hollow pewter
trinkets—many of them obviously children's toys—found preserved in
the riverbed of the Thames. Hollow-cast figurines of knights datable,
from their depiction of armor, to c. 1300, presumably for boys; miniature metal tableware and pottery ostensibly for girls; lead-alloy hollow
heads—including one that may be a Christ figure, a grotesque, and two
that resemble a "caricatured Jewish head" with pointed hat, all of which
may have been puppet heads;[3] one remarkable hollow-metal miniature

Comments on earlier versions of this essay have improved it considerably. I am particularly grateful to Judith Anderson, Constance Furey, Shannon Gayk, Frank Grady,
Shawn Hughes, and Elizabeth Scala, and to audiences at Purdue University and at the
University of Missouri, Columbia. Special thanks to Peter Travis, and the anonymous
reader for *SAC* for helpful comments and suggestions.

[1] *Magic in the Middle Ages* (Cambridge: Cambridge University Press, 2000), 107.

[2] Philippe Ariès famously denied childhood to the medieval period. The bibliography
disputing this claim is increasingly vast. See, particularly, N. Orme, *Medieval Childhood*
(New Haven: Yale University Press, 2001).

[3] Here quoting Geoff Egan. Hazel Forsyth with Geoff Egan, *Toys, Trifles, and Trinkets:
Base Metal Miniatures from London 1200 to 1800* (London: Museum of London Unicorn
Press, 2005), 142.

bird or fledgling, originally with moving parts that "enabled the bird to bob and its tongue to go in and out";[4] and significantly, a mold clearly used to produce quantities of toys. On the basis of these findings, Geoff Egan of the British Museum and Hazel Forsyth of the Museum of London hypothesize the mass-production of lead-alloy playthings, "more for a mass market than [as] the privileged treasures of a rich elite."[5] These artifacts suggest not only that childhood existed during the Middle Ages but also that considerable technological skill was dedicated to its entertainments. They also make one wonder why social historians have been so quick to assume a Middle Ages without children or childhood play—an idea that is, relative to the evidence, "virtually baseless," as Egan puts it.[6] On the one hand, these little nothings of medieval social and cultural production, the toys, gadgets, and frivolous entertainments surviving from the period whether in the mud of the Thames or in the pages of medieval romance have been catalogued in the work of such scholars as Kieckhefer, Scott Lightsey, or William Eamon.[7] On the other hand, such productions are rarely featured in technological histories, despite the evidence they give of developments in technology.

Weberian sociology reserves technological advance for those things associated with production, not leisure, for usable, not "frivolous," items. Histories of medieval technology stress the innovative power of flying buttresses, windmills, or cannons, yet ignore the drolleries of medieval romance, implicitly viewing them as trivial, not unlike the delicate ceramic glazes or Ming vases fashioned by Asian artists. Max Weber is of course the author of the powerful story of modern disenchantment, positing the historical transformation from a premodern

---

[4] Ibid., 143.

[5] Ibid., 59. Egan continues, "The best of the latest work on medieval childhood now fully acknowledges playthings in the sense used in this volume as a reality. There remain others who are skeptical or simply uninformed from archaeological sources." And, on the question of the mass market: "Of course, those without any spare money would not have been able to afford such trifles, but within towns there would have been many families for whom the occasional indulgence of a few pence on their children would have been easily expendable."

[6] Ibid., 58. As Egan and Forsyth point out, an earlier inability to recognize these artifacts as, in fact, toys has much to do with assumptions made about the absence of childhood during the time.

[7] In addition to Kieckhefer's *Magic in the Middle Ages*, see Lightsey, "Chaucer's Secular Marvels and the Medieval Economy of Wonder," *SAC* 23 (2001): 289–316, and *Man-made Marvels in Medieval Culture and Literature* (New York: Palgrave, 2007); William Eamon, "Technology as Magic in the Late Middle Ages and the Renaissance," *Janus* 70 (1983): 171–212.

magical sense of wonder in the world to a modern understanding of the world as accessible to calculation.[8] Medieval toys seem disqualified on two counts: not only are they items of play, but they date from the time before widespread technological reckoning.

To be sure, there is much to recommend the story of disenchantment, much that resonates with the trackings of culture over the *longue durée*. Yet Weber's work cannot help us to assess the productive impulse of this mass market in medieval toys. Criticism of Weber is not new: his earliest Marxist critics, including Christopher Hill and R. H. Tawney, pointed out the errors in his account of Protestantism; more recently Afshin Matin-Asgari, Wolfgang Schluchter, and others have critiqued Weber's statements about non-Western cultures as predicated on slim knowledge of Islam in its various historical settings.[9] In a survey of the field of Islamic Studies, Matin-Asgari points out the ambitious reach of these problems and calls for a rethinking of Weber's "deeply ethnocentric" fallacy: "defin[ing] societies, or historical eras, primarily in terms of their cultural 'ethos,' often articulated in religion," deserves to be rethought, especially since it is ultimately predicated upon a "rigid and stagnant [view of] 'non-Western' cultural and religious norms."[10] To make the obvious point: even when construed dialectically, Western "disenchantment" depends upon more fully enchanted (and religiously primitive) times and places (the Middle Ages; the "East"). Despite their differences, these cultures occupy the same place in Weber's thought; inherently premodern, they are characterized by a singular unwillingness to view the world in calculable terms.

With regard to the Middle Ages, however, consider the following from Isidore of Seville: "Take calculation from the world and all is enveloped in dark ignorance, nor can he who does not know the way to reckon be distinguished from the rest of the animals."[11] The philosophical debates of the twelfth century—the dialectics of scholasticism in

[8] See, for example, Max Weber, "Science as Vocation," in Weber, *From Max Weber: Essays in Sociology*, ed H. H. Gerth and C. Wright Mills (New York: Oxford University Press, 1981).

[9] Afshin Matin-Asgari, "Islamic Studies and the Spirit of Max Weber: A Critique of Cultural Essentialism," *Critique: Critical Middle Eastern Studies* 13, no. 3 (2004): 293–312. Toby E. Huff and Wolfgang Schluchter, eds., *Max Weber and Islam* (New Brunswick: Transaction Publishers, 1999).

[10] Ibid., 310.

[11] *The Etymologies of Isidore of Seville*, trans. Stephen A. Barney et al., with the collaboration of Muriel Hall (New York: Cambridge University Press, 2006).

the quarrel over universals, for instance—suggest a deep propensity for questioning and reckoning, if not for precisely the kind of calculation that Weber has in mind. Medieval thinkers were not as preoccupied as were later natural scientists with calculating the vital life force. The infinite God, and not a calculable life force, was for them the source of human vitality; this distinction inhabited Weber's writings on the nature of medieval enchantment. But medieval scholastics were equally interested in reckoning evidence from the world, even as their calculations directed them toward different conclusions.

Wonder and enchantment are not without their darker sides.[12] Witness the evidence of medieval toys described earlier: the toy as stereotypical Jewish head, the apparently gendered arrangements of domestic and military playthings, remind us that childhood, whatever its magical delights, also constitutes a training ground for later ideological beliefs. Yet childhood enchantments tend to be read more optimistically than their adult counterparts, regularly linked, in the affective register, to an absorption with matter and a delight in the natural world. Raymond Williams most famously made the point: his evocative description of the "feeling of childhood" associates it with the "feeling of the country" and with the very old days of England, each the time before the commodification of people and things.[13]

Kieckhefer's metaphor of medieval romance as a vast toy shop implicitly argues this case: the magical fancies that delighted adult audiences during the Middle Ages are ancestor to the modern playthings of childhood. Nor is he alone: such romances as *Guy of Warwick* were, of course, recast and popularly marketed as children's literature during the eighteenth century and beyond; the attitudes of a medieval "age of faith" are regularly said to converge upon the habits of magical thinking operative before the "age of reason," whether understood culturally or subjectively—that is, whether that age applies to the putatively more secular period known as the Enlightenment or to the age of a particular individual in the acquisition of seven years. To assume that medieval enchantment survives modernity via the delights of childhood casts

---

[12] Recent work on medieval romance has made this case forcefully. See my *Sovereign Fantasies: Arthurian Romance and the Making of Britain* (Philadelphia: University of Pennsylvania Press, 2001); see also Geraldine Heng, *Empire of Magic* (New York: Columbia University Press, 2006).

[13] Raymond Williams, *The Country and the City* (New York: Oxford University Press, 1973), 297–98.

Western history as a *Bildungsroman*, a narrative of maturation that implicitly renders medieval childhood an oxymoron. If modern childhood is defined by its preservation of an enchantment identified with the Middle Ages *tout court* (and is thus a feature of *adult* medieval subjectivity), how are we to make sense of the category of the medieval child? How, after all, would one distinguish the enchantments of childhood within a period marked in principle by an enchanted sensibility? That is, the long-standing association of the medieval period with enchantment may have helped produce the assumption that childhood was culturally impossible for it. A Middle Ages without childhood can of course usefully serve the developmental-historical view of the rise of scientific calculation, one that relocates the future of enchantment in the sensibilities of the modern child, a view that not incidentally seems to evacuate the complications of history and childhood both.

Recent reassessments of Weber's account of disenchantment trouble the standard reading of the opposition between enchantment and disenchantment in his work, stressing the importance of absorption and delight for a material (and ethical) engagement with the world. Jane Bennett and Alan Sica have each argued that modern experiences of enchantment are more crucial to Weber's story of disenchantment than has heretofore been recognized. Weber, they each argue, preserves enchantment in the nooks and crannies of disenchanted culture. Magical elements remain, in the words of Sica, "fragmented but still powerful."[14] As Bennett puts it, "Disenchantment does not mean that we live in a world that has been completely counted up and figured out but rather that the world has become calculable in principle. It is quite possible for one to experience aspects of nature that currently defy understanding and still affirm the principle of the scientific calculability of the world. In [Weber's] disenchanted world, the principle of calculability tends to overrule, even if it does not overpower, experience."[15] The development-

[14] Alan Sica, *Weber, Irrationality, and Social Order* (Berkeley and Los Angeles: University of California Press, 1988), 168.

[15] Jane Bennett, *The Enchantment of Modern Life* (Princeton: Princeton University Press, 2001), 59. Bennett stresses that, under the conditions of modernity, "the principle of calculability tends to *overrule*, even if it does not *overpower*, experience" (emphasis mine). While both verbs allude to dynamics of power, "rule" attends more specifically to strategies of sovereign, institutional, and bureaucratic ordering, to governmentality and regulation. "Power," while able to encompass all of the above, also alludes to the phenomenological, affective element of experience, the ways in which the human subject is moved, her attachments formed by way of interest, curiosity, absorption, and delight. This deployment of phenomenological approaches—important to the work of theorists

alist uses made of Weber have often played against these subtleties. For Bennett, such residual enchantment is crucial for the affective impulse of ethics; she links absorption with matter to a materialist care for the world, reminding us that such structures of feeling motivate our willingness to devote our limited mortal resources to the people and things of the world.

Medieval romance regularly engages enchanted sensibilities in an expansive array of the people and things of this world; recent work on medieval romance has similarly considered the ethical implications of such enchantments.[16] Chaucer's *Squire's Tale*, I will argue here, is essentially concerned with these same issues, and offers an especially fine site for considering Bennett's claim. Enchanting technological invention, the delights of magical drolleries, birthday gifts given to faraway Mongol emperor Genghis Khan (Cambyuskan), emerge as compelling in ways that allude to the ethical mode. By way of its references to a series of usable little items—magical and technological—this romance crosscuts disenchanted rationalism with the kind of enchanted absorption in the new and unusual, a wonder familiar to readers of romance but here considered in contradictory and complex terms. Depicting enchanted wonder in the new as both problem and opportunity—as productive for *both* traumatic pain and for a compassionate engagement with the world—the tale raises philosophical issues important to medieval metaphysics of creation. If, as Marshall Leicester has compellingly shown, Chaucer's poetry regularly places the disenchanted self on full display, *The Squire's Tale* reveals the poet's interest in the uses of fascination and delight for compassionate engagement with the world.[17]

---

like Deleuze and Guattari—offers a way to rethink the condescension with which enchanted sensibilities have long been viewed. In her retheorization of an "enchanted materialism," Bennett, for example, points to the importance of attachment for ethics, a point that resonates with other recent efforts at rethinking ethics in psychic and phenomenological terms.

[16] If readers of medieval romance found plenty of ways to be enchanted, medievalists have as often been wary of the enchanting aspects of medieval texts. Critics tend either to critique the enchantments of romance as religious mystification or colonizing fantasy, or to emphasize the disenchanting strategies of medieval texts.

[17] In a deservedly influential reading of Geoffrey Chaucer's poetry, Marshall Leicester deploys a nuanced version of Weber's notion—one directed at social rather than technical registers—to argue convincingly for that poet's disenchanted account of the agency of the subject in the fourteenth century. Leicester cites Chaucer's corpus as historical evidence of disenchanted sensibilities, arguing that it clearly depicts the fourteenth century as an era "in which not only the structures of the Church . . . , but gender roles, and estates (such as wives and knighthood, and, more generally, subjectivity itself) [were] deeply affected by a pervasive disenchanted scrutiny." He thus casts Chaucer as a "disenchanted agent," the pilgrims from his *Canterbury Tales*, the "sufferers and agents

The Squire's Tale aims at both. Twinning enchanted desire with technical curiosity, Chaucer's tale highlights both the productive power of the newfangled and the ways that even destabilizing experiences of novelty might ultimately lead us back to where we started. "Newefangelnesse" is, for one thing, an attribute that the poet explicitly associates not with technologies of flying machines—technologies, thanks to Leonardo's Sketch Book, long linked to Renaissance innovation—but with the incontrovertibly medieval sensibilities of (so-called) courtly love. Whereas the tale's *Prima Pars* details the court's delight in and debate over the fascinations of an innovative gadget, the *Pars Secunda* tells what seems only tangentially related, the story of a brokenhearted falcon, abandoned by her beloved tercelet for the newfangled attractions of a common kite.[18]

Why, after all, does Chaucer link failed love with innovative technology? And why is the former, rather than the latter, associated with a love for the new? Taken together, these two narratives delimit the problematics of an enchantment with novelty here: newfangled things fascinate and motivate, as the mechanical horse does for Cambyuskan's court; yet that very fascination, as the brokenhearted falcon testifies, limns the repetitive pains of desire. On the one hand, as we shall see, *The Squire's Tale* makes legible the psychoanalytic insight: the new may herald—in disguise—the return of something very old. On the other hand, drolleries like the flying horse startle and stun the senses, presenting viewers with unassimilable experience of a radical kind.

Such a collocation might contribute to recent accounts of the revolutionary potential of the novel event precisely as an experience of radical rupture, a point influentially argued by philosopher Alain Badiou. Badiou's account is indebted to Jacques Lacan's rereading of sublimation, particularly Lacan's theorizations of the significance of creation *ex nihilo*. And Lacan's account of creative production, detouring as it does through scholastic philosophy and troubadour poetry, offers an analyti-

---

of a culture whose cover is blown." Leicester, *The Disenchanted Self: Representing the Subject in the Canterbury Tales* (Berkeley and Los Angeles: University of California Press, 1990), 28.

[18] All references to Chaucer's poem are taken from Larry D. Benson, gen. ed., *The Riverside Chaucer*, 3rd ed. (Boston: Houghton Mifflin, 1987). Of course, as we will see, the first narrative is instrumental with regard to the second. The second is made possible by the magical technologies described in the first: Cambyuskan's daughter Canacee can, with the magic ring and mirror, now understand the tale of unhappy love that the wounded falcon tells her.

cal purchase on the vicissitudes of medieval notions of creativity, one with implications for a fuller understanding of both the problems and possibilities inhabiting our attachments to new things. Before turning to Chaucer's tale, then, we need to assess an insight from contemporary theory about which medieval culture seems well aware: that even as it is filled with utopian promise, novelty can also refigure the compulsions of the death drive, serving as a screen for impossible desires.

Novelties *ex nihilo*

Recent interest in the cultural function of novelty seems to come from an understandable longing for change. Influential theorizations of cultural change range from social science and systems theory—such as Malcolm Gladwell's *New York Times* bestseller *The Tipping Point*[19]—to philosophy, as in Alain Badiou's "new universalism."[20] Gladwell, interested in isolating the factors that make an innovation "stick," frames his central question in part by way of epidemiology: What constitutes the "tipping point," when small improvements lead to massive cultural change? Gladwell wants to offer a how-to guide for cultural change, and his examples are quotidian—smoking, the sudden hipster popularity of the heretofore terminally uncool Hush Puppies, the relation of graffiti to New York City crime statistics, or the transformative splash made by children's television programs. Badiou, less concerned with the historical or sociological aftermath of innovation than he is with the revolutionary force of what he calls the Event, emphasizes the disorienting power of novelty as a radical experience of discontinuity, one capable of producing a new Universalism. The event functions formally for Badiou, a singular, shattering occurrence emblematized by the narrative of Paul on the road

[19] *The Tipping Point: How Little Things Can Make a Big Difference* (Boston: Little, Brown, 2000). Also relevant here is Joel Mokyr's distinction between "micro" and "macro" innovations; *The Lever of Riches: Technological Creativity and Economic Progress* (New York: Oxford University Press, 1992). Mokyr's learned and ambitious account of technological change has much to recommend it, particularly his willingness to construe the oscillating movement of progress through a variety of periods. His notion of progress, however, rests upon neoliberal economic assumptions about the benefit and nature of economic growth that can only be assessed in relation to colonialist expansion. His understanding of the emergence of the Western Europe over Asian and Islamic cultures does not explicitly engage the role that Western expansionism played, particularly in the case of Islam.

[20] Alain Badiou, *Saint Paul: The Foundation of Universalism*, trans. Ray Brassier (Stanford: Stanford University Press, 2003). See particularly Badiou's comments on Paul's role as "inventor" (5–6), and on the "event" (16–30).

to Damascus—where the former Pharisee becomes a new man, rendering Christianity as the new law capable of dissolving the former identities and loyalties, of slave or free, Greek or Jew, woman or man. To be sure, the status of the new in Pauline Christianity, as Badiou acknowledges, is paradoxical, regularly serving not (only) hopes for a new and better universal, but also founding Christian supersessionism, as in Paul's notion that the new and living law of Christ supersedes the old, apparently dead law of Moses and the Prophets. Certainly Badiou makes legible the revolutionary potential of the (singular) event as a destabilizing formalization capable of demanding that we abandon old forms and old pieties.

Yet from a psychoanalytic point of view, Badiou's example of Paul's new law emerges as—even formally—a bit more complicated than he lets on: Paul's account of radical innovation embeds a *renewal* of Jewish law as much as it constitutes a shattering experience of something not yet seen or imagined. As a number of critics of Badiou have pointed out, the radical rupture of a universal Christianity is twinned, in Paul, with residual features of Jewish community and identity. This is a problem for Badiou's philosophy to the extent that he underemphasizes his Lacanian debts: insofar as novelty is understood as *absolute* rupture, as utterly different from (even diametrically opposed to) historical repetition, it is, from a Lacanian perspective, misrecognized as such. This is because experiences of the radically new can trick us, constituting the disguised (or repressed) return to something very old. As Aranye Fradenburg puts it, "The Real's return always generates the effect of the stunningly new."[21]

To be sure, the formal features of Badiou's "new universalism" are fundamentally philosophical rather than psychoanalytic (and indeed, he argues that it is philosophy, not psychoanalysis, that can best account for it); his account of rupture is nonetheless indebted to Lacan's understanding of the absence at the heart of creation *ex nihilo*. Yet where Badiou emphasizes the singularity (or oneness) of the event, Lacan's rereading of the tradition of creation *ex nihilo* emphasizes this *nihil*—that very nothing important to medieval accounts of divine creative power—as the *sine qua non* of sublimation itself. And in a move anticipated by Chaucer's *Squire's Tale*, Lacan considers creation *ex nihilo* alongside the repetitious patternings of what has come to be called the discourse of courtly love.

---

[21] "Simply Marvelous," *SAC* 26 (2004): 1–26 (16).

In his much-discussed lecture, "Courtly Love as Anamorphosis," Lacan argues that the discourse of courtly love historically appeared as if *ex nihilo*. This statement highlights Lacan's paradoxical notion of the subject (and subjectivization) as, at once, historical and universal. For Lacan, courtly love occupies a doubled and paradoxical history: it is an innovative social consensus (as Fradenburg puts it, "a breakaway moment in the history of the signifier") that emblematizes a recurring, "universal" structure of subjectivity.[22] By highlighting courtly love as emerging *ex nihilo,* Lacan alludes to the belief that creation *ex nihilo* accrues solely to the Divine, with human making constituting a secondary rearrangement of things already made. God—preeminent creator, artisan, maker—produces out of nothing; human making, in contrast, can only rearrange, recompose, rework those things already in the world, just as Adam and Eve, themselves divinely created from nothing but dust, fashioned coverings from fig leaves found in Eden, the perfect garden already made by God. Their modesty, while certainly "new" in postlapsarian Eden, constitutes not an innovative push forward, but that "fall" backwards from which humankind has never recovered, the exemplary definition of human degeneration. The Franciscan theologian Bonaventure (1221–1275) offers an emblematic version of the limitations posed to humanity's claim to the new: "The soul is able to make new compositions [of what it receives from the external world], but not new things."[23] Hugh of St. Victor (1096–1141) makes a similar point, one that Bonaventure will develop further, delineating a hierarchy of creative agents: God (who operates *ex nihilo*), nature (operating *ens in potentia*), and human artists (who produce *ens completum*), following after nature. Human artifice is, in this view, a means of forming things "mechanical, that is adulterate," as Hugh puts it.[24] In contrast to the mechanical, adulterated, inferior composite creations made by human artisans, there is of course God's perfect, original, and originating cre-

---

[22] *Sacrifice Your Love: Psychoanalysis, Historicism, Chaucer* (Minneapolis: University of Minnesota Press, 2002), 15. On the "newness" of courtly love and its relation to historical rupture, see 18–19.

[23] "Anima enim facit novas compositiones, licet non faciat novas res; et secundum quod fingit interius, sic etiam depingit et sculpit exterius" (III S. 37. Dub 1), quoted in E. J. M. Spargo, *The Category of the Aesthetic in St. Bonaventure* (New York: Franciscan Institute, 1953), 111. Michael Camille glosses Bonaventure as follows, "[Bonaventure] lists chimeras and other fanciful creations of composite art as emblems not of creativity but of mere synthesis." *The Gothic Idol: Ideology and Image-Making in Medieval Art* (Cambridge: Cambridge University Press, 1989), 40.

[24] *Didascalion* I, chap. 9, as cited by Camille, *The Gothic Idol,* 35.

ation.[25] For Aquinas, the astonishing newness of creation exists despite the eternity of universals as essences of things; it remains linked to divine will, to a power outside human time, and thus is knowable only through revelation.[26] Accordingly, human creative capacity has limited, derivative access to newness. As for Bonaventure, the newness produced by human making constitutes mere repetition, a synthesis or reworking of things already created. Human innovation is thus imitative, not originary, a humbler, second-order power able to rearrange preexisting creation in new ways, but unable really to *invent* new things.

Lacan remains interested in the paradox at the heart of this Thomistic argument: for him, as for Aquinas, newness exists despite the existence of universals, God (for Aquinas) and the Real (for Lacan). [27] Medieval orthodoxies of creation will prove important throughout Lacan's Seminar VII, particularly in the lecture "On Creation ex nihilo," where "knowledge of the creature and of the creator" will be central to his thinking.[28] And here he turns forcefully to a metaphor of creativity long important to Judeo-Christian tradition, the metaphor of the potter: "According to a fable handed down through the chain of generations, and that nothing prevents us from using, we are going to refer to what is the most primitive of artistic activities, that of the potter."[29] This example alludes to the biblical traditions from the books of Jeremiah and Isaiah, whereby the relation of potter to the clay he molds figures

---

[25] The implications of this tradition for rhetorical *inventio* will be clearer in my reading of the tale below.

[26] Aquinas writes: "The newness of the world cannot be demonstrated on the part of the world itself. For the principle of demonstration is the essence of a thing. Now everything according to its species is abstracted from "here" and "now"; whence it is said that universals are everywhere and always. Hence it cannot be demonstrated that man, or heaven, or a stone were not always. . . . But the divine will can be manifested by revelation, on which faith rests. Hence that the world began to exist is an object of faith, but not of demonstration or science." *Summa Theologiae, Vol. 1: Christian Theology,* trans. Thomas Gilby (Cambridge: Blackfriars; New York: McGraw-Hill, 1964), 1.46.2.

[27] Erin Labbie reads Lacan's work precisely as tracking the complex dynamic of the "universal" with the "particular" by way of the structuring principle of the Real, a universal mode capable of crossing and accommodating various particular changes and shifts in signification over time. Her cogent account makes clear the myriad ways in which Lacan's theorization of an apparently "universal" subject takes considerable inspiration from the "quarrel of the universals" of the scholastics, and is thus particularly indebted to Thomistic and Boethian philosophical traditions, traditions that, Labbie argues, Lacan "turns on their head." See her *Lacan's Medievalism* (University of Minnesota Press, 2006), "Introduction," 1–34 (18).

[28] *The Ethics of Psychoanalysis, 1959–1960: The Seminar of Jacques Lacan, Book VII,* ed. Jacques-Alain Miller, trans. Dennis Porter (New York: W. W. Norton, 1992), 115–27.

[29] Ibid., 119.

the relation of God to Israel, of Creator to creature: "Can I not deal with you, Israel, says the Lord, as this potter deals with his clay? You are clay in my hands, like the clay in his, O house of Israel."[30] Here, then, is a dominant metaphor for the creation: the divine artisan molds dead matter into living creature. He is the potter; we are the clay, the work of his hands.

Reference to the potter simultaneously raises human creative acts and the orthodox view of human creatureliness, of God's preeminent position as creator; it also for Lacan gestures to the emptiness at the heart of the Real, a place occupied by the Lady in the courtly love relation. But, as an artifact that physically encircles an empty space, the vase can also make it clear that Lacan's "nothing" has a *positive* valence; it alludes to a structural emptiness—such as that around which the human potter forms the vase. "Nothing" is thus not simply nothing, and recalls the *nihil* identified with God's creative extravagance. "Nothing" is also, however, simply nothing, gesturing toward the material impossibility at the heart of this belief (that matter, in other words, can neither be created nor destroyed).[31]

This view of creation plays into Lacan's understanding of sublimation, of the place of the Thing (Freud's *das Ding*) in his reading of courtly love. In "Courtly Love as Anamorphosis," as Fradenburg and Nancy Frelik have each made clear, Lacan plays with the echoes between sublimation and sublime, arguing that processes of sublimation impinge upon the structures of social and cultural elevation and value alluded to, in, and through the category of the Sublime, particularly in its godlike capacity as the unrepresentable, the ineffable, the impossible.[32] Courtly

[30] Jeremiah 18:6. In Isaiah, the link to God's preeminence as the source of all created matter is more explicitly at issue (see, for instance, Isaiah 45:8–11), a point also, if more obliquely, taken up elsewhere in the wisdom literature. The image of God as artisan, as potter, will be important to Christian theology in the post-Reformation period as well. Citations are taken from *The New English Bible* (New York: Oxford University Press, 1961).

[31] "Nothing" can neither be created nor destroyed—nothing is there for God to work with in the first place; and in Lacanian terms, it remains at the heart of the symbolic order. Nothing is, thus, the formal heart of all creativity—resonating with Badiou's impulse to turn to form—although for Badiou the crucial integer is 1, not 0.

[32] Fradenburg, *Sacrifice Your Love*, 18–20. Nancy Frelick writes, "For Lacan, the creation of courtly love is analogous to the appearance of the image in anamorphotic art. He makes use of this analogy in order to evoke, in a dramatic way, the almost magical appearance of an image, as if from nowhere, as if from the Real. He also stresses the self-conscious play of illusion in anamorphotic art which highlights the primacy of the signifier in a manner analogous to the play on conventions and artifice in Courtly love." "Lacan, Courtly Love, and Anamorphosis," in *The Court Reconvenes: Courtly Literature*

love elaborates a cultural value that signifies desire beyond its own limits or productions; desire, always pursuing the impossibility of its own permanent satisfaction (the desiring subject prostrate before the Thing as cruel and inhuman partner who coldly refuses to be won), and thus always alluding to something more, something beyond, something impossible of representation or achievement. There is, at the heart of this transaction, a little bit of nothing; the impossible (and/or prohibited) love object occupies the space of the Thing, a void, a vacuole, an absence (mis)recognized as cold, inhuman refusal. The signifier comes then to the rescue, headed for the Thing but detouring around the void, preserving the empty space of the Thing sublimed.[33] Creative production comes out of, even as it circles, this nothing at the heart of the Thing. Lacan's account of creation *ex nihilo* suggests, then, that new creative productions require a space of nothing they circle and preserve. It suggests, moreover, that certain little nothings like the vase, or the lyrics of courtly love, or a mechanical horse, can function as representative of the "existence of the emptiness at the center of the real that is called the Thing."[34]

The Squire's Tale links such drolleries to impossible loves so as to suggest the *proximity*, rather than the absolute difference, between nothing and something, rupture and return, novelty and repetition. While productive of startling experiences, the little nothings of Chaucer's exotic romance, as critics have made clear, would have been quite well known to a medieval audience, familiar, precisely, as fascinating novelties. *The Squire's Tale* offers, that is to say, a typically ambivalent medieval account of newness and newfangledness, one that nonetheless suggests the culture's considerable enchantment with innovation. Part 1 of the tale depicts courtly fascination with a series of fabulous birthday gifts given to Cambyuskan and to his daughter Canacee. A mechanical horse of brass that can, with the turn of a pin, transport its rider beyond the bounds of the natural world is the most prominent, and Chaucer's Squire castigates the "lewedness" of Cambyuskan's courtiers, who are

---

Across the Disciplines, ed. Barbara K. Altmann and Carleton W. Carroll (Rochester, N.Y.: D. S. Brewer, 2003), 107–14 (111).

[33] Medieval traditions of love, Lacan argues, make it clear that the Thing, which cannot be approached directly, is fundamentally veiled; we can only draw near by way of detour, encircling, or bypass. A means of approaching the love object yet never attaining her, courtly love makes "the domain of the vacuole stand out," "at the center of the signifiers" of its discourse. Lacan, "Courtly Love as Anamorphosis" (152, 150).

[34] In Bill Brown's gloss. "Thing Theory," *Critical Inquiry* 28 (2001): 1–22 (2).

unable to explain how the gadget works and ascribe it instead to the stuff of legend. Critics have regularly read this aspect of Chaucer's text as a critique of the naïveté of enchanted sensibilities. Scott Lightsey finds here a disenchanted version of an earlier romance admiration for *mirabilia*.[35] Yet such readings cannot account for the tale's own considerable absorption with newness and fresh-feeling: as John Fyler points out, taken together, the birthday gifts (which include a magical ring, a mirror, and a sword, as well as the mechanical horse) offer cosmological renewal, "a means of reintegration, of recapturing a lost world of freshness, transparency, and clarity."[36] Linking the tale even more directly with innovation, Alan Ambrisco emphasizes Chaucer's investment in the new immediacy of the English language, as a fantasy, he argues, of "flawless" communication.[37]

As this critical tradition makes clear, the tale offers contradictory evidence on the status and meaning of the new. None of these accounts entirely explains that status, particularly given the fact that the poet explicitly associates "newefangelnesse" neither with romance *mirabilia* nor with language, but, in Part 2 of the tale, with a traumatic experience of love. In Part 2, a brokenhearted peregrine falcon abandoned by her beloved tercelet explicitly deplores newness, lamenting a love of "novelries."

Canacee's Novelties

Juxtaposed with the intriguing novelties given both to Cambyuskan and to Canacee is the starker, darker story of the self-mutilating peregrine. Thanks to the gift of a magical ring, Canacee can cross the linguistic gulf between humans and birds, gaining access to the bird's sad tale. This is certainly a new, and stunning, linguistic medium. Canacee's excited interest in her gifts—"swich a joye she in hir herte took / Bothe of

[35] Lightsey, "Chaucer's Secular Marvels." Morton Bloomfield identifies *The Squire's Tale*'s ingenuity not with things medieval but with the "new spirit of the Renaissance." "Chaucer's *Squire's Tale* and the Renaissance" *Poetica* 12 (1979): 28–35 (28). Many critics have remarked on the attractions of the tale's own ingenuity, linked to a range of discourses about its marvels: a composite romance with influences traceable to French, Arabian, and classical Greek sources and analogues.

[36] John Fyler, "Domesticating the Exotic in the *Squire's Tale*," *ELH* 55 (1988): 1–26. "But the sword, capable of both healing mayhem and wreaking it, epitomizes the problematic quality of the others as innocent gifts in a world of experience" (3).

[37] Alan S. Ambrisco, "'It lyth nat in my tonge': Occupatio and Otherness in the *Squire's Tale*," *ChauR* 38 (2004): 205–28.

hir queynte ryng and hire mirour, / That twenty tyme she changed hir colour" (V.368–70)—awakes her early, leading her to the garden ramble during which she encounters the peregrine in the first place. Yet this gadget enables a very old story of infidelity and pain: the lovesick, self-mutilating falcon has been abandoned by her tercelet, who, too easily seduced by newfangledness, turned to the love of a scavenger kite. From the point of view of the peregrine, desire for the new comes bearing the marks of the death drive.

Such pain is literalized in the bird's body. As the falcon tells her tale, she has "Ybeten . . . hirself so pitously" that "the rede blood / Ran endelong the tree ther-as she stood" (V.414–16). The scene is dramatic, with the wetness of the peregrine's red blood running down along the branches and bark of the dry, white tree in which she sits (V.409). The peregrine opines that men and birds unhappily share a powerful attraction to novelties, superficial things that distract them from loves of real value.

> Men loven of propre kynde newefangelnesse,
> As briddes doon that men in cages fede.
> For though thou nyght and day take of hem hede,
> And strawe hir cage faire and softe as silk,
> And yeve hem sugre, hony, breed and milk,
> Yet right anon as that his dore is uppe
> He with his feet wol spurne adoun his cuppe,
> And to the wode he wole and wormes ete;
> So newefangel been they of hire mete,
> And loven novelries of propre kynde,
> No gentillesse of blood ne may hem bynde.
>
> (V.610–20)

The peregrine laments an indiscriminate love of the new: men "loven novelries of proper kynde." The formulation, twice repeated, marks novelties "of propre kynde," literally of a characteristic nature; and the syntax could be read to suggest both that it is the special, and deplorable, characteristic of men to "loven novelries" (an attribute of humankind frequently noted in both medieval and early modern literature), and that newfangled things are loved for the characteristic of newness they bear. In its context here, the familiar image registers pain and discontent in ways that converge on social class: just as birds like the tercelet spurn their rare cup, slumming after the ignobility of common worms, so is she, noble raptor, thrown over for a common kite.[38] Rather than signify value, "newefangelnesse" emerges as the stuff of smoke and mirrors, empty attraction to newness for its own sake.

Chaucer has used this image of the captive bird before, and to somewhat different ends. In Book 3, metrum 2 of his *Boece*, a caged songbird (not, notably, a "noble" tercelet) similarly despoils food with dirty feet, yearning to return to the freedom of the woods. In that context, the bird's desire serves as an example of the natural order, the fact that all things in this world (like lions, like saplings, and like birds) adhere to their natural place, their "propre kynde."[39] Importing this image into *The Squire's Tale*, Chaucer changes the gender of the captive bird (a she, in *Boece*, twittering "with swete voys"); he also shifts the emphasis from the caged bird's desire for freedom (she "seith the / agreables schadwes of the wodes, sche defouleth / with hir feet hir metes ischad, and seketh / mornynge oonly the wode" [3, m. 2, lines 27–30]) to the male bird's appetite for worms. By changing the caged bird's gender, Chaucer emblematizes the love of the new as, on the one hand, a particularly masculine propensity; the "men" of line 610 now seems gender specific. Yet the representation of desire shifts, too: desire for a life in the natural woods, a desire for life beyond the constraining limits of the cage, is recast as a desire to possess whatever object is lacking, whether or not the object in question is worthy. The notion that woodland songbirds naturally long for freedom translates into the propensity of men to yearn after unavailable things. Chaucer recasts yearning for a specific kind of liberation into a more complex account of desire, one in which the contextual and relational features prove determining: it is the unavailability of objects, rather than their inherent worth, that renders them desirable. By associating this form of desire with men's love of newfangledness, Chaucer underscores both the contextual and the ambivalent features of his account of novelty.[40]

[38] Among the discontents of culture registered here may be the limiting boundaries of class that the Falcon perhaps inadvertently recommends. According to the logic of courtly love, of course, the falcon should be sublimed, set apart and irreplaceable; she is shown to be one elevated object in a set of signifiers exchanged and commodified.

[39] I am grateful to Frank Grady for drawing my attention to the similarities between these passages.

[40] There is still more to be said about this odd passage, particularly about the special emphasis here on the caged bird's desire for "worms." Worms are hardly newfangled from a songbird's perspective; here again, they emerge as new because they have been so long deferred. The old becomes the new under certain circumstances—and repetition prevails, functionally as well as rhetorically (this is, after all, a reused image).

As in her own self-mutilating acts, moreover, the peregrine's remarks display the sacrificial impulse embedded in the entire structure: just as she forfeits safety and bodily ease for the self-abuse she heaps upon her now bloody breast, so do the men and birds who "loven novelries," give up elevated circumstance—sumptuous silks, cups filled with milk and honey—rejecting the elegant cage and cup in favor of dirt and worms. Another possible irony here: raptors like the tercelet are birds of prey; unlike the caged songbirds of the metaphor, they do not "of propre kynde" desire worms at all. Associating the love of newfangledness with a desire to eat worms, the peregrine both registers her contempt for the tercelet's bad taste and undermines the usual association of the new with glittery attraction: rather than a fondness for frivolity, the love of novelty can debase, motivating not the acquisition of luxury but its sacrifice. This means that if the peregrine, by extension, deplores the tercelet's choice, she also and at the same time makes it clear that the pull of the newfangled is powerful enough to lure one to sacrifice easy pleasure for it.

Here, then, we see that desire for the new can prompt the sacrifice of pleasure in favor of what Slavoj Žižek calls enjoyment (or pleasure in unpleasure). With regard to sacrifice as a form of desire, Fradenburg points out that sacrificial discipline (whether of the peregrine or her erstwhile lover) "enhances *jouissance*; it multiplies and extends its possibilities."[41] In refusing elevated objects, the tercelet extends desire in all its forms, eventuating in the peregrine's story and Canacee's creative response to it. The desire of the peregrine, still directed toward her tercelet but now barred from its fulfillment, erupts in self-mutilation and in poetry both, and she tells her moving story in lovely lines of verse. The tercelet's flirtation with the new keeps the peregrine's satisfaction deferred, her desire engaged even more now on its newly impossible object. As absent love object, quite literally a "cruel" as well as an "inhuman partner," the tercelet constitutes the space, the hole around which the peregrine's story detours. His flirtation with novelty produces the *nihil* out of which she creates.[42] This suggests that a desire for nov-

---

[41] This is not how we are accustomed to thinking about it: "The intimacy between desire and the law is not one we readily acknowledge. We are so accustomed to pitting morality against desire that it is simply hard to believe that morality is a form of desire, or desire is what morality is." *Sacrifice Your Love*, 7.

[42] The gendered roles are reversed here to some degree: for Lacan, the "nothing" sublimed in courtly love, the "hole," is sexual as well: indeed, much of Lacan's interest in courtly love has to do with the erotics of the structure. The constraints of space prohibit a more detailed consideration of this point.

elty prompts sacrifice precisely because sacrifice multiplies and extends possibility: the tercelet's desire for the new reverberates outward, generating all kinds of creative productions.

The absent tercelet, that is, constitutes the emptiness around which the peregrine's story detours, and it produces both the falcon's self-mutilation as well as her poetic refrain. By adopting a central narrative of loss in love, the tale's second part keeps us mindful not only of the complex simultaneity of novelty with painful repetition, but of the ways this contradictory structure makes legible, to borrow Sarah Kay's formulation, "the emergence of the literary object."[43] Indeed the peregrine's poetic peregrinations invoke a long tradition: faithless lovers fawn after new loves, leaving their former partners with nothing; this is, of course, old news, as those references make clear. These are also stories that Chaucer has himself told before, repeatedly: in *The Legend of Good Women*, we hear of Jason's desertion of Medea (see *LGW* 1580–1679) and in *Troilus and Criseyde*, briefly, of Paris's desertion of Oenone for Helen (I.652–56), but more forcefully, of course, of Troilus's love for the ultimately faithless Criseyde. If, as Alan Ambrisco argues, *The Squire's Tale* is Chaucer's reflection on the linguistic innovations of English, at moments like these the tale remains interested in the ways in which even "new" languages fall back on older forms, nearly automatic in their force; innovative poets—like the peregrine, like Chaucer—still and nonetheless traffic in well-worn phrases, returning us to familiar and arresting images, or predictable plots.

Old and new, repetition and rupture, remain twinned throughout. It is not at all coincidental that as we carry on in Part 2, the (old, repetitive) problems engendered by love remain entirely productive for newfangled things. Even the peregrine who disdains novelties requires new salves to heal her wounds.

> But Canacee hom bereth hire in hir lappe,
> And softely in plastres gan hire wrappe,
> Ther as she with hire beek hadde hurt hirselve.
> Now kan nat Canacee but herbes delve
> Out of the ground, and make salves newe
> Of herbes preciouse and fyne of hewe
> To heelen with this hauk . . .
>
> (V.635–41)

[43] *Courtly Contradictions: The Emergence of the Literary Object in the Twelfth Century* (Stanford: Stanford University Press, 2001).

For all its sacrifice of luxury, the new here also registers as ingenuity capable of refashioning common things to healing ends. Base matter— roots dug out of the same dirt that carries the common worm—offers up elevated treasures: precious herbs, beautifully fine. (This is of course a conventionally Bonaventuran example of human artifice.) Desire now multiplies and extends toward Canacee, whose healing ministrations absorb her completely ("Fro day to nyght / she dooth hire bisynesse and al hire myght" [641–42]). Even sumptuousness returns in an elegant "mewe" that Canacee fashions as a sanatorium, adorned with blue velvet and painted ornamentation, the mark of a generosity designed to heal, protect, and console her newfound friend. And if the peregrine's pain is produced by the other's captivation by novelty (the tercelet's faithlessness), the other's captivation with new things (Canacee's enthusiasms with magic) also structures the very possibility that her lamentable story will get either a hearing or a reparative response. Insofar as magic makes possible a heretofore impossible intercourse, insofar as Canacee's excitement over her newfound little nothings impels her walk, readying her ear for "every thyng / That any fowel may in his leden seyn" (V.434–35) that she will newly hear, the tale links the new to a creative ability to extend oneself for another, to what Elaine Scarry calls the world-creating capacity of the imagination, here specifically in the care for the suffering and injured. Here we see, that is, a hint of the utopian hope that surrounds all new technologies of communication. Human ears and lips, touched as if by magic, are rendered more fully capable of hearing and responding to the sufferings of others, however "fremde," strange they may be. Canacee can respond to the peregrine's piteous cry because her senses are newly transfigured; she knows what remedy to supply because her acquaintance with the natural world has been expanded and enlivened.

Of course, from one view, the tercelet's hope in newfangledness is utopian, too, particularly insofar as the newfangled serves as a screen for those desires, like utopia, impossible to fulfill. This is to say that this triangulation brings Canacee together with the tercelet through and across the body of the peregrine, thus revealing the deeply, even madly, ambivalent nature of Chaucer's cultural relation to newness here: the absorption that motivates the smiling face of empathy is the other side of novelty's lascivious grin. While these complications are less obviously at stake in the tale's *Prima Pars*, there too we see the way desire and compulsion—rupture and repetition—might be twinned. If in Part 2 the living creature threatens death and deadliness, in Part 1 dead metal takes on the appearance of the living thing.

The Ambition of Gadgets

Chaucer's *Squire's Tale* describes a number of enchanting objects. But it is the advent of the flying horse of brass that garners the most attention, constituting something of a breakaway moment in the history of Cambyuskan's court:

> For it so heigh was, and so brood and long,
> So wel proporcioned for to been strong,
> Right as it were a steede of Lumbardye;
> Therwith so horsly, and so quyk of ye,
> As it a gentil Poilleys courser were.
> For certes, fro his tayl unto his ere
> *Nature ne art ne koude him nat amende*
> *In no degree, as al the people wende.*
> But everemoore hir mooste wonder was
> How that it koude gon, and was of bras . . .
> (V.191–200; my emphasis)

Combining liveliness with mechanization, the horse apes nature ("so horsly . . . As it a gentil Poilleys courser were") even as it breaks natural bonds ("how that it koude gon, and was of bras"). Chaucer's neologism, "horsly," charmingly encodes the novel effect of the artifact come to life: the toy, as horsey as ever nature made, communicates a quickness of intelligence even while it stands mute before the court's gaze. As an artifact whose form cannot be amended either by nature or by artisanal skill, the horse outstrips medieval categories of production available for humanity: repudiating the possibility of amending the object by way either of Nature or Art, the Squire excludes the two second-order creative powers that, according to medieval scholastics, follow after God's creative force. For all its mechanization, the gadget alludes to a power of creation beyond human or nature. An extravagant gift from places unseen, this little nothing appears as if *ex nihilo*.

In describing the mechanical gadget as "quyk of ye," Chaucer emphasizes the doubleness of the object's "social life":[44] on the one hand, the descriptor refers to the court's visual consumption of the horse—its liveliness seems to them lifelike; on the other—as a phrase regularly used to signify vigor and vitality—it raises an impossible possibility: a metal horse with vibrant "health." Or better, the horse's liveliness is analogical for a mechanized type of sentience: a subject in the invisible thrall of the death drive. From the point of view of Lacanian theory, this combination of living vitality and empty metal offers an example of what Rosalind Krauss calls the "optical unconscious," automaton as screen object, both concealing and revealing the subjectivization of the subject before the power of invisible forces, like the real or the unconscious. In his own discussions of automata, Lacan refers to Aristotle, where the term is normally translated as "chance"; he pairs it with *tuché*, or fate, a term that Lacan elsewhere glosses as "the encounter with the real." The automaton emerges as a figure harboring a specter of the Real, the mechanized features of the living thing under the deadening sway of compulsion. Daniel Tiffany remarks, following Krauss, that such a toy serves as "a spectacular device that discloses, in the name of science, the immaterial foundation of the object—the invisibility of the real."[45] Life figured in dead metal.[46]

[44] Arjun Appaduri, ed., *The Social Life of Things: Commodities in Cultural Perspective* (Cambridge: Cambridge University Press, 1988). Sentient objects are of course crucial to the economies of signification structured by courtly love: the circulation of people as objects and signifiers. Fradenburg again: "Courtly love discourse enacts the economy of 'feudal' subsistence 'seen from the perspective of the Thing'—meaning, among other things, seen as a matter of life and death, as counting absolutely. As a corollary it performs in the theaters of exchange the loss of the artifact that is interdependent with its creation, true whether the artifact in question is an abstract instrument (the euro) or the recollected subject. Courtly love sublimes the very *relationship* between *jouissance* and the movements of the signifier that generate kinship systems, economies, and desiring subjects" (23).

[45] Daniel Tiffany, *Toy Medium: Materialism and the Modern Lyric* (Stanford: Stanford University Press, 2000), 82. See also Lacan, "Of the Network of Signifiers," "Tuché [fate] and Automaton," and "The Split between the Eye and the Gaze," *The Four Fundamental Concepts of Psychoanalysis: The Seminar of Jacques Lacan, Book XI*, ed. Jacques-Alain Miller, trans. Alan Sheridan (1977; New York: W. W. Norton, 1998). My thinking is indebted to Rosalind Krauss, *The Optical Unconscious* (Cambridge, Mass.: MIT Press, 1993), esp. 71–72.

[46] Lightsey writes: "Chaucer merges the awe inspired by the literary *mirabilia* of romance with curiosity about the mechanical marvels that were a part of late-medieval court life. The text not only confronts the reader with a romance marvel but depicts this supposedly supernatural motif as an object of rational inquiry. Chaucer often appears to invite readers to experience marvels as products of human artifice rather than as supernatural phenomena." "Chaucer's Secular Marvels," 316. In his book, *Manmade Marvels*,

Even as a novel event, then, the horse of brass alludes to mechaniza-tion. But it also—here again the ambivalence noted in Part 2 of the tale—offers the promise of freedom, an ability to break through the physical limits of the natural world:

> This steede of bras, that esily and weel
> Kan in the space of o day natureel—
> This is to seyn, in foure and twenty houres—
> Wher-so yow lyst, in droghte or elles shoures,
> Beren youre body into every place
> To which youre herte wilneth for to pace,
> Withouten wem of yow, thurgh foul or fair;
> Or, if yow lyst to fleen as hye in the air
> As dooth an egle whan hym list to soore,
> This same steede shal bere yow evere moore,
> Withouten harm, til ye be ther yow leste,
> Though that ye slepen on his bak or reste,
> And turne ayeyn with writhyng of a pyn.
>   (V.115–27)

This description, spoken by the visiting knight who brings the gift to court, simultaneously foregrounds safety and liminality: even a sleeping rider is safe, flying between earth and sky, on the brink of danger and excitement, breaking the bonds of time and space. The description cer-tainly alludes to the hyper-excitement (and transgressive power) of ex-perimentation, the fantasy of safely overcoming the impossible, breaking the physical limits of daily life and of the natural body.

The horse is, however, a "gyn" (a term with a wide semantic range during the period) and as such, as Lightsey points out, is of an ambigu-ous character. But "gyn" was a term with an even wider semantic range than Lightsey emphasizes; the *MED* notes various usages, from the Old French *gin*, or *engien*, linked to the Latin, *ingenium;* it is etymologically linked to the modern word *engine*. *Gyn* and *engyn* (and their French and Latin cognates) occur frequently in romance (*ingenium* is an important word to Geoffrey of Monmouth, particularly in relation to his own cre-ative production, and the ambiguities of its meaning in the *Historia*

Lightsey de-emphasizes this question of what we might call the tale's investment in "disenchantment" (74–80).

Regum Britannie have been usefully debated by critics).[47] The potential for deceit, the ambiguity of motive and purpose, inherent in the word could equally apply to feats of engineering and to linguistic creations, to mechanical contrivances and philosophical ingenuities. In this regard, in view of these links between artifact and art, we might recall that fables of "Virgil, the Necromancer"—stories of the magical, mechanical ingenuities that Virgil was purported to have made—flourished particularly in the late fourteenth century, and at the time of Chaucer's writing.[48] Poetic maker as magician as engineer. That is, if romance helped materially to produce gadgets (as Lightsey compelling shows), it might itself be figured as a gadget encoding the very same ambiguities of meaning and purpose, with its own fine array of gadgets, bells, and whistles.

The tale emphasizes the energetic efforts of this sophisticated court to sort through the meaning and workings of the impossible thing before them: "It was a fairye"; "They murmureden as dooth a swarm of been, / And maden skiles after hir fantasies" (V.201; 204–5). It is true, as many have argued, that Chaucer's Squire explicitly disdains the enthusiasms of Cambyuskan's courtiers; their debate and "jangle," he implies, shows a fuzzy-headed fascination with magic, leading many to read the tale as a demystification of wonder in favor of the rationality of science. Yet, as Lightsey suggests, following Mary Campbell's work, wonder and science are more closely related here than many readings of *The Squire's Tale* acknowledge.[49]

Furthermore, whatever the dramatic features of Chaucer's Squire's attitude, the description of the court's response emphasizes not the special stupidity of this particular group, but the commonness of such puzzlement before subtle things: "As lewed peple demeth comunly / Of thynges that been maad moore subtilly / Than they kan in hir lewednesse comprehende; / They demen gladly to the badder ende" (V.221–24). If we can read here the Squire's self-satisfied superiority, we can also read the courtiers' predicament in trying to recover from the fascination

[47] Martin Shichtman and Laurie Finke, "Profiting from the Past: History as Symbolic Capital in the *Historia Regum Britanniae*," *Arthurian Literature* 12 (1994): 1–35; Michelle Warren, *History on the Edge: Excalibur and the Borders of Britain, 1100–1300* (Minneapolis: University of Minnesota Press, 2000); Ingham, *Sovereign Fantasies*.

[48] On fables of Virgil the Necromancer, see John Spargo, *Virgil the Necromancer: Studies in Virgilian Legend* (Cambridge, Mass.: Harvard University Press, 1934).

[49] Mary Campbell, *Wonder and Science: Imagining Worlds in Early Modern Europe* (Ithaca: Cornell University Press, 1999).

produced by this radically anomalous event, in trying to make sense of the (as yet) nonsensical, or to assimilate the radically new. And if the courtiers are ignorant of the automaton's mechanics, they are certainly not unlearned: the text repeatedly emphasizes the array of authorities referred to in their debate from the widest range of the Liberal Arts: poetry (stories of Pegasus and of the Trojan horse), philosophy (Aristotle), and the science of optics (Alhazan and Witello, authorities on optics and on perspective), all authorities known in the West. Taken as a whole, the scene repeatedly draws attention not to the insufficiency of this particular audience of knowers but to an experience of epistemological poverty as such, of the difficulty (altogether common) of knowing what to make of something never before seen or experienced.

Criticism, too, has seemed to embrace this flying horse as imaginative enigma, despite evidence to the contrary. In a fascinating but largely overlooked essay, Marijane Osborn argues that the Squire's steed of brass is in fact an astrolabe, one equipped with a governing horse's head (operated by the turning of a pin) at its top.[50] Osborn persuasively links the Squire's description to similar descriptive moments in *A Treatise on the Astrolabe*, patiently explaining the precise workings of the mechanical contraption.[51] From the larger vantage of Chaucer's corpus, then, even this new thing is not so new after all; a literal repetition, the Squire's "steed of brass" is a well-wrought urn that Chaucer has wrought before. Even those novel items that stun and startle the senses remain entangled with earlier figures and forms. Furthermore, the fact that recent criticism on the tale, including analyses of its man-made marvels, continues to overlook the horse as astrolabe despite Osborn's reading suggests the critical afterlife of the very epistemological difficulty experienced by Cambyuskan's courtiers.

The problem of the court's "lewedness" alludes, then, not to the failings of a particularly unsubtle, or easily fascinated, audience before the

---

[50] Marijane Osborn, "The Squire's 'Steed of Brass' as Astrolabe: Some Implications for *The Canterbury Tales*," in *Hermeneutics and Medieval Culture,* ed. Patrick J. Gallacher and Helen Damico (Albany: State University of New York Press, 1989), 121–31.

[51] From *A Treatise on the Astrolabe* (*Riverside Chaucer*): "Thyn Astrolabe hat a ring to putten on the thombe of thy right hond in taking the height of thinges" (I, 1). "Than is there a large pyne in manere of an extre [axel tree], that goth thorugh the hole that half the tables of the clymates and the riet in the wombe of the moder; thorugh which pyn ther goth a litel wegge, which that is clepd the horse, that steynth allthese parties to-hepe" (I, 14). Further assessment of the implications of this connection must be deferred at present. I am grateful to Peter Travis for drawing my attention to Osborn's work.

transformative power of novelty—even if that is the Squire's own unsubtle conclusion—but to the arresting power of fascination (wonder is, after all, the way desire looks from the perspective of the death drive) and to the problem (both epistemological and ethical) of what to make of, and what to do with, new things. Confronted with the incredible, the courtiers bring all their best learning to bear on the problem; they cannot, however, solve it with the knowledge available to them. Certainly their energetic response—like Canacee's—shows a renewed engagement in the material details of the world before them. That said, their wonder has different effects from hers. While the horse begs for experimental testing, neither rational debate nor fascinated wonder changes the court's behavior. Despite precise instruction as to how one might ride it, the horse is taken instead to Cambyuskan's tower, stockpiled "among his jueles leeve and deere" (V.341), while this king who is earlier described as "hardy" and "wys" as well as "riche" (V.19), "Repeireth to his revel as biforn" (V.339). Despite the clearly disruptive nature of the event, nothing much changes at Cambyuskan's court.

In *The Squire's Tale*, then, novelty oscillates between old patterns and startling ruptures, alluding both to the frustrations of desire and to human ingenuity in the production of new things and new relations.[52] Chaucer's tale renders "newefangelnesse" as inherently paradoxical, a feature of creative production that simultaneously produces breakaway moments, even as it partakes of older, repetitive forms. We should note, moreover, that both Canacee's remarkable discovery of a talking bird and the court's equally remarkable experience of a flying mechanical horse suggest the possibility for a fundamental restructuring of perception and expectation that Badiou identifies with the event. That restructuring may well be *necessary* for a "new universalism," as Badiou argues, but by offering Cambyuskan's response to the flying horse as a counter-example, Chaucer's poem suggests that the event is not *sufficient* to pro-

---

[52] Here the structure of courtly love, in other words, sublimes the Thing (Das Ding) even as the new things produced seem themselves to promise relief, however temporary, from the deadliness of pain, loss, mutilation. Recent accounts of "thing theory" have parsed precisely this difference between the object and the Thing. Alluding both to Lacanian accounts of the Thing as well to particular objects that can front those moves, Bill Brown notes that the Thing "lies beyond the grid of intelligibility, outside the order of objects" as a "relief from ideas." "This is also why," he continues, "the Thing becomes the most compelling name for that enigma that can only be encircled and which the object (by its presence) necessarily negates." I would argue, in contrast, that some objects, like the automaton, place us ineluctably before it. Brown, "Thing Theory," 11–12.

duce change. As far as we can tell, Cambyuskan seeks neither knowledge nor action; he trades the stupefaction of the event for the stupefaction of drunkenness. Canacee and the peregrine, in contrast, engage their initial scene of fascination by crafting lines of poetry, thinking, planning, even digging in the dirt so as to craft new things used to compassionate ends. To be sure, the peregrine's future is left open: Will the magical bird in her sumptuous enclosure become one of *Canacee's* collectibles, on a par with Cambyuskan's tower filled with jewels and gadgets? The tale's incompletion offers no answer.

But in avoiding an answer, *The Squire's Tale* also implies that the event demands, to some degree, a willingness to entertain, rather than immediately to resolve, the double-face of newness. This is an ethical demand that authorizes pleasure in the wonder of the world even as it takes on the problem of what relations—whether compassionate or consumptive—such pleasure might itself authorize and produce. The technological know-how with which the tale is fascinated depends upon an attachment to a creative rationality from which enchanted desire can never entirely divorce itself.[53] In its elaboration of such an ambivalent view of novelty, romance operates as a kind of double-helix entwining old with new, an engine driven by and driving the desire to feel afresh, to begin again. This doubleness may well be why romance seems blind to its own well-documented (even luridly overdetermined) excesses. And it is here that we might reconsider the exoticism of the tale—its setting in "Tartarye," at the court of Genghis Khan and with that court's response to gifts from the King "of Arabe and of Inde." And so I turn, finally, to the view of enchantment and disenchantment as a means of reconsidering the history of relations between Europe and what was constructed, in the Middle Ages, as the East.

Conclusion: Exotic Calculations

Cambyuskan's court, like Asian courts generally, had a reputation for sophistication and cosmopolitanism, in marked contrast to England,

---

[53] Scholars have, moreover, linked Cambyuskan's horse rather directly to the matter of poetry. Reading of the classical sources to which Chaucer's poem alludes, Craig Berry describes the automaton as "an amazing piece of technology, and as a model of poetic inspiration which elides the difference between engineering and artistry," "a model well-suited to a poet who served as Clerk of the Works and wrote *The Treatise on the Astrolabe*" (292). If Lightsey positions poetry as a contributing cause to mechanical productions, Berry here emphasizes the similarities—not the differences—between the making of things and the making of poetry. Berry, "Flying Sources: Classical Authority in Chaucer's *Squire's Tale*," *ELH* 68 (2001): 287–313.

something of a backwater even in Europe. From the twelfth century onward, the "east" was an important source of knowledge about philosophy, natural science, mechanics, and the source of a host of fascinating gadgets such as water clocks or table fountains. It is well known by now that many of the gizmos and gadgets described in romance have intriguing links to "Eastern" culture—Joseph Needham surmises that mechanized timekeepers from China may have inspired the development in Europe of mechanical clocks through a process he terms "stimulus diffusion"[54]—and, as *The Squire's Tale* makes clear, in romances these cross-cultural settings are regularly noted.

Medieval romance has long been positioned amid the intercultural interactions of Islam with Christianity; yet medieval cooperation among various peoples of the book has been identified not with romance, but with what Sheila Delany has called the "rational scholarly approach." Delany and others have identified such "rationality" with the work of the School of Toledo, and with the intellectual indebtedness of scholasticism to Arabic texts and traditions. Delany in fact opposes the respect for Islam within theological and political treatises, to an older "mythic" "patristic and popular orientalism . . . embodied in stories of sexual desire."[55] To be sure, much recent work on medieval romance (including my own) has emphasized the conquering impulse of these texts. Yet if romances regularly narrate stories of conquest by way of stories of sexual desire, they also, as we see here, pair desire with intriguing accounts of technology and its fascinations. Given the full range of such references, Delany's opposition between "rational/scientific" and "mythic" realms of culture seems overdrawn. The romance genre's enchantment with new things might prove indexical for a different story about medieval enchantment from the one currently on display.

Max Weber, we recall, linked the "rule" of rationality over the power of "enchantment" with *modern* Western culture: "Western civilization," Weber writes, "is distinguished from every other by the presence of men with a rational ethos for the conduct of life. Magic and religion are found everywhere; but a religious basis for conduct that, when consistently followed, had to lead to a specific form of rationalism is again peculiar to Western civilization."[56]

[54] See Needham, *Science and Civilization in China*, vol. 4, part 2 (Cambridge: Cambridge University Press, 1965).

[55] Sheila Delany, *The Naked Text: Chaucer's "Legend of Good Women"* (Berkeley and Los Angeles: University of California Press, 1994), 186.

[56] Max Weber is quoted in Huff and Schluchter, eds., *Max Weber and Islam*, 76.

This seems an apt description of what Delany would term the putatively "tolerant" rationalism of the scholars and scholastics. Yet Chaucer's tale argues—*pace* Weber and Delany both—that Europe's enchantments with the considerable achievements of Islamic and Asian cultures were rational and amorous in equal measure. The "rational/scientific" realm is as compromised by desire and aggression as is its "mythic" twin. Desire and thought emerge, explicitly in romance, as more proximate than opposed. Chaucer's tale invites us to consider such enchantments as problem and opportunity both, drawing us into an ethical uncertainty that he here refuses to settle. And insofar as romance regularly insists upon the doubleness of these enchanted novelties, the genre registers the paradoxical nature of desire. It allows us to see that the fascination with body and matter that motivates conquest and consumption can never entirely be divorced from that version of delight that marks the beginning of human invention, and inhabits our attachments to one another.[57]

[57] Cultures throughout history regularly (and understandably) evince ambivalence about technology; medieval accounts of its promise and perils should not compromise our understanding of the ambitions of such fascinating gadgets. No small part of the medieval/antitechnological attitude emerges not from the medievals themselves, but from some of the founders of the discipline of medieval studies. I am thinking particularly of Henry Adams's "The Virgin and the Dynamo" (1900), which pits what Adams saw as an organic, religious, medieval sensibility (emblematized for him in the cathedral of Chartres, dedicated to the Virgin Mary) against what he termed a modern, industrialized, and dehumanizing spirit of the twentieth century. See also Lynn White's effort to refute Adams, "Dynamo and Virgin Reconsidered," *American Scholar* 27 (1958): 183–94.

Desire in the *Canterbury Tales*:

Sovereignty and Mastery Between the Wife and Clerk

Elizabeth Scala
University of Texas at Austin

F ROM THE BEGINNING of *The General Prologue,* Chaucer makes it clear that desire is, everywhere in the *Canterbury Tales,* his most central and abiding concern. Where individual tales speak to the particular desires of their tellers, the poem's memorable opening sentence frames the entire fiction as a function of desire in its deferred predicate: "[folk] longen."[1] This syntactic delay also incites the audience's desire across its first eleven lines as it explains the effects of a changing landscape and newly awakened natural world. In setting the season for an Eastertide ride to Canterbury, Chaucer situates the pilgrimage as an effect of collective human desire as he simultaneously conceals why each figure is on the pilgrimage behind a variety of implied but unstated motives.[2] And desire gets things going in more ways than one. Beyond accounting for a way of understanding what lies "behind" each narrator's speech, desire inhabits the very language of the tales in larger and more abstract terms. The conscious means by which speakers pursue various desires and goals within their stories is underwritten by the structure of unconscious desire assumed with language when the subject enters the com-

For their perceptive readings and helpful comments, I want to thank my steady group of critical interlocutors: Douglas Bruster, Patricia Clare Ingham, Daniel Birkholz, and Brooke Hunter. I owe thanks also to the persistent resistance of Frank Grady and to the essay's anonymous readers.

[1] *The Riverside Chaucer,* gen. ed. Larry D. Benson (Boston: Houghton Mifflin, 1987), I.12; all quotations are taken from this edition and will be referenced parenthetically by fragment and line number.

[2] For a compelling discussion of the importance of and differences between group and individual desire in relation to *The Wife of Bath's Tale,* see [Aranye] Louise Fradenburg, "The Wife of Bath's Passing Fancy," *SAC* 8 (1986): 31–58.

plex and socially structured world of symbolization. Most fully elaborated as the emergence of the subject in the psychoanalytic theory of Jacques Lacan, desire accounts for what fundamentally eludes and constitutes the subject as such. The subject comes into being as a separate entity by losing the (imagined) unity with the original object of desire, the body of the mother. This loss, for what one never actually possessed, forever haunts the subject and stalks its fantasies of satisfaction.

Marked by an irrecuperable loss, the subject desires infinite substitutions for this originary object.[3] It is as axiomatic for Plato as for Lacan that desire is lack, for, as Socrates asks Aristomachus in the *Symposium*, how can one desire that which one possesses?[4] Language inserts the subject into the world of symbolization by speaking desire, an acknowledgment and recognition of lack in terms that mystify what is lacking—the subject's relation to the Real (the realm of what lies beyond signification).[5] Through displacement and metonymy, the path desire traces is by its nature indirect, as it substitutes linguistic signifiers for the "thing" that has been lost. As Judith Butler explains, "In this way the aims of desire are not transparently represented in the objects . . . it seeks; indeed, its aims are cloaked or displaced in such a way that what one desires is radically other. . . . The subject may well be the last to know, if he or she ever does, what it is that he or she desires."[6] While explaining the advent of desire in the subject through the substitutive logic of language, this Lacanian model posits a fundamental *disconnection* between language (even the explicit articulation of wanting) and the ob-

[3] This lost and never-possessed object is, of course, Lacan's *objet petit a*, "the object which can never be attained, which is really the cause of desire rather than that toward which desire tends." See Dylan Evans, *An Introductory Dictionary of Lacanian Psychoanalysis* (New York: Routledge, 1996), 125.

[4] I refer, of course, to Plato's *Symposium*; see *Plato*, vol. 3: *Lysis, Symposium, Gorgias*, ed. and trans. W. R. M. Lamb, Loeb Classical Library 166 (Cambridge, Mass.: Harvard University Press, 1925).

[5] Jacques Lacan, "The Mirror Stage as Formative of the *I* Function, as Revealed in Psychoanalytic Experience," in *Ecrits: A Selection*, trans. Bruce Fink (New York: W. W. Norton, 2003), 3–9. For an excellent introduction to Lacan, see Elizabeth Grosz, *Jacques Lacan: A Feminist Introduction* (New York: Routledge, 1990).

[6] For Judith Butler's seminal account of the centrality of desire in Hegelian and post-Hegelian thought, which includes the work of Lacan, see *Subjects of Desire: Hegelian Reflections in Twentieth-Century France* (1987; rev. ed., New York: Columbia University Press, 1999), esp. 186–204. The quotation above comes from her synoptic essay on "Desire," in *Critical Terms for Literary Study*, ed. Frank Lentricchia and Thomas McLaughlin, 2nd ed. (Chicago: University of Chicago Press, 1995), 369–86 (380).

jects and others that supposedly lie "beyond" it. While one's desire is spoken in language, desire names a relation to lack (rather than a particular object). In Lacan's by-now-familiar formula," "Desire is the desire of the Other," which means both that the subject wishes to be the object of another's desire *and* wishes to be recognized by another.[7] Thus, beyond its complex articulation of the way desire grounds the subject itself, Lacan's formulations also insist upon the *social* nature of desire, its origin in our real and imagined relation to others.

Two pilgrims overtly engaged in a debate over the correct (feminine) form of desire are Chaucer's Wife of Bath and Clerk. The Wife makes feminine desire her explicit subject by subjecting a recreant knight to the task of finding "what thyng it is that wommen moost desire" (III.1007). The Clerk more cannily deflects the Wife's question in his exemplification of patient Griselda, the wife who can subordinate herself completely to the desire of another. These ideal images in the Wife's and Clerk's Tales, the magical old woman and the humble, desire-less wife, figure ideal self-images projected by the Wife and Clerk, respectively.[8] But as Butler has just warned us about the unconscious workings of desire beyond the objects we putatively seek, the Wife and Clerk may "well be the last to know, if he or she ever does, what it is that he or she desires." It will take more than these pilgrims' own words on the matter, therefore, to understand what they have to tell us about the nature of their debate as well as the larger workings of desire in the *Canterbury Tales*.

The imperfectly disguised manner in which desire inheres in the signifier, for example, confounds the Franklin's Dorigen, whose words "in pley" tell Aurelius in no uncertain terms how impossible it would be for her to return his affection. Following an absolute rejection—"Taak this for fynal answere as of me" (V.987)—she offers him this consolation: "whan ye han maad the coost so clene / Of rokkes that ther nys no stoon ysene, / Thanne wol I love yow best of any man" (V.995–97). His response, "Madame . . . this were an inpossible!" (V.1009), only makes clearer her point (the event's impossibility) and her intent (of loving only her husband). By giving as a condition a task that cannot be accomplished, she says that she will *never* love him, and his lament proves

[7] Jacques Lacan, *The Four Fundamental Concepts of Psychoanalysis*, ed. Jacques-Alain Miller, trans. Alan Sheridan (New York: W. W. Norton, 1981), 235.
[8] For Lacan's seminal account of the formation of the ego in relation to its images, see "The Mirror Stage as Formative of the *I* Function."

that he has perfectly understood her intent. And yet, we could ask, doesn't Dorigen want the coast cleaned? Captivated by the danger that they signify for her absent husband, she complains of "thise grisly feendly rokkes blake" (V.868). What the Franklin calls "hire derke fantasye" (V.844) amounts to an obsession with a clean coast that sets the tale's plot in motion. Her playful speech with Aurelius expresses, then, undivided love for her husband, her intent to remain faithful to him, disdain for Aurelius's suit, *and*, most significantly, her very deepest desire. In her obsession over the rocks and her wish to have them removed, we can say that Dorigen also wants to be able to give Aurelius her love, however paradoxical it may seem. By no means transparent, the logic of desire grounds the logic of narrative, with all its swerves and surprises. It is spoken in the language that makes up the symbolic order out of which desire arises.[9]

Charging the relationship between the Wife and Clerk in Fragments III and IV are the antics of fictional wives and clerks in the increasingly violent comedies of Fragment I. According to the Miller's fabliau logic, married women attract clerks as well as provoke their ire and ridicule. We see this provocation as he details the erotic interest clerks Nicholas and Absolon naturally display for the carpenter's young wife, Alison (a fictional namesake, of course, to the Wife of Bath). The Wife of Bath's Prologue explains the "naturalness" of the charged desires between wives and clerks in the fabliaux. Astrological forces lead her to conclude:

> And thus, God woot, Mercurie is desolat
> In Pisces, wher Venus is exaltat,
> And Venus falleth ther Mercurie is reysed.
> Therfore no womman of no clerk is preysed.
> The clerk, whan he is oold, and may noght do
> Of Venus werkes worth his olde sho,
> Thanne sit he doun, and writ in his dotage
> That wommen kan nat kepe hir mariage!
>
> (III.703–10)

---

[9] *The Franklin's Tale* appears as a story organized against ideas of mastery: "Whan maistrie comth, the God of Love anon / Beteth his wynges, and farewel, he is gon!" (V.765–66). In an essay on mastery in *The Franklin's Tale* relevant to my purposes here, John Pitcher argues that "the master is Chaucer's magician, he who grasps the logic of the subject's desire in fantasy" (77). See John A. Pitcher, "'Word and Werke' in Chaucer's *Franklin's Tale*," *Psychology and Literature* 49 (2003): 77–109.

Cosmic determinism naturalizes a rivalry between clerks and wives, which then gives way to more practical explanations in the sexual frustration of the older clerk, his inability to "do / Of Venus werkes worth his olde sho." Such physical desires and the impotence preventing their fulfillment provoke the stories about women found in texts like Jankyn's "book of wikked wyves" (III.685). The Wife concludes, "For trusteth wel, it is an impossible / That any clerk wol speke good of wyves, / But if it be of hooly seintes lyves, / Ne of noon oother womman never the mo" (III.688–91). But in marking such sexual frustration, the Wife suggests that the Clerk has desires he fails to acknowledge.

Readers have taken the Clerk's tale as a direct retort to the Wife's claim, made especially pointed when he refers to her by name in the Envoy. Ostensibly perceiving the Wife's statement as a challenge, the Clerk tells a story of an impossibly good wife in his tale of patient Griselda. Both the prologue and Envoy to *The Clerk's Tale* make the Wife's "impossible" quite possible as they locate the story in a particular "clerkly" origin, Petrarch, and address the Wife of Bath "and al hire secte" respectively (IV.1171). This rivalry has greater stakes than the dramatic context or materialist narrative of the pilgrimage alone.[10] The desire of clerks and wives witnessed in these tales—desire that appears in such radically different forms—figures the very desiring discourse and its dislocations that produce the *Canterbury Tales* in the first place. In shifting from the ordinary sense of desire to the more linguistically constitutive one at stake here, the significance of the particular object of desire gives way to the persistence of desire itself and the telling symptom in which it is manifested.

That symptom arises in a narrative similarity shared by the Wife and Clerk that has not been noted before, most likely because of their argumentative posture.[11] Chaucer's Wife and Clerk sketch idealized rep-

---

[10] One of the most recent essays on *The Clerk's Tale* repositions its rhetoric in relation to the Wife of Bath and her "sumptuous material world," against which the Clerk argues in increasingly subtle ways. Andrea Denny-Brown reads the dressing and undressing of Griselda in the context of the historical significance of material goods and objects, and particularly sartorial legislation and infraction, to the ultimate critique of the "superfluity, frivolity, and love of novelty with not only the common 'peple' of his tale but also the *nouveaux riches* [sic] merchant class and its spendthrift 'arch' wives"—a critique pointedly relevant, in yet another way, to the Wife of Bath. See "*Povre* Griselda and the All-Consuming *Archewyves*," *SAC* 28 (2006): 77–115 (80).

[11] The conflict between Wife and Clerk in this matter is perhaps largely overdetermined. Not only does the Wife's idealization of the crafty old woman and cannily judicious Guenevere contrast sharply with the Clerk's perfectly passive Griselda, but the conflict begins even before her Prologue. Chaucer sets the Wife and Clerk at odds through the depiction of wives and clerks in such fabliaux as *The Miller's Tale* and still

resentations of female behavior dramatically at odds with each other. The Wife depicts an actively aggressive woman who is responsible for the redemptive and transformative "magic" in her tale. The Clerk, on the other hand, idealizes a passive woman whose inhuman constancy is rewarded in the end.[12] Where these feminine depictions and their attendant fictions suggest radical opposition, the Wife and Clerk respond to their tales in surprisingly similar ways. Both pilgrims' closing gestures withdraw from the powerful position of mastery that each of their tales has advanced. The recoil of these two narrators is striking, magnified only by the critical attempts to explain the ends of each performance. The Wife of Bath's diverse arguments for the necessity of female dominance culminate, for instance, in a fairy-tale ending (that includes marriage and feminine submission) from which she withdraws back into belligerence in the space of a mere eight lines (III.1257–64).[13] Likewise the Clerk proffers an idealized image of female submission that proves heroically dominant at the end of his tale. In a more prolonged fashion, he recoils from the power Griselda exerts over Walter in eleven stanzas of Petrarchan apology and allegorization. Even more excessively, the Clerk adds an antifeminist harangue that closes the debate and provides his ironically caustic Envoy (IV.1142–1212). In these conclusions, the Wife's and Clerk's tales both reveal a narrative *jouissance*, an ecstasy of pleasure that abruptly turns to un-pleasure, provoking their aversion. What is it that the Wife and Clerk glimpse in their fictions?

Attempts to explain the tales' closing gestures have treated them in isolation, thus failing to recognize the shared structure at work in their

---

earlier, in their contrasting descriptions in *The General Prologue* as "mirror opposites," which are from the beginning "destined to clash." See John A. Alford, "The Wife of Bath versus the Clerk of Oxford: What Their Rivalry Means," *ChauR* 21 (1986): 108–32 (109). Even further, Alford argues, they must be understood in terms of each other and each other's discourse. They "come directly from the tradition of the allegorized liberal arts" in which the Clerk is "Logic personified," while the Wife speaks as "Dame Rhetoric" (110). Thus, Alford concludes that "the conflict between the Wife and the Clerk is not personal but historical . . . rooted in the recurrent tension between two modes of discourse, rhetorical and philosophical" (109).

[12] On the identifications of these narrators with their heroines, see Warren Ginsberg, "The Lineaments of Desire: Wish-Fulfillment in Chaucer's Marriage Group," *Criticism* 25 (1983): 197–210. On the Clerk's identification with Griselda, see Carolyn Dinshaw, *Chaucer's Sexual Poetics* (Madison: University of Wisconsin Press, 1989), 135–36.

[13] Penn R. Szittya also points to the Wife's renunciation of power at the end of the romance in "The Green Yeoman as Loathly Lady: The Friar's Parody of the Wife of Bath's Tale," *PMLA* 90 (1975): 386–94 (392).

performances. Opposed in philosophic ideas and feminine ideals, Wife and Clerk both work to conceal a similar recognition. In René Girard's formulation, both tales "defend the same illusion of autonomy," or what the Wife and Clerk call "sovereignty."[14] But in offering a particular account of sovereignty, each tale depends on a mastery that ultimately disrupts their neat identification with these ideal heroines. Into the fictions of autonomy that each figure has offered, such mastery inserts an other that gives the lie to the fantasy of sovereignty each story proffers. In their structural similarity, then, the Wife's and Clerk's tales momentarily reveal a desire—much like Dorigen's—for what each speaker seems most desperate to deny. The Wife's rhetoric of mastery and exemplary female sovereignty covers over a wish to submit to masculine power, while the Clerk's ideal of passive suffering, Christ-like in its exemplification, is driven by a disavowed desire to dominate, seemingly un-Christian in its very aspiration.[15] For all their supposed difference, the Wife and Clerk reveal the same division in the structure of desire, the desire for (and to be) the Other's desire, that unravels the neat close of their fictions and provokes a number of ironic readings of those endings. This shared structure suggests an identification between the two figures and between their tales that rewrites our conception of the "marriage group" as a simple debate in these fragments.[16] This identification, in turn, disrupts the very opposition between wives and clerks that readers of Chaucer's poetry have all too easily accepted and shifts our attention to the productive value of desire—even if desire means "lack"—for the *Canterbury Tales* as a whole.[17]

[14] Girard's quasi-Hegelian formulation of mimetic desire and triangulation looks to account for the way desire arises through social relations rather than in imitation of one's originary and imaginary relation with the other, the *objet petit a*. See René Girard, *Deceit, Desire, and the Novel*, trans. Yvonne Freccero (Baltimore: Johns Hopkins University Press, 1965).

[15] Lynn Staley, "Chaucer and the Postures of Sanctity," in *The Powers of the Holy: Religion, Politics, and Gender in Late Medieval English Culture*, ed. David Aers and Lynn Staley (University Park: Pennsylvania State University Press, 1996), esp. 233–59.

[16] The "marriage group," a heuristic collocation of tales that respond to the ideas about gender in Jerome's *Adversus Jovinianum*, is typically attributed to George Lyman Kittredge's essay, "Chaucer's Discussion of Marriage," *MP* 9 (1912): 435–67, but it originally comes from Eleanor Prescott Hammond, *Chaucer: A Bibliographical Manual* (New York: Macmillan, 1908), 256. For a fuller discussion, see my forthcoming essay, "The Women in Chaucer's Marriage Group," in *MFF* 44 (2009): 50–56.

[17] For a recent discussion of the unhelpful opposition staged between Deleuzian and Lacanian accounts of desire, see Kristyn Gorton, *Theorising Desire: From Freud to Feminism to Film* (New York: Palgrave Macmillan, 2008).

Evading the End

Where Chaucer's *Tales* originate in a human desire embedded and obfuscated by the artifice of its opening sentence, the individual tales' conclusions typically resound with the satisfaction of a narrative crescendo. *The Miller's Tale* provides an exaggerated example of such an ending. The Miller's voice comes crashing down upon his conclusion—"This tale is doon, and God save al the rowte!" (I.3854)—much like the carpenter hanging from the rafters in the denouement of the Miller's comedy. The Wife's speedy ending appears less a departure from the Miller's tidy conclusion than the Clerk's multiple endings, which include Petrarchan moral and antifeminist song. Where the Wife's tale closes with the transformation and happy marriage of beautiful, young, and faithful lady with reformed knight (III.1250–58), the Clerk's ends with the re-exaltation of Griselda and her emotional reunion with her lost children (IV.1079–1127). Both endings offer explicit satisfaction to their protagonists and, presumably, to their narrators as well. The Clerk's prospective vision goes so far as to suggest the future happiness and security that motivated the tale in the first place. Walter's son, we are told, eventually "succedeth in his heritage / In reste and pees, after his fader day" (IV.1135–36). These endings are conventional in that they resolve the conflicts each tale stages. Problems arise, then, only from their own narrators' inability to accept them. Much like the Franklin's Dorigen, these narrators speak in excess of their meaning, beyond the satisfaction each tale has wrought. The Wife and Clerk continue, almost fearful that their points have not been made clearly enough. But we might read them as anxious acknowledgments that they have been made all *too* clearly. Like Dorigen's words uttered "in pley" (V.988), words that assuage the harsh refusal of Aurelius's suit too directly, these conclusions have provoked, even necessitated, critical intervention.

While these endings are foregrounded by critical attempts to supervene them, such evasive readings only repeat the tales' own evasive and resistant gestures.[18] For instance, just as the Wife offers the transforma-

---

[18] Charlotte Morse and William McClellan, in very different ways, challenge us to rethink our response to and what we supposedly know about *The Clerk's Tale*. In its uncanny scene of domestic violence, we have to avert our eyes, and this aversion leads to highly critical responses to the tale: we historicize it, we allegorize and dehumanize it, as we make it into something "as for oure excercise" (IV.1156). See Morse, "The Exemplary Griselda," *SAC* 7 (1985): 51–86, and McClellan, "'Ful Pale Face': Agamben's Biopolitical Theory and the Sovereign Subject in Chaucer's *Clerk's Tale*," *Exem-*

tive, happily-ever-after ending—"And thus they lyve unto hir lyves ende / In parfit joye" (III.1257–58)—she returns, even before she can finish the sentence, to the Prologue's masterful terms she had finally seemed to transcend:

> . . . and Jhesu Crist us sende
> Housbondes meeke, yonge, and fressh abedde,
> And grace t'overbyde hem that we wedde;
> And eek I praye Jhesu shorte hir lyves
> That noght wol be governed by hir wyves;
> And olde and angry nygardes of dispence,
> God sende hem soone verray pestilence!
>
> (III.1258–64)

The "parfit joye" produced at the end of the Wife's tale as proof that female sovereignty makes for perfect male felicity in marriage is short lived. What could be a two-line conclusion (by ending, that is, at line 1259's "fresh abedde") runs on for almost ten, following an associative chain of thought that brings the Wife back to the marital reality she knows firsthand. Her characters' "parfit joye" inspires thoughts of her own intimate pleasures: "Housboundes meeke, yonge, and fressh ab-edde." Similarly the continuation of such joy "unto hir lyves ende" also invokes an "end" with which she is only too familiar. She has already been to that end with at least four, if not five, of her husbands and "welcome the sixte, whan that evere he shal" (III.45). Her comic prayer to outlive these "meeke, yonge, and fresh" men raises the specter of death, which is what she wishes on those husbands resistant to her superior knowledge. At one point the Wife calmly concluded her Breton *lai* with the mutual satisfaction of reformed knight and transformed lady: "A thousand tyme a-rewe he gan hire kisse, / And she obeyed hym in every thyng / That myghte doon hym plesance or likyng" (III.1254–56). But such bliss, contingent finally upon female obedience, quickly moves to the kind of preemptive curse more familiar from her Prologue.

The situation is not particularly hard to explain given the resemblance of the Wife to the wily hag of the tale. As a projection of the Wife's ideal self-image, the hag can position herself, through shrewd

---

plaria 17 (2005): 103–34. As a last resort, I suppose, we might ironize the Clerk's narration—even before the satiric Envoy—or Chaucer's depiction of the Clerk himself and so release him from all authority.

argumentation (or the enchantments of fiction), to be transformed by the "maistrye" ceded to her by her new husband. That moment of release—from ugliness, from the rash promise that forces their marriage, from the charges of age, poverty, and hideousness he levels—also provokes anxiety, indexing the desire at work in the tale as well as ultimately undoing all for which she has to this point worked. Attaining mastery over the man in deed, rather than in mere word, and in earnest, rather than in naive repetition of what she "rowned . . . in his ere" (III.1021), produces the best marital arrangement in the Wife's fictive world. It consolidates the hag's marriage, guaranteeing her love and fidelity: "we be no lenger wrothe, / For, by my trouthe, I wol be to yow bothe—/ This is to seyn, ye, bothe fair and good" (III.1239–41). The reward delights the husband: "For joye he hente hire in his armes two. / His herte bathed in a bath of blisse" (III.1252–53). Such physical affection also delights the Wife/wife, who has entered into the terms of conventional marriage in idealized form. Giving women what they want will always end in men's happiness: "happy wife, happy life," she might more economically say. But the ideals espoused here are also placed into conventional terms that the Wife has a harder time assimilating. Like the wedding vows themselves, which solicit a promise to love, honor, and obey from the woman, and which ensure the legal rights a husband attains in marriage, she promises to love and "be also good and trewe" (III.1243) in a way that returns to him ultimate power over her: "Dooth with my lyf and deth right as yow lest" (III.1248).[19] Just after he *bathes* in the *bath* of bliss—a telling resignification of the Wife's identity at this critical juncture—and kisses her continually, she must answer in proper wifely fashion: "And she *obeyed* hym in every thyng / That myghte doon hym plesance or likyng" (III.1255–56; my emphasis).[20] Happy life indeed!

The end of the tale thus shifts from argument and opposition ("we be . . . wrothe"), from a marriage won through guile and female mastery, to elaborating man's "real" happiness in marriage. The image of the tale's characters with which the Wife closes also forms the conclusion to her

---

[19] Not coincidentally, Griselda offers similar sentiments to Walter under very different and far less joyful conditions throughout her trials. She claims that she and her child are his to do with as he pleases: "ye mowe save or spille / Youre owene thyng; werketh after youre wille" (IV.503–4). But her marriage and all her action is produced under the sign of his "luste" (IV.659–65).

[20] This uncharacteristic lexical redundancy, "bathing in a bath of bliss," reinscribes her name, perhaps testifying to the fiction of identity at stake here.

argument: the recipe for happy, contented husbands. We end not with female mastery or sovereignty but with an image of *male* bliss, *his* "plesance or likyng." One can see this tale's conclusion in terms of mutual sovereignty or shared mastery, but the Wife actually shows men what they need to relinquish so as to gain complete happiness and obedience from their wives. If she reveals the conditions under which men and women ultimately give up their claims of mastery over each other, as the Franklin's Dorigen and Arveragus also attempt, she ends with the lady offering the power of life and death to the knight. An acute observer attentive to the masterful terms of worldly and spiritual matters, the Wife hears the rhetoric of romance afresh at the end of her own tale. A keen reader of texts ("Who peyntede the leon, tel me who? [III.692]), she proves no less so for her own. Typically we laugh at the Wife's annoyed response to her idealized romance story, chalking it up to Chaucer's vibrant characterization.[21] As with many of the digressions, illogicalities, and falsehoods used locally and to comic effect in her Prologue, this obstreperous and abrupt ending characterizes her discourse as stereotypically "feminine" precisely because self-contradictory. It makes her sound like "herself," a characterization that may in fact obscure our realization of how much like *every* self she sounds, since desire is located and revealed, precisely, at such points of discontinuity.[22]

If we enjoy the comic reversal by which *The Wife of Bath's Tale* returns to the forceful rhetoric heard in the Prologue, the ending of *The Clerk's Tale* provokes a more heated debate about its endgame. As one reader puts it, multiple "closing frames of the *Clerk's Tale* offer shifting evaluations . . . [that] are marked by changes in the clerkly voice of the narrator, and his ostensible audience of address."[23] In far more dramatic fashion, the Clerk's Envoy has caused a variety of critical responses, not the least of which concerns the textual status of its ending. Long read as caustic irony within the frame narrative of the *Tales*, and, to its critical admirers, "a passable display of wit, a heartily ironic tribute to the Wife of Bath, and a vivacious and sarcastic song," the Clerk's Envoy has com-

---

[21] For examples of the rather commonplace reading of the Wife's shift at the end of her tale, see Fradenburg, "Passing Fancy," 55; H. Marshall Leicester, *The Disenchanted Self: Representing the Subject in the Canterbury Tales* (Berkeley and Los Angeles: University of California Press, 1991), 155; Ginsberg, "Lineaments of Desire," 196–98.

[22] Butler, *Subjects of Desire*, 186.

[23] Lesley Johnson, "Reincarnations of Griselda: Contexts for the *Clerk's Tale?*" *Feminist Readings of Middle English Literature: The Wife of Bath and All Her Sect*, ed. Ruth Evans and Lesley Johnson (London: Routledge, 1994), 209.

plicated our responses to the unobtrusive pilgrim Harry Bailly has introduced *as a wife*: the Clerk "ryde[s] as coy and stille as dooth a mayde / Were newe spoused, sittynge at the bord" (IV.2–3).[24] The standard printed version of *The Clerk's Tale* in *The Riverside Chaucer* displays its ambiguous textual situation through a number of formatting choices that make for a story with a markedly different *mise-en-page* from the majority of other Canterbury tales. It is broken into sections with Latin incipits and explicits, and it has a prologue and formal envoy in different verse forms with at least one rubric. But the Envoy also remains problematic at the level of structure and narration as well. Readers have found its tone glib and far out of character for its otherwise erudite speaker.[25]

The Envoy ambiguously attached to the Clerk's tale might be too easily read as an addition to the story that ruins its elegant allegory. Separated from the tale by a rubric, this feature puts the Envoy's textual status in doubt even as it attempts to clarify that status.[26] And if the Envoy's final line—"And lat hym care, and wepe, and wrynge, and waille!" (IV.1212)—were not immediately picked up by the Merchant and transformed into the opening of his own prologue—"Wepyng and waylyng, care and oother sorwe / I knowe ynogh, on even and a-morwe" (IV.1213–14)—it might have been cancelled long ago by editors as a crudely antifeminist interpolation.[27] The scribes of the manuscript tradition may perhaps be warding off just such a cancellation by marking the passage now at IV.1177 as "Lenvoy de Chaucer," signing its author's name.

---

[24] Steven Axelrod, "The Wife of Bath and the Clerk," *Annuale Mediaevale* 15 (1974): 109–24 (113). Axelrod's essay recuperates the Clerk "for the witty, spirited, flawed and attractive human being he is" (113). Dinshaw has also made much of the Clerk's position as a newly spoused wife (*Chaucer's Sexual Poetics*, 135).

[25] The Clerk's Envoy has been reckoned a problem by a number of readers, including Thomas J. Farrell, "The 'Envoy de Chaucer' and the *Clerk's Tale*," *ChauR* 24 (1990): 329–36, and Howell Chickering, "Form and Interpretation in the *Envoy* to the *Clerk's Tale*," *ChauR* 29 (1995): 352–72.

[26] The rubric introducing the Clerk's Envoy is attested in most of the base manuscripts of the *Canterbury Tales*; see Farrell, "Envoy de Chaucer," 329, and John M. Manly and Edith Rickert, eds., *The Text of the Canterbury Tales, Studied on the Basis of All Known Manuscripts*, 8 vols. (Chicago: University of Chicago Press, 1940), 3:528–37. In their view Chaucer revised the ending of *The Clerk's Tale*, at which time he added the Envoy to link directly to the Merchant's prologue.

[27] Following line 1212 stands what is called "the Host's stanza," which, according to the *Riverside* notes, "is generally held to have been written early and canceled when Chaucer wrote new lines for The Merchant's Prologue containing an echo of 1212 [see Manly and Rickert, note 26 above]. It is found in Ellesmere, Hengwrt, and 20 other MSS" (884).

The change in verse form in the Envoy may also make necessary that authorial signature. Introducing "a song to glade yow" after the "ernestful matere" of his tale (IV.1174–75), the Clerk switches from his elevated rime royal stanzas to the form of the double ballade (six-line stanzas with only three rhymes).[28] Formally different from most others in the Canterbury collection, *The Clerk's Tale*'s differences from itself are most significant. These differences are embodied in the name of the author, signed as rubric to the Envoy's beginning, a signature ostensibly offered to guarantee the authority of the text. But the imposition of an authorial signature, even if only in the manuscript apparatus, here works the opposite way as well by breaking the fiction of the speaking character and marking all too clearly the absence of a consistent voice in the Clerk's performance.[29] Ironically, if the scribes were looking to preserve an authentic part of the Clerk's speech at the end of his story—a desire in which the modern editor also participates—they do so by indicating Chaucer's name rather than the fictional speaker's. Preserving the text as Chaucer's, they disrupt his fiction of the Clerk's discourse.

Despite these problems, the Envoy remains, and it remains to be explained by readers of the Clerk's allegory. Beyond the various arguments preserving, assimilating, and nullifying the Envoy are those justifying the Clerk's sarcasm and integrating its ironies into the argument of the tale as a whole. John Ganim, for instance, argues for "the festive nature of the envoy" and thus participates in a critical trend that separates the Envoy from the tale. Reading it as independent lyric, Ganim returns it to the conditions set by the Clerk's own Prologue. In the Envoy, filled with "comic sexual reversals, . . . Harry's mastery of the proceedings and his sense of how stories are meant to be understood . . . is made fun of, certainly as much as the Wife of Bath's ideas on marriage are ironically praised." Ganim reads the Envoy as a decided shift to the sort of performances, "song, minstrelsy, student prank—[that] dramatize th[e] failure" of the tale for the contest's judge.[30] It is too difficult and demanding for the likes of Harry Bailly, who wants no preaching or scholarly terms but only "pleyn" language (IV.19). Separating the

---

[28] The most elaborate analysis of these metrics, particularly in the Envoy, is found in Chickering, "Form and Interpretation."

[29] On the textual tradition of the Envoy and the Chaucerian signature by which it is introduced, see Farrell, "Envoy de Chaucer."

[30] John Ganim, *Chaucerian Theatricality* (Princeton: Princeton University Press, 1990), 82, 84.

Envoy from the tale, then, Ganim attaches it more securely to the prologue and changes its immediate audience from that named, "for the Wyves love of Bathe / . . . and al hire secte" (IV.1170–71), to the Host. If such a separation is meant to allow us to read beyond the dramatic principle or a marriage group—beyond a conflict with the Wife herself—this reading only widens, by including the rest of the pilgrim company, its dramatic context. Even as a separate poem, then, the Envoy is directed toward a larger dramatic audience.

Registering a similar difference at the end of *The Clerk's Tale*, Elizabeth Salter hears the voice of the tale's conclusion *as* the Clerk's. In her extremely influential study, Salter writes, "If, during the *Tale*, we have sometimes been uncertain about the exact identity of the narrator, we are now clearly intended to understand that the voice we hear is that of the Clerk, speaking familiarly to his fellow-pilgrims, establishing a second *raison d'être* for his story—an outer frame of reference."[31] The two voices Salter hears in the *Tale* follow the two registers, allegorical and verisimilar, in which Chaucer seeks to write and which he sets in open competition. The Clerk's story emerges, in Salter's words, as caught "between two worlds" and two very different styles, demanding opposing kinds of audience response that cannot be reconciled: "the one expressing itself in austere modes, with controlled religious echoes, the other in lively language, critical, sentimental, dramatic."[32] In this way she explains the Envoy's humor and the Clerk's self-abasing ending to his story as a "skillfully managed return to the miscellaneous crowd of pilgrims on the road to Canterbury." The Envoy continues with its humor by "recommend[ing], tacitly, those very virtues and behaviour [prudence, humility, innocence, reverence] they seem to scorn." Thus, according to Salter, if Griselda cannot be believed in any realist sense, the Envoy makes her "a more acceptable, less preposterous creation than the Wife of Bath and 'archewyves' of her kind."[33] Yet we might note even further that, much as in the ending of *The Wife of Bath's Tale*, the Clerk's humor and shift in tone return us to its narrator's own anxious uncertainty. Read as a continuation of the tale, a reinscription into the marriage debate, or part of the linking framework of the entire poem, the Envoy has made Chaucer's readers uncertain as to what it "is" as well as the Clerk's control over the discourse in it.

[31] Elizabeth Salter, *Chaucer: "The Knight's Tale" and "The Clerk's Tale"* (London: Edward Arnold, 1962), 62–63.
[32] Ibid., 62.
[33] Ibid., 64, 65.

Discourses of Mastery

The Wife's bid for mastery and her practical argument for its foundation in nature and divine creation get complicated by the tale she chooses to tell. While her Prologue makes an openly hostile rebuttal to clerical judgments about women that borders on diatribe, the unexpectedly nuanced and idealist Arthurian romance she tells offers a more sophisticated articulation of the mutual bliss attained through women's sovereignty in marriage. In these claims I have very consciously moved from one of the Wife's operative terms, *maistrie*, to another, *sovereynetee*, because of the importance of both words and their sometimes unexamined relations.[34] The elision of sovereignty and mastery emerges from the general discourse of power and the hierarchies it generates. A sovereign has power or mastery over others, as does Arthur in *The Wife of Bath's Tale* or Walter in *The Clerk's Tale* over their subjects. But no one holds power over the sovereign, who has complete self-determination. This is why the old woman in the Wife's tale must clarify the power she has gained from the knight: "Thanne have I gete of yow maistrie . . . / Syn I may chese and governe as me lest?" (III.1236–37). Her control in this situation is actually self-control, the ability to "chese" herself. As her husband has shown: "For as yow liketh, it suffiseth me" (III.1235). So too in *The Clerk's Tale* do Walter's subjects try to explain marriage not as constraint but as "soveraynetee, noght of servyse" (IV.114). Their part is clearly more difficult. But Walter's acceptance of this bond "of soveraynetee" is immediately turned into a dramatization of his self-determination in the scenes of subordination (of his subjects and of Griselda) to his will.

The ease with which the idea of sovereignty (self-determination)

[34] Donald C. Green, "The Semantics of Power: *Maistrie* and *Soveraynetee* in *The Canterbury Tales*," *MP* 84 (1986): 18–23. Green discusses these terms and four others (*servage, servyse, governaunce,* and *assente*), with particular attention to the Wife and Clerk, to reread sovereignty (contra the Wife) as subordination to a role and/in a proper order. He writes, "Chaucer has made a careful distinction between the individually defined relationships of *maistrie* and *servyse* on the one hand and the role-defined relationships of *soveraynetee* and *servage* on the other" (23). The Wife, who conflates mastery with sovereignty, performs a heresy in Green's reading: "It is significant, then, that the term *maistrie* does not occur in the *Clerk's Tale*. Walter's sovereignty is acknowledged from the beginning, and the story is not about winning or losing mastery; rather, it is about assent to that higher sovereignty whose yoke, if Griselda's example is to be believed, may not be blissful at all times but which leads to ultimate bliss" (23). For a more recent and completely skeptical reading of the tale, see Susanne Sara Thomas, "The Problem of Defining *Soveraynetee* in the *Wife of Bath's Tale*," *ChauR* 41 (2006): 87–97.

slides into a discourse of mastery (control over another) has always been a problem in and for the Wife's story. Her critical readers have found it difficult to define the sovereignty the Wife advocates because it looks so much like mastery over another plain and simple.[35] Similarly difficult for readers, and for the Clerk himself, is Walter's compulsive desire for mastery over his wife.[36] While "some men preise it for a subtil wit," the Clerk finds Walter's trial of Griselda both unnecessary and unendurable, opinions that interject some rather glaring first-person commentary into the tale: "But as for me, I seye that yvele it sit / To assaye a wyf whan that it is no nede, / And putten hire in angwyssh and in drede" (IV.460–62). While "mastery" is a word that neither the Clerk nor Walter uses to describe his desires or Griselda's subjected condition, the idea of Walter's mastery looms large over the tale and Griselda's sworn obedience to him.[37] It is heard in the tale's beginning when Walter assents to the idea of marriage, to which, he claims, "I nevere erst thoughte streyne me" (IV.144), as well as in the testing scenes in which he invokes Griselda's promises of perfect obedience by reminding her of the state to which he has raised her. He begins: "Grisilde . . . that day / That I yow took out of youre povere array, / And putte yow in estaat of heigh noblesse—/ Ye have nat that forgeten, as I gesse?" (IV.466–69). Walter's mastery over Griselda, his people, and the institution of marriage itself is woven into the first movement of the story, in which the Marquis's loving subjects suggest a marriage in order to ensure the continuity of his lineage and rule.[38] As many critics have elaborated in the

[35] See Thomas, "Problem of *Sovereynetee*," 89, and Susan Crane, *Gender and Romance in Chaucer's Canterbury Tales* (Princeton: Princeton University Press, 1994), 123–26.

[36] For an extensive study of this situation as one reflecting the issue of Lombard tyranny with which Chaucer came into contact on his Italian voyages, see David Wallace, *Chaucerian Polity: Absolutist Lineages and Associational Forms* (Stanford: Stanford University Press, 1997), 261–98. For a more general discussion of the tale's commentary on tyranny in relation to English politics, see Carol Falvo Heffernan, "Tyranny and *Commune Profit* in the *Clerk's Tale*," *ChauR* 17 (1983): 332–40, as well as Staley's "Postures of Sanctity."

[37] Significantly, the Clerk uses the term "maistrie" only once, just before the Envoy, when he speaks specifically about the Wife of Bath herself, "Whos lyf and al hire secte God mayntene / In heigh *maistrie*" (IV.1171–2: my emphasis).

[38] In this way, Walter demonstrates the paradoxical operations of what Fradenburg calls "sovereign love," which offers "a relation of social and economic 'necessity' . . . refigured as volitional." See [Aranye] Louise Fradenburg, *City, Marriage, Tournament: Arts of Rule in Late Medieval Scotland* (Madison: University of Wisconsin Press, 1991), 85. I am indebted here to Fradenburg's analysis of the Song of Songs and her conception of the uses of marriage for the articulation of sovereignty, particularly her chapter "Sovereign Love."

work cited throughout this essay, the analysis of marriage in *The Clerk's Tale* never fully escapes its political function. Marriage remains consistently *un*related to personal pleasure (in sharp distinction to what the Wife of Bath thinks) and stands in opposition to the "lust present" (IV.80) upon which Walter's youthful attention is fixed. The Clerk thus blames him for a failure to consider "[i]n tyme comynge what myghte hym bityde," as Walter instead focuses on immediate pleasures, "for to hauke and hunte" (IV.79, 81). Divorced from pleasure, marriage for Walter signifies prudence and responsive responsibility to his people.

However, marriage also gets framed as a pledge of obedience *from* his people and is therefore implicated in the sovereignty he holds over them. Much as he will with Griselda, Walter exacts a promise "[a]gayn my choys . . . neither [to] grucche ne stryve" from his subjects (IV.170). In fact, in the story's opening Walter's subjects foreshadow the humble position Griselda will assume in the very next part of the tale, when they promise their obedience to his pleasure upon their knees:

> With hertely wyl they sworen and assenten
> To al this thyng—ther seyde no wight nay—
> Bisekynge hym of grace, er that they wenten,
> That he wolde graunten hem a certein day
> Of his spousaille, as soone as evere he may;
> For yet alwey the peple somwhat dredde,
> Lest that the markys no wyf wolde wedde.
>
> He graunted hem a day, swich as hym leste,
> On which he wolde be wedded sikerly,
> And seyde he dide al this at hir requeste.
> And they, with humble entente, buxomly,
> Knelynge upon hir knees ful reverently.
> Hym thonken alle; and thus they han an ende
> Of hire entente, and hoom agayn they wende.
>
> (IV.176–89)

This kneeling throng, "with humble entente" and "buxomly" as a wife (with a visual though nonetymological association to *uxor*), presages Griselda's actions before the Marquis only one hundred lines later:

> The markys cam and gan hire for to calle;
> And she set doun hir water pot anon,

> Biside the thresshfold, in an oxes stalle,
> And doun upon hir knes she gan to falle,
> And with sad contenance kneleth stille,
> Til she had herd what was the lordes wille.
>
> (IV.289–94)

The Marian imagery of buxom maid on knees waiting to hear the Lord's will has overshadowed the secular and ideological dimension of Griselda's state, her reproduction of (and symbolic substitution for) the people's political position in relation to Walter's governance.[39] Insofar as Griselda's promise to obey her husband and to follow his will figures the assent of Walter's people to his rule, marriage in *The Clerk's Tale* forges perfect, idealized political relationships—or at least it should.[40]

More than mere romance such as the Wife offers, then, *The Clerk's Tale* presents marriage as always signifying something beyond itself. Individual motives drive no figure in this story, save Walter's strange desire to test his wife. His people, on the other hand, desire only political continuity and stability, what they call living "in sovereyn hertes reste" (IV.112). Similarly, Griselda marries the Marquis for no personal gain or pleasure, but out of obedience to her "Lord," which variously refers to her father, to Saluzzo's ruler, and to God. Marriage thus figures, quite literally, Walter's relation to his people and his right to rule. In both Walter's assent to his people's concern for an heir and in the choice he makes for a wife, the Clerk dramatizes the political figurations of marriage that exceed the pleasures or personal desires anatomized by romance and the Wife of Bath's Prologue.

But within the Clerk's political economy, Walter's choice not only displays his benevolent rule, but it also exacts a price from the audience for whom it is publicly performed. Even before revealing Griselda as his

[39] McClellan reads *The Clerk's Tale* as "enact[ing] a kind of primal scene of sovereign power, showing how it exerts itself over those it subjects" ("'Ful Pale Face,'" 107). Reading Walter and Griselda quasi-allegorically in Giorgio Agamben's terms of "sovereign power" and "bare life," respectively, McClellan shows how their marriage translates Griselda into a political subject. "At the same time, Walter subjects Griselda to the most abject treatment and outrageous demands, to which she gives silent 'assente'" (107), illuminating the paradox of sovereignty and the agency of its subject(ions). Such a reading also makes *The Clerk's Tale* into an explicitly political drama.

[40] McClellan also returns to this point, "the secret contract of obedience between sovereign and subject. . . . As Agamben maintains, the oldest secret of sovereign power is that obedience precedes every institution of power. . . . Chaucer shows us how the sovereign coerces the human subject to 'assente' to the demand of obedience" ("'Ful Pale Face,'" 126).

chosen bride, he demands a promise of obedience from his subjects: "What wyf that I take, ye me assure / To worshipe hire, whil that hir lyf may dure, / In word and werk, bothe heere and everywheere, / As she an emperoures doghter weere" (IV.165–68). His choice of a simple, low-born maid not only appears prudent, but it also offers the opportunity for testing his subjects' loyalty and obedience. Indeed, the choice itself is staged for his subjects as the "retenue [of] the bachelrye" (270) follows Walter into Griselda's village, while she, around whom the drama is constructed, waits unaware of her role in his elaborate wedding plans. Griselda's consent to follow Walter's will, "in werk ne thoght . . . [never to] disobeye" (363), is only as important as the consent of his people to "swere . . . [never] / Agayn [his] choys . . . neither [to] grucche ne stryve" (169–70). In fact, the parallel terms in which each must make its promise to Walter, by full assent, only renders the political function of marriage all the more clear. To Walter's demands Griselda must: "be . . . redy with good herte / To al my lust, and that I frely may, / As me best thynketh, do yow laughe or smerte / And nevere ye *to grucche* it, nyght ne day?" (IV.351–54; my emphasis). With similar language, Walter exacts the same promise from his subjects before he consents to wed: "this shal ye swere: that ye / Agayn my choys shul neither *grucche* ne stryve" (IV.169–70; my emphasis). Thus, Walter marries to satisfy *and* to subdue his subjects. He turns their request for his marriage from a constraint placed upon his will into an exercise of will, and in the end his correction of his subjects, "the stormy peple" who shift their sworn allegiance from Griselda to the idea of a new wife, shows how much they stand in need of such correction.

Not so with Griselda herself. Instead, as a number of feminist readers have recognized, she subdues Walter.[41] Indeed, as we shall see, the satisfaction Griselda offers to Walter's curious desire "hir sadness for to knowe" results in a similar alignment of satisfying and subduing her husband. Such a performance contravenes the Wife's discussion of marriage, particularly her subtle understanding of the economics of desire governing its operations. For the Wife, marriage turns upon someone's desire, typically her own. The Clerk's abstract ideas of marital union and its figural significance—played out not only in the allegorizing end-

---

[41] See Elaine Tuttle Hansen, *Chaucer and the Fictions of Gender* (Berkeley and Los Angeles: University of California Press, 1992), and Jill Mann, *Geoffrey Chaucer* (Atlantic Highlands, N.J.: Humanities Press, 1991); revised as *Feminizing Chaucer* (Woodbridge: D. S. Brewer, 2002).

ing of the tale but also at the literal level of the story in the political figurations elaborated above—could not be further from the Wife's completely human and corporealized assumptions about marriage and its relation to personal desire.

Of course it is the human actions of Walter at the tale's literal level that provide the most difficulty for the Clerk and that trigger his well-known interjections of opinion into the fiction. Walter's "lest / To tempte his wyf" causes embarrassment for the Clerk even as it fuels the story of Griselda's unendurable and exemplary patience (IV.619–20). But Walter's monstrous "acts"—dramatized child murders and spousal abandonment—are matched by the unfathomable monstrosity of Griselda herself, whose maternal and human feelings have been called into question.[42] In fact, one could charge the Clerk's recoil from his tale, his speedy transition into the satiric song of the Envoy, upon her as well. But to see Griselda as monster rather than Walter, the Wife might argue, amounts to a form of feminist heresy as well as the vanishing point of the tale's figural and thus moral significance. Whether a success or a failure, the Clerk's exemplum of patience extols its virtue by taking the narrative to the limit, perhaps even threatening to exceed such limits and thus to know no limit at all. She "wol no thyng, ne nyl no thyng" (IV.646); she will do and say nothing, no matter how gross the cruelty of Walter's design. But at this limit Griselda explodes the very concept of limits; her passivity in the face of all Walter can devise for her becomes, like Christ's, the greatest *action*, as an act of will, to which the tale can bear witness.[43]

Because *The Clerk's Tale* works to oppose the Wife's in order to argue

---

[42] Modern readings of *The Clerk's Tale* criticize Griselda's behavior as much as Walter's. See Robert Emmett Finnegan, " 'She Should Have Said No to Walter': Griselda's Promise in the *Clerk's Tale*," *ES* 4 (1994): 303–21, and, more recently, J. Allen Mitchell, "Chaucer's *Clerk's Tale* and the Question of Ethical Monstrosity," *SP* 102 (2005): 1–26. Even McClellan's recent reading of the "aenigma of Griselda" as a Lacanian "negative subject," one who cannot say no, falls back on this distinction when he writes that her inability to say no, her power to be completely obedient to the will of another even to the point of death, was "meant to show us just how monstrous the situation really is" (" 'Ful Pale Face,' " 130). The critical tradition of reading the tale in terms of the monstrosity of its characters is long-standing and has been assessed as such. See, for example, James Sledd, "The *Clerk's Tale*: The Monsters and Critics," *MP* 51 (1953): 73–82.

[43] Linda Georgianna, "The Clerk's Tale and the Grammar of Assent," *Speculum* 70 (1995): 793–821. Lynn Staley compares Griselda specifically to the intimidating Jesus figure of the mystery plays. She writes, "His silence, his dignity under torture, his willing assumption of suffering, and his understanding of the dynamics of power are attributes of absolute authority" ("Postures of Sanctity," 254).

for passive suffering as the more powerful role for women in marriage, and because it figures the most sublimely heroic model of human behavior possible, we might find even more shocking the Clerk's recoil from its achievement. The Clerk's success, it would seem, comes at a heavy price. Griselda's strength in the face of her own rejection, Walter's request that she "voyde anon hir place" (IV.806), as well as her forbearance to arrange his new bride's accommodations, quickly turns into a machinery that threatens to permit the most heinous and inhuman of actions: an incestuous union of father and daughter. Though Griselda is completely unaware of the drama Walter scripts, the narrative tension staged for the Clerk's audience is almost palpable. In these final moments, we see Walter continually upping the ante "to the outtreste preeve of hir corage" (IV.787). Beyond murder and divorce, the Marquis would also have Griselda return as the servant of a new bride, who also happens to be her daughter. Like the dramatic spectacle staged at the opening of the tale for Walter's wedding, but with a far more uncomfortable effect, these intricated plans are set to bring final resolution to matters in Saluzzo and restoration to Griselda and to the audience watching her perform.

Griselda's refusal to break her promise of perfect obedience to Walter's will propels him to potentially horrific ends. Refusing to stand in the way of Walter's will, she will assist in Walter's marriage to his own daughter. Griselda's monstrosity, should the tale be said to contain this, has been configured as a lack of womanly or maternal resistance to Walter's designs. Caught between virtue and neglect, her lack of resistance drives Walter to the altar of incest and provokes an impending scene of pollution that he alone must forestall. Walter stops matters with the very same words he used earlier in the tale to exact Griselda's promise of obedience in marriage: "This is ynogh, Grisilde myn" (IV.1051; cf. IV.365). Where such a statement once halted the flow of her words, a promise "[i]n werk ne thought, I nyl yow disobeye, / For to be deed, though me were looth to deye" (IV.363–64), by the end of the tale those words must stop more than speech. They must prevent the act that would prove the absolute limitlessness of Walter's power by violating one of human civilization's primary laws.

If Walter is finally satisfied with Griselda's constancy, despite or actually because "he so ofte had doon to hire offence" (IV.1046), that satisfaction subdues—and conquers—him as it positions him to do the unthinkable in making his daughter his bride. Griselda's patience forces him to curtail his will and to relinquish his fiction of remarriage before it becomes a different story entirely. At the end of the incestuous fiction staged before her, Griselda triumphs over Walter's plot by making him give up the position of complete mastery he has so happily exercised at all other points throughout the story.[44] Griselda thus gives the lie to "sovereignty," the Marquis's absolute self-determination, by turning Walter's power inside out, extending its limits beyond his own seemingly "limitless" desires.

In the midst of Griselda's greatest trial, the Clerk unleashes an animus (possibly against Walter as much as her) on the "stormy peple" (IV.995), who were so easily swayed by the allure of a new and more noble bride. One could say that their responses throughout the tale were the ones Walter had been tempting his wife to exhibit:

> O stormy peple! Unsad and evere untrewe!
> Ay undiscreet and chaungynge as a fane!
> Delitynge evere in rumbul that is newe,
> For lyk the moone ay wexe ye and wane!
> Ay ful of clappyng, deere ynogh a jane!
> Youre doom is fals, youre constance yvele preeveth;
> A ful greet fool is he that on yow leeveth.
>
> (IV.995–1001)

The steadfast Griselda, "sad and constant as a wal" (IV.1047), provides the contrast for this image of the jangling and changeable "peple," "ful of clappyng." But they also bear an archetypal feminine resemblance to the "archewyves" in the Envoy, who are urged, "Ay clappeth as a mille" (IV.1200). Even more, besides the noise of "clappyng" common to both passages, the image of the moon with its changeable cycle is one of the most persistent images of femininity, elaborated early in the *Canterbury Tales* in the Knight's depiction of Diana's temple (I.2077–78). Much like the gossiping of wives seen in the Wife of Bath's Prologue, the crowd's "rumbul" echoes women's language, heard when Midas's wife "bombleth in the myre" (III.972) to satisfy her irresistible urge to tell his secret. This subtle feminine characterization of Walter's people refigures them into the form of a bad wife, one that specifically recalls Alison of Bath, who stands as an ostentatious and hyperbolic version of the wife Griselda refuses to become.

[44] Mann, *Geoffrey Chaucer*, 146; Hansen, *Fictions of Gender*, 203.

Passivity and the Desire for Mastery

Nobile vincendi genus est paciencia.[45]
"Patience is a noble form of conquering."

The Clerk's Tale unleashes a number of transferred effects here, at the point at which Griselda turns from victim of Walter's tests to victor over his incestuous plot. This movement shapes the Clerk's proof of his implicit argument, ostensibly setting to rest all the division and discord unleashed by the tale and the fictions maintained by Walter's test of both his wife and his people. Conflating ideas of passivity and passion, as Linda Georgianna has shown, Griselda's passive suffering triumphs in an intently active way.[46] She writes, "For all of his seeming power and authority, Walter becomes increasingly *re*active, following rather than directing Griselda's assent" (815). Even further, Griselda's passion amounts to a mastery that the tale formerly seemed to resist; in the telling words of Lynn Staley, "Griselda appears less victim than master of the man who apparently masters her."[47]

We might wonder here why the Clerk does not end on his note of triumph. Was this not "ynogh"? Even further than the Wife's, the Clerk's tale reaches beyond fairy-tale endings that sees a "pitous day" result in a "blisful ende" (IV.1121): "For moore solempne in every man-

---

[45] From a gloss to a proverb in the *Disticha Catonis*, cited by Jill Mann, " 'He Knew Nat Catoun: Medieval School Texts and Middle English Literature," in *The Text in the Community: Essays on Medieval Works, Manuscripts, Authors, and Readers*, ed. Jill Mann and Maura Nolan (Notre Dame: University of Notre Dame Press, 2006), 41–74 (59).

[46] "Grammar of Assent," esp. 803–5. Georgianna's stricter historicism articulates the active will of Griselda's passive suffering and also uncovers a latent Protestant critical ethic in the readings of Griselda. In her view, the Clerk fails to understand Griselda's story and reads it, much as modern critics have, in too rational terms. Georgianna calls for an emotive, numinous experience of reading the tale's pathos, an articulation that leaves the higher historicist claim somewhat troubled. She would see the critical (mis)-reading of passivity in negative terms (i.e., the critical rebuke of Griselda for neglect of her children) as a purely historical problem: "Passivity as a psychological abnormality found especially in females is a modern, post-Freudian usage" (803 n. 22). But the narrator's own misunderstanding of his tale, which she posits on 814–15, makes it less so. *The Clerk's Tale* appears to dramatize the difference between such renderings of passivity, showing Griselda's passive will as different from itself. A similar deconstruction of the idea of "sadness," a term, like "passive" here, strongly policed by philologists as completely separate from its modern emotional signification, would also seem to be in play. And of course what Georgianna's historicism can nowhere address is the salvific fantasy of symbolic plentitude such a reading offers via identification with Griselda herself.

[47] Staley, "Postures of Sanctity," 254.

nes syght / This feste was, and gretter of costage, / Than was the revel of hire mariage" (IV.1125–27). Much of this close to *The Clerk's Tale* repeats with excess the opening drama of Walter's wedding, retranslating Griselda from another "povre estaat" back into "richesse," "ther she was honored as hire oughte" (IV.1120). In echoing the opening "revel of hir mariage," this "moore solempne" close must also exceed its "costage" to form a fitting and final conclusion. It must repeat with a difference: as a renewal of the marriage drama, it marks both points of origination and conclusion as such. Yet as a final end, it must also denote its singularity, its unrepeatability—it "ys ynogh" and more. This should be his tale's proper end, and yet the Clerk continues beyond this point to assure us, with the certainty of history, that all turned out for the best.

In this elaborate allegorizing, the Clerk may position marriage far beyond personal pleasure or desire, but not so for *The Clerk's Tale*. His unstoppable speech and nervously concluding "song" reveal a number of desires in his narrative both proclaimed and disavowed. Even as he offers the reason for Griselda's test and fills the lack the story answers, his proliferating words betray their insufficiency. More information than seems needed follows: their daughter's marriage, Janicula's death, their son's succession are all foretold. But the factuality of these events cannot conclusively interpret and evaluate the story. He then offers the meaning Griselda's story does *not* hold: "This storie is seyd nat for that wyves sholde / Folwen Grisilde as in humylitee, / For it were inportable, though they wolde . . ." (IV.1142–44).

But the Clerk's denied reason for telling the story provides no final word or conclusive *raison d'être*. And that lack of finality or conclusion, it seems, propels him to keep speaking, to beg for another word, just a bit more of his audience's attention: "But o word, lordynges, herkneth er I go" (IV.1163); "I wol . . . / Seyn yow a song to glade yow" (IV.1173–74); "Herkneth my song that seith in this manere" (IV.1176). These pleas to his audience repeat, and thus ultimately show the failure of, his invocation of Petrarch's purpose, which is itself introduced in similar terms: "Herkneth what this auctour seith" (IV.1141). With a more opaque motive than would appear for the Wife's, *The Clerk's Tale* also nervously withdraws from its own triumphant end. These self-fracturing endings are not some symptom of a failure with these idealizations; indeed, on its own each succeeds brilliantly. But the recoil of the once-triumphant narrators ultimately articulates the desire, and thus the lack, that drives them toward narration in the first place. In this sense, then, the Clerk's aggression against the Wife in the Envoy to his tale is not so much a hostility to the content of her tale as much as it is his attempt to control the circulation of the signifier between them and who properly "owns" it. Seeking the recognition always at the heart of desire, he wants to be sure that she knows that he has had the last word.

Yet where the Wife's and Clerk's tales offer radically different idealizations of femininity, to an uncanny degree they work and speak alike within their fictions. If a hideous, undesirable (yet magical) crone in a fanciful Arthurian romance appears too unlike the "exemplary" Griselda, we have only to turn to the powerful mobility of these figures to see their connection. The hag changes her own form, appearing repulsive on her wedding night only to reward her husband with what she knows he wants in a mate. We are even led, retrospectively, to attribute to her the abrupt vision of dancing ladies that lures the questing knight into her company in the first place. Similarly mobile, Griselda is "translated" by marriage to Walter out of her inferior social position at the opening and close of her tale. Her transformation differs from the hag's as much as the genre of the Clerk's story trumps the ostensible frivolity of romance. Yet Griselda's translation ultimately marks an essential lack of change, her stability from her first words out of the "oxes stalle" in which she is found, throughout her trials by Walter's cruel design, to the final denouement. Griselda's initial translation works as a kind of revelation, a shift in appearance (much like the hag's) that articulates an essential inscription of value.

Despite what may *seem* to us their differences, in the end Griselda and the old woman offer the very same argument in their tales; the hag does so explicitly in her pillow lecture while Griselda does so implicitly by her constancy. These female figures, of course, give the lie to the assumed value of inherited wealth and station. Both subvert the social conditions of aristocratic privilege upon which so much of the discourse of the *Canterbury Tales* is founded. They offer in its place a moral order of heritability: "Crist wole we clayme of hym oure gentillesse" (III.1117). As the hag puts it to the knight she rebukes: "Looke who that is moost vertuous alway, / Pryvee and apert, and moost entendeth ay / To do the gentil dedes that he kan; / Taak hym for the grettest gentil man" (III.1113–16). Much like the narrators recoiling at the end of their respective tales, we may be shocked to learn that, in more ways than one, the Wife and Clerk have told the very same story.

Narrative Desire

A tale where the limitless desire for sovereignty must be curtailed by one who lacks any desire whatsoever, the Clerk's performance provokes a number of questions about its narrator's desires and those of his presumed audience. With whom should we align the Clerk's desire? Although the question orients us toward the figures in his tale, to a choice between Walter and Griselda, the real answer appears to be the Wife of Bath. To attain the sovereignty and autonomy to which the Wife and Clerk aspire through their tales (and which anyone engaged in Bailly's competition implicitly seeks), they must lay themselves open to the mastery they have supposedly abjured. In this way they define themselves not by sharing any similar appetite (in this they remain opposed), but by and through the Other's desire—the working of the Symbolic order to which they must submit.[48] Both narrators align themselves with feminine heroes idealized by their tales, the hag/lady and Griselda, figures that inhabit the place of the Other's desire for each of them. And each tale ultimately narrates the assumption of this desire for the Other. Desiring an Other they imagine and formulate in radically different terms, the Wife and Clerk desire to be the object of the Other's desire.

These terms undo the confusion between sovereignty and mastery at the end of the Wife's tale and rescript them into a fiction of subjectivity and its attendant (mis)recognitions. Given the "sovereynetee" to decide for herself, the hag asks her husband to qualify his choice: "Thanne have I gete of yow maistrie" (III.1236). The hag/Wife defines her sovereignty in terms of mastery over her husband, and thus gives the lie to the subject's own fiction of autonomy and self-determination. Gaining sovereignty, the power of self-determination, is a fiction of subjectivity,

---

[48] I should note the way the self-sufficient Walter paradigmatically assumes the desire of the Other in *The Clerk's Tale*. Walter's desire to marry, we will recall, comes from elsewhere; it originates with his people's desire and their concern for the "tyme comynge" (IV.79). He claims to have "nevere erst thoughte streyne me," but he immediately orchestrates a wedding that proves his beneficence and forethought. Walter similarly constructs his choice for a wife as other to the desire of the people for one "[b]orn of the gentilleste" appropriate to his "honour" (IV.144; 131, 133). He works according to a logic beyond the aristocratic form by which his people presume to find him a suitable match.

which demands far more mastery as well as the others mastery necessitates. To become a "self," one must also become a subject, which means recognizing and identifying with the Other. In fact, the misrecognition of the conditions of mastery as sovereignty is one of the primal fictions of the subject out of which desire, and the language that aims to fulfill it, emerges.

Such a reading thus turns the Clerk, through his identification with Griselda's desire, into one who desires complete mastery: "But as ye wole youreself, right so wol I" (IV.361). It also turns the Wife into the one subjected to an absolute master to whom she relinquishes all control. Seen in this way, the Wife and Clerk surprisingly inhabit the desires of each other's stories insofar as the raped maiden functions as a version of the passive Griselda and as Walter appears as a more exalted exemplar for the bachelor knight who deserves redemption. If the Wife's and Clerk's tales center on ideal images, then, these projections come with a cost, which is the fundamental alienation that the assumption of identity (and language) incurs. For the Clerk in particular, who so wishes to universalize his ideal as a model for human rather than feminine or wifely behavior, that cost is pressing. Difficult to calculate, these costs do not appear as such on the surface but stalk these ideal images in abjected form as raped maiden and voracious husband.

Ultimately, it may be no surprise to find out that the Clerk envies Walter's sovereign will, particularly insofar as it can be admired in the opening scene of the tale, before Griselda demystifies its lack. Such power subtends the meek and threadbare Clerk's desire.[49] More shocking is the recognition of the Wife's analogous fantasy of submission to a worthy man, a desire that positions her somewhat uncomfortably as the silent maiden and accounts for the rape opening her unique version of this traditional tale.[50] Such associations (and the extreme versions of

[49] We might read in this context the Clerk's one resounding criticism of the noble Walter. After delineating his conventionally noble attributes, the Clerk abruptly objects: "I blame hym thus: that he considered noght / In tyme comynge what myghte hym bityde" (IV.78–79). Such a curiously, even awkwardly, articulated evaluation in the Clerk's own voice amounts to the kind of performative utterance that does and means far more than it says. Not only symptomatizing the Clerk's veiled desire to dominate in advance of the story, his "blame" aligns him further with Walter's power, much of which operates in terms of performative utterances and orchestrates dramas Walter stages for an internal audience.

[50] In her discussion of the sources and analogues to *The Wife of Bath's Tale*, Helen Cooper writes, "The rape that opens the tale has no parallels in these other English versions, though similar adventures are on occasion credited (or discredited) to Gawain in some French romances" (159). *Oxford Guides to Chaucer: The Canterbury Tales* (Oxford: Oxford University Press, 1986).

the desire they articulate) make it much clearer why the Wife and Clerk recoil from a recognition of what they have accomplished in their tales. Their fictions witness the structure of desire underwriting them, their so-called rivalry, and the storytelling game more generally. At the very least, such associations may lead us to rethink the marriage group and the connections within these fragments of the *Canterbury Tales*. Looking at them in terms of sovereignty/mastery, and thus as what we might more playfully restyle an "S/M group," gives us a more precise picture of what the *Canterbury Tales* sees at stake in marriage and the stories told about it.

The fiction of the "marriage group" is a fiction of men arguing with women. But in using marriage to signify beyond the social contract, toward the more foundational importance of mastery in our originary fiction of autonomy and selfhood, Chaucer raises the stakes of marriage. The "marriage group" thus exceeds the Wife of Bath, which is why so many other tales—the Shipman's, the *Tale of Melibee*, the Nun's Priest's, the Manciple's—can be continually included within its bounds. The "marriage group" is not merely a group of tales responsive to Jerome's *Adversus Jovinianum* or a spectacle of dramatic interaction, but a sharper means of talking about desire, recognition, and social identity, the very subjects of the *Canterbury Tales* itself.

The Scribe of Bodleian Library MS Bodley 619 and the Circulation of Chaucer's *Treatise on the Astrolabe*

Simon Horobin
Magdalen College, Oxford

W HO WERE THE EARLY READERS of Chaucer's *Treatise on the Astrolabe?* The dedication of the work in its prologue to Chaucer's ten-year-old son Lewis indicates its immediate intended audience, but references elsewhere in the text suggest that it was also aimed at a wider readership. In the prologue Chaucer addresses "every discret persone that redith or herith this litel tretis," begging them to excuse his "rude endityng" and "superfluite of wordes."[1] That Chaucer's work was indeed widely read throughout the fifteenth century is apparent from the large number of surviving witnesses: a total of thirty-three manuscripts or fragments survive, the largest number for any Chaucerian text after the *Canterbury Tales.* Embarrassed by the apparent popularity of a work that seems so foreign to our modern view of Chaucer's attractions scholars have sought to explain away this situation as an aberration. E. T. Donaldson, for instance, proposed that the survival of a large number of manuscripts was the result of the dullness of its content which ensured that they were not harmed by overuse.[2] More recently there has been a resurgence of interest in this text, its status as a translation, its audience and reception. Scholars have particularly emphasized its reception within the fifteenth-century scientific community, and the tendency of scribes and compilers to expand upon Chaucer's unfinished treatise, and to copy it alongside

---

[1] *Treatise on the Astrolabe*, Prologue 33–36. All quotations from the text of the *Treatise* are taken from *A Variorum Edition of the Works of Geoffrey Chaucer, Volume I: The Prose Treatises, Part One: A Treatise on the Astrolabe*, ed. Sigmund Eisner (Norman: University of Oklahoma Press, 2002).

[2] E. T. Donaldson, "The Manuscripts of Chaucer's Works and Their Use," in *Geoffrey Chaucer*, ed. D. S. Brewer (London: Bell, 1974), 85–108.

other related astronomical works.[3] Of particular importance in this reconsideration of the text and its audience are the manuscripts themselves, and the evidence they provide for the text's readership. In this essay I aim to reconsider the evidence for the copying and consumption of one such manuscript to show how study of these numerous primary witnesses can shed important light on questions of audience and reception.

Bodleian Library MS Bodley 619, a copy of Chaucer's *Astrolabe* traditionally dated to the early fifteenth century, is an important witness to the early academic circulation of Chaucer's work. Its text of the treatise belongs to the superior alpha tradition, a text characterised by a particular order of the conclusions and the omission of all the probably spurious supplementary conclusions. Bodley 619 is considered by most editors to be the best surviving witness to that text, although it differs from all other alpha witnesses except one in the inclusion of supplementary conclusion 46.[4] The excellence of its text led to its use as a base text for the editions of F. N. Robinson, the *Riverside Chaucer* and the Variorum series.[5] The only other contender for base text is Cambridge University Library MS Dd.3.53, another early and accurate witness to the superior alpha textual tradition. This manuscript was adopted by W. W. Skeat and J. H. Fisher as the base text for their editions of the *Astrolabe*, although this preference was based more upon its inclusion of diagrams than the superiority of its text.[6]

The excellence of its text and the accuracy of its arithmetic have led many scholars to suggest that Bodley 619 was produced and read by learned astronomers. This view has been encouraged by the identification of the scribe of Bodley 619 himself as an astronomer with connec-

[3] See Edgar Laird, "Geoffrey Chaucer and Other Contributors to the *Treatise on the Astrolabe*," in *Rewriting Chaucer: Culture, Authority, and the Idea of the Authentic Text 1400–1602*, ed. Thomas A. Prendergast and Barbara Kline (Columbus: Ohio State University Press, 1999), 145–65.

[4] For a description of the text of Bodley 619 and a discussion of the textual tradition of the *Astrolabe*, see Eisner ed., *Variorum Edition*, 48–49.

[5] F. N. Robinson, ed. *The Works of Geoffrey Chaucer*, 2nd ed. (Oxford: Oxford University Press, 1957); Larry D. Benson, gen. ed., *The Riverside Chaucer* (Oxford: Oxford University Press, 1988). The Variorum text is based on a conflation of two manuscripts: Bodley 619, the best witness to the alpha tradition, and Bodleian Library MS Digby 72, the best representative of the inferior beta tradition. In basing his edition on Bodley 619, Eisner made 166 emendations to its text. See his discussion of the choice of base manuscript in *Variorum Edition*, 40–43.

[6] See *The Complete Works of Geoffrey Chaucer: Volume III*, ed. W. W. Skeat (Oxford: Clarendon Press, 1900), lvii, and *The Complete Poetry and Prose of Geoffrey Chaucer*, ed. John H. Fisher (New York: Holt, Rinehart and Winston, 1977), 971.

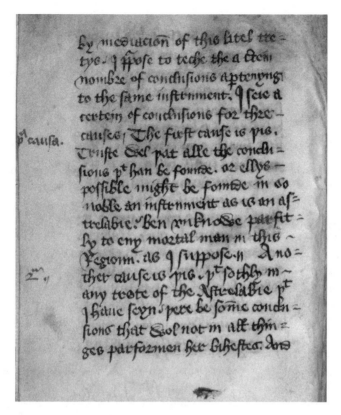

Bodleian Library MS Bodley 619, fol. 1v. Reproduced by permission of the Bodleian Library, University of Oxford.

tions to Merton College, Oxford, a major centre of astronomy in the fifteenth century. This suggestion appears to have originated with M. H. Liddell in his edition of the treatise for the Globe Chaucer, where he claims that "MS. Bodley 619 . . . bears evidence of having been written by an Astronomer of Merton College."[7] The claim was subsequently repeated by P. Pintelon and F. N. Robinson, while J. A. W. Bennett's discussion of the relationship between Chaucer's works and the Merton school of astronomers also drew upon this identification: "The Astrolabe of Chaucer itself became an Oxford text inasmuch as at least one copy

[7] *The Works of Chaucer*, ed. Alfred W. Pollard, H. Frank Heath, Mark H. Liddell, and W. S. McCormick (London: Macmillan, 1928), liii.

111

of it (MS.Bodley 619) was made by an Oxford astronomer."[8] The reason for attributing the copying of Bodley 619 to a Merton astronomer is a marginal note that appears on folio 15r in the scribe's hand which reads: "nota þat þese 5 sterres be meridional fro þe ecliptis and septemonal fro þe equinoctis Astrolabium colleg[ii] de Merton." Merton College Oxford was the centre of astronomical studies in England, perhaps even in Europe, in the Middle Ages, so that reference to it in this text might not appear surprising. However a direct link with Merton is strengthened by the fact that an astrolabe listed in the college inventory during the fourteenth century, and still there today, matches this description in having the same five stars north of the equator and south of the ecliptic named in the note. While many scholars have used this note as evidence for a direct connection between the scribe of the manuscript and Merton College, J. D. North is more cautious about drawing such a conclusion, though he does agree that the author of the note had probably seen the Merton astrolabe: "It seems very probable that the writer, Mertonian or not, knew the large Merton instrument."[9] Further support for a connection between the text of Bodley 619 and the Merton astrolabe is offered by Sigmund Eisner, who notes that both the Merton astrolabe and the marginal note mistakenly indicate that the star Cor Leonis had a negative latitude, where other medieval astrolabes correctly show that in the fourteenth century the latitude was positive. The combination of the excellence of the text of Bodley 619, including its very precise arithmetic, with the presence of this marginal note, has led to the view that its scribe was an interested and experienced practitioner of astronomy, as shown by Pintelon's view that the manuscript was the work of a "learned scribe," who was responsible for the added commentary and the "very clever conjectural addition" in Conclusion 26.

These comments rest on the assumption that the scribe of the manuscript was also responsible for composing this note, but it is of course possible that he simply reproduced a note that appeared in his exemplar. Pintelon's comments further assume that the production of an accurate copy of Chaucer's text requires scientific learning, overlooking the possibility that such a copy might be achieved by a professional scribe accurately reproducing a high-quality exemplar. That this scenario might lie behind Bodley 619 is suggested by the textual problems that surround

[8] J. A. W. Bennett, *Chaucer at Oxford and at Cambridge* (Oxford: Clarendon Press, 1974), 75.

[9] J. D. North, *Chaucer's Universe* (Oxford: Clarendon Press, 1988), 39 n. 2.

its copy of conclusions 38–40. Here, Bodley 619 becomes much less accurate so that editors have been forced to correct it heavily using another witness. From this point on, the text of Bodley 619 agrees closely with two other manuscripts, Cambridge University Library MS Dd.3.53 (Dd[1]) and Bodleian Library MS e Musaeo 54 (M[1]), and Liddell argued that this is due to a change of exemplar. This reduction in textual quality casts some doubt on the theory of the learned astronomer scribe, who might have been expected to have improved the quality of this inferior text. What this change implies is that the quality of the text was governed by the quality of the exemplar rather than the learning of the scribe. Within the alpha tradition, Bodley 619 is most closely related to British Library MS Additional 29250, a late fifteenth-century copy in a mixed secretary hand. As well as sharing numerous variants with Bodley 619, Additional 29250 also contains conclusion 46, not found in any other extant witness. The close textual relationship between these two manuscripts helps to emphasize the accuracy of Bodley 619 since Additional 29250 contains nearly twice as many variants as its textual twin. Of the 192 variants identified by Eisner in Bodley 619, 150 are also found in Additional 29250. This situation led Derek Price to argue that Additional 29250 was copied directly from Bodley 619, a conclusion with which Eisner concurs.[10] While this is a reasonable suggestion, it once again ignores the possibility that these variants derive from a common ancestor. The small number of examples of surviving manuscripts where one served as exemplar for the other makes this appear the likelier suggestion.[11] If we accept descent from a shared exemplar as the more likely scenario, then we may make further deductions about the copying abilities of our scribe. If 150 of his 192 variant readings can be attributed to his exemplar, then it is apparent that this was a very accurate and faithful copyist. The fact that he did not correct any of these inherited errors, however, implies that he was not an astronomer but rather a highly competent professional copyist. This view

---

[10] See Eisner, *Variorum Edition*, 54: "Since Ad[2] shares 150 of Bl[1]'s 192 variants, Price is likely right that Ad[2] was copied from Bl[1]." For Price's view, see his unpublished notes "On Astrolabe MSS" appended to Harvard University Library MS Houghton Library English 920.

[11] Richard Beadle has commented on the "decidedly small" number of instances of the survival among Middle English manuscripts of both exemplar and copy in "Geoffrey Spirleng (*c*.1426–*c*.1494): A Scribe of the *Canterbury Tales* in His Time," in *Of the Making of Books: Medieval Manuscripts, Their Scribes and Readers, Essays Presented to M. B. Parkes*, ed. P. R. Robinson and Rivkah Zim (Aldershot: Scolar Press, 1997), 116–46 (119 and n.7).

gains support from J. D. North, whose analysis of the text of this manuscript has led him to question the view that the scribe was a learned
practitioner of astronomy, and to claim that "no self-respecting astronomer of any century" would have accepted some of its figures. North's
skepticism toward the text of Bodley 619 leads him to argue that editors
should favor those manuscripts used by Skeat as his base text in preference to that of the "unknown Merton astronomer (if such he was) responsible for the manuscript (Bodley 619) that Liddell accepted as the
basis of the Globe edition."[12]

As well as sharing a similar text, Additional 29250 also contains the
marginal note associating Bodley 619 with Merton College, suggesting
that the note also derives from a common exemplar and may not be
relevant to the provenance of the manuscript or its scribe. The note
forms part of a set of learned Latin commentaries designed to correct
certain statements that Chaucer made in his treatise, recorded in both
Bodley 619 and Additional 29250 and no other manuscript. For instance, alongside line 174, both manuscripts include a gloss noting that
Chaucer's statement that "the sonne dwellith therfore nevere the more
ne lasse in oon signe that in another" is untrue: "Nota quod hoc falsum
est."[13] The gloss continues with a correct explanation that the sun is
longer in the summer signs than in the winter signs. Eisner has noted
that while this comment is essentially correct, it was miscopied by the
scribe, who wrote "hoc" for "hac" and "solis" where we would expect
"sicut."[14] Copying errors of this kind strongly suggest that this commentary was found in the scribe's exemplar and that it was not his own
learned response to the text. Other glosses added in these manuscripts
contain extracts from Chaucer's principal source text for the *Treatise*,
Messahala's *Compositio et operatio astrolabii*. For example, at line 440, Bodley 619 includes an additional passage translated from Messahala 2.30.
It is of course possible that additional passages from Messahala included
in this way could be authentic additions, although most scholars consider
them to be evidence of an attempt to improve on Chaucer's text by
returning to its source. Edgar Laird has even argued that the language
of the gloss shows the scribe attempting to imitate Chaucer's diction.[15]

---

[12] North, *Chaucer's Universe*, 74.

[13] These glosses are quoted from Eisner, *Variorum Edition*.

[14] See Eisner, *Variorum Edition*, 132.

[15] "This is fairly clearly a case of a scribe's improving a writer's text by going to the
writer's source." Laird argues that the use of "Nota" to claim the reader's attention and
the use of the rare but distinctively Chaucerian word "mediacioun" indicates that the

In addition to this vernacular rendition of Messahala, there are two other additions, at lines 458 and 1066, where additions quote directly from Messahala's Latin text, while another addition, at line 568, includes a reference to a *Treatise on the Quadrant*. While additions of this kind clearly point to a learned response to Chaucer's text by a reader familiar with its sources, it is not necessary to assume that these additions are the work of the scribe, while the appearance of all these passages in Additional 29250 would seem to militate against such a conclusion.[16] One further piece of evidence frequently cited in support of the Bodley 619 scribe's astronomical learning is the inclusion of lines 935–39. Skeat noted that this sentence, missing in all other manuscripts, is necessary for the sense and so must be genuine. Pintelon, drawing on Skeat's observation, argued that these lines are the result of a "very clever conjectural addition" by the scribe who noted the omission. This is a possible explanation of the manuscript evidence, but a more likely interpretation is that the scribe of Bodley 619 has simply reproduced his exemplar faithfully where others have omitted the lines as the result of eyeskip. That the passage is genuine is implied by the sense, and the likelihood that it appeared in the Bodley scribe's exemplar is suggested by its appearance in Additional 29250, a fact not noted by Skeat.

The excellence of the Bodley text and the learning of its scribe are further undermined by its inclusion of the supplementary conclusion 46, which describes how the astrolabe may be used to discover the zodiacal position of the moon. Eisner points out that the author of this spurious addition shows only a very general knowledge of the effects of the sun and moon on the tides, and, given the lack of consideration of the position of the sun and the irregularities of the coastline, the resulting calculations would be at best rough ones. Other editors have also printed the conclusion while simultaneously questioning the usefulness of the procedure it outlines. Skeat wrote that "it may be doubted whether this proposition is of much practical utility," and J. R. Reidy states that "this procedure seems pointless."[17]

So far I have sought to question the scholarly consensus that has attributed the copying of Bodley 619 to a learned astronomer with con-

---

scribe was attempting to imitate the diction and style of Chaucer's translation. See Laird, "Geoffrey Chaucer and Other Contributors," 153.

[16] Laird's reading of the gloss in note 15 is based on Skeat's edition of the *Astrolabe* and he is therefore unaware that it also appears in Additional 29250.

[17] See Skeat, *Complete Works*, 59–60, and *Riverside Chaucer*, 1102.

nections to Merton College, Oxford, on the basis of its textual affiliations and the accuracy of the text it transmits. In what follows I want
to offer an identification of its scribe on the basis of an analysis of his
handwriting, punctuation, spelling, and copying habits.[18] I will begin
by considering the paleographic evidence upon which such an identification can be made. The distinctive features of the scribe's hand include
the following: triangular single compartment **a** (fig. 1 line 7 *þat*) alongside more common two compartment **a** (fig. 1 line 4 *same*), tapered and
slanting **f** and long-s (fig. 1 line 6, *first, cause*), B-shaped kidney **s** finally
(fig. 1 line 6 *þis*) alongside 8-shaped **s** (fig. 1 line 8 *ellys*) and 6-shaped
s (fig. 1 lines 16–17 *conclusions*). This last form is common in initial
position (fig. 1 line 9 *so*) where it is used alongside long-s (fig. 1 line 4
same). Other distinctive characteristics not illustrated here include
upper-case **D** with a sharp left foot (see f. 8v line 4, *December*) and a
spiky upper-case **N** (fol. 21r line 3 *Nota*). This combination of striking
paleographic characteristics is typical of the writing style of the prolific
professional scribe Stephen Dodesham as characterized by A. I. Doyle
in his analysis of the more than twenty manuscripts attributed to his
hand.[19] In addition to the paleographic features described above, Dodesham employs a collection of characteristic non-alphabetic graphs: punctuation and space-fillers. In Figure 1 we can see a distinctive form of the
punctus in which it is extended by a curved stroke rising to the right as
a virgula (line 16), similar to the upper stroke of his punctus elevatus
(line 11). Another distinctive habit is the use of a hyphen to fill the
remainder of the line when the text does not fill the space (fig. 1, lines
5, 8, 12, 14). Commonly appearing at the end of sections of text is
Dodesham's 9-like positura (see fol. 30r, line 12), often with a clockwise
loop at the foot (see fol. 30r, line 10). A distinctive feature of his spelling
practices also noted by Doyle is the use of **v** where we would expect to
find **w**, eg *ovne* "own," a feature also noted by Brendan Biggs in his
analysis of Dodesham's spelling habits.[20] This practice is consistently
employed throughout the Bodley manuscript. In an analysis of Dodesham's spelling practices in his copy of the English translation of the

---

[18] I am very grateful to Dr A. I. Doyle for confirming this identification and for many
helpful suggestions.

[19] A. I. Doyle, "Stephen Dodesham of Witham and Sheen," in *Of the Making of Books:
Medieval Manuscripts, Their Scribes and Readers, Essays presented to M. B. Parkes*, ed. P. R.
Robinson and Rivkah Zim (Scolar Press: Aldershot, 1997), 94–115.

[20] B. Biggs, "The Language of the Scribes of the First English Translation of the
Imitatio Christi," *LeedsSE* n.s. 26 (1995): 79–111.

Imitatio Christi, now Dublin, Trinity College MS 678, Biggs compared the spellings found in this manuscript with twelve other manuscripts in Dodesham's hand. While there is a certain amount of linguistic variation across this substantial oeuvre, the overall impression is of considerable consistency. A comparison of Biggs's data taken from these thirteen manuscripts copied by Dodesham with Bodley 619 reveals the same linguistic preferences in the Bodley manuscript. Typical features of Dodesham's spelling practices found in Bodley 619 include: *hem* "them," *her* "their," *many, eny* "any," *moch, ben, wol, though, yit* "yet," *thorugh, youen* "give" (past participle).

Stephen Dodesham is the most prolific fifteenth-century English scribe yet identified, responsible for more than twenty surviving manuscripts. As well as copying works in Latin and religious and devotional works in the vernacular, including three manuscripts of Nicholas Love's *Mirror of the Blessed Life of Jesus Christ*, Dodesham was also responsible for a number of high-quality copies of secular works in Middle English, including three copies of Lydgate's *Siege of Thebes* and two manuscripts containing Benedict Burgh's *Parvus* and *Magnus Cato*. Bodley 619, however, is the first manuscript containing a work by Chaucer to be identified as the work of this important scribe. Doyle's analysis of Dodesham's extensive and prolific output enabled him to reconstruct episodes in the scribe's career, as well as to suggest tentative dates for some of his productions. Dodesham's earliest datable work suggests that his copying career began in the 1430s, or possibly even earlier, and he remained an active copyist until his death in 1482.[21] Among the earliest manuscripts in his hand are the three copies of Lydgate's *Siege of Thebes*, whose content and appearance imply that he began working as a professional lay scribe active in the London book trade.[22] A. S. G. Edwards's study of

[21] Doyle, "Stephen Dodesham," passim, and see also the brief discussion of Dodesham's copying career in *Aelred of Rievaulx's De Institutione Inclusarum: Two English Versions*, ed. John Ayto and Alexandra Barratt, EETS o.s. 287 (London: Oxford University Press, 1984), xxix–xxxii.

[22] The three texts of Lydgate's *Siege of Thebes* copied by Dodesham are: Boston Public Library f.med.94; Cambridge University Library Additional 3137; and New Haven, Yale University Library Beinecke 661. Kathleen Scott has linked one of the decorators who worked on both the Boston and Beinecke manuscripts of the *Siege of Thebes* with a London shop of the 1420s. See A. S. G. Edwards, "Beinecke MS 661 and Early Fifteenth-Century English Manuscript Production," *Yale University Library Gazette* 66 Suppl. (1991): 181–96 (188 and n. 37). Scott thinks it likely that the CUL manuscript belongs to the same period, although its fragmentary state makes a definite identification impossible.

the Lydgate manuscripts copied by Dodesham has shown that he drew on different exemplars of this text and employed various models of *ordinatio*, suggesting that they were produced in an ad hoc manner rather than in a bookshop, where access to a single exemplar and use of a standard format might be expected.[23] By the late 1460s, Dodesham had become a Carthusian monk, and in a record of 1469 of the *cartae* of that order he is named as a member of the Carthusian house at Witham, Somerset. A subsequent record of 1471 describes him as a professed monk of the house at Sheen, indicating that he had by this date moved to the Surrey house, where he died in 1482. A number of his copying commissions can be associated with his period as a Carthusian, including a copy of the pseudo-Augustine *Sermones morales ad fratres suos in heremo,* copied while at Witham, a Latin choir Psalter containing a Carthusian liturgical calendar, and at least one of his three surviving copies of Nicholas Love's *Mirror of the Blessed Life of Jesus Christ*, Glasgow University Library Hunterian MS T.3.15 (77), which contains a signature in a different hand stating that it belongs to the Charterhouse at Sheen and dating its copying to 1474–75.[24] Whether the two further deluxe copies of Love's *Mirror* were copied during his period of lay or monastic employment is not known; the breadth of appeal and readership of this text make either possible.

This identification of the scribe of Bodley 619 as the professional lay scribe and subsequently Carthusian monk Stephen Dodesham enables us finally to dismiss the long-held and widespread belief that the manuscript was copied by an Oxford astronomer. The attribution of the copying of this manuscript to a professional scribe like Dodesham fits well with the hypothesis posited above that the accuracy of the text and its learned commentary are the result of faithful copying of a high-quality exemplar. But it raises a new set of important questions: When did Dodesham copy the manuscript? Was it during his career as a professional lay scribe or after his profession as a Carthusian monk? How did he get access to such a good copy of the treatise, and for whom did Dodesham copy the manuscript?

The high quality of its text of Chaucer's *Astrolabe*, a work apparently

---

[23] Edwards, "Beinecke MS 661," 187–89.

[24] The inscription is quoted in full by Doyle, "Stephen Dodesham," 96. For images of the Hunterian MS, see "The World of Chaucer," exhibition hosted on the Web site of Glasgow University Library Department of Special Collections: http://special.lib.gla.ac.uk/exhibns/chaucer/index.html.

written by Chaucer in 1391 and preserved in other manuscripts of the first quarter of the fifteenth century, might suggest that this is one of Dodesham's early commissions as a professional lay scribe. The London focus for the earliest copying, circulation, and readership of Chaucer's works would also fit with this period in Dodesham's career, when he was copying secular works for the London book trade. Edgar Laird has recently argued that the readers of Chaucer's *Treatise on the Astrolabe* comprised a similar group as the audience of his poetic works. Rather than seeing the *Astrolabe* as a purely technical work destined for a coterie of expert astronomers, Laird emphasizes the work's broader appeal as well as its potential usefulness for readers without specialist knowledge, struggling with the astronomical allusions in his poetry.[25] The copying of this manuscript by Dodesham may therefore provide further support for Laird's argument, indicating that this text was circulating within the same literary circles as such secular works as Lydgate's *Siege of Thebes*. This work is explicitly intended as a continuation of Chaucer's *Canterbury Tales*, and its use of astronomical allusions might require explanation for the uninitiated just as Laird has suggested for Chaucer's works.

The primary audience of Chaucer's *Astrolabe* is of course a ten-year-old boy, and it is possible that Bodley 619 was intended to be used in the education of a child of similar age, as is further implied by its use of the title "Brede and Milke for Children," a heading found in three other manuscripts. A similar audience is implied by another of Dodesham's productions, surviving as Glasgow University Library Hunter MSS U.4.17 (259) and U.4.16 (260) but originally a single manuscript. This manuscript contains a verse paraphrase of the *Parvus Cato* and *Magnus Cato* by Benedict Burgh, works used to educate the young in Latin and etiquette. These texts are followed by a copy of Lydgate's *Dietary* with its basic advice on healthy eating, further implying an audience of youthful learners. Doyle has speculated that the large size of the writing in this volume may have been designed to make the volume more easily legible by readers beginning their education.[26] Dodesham produced a second copy of the *Parvus* and *Magnus Cato*, Bodleian Library Eng. Poetry e.15, where the text appears alone in a smaller and more utilitarian format more reminiscent of Bodley 619. So it may be that Dodesham's copy of

---

[25] Edgar Laird, "Chaucer and Friends: The Audience for *The Treatise on the Astrolabe*," *ChauR* 41 (2007): 439–44.

[26] Doyle, "Stephen Dodesham," 104.

the *Astrolabe* was designed to be used for elementary education in a household in a similar way as the copies of Burgh's translations.

However, there are important differences that appear to contradict this interpretation. In comparison with the large size of the writing in the Hunterian manuscripts, Bodley 619 is a small manuscript, with leaves measuring 140mm x 90mm with a writing space of 90mm x 60mm. The text is written throughout in a compact hand with no apparent concession to the elementary reader. Where the Hunterian manuscripts employ a clear and elegant *ordinatio*, with a decorative hierarchy that makes the volume easily navigable, the Bodley manuscript is much less clearly and expansively laid out. The possibility that Bodley 619 was commissioned by a wealthy household is also contradicted by its plainness and lack of decoration or illustration. This is particularly apparent when it is compared with Dodesham's other commercial commissions, such as the copies of Lydgate's *Siege of Thebes* and possibly the copies of Love's *Mirror*. These manuscripts were decorated and illuminated by professional metropolitan limners whose work has been identified in other deluxe manuscripts.[27] By comparison, Bodley 619 is a decidedly utilitarian manuscript with no such decoration. Gaps have been left by the scribe for the inclusion of decorated capitals at a later stage, although these were never executed, while headings have been written by the scribe in rubric. I have already noted that the manuscript does not include any of the illustrations that are found in other early copies of the *Astrolabe* and that we might expect any self-respecting London patron to have considered a crucial component in such a commission.

Given this, it might be better to consider this manuscript to have been produced after Dodesham's profession as a Carthusian. Support for the hypothesis that the manuscript was copied comparatively late in Dodesham's career is found in a comparison of the handwriting in Bodley 619 with other instances of his writing. The several datable manuscripts in Dodesham's hand allow us to identify certain changes in the preference for individual letterforms, enabling a tentative chronology for his works to be constructed. The earliest datable manuscript is Karlsruhe, Badische Landesbibliothek, MS Sankt Georgen 12, containing part of the *Sanctilogium salvatoris*, copied for Sion Abbey on behalf of

[27] For the *Siege of Thebes* manuscripts, see note 22 above. Kathleen Scott also notes that while Hunter T.3.15 (77) was copied at Sheen, there is no need to assume that the decoration was also carried out in-house. See Kathleen L. Scott, *Dated & Datable English Manuscript Borders, c. 1395–1499* (London: Bibliographical Society, 2002), 94–97.

Margaret Duchess of Clarence, who died in 1439. Dodesham's last datable work is Hunter T.3.15 (77), dated internally to 1474–75, some thirty-five years later. Comparing Dodesham's *anglicana formata* in these two volumes, Doyle noted certain changes in the scribe's preferences for individual letterforms. In the Karlsruhe MS, Dodesham prefers initial and medial long r and 8-shaped s, whereas in the Hunterian MS short r and kidney-shaped s are preferred. The scribe's handwriting in Bodley 619 is more closely affiliated with the Hunterian MS than the Kalsruhe MS, with short r and kidney-shaped s much more frequent than long r and 8-shaped s. Long r does appear, but very infrequently, while 8-shaped s is also rare. This suggests that Bodley 619 was copied comparatively late in Dodesham's career, although a more detailed analysis of his entire output would be required to verify this hypothesis.

A number of extant copies of Chaucer's *Astrolabe* can be associated with religious houses, so it is not difficult to imagine a Carthusian monk getting access to an exemplar and having an interest in such a work. Other copies with similar associations include Bodleian Library MS Bodley 68, which contains an ownership inscription in the hand of its scribe, Iohanni Enderby de Louth capellano, perhaps a member of the Cistercian house at Louth Park in Lincolnshire. Bodleian Library MS Ashmole 360 is also signed by its scribe, who names himself Fr John Pekeryng, while Bodleian Library MS Ashmole 393 was copied by Henry Cranebroke, a Benedictine monk of Christ Church Canterbury (d. 1466). A recently discovered fragment of the *Astrolabe* appears as part of a collection of scientific texts in Latin whose copying and fifteenth-century ownership can be linked with Thurgarton Priory, a house of Augustinian canons in Nottinghamshire.[28] References within this manuscript to "my astrolabe" and "the large astrolabe" indicate that the canons at Thurgarton owned at least one astrolabe and possibly more. That it was not unusual for an Augustinian house to possess an astrolabe is further witnessed by records of ownership of these and other astronomical instruments by the Augustinian canons of York and Leicester. Each of these manuscripts of the *Astrolabe* appears to have been copied for personal use, and the comparatively utilitarian appearance of Bodley 619, combined with its diminutive size, might indicate that it too was intended for its scribe's personal study.

---

[28] This manuscript is London, Royal College of Physicians MS 358. For a description of its identification and a discussion of its provenance, see Catherine Eagleton, "A Previously Unnoticed Fragment of Chaucer's *Treatise on the Astrolabe*," *JEBS* 6 (2003): 161–73.

The catalogue of books owned at Sion Abbey includes books containing scientific treatises demonstrating interest in astronomy in such institutions. Cambridge University Library MS Hh.6.8, formerly owned by Sion, contains tables for the latitude of Toledo, astronomical tables and notes, and a translation of Messahala's *Compositio et operatio astrolabii*, Chaucer's major source for the *Astrolabe*. The reference to a "tractatus de spera" in another volume listed in the catalogue is probably to another text used by Chaucer: Sacrobosco's *Tractatus de sphaera*.[29]

A third possible explanation of the circumstances surrounding the copying of Bodley 619 is linked to the Oxford connection discussed above. While I have argued that the scribe himself was not a learned astronomer connected to Merton College, Oxford, commercial scribes were active in copying books for the University of Oxford in the fifteenth century, employed in a similar freelance manner as found among the scribes working in the London book trade.[30] This is well demonstrated by the copying career of the continental scribe Henry Mere, who copied royal charters in addition to books for the Oxford book trade, as well as manuscripts for Christ Church Priory Canterbury.[31] A. I. Doyle has noted similarities between Dodesham's hand and those found in other royal charters, such as the foundation charters of King's College Cambridge and Eton College, suggesting that Dodesham received his training among scribes of the royal chancery.[32] Like Mere, Dodesham may have also undertaken paid work for the Oxford book trade; perhaps Bodley 619 was a commission undertaken for an astronomer associated with Merton College? Interestingly, Henry Mere himself undertook scribal work for Merton College, contributing a single volume to a four-volume set of the postils by Hugh of St. Cher commissioned by Henry Sever, Warden of Merton. This manuscript is still in the college library, where it is Merton College MS 150. A possible patron that might help to explain the connection between Dodesham and Merton College is John Blacman. Blacman was admitted as a student at Merton in 1437,

---

[29] For the Sion Abbey catalogue and manuscripts associated with Carthusian houses, see Vincent Gillespie, *Sion Abbey, with the libraries of the Carthusians* edited by *A. I. Doyle*, Corpus of British Medieval Library Catalogues 9 (London: British Library, 2001).

[30] See M. B. Parkes, "The Provision of Books," in *The History of the University of Oxford Volume II: Late Medieval Oxford*, ed. J. I. Catto and Ralph Evans (Oxford: Clarendon Press, 1992), 407–83.

[31] The copying career of Henry Mere is described in M. B. Parkes, "A Fifteenth-Century Scribe: Henry Mere," *Bodleian Library Record* 6 (1957–61): 654–59, repr. in M. B. Parkes, *Scribes, Scripts, and Readers: Studies in the Communication, Presentation, and Dissemination of Medieval Texts* (London: Hambledon Press, 1991), 249–56.

[32] Doyle, "Stephen Dodesham," 114.

graduating MA in 1439, when he became a fellow. He resigned his fellowship in 1443 in order to take up a fellowship at the newly founded Eton College, where he served as precentor from 1444 to 1452. In 1452, he became warden of King's Hall Cambridge, resigning his Eton fellowship in the following year. In 1457 or 1458, Blacman resigned from his various livings and was admitted to the London Charterhouse. In 1465, he moved to Witham Charterhouse, where he acquired a substantial library; in 1474, he donated a large number of volumes to the Witham library. Among his donation to the Witham Charterhouse was a two-volume copy of Nicholas de Lyra copied by Henry Mere. Parkes considers this evidence that Blacman commissioned Mere to copy the work for him, indicating that Blacman did indeed draw upon freelance scribes like Mere and Dodesham. As we have seen, Dodesham was a member of Witham Priory in the late 1460s and their period of residence must have overlapped for at least several years before Dodesham's transfer to Sheen. In his discussion of Blacman's library and its reflection of his developing interests, Lovatt notes of Blacman's decision to move from the London Charterhouse to Witham that Dodesham's presence at the Somerset house might have attracted someone with Blacman's "particular intellectual and bibliographical concerns." That Blacman kept up his interest in his former studies at Oxford and the work of his former colleagues is apparent from the inclusion in his library of a copy of astronomical tables calculated according to the meridian of Oxford by a former Merton fellow, William Rede. There are also direct connections between Blacman's library and Dodesham's productions: an inscription attributing a copy of *Sermones morales* to Dodesham is in the hand of the same monk of Witham who added ex-libris inscriptions to other books and a portion of the list of gifts to the Charterhouse by John Blacman.[33] These connections may be no more than coincidence, but they at least indicate one method by which a professional scribe and subsequently Carthusian monk of Witham Priory could have come to copy an excellent text of Chaucer's *Astrolabe* with Mertonian connections.

Bodley 619 does not contain a coat of arms, nor are there any indications of early ownership. The earliest ownership mark is an inscription on folio 69v in a hand of the early sixteenth century that reads: "Constat More de Mychelmalvarn monech." M. C. Seymour has suggested that

---

[33] This identification is made in Doyle, "Stephen Dodesham," 94. For a discussion of Blacman and his library, see R. Lovatt, "The Library of John Blacman and Contemporary Carthusian Spirituality," *Journal of Ecclesiastical History* 43 (1992): 195–230.

this More was the Christopher Aldewyn who received £10 after the surrender of the Benedictine Priory of Great Malvern in 1539 and who is
described as alias More, scholar at Oxford.[34] The Oxford connection
implied by this identification serves to reinforce the Oxford provenance
I have been suggesting, while also helping to explain how the manuscript came into the hands of a Benedictine monk of Great Malvern.

Whichever of these possible scenarios is accepted as an explanation
for Dodesham's copying of Chaucer's *Astrolabe*, it is clear that identification of the scribes responsible for the copying of these manuscripts
can help to shed important new light on questions concerning the reception and circulation of Chaucer's treatise. Chaucer's *Astrolabe* has long
been neglected by students of Chaucer's works in favor of his more canonical poetical works. The recent renaissance of interest in this text
and its audience has considerably expanded our understanding of the
circulation of Chaucer's treatise, although there is still much work to be
done on the numerous surviving primary witnesses. The recent discoveries of an extract of the text and an erased fragment in two fifteenth-
century scientific anthologies have alerted us to the possibility that
further witnesses of the text may remain to be identified.[35] In their attempts to identify Chaucer's readers, scholars have often focused on the
manuscripts of the *Canterbury Tales* and *Troilus and Criseyde*, although
their lack of coats of arms or early ownership inscriptions often frustrates
efforts to identify their original owners. In contrast, the manuscripts of
Chaucer's *Astrolabe* contain a number of scribal signatures and fifteenth-
century inscriptions and remain a valuable source of evidence for Chaucer's reception that remains largely untapped.[36]

---

[34] M. C. Seymour, *A Catalogue of Chaucer Manuscripts, Volume I: Works before the Canterbury Tales* (Aldershot: Scolar Press, 1995), 107. For the original reference, see "Houses
of Benedictine Monks: Priory of Great Malvern," in *The Victoria History of the County of
Worcester: Volume 2*, ed. J. W. Willis-Bund and William Page (1906; Folkestone: Institute of Historical Research, 1971), 136–43.

[35] The new fragment is preserved in Trinity College Cambridge MS R.14.52 and is
identified in Edgar Laird, "A Previously Unnoticed Manuscript of Chaucer's *Treatise on
the Astrolabe*," *ChauR* 34 (2000): 410–15. Laird's edition of this extract of the *Astrolabe*
is available in *Sex, Aging, and Death in a Medieval Medical Compendium: Trinity College
Cambridge MS. R.14.52, Its Language, Scribe, and Texts*, ed. M. Teresa Tavormina (Tempe:
MRTS, 2006). For the erased fragment in London, Royal College of Physicians MS 358,
see Eagleton, "A Previously Unnoticed Fragment."

[36] Research for this article was carried out as part of a project entitled "The Identifi-
cation of Scribes Responsible for Copying Major Works of Middle English Literature,"
co-directed by the author and Professor Linne Mooney of the University of York. The
Project is supported by a four-year grant from the UK Arts and Humanities Research
Council and aims to examine all the manuscripts containing the works of Chaucer,
Gower, Langland, Hoccleve, and Trevisa.

English Historical Narratives of Jewish Child-Murder, Chaucer's *Prioress's Tale*, and the Date of Chaucer's Unknown Source

Roger Dahood
University of Arizona

SCHOLARS HAVE LONG RECOGNIZED that *The Prioress's Tale* is a version of the Chorister class, sometimes called the Boy Singer class, of Marian miracle stories. In *The Prioress's Tale*, Jews in an Asian city murder a Christian schoolboy, the "litel clergeon," for singing the *Alma redemptoris mater* in the Jewry. A "greyn" that Mary places on his tongue miraculously causes him to continue singing until Christians discover the crime, the authorities execute his murderers by drawing and hanging, and an abbot removes the grain. Monks then inter the boy's corpse in a marble tomb.

In the first decade of the twentieth century, Carleton Brown distinguished three groups among the Chorister tales, which he labeled A, B, and C. *The Prioress's Tale* is number 6 in Group C.[1] The Chorister stories

This essay has evolved from two conference papers, the first delivered in Kalamazoo in 2007 at a session organized by Georgiana Donavin in honor of Dhira Mahoney, and the second in Swansea in 2008 at a New Chaucer Society session organized by Geraldine Heng and Kathy Lavezzo. The essay has benefited from comments at various times by Carl T. Berkhout, H. A. Kelly, Lister Matheson, Peter E. Medine, Donald R. Nickerson, Glending Olson, and M. Teresa Tavormina. I am grateful to Cynthia White for consultation in translating the Latin from the Gloucester chronicle.

[1] Carleton Brown, *A Study of the Miracle of Our Lady, Told by Chaucer's Prioress*, Chaucer Society, Second Series, 45 (London, Oxford, and New York: Chaucer Society, 1910); Brown, "The Prioress's Tale," in *Sources and Analogues of Chaucer's Canterbury Tales*, ed. W. F. Bryan and Germaine Dempster (New York: Humanities Press, 1941, repr. 1958), 447–85. Laurel Broughton, "The Prioress's Prologue and Tale," in *Sources and Analogues of the Canterbury Tales*, ed. Robert M. Correale and Mary Hamel, 2 vols. (Cambridge: D. S. Brewer, 2002–5), 2:583–647, retains Brown's groupings but labels six additional analogues NA1–NA6. Anthony Bale, *The Jew in the Medieval Book: English Antisemitisms, 1350–1500* (Cambridge: Cambridge University Press, 2006), 169, prefers to focus on "disagreement and variation" among the Chorister stories and see the "story's discursive

have strong ties to England. Many versions, especially those of Group C, survive in manuscripts of English provenance, and six versions have an English setting.[2] Indeed, C9, from fifteenth-century Spain, is set in Lincoln. Chaucerians have not fully appreciated the implications of this late Spanish version for study of *The Prioress's Tale*.

The present essay explores the possibility that *The Prioress's Tale* combines Chorister features with features from non-Marian English narratives in which Jews are said to crucify Christian boys in mockery of Christ's Passion. I begin my analysis by revisiting the question, long thought to be settled, of whether *The Prioress's Tale* owes a debt to the history of Hugh of Lincoln, a Christian boy for whose supposed crucifixion in 1255 Henry III executed nineteen Lincoln Jews.[3] As we shall see, evidence from a number of sources suggests that boy-crucifixion stories,[4] whose origins scholars have traced to twelfth-century England, partially merged with the Chorister tradition in England in response to distinctive historical stimuli. We can identify the stimuli from the testimony of *The Prioress's Tale* and its Spanish cousin. I conclude by proposing a *terminus a quo* for the kind of Chorister narrative Chaucer draws on and suggesting that Hugh of Lincoln played a more central role in the genesis of *The Prioress's Tale* than has hitherto been supposed.

Group A and B stories, Brown observed, survive from the thirteenth century, but the earliest C analogues of which Brown was aware at the time he distinguished the groups date from the early fourteenth century. Because the victim's death and burial occur exclusively in Group C, Brown reasoned that they are a late development. He further hypothe-

---

development as a defining hermeneutic rather than as an inconvenient obstacle to establishing Chaucer's true source." Bale rejects Brown's classification and lists the analogues in chronological order. As my essay demonstrates, however, Brown's classification remains a useful framework for studying the Chorister story's evolution.

[2] In his study of 1910, Brown used roman numerals within the groups. In his 1941 study, limited to Group C, he used arabic numbers. I have used arabic numbers only. The versions in English manuscripts number at least sixteen: A10, B4, C1–C8, C10, and NA2–NA6. Those with an English setting include A1, A3, A5, A7, C9, and NA1.

[3] The standard modern treatment of Hugh's death and its aftermath is Gavin I. Langmuir, "The Knight's Tale of Young Hugh of Lincoln," *Speculum* 47 (1972): 459–82; repr. in *Toward a Definition of Antisemitism*, ed. Gavin I. Langmuir (Berkeley and Los Angeles: University of California Press, 1990), 237–62.

[4] The term "mock crucifixion," sometimes used to designate boy-crucifixion stories, is potentially misleading and I have avoided it, for in the stories I will discuss the incidents were believed to involve real crucifixion of living Christian boys.

sized that the death and burial derive from the history of Hugh,[5] for the Prioress invokes Hugh in her final stanza:

> O yonge Hugh of Lincoln, slayn also
> With cursed Jewes, as it is notable,
> For it is but a litel while ago,
> Preye eke for us, we sinful folk unstable . . .
>   (VII.684–87)[6]

Brown's evidence proved flawed, however, and his hypothesis untenable. In the 1930s, Albert C. Friend discovered a C analogue from around 1215, complete with the death and burial of the victim. The 1215 analogue, since designated C1, is the earliest of all the precisely datable analogues, A, B, and C. The death and burial cannot be a late development and cannot derive from Hugh, who died in 1255, which C1 antedates by some forty years. In 1941, Brown withdrew his hypothesis, and the idea that Hugh could be a source of *The Prioress's Tale* has been discounted ever since.[7]

Yet close examination shows that although the evidence of C1 rules out Brown's hypothesis, it does not rule out Hugh of Lincoln as a source of *The Prioress's Tale*. The left-hand column of Table 1 lists twenty-six plot features from pre-Chaucerian English narratives of Jewish child-murder. In all cases the victims are Christian boys, some said to have been horribly tortured before death, and some said to have been crucified. Features 20–26 are absent from *The Prioress's Tale* and all other Chorister stories but will figure later in my analysis. Features 1–15 appear in *The Prioress's Tale* and in the anterior Chorister tradition. They constitute the tale's Chorister legacy. I have marked them with capital X in the table.[8] Features 16–19, marked with lower-case x, occur in *The*

---

[5] Carleton Brown, "Chaucer's *Prioresses Tale* and Its Analogues," *PMLA* 21 (1906): 486–518 (508–17); Brown, *A Study*, 97–99.

[6] Quotations of *The Prioress's Tale* are from Larry D. Benson, ed., *The Canterbury Tales, Complete* (Boston and New York: Houghton Mifflin, 2000).

[7] Brown, "The Prioress's Tale," 451–57; Broughton, "The Prioress's Prologue and Tale," 591–92, alludes to Brown's retraction and quotes his observation that the ending of Group C stories may reflect "earlier stories of Jewish atrocities which were circulating in England."

[8] All except features 7 and 15 appear in C1. Feature 7, the cut throat, is extant in analogues from as early as the thirteenth century (A6 and B2). C1 identifies the mother only as *vetulam pauperem* "a poor old woman," not specifically, as feature 15 requires, a widow, but C2, from the early fourteenth century, refers to a story *de filio vidue* "about the son of a widow"; Broughton, "The Prioress's Prologue and Tale," 617, 621.

Table 1: Twenty-six Plot Features from Stories of Jewish Child-Murder

Plot Feature	Chorister Stories (ante *PriT*)	*PriT* (c. 1390)
1 Child-murder	X	X
2 Christian boy as victim	X	X
3 Christian boy victim is a clerk	X	X
4 Victim sings *Alma redemptoris* in the Jewry	X	X
5 Jews as conspirators/murderers	X	X
6 Victim's mother searches for missing boy	X	X
7 Victim's throat cut in Jewry or Jew's house	X	X
8 Victim's corpse thrown into a privy	X	X
9 Virgin Mary or God miraculously intervenes	X	X
10 Victim continues singing *Alma* after death	X	X
11 Mother discovers victim's body in Jew's house	X	X
12 Secular authority intervenes against the Jews	X	X
13 Secular investigation establishes Jews' guilt	X	X
14 Clergy reverently inter the victim in church	X	X
15 Victim's mother is a widow	X	X
FEATURES 16–19 ABSENT FROM CHORISTER STORIES BEFORE *THE PRIORESS'S TALE*		
16 Jews drawn and hanged		x
17 Clergy inter victim in a marble tomb		x
18 Murder occurs in unfrequented or secret place in alley		x
19 Clergy who inter the victim are an abbot and his monks		x
FEATURES 20–25 ABSENT FROM ALL CHORISTER TALES		

Table 1 (Continued)

Plot Feature	Chorister Stories (ante *PriT*)	*PriT* (c. 1390)
20 Extra-local Jews assemble, decide on the ritual murder		
21 The murder occurs at Easter		
22 Victim allegedly crucified		
23 Jews engage in cannibalism		
24 Corpse cannot be buried, etc., until the crime is known		
25 Rival clergyman tries to claim corpse for his church		
26 Miracles of healing associated with victim's corpse		

Prioress's Tale but are absent from Chorister tales before Chaucer. For antecedents of these features we must look beyond the Chorister tradition.

The Prioress's allusion to Hugh of Lincoln points us to antecedents for features 16 and 17, the execution of the Jews by drawing and hanging and the marble tomb. A thirteenth-century Anglo-Norman poem, the contemporary Saint Albans chronicle of Matthew Paris, the Burton chronicle, the Waverley chronicle, and a slightly later London chronicle from about 1270 all report the drawing and hanging of Lincoln Jews for Hugh's death.[9] *Castleford's Chronicle*, probably from Yorkshire and on internal evidence completed not before 1327, also reports the drawing and hanging.[10] The record thus shows the drawing and hanging of the

[9] "Hugo de Lincolnia," in *Hugues de Lincoln: Recueil de Ballades Anglo-Normande et Ecossoises Relatives Au Meurtre de Cet Enfant Commis par les Juifs en MCCLV*, ed. Francisque Michel (Paris and London: Silvestre [Paris]; Pickering [London], 1834), 3–16 (15–16); Matthew Paris, *Chronica Majora*, ed. Henry Richards Luard, Rolls Series 57, 7 vols. (1872–83; Wiesbaden: Kraus Reprint, 1964), 5 (1880): 519; *Annales Monastici*, ed. Henry Richards Luard, Rolls Series 36, 5 vols. (London: Longman, Green, Longman, Roberts, and Green, 1864–69), 1:345–46, 2 (1865): 348; *De Antiquis Legibus Liber: Cronica Maiorum et Vicecomitum Londiniarum*, ed. Thomas Stapleton, Camden Society, vol. o.s. 34 (London, 1846), 23; Neil R. Ker and Alan J. Piper, *Medieval Manuscripts in British Libraries*, 4 vols. (Oxford: Clarendon Press, 1969–92), 1:22, supply the date for the last.

[10] The chronicle survives uniquely in Göttingen, Niederdersächsische Staats- und Universitätsbibliothek, MS. 2 Cod. hist. 740, from the fifteenth century. Discussion of the date and provenance of the manuscript and the chronicle may be found in the "Introduction" to Caroline D. Eckhardt, ed., *Castleford's Chronicle or the Boke of Brut*, 2

Jews to be a core feature of Hugh narratives well into the third decade of the fourteenth century. As for feature 17, the early chronicles say nothing of a marble tomb. In the 1290s, however, thirty or forty years after the early chronicles were written, in the south choir aisle of Lincoln cathedral Edward I commissioned for Hugh an impressive shrine enclosing a tomb of Purbeck marble. The archaeological remnants of the tomb survive to this day.[11] The Prioress's closing invocation of Hugh of Lincoln points strongly to the history of Hugh as the source for the execution of the murderers by drawing and hanging and for the marble tomb of the "litel clergeon."

Antecedents of features 18 and 19 occur in tales from twelfth-century England. Thomas of Monmouth's mid-twelfth-century life of Saint William of Norwich, thought to be the ancestor of all boy-crucifixion stories from medieval Europe,[12] may be the ultimate source of feature 18. According to Thomas, the Jews' henchman and William walk together *diuertentes eos per priuata diuerticula* ["turning aside through private by-ways" or "by-ways out of public view"] to get to the Jew's house where the alleged crucifixion occurs.[13] If elements of the two traditions were beginning to mingle by the later thirteenth century, it is possible that via some no-longer-traceable stages, this henchman evolved into the hired murderer who in *The Prioress's Tale* ". . . in an aleye hadde a privee place" (VII.568).

The trail for an antecedent to feature 19—that is, the abbot and monks who inter the litel clergeon's corpse—again leads to twelfth-century England, this time to the child-murder legends of Harold of

---

vols. (third volume yet to be published) EETS 305, 306 (Oxford: Oxford University Press, 1996), 1:xi. The pertinent text appears in 2:1001–4.

[11] David Stocker, "The Shrine of Little St Hugh," in *Medieval Art and Architecture at Lincoln Cathedral*, ed. T. A. Heslop and V. A. Sekules, British Archaeological Association Conference Transactions 8 (Leeds: British Archaeological Association, 1986), 109–17, provides a thorough account of the remnants and a reconstruction drawing of the shrine. Joe Hillaby, "The Ritual-Child-Murder Accusation: Its Dissemination and Harold of Gloucester," *Jewish Historical Studies: Transactions of the Jewish Historical Society of England* 34 (1994–96): 69–109, reproduces a photograph of the tomb (95).

[12] Gavin I. Langmuir, "Thomas of Monmouth: Detector of Ritual Murder," *Speculum* 59 (1984): 820–46; repr. in *Toward a Definition of Antisemitism,* ed. Langmuir, 209–36; John M. McCulloh, "Jewish Ritual Murder: William of Norwich, Thomas of Monmouth, and the Early Dissemination of the Myth," *Speculum* 72 (1997): 698–740.

[13] *The Life and Miracles of St. William of Norwich, by Thomas of Monmouth*, ed. and trans. Augustus Jessopp and Montague Rhodes James (Cambridge: Cambridge University Press, 1896), 19.

Gloucester and Robert of Bury. In both cases the early witnesses say nothing of boy-crucifixion.[14] The earliest account of Harold appears in the chronicle of Saint Peter's abbey of Gloucester.[15] Walter Froucester or Frocester (d. 1414), abbot of Saint Peter's, who probably compiled the chronicle in the late fourteenth or early fifteenth century, appears to have relied for his account of Harold on a much earlier but no longer extant source.[16] The chronicle reports that in March 1168 the Gloucester monks, under the direction of Abbot Hamelin (d. 1179), honorably carried into the abbey church and buried there the corpse of a Christian boy called Harold, on whom local Jews had inflicted tortures and whom they had murdered, mainly by roasting alive.[17] The chronicle says *cruciatus*, "tortured," not *crucifixus*, "crucified."[18] A reference under the year

---

[14] The first explicit statement that in twelfth-century Gloucester a boy was crucified comes from a thirteenth-century Peterborough chronicle, as noted in my main text. The first explicit statements for Robert appear in works by John Lydgate (c. 1370–1449/50?) and William Worcester (1415–1480x85). The proximity of Bury to Norwich nonetheless makes likely that crucifixion by then had long since become part of Robert's story. I have taken the dates for Lydgate and Worcester from articles by Douglas Gray and Nicholas Orme in the *Oxford Dictionary of National Biography* (hereafter *ODNB*) online, respectively http://www.oxforddnb.com/view/article/17238 and http://www.oxforddnb.com/view/article/29967, accessed March 6, 2009. Hillaby, "The Ritual-Child-Murder Accusation," 74, gathers the references to Harold; Bale, *The Jew in the Medieval Book*, 107–8, 111–12, the references to Robert.

[15] Saint Peter's was a Benedictine monastery before the dissolution. In 1541, Henry VIII made it a cathedral; David Knowles and R. Neville Hadcock, *Medieval Religious Houses, England and Wales*, 2nd ed. (London: Longman Group, 1971), 66.

[16] For a discussion of the chronicle's date and authorship and, where Froucester's work can be checked, his faithfulness to his sources, see Christopher N. L. Brooke, "St. Peter of Gloucester and St. Cadog of Llancarfan," in *The Church and the Welsh Border in the Central Middle Ages*, ed. D. N. Dumville and C. N. L. Brooke, Studies in Celtic History 8 (Woodbridge, Suffolk: Boydell, 1986), 50–94 (51, 54, 56–57, 64). There is little reason to suppose that Froucester's account of Harold's death and burial diverges substantially from his source.

[17] *Historia et Cartularium Monasterii Sancti Petri Gloucestriae*, ed. W. H. Hart, Rolls Series 33 (London: Her Majesty's Stationery Office, 1863–65), 1:20–22. Hillaby, "The Ritual-Child-Murder Accusation," 77, argues from internal inconsistencies that the episode occurred in 1167. For Hamelin's death date, I have relied on David Knowles, C. N. L. Brooke, and Vera C. M. London, eds., *The Heads of Religious Houses, England and Wales, 940–1216* (Cambridge: Cambridge University Press, 1972), 53.

[18] The reading *cruciatus* appears in the printed text in Hart, ed., *Historia et Cartularium Monasterii Sancti Petri*, and also in the text in Gloucester, Gloucester Cathedral Library, MS 34, fol. 7v, which Hart did not use. Neither has *crucifixus*. Brooke, "St. Peter of Gloucester," 51 n. 3, judges Gloucester MS 34 the best of the three known manuscripts of the chronicle. I am grateful to the Reverend Canon David Hoyle for granting me access to the manuscript, and to him and his office staff for extending warm hospitality during my visit.

1161 to an anonymous boy crucified at Gloucester at Easter appears in a Peterborough chronicle probably compiled after 1273.[19] The reference suggests that a version of Harold's story had reached the east of England by the later thirteenth century, and that it had by then become a story of boy-crucifixion. Of Robert of Bury we have only sketchy knowledge. Jocelin of Brakelond (fl. 1173–c. 1215) says that Robert was martyred (*martirizatus*) in 1181 and buried *in ecclesia nostra* "in our church," that is, the abbey church, which also contained Robert's shrine.[20] Jocelin's contemporary, Gervase of Canterbury (c. 1145–1210 or later), adds that Jews martyred Robert at Easter.[21] It is probably safe, relying on the precedent of Hamelin and the monks of Gloucester, to infer from Jocelin's statement that the abbot and monks of Bury performed Robert's interment.[22]

[19] "In hoc Pascha quidam puer crucifixus est apud Gloucestriam." *Chronicon Petroburgense*, ed. Thomas Stapleton, Camden Society, o.s. 47 (London, 1849), 3.

[20] Jocelin's full sentence reads, *"Eodem tempore fuit sanctus puer Robertus martirizatus, et in ecclesia nostra sepultus, et fiebant prodigia et signa multa in plebe, sicut alibi scripsimus."* [At this same time the holy boy Robert suffered martyrdom and was buried in our church, and many signs and wonders were performed among the common folk, as I have set down elsewhere.] It is thought that the final clause of the passage refers to a hagiography of Robert, now lost. I have taken the text and translation from Jocelin of Brakelond, *The Chronicle of Jocelin of Brakelond Concerning the Acts of Samson Abbot of the Monastery of St. Edmund*, ed. H. E. Butler, Medieval Classics (London: Thomas Nelson and Sons, 1949), 16. For a more recent translation based on Butler's Latin text, see Jocelin of Brakelond, *Chronicle of the Abbey of Bury St Edmunds*, trans. Diana E. Greenway and Jane E. Sayers, Oxford World's Classics (Oxford: Oxford University Press, 1989), 15.

[21] S.v. A.D. 1181: *"Martyrizatus est hoc anno ad Pascha apud Sanctum Ædmundum a Judæis puer quidam Robertus nomine . . ."*; Gervase of Canterbury, *The Historical Works of Gervase of Canterbury: The Chronicle of the Reigns of Stephen, Henry II, and Richard I*, ed. William Stubbs, Rolls Series 73, 2 vols. (London: Longman, 1879), 1:296. For Gervase's dates, I have relied on the article by G. H. Martin in the *ODNB;* http://www.oxforddnb.com/view/article/10570, accessed March 6, 2009.

[22] Harold's and Robert's burials antedate Gregory IX's *Decretals* (promulgated in 1234) and later additions to canon law that prohibit monastic performance of pastoral duties. Henry Ansgar Kelly, "Sacraments, Sacramentals, and Lay Piety in Chaucer's England," *ChauR* 28 (1993): 5–22 (18 n. 44), cites the *Ordinary Gloss* of Bernard of Parma (published in the mid-1260s): "Nota quod monachi curam populi habere non debent." The quoted passage appears at col. 1311 of the *Corpus iuris canonici* (Rome, 1582; repr. Lyons, 1606), vol. 3, cited in Kelly, "Sacraments," n. 8. There is evidence that after the ravages of the plague in the 1340s, English Benedictines had permission to serve parish churches; Cuthbert Butler, *Benedictine Monachism: Studies in Benedictine Life and Rule*, 2nd ed. (1924; repr. Cambridge: Speculum Historiale, 1961), 417. Relaxation in *The Prioress's Tale* of the prohibition of monks performing burial duties would have perhaps seemed unsurprising to Chaucer and his late fourteenth-century English audiences, especially because the monks perform the burial in their own abbey and implicitly with the abbot's participation. For the reference to Butler, I am indebted to Margaret Jennings.

Two further boy-crucifixion stories require notice in this survey. The earlier one, in which the victim is a French boy living in Winchester, appears in the chronicle of Richard of Devizes, and the later one tells of the death of Adam of Bristol. Richard of Devizes completed his chronicle at Winchester before 1198. Although in many details Richard's narrative is idiosyncratic, it alleges notably that the Jews of Winchester crucified, cut the throat of, and cannibalized their anonymous victim at Easter.[23]

The story of Adam of Bristol, a Christian boy said to have suffered crucifixion at the hands of Jews in the twelfth century, is a thirteenth-century creation. Adam is at best distantly related to the other boy-crucifixions. The only feature peculiar to boy-crucifixion stories Adam shares with the rest is murder by boy-crucifixion. Also, Adam unlike the others is a Marian tale. Mary and Jesus miraculously comfort Adam in his travail, and angels stand guard over his lifeless corpse.[24]

Table 2 shows aggregated and marked with capital X the shared features discussed so far. All nineteen features in *The Prioress's Tale* have antecedents in the Chorister, the boy-crucifixion, or both traditions. The table also marks with capital O features 20–26, features associated with boy-crucifixion stories but absent from the Chorister tradition. Five appear in the life of William, three in Harold, four in Robert, three in Richard, one in Adam, and all seven in one or more versions of Hugh.

The distribution of features enables a number of straightforward conclusions. First, *The Prioress's Tale* participates in two partially overlapping but independent story traditions of Jews murdering Christian boys: the Chorister and the boy-crucifixion traditions. Second, in the Chorister stories, the Virgin Mary is central and crucifixion is absent. In the boy-crucifixion stories, boy-crucifixion is central, and from all but Adam of Bristol the Marian elements are absent. To put it another way, the Chorister stories are Marian and not boy-crucifixion tales,

---

[23] Richard of Devizes, *Chronicon Richardi Divisensis de Tempore Regis Richardi Primi*, ed. and trans. John T. Appleby (London and New York: Thomas Nelson and Sons, 1963), 64–69 (68–69). Appleby discusses the chronicle's provenance and date of completion, xv, xviii.

[24] Robert C. Stacey, "From Ritual Crucifixion to Host Desecration: Jews and the Body of Christ," *Jewish History* 12 (1998): 11–28, assigns the composition a *terminus a quo* in the second quarter of the thirteenth century (15) and provides a useful summary of the story. For an edition of the Latin, see Christoph Cluse, " 'Fabula Ineptissima': Die Ritualmordlegende Um Adam von Bristol nach der Handschrift London, British Library, Harley 957," *Aschkenas: Zeitschrift Für Geschichte und Kultur der Juden* (Vienna) 5 (1995): 293–330, starting at 305.

Table 2: Aggregate of Plot Features from Chorister and Boy-Crucifixion Stories. X Marks Features Common to the Chorister and Boy-Crucifixion Stories. O Marks Features Exclusive to Boy-Crucifixion Stories.

Plot Feature	William (c. 1150)	Harold (1168)	Robert (1181)	Richard (a. 1198)	Chor. (1215–a. *PriT*)	Adam (p. 1225)	Hugh (1255)	*PriT* (c. 1390)
1 Child-murder	X	X	X	X	X	X	X	X
2 Christian boy as victim	X	X	X	X	X	X	X	X
3 Christian boy victim is a clerk					X		X	X
4 Victim sings *Alma redemptoris* in Jewry					X			X
5 Jews as conspirators/murderers	X	X	X	X	X	X	X	X
6 Victim's mother searches for missing boy					X		X	X
7 Victim's throat cut in Jewry or Jew's house				X	X	X	X	X
8 Victim's corpse thrown into privy					X	X	X	X
9 Virgin Mary or God miraculously intervenes					X	X		X
10 Victim continues singing *Alma* after death					X			X
11 Mother discovers victim's body in Jew's house					X		X	X

	1	2	3	4	5	6	7
12 Secular authority intervenes against the Jews				X		X	X
13 Secular investigation establishes Jews' guilt				X		X	X
14 Clergy reverently inter victim in church	X	X	X	X		X	X
15 Victim's mother is a widow				X			X
16 Jews drawn and hanged						X	X
17 Clergy inter victim in a marble tomb						X	X
18 Murder occurs in secret or unfrequented place in alley	X						X
19 Clergy who inter the victim are an abbot and his monks		X	X				X
20 Extra-local Jews assemble, decide on the ritual murder	O	O	O			O	
21 The murder occurs at Easter	O	O	O			O	
22 Victim allegedly crucified	O	O	O		O	O	
23 Jews engage in cannibalism			O			O	
24 Corpse cannot be buried, etc., until the crime is known		O	O			O	
25 Rival clergyman tries to claim corpse for his church	O					O	
26 Miracle(s) of healing associated with victim's corpse	O	O	O			O	

135

and the boy-crucifixion tales are predominantly not Marian. Third, *The Prioress's Tale*, as Brown recognized, is fundamentally a Chorister story. Although it shares a number of features with the boy-crucifixion narratives, these are incidental to the plot. The Jews in *The Prioress's Tale* show no interest in crucifixion or ritual murder of any kind. They are motivated by a desire to put an end to perceived sacrilege, the boy's singing, which Satan tells them is "'agayn youre lawes reverence'":

> Fro thennes forth the Jues han conspired
> This innocent out of this world to chace.
> An homycide therto han they hyred . . .
>
> (VII.564–67)

The murderer unceremoniously cuts the boy's throat and casts the body into a privy:

> And as the child gan forby for to pace
> This cursed Jew hym hente, and heeld hym faste,
> And kitte his throte and in a pit him caste . . .
> Where as thise Jewes purgen hire entraille.
>
> (VII.569–73)

The foregoing analysis confirms that *The Prioress's Tale* springs chiefly from the Chorister tradition but exhibits features with antecedents found only in a broader narrative context, a cluster of non-Chorister, non-Marian, boy-crucifixion stories rooted in twelfth- and thirteenth-century English history. Probably from Hugh of Lincoln came the drawing and hanging of the Jews and the marble tomb; probably from Harold of Gloucester, Robert of Bury, or both, came the abbey burial; and perhaps from William of Norwich came the secret alley. At the center of the cluster is the history of Hugh of Lincoln. The Prioress herself points us directly to Hugh and invites us to read the story of the "litel clergeon" in the light of Hugh's.

It remains to draw out some perhaps less evident implications of this study. The tables show that William's, Harold's, Robert's, Richard's, and the pre-Chaucerian Chorister stories exhibit five features in common. If we include the highly idiosyncratic story of Adam of Bristol, the number rises to seven. The shared features may be the traces of a very early relationship between the boy-crucifixion and Chorister groups, but whether there was a relationship, and what its nature might have been, are questions that in our present state of knowledge remain obscure. The evidence of Richard of Devizes perhaps hints that the cut throat entered the Chorister tradition from a boy-crucifixion story circulating in the late twelfth century. As we have seen, the cut throat makes its earliest extant Chorister appearances in the thirteenth century (note 8 above). The presence of the Virgin Mary in Adam of Bristol suggests that as early as the second quarter of the thirteenth century features from boy-crucifixion and Marian, possibly Chorister tales could coalesce into a story distinct in plot from mainstream boy-crucifixion and Marian miracle narratives.[25]

In 1255, with the death of Hugh, the number of shared features among pre-Chaucerian tales rises to eleven. This dramatic increase is compatible with a hypothesis of increasing association of the Chorister and boy-crucifixion tales during the thirteenth century. Hugh's interment in 1255 in Lincoln cathedral, or, to give its full name, the Cathedral Church of Saint Mary of Lincoln, might well have evoked the closer association. It is, however, the Prioress's invocation of Hugh in the late fourteenth century that provides the first explicit linking of the traditions.[26] The placement of "also" in rhyme position stresses a parallel between Hugh's fate and the fate of the Prioress's "litel clergeon":

> O yonge Hugh of Lincoln, slayn also
> With cursed Jewes . . .
>
> (VII.684–85)

The imputed similarity between Hugh's death and that of the "litel clergeon," the incorporation of drawing and hanging of the Jews, and especially the incorporation of the marble tomb from Hugh's story into that of the "litel clergeon" indicate that assimilation of boy-crucifixion to Chorister miracle narratives had continued at least to the last decade of the thirteenth century.

---

[25] The disposal of the body in a privy, which first occurs among the boy-crucifixions in Adam, may have been suggested by the story of William in which the Jews consider, but divinely inspired advice leads them to reject, throwing the body into a privy (*The Life*, ed. and trans. Jessopp and James, 24).

[26] Sumner Ferris, "Chaucer at Lincoln (1387): The *Prioress's Tale* as Political Poem," *ChauR* 15 (1981): 295–321 (297–99, 316), finds a number of additional allusions to Lincoln and Lincoln Cathedral in the tale. These allusions must be inferred, but especially appealing is Ferris's argument that a fourteenth-century audience would recognize Lincoln in a reference to Saint Nicholas (VII.514). The Anglo-Norman name for Lincoln is "Nichole."

Might it be possible to identify a catalyst for the Chorister tradition's apparently late assimilation of features 16–19 from boy-crucifixion tales? Analogue C9, composed by Alphonsus a Spina in Salamanca sometime between 1458 and 1460 as part of his *Fortalitium fidei contra Judeos, Saracenos, aliosque Christiane fidei inimicos*, provides a clue. C9 is set in Lincoln and represents the schoolboy's murder as a principal cause of the 1290 expulsion:

In Lincoln . . . [a] certain poor widow had a son. . . . And [because of the murder and other Jewish crimes against Christ and Mary] the king of the realm . . . ordered that on an assigned day, all the Jews found in the kingdom would be killed. Those who thought better of it were despoiled of all their goods, and baptized and expelled from the entire kingdom of England. From that time no Jew ever lived, nor lives, nor dared to appear there.[27]

The Prioress's Tale and C9 comprise what can be called a Lincoln subgroup within Group C. The existence of the subgroup raises four questions: whether C9 is independent of *The Prioress's Tale*, why and when the connection between Lincoln and the Chorister tradition originated, and why a Chorister story intimately tied to Lincoln and the expulsion should have found its way to Spain.

C9 is almost certainly independent of *The Prioress's Tale*. As Brown noted long ago, Alphonsus would have been unlikely to have had access to the *Canterbury Tales* or have had the ability to read Middle English.[28] Also, *The Prioress's Tale* and C9 differ markedly in focus and details. The two analogues are thus independent witnesses to late developments in the Chorister tradition and, as we shall now see, to the emergence of the Lincoln subgroup probably around the turn of the fourteenth century.

Hugh's shrine is one of a number of projects in which David Stocker finds evidence of King Edward's "strong interest in emphasizing both the alleged criminality of the English Jewry and the Crown's position as principal defender of the English Christians."[29] The shrine seems to have prominently displayed the royal arms. As Stocker observes, "The political implications of this explicit connection between the Crown and the Saint . . . would not have been lost on contemporaries."[30] Stocker dates the

---

[27] I have adapted the extracts from the translation by Priscilla Throop in Broughton, "The Prioress's Prologue and Tale," 632–36.
[28] Brown, "Chaucer's *Prioresses Tale*," 512n.
[29] Stocker, "The Shrine," 116.
[30] Ibid., 115.

design of Hugh's shrine to between 1290 and 1295 and suggests that completion of the project from start to finish may have taken a decade.[31] C9 gives the Chorister tale a Lincoln setting, includes the marble tomb,[32] and cites the Lincoln singer's death as a primary reason for the expulsion. The presence of the marble tomb in C9 and *The Prioress's Tale*, and the explicit connection C9 makes between Lincoln, the Chorister murder, and the expulsion, probably indicates that the subgroup formed in response to Edward's enshrinement of Hugh as an icon of the expulsion. Ancestral versions of *The Prioress's Tale* and C9 therefore probably date to sometime between the early 1290s and Edward's death in 1307.

There is additional evidence of a *terminus a quo* for the Lincoln subgroup between the 1290s and 1307. The Prioress's opening stanza characterizes Jews, usury, and rulers who sustain them as hateful to Christ and Christians:

> Ther was in Asye, in a greet cite,
> Amonges Cristene folk a Jewerye,
> Sustened by a lord of that contree
> For foule usure and lucre of vileynye,
> Hateful to Crist and to his compaignye. . . .
>
> (VII.488–92)

The Prioress's closing stanza invokes Hugh of Lincoln and, by extension, boy-crucifixion. Usury and boy-crucifixion are remote from the central concerns of pre-Chaucerian Chorister stories, and indeed they have no evident connection to the death and miraculous singing of the Prioress's "litel clergeon." These very concerns, however, determined royal policy toward Jews during Edward's reign.[33] The Prioress's open-

---

[31] Ibid., 114–15.

[32] According to Alphonsus, the little boy was buried "in sepulcro marmoreo"; Broughton, "The Prioress's Prologue and Tale," 637, line 76.

[33] Robert C. Stacey, "Parliamentary Negotiation and the Expulsion of the Jews from England," in *Thirteenth-Century England VI: Proceedings of the Durham Conference 1995*, ed. Michael Prestwich, R. H. Britnell, and Robin Frame (Woodbridge, Suffolk, and Rochester, N.Y.: Boydell, 1997), 77–101, esp. 93–101; Stacey, "Anti-Semitism and the Medieval English State," in *The Medieval State: Essays Presented to James Campbell*, ed. John R. Maddicott and David M. Palliser (London, and Rio Grande, Ohio: Hambledon Press, 2000), 163–77 (174–77), and, on eliminating Jews by conversion, Stacey, "The Conversion of the Jews to Christianity in Thirteenth-Century England," *Speculum* 67 (1992): 263–83. For a broader analysis of the causes, in which, nonetheless, Edward's concern to curb Jewish usury is prominent, see Robin R. Mundill, *England's Jewish Solution: Experiment and Expulsion, 1262–1290* (Cambridge: Cambridge University Press, 1998), 108–24, 249–85.

ing stanza implies that no Christian ruler can tolerate Jews or Jewish usury within his kingdom. Her closing stanza, by appeal to English history, reaffirms the tale's lesson that a Jewish community within a Christian one is a deadly menace to the Christians. Such reasoning contributed to Edward's decision to expel the Jews. Three-quarters of a century before C9, *The Prioress's Tale* testifies to the Chorister tradition's assimilation of the events in Lincoln and the expulsion.

That fifteenth-century Spain should produce a Chorister analogue with a Lincoln connection is not surprising. It may be that Chaucer's patron John of Gaunt (d. 1399), whose enduring ties to Lincoln and activities in Spain are well known, brought a version of C9 to Spain in the later fourteenth century.[34] We should not, however, overlook the possibility that an ancestral version of C9 reached Spain significantly earlier. Eleanor, Edward's queen, was the daughter of Ferdinand III of Castile. Eleanor died near Lincoln on November 28, 1290, not a month after the expulsion took effect, and her viscera lie in a sepulcher topped with her effigy at the east end of Lincoln Cathedral.[35] The coincidence of the expulsion, Eleanor's death, and Edward's memorializing of Eleanor and Hugh at Lincoln is difficult to ignore. We may conjecture that between the early 1290s and 1307 a Chorister tale tying the expulsion to Hugh followed the news of Eleanor's death into Spain.

By invoking Hugh, the Prioress calls attention to the half of her tale's genealogy that modern scholarship has tended to dismiss, that is, the non-Marian, historical English narratives of Jews crucifying English Christian boys. She also reminds us of the historical context from which her version of the Chorister tale emerged: the expulsion of 1290. A story that presents itself as Asian turns out to be deeply informed by events in England of the twelfth and especially the late thirteenth century. Some seventy and more years after the discovery of C1 relegated Hugh of Lincoln to the margins of *Prioress's Tale* study, it is now perhaps time to move him back closer to the center.

---

[34] From 1371, when he married Constanza of Castile, daughter of the murdered Pedro I, until 1387, John was pretender to the crown of Castile. For a brief account of John's career, see Simon Walker, "John, duke of Aquitaine and duke of Lancaster, styled king of Castile and León (1340–1399)," *ODNB;* http://www.oxforddnb.com/view/article/14843, accessed November 26, 2008.

[35] Edward had ordered the Jews to leave England by November 1, 1290. For a useful summary of Eleanor's life, see John Carmi Parsons, "Eleanor (1241–1290)," *ODNB;* http://www.oxforddnb.com/view/article/8619, accessed November 24, 2008.

Composing the King, 1390–1391:

Gower's Ricardian Rhetoric

Kurt Olsson
University of Idaho

I N ACCOUNTS OF THE MIDDLE YEARS of Richard II's reign, contemporary chroniclers record a lively series of encounters between the king and those who had become increasingly concerned about the conduct of his rule and the future of the realm. John Gower may have shared those concerns, but in the Prologue of the original *Confessio Amantis* his report of meeting the king on the Thames does not touch on them. Gower sets the scene: "As I be bote cam rowende," he writes, "My liege lord par chaunce I mette; / And so befell, as I cam nyh, / He bad me come in to his barge" (Prol. 40*, 42–44*).[1] Having already declared his intention to "make / A bok for king Richardes sake" (Prol. 23–24*), Gower not surprisingly centers this account on the "kinges heste":

> And whan I was with him at large,
> Amonges othre thinges seid
> He hath this charge upon me leid,
> And bad me doo my besynesse
> That to his hihe worthinesse
> Som newe thing I scholde boke,

---

[1] All quotations from Gower are from *The Complete Works of John Gower*, ed. G. C. Macaulay, 4 vols. (Oxford: Clarendon Press, 1899–1902); translations of *Vox clamantis* are from Eric W. Stockton, trans., *The Major Latin Works of John Gower: The Voice of One Crying and The Tripartite Chronicle* (Seattle: University of Washington Press, 1962). I follow Macaulay in using an asterisk to designate original, first-recension lines that Gower subsequently replaced in later versions of the poems. Aside from a few instances in the *Vox clamantis*, in this study I draw only upon such passages in the *Confessio* Prol. 24–92*, and epilogue, 8.2971–3069*.

> That he himself it mihte loke
> After the forme of my writynge.
>
> (Prol. 46–53*)

In this meeting, the conversation, as far as we are told, was not political, but literary, and the poet provides no evidence that among "othre thinges seid" he repeated his own earlier advice—from the epistle to a younger Richard that he had incorporated in the *Vox clamantis*—about conduct supporting or detracting from effective rule. Nor does he hint that the king encouraged him to do so, to speak his mind or elaborate on what he had previously written. Richard simply wants "som newe thing." That sets the poet's task, and Gower responds deferentially, exactly as is expected of him: "And elles were I nought excused, / For that thing may nought be refused / Which a king himselve bit" (Prol. 73–75*). This is a case of hard patronage. The poet has no choice but to comply, and comply with grace.

The story of the poet being thus engaged by his king does not end with this narrative, of course, but extends through the entire work to its closing, the presentation of the "povere bok" unto the king's "hihe worthinesse" (8.3050–51*), and before Gower finishes with it, he adroitly comments on Richard's history. Many stories informed the content and rhetorical strategy of his response. Possibly included in that number is the famous report—in part another Thames narrative—preserved in the *Westminster Chronicle* and elsewhere, of a day in March 1385, when Archbishop Courtenay upbraids Richard for his complicity in the plot to murder his uncle, John of Gaunt. Richard's action has weakened accepted laws and imperiled the kingdom, the archbishop argues, because it sets a precedent, enabling a king, whenever he wishes, to murder in secret anyone toward whom he bears ill will. Richard's response tells us what *he* thinks: first, at Westminster, he "leapt to his feet with a volley of threats" at the archbishop, and later that day, when they meet on the Thames and Courtenay, unwilling to let the earlier matter rest, repeats his charges, he "drew his sword and would have run the archbishop through on the spot."[2] Although Gower does not rise to

---

[2] ". . . rex iratus versus archiepiscopum iloco surrexit et minas ei intulit." ". . . rex extracto ense archiepiscopum iloco perfodisset." *The Westminster Chronicle, 1381–1394*, ed. and trans. L. C. Hector and Barbara F. Harvey (Oxford: Clarendon Press, 1982), 116–17. For a discussion of relationships between the two Thames narratives—Gower's and the Westminster chronicler's—see Frank Grady, "Gower's Boat, Richard's Barge, and the True Story of the *Confessio Amantis*: Text and Gloss," *TSLL* 44 (2002): 1–12.

this level of drama in his own report, it is precisely on stories of this kind—with speeches detailing political conflict, and Richard's reactions disclosing aspects of character—that he will build his case, his invention, regarding the king. This brings us back to his Thames narrative. Never, in his literary career, has Gower sought merely to please. He speaks truths to power, and he does not forget truths he has spoken. On this occasion Gower remains political, and though his "herte is . . . glad" (Prol. 55*) to do the king's bidding, he may have more to say than he is prepared to disclose in the opening report. If the archbishop, powerful in his own right, has failed with the king in his strategy of truth telling, how then might the poet, a man of humbler status but with a history of plain speaking, succeed in his? That the king should have invited the poet onto the royal barge suggests a prior acquaintance, and that aspect of the narrative serves Gower's credibility. But new rules have been set. If he wants to speak his mind, he now must do so while also pleasing the king.

The panegyric to Richard's high worthiness in the original epilogue of the poem hardly serves that double purpose, as Gower himself may have acknowledged in canceling the tribute soon after it appeared. In large part, this ending is a pastiche of the right things to say, things that a king would think fitting and "worthy" of him, the dignity of the crown, and his place in a succession of kings. But the panegyric continues to trouble critics, especially because its "over-sanguine" praise seems to betray double speech in a poet who elsewhere in this work so strongly indicts flatterers of kings. Before we finish, we shall return to that vexing tribute, as well as the possible reasons for Gower's revising it. Here it will be more useful simply to indicate the sequence of Gower's alterations of passages pertaining to the king not only in the epilogue but also in the Prologue of the work. Macaulay argued that the poem appeared in three recensions. Unique to the first version, published in 1390, is the combination of the report of the meeting on the Thames, the dedication, and Gower's concluding tribute. In the second version (June 21, 1390–91), the poet drops from the epilogue the extended praise of Richard and, in a replacement passage, turns to a mode approaching plain-speaking, showing how kings—and without much question, he is referring to Richard in particular—go wrong in their conduct of government. In the third and final version (June 21, 1392–93), Gower cancels the report of the meeting on the Thames and the dedication to Richard and, in substituted lines, describes the poem as a "bok for Engelondes sake," now to be sent to Henry of Lancaster for correction.[3] The two versions of the epilogue apply different rhetorical strategies to "readings" of the king. The material basis of both—and my subject for the greater part of this inquiry—lies in portions of the original work that remained unchanged through the poem's three recensions.

In the unrevised parts of the work, Gower also presents something new to the king's worthiness, and he does so in a new style. Years before, he claimed, or prayed, that the "plain instruction" of his epistle to Richard in the *Vox* would serve the king well in later years.[4] He now knows that to speak truths to good effect may require more than merely stringing together a series of warnings, as he had done in the paratactic mode of the Latin poem. He also knows that to speak as baldly as he had done there—"Let no empty glory puff you up, I beg of you, O king," or "Do not let an angry impulse suddenly rush upon you, O king"[5]—would be sheer folly, especially given Richard's temperament and new impatience: he will no longer tolerate being treated as a "boy king."

Instruction for Richard still abounds in the *Confessio* of course, but it is rarely plain and never so direct. Thus, when Gower shows how "a king himself schal reule," he does so primarily through Amans's confession. By this means, Elizabeth Porter remarks, he can "gracefully . . . disarm his royal patron" and thereby teach him more effectively.[6] In this essay, I will not consider Amans, for he contributes nothing in that

[3] The revised Prologue also appears in some copies of the second recension. Macaulay, *Works of Gower*, 2:xxi–xxvi, cxxvii–cxxix. Here I draw upon Macaulay's generally accepted description and chronology of the three versions of the poem. While in recent decades questions have been raised about his findings (see especially Peter Nicholson, "Gower's Revisions in the *Confessio Amantis*," *ChauR* 19 [1984]: 123–43), the questions remain open and do not affect the basic tenets of my argument.

[4] "Hic . . . intendit ad presens regnaturo iam Regi nostro quondam epistolam doctrine causa editam scribere consequenter, ex qua ille rex noster, qui modo in sua puerili constituitur etate, cum vberiores postea sumpserit anos, gracia mediante diuina, in suis regalibus exercendis euidencius instruatur." *Vox clamantis*, *Complete Works of John Gower*, ed. Macaulay, vol. 4, 6.8, header.

[5] "Gloria nulla, precor, te, rex, extollat inanis." "Mocio, rex, in te subito non irruat ire." *Vox clamantis*, 6.11.789, 801; Stockton, trans., *The Major Latin Works of John Gower*, 238.

[6] Elizabeth Porter, "Gower's Ethical Microcosm and Political Macrocosm," in *Gower's Confessio Amantis: Responses and Reassessments*, ed. A. J. Minnis (Cambridge: D. S. Brewer, 1983), 135–62 (146); in Porter's view, Gower seeks to educate the king in ethical self-governance by identifying himself with Amans, who is, she remarks, "a surrogate for Richard II" (146–47, 159–60); see also James Simpson, *Sciences and the Self in Medieval Poetry: Alan of Lille's Anticlaudianus and John Gower's Confessio Amantis* (Cambridge: Cambridge University Press, 1995), 280–81.

section of the work where this truth-speaking poet steps forward to confront, with help from Genius's "Aristotle," the highly charged political realities of Richard's reign. For good reason, Gower has skirted the king's history in the Thames narrative, but now, in the context of representing a regal education in Book VII, he may legitimately respond to critical issues that had recently threatened Richard's rule.[7]

The events of 1386–88 that culminated in the Merciless Parliament may have chastened Richard, but they seem not to have transformed him. Certainly he sought to project a new image in 1389, when he declared that he was "of sufficient age to gouerne" and would henceforth "take þe gouernauns" of the kingdom upon himself,[8] but he had yet to achieve, as Lynn Staley aptly expresses it, a "mature regal identity."[9] It is to that problem that Gower now responds by joining, through this poem, a major contemporary "conversation" about the nature of regal power and kingship itself. "For Richard and for those around him," Staley writes, "kingship appeared to lack a defining rhetoric,"[10] and that is where Gower seems intent on making a contribution.

Discovering and articulating a "defining" rhetoric itself requires a rhetoric, a means of broaching what may be disquieting truths for the king and those associated with him. Addressing an irascible, excitable king and a readership unsettled in its perception of what kingship means leads the poet to speak "derkly," to argue by means of analogies or

[7] On the importance of Book VII in Gower's design, see Russell A. Peck, *Kingship and Common Profit in Gower's "Confessio Amantis"* (Carbondale: Southern Illinois University Press, 1978), 140; R. F. Yeager, *John Gower's Poetic: The Search for a New Arion* (Cambridge: D. S. Brewer, 1990), 196–216; and Simpson, *Sciences and the Self*, 198–229. In the present study, I will reexamine a common perception that the "advice on ruling" in this book "is very general" and seems not to be directed at "any specific ruler" (Peter Nicholson, *Love and Ethics in Gower's "Confessio Amantis"* [Ann Arbor: University of Michigan Press, 2005], 348). Larry Scanlon makes a similar point on the grounds that the poet, in his revisions, retained "essentially the same poem," while changing the dedicatee" (*Narrative, Authority, and Power: The Medieval Exemplum and the Chaucerian Tradition* [Cambridge: Cambridge University Press, 1994], 252). Yeager takes a different tack: Book VII, he argues, was designed "as a direct address to the king—initially to Richard II, probably, but certainly to Henry IV" (*Gower's Poetic*, 268). My hypothesis is closest to Yeager's, though with the kings reversed: in the first instance, Gower composes this book with reference to the reigning king; that orientation has a direct bearing on how he identifies meaningful questions and constructs arguments.

[8] John Capgrave, *John Capgrave's Abbreuiacion of Cronicles*, ed. Peter J. Lucas, EETS o.s. 285 (Oxford: Oxford University Press, 1983), 196.

[9] Lynn Staley, *Languages of Power in the Age of Richard II* (University Park: Pennsylvania State University Press, 2005), 117.

[10] Lynn Staley, "Gower, Richard II, Henry of Derby, and the Business of Making Culture," *Speculum* 75 (2000): 68–96 (69); Staley, *Languages of Power*, 76, 1.

parallels still directly pertaining to the king, in a mode resembling that adopted by the biblical prophet Nathan in a classic encounter with King David. John Bromyard summarizes that encounter and analyzes Nathan's approach:

When the prophet Nathan wished to rebuke king David for adultery and homicide, he carefully set forth an exemplum about a rich man who had many sheep and a poor man who had only one, which the rich man killed for a wayfarer, a stranger. Nathan then said to the king, "How would you judge this case?" The king answered, "As the Lord lives, the man who did this is the child of death." And the prophet said to him, "You are that man." Note that if Nathan had chastised him openly, without the exemplum, perhaps the king, indignant, would have responded haughtily and without remorse. But because of this excellent exemplum, the king willingly came to a conclusion as if by his own judgment and, to his benefit, admitted the charge, saying "I have sinned against the Lord."[11]

Like Nathan, Gower uses analogy to elicit judgment on a presumption of kingly power, and like Bromyard, he sets *correctio* or a readjusting of perception as his goal. But rather than press for a verdict on this or that particular action, Gower works from patterns in Richard's conduct over the course of a decade to identify and address underlying and continuing problems in the governance of the realm. His arguments are issue-based, exploratory, complex, and ultimately practical, and his end is not to indict or judge the king, but to "compose" him, shaping for him a "worthi" regal identity (VII.1708). It would have been pointless, even dangerous, for Nathan to level charges against the king openly, given his likely response, or to patronize him with needless instruction about what he already knows or can readily infer. At the Salisbury parliament in 1384, the earl of Arundel so insults the young Richard when he complains that "this country, which . . . began long ago through bad government to lose strength" now faces "enormous setbacks," "crippling

[11] John Bromyard, s.v. *correctio*, *Summa Praedicantium* (Venetiis: apud Dominicum Nicolinum, 1586), 16.13 (fol. 156r): "Quando [Nathan propheta] voluit regem David de adulterio, et homicidio corripere, caute proposuit exemplum de divite, ui habebat oues plurimas, et de paupere, qui non habuit, nisi unam, quam dives pro peregrino sibi aduenicute occidit; Ait ergo regi. Responde mihi iudicum, qui respondit, vivit dominus, quoniam filius mortis vir, qui fecit hoc, cui propheta, tu es ille vir: Ecce si aperte sine exemplo eum reprehendisset, forsitan Rex indignans superbe, et sine correctionis effectu respondisset; Quia vero pulchro exemplo, et quasi ex iudicio proprio concludit, gratanter, et salubriter reprehensionem admisit, dicens, peccavi domino" (my translation).

losses," and imminent collapse. As might be expected, the king, in a fury, retorts, "If it is to my charge . . . that you would lay this . . . you lie in your teeth. You can go to the Devil!"[12] The earl fails to anticipate this likely response. By contrast, Gower, at the time he published the *Confessio*, would have known that a mode like that adopted by the prophet promised to be more effective. His arguments are literary, and left behind, most notably, are the simple, unqualified, admonitory do's and don'ts of the *Vox*.

Truth and Power

Gower creates this issue-based rhetoric in the portion of Book VII— about two-thirds of the whole—devoted to explaining five virtues or "pointz" of an ethical Policie—Trouthe, Largesse, Justice, Pite, and Chastite—as forming the basis of sound rulership. Using the common phrasing and cadence of binding pledges like those of the coronation oath, Gower insists that a king "undertake / To kepe and holde in observance" these virtues "As for the worthi governance / Which longeth to his Regalie" (VII.1706–9). In this essay, I will concentrate on the first and "chief" of the virtues, Trouthe, and the issue of its relationship to and potential conflict with regal power. Upon *trouthe*, the poet concludes, "the ground is leid / Of every kinges regiment" (VII.1980–81). That, rhetorically, is a bold assertion, and proving it is a daunting task. Truth is little valued in the Ricardian court—those who spoke it had been banished, and those who speak it are not yet preferred—and power obviously still holds much greater allure for Richard, especially in a form Gower will introduce in his sole exemplum of *trouthe*, a new version of the tale of Darius's three counselors. Significantly altering this tale from its source in 3 Esdras and his own synopsis of it in the *Mirour de l'Omme* (22765–800), Gower interjects into its opening argument an idea about kingly power that had come to dominate Richard's court in the 1380s. Taking or saving a life may be power enough for a king, but Arpaghes, Gower's first speaker, claims much more. A king may do whatever he pleases because his power "stant so, / That he the lawes overpasseth." Nothing can stop him, for "as the gentil faucon soreth, / He fleth, that noman him reclameth" (VII.1838–39, 1842–43).

[12] ". . . regnum istud a diu propter malum regimen cepit languescere." "Quod si tu michi imponas, et mei culpa sit ut malum regimen habeatur in regno, in faciem tuam mentiris. Vadas ad diabolum!" *Westminster Chronicle*, 68–69.

This notion that a king is above the law—"he the lawes overpas-seth"—had been impressed upon Richard at least by the mid-1380s. Just before his encounter with Archbishop Courtenay over the plot against John of Gaunt, Richard is confronted by the duke himself, who, as we might expect, also rebukes him "with some harshness and sever-ity" for his involvement in the plot. But the basis and outcome of Gaunt's argument are different. Whereas the archbishop argues that a king is accountable to the law, Gaunt argues, to the contrary, that it is "shameful for a king in his own kingdom, where he was lord of all, to avenge himself by means of private murder when he was himself above the law and had the power to vouchsafe life and limb with a nod, or, if he were so minded, to take them away."[13]

Richard's response is unexpected. He "answered him amiably, giving him, in mild and soothing language, a positive assurance that he would see to it that in future there should be improvement and reform."[14] This exchange is notable in revealing a mildness and rare deference in Rich-ard, especially when he has been severely reprimanded for something he has done. His response may be attributed not only to the duke's stature, but to his adroit handling of the case. As others "went in constant fear [of the duke] because of his great power, his admirable judgement, and his brilliant mind,"[15] so there may be in Richard a like fear of his very powerful uncle. Just as important, however, is Gaunt's argument. With-out the moral stridency evident in the archbishop's later censure, this argument includes reproach, but it palliates that by simultaneously af-firming the king's supreme power. His claim that the king is above the law, without the complement of the archbishop's counterclaim, would have been regarded by most, if not all, late medieval political thinkers as ultimately untenable. Even Giles of Rome, sometimes thought to be "a unique medieval advocate of absolute monarchy,"[16] challenges it, joining other legal authorities in arguing that the better doctrine is the

---

[13] ". . . inhonestum est regem in suo regno, cum sit dominus omnium, se privato homicidio vindicare, cum ipse sit supra legem, cujus est posse vitam tribuere and mem-bra eciam, et si voluerit ea tollere potest ad nutum." Ibid., 114–15.

[14] "Cui rex mollia verba et suavia benigne refudit, asserens indubitanter ea que antea minus juste sunt gesta operam daret deinceps in melius reformare." Ibid.

[15] ". . . duce Lancastr' propter ejus magnam potenciam, prudenciam commendabilem et suum ingenium tam preclarum semper timebant." Ibid., 112–13.

[16] For discussion of this characterization, see Richard H. Jones, *The Royal Policy of Richard II: Absolutism in the Later Middle Ages* (Oxford: Basil Blackwell, 1968), 155.

paradoxical one that the king is both above and under the law.[17] Gower had drawn upon that very distinction while advising the king in the *Vox*: "You are above the laws, but live as a just man under them."[18] In the *Confessio*, he waits to introduce it until later in Book VII, there subscribing to a doctrine succinctly stated by Henry Bracton: "The king himself must not be under man, but under God and the law, because the law makes the king."[19] Arpaghes, like Gaunt in his encounter with Richard, affirms only half of Bracton's teaching. His notion that the "king hath pouer over man" (VII.1827), pursued to its conclusion and without the qualification that the king is also "under God and the law," is internally consistent. As Bracton, on this side of his own argument, recognizes "the unique position of the king against whom Law could not legally be set in motion,"[20] so Arpaghes concludes: "noman him reclameth; / Bot he al one alle othre tameth, / And stant himself of lawe fre" (VII.1843–45).[21]

In his tale of Darius's counselors, Gower thus initially presents what

---

[17] Jean Dunbabin, "Government," in *The Cambridge History of Medieval Political Thought, c. 350–c. 1450*, ed. J. H. Burns (Cambridge: Cambridge University Press, 1988), 485, notes that Giles's advocacy of a strong monarchy was far from unique in the period: some writers echoed his "belief that the just prince's powers should be unlimited"; others "arrived at the same conclusion independently." The term "just" is a key qualifier in this statement; it identifies a significant restriction of the prince's power and reintroduces the paradox of the king being both above and under the law. It is Giles's position, simply, that "lawe positif is vnder þe prince as lawe of kynde is aboue hym." Giles of Rome, *The Governance of Kings and Princes: John Trevisa's Middle English Translation of the "De Regimine Principum of Aegidius Romanus,"* ed. David C. Fowler, Charles F. Briggs, and Paul G. Remley (New York: Garland, 1997), 3.2.29 (p. 377).

[18] "Tu super es iura, iustus set viue sub illis." *Vox clamantis*, 6.8.613; trans. Stockton, 234.

[19] "Ipse autem rex non debet esse sub homine sed sub deo et sub lege, quia lex facit regem." Henry of Bracton, *De legibus et consuetudinibus Angliae*, 2.33, ed. George E. Woodbine, in *Bracton Online* (Harvard Law School Library, 2003), http://hlsl5.law.harvard.edu/bracton/; trans. Ernst Kantorowicz, *The King's Two Bodies: A Study in Mediaeval Political Theology* (Princeton: Princeton University Press, 1957), 156. See also Bracton, *De legibus*, 2.306. Robert S. Hoyt notes the appearance of this teaching in the coronation oath. "The Coronation Oath of 1308," *EHR* 71 (1956): 253–83 (370).

[20] Kantorowicz, *King's Two Bodies*, 147.

[21] Gower provides his retrospective interpretation of the claim presented by Arpaghes while treating Justice, the third point of Policie, and his opening lines closely echo the words not only of Arpaghes but also of John of Gaunt in chastising Richard: a king's "pouer stant above the lawe," Gower writes, "To yive bothe and to withdrawe / The forfet of a mannes lif" (VII.2719–21). Then, however, he states the qualification, one withheld from his treatise on Truth: "The myhtes of a king ben grete, / Bot yit a worthi king schal lete / Of wrong to don, al that he myhte" (VII.2725–27). In his person, "his astat is elles fre / Toward alle other" except God, "Which wol himself a king chastise, / Wher that non other mai suffise" (VII.2732–33, 2735–36).

contemporary thinkers considered a half-truth, and by doing so when Richard still sought to create for himself an imposing regal image, he gains a foothold in argument. Over the remainder of the exemplum, nonetheless, he interrogates the notion, as well as the premise underlying Gaunt's further claim that one must avoid private murder because it is an act beneath the majesty of a king, unseemly and shameful to his dignity.[22]

The Oath and the Crown: Trouthe in Richard's History

Gower's questions derive from his more particular assertion, in the introduction to the tale, that the ground of kingship is steadfast character, or a truth "withinne," where "a worthi king" begins "To kepe his tunge and to be trewe" (VII.1739). This *trouthe* is manifested in a king's pledges, beginning with the coronation oath, and celebrated in his crown. Committed to being "true" or keeping faith—the root, as remarked in the *Secretum Secretorum*, of the "congregacion of men, inhabitacion of citees, of peple comvnicacion, and of kynges dominacion"[23]—a worthy king will "Avise him . . . tofore, / And be wel war, er he be swore" (VII.1741–42) and not retreat from, challenge, or "debate" the words of his regal pledges after he has sworn them, for "afterward it is to late" (VII.1743). Swearing oaths too quickly, and debating and breaking them too readily, however, had marked Richard's recent history, in actions that also implicated the coronation oath. To be sure, as the Merciless Parliament drew to a close, following a mass and "a splendid speech" by the archbishop of Canterbury "concerning the form and

---

[22] This has consistently been Gaunt's position through the early years of the reign. The public record he ordered on the occasion of Richard's coronation was designed, for example, "as a memorial of royal dignity to be kept before the eyes of the king himself." Patricia Eberle, "Richard II and the Literary Arts," in *Richard II: The Art of Kingship*, ed. Anthony Goodman and James Gillespie (Oxford: Clarendon Press, 2003), 231–53 (234).

[23] "The 'Ashmole' Version, The Secrete of Secretes," in *Secretum Secretorum: Nine English Versions*, ed. M. A. Manzalaoui, vol. 1, EETS o.s. 276 (Oxford: Oxford University Press, 1977), 43; see also *Secretum Secretorum, in Roger Bacon's redaction of the Latin*, ed. Robert Steele (Oxford: Clarendon Press, 1920), 57. On this "bedrock assumption" of "a juridical world," see Morris Arnold, "Towards an Ideology of the Early English Law of Obligations," *Law and History Review* 5 (1987): 505–21 (510); cited by Richard Firth Green, *Literature and Law in Ricardian England: A Crisis of Truth* (Philadelphia: University of Pennsylvania Press, 1999), 324, in a discussion of this passage from the *Confessio*.

danger of oath-giving,"[24] Richard solemnly renewed that "oth which he had mad before . . . in his childhood,"[25] now specifically in response to the recent "uprooting concerns" of the realm.[26] But the question of steadfastness remained. By calling us back to the oath, Gower identifies a critical desideratum for the recasting of the royal image, and it is important enough that he will return to it in another formulation at the end of his exemplum.

The *trouthe* upon which the kingly oath is based has other distinctive features identified in the poet's reading of the crown, a subject of special fascination to Richard as the key signifier of his power and "hihe worthinesse."[27] That the crown should represent power the poet accepts as a given. The first of its attributes, its gold, "betokneth excellence," Gower writes, "That men schull don [the king] reverence / As to here liege soverein" (VII.1751–53). But this excellence also has another dimension: "Hou that a king himself schal reule / Of his moral condicion," Gower had earlier remarked, "is the chief of his corone" (VII.1654–55, 1658), and now he extends that ethical principle to Policie: as the king surpasses others in power, so he should rise above them in virtue, "And that mai wel be signefied / Be his corone and specified (VII.1749–50). In thus conjoining power and virtue, Gower follows leading medieval political thinkers, including Giles of Rome, who had remarked that the prince "schal be as it were an half god; for as he passeþ oþere men in

---

[24] "Finita missa, archiepiscopus Cantuariensis de forma et periculo iuramenti optimam collacionem promulgauit." Thomas Favent, *Historia siue narracio de modo et forma mirabilis parliamenti*, ed. May McKisack, Camden Miscellany 14 (London: Camden Society, 1926), 24; trans. Andrew Galloway, *History or Narration Concerning the Manner and Form of the Miraculous Parliament at Westminster*, in *The Letter of the Law: Legal Practice and Literary Production in Medieval England*, ed. Emily Steiner and Candace Barrington (Ithaca: Cornell University Press, 2002), 251. On the centrality of the oath for judging as well as guiding the king, see Hoyt, "Coronation Oath," 367–68; Percy Ernst Schramm, *A History of the English Coronation*, trans. Leopold G. Wickham Legg (Oxford: Clarendon Press, 1937), 213; Gower's allusions to the oath are briefly discussed by Ann W. Astell, *Political Allegory in Late Medieval England* (Ithaca: Cornell University Press, 1999), 90–91.

[25] Capgrave, *Abbreuiacion of Cronicles*, 195.

[26] For a brief elaboration, see Favent, *Historia mirabilis parliamenti*, ed. McKisack, 24, and trans. Galloway, *History*, 251.

[27] Richard's curiosity about his own place among English kings inspired research into the historical, political, and religious significance of the regalia. William Sudbury testifies to this point in *De primis regalibus ornamentis regni Angliae*, in *Ricardi de Cirencestria Speculum historiale de gestis regum Angliae*, ed. John E. B. Mayor (London: Longman, Green, Longman, Roberts, and Green, 1863–69), 2:38. For a brief discussion, see Eberle, "Richard II and the Literary Arts," 239–40.

dignite and in my3t, so [he] scholde passe hem in goodnesse."[28] This teaching is assumed in Gower's discussion, but, as we shall see, it does not adequately describe its conclusion.

In reading the crown more specifically, Gower, drawing upon an analogy introduced in the coronation service, discovers in the stones of the crown "Signes" of precious virtues,[29] here fittingly represented as aspects of truth (*MED* s.v. *trouthe* 3a, 4b, 5a, 5b). The jewels' hardness signifies the king's constancy, "So that ther schal no variance / Be founde in his condicion" (VII.1758–59); their strength his "honeste" in upholding "trewly his beheste / Of thing which longeth to kinghede" (VII.1764–65), and their bright color his integrity or good name, which shines forth in "The Cronique of this worldes fame" (VII.1769).[30] These aspects of *trouthe*—constancy, honesty, and integrity—bear upon Gower's final observation about the crown, a perception that its circular shape is a token of the land the king rules, "That he it schal wel kepe and guye" (VII.1774). Gower thus arrives at the principal obligation of

[28] Giles of Rome, 3.2.15, p. 351. Giles further argues that a "principate" is best when the king integrates power and virtue, for then with "ri3tful desire" he "may do moche good"; by contrast, a "principate" is worst, becoming a "tyraundise . . . most noyful and greuous," when the king seeks power alone, for then with "evel desire . . . he may do moche harme" (3.2.7, p. 335).

[29] As the archbishop places the crown on the king's head, he prays that God may "Blesse and sanctifie this Crowne, That as the same is adorned with divers pretious Stones, so this thie Servant that weareth it, may be filled with thy manifold graces, and all pretious Vertues [bene + dic et sanctifi + ca coronam istam. quatinus sicut ipsa diuersis preciosisque lapidus adornatur. sic famulus tuus gestator ipsius multiplici preciosarum uirtutum munere tua largiente gracia repleatur]." *Liber Regalis*, ed. Leopold G. Wickham Legg, *English Coronation Records* (Westminster: Archibald Constable, 1901), 96, trans., 261. The *Liber Regalis* represents the fourth recension of the coronation service, probably introduced at the coronation of Edward II in 1308. For background, see Schramm, *A History of the English Coronation,* 74–89, 203–13; L. B. Wilkinson, "Notes on the Coronation Records of the Fourteenth Century," *EHR* 70 (1955): 581–600; and Hoyt, "Coronation Oath," 362–70. At the end of the decade, the author of *Richard the Redeles*, possibly also inspired by this service, ordered a new reading of the precious stones to an end resembling Gower's. *Richard the Redeles*, Passus 1.32–48, in William Langland, *The Vision of William concerning Piers the Plowman . . . together with Richard the Redeless*, ed. Walter W. Skeat (1886; repr. London: Oxford University Press, 1968), 1:607.

[30] A good king earns his "goode name" by the "gode governance of his lande and cuntrey," and to achieve both he "desirebe in troube for to have gode counseyle" (*MED* s.v. *trouthe* 12a). By contrast, the tyrant courts praise to augment his power and image, but in the absence of *trouthe* attracts flattery, "yvel counsayle," and eventual ignominy. This teaching of "Aristotle" in the *Secretum* is succinct: "Desire goode fame. For reson thurgh good fame chesith trouthe." See both "Decretum Aristotelis: Þe Secrete of Secretes, and Tresore Incomperable" and "The 'Ashmole' Version," in *Secretum Secretorum: Nine English Versions*, ed. Manzalaoui (212, 35); see also *Secretum Secretorum* (Bacon redaction), 46.

kingship—what a king swears to do in *trouthe* as he is crowned, and then presumably does.

Gower thus sets a standard of high worthiness. These same categories of judgment appeared in another form in the chronicles, there emerging as recurrent topics in the evaluation of the king's conduct.[31] In the 1380s, Richard, paying greater attention to kingliness than to kingship, tried to establish by appearances that he was "Above alle othre . . . principal / Of his pouer" (VII.1746–47). As the chronicles testify, his aspiration manifested itself, often reactively, in increasingly troubling displays of inconstancy or "variance . . . in his condicion," oath-breaking, posturing for the sake of "worldes fame" at the expense of integrity, and myopic self-absorption to the neglect of sworn duties.[32] The new royal identity Gower sets out to fashion becomes palpable and more compelling because it arises out of instances available to us in these reopened histories, and a few aggregated examples will begin to suggest the behavioral patterns to which he is responding. Thomas Walsingham testifies that Richard's inconstancy, *inconstancia regis*, "became known far and wide" as early as 1383.[33] Over the course of the decade, that charge, referring here to a young king who foolishly changed his mind, shifted to a question of disposition, to the king's "ungovernable temper."[34] That is manifested not only in his outbursts of rage, but in impetuous, seemingly capricious decision making as when, in a memorable instance in 1386, he declared in a fit of pique that he would turn to "our cousin of France" for support against his subjects, who were, he had rashly determined, not merely resistant and fractious, but, in effect, "our enemies."[35]

[31] On the question of the value of the chronicles in portraying Richard's character, see John Taylor, "Richard II in the Chronicles," in *Richard II: The Art of Kingship*, ed. Anthony Goodman and James Gillespie (Oxford: Clarendon Press, 2003), 15–35; G. H. Martin, "Narrative Sources for the Reign of Richard II," in *The Age of Richard II*, ed. James L. Gillespie (New York: St. Martin's Press, 1997), 51–69.

[32] These patterns, the contraries of the "virtues" signified by the crown, were well known to contemporaries, and Gower's readers could have readily made the connection. For a theoretical discussion of subtexts like this one, where "memory is necessarily summoned up," see Michael Riffaterre, "The Mind's Eye: Memory and Textuality," in *The New Medievalism*, ed. Marina S. Brownlee, Kevin Brownlee, and Stephen G. Nichols (Baltimore: Johns Hopkins University Press, 1991), 29–45 (30).

[33] ". . . longe lateque innotuit." Thomas Walsingham, *The St Albans Chronicle, Vol. 1: 1376–1394: The Chronica Maiora of Thomas Walsingham*, ed. and trans. John Taylor, Wendy R. Childs, and Leslie Watkiss (Oxford: Clarendon Press, 2003), 690–91.

[34] Jones, *Royal Policy*, 71; see also Taylor, "Richard II," 28–29.

[35] "Iam plene consideramus quod populus noster et communes intendunt resistere, atque contra nos insurgere moliuntur, et in tali infestacione melius nobis non uidetur quin cognatum nostrum regem Francie et ab eo consilium et auxilium petere contra

In 1387, Richard was repeatedly charged by the lords, and the Appellants in particular, with failing to keep his promises with them.[36] A year earlier, he agreed by oath to abide by the decisions of the reforming commission,[37] but soon afterward, prompted by his favorites, regrets "having taken this step," declaring "that he had been coerced into it; and it had been no part of his intention . . . to delegate the whole of his royal power to others and to retain virtually none at all for himself."[38] Ten months later he established his panel of judges to challenge the commission's existence. Caught between the lords and his favorites, he may swear and then break oaths because "necessite axe it,"[39] but in making promises he cannot keep, he compromises "the dignyté and magisté"[40] he seeks to display. The "derogacion to his honour" lies in his failing to grasp a difficult paradox: his "free condition" and "dominacion" depend upon holding "trewly his beheste."

Attracted more to the symbols than to the realities of governing, Richard spends lavishly and courts praise to win support and augment his kingliness. To many, "his lust for glory"[41] appeared to take precedence over a desire, or aspiration, to rule well. He invites flattery even as he bestows it. From "a desire to create a courtier nobility in his image,"[42] for example, he raises Michael de la Pole to an earldom, maintaining that the more he honors such men, "the more our crown is adorned with . . . precious stones."[43] Such image-building involves ceremonial or formalized shows of majesty, which Gower for their excesses derogatorily terms "pompe" in the second recension of his poem, and this also extends to displays of might. Having summoned the three principal Appellant lords to explain their march on London in 1387, Richard enters Westminster Hall "regalibus ornans se insigniis, toga uidelicet et

insidiantes, et nos eis submittere quam succumbere subditis nostris." *Knighton's Chronicle, 1337–1396,* ed. and trans. G. H. Martin (Oxford: Clarendon Press, 1995), 356–59.

[36] *Westminster Chronicle,* 216–17, 226–29.

[37] *Knighton's Chronicle,* 370–71.

[38] ". . . penituit se fecisse hoc factum, asserens se ad hoc coactum fuisse, nec fuit intencionis sue, ut dixit, omnem potestatem suam regale aliis delegare et sibi quasi nullam penitus reservare." *Westminster Chronicle,* 186–87.

[39] *The Secrete of Secretes,* in *Three Prose Versions of the Secreta Secretorum,* ed. Robert Steele, EETS e.s. 74 (London: Kegan Paul, Trench, Trübner, 1898), 19.

[40] "The 'Ashmole' Version," in *Secretum Secretorum,* ed. Manzalaoui, 43.

[41] "Rex autem, glorie cupidus . . ." *Westminster Chronicle,* 138–39.

[42] Nigel Saul, *Richard II* (New Haven: Yale University Press, 1997), 248.

[43] *Reports from the Lords Committees Touching the Dignity of a Peer of the Realm,* 5 vols. (London, 1820–29), 5:64–65, as quoted by Saul, *Richard II,* 248.

ceptro,"[44] and when the lords arrive, approaching the king "with humble face and mien"[45] and displaying the due reverence that Archbishop Courtenay had advised, Richard, as Thomas Walsingham pictures the scene, does what he, in turn, must do in this public place—he rebukes them, declares his might, and even shows them that his wrath is, or easily could become, death.[46] Thus he mocks their insolence: "Did you imagine you could frighten me by such presumption of yours? Do I not have soldiers who, if I had wished, would have rounded you up like cattle, and slaughtered you? Indeed, I have no more regard for any of you in this matter than I have for the lowest servant in my kitchen."[47] This scene is simply about affirming a regal and thereby dangerous presence. But more follows. Having shown his wrath, Richard quickly dispels its intended effect by amicably leading the lords into his chamber and graciously hosting them.[48] Each response is pursued in earnest, but the latter exposes a quality of play-acting in the former, of merely doing what is expected. So also later, when threatened with deposition by the Appellants, he yields to their demands but, as he insists, "without prejudice to his crown and royal dignity."[49]

Richard's preoccupation with maintaining his regal dignity or, as Gower later puts it, remaining "evere briht and feir, / Withinne himself and noght empeired" (VIII.3010–11*), leads to neglect, a failure to uphold his coronation oath, beginning with its first clause, "to grant and keep and by his oath confirm to the people of England the laws and customs granted by the ancient kings of England, his lawful and religious predecessors."[50] He has, in short, failed to "kepe and guye."

[44] Walsingham, *St Albans Chronicle*, 834–35.
[45] ". . . sub humillimo uultu et gestu . . ." *Knighton's Chronicle*, 412–13.
[46] "Est mors ira tua." *Vox clamantis*, 6.8.615, trans. Stockton, 234.
[47] "Putastisne me terruisse cum tanta uestra presumpcione? An non armatos habeo, si uoluissem, qui uos circumseptos ut pecudes mactauissent? Profecto de uobis omnibus non plus in hac parte reputo quam de coquine mee infimo garcione." Walsingham, *St Albans Chronicle*, 836–37. Knighton, while not including this speech, introduces its elements elsewhere. The analogy of rounding up cattle is ascribed to "one of those close to the king [quendam de hiis qui adherebant regi]," and the reference to the scullion is best known from another context: when told to dismiss Pole and Fordham, Richard reacts in a fury, "dicens se nolle pro ipsis nec minimum garcionem de coquina sua ammouere de officio suo." *Knighton's Chronicle*, 406–7, 354–55.
[48] Walsingham, *St Albans Chronicle*, 836–37. See also *Knighton's Chronicle*, 414–15: "And then he rose and took the lords with him to his chamber, and they drank with him, and so departed [Et surgens adduxit eos secum in cameram, et biberunt cum eo et sic discesserunt]."
[49] ". . . salva corona sua ac eciam regia dignitate." *Westminster Chronicle*, 228–29.
[50] ". . . concedendo et seruando cum sacramenti confirmacione leges et consuetudines ab antiquis iustis et deo deuotis Regibus Anglie progenitoribus ipsius Regis plebe regni

Such displays, many of which exhibit what Nigel Saul terms "situation dependent behavior,"[51] obviously reflect the unsureness of a young king who is struggling to be kinglike. But Gower also sees them combined in a "moral condicion," which now, in his fiction, he sets out to delineate and transform. In a recent interpretation of Chaucer's "Lak of Stedfastnesse"—a poem probably written at about the same time[52]—David Wallace has imagined a Richard unlike the one portrayed in the chronicles. Reading the line urging the king to "wed thy folk agein to stedfastnesse," Wallace writes, "Chaucer imagines the 'folk' as collective bride to Richard's 'stedfastnesse,' the virtue that holds *voluntatis arbitrium* in check."[53] Gower would certainly agree that *stedfastnesse* checks willfulness, but for him the virtue remains a prospect idealized in the crown but not yet realized by the king. The "moral condicion" he will address in his exemplum centers on that question, even as it extends to the implied charges in the famous warning to Richard in 1386 by the duke of Gloucester and the bishop of Ely: a king may legitimately be "put down . . . from his royal seat," they argue, if he, "upon some evil counsel, or from willfulness and contempt, or moved by his violent will, or in any other improper way, estrange himself from his people, and will not be governed and guided by the laws of the land, . . . and the wholesome counsel of the lords and nobles of the kingdom, but wrongheadedly, upon his own unsound conclusions, follows the promptings of his untempered will."[54]

Anglie concessas." *Processus factus ad Coronacionem domini Regis Anglie Ricardi secundi*, ed. Legg, *Coronation Records*, 147, trans., 166.

[51] Saul, *Richard II*, 202.

[52] For the dating of the poem, c. 1388–90, I follow Paul Strohm, *Hochon's Arrow: The Social Imagination of Fourteenth-Century Texts* (Princeton: Princeton University Press, 1992), 65–74.

[53] David Wallace, *Chaucerian Polity: Absolutist Lineages and Associational Forms in England and Italy* (Stanford: Stanford University Press, 1997), 297.

[54] ". . . si rex ex maligno consilio quocumque uel inepta contumacia aut contemptu seu propterua uoluntate singulari, aut quouis modo irregulari se alienauerit a populo suo, nec uoluerit per iura regni et statuta ac laudabiles ordinaciones cum salubri consilio dominorum et procerum regni gubernari et regulari, set captiose in suis insanis consiliis propriam uoluntatem suam singularem proterue exercere, extunc licitum est eis . . . ipsum regem de regali solio abrogare." *Knighton's Chronicle*, 360–61. Voiced in this veiled threat are early indications of what will surface many years later at Richard's deposition, when the king is charged, as in the well-known sixteenth article, with refusing to uphold the laws and customs of the realm, "set secundum sue arbitrium Voluntatis facere quicquid desideriis ejus occurrerit." *Rotuli Parliamentorum*, ed. J. Strachey, 6 vols. (London, 1767–77), 3:419. In the exemplum that follows, Gower caricatures the effects of a king's doing whatever he likes, according to "the promptings of his untempered will."

Willfulness Exemplified

Let us return, then, to the exemplum and what will now emerge, a twist to Bracton's classic teaching that "the will of the prince has the force of law."[55] The tale centers on the responses of Darius's three favored advisers to his question "Of thinges thre which strengest is, / The wyn, the womman or the king" (VII.1812–13). Arpaghes had argued that the king "alle othre tameth," but the next speaker, Manachaz, challenges his tenet that the king is strongest by virtue of his power over man, God's noblest creature in that he "reson can." Wine is a far greater power because it takes that reason away. On this subject, Gower changes the focus of the argument presented in 3 Esdras. The unnamed counselor in the biblical text, after exclaiming "how doth wine preuaile ouer al men that drinke! it seduceth the minde," shows how "euerie mind" so seduced deteriorates by stages, becoming dazedly cheerful, self-assured, loose-tongued, grasping, and finally bellicose, along the way forgetting sorrow, duty, restraining authority, and friendship (3 Esdras 3.18–23).[56] Gower leaves this progression and instead has Manachaz focus on radical transformations, on wine turning man, in drunken fantasy or reality, into his opposite. Thus, in fantasy, it "makth a lewed man a clerk," and in reality, "fro the clerkes the clergie / It takth aweie" (VII.1858–60). No good comes of wine in any of the paired cases in this series: the drunken person either turns into something worse or is merely deluded into thinking he has become something better. Gower's interest, however, is focused not merely on wine but more importantly on its effect, on an illusion of power that claims "mannes herte," intoxicating him, rendering his will incapable of reasonable intention, and emboldening him to suppose that he can now do anything he fancies. He is of "lawe fre."

Gower's last speaker, Zorobabel, humorously explores that effect and

[55] "Quod principi placet legis habet vigorem." Bracton, *De legibus*, 2.305, trans. Samuel E. Thorne, *Bracton Online*.

[56] Biblical quotations are from the Douay-Rheims version, which is most familiar to modern readers in the revision of Bishop Richard Challoner (1749–52). 3 Esdras presents a special case. In the original Douay-Rheims version (as in the Vulgate), this book was included with other noncanonical texts in an appendix ("extra scilicet seriem Canonicorum Librorum"). Challoner also appended these texts, but he did not revise or "modernize" them. Passages here quoted from 3 Esdras are therefore presented as they appeared in the unrevised 1610 edition of the Douay-Rheims Old Testament, second volume; I have used the Project Gutenberg online version (http://www.gutenberg.org/dirs/8/3/0/8300/8300-8.txt).

poses an alternative in two capsule tales also proving the surpassing strength of women. In the first of these, the courtesan Apeme displays "maistrie" over Cyrus, no longer, as in Esdras, a "meruelous king," but a "king tirant," who, in a newly devised scene, is introduced in his most dreaded pose—"hotest in his ire / Toward the grete of his empire" (VII.1887–88). Apeme is there, sitting, as suits her, "upon his hihe deis" (VII.1886), and when she catches his eye Cyrus undergoes a wondrous change: "only with hire goodly lok / Sche made him debonaire and meke" (VII.1890–91). The formidable Cyrus, "overlad" and with remarkable "variance . . . in his condicion," now becomes the weak subject of another's capricious will: "And be the chyn and be the cheke / Sche luggeth him riht as hir liste, / That nou sche japeth, nou sche kiste, / And doth with him what evere hir liketh" (VII.1892–95).

This tale of seduction hardly seems relevant to Richard,[57] but Gower has transformed it into a rhetorical figure, striking in the application. Like Cyrus, Richard is a figure of contrasts, one who, upon his high dais, explodes in rage toward the great of his kingdom, but who then, easily distracted, meekly submits to what others, mightier than he, dictate. George Stow has noted in the historical record abundant evidence of these contrasting aspects of the English monarch. On the one side is the disposition of a potential tyrant—arrogant, overbearing, "vindictive," petulant, rash, and prone to "violent displays of temper." On the other side is a "weak-willed, impressionable and youthful . . . personality," "too much devoted to luxury," extravagant, "capricious in . . . manners," and easily manipulated.[58]

Apeme plays a significant role in this analogy as the figure of a *fikel-*

[57] Gower knows when such a narrative about a king's trifling, lecherous game with his wanton concubine, proving the power of women, could have literal historical currency. Although in his *Mirour* he did not recount or even mention the story of Apeme in summarizing the exemplum from Esdras, his very selective final comment in the summary focuses on what "is visible nowadays"—here, most likely, he is alluding to the case of Alice Perrers and Richard's grandfather, Edward III—as proof that "women can tame the king." He drops that allusion entirely in the *Confessio*, reintroduces the Esdras story of Apeme, adds the contrasting case of Alceste, and turns this segment of the exemplum to an entirely new purpose—one that is clearly more applicable to Richard. This is not to say of course that contemporary readers could not have seen a possible allusion; it is simply to say that Gower now seems intent in his refinements of the complete exemplum, including this segment, on pursuing another end.

[58] George B. Stow, "Chronicles Versus Records: The Character of Richard II," in *Documenting the Past: Essays in Medieval History Presented to George Peddy Cuttino*, ed. J. S. Hamilton and Patricia J. Bradley (Woodbridge, Suffolk: Boydell and Brewer, 1989), 155–76 (156–60).

nesse that, in the larger argument, will be offset by the *trouthe* of Alceste, the subject of Gower's second, newly added capsule tale and the means by which his Zorobabel will effect the transition to a fourth possible answer to Darius's opening question.[59] These two figures, Apeme and Alceste, exemplify women's *maistrie* in contrasting modes; more generally, they epitomize opposed ways of perceiving, defining, and exercising power. Apeme's prototype is the best-known figure of such fickleness or "lak of stedfastnesse" in the period, the Boethian figure of Fortune. Gower's brief narrative and the relevant sections of Boethius's work are in obvious respects very different. Whereas Gower's tale is "game," a comic narrative of dalliance at court, Boethius's tale is entirely "ernest," the story of a man unjustly condemned, imprisoned, and about to be executed for crimes against the state. On the one hand, Apeme wantonly plays Cyrus for a fool in a sport that would appear to have no end—the story provides no closure, but suggests endless variation on a theme, for Cyrus seems singularly unaware not only of the ridicule to which he is exposed, especially among the "grete" who have just been subjected to his ire, but also of where his behavior tends. On the other hand, Fortune has now done her worst to Boethius, and his complaint about her launches his story: "Fortune cloudy hath chaunged hir deceyvable chere to meward."[60] The differences are manifested also in the mode of presentation. In Boethius's work, Fortune is glossed variously by complaint, character analysis, warning, and even vindication: "Sche hath rather kept, as to the-ward, hir propre stablenesse in the chaungynge of hirself" (II.pr.1.53–55). Gower provides no such gloss.

---

[59] Zorobabel, having told the story of Alceste, pays his ultimate tribute to women, remarking, "Hou next after the god above / The trouthe of wommen and the love, / ... / Is myhtiest upon this grounde" (VII.1945–46, 1948). This statement clearly refers to Alceste. In its light, she and women like her become, as Patrick Gallacher remarks, a synecdoche for *trouthe* (*Love, the Word, and Mercury: A Reading of John Gower's "Confessio Amantis"* [Albuquerque: University of New Mexico Press, 1975], 102). But if we allegorize Zorobabel's speech in that way, how, then, do we account for Apeme, a figure so often forgotten in Gower scholarship? The poet presents her in parallel to Alceste as another, but contrasting, exemplar of women's strength. For what, then, does she become a synecdoche? My hypothesis that she epitomizes *fikelnesse* draws upon a conventional pairing of co-equivalent terms in the period, as in Chaucer's lament that "Trouthe is put doun" in "Lak of Stedfastnesse": "The world hath mad a permutacioun," he writes, "Fro right to wrong, fro trouthe to fikelnesse" (15, 19–20). This and all subsequent quotations from Chaucer are from *The Riverside Chaucer*, 3rd. ed., gen. ed. Larry D. Benson (Boston: Houghton Mifflin, 1987).

[60] Boethius, *The Consolation of Philosophy*, trans. Chaucer, *Boece*, I.m1.26–28 (hereafter cited in the text).

The differences of tone and mode in Gower's narrative serve a particular purpose. The poet has moved inward, drawing upon this analogy
involving the dynamic interplay of seduction, cruelty, desire, self-indulgence, and trifling imitation to explore what happens when power in-
toxicates or, as Esdras had put it, "seduceth the minde." Whereas
Boethius's Fortune "casteth adoun kynges that whilom weren ydradd"
(II.m.1.7–8), Apeme, in this single incident, lures Cyrus away from his
pose as a dreaded "king tirant" and draws him into fatuous play-acting
that augurs his undoing. Acceding to "what evere hir liketh," he doc-
ilely follows her cues, sighing when she "loureth" and exulting when
she "gladeth," to win favor and partake of the power she enjoys, and
yet his effort, more than inept, is futile, for Apeme, in her own "ful
flaterynge famylarite," does not "duelle stable" (*Boece* II.pr.1.17, 114).
Everything to her is "game": she "leygheth and scorneth" the behavior
she inspires (*Boece* II.m.1.12–13), and as she "pleyeth," capriciously
making of Cyrus a public spectacle, she "prooeveth hir strengthes." This
powerful king, thus trivialized in the desire he foolishly pursues, remains
a "greet wonder" only in the sense of being so sensationally "overthrowe
in an houre" (*Boece* II.m.1.15–18).

In this light, Gower's political analogy takes on added significance.
The young Richard has been drawn to Fortune and one of her gifts, the
"goodly lok" of power. In a moral, psychological sense "overlad / With
hire which his lemman was" (VII.1898–99), he heedlessly sports with
her to make that power his own, but this engagement is, as it had been
for Cyrus with Apeme, a game without a future: the kind of power he
desires "may nat ben withholden at a mannys wille" (*Boece* II.pr.1.78–
79). Just as Cyrus, besotted by his mistress and currying her favor, does
whatever pleases her, so Richard, seduced by the power he craves, imitates and flatters those who possess or appear to understand it on either
side of the controversies surrounding his rule. In the miming, however,
he manifests what Chris Given-Wilson has described as "the one clear
message" in contemporary accounts of him, that he "was far too impressionable"[61]—or as Gower himself puts it, he was "quite easily led."[62]
Thus "lugged" about while seeking a power that eludes him, Richard
forgets, if he has ever heard, Philosophy's famous warning: "Yif thou
committest and betakest thi seyels to the wynd, thow schalt ben scho-

---

[61] Chris Given-Wilson, *The Royal Household and the King's Affinity: Service, Politics, and Finance in England, 1360–1413* (New Haven: Yale University Press, 1986), 187.
[62] ". . . satis est docilis . . ." *Vox clamantis*, 6.7.570, trans. Stockton, 232.

ven, nat thider that thow woldest, but whider that the wynd schouveth the" (*Boece* II.pr.1.100–4).

The tale of Apeme, then, figures in Cyrus a younger Richard. Revealing the effects of power on an inconstant king who, to borrow Brunetto Latini's words, "se torne a chascun vent,"[63] the exemplum is designed to redirect thinking away from a notion, marginally understood, that "quod principi placet legis habet vigorem," to a new conception of regal power and independence better suited to one "of sufficient age to gouerne."

In the likeness with Cyrus, as a matter of fact, there is a key underlying difference. Richard exhibited the behavior figured in this parallel especially during his "boyish reign." Cyrus, by contrast, is, as a "king tirant," a man, and yet he is one who has refused to "put away the things of a child." Richard in reality now has a choice, rejected by Cyrus, to cast off the child and become an adult, in short to do what in 1389 he claimed the license to do. This involves more of course than declaring his majority; it approximates the choice to which the entire *Confessio* builds, a choice offered to Amans at confession's end: "Yit is it time to withdrawe, / And set thin herte under that lawe, / The which of reson is governed / And noght of will" (VIII.2133–36).

Gower confronts Richard with that decision even through the very humor and theatricality of his narrative, for in its world he has deftly imagined and recast the mirth—the *iocus* and *ludus*—that he had earlier attributed to the court of Richard's youth: "To boys, evils are not wrongdoing but joking, not dishonor but glorious sport."[64] In that earlier reality and now in the fiction, everything turns comically frivolous, heedlessly self-indulgent, disingenuous, and idle. Whether sighing or grinning, Cyrus is not what he seems; he is merely a person responding to cues, acting, and acting foolishly. The younger Richard, titillated by the *gloria ludi* and the risks and exhilaration of power underlying it, was then, as Cyrus is now, easily diverted from the state's business. What then do these kingly figures—Cyrus and Richard—return to after the diversion? There is for them only the *furor* of their power: there is no business of state, nothing truly "ernest," for even the anger is empty "game." Missing in the vacuum is *trouthe*.

---

[63] Brunetto Latini, *Li Livres dou Tresor,* ed. Francis J. Carmody (Berkeley and Los Angeles: University of California Press, 1948), 2.88 (p. 269).

[64] "Non dolus, immo iocus, non fraus set gloria ludi, / Sunt pueris. . . ." *Vox clamantis*, 6.7.571–72*, trans. Stockton, 232.

Gower's most pointed critique of the sadly comic, childish delusions of power epitomized in this narrative is formulated in his second tale, the story of a manifestly grown-up Alceste. This story, representing none of the whimsicality of choice and action of the preceding tale, advances steadily and inexorably to its very different conclusion. It is a story simply told—Admetus lying on his deathbed, Alceste hearing Minerva's answer to her prayer, "That if sche wolde for his sake / The maladie soffre and take, / And deie hirself, he scholde live" (VII.1929–31), her choosing that course "with al hire hole entente," returning home, telling her husband "what her liste," and facing the immediate consequence: "And therupon withinne a throwe / This goode wif was overthrowe / And deide, and he was hool in haste" (VII.1941–43). With Alceste, there is no wavering, no vacillation, no yielding, willy-nilly, to sudden, variable, possibly opposed cues from those surrounding her. She is alone, an adult left to her decision. The simple, direct accounting of her transaction—giving up her life so that Admetus may live—underscores the paradox that the greatest power, embodying "alle grace," lies in decisive, principled acts of submission to a stabilizing *trouthe*, not in the aggressive and capricious acts of a seemingly "absolute" but ultimately enfeebled will. Cyrus, despite his apparent strength, betrays great weakness in so readily yielding to his every impulse, to a tyranny of desire, futilely courting a power whose "propre stablenesse," as we have seen, lies "in the chaungynge of hirself." By contrast, Alceste, upholding *trouthe* in marriage (*MED* s.v. *trouthe* 1b), denies herself to save Admetus, and in the boldness and finality of that act, she exhibits peerless strength. By her example, Gower thus comes to redefine kingly power. To be a king, the analogy suggests, requires a surrender of personal desire to a restraining, yet liberating virtue, the ground "Of every kinges regiment." In a *trouthe* that humbles yet does not debase lies the "myhtiest" strength of kings.[65]

[65] By drawing the story of Alceste into this argument and unfolding it separately, Gower clearly demarcates choices, certainly between love dalliance and marriage—a subject he will return to later in Book VII and again in his late poems—but also, in this political allegory, between two radically different "styles" of kingship. In his matter-of-fact treatment of Alceste, Gower excludes any mention of how "Ercules," in Chaucer's words, "rescued hire, parde, / And brought hyre out of helle ageyn to blys" (*LGW*, G 503–4). One may surmise by this omission that Gower refuses to sentimentalize; a reference to such an ending would significantly diminish the momentousness of Alceste's decision. At the same time, in the analogy of the king, the poet is not talking literally about dying (and thereby no longer ruling), but pointing to sacrifice of another order—the necessity of checking desire, or "dying" to one's personal wishes, while pur-

Gower could have taken his reading of Alceste's tale further. Her virtue is manifested in an act of self-sacrifice whose terms have been set by Minerva, a goddess whose own truth and grace enable Alceste to bestow grace on Admetus. Presumably, a king, in the depth of his commitment to *trouthe* and the divine power that expresses it perfectly, will gain an analogous power to confer grace on his subjects. We may now anticipate Gower's centering his argument on "the god above" as the ultimate Truth and source of grace, for that is where Zorobabel closes the argument in Esdras: "The earth is great and heauen is high: & the swift course of the sunne turneth the heauen round into his place in one day. Is not he magnifical that doth these thinges, and the truth great, and stronger aboue al thinges? . . . there is no vniust thing in the iudgement therof, but strength, and reigne, and power, and maiestie of worldes. Blessed be the God of truth" (3 Esdras 4.34–35, 40–41).

Gower's tribute, however, does not rise to this level. He rejects a style resonating with the psalm-like qualities of the speech in Esdras and refuses to call upon the string of terms—"strength, and reigne, and power, and maiestie of worldes"—that would have drawn the story back to his subject of kingship, raising it to a height suited to its dignity. He concludes much more simply. His summation—truth is mightiest "of erthli things" and "Mai for nothing ben overcome" (VII.1953, 1958)— precedes a series of down-to-earth, humble, plainly spoken aphorisms (VII.1959–69): Truth may suffer for a time, but at last it will be known. One who is true will never regret it. However a case unfolds, in the end truth is free from shame. What is truthless may not be free from shame. Shame hinders every person. So it is proven, there is no might without truth in any degree.

These proverbial statements, focused on truth in its earthly manifestations, obviously do not convey the charged rhetoric of a peroration, the sort of rhetoric that helped Zorobabel claim the victor's prize in the debate recounted in Esdras. Why, then, are these "homely" truths drawn into Gower's case, and why especially in this form?

---

suing the essential, sovereign virtue. A parallel in the *Mirour de l'Omme* may clarify the point. There, in chastising a negligent bishop, Gower introduces the case of Codrus, the last king of Athens, to whom Apollo offers a choice—either to die or to let his people fall. Codrus dies to save them. Gower then asks, "D'un tiel paien qant penseras, / Responde, Evesque, quoy dirras?" (20005–6). In the analogy, this question, reminiscent of Nathan's question of David in its form, is not a call to martyrdom, but an admonition, in accordance with a sworn commitment, to serve others before oneself.

Informing the *Pleine Trouthe*

Answers to these questions may derive from principles Gower articulated in discussing Rethorique in the preceding section of Book VII. There he reflects on speeches from the ancient Roman trial of Catiline, where Silanus argues that the conspirators should be put to death, and Julius Caesar argues that they should not. Gower takes from his source, Brunetto Latini, only as much as he needs regarding the debate to differentiate the rhetorical modes of these two speakers. On the one hand, Silanus "ferst his tale tolde, / To trouthe" (VII.1607–8). He speaks plainly because identifying facts, applying a baldly stated "lawe," and coming to a simple judgment—"tresoun scholde have / A cruel deth" (VII.1610–11)—serve his purpose. On the other hand, Caesar, to win Catiline's pardon, proceeds very differently. He "the wordes of his sawe / Coloureth" (VII.1624–25) in order to "excite / The jugges thurgh his eloquence / Fro deth to torne the sentence / And sette here hertes to pite" (VII.1618–21).

At various points in the *Confessio,* Gower credits those who speak "With trewe hertes and with pleine" (Prol. 184), and here we might expect him to privilege Silanus's rhetorical approach.[66] He does not. The choice he describes is not a simple one, between plainly voicing truths and, in a "rhetoric" narrowly conceived, coloring words so that, "wel spoke at mannes Ere," they please though "ther is no trouthe there" (VII.1551–52).[67] He credits Caesar with speaking "wordes wise" and accepts his having to tell his "tale" differently because his rhetorical purpose differs. Ultimately the poet shows no preference for either rhetorical mode: these two speakers "Made ech of hem his Argument," and "Ther mai a man the Scole liere / Of Rethoriqes eloquences" (VII.1628, 1630–31). In later discussing *trouthe,* in fact, Gower adopts Caesar's strategy because the politically charged questions he is addressing demand it. He also knows his further obligation: even in this mode of coloring his words, he must "knette upon conclusioun / His Argument

---

[66] Götz Schmitz, "Rhetoric and Fiction: Gower's Comments on Eloquence and Courtly Poetry," in *Gower's "Confessio Amantis": A Critical Anthology,* ed. Peter Nicholson (Cambridge: D. S. Brewer, 1991), 117–42 (129).

[67] For a useful discussion of key topoi of opposition between truth telling and rhetoric, see the first of six lectures delivered by Michel Foucault at the University of California at Berkeley, October–November 1983, and collected under the title *Discourse and Truth: The Problematization of Parrhesia,* ed. Joseph Pearson, 1985, http://www.foucault.info/documents/parrhesia/.

in such a forme, / Which mai the pleine trouthe enforme / And the soubtil cautele abate" (VII.1636–39).

How, then, in a potentially hostile setting does he begin to "inform" that plain truth to effect a good result? In the Latin verses introducing Rethorique, he focuses on definitive value: "Fair words at first are pleasing in a speech, / But in the end what pleases is the truth" (VII.5.1–2).[68] Brunetto's advice in his treatment of the Catilinian debate focuses on exordial questions, on how one introduces subjects. When approaching a controversial topic, a speaker must begin with what engages, even pleases, his hearers and gains their immediate approbation, and then build the rest of his case cautiously, striving to retain his hearers' goodwill throughout. Each stage of argument therefore requires its own introduction, its own act of conciliation,[69] and this could mean, paradoxically, that a speaker, in getting closer to the truth, may also have to get farther from it, introducing "fable" at deeper and deeper levels to achieve his end. Gower faces that prospect in the *Confessio* as a whole, starting with the Thames narrative. He also faces it in its parts. In the discourse on Trouthe, the opening tribute to the crown and Arpaghes' later eloquent defense of regal power are ingratiating gestures helping to ensure the poet's steady progress, without objection, to a point of judgment at the end.

Truth and Shame

Gower's closing praise of the virtue, though seemingly understated, has been precisely framed at the deepest level of fable by his paired capsule narratives. Through that point in his narrative, Gower has followed Brunetto Latini's advice to color "the wordes of his sawe" when the nature of his subject demands it, but he also knows that having thereby prepared his readers to accept the truth, he must finally speak it openly. But why, then, does the "pleine trouthe" that this argument supposedly informs *set* truth, the regal virtue, against shame? In the preceding argu-

---

[68] "Compositi pulcra sermonis verba placere / Principio poterunt, veraque fine placent" (VII.5.1–2). Trans. Siân Echard and Claire Fanger, *The Latin Verses in the "Confessio Amantis": An Annotated Translation* (East Lansing, Mich.: Colleagues Press, 1991), 79.

[69] "Then begin to soften the hearts of the listeners somewhat, and little by little begin to touch upon the matter of your purpose." Brunetto Latini, *The Book of the Treasure (Li Livres dou Tresor)* 3.29, trans. Paul Barrette and Spurgeon Baldwin (New York: Garland, 1993), 301; see also 3.20, p. 298 (cf. *Li Livres dou Tresor,* ed. Carmody, 336, 340).

ment, *schame* is mentioned only once, specifically in a transitional passage between the tales of Apeme and Alceste. Genius there declares that by inspiring the "jolif peine" of love, women "make a man to drede schame, / And honour forto be desired" (VII.1906–7). This statement seems strangely out of place in the context, for neither story is about a woman's love so affecting a man. Nevertheless, in an application that leaves behind the pieties of Venus's priest, the terms *schame* and *honour* describe the respective subjects of these two narratives and ultimately frame the question demanding judgment. Of particular note in the present context is Cyrus. Caught up in what pleases him, he is impervious to dread and indifferent to shame, and honor, a facet of truth exemplified by Alceste (*MED* s.v. *trouthe* 3a), is a virtue beyond his scope. His shame, exhibited in a laughable want of kingliness, threatens not only to hinder but to unmake him.

In ridiculing a king blinded to his want of kingliness and seemingly inevitable disgrace, this tale not only informs Gower's culminating "pleine trouthe" but also appears to lend point to the notion of shame that John of Gaunt applied to Richard in chastising him years before. It does that, but it also does more. Whereas the duke had seen young Richard's shame—his lack of kingliness—as a failure to recognize his greatness, Gower sees Cyrus's shame—his *presumption* of greatness—as a failure to recognize limitation. That is the greater danger, and it is the temptation to which Richard, in the years following Gaunt's counsel, has apparently succumbed. What for Gaunt was a problem of regal dignity, of seemliness, is for Gower a more serious problem of will, for, as Bracton had argued and the poet has now vividly shown, "there is no king where arbitrary will rules and not law."[70] Presumably standing "himself of lawe fre"—and thereby able as a "king tirant" to do what he pleases, even to subject himself to the playful, enervating, humiliating caprice of his mistress—Cyrus is, in reality, newly bound by whims of desire. His choices are either no longer his own—he needs cues—or they are trifling. And in that demeaning illusion of greatness, he is oblivious to the prospect of ridicule, starting with the lords who have just suffered his wrath.

In down-to-earth counsel, Gower thus confronts Richard, a king who is eager "to have from everybody the deference properly due to his king-

---

[70] "Non est enim rex ubi dominatur voluntas et non lex." Bracton, *De legibus*, 2.33.

ship,"[71] with a choice between *trouthe* and a *schame* that should be "loth-ere" or more hateful to him than any other threat to his regality, precisely because *what causes this shame has also destroyed the very capacity to detect it*. Gower, for his part, has thus "informed" and given shape to the plain truth by means of his two short fictions. The king is seemingly left with a single choice, and the poet, in pointing to that conclusion, may envision Richard coming to it "as if by his own judgment."

That outcome is not assured, of course. Gower has made his case regarding *trouthe*, but he cannot know how Richard will respond. Later, however, the poet draws upon that argument in the two versions of his epilogue, and the revision may indicate his perception of Richard's response to the original work. In conclusion, I will consider those endings as they pertain to the king.

The Two Epilogues

Gower's discussion of *Trouthe*, "the vertu soverein of alle" (VII.1776), provides not only a framework and an underlying terminology for his treatment of the remaining four virtues of Policie, but also, to the point of the present inquiry, a grounding for his last major task, suitably approaching the king with the finished poem. As I have noted, Gower begins the original epilogue focused on tribute. Praying for God's favor—"Upon mi bare knees I preye, / That he my worthi king conveye" (VIII.2985–86*)—he defers completing the thought, or his petition, for nearly fifty lines, devoting the intervening lines instead to detailing Richard's worthiness. Therein lies a curiosity. In Richard, we read, "hath evere yit be founde / Justice medled with pite, / Largesce forth with charite" (VIII.2988–90*). That is well and good, and yet the praise is tempered by the "evere yit," which projects an unsureness, an uncertainty about how Richard may act in the future. The subsequent praise of individual virtues contains a like ambiguity. Richard is of good disposition "Touchinge of pite," but the point is made by negation: "he yit nevere unpitously / Ayein the liges of his lond, / For no defaute which he fond, / Thurgh cruelte vengaunce soughte" (VIII.2994–97). During the 1380s, even when "hotest in his ire," Richard did not pursue

---

[71] ". . . appetensque ab omnibus prout regi decuit venerari." *Westminster Chronicle,* 138–39.

vengeance "unpitously,"[72] to be sure, but the "yit nevere," like the earlier "evere yit," suggests a line he could cross at any time. Richard still has choices, undoubtedly, and these have been identified and recast in narrative settings throughout the *Confessio*. The essay on *trouthe* contributes its own unique perspective to this discussion, illustrating how Gower, even through the fabling of his earlier arguments, informs—or identifies the question underlying—the "pleine trouthe." In this case, the fabling affords a perspective on contingency, the danger of *fikelnesse*, and the pressing need for a stable disposition if one is to achieve "hihe worthinesse."

The king's past habitual behavior warrants the same kind of attention. We read, for example, that Richard has risen above misfortune as an exemplary ruler must: like the sun "bischadewed" by clouds, he has remained "evere briht and feir, / Within himself and noght empeired" (VIII.3010–11*). This could mean that he is not only supreme but self-possessed, constant, and even-tempered, and such a reading suits a panegyric. Alternatively, however, it could indicate that he is inclined to "estrange himself from his people," indifferent to matters of governing, and preoccupied with his own majesty. The meaning of this powerful image may, in short, be debated, and it appears to have been Gower's intent to make it one of the subjects of the epilogue that could inspire conversation grounded in "slow time" and reflection and designed to cultivate the kind of discernment that the entire *Confessio*, in its content, style, and leisurely unfolding, has been intent on effecting.

The discourse on *trouthe* sets the terms of debate for this and other questions arising in the panegyric. When the poet returns to his prayer and identifies its subject, he states his greatest concern even as he affirms his lasting goodwill toward the king: "And so to make his regne stable, / With al the wil that I mai yive / I preie and schal whil that I live" (VIII.3036–38*). As the encomium even through the praise identifies points of possible instability in the reign, indeed in the king, so it summons up from memory the discussion of *trouthe* as framing an apt response. In particular, this final plea in composing the king, a statement urging Richard to "make his regne stable," carries the lessons about a virtue that is critical to habitual, not fleeting, worthiness.

The rhetorical strategy of the encomium seems to be promising, but

---

[72] For further discussion, see Andrew Galloway, "The Literature of 1388 and the Politics of Pity in Gower's *Confessio Amantis*," in *The Letter of the Law*, ed. Steiner and Barrington, 67–104 (92–93).

if it is, why, then, did Gower revise this segment of the poem so soon after it appeared? Scholars have debated what happened within a period of no more than eighteen months—between the appearance of the original version of this poem in calendar year 1390 and of this revision completed by June 21, 1391—to have caused such an apparently precipitous change in the poet's outlook, leading him to excise his commendation of the king and add newly written replacement lines describing what can go wrong with a king's rule and implicitly has gone wrong with Richard's.[73] Gower's revision of the epilogue provides no evidence of a radical change of allegiance or of sudden alarm, a reaction to any one thing the king has recently done. That has not been his orientation in the work: instead, he has consistently reflected on and offered measured critiques of complex, long-standing patterns of behavior. In that light, the revision may represent a comment as much on what Richard has not done as on what he has done: it could express Gower's growing concern that Richard remains entrenched in old habits, that he has not yet stepped forward to exhibit the kind of *trouthe* that grounds a rule or empowers a king to "kepe and guye." Still, Gower appears to believe that change, or a refocusing and maturation, is possible and that his own fictive re-creation of the king could have a positive effect: that is suggested by the retention of the Thames narrative in the second recension of the poem.

In the revised epilogue, nonetheless, Gower approaches the reign differently. He no longer speaks so prevalently in figures but also becomes a prelector interpreting his own work.[74] Here he applies the same principle he applied in the body of the poem, where, after using fables or "colors" to inform the plain truth, he had left subtlety and rhetorical "cautele" behind. Now, having rejected the original epilogue, he will speak directly and freshly "knette upon conclusioun / His Argument" about the king. Thus, whereas he begins the relevant section of both epilogues in the same posture of prayer—"Uppon my bare knes y preie"

[73] Peter Nicholson, "The Dedications of Gower's *Confessio Amantis*," *Medievalia* 11 (1985): 159–80 (161); John Hurt Fisher, *John Gower: Moral Philosopher and Friend of Chaucer* (New York: New York University Press, 1964), 118, 120; and George B. Stow, "Richard II in John Gower's *Confessio Amantis*: Some Historical Perspectives," *Medievalia* 16 (1993): 3–31 (15, 23).

[74] Joyce Coleman ("Lay Readers and Hard Latin: How Gower May Have Intended the *Confessio Amantis* to Be Read," *SAC* 24 [2002]: 209–35 [216]) suggests that clerks in royal, ecclesiastical, and noble households may have served in such a role as public readers of the *Confessio*. Here Gower takes that role upon himself, within the poem.

(VIII.2985*, 2985)—in the revision he asks that God "this lond in siker weie / Wol sette uppon good governance" (VIII.2986–87). With this shift in focus, Gower speaks not only of the king but of other estates, and in the process he gathers evidence to show an England not yet set "in siker weie" upon good governance. Because "Above alle othre on erthe hiere" a king "hath the lond in his balance" (VIII.3056–57), the blame for the current state of affairs must fall squarely on Richard.

The tenets of the discourse on *trouthe* now become more explicit and, in the circumstances, especially relevant, for "Men sein that trouthe hath broke his bond / And with brocage is goon aweie" (VIII.3032–33). Richard has failed "uppon his covenant" to "Governe and lede in such a wise, / So that ther be no tirandise, / Wherof that he his poeple grieve" (VIII.3074–77). The implied "naming" of Richard occurs in the effects of his defection: his people do not see "the weie / Wher forto fynde rightwisnesse" (VIII.3034–35), and "pleigneth sore, / Toward the lawis of oure lond" (VIII.3030–31). Richard, in the meantime, "takth his lust on every side / And wil nought go the righte weie" (VIII.3090–91), and though, Gower warns, the "pompe which he secheth here" (VIII.3095) is short-lived, his "more exalted style" of rule,[75] as well as his augmented power, sets him on a trajectory toward "tirandise."

In concluding this revision, Gower strikes at Richard's profound desire for a suitable, lasting memorial, a legacy among kings. Later, Richard boasted in the epitaph he commissioned for his tomb that "Verax sermone—fuit, et plenus ratione," that his speech was "trewe and plein" and his judgment sound. But even more, he wanted to be remembered as a king who struck awe of a particular kind in his enemies, his people, and perhaps even readers of the historical record: "Quemvis prostravit— regalia qui violavit."[76] A decade before the engraving of this inscription—in breaking the bonds of truth, pridefully taking "his lust on every side," foolishly seeking transitory pomp, and rejecting his covenant to govern his people justly—Richard writes a memorial countering the one Gower proposed in 1390–91 for a worthy king. To the poet, the king under whom "The poeple schal nought ben oppressid"

---

[75] Saul, *Richard II*, 438; see also Patricia Eberle, "The Politics of Courtly Style at the Court of Richard II," in *The Spirit of the Court: Selected Proceedings of the Fourth Congress of the International Courtly Literature Society*, ed. Glyn S. Burgess and Robert A. Taylor (Cambridge: D. S. Brewer, 1985), 168–78.

[76] *An Inventory of the Historical Monuments in London*, 5 vols. (London: Royal Commission on Historical Monuments, 1924–30), 1:31.

(VIII.3103) will win not merely a good name in the chronicle of this world's fame but something much greater: "his name schal be blessid, / For evere and be memorial" (VIII.3104–5). Richard's ultimate presumption, against the standard of Gower's revised epilogue, is thinking that he can force upon his people a "good name"—a name of his own devising, expressive of kingliness and absolute regal power—while forgetting that the king who aggrieves his subjects may "nought achieve / That longith to his regalie" (VIII.3078–79).

How, then, may Gower see this revised epilogue being read? No longer referring to his relationship with the king, he expressly identifies a new audience: "So preye y to my lordis alle / . . . / That y mot stonden in here grace" (VIII.3129–31). Here again he repeats lines from the original text, but with telling variations. Earlier he wrote that he could not "purchace / Mi kinges thonk as by decerte, / Yit the Simplesce of mi poverte / . . . / Desireth forto do plesance" (VIII.3044–48*), but now, for "my lordis," he writes that he cannot

> purchace
> Here worthi thonk as by decerte,
> Yit the symplesse of my poverte
> Desireth forto do plesance,
> To hem undir whos governance
> I hope siker to abide.
>
> (VIII.3132–37)

Whereas the poet may still think reform possible and may still aspire to advise the king, this version of the epilogue appears to shift the "presentation" and to some degree the "allegiance" to "my lordis alle." Nevertheless, speaking to the king remains a necessity. Indeed, this change may tell us no more than that Gower seeks help from these well-positioned readers and patrons as intermediaries in presenting his ideas to Richard.[77] Such a notion for the reception of his book may have evolved from an analogous ideal of princely counsel that Gower has persisted in advocating, despite its potential abuses, as necessary in a

---

[77] Gower's also dedicating the original poem to Henry of Lancaster, then Earl of Derby, in Latin verses following the epilogue may provide an instance of this strategy. That dedication, Nicholson argues, reflects not "a defiance or a rejection" of Richard, but a simple intent to honor the king's "prominent but loyal cousin" ("The Dedications," 161, 170). Beyond the praise, Gower may also have sought Henry's mediating support in a discourse community surrounding the king.

world of contingencies: "conseil passeth alle thing / To him which then-kth to ben a king" (VIII.2109–10). Such an ideal, whether involving official advisers or informed readers, carries reciprocal obligation, on the one hand that "unto him which the heved is / The membres buxom scholden bowe" (Prol. 152–53), and on the other, that "he scholde ek her trowthe allowe, / With al his herte and make hem chiere" (Prol. 154–55). This model may have inspired Gower's effort to engage readers, especially "hem that now be grete" (Prol. 78), in conversation about the book that could benefit the king, presumably "wys himself," with something like "the wisdom more of tuelve" (Prol. 157–58). Unfortunately, however, if this informed Gower's strategy in redirecting the poem, it ultimately did not succeed with Richard, perhaps for the very reasons Gower has now identified in his new portrayal of the king.

Gower is not a seer, though his statements about *trouthe* may read like a prophecy, uncannily accurate, of his king's coming to an end like the one depicted in post-deposition chronicle accounts, helpfully summarized by G. H. Martin as that of a "man left to die in prison because no one could trust his word."[78] But the poet cannot know what will eventually happen to Richard, nor can he anticipate immediate responses to his poem. What he does understand are human choices, and that knowledge includes a keen sense of where choices lead. For that very reason, however, it may be said that while this poem begins with Richard and he remains its "occasion," it does not end with him. Gower, deeply involved in political events immediately preceding the publication of the *Confessio*, rose to the occasion of assessing the meaning of regal power and imaginatively recasting it. With the third version of the poem, however, he excises the last vestige of the framing story directly involving Richard. In the lines replacing the Thames narrative, he celebrates old books written not only "to magnefie / The worthi princes that tho were," but also to describe others "that deden thanne amis / Thurgh tirannie and crualte, / Right as thei stoden in degre" (Prol. 45–46, 48–50). The poet's effort in this work to compose a living king, shaping for him a "worthi" regal identity at a critical juncture of his reign, has now come to an end. These new lines describe an alternative, a place into which that king has been writing himself, among those who abused their power and "degre." But though Richard is no longer featured in the work, Gower's argument retains its vitality in providing a

[78] Martin, "Narrative Sources," 61.

"new" framework to guide evolving discussion about kingship through the remainder of the reign and beyond. Indeed, this poem's continuing relevance for Henry IV is not far to seek. Beyond its having been dedicated to and acknowledged by him much earlier, the work speaks to questions he still must deal with as a king. Henry was intimately acquainted with Richard's reign, of course, and major issues deriving from that history, pointedly addressed by Gower, endured. In his father, Henry shared with Richard a powerful mentor whose teachings about regal power and royal "dignite" the poet had effectively interrogated in this work. In the *Confessio*, Gower asks vital questions, and he shows readers, whether royal or not, that he can arrive at and defend his answers with literary power, imagination, and grace.

Harley Lyrics and Hereford Clerics:

The Implications of Mobility, c. 1300–1351

Daniel Birkholz
University of Texas at Austin

Wiþ longyng y am lad,	*afflicted*
on molde y waxe mad,	*earth*
a maide marreþ me;	
y grede, y grone, vnglad,	*lament*
for selden y am sad	*seldom; sober, unmoved*
þat semly forte se.	*fair one*
Leuedi, þou rewe me!	*beloved; have pity on*
To rouþe þou hauest me rad.	*sorrow; brought*
Be bote of þat y bad;	*remedy*
my lyf is long on þe.	*depends on*

The Lover's Complaint
(G. L. Brook, *The Harley Lyrics*, #5.1–10)[1]

THIS ESSAY IS ABOUT POETRY, community, and medieval literary history. To be more precise, it is about the poetry *of* community, and how communities (past and present) shape and locate themselves through the medium of poetry. Such group articulation involves more than just the composition of text. At least as important are the circula-

My thanks, for their suggestions, to Samuel Baker, Kristin Cole, Brooke Hunter, Coleman Hutchison, Julia Mickenberg, Carter Revard, Elizabeth Scala, Joey Taylor, and Marjorie Curry Woods; also, for their generosity, to my *SAC* reviewers. I am grateful to audiences at UC-Santa Barbara, the University of Minnesota, and the University of Texas. Rita Copeland and David Wallace may remember how all of this began.

[1] Lyric citations are from G. L. Brook, ed., *The Harley Lyrics: The Middle English Lyrics of Ms. Harley 2253* (Manchester: Manchester University Press, 1948) (hereafter *HL*). In my renderings of these poems' concentrated, sometimes "obscure" early Middle English (7), I have mixed the literal and the idiomatic, at times providing multiple translations to communicate tonal or semantic alternatives. I have not normally attempted to reproduce metrical, alliterative, or rhyming schemes. For MS location of poems and cross-referencing by edition, see the Appendix.

tion, grounding, and evaluation of poetry, which is to say, its incorporation by authorized social bodies. It is by no means incidental that the poems this essay treats are on their way to being forgotten. Thus, these pages also concern how, under the pressure of historicist methodological tastes (New and old), one kind of literary anonymity, the anonymity of unestablished authorship, can breed another: the anonymity of provincial inconsequence. Below I will examine how the cultural meanings and artistic valuation of some reportedly slight medieval poems have been affected by trends in postmedieval literary study. All texts are subject to the vagaries of reception, but the poems I study here have found themselves unusually susceptible to changes in historiographical fashion.

To assert that literary history helps constitute the object of its own study is a nod toward recent critical trends. Where this essay departs from previous work is in the connections it traces between movements in critical taste (instituted diachronically, across generations of scholarly readers) and movement in the material geographical sense (articulated horizontally, across expanses of topographical space). Key manifestations of the latter include the travel of human bodies as well as the circulation of textual artifacts, modes, and effects, while comprising the former are more nebulous and historically contingent forms of literary spatialization. As recent work in theoretical geography has demonstrated, all human cultures engage perennially in the construction, organization, and representation of space. Geography, in other words, is one of the basic categories through which social power is negotiated. Operating dialectically with any society's material geographies is a plethora of imaginative geographies, prominent among which are those encoded or produced in literary discourse.[2] Based in the first half of the fourteenth century, but extended over time, this essay offers a case study in the intersection of geography and literature. Patterns of medieval mobility—human, textual, and imaginative—will be shown, in their interlocked dynamics, to offer new perspectives on the geographical assumptions (what is "cosmopolitan"? what is "provincial"?) that have helped drive modern assessments of premodern poetic achievement.

---

[2] As a starting point, see Henri Lefebvre, *The Production of Space*, trans. Donald Nicholson-Smith (Oxford: Blackwell, 1991). Edward W. Soja, *Postmodern Geographies: The Reassertion of Space in Critical Theory* (New York: Verso, 1992), stands out among Lefebvre's explicators. Raymond Williams's *The Country and the City* (Oxford: Oxford University Press, 1975) provides an excellent introduction to literature and geography in the context of English history.

This assertion contains a certain amount of protestation, one lover's special pleading on behalf of a beloved corpus of texts. But the argument has broader purchase insofar as this case demonstrates how judgments of literary merit can become caught up within an evolutionary model of cultural history, one that privileges metropolitan notions of development.

Above I chose the term "forgotten" to describe one possible fate awaiting the poems I examine here. The fond hope or "longyng" (Brook #5.1) of this essay is that such a future might be averted. To embark on any project of literary-historical recovery is both to commit an act of conspicuous love ("my loue is on þe liht" [my love has alighted on you], 22) and to seek redress for past wrongs of devaluation. As the poet of my epigraph pleads, "Be bote of þat y bad" [Grant the remedy that I require].[3] This essay itself amounts to a lover's complaint, the particular species of whose desire is to impose its own, remapped version of the literary past. Previous essays in these pages have established the seminal role that pleasure plays in medievalist scholarship, our collective desire for the emotional matter of the past.[4] "Love" as shorthand for the antiquarian drive, meanwhile, holds the status of cultural convention. "Love" also serves as a vehicle by which medieval texts themselves (literary, philosophical, theological, political) give expression to their most cherished ethical propositions. In short, "love" in a medieval context seems always to represent something else.

Delightful Promise

Community, mobility, love: the following pages track the interaction of these abstractions in the celebrated but now seldom-studied Harley Lyrics, a set of poems that has never been featured by this journal. The Harley Lyrics are named for British Library MS Harley 2253, a literary anthology or miscellany produced about 1340. The Harley Manuscript contains more than 120 texts. It employs three languages (Anglo-Norman, Middle English, Latin) and multiple genres: fabliau to devotional text, romance to political song.[5] The book's fame rests chiefly on its

---

[3] Or, to retain the alliteration: "Be the balm I have bidden you to be" (9).

[4] L. O. Aranye Fradenburg, "Simply Marvelous," *SAC* 26 (2004): 1–26; Nicholas Watson, "Desire for the Past," *SAC* 21 (1999): 59–97.

[5] N. R. Ker, *Facsimile of British Museum MS. Harley 2253*, EETS o.s. 255 (London: Oxford University Press, 1965). For updating, see Susanna Fein, ed., *Studies in the Harley Manuscript: The Scribes, Contents, and Social Contexts of British Library MS Harley 2253* (Kalamazoo: Medieval Institute, 2000).

collection of Middle English lyrics, more than thirty in all.[6] Most of these are amorous in theme; most are preserved here uniquely; and together they comprise "most of the best" English lyrics before the age of Chaucer.[7] The Harley Manuscript was assembled, and the latter two-thirds of it copied, by a scribe who is said to have possessed "a genius for compilation" approaching that of Chaucer's,[8] and who also had a coordinating hand in two other multilingual manuscript compendia.[9] According to Carter Revard, this main "Harley scribe" spent a career (1314–49) copying land charters in the vicinity of Ludlow, a town halfway between Hereford and Shrewsbury on the Welsh March.[10] Beyond his periodic work as legal scrivener and literary copyist, the Harley scribe's professional employment appears to have been as a parish or household chaplain, and/or tutor, in which capacity he will have been affiliated with one or another prominent local family.[11] Strong ties also

[6] The body of poems regarded as Harley Lyrics is conventionally numbered at 32 (15 secular, 17 religious), but some scholars include nine additional pieces that are political or satirical in nature. There are good semantic and material grounds for this decision, but as a literary-historical phenomenon the phrase "Harley Lyrics" remains synonymous with Brook, whose "slim, definitive edition" has become "something of a classic"; Fein, "Introduction: British Library MS Harley 2253: The Lyrics, the Facsimile, and the Book," in Fein, *Studies*, 1–20 (6, 7, 10, 5).

[7] Carter Revard, "From French Fabliau Manuscripts and MS Harley 2253 to the *Decameron* and the *Canterbury Tales*," *MÆ* 69.2 (2000): 261–78 n. 36. Such assessments have long been standard; see Brook, *HL*, Preface, and Fein, "Introduction," 4–5.

[8] Carter Revard, "*Gilote et Johane*: An Interlude in B.L. Harley 2253," *SP* 79 (1982): 122–46 (138); E. J. Hathaway, P. T. Ricketts, C. A. Robson and A. D. Wilshire, eds., *Fouke le Fitz Warin* (Oxford: Blackwell, 1975), xliv.

[9] These earlier compilations are London, British Library MS Royal 12.c.xii (c. 1320–40) and MS Harley 273 (c. 1314–28). Royal 12.c.xii's major items include redactions (probably by the Harley scribe himself) of the AN romance *Fouke le Fitz Waryn* and the ME *Short Metrical Chronicle*, but overall this book is "even more of a miscellany than Harley [2253]"; Ker, *Facsimile*, xx. For comprehensive treatment, see Hathaway et al., eds., *Fouke le Fitz Waryn*. Harley 273 is an administrative and devotional compendium that the main Harley scribe came to treat "as his book," though it was "more gathered than copied by him"; Revard, "Scribe and Provenance," in Fein, *Studies*, 21–109, esp. 67–73.

[10] Revard (esp. "Scribe and Provenance") has displaced Ker and Hathaway as the definitive voice on the Harley scribe and his context. For earlier iterations of his provenance argument, see "The Scribe of MS. Harley 2253," *N&Q*, n.s. 29 (1982): 62–63; "Three More Holographs in the Hand of the Scribe of MS. Harley 2253 in Shrewsbury," *N&Q*, n.s. 28 (1981): 199–200; and "Richard Hurd and MS. Harley 2253," *N&Q*, n.s. 26 (1979): 199–202.

[11] Like Revard, Ker and Hathaway discuss the secular-household orientation of Royal and Harley, yet both regard such a context as "only [partly] applicable for the Harley/Royal compiler, who seems to have moved in an episcopal milieu, though his parents may have belonged to the baronial world"; Hathaway et al., eds., *Fouke le Fitz Waryn*, xl–xliv; Ker, *Facsimile*, xx–xxiii.

appear to have obtained between this Ludlow-based copyist and Hereford Cathedral, specifically its bishops, although provenance experts disagree about the precise nature of the Harley scribe's attachment to diocesan leadership.[12] As we shall find, the geographical mobility of those involved in our lyrics' compilation—a process that includes their transmission *to* a Ludlow copying—has implications for what manner of community may be imagined for these poems.

As if to confirm their host manuscript's hybrid provenance, the Harley Lyrics operate in a register that is at once secular and religious. Not just overall, but within numerous individual poems, we witness an intermingling of the two realms, much as medieval lay and clerical audiences tend to be blended. Sometimes this occurs in a single breath. The lyric whose opening provides my epigraph, for example, concludes with the assertion that "heuene y tolde al his / þat o nyht were hire gest" [heaven, I am certain {told/assured}, would be all his, who for a single night were her guest] (Brook #5.39–40; cf. #7.82–84). Lyric taxonomists class *The Lover's Complaint* as secular—safely so, it would seem, given its speaker's "longyng," "grone"-ing, and brazen substitution of a carnal "heuene" for a spiritual one. It may be debatable just how sustainable such division is, but certainly the classification of some lyrics as "secular" and others as "religious"—so too for the categories "popular," "courtly," and "learned"—has figured prominently in editorial initiatives and the accounts of literary history that derive from them.[13] "Religious" lyrics far outnumber their "secular" counterparts in the early Middle English corpus, to the extent that the secular lyrics preserved in Harley 2253 account for some half of those extant. The Harley Lyrics are also unusual for their French influence, but these are not limp derivatives. Better to speak of cultural alloy: the Harley Lyrics recast continental conventions and generic models into an insular, alliterative, colloquial, even "homey" mode.[14] Like so much early vernacular writ-

---

[12] See Ker, *Facsimile,* and Hathaway et al., eds., *Fouke le Fitz Waryn.* Revard ("Scribe and Provenance," 26–28) dismisses the "romantic speculation" linking Harley to episcopal circles, but allows that its copyist "had reason to copy seal-mottoes of Hereford bishops Swinfield and Orleton into a book of his [Royal 12.c.xii] during the 1320s."

[13] For the history and implications of such categorization, see Fein, "Introduction," 5–7.

[14] For an international context, see Peter Dronke, *Medieval Latin and the Rise of European Love-Lyric* (Oxford: Clarendon Press, 1968), esp. 112–25; Brook, *HL,* 7–8, 18–21; R. H. Robbins, *Secular Lyrics of the XIVth and XVth Centuries* (Oxford: Clarendon Press, 1952), xviii, lii; and E. K. Chambers, "Some Aspects of Mediaeval Lyric," in *Early English Lyrics: Amorous, Divine, Moral, and Trivial,* ed. E. K. Chambers and F. Sidgwick

ing, the Harley Lyrics are indebted to ecclesiastical learning and Latin rhetoric; hence their staple passages of point-by-point bodily description and their "touches of pedantic symbolism." Such formal and hermeneutic details provide "evidence of clerical authorship,"[15] notwithstanding the lay-household orientation of the book they inhabit. Similarly, notwithstanding their grounding in a Marcher locale, their cosmopolitan poetics call into question their traditional characterization along provincial lines—that is, as verses of a "serene western type," coaxed into expression by continental impetus, perhaps, but "[written] down amongst the apple-blossoms" of Herefordshire.[16]

The manifest "excellence" of the Harley Lyrics, according to G. L. Brook, is "largely due to the fitness of Middle English to be a lyrical language"; it has a sound-landscape "more sonorous than modern English." This is why I began with a poetic invocation rather than a theoretical or literary-historical proposition.[17] The historicist portion of this essay shall argue that the textual phenomenon of the Harley Lyrics— their unique currency "by west" (Brook #5.37)—may be regarded as a consequence of the geographical mobility that marks the careers of certain West Midlands secular clerks c. 1300–1351. I intend this claim as a critical contribution in its own right, but seen in functional terms, it is merely incidental. For the historicist maneuver of tying Harley Lyrics to Hereford clerics enables another, less circumscribed intervention. The larger goal of this essay shall be to account for the ambivalent place of the Harley Lyrics in English literary history, the way they defy location in the grand narrative of vernacular development that finds its self-evident turning point in the late fourteenth century, in and around an increasingly hegemonic metropolis. Still—somewhat counterintuitively—the Harley Lyrics retain canonical status, or at least its vestiges.

(New York: October House, 1967 [1907]), 257–96 (274–78). Alliteration is less a feature of Harley's religious lyrics than of its secular lyrics and political poems; cf. M. Theresa Clare Hogan, "A Critical Study of the Middle English Lyrics of B.M. MS. Harley 2253" (Ph.D. diss., University of Notre Dame, 1962), ix.

[15] Chambers, "Aspects," 277–78; Brook, *HL*, 19–20, 25–26. As Julia Boffey notes, early lyric provenances are "predominantly clerical"; *Manuscripts of English Courtly Love Lyrics in the Later Middle Ages* (Woodbridge, Suffolk: D. S. Brewer, 1985), 95, 127.

[16] In their "sincerity and wholesome conviction," Chambers believes, the Harley poems strike "a distinctively English note"—thankfully free of "Gallic irony"; "Aspects," 275–79.

[17] Brook, *HL*, 20. For lyric as a mode of "incantation," "fundamentally an attempt to approximate the condition of music," see Daniel Albright, *Lyricality in English Literature* (Lincoln: University of Nebraska Press, 1985), viii–x.

They may not figure much in recent journals (or press catalogues, or conference programs),[18] but they have had their champions. R. H. Robbins calls them "the greatest achievement of all Middle English poetry."[19] An overstatement, perhaps, yet the quaint provincialism of the upstate professor's notion may be something less than self-evident, and his intervention more than merely partisan. This essay maintains that the persistent critical marginality of the Harley Lyrics is less a function of pre-plague spatial relations and their attendant literary realities than a result of the changed cultural configurations—geopolitical, linguistic, and scholarly—that would prevail subsequently.[20]

It is probably not coincidental that most of those sharing Robbins's taste for medieval lyric came of age in the wake of the New Criticism. In the early to mid-twentieth century, thick anthologies were published in which individual lyrics, grouped by type, appear all but untethered from manuscript setting and historical context. Such editions remain standard for many of the poems they compile.[21] Certain assumptions about the transhistorical essentials of a "lyric mode" continue to influence the scholarly reading of medieval lyric poetry. Moreover, the uni-

[18] Fein observes that the Harley Lyrics "have provided steady grist for generations of philologists, critics, and dissertation writers" (4168), but her wonderfully comprehensive bibliography reveals a declining incidence of treatment; "The Lyrics of MS Harley 2253," in *A Manual of the Writings in Middle English, 1050–1500*, vol. 12, ed. Peter G. Beidler (New Haven: Connecticut Academy of Arts and Sciences, 2005), 4168–4206, 4311–61. The recent attention paid to the book's neglected political/historical and non-English pieces—especially when these are referred to as Harley "Lyrics"—disguises the fact that the amorous ME poems championed by a previous generation have not much participated in this revival.

[19] Robbins, *Secular Lyrics*, xvii. The surest sign of these poems' quasi-canonical status may be that *The Norton Anthology of English Literature Vol. I*, 8th ed. (New York: W. W. Norton, 2005), includes just a single Harley Lyric (Brook #4, *Alysoun*) in its 484-page medieval section. Other anthologies reserve slightly more room; see J. B. Trapp, Douglas Gray, and Julia Boffey, eds., *Medieval English Literature*, 2nd ed. (New York: Oxford University Press, 2002), whose 20 lyrics (among 594 pp.) include two drawn from Harley (Brook #4; #11, *Spring*). By contrast, Elaine Treharne, ed., *Old and Middle English, c. 890–c.1400: An Anthology*, 2nd ed. (Oxford: Blackwell, 2004), devotes 50 of 650 pages to the Harley MS—eight lyrics, a political song, and the romance *King Horn*.

[20] For a characterization of the Harley Lyrics as definitively "extra-canonical"—the "dearth of critical responses" bespeaking their "exclusion . . . from the canon," see Gayle Margherita, *Romance of Origins: Language and Sexual Difference in Medieval English Literature* (Philadelphia: University of Pennsylvania Press, 1994), 8–12, 64–72.

[21] See Siegfried Wenzel, *Preachers, Poets, and the Early English Lyric* (Princeton: Princeton University Press, 1986), 209–10, who laments that modern anthologies usually neglect to present lyrics "in their immediate context." For example, see Maxwell S. Luria and Richard L. Hoffman, eds., *Middle English Lyrics* (New York: W. W. Norton, 1974).

tary coherence, brevity, and "non-referential quality" of lyric poems (their apparent "non-engagement with an outside world") have seemed to invite the application of myopic "close reading" practices while discouraging other approaches.[22] It is precisely the appropriateness of lyric genres to New Critical methodologies, therefore, that may best account for the Harley poems' conspicuous absence from the projects of recently minted critics—those weaned on Stephen Greenblatt instead of Cleanth Brooks, as it were.

The Harley Lyrics have slipped in disciplinary standing for reasons that are essentially methodological. But the profession-wide dynamics of canon realignment during the past few decades (that is, the jettisoning of early texts from the canonical fringe) do not play so crucial a role here as might be expected. That the Harley Lyrics no longer enjoy landmark status has more to do with their degree of susceptibility (low, it is supposed) to regnant practices in literary interpretation—specifically, the historicist methods that until recently have dominated medievalist research.[23] The increasing marginality of the poems relates directly to their once-opportune but now "frustrating" ahistoricity.[24] What began as a dilemma of diachronic genealogy has become transmuted into a problem of synchronic contextualization. The precarious hold the Harley Lyrics have on a place in the medieval canon thus appears, early and late, to be a function of their elusiveness: first in developmental and then in social-material terms. Literary historiography has never known quite what to do with them—or more to the point, how to place them. Fortunately, these poems grapple with matters of geographical ambivalence themselves. Addressing such moments may teach us how to bridge the fault lines upon which Harley criticism is built.

The Harley Lyrics are disconcerting to literary historians due to their

---

[22] Cf. Helen Barr: "The legacy bequeathed to literary studies by practical criticism and new criticism has left a residue in which 'close reading' is associated with socially deracinated study"; *Socioliterary Practice in Late Medieval England* (Oxford: Oxford University Press, 2002), 1–9. See Albright, *Lyricality*, ix, 27, and Boffey, *Manuscripts of English Courtly Love Lyrics*, 3, for lyric nonreferentiality, brevity, and coherence.

[23] For historicism as an "unassailable reading strategy" that "has become so dominant, even hegemonic, in medieval studies that at times it seems stifling, even repressive, to other methodological practices," see Elizabeth Scala, "The Ends of Historicism: Medieval English Literary Study in the New Century," *TSLL* 44, no. 1 (2002): [iv].

[24] For lyric as the "most frustrating" of literary genres, see Albright, *Lyricality*, ix. Such observations echo throughout commentary on medieval lyric in general and the Harley Lyrics in particular.

"sudden" appearance out in the provincial "backwater" of Hereford-shire. Even more troubling, they are "[not] enduring" in formal or aes-thetic influence.[25] Robbins outlines the conundrum: the strain of vernacular lyric preserved in Harley "comes without warning and leaves as suddenly," such that "after the Black Death, Middle English lyric seems to start out afresh." As E. K. Chambers laments, "the delightful promise of the [Harley] manuscript is, alas! not maintained."[26] The "old historicist" misgivings of early- to mid-twentieth-century scholars, con-cerning the obscure origins and negligible influence of the Harley Lyrics, have their New Historicist counterpart in the unconsummated docu-mentary desires of late-century critics. Where vertical formal linkages preoccupied the former, the latter unite in their yearning for horizontal contextual certainty—that is, for secure placement of Harley 2253 in some tangible, animating milieu.

The seeming resistance of the Harley Lyrics to historicism has much to do with the fraught history of lyric as a genre. But the crux of the matter involves what might be called these poems' "Age of Chaucer" problem. Despite the efforts of those who agitate on their behalf, the Harley Lyrics do not lay demonstrable groundwork for late fourteenth-century metropolitan literary English,[27] or even, to any significant de-

[25] Robbins, *Secular Lyrics*, lii. Robbins and Chambers ("Aspects," 273) both choose the term "sudden" to describe the Harley Lyrics, but see also R. H. Robbins, ed., *Histor-ical Poems of the XIVth and XVth Centuries* (New York: Columbia University Press, 1959), xxxiii ("conventions such as these did not grow up overnight"). Scholars from Williams, *The Country and the City*, to R. H. Hilton, *A Medieval Society: The West Midlands at the End of the Thirteenth Century* (New York: Wiley & Sons, 1966), 168, have referred to the region's persistent "backwater" status. See also Derek Pearsall, *Old English and Middle English Poetry* (London: Routledge & Kegan Paul, 1977), 120, for an emphasis on arti-fact loss rather than artistic ineffectualness. For lyric non-survival, see Boffey, *Manu-scripts of English Courtly Love Lyrics,* 134; Brook, *HL,* 1.

[26] Robbins, *Secular Lyrics*, lii, liv; Chambers, "Aspects," 278.

[27] Cf. Robbins: "There is not a single later lyric that shows any influence of [this anthology]"; *Secular Lyrics*, lii. For an opposing argument—that Chaucer knew the idiom of vernacular lyric as exemplified in Harley 2253—see E. Talbot Donaldson's "Idiom of Popular Poetry in the Miller's Tale" (1951), repr. in *Speaking of Chaucer* (New York: W. W. Norton, 1970), 13–29. Donaldson finds semantic congruences, but what this mostly achieves is to show why *Alysoun*, whose love-object seems to prefigure Alison of the *MilT*, is the most anthologized Harley Lyric. Revard is an especially fervent proponent of the Harley scribe's Chaucerian literary credentials ("Scribe and Prove-nance," 73; *"Gilote et Johane"*), but cf. Thorlac Turville-Petre, *England the Nation: Lan-guage, Literature, and National Identity, 1290–1340* (Oxford: Clarendon Press, 1996), 211, and Fein, "Introduction," 8. Tellingly, even Margherita's "extra-canonical reading" (*Romance of Origins*, 61–80) makes constant reference to Chaucer studies.

gree, for the alliterative verse that would flourish along the Welsh March.[28] This lack of party affiliation with the period's major literary properties leaves the poems in Harley 2253 historiographically unprotected, especially as lobbying interests are pooled under "a loose rubric of [Ricardian] periodization."[29] From the perspective of texts outside this economy, medieval England's leading literary brands blend into a corporate conglomerate whose market-share threatens to choke out competition.

The inability of midcentury lyric partisans to secure the Harley Lyrics a definitive place in the master narrative of national vernacular development—that tenacious account in which Chaucer serves alternately as culmination and progenitor—has left them with uncertain standing in the field. Obscured by the logic of epochal divide, the lyrics preserved in Harley 2253 come to be associated not with the kind of headwater vitality their supporters might desire, but instead with a side-pool stagnancy, or at best a tributary evanescence. The elegiac tone of much writing on the Harley Lyrics ("alas!") speaks to the ingrained habit of reading these poems in terms of formal impact, or rather their lack thereof. The failure of the Harley Lyrics to consolidate a position of literary-historical relevance—to translate "delightful" promise into "enduring" influence—relegates them to the cultural periphery. But then it is precisely our presumption of their displacement from the sites of medieval literary urbanity that has convinced us of the outland nature of these texts to begin with.

Community, mobility, love—and peripheral status. How, without resorting to apple-blossom nostalgia, can we account for the literary-historical anomaly that is the Harley Lyrics? Any articulation of community requires that body's placement in a wider social *and spatial* field. If geographic commonalities and differences—matters of origin, residence, travel, topophilia—serve as a prime axis along which human identity

[28] Langland (Worcs.) and the *Pearl*-poet (Ches.) may have known Harley texts, but even here links are tenuous. Many count the *Song of the Husbandman* among *Piers Plowman*'s precursors in a western alliterative "literature of social unrest"; cf. Janet Coleman, *Medieval Readers and Writers, 1350–1400* (New York: Columbia University Press, 1981), 79–84. Pearsall sees Harley complaint traditions as extending to other late alliterative poems; *Old English and Middle English Poetry*, 160, 172, 185.

[29] Robert R. Edwards, " 'The Metropol and the Mayster-Toun': Cosmopolitanism and Late Medieval Literature," in *Cosmopolitan Geographies: New Locations in Literature and Culture*, ed. Vinay Dharwadker (London: Routledge, 2001), 33–62 (42–43, 59); cf. John Burrow, *Ricardian Poetry: Chaucer, Gower, Langland, and the Gawain-Poet* (London: Routledge & Kegan Paul, 1971).

is expressed, how, then, do dynamics of spatiality affect the poetics of community? What would it mean to recover the Harley Lyrics?

The fundamental geographical orientation of these poems may be seen in their activation of two touchstone categories: first, that of an abstracted western "lond" [country, landscape], to which Harley narrators frequently express their longing to return; and second, the fetishized figure of the embowered lyric maiden, or local "leuedi" [lady, beloved], who is anxiously placed within, even collapsed into, that "lond." The community brought into being through such declamatory magic is mobile yet rooted: widely perambulating, but circumscribed in membership; textually anonymous, but located institutionally. In essence, my method in this project is to place the surprising lyrics of Harley 2253 beside some of their era's more agile clerical lives. This biographical gesture offers to resolve a long-standing literary-historical dilemma: Where did the Harley Lyrics come from, before going where they went? In less parochial terms, less narrowly medievalist and historicist, my hope is that such a move will help us better perceive how cultural products, like cultural agents, defy assignment to any singular, static location and instead attenuate across space—and for that matter, time.

We shall find that in geographical character and hermeneutic mooring the Harley Lyrics are fundamentally regionalist but also intrinsically cosmopolitan. What is unusual is that they manage to strike both regional and cosmopolitan identities while being little concerned with the form of geographical community usually imagined as negotiating between these poles: that is, "England the Nation" (to cite the title of one study that has sought, via this master category, to characterize vernacular production in these years).[30] This essay argues that the Harley Lyrics embody not a proto-"national" vernacularity, predictive of later English literary character, but rather a hybrid cosmopolitan/regional vernacularity. In this they differ from accepted English medieval literary norms—which tend to derive from the triumphant *late* fourteenth century—as

---

[30] Turville-Petre's influential study of "language, literature, and national identity, 1290–1340," concludes with Harley 2253, which as a compilation helps "point the way ahead" to Chaucer and his "status as a national poet." However, because in his view "love-lyric is surely the [genre] least concerned with society and its structures" and because here "love is located," the Harley Lyrics "make no claim to national cultural significance." Finding lovers who "can ignore all values except [their] passion," Turville-Petre becomes free to privilege the terms by which community is imagined in the political and historical pieces. *England the Nation*, 206–17.

well as from prevailing postmedieval paradigms of literary cosmopolitanism.[31]

Familial Sense and Regional Sensibility

The "literary worth" of the Harley Lyrics has been said to "arise from qualities which are independent of the time when they were written."[32] My own Harley encounters are backdropped by the careers of a group of secular clerks from western England in the half-century prior to the Black Death (1348–51). These bureaucrats have left substantial documentary trace, but their identities emerge for us mostly through their official relationships: to home diocese, cathedral chapter, and especially patron-bishop. Exactly where and when the lyrics in Harley 2253 were composed remains unclear. What is certain is that they circulated in the region—although not as a body—during the early fourteenth century.[33] This period of gestation and transmission coincides with the eventful episcopates of two Hereford bishops: Richard Swinfield (1283–1317) and Adam Orleton (1317–1327), later bishop of Worcester (1327–33), then Winchester (1333–45).

Richard Swinfield was a "bountiful patron of learning," who was friendly with minstrels and Franciscans, two early orders of mobile vernacular poet. But he was himself a "stay-at-home prelate," more concerned with pastoral care than with national politics or church councils.[34] Still, Swinfield did not hole up at his cathedral palace: both his Register and an extant household roll have him seldom at Here-

---

[31] For an overview unusually well attuned to historical difference, see Vinay Dharwadker, "Cosmopolitanism in Its Time and Place," in *Cosmopolitan Geographies*, ed. Dharwadker, 1–13.

[32] Brook, *HL*, 23. See, similarly, Bonnie Israel Duncan, "Middle English Poems in Harley Ms. 2253: Semiosis and Reading Scribes" (Ph.D. diss., University of Iowa, 1988), 13–17.

[33] See Frances McSparran, "The Language of the English Poems: The Harley Scribe and His Exemplars," in Fein, *Studies*, 391–426. For interpretive and codicological significance, cf. Fein, "A Saint 'Geynest under Gore': Marina and the Love Lyrics of the Seventh Quire," in Fein, *Studies,* 351–76 (367–69), and Marilyn Corrie, "Harley 2253, Digby 86, and the Circulation of Literature in Pre-Chaucerian England," in ibid., 427–44.

[34] Leslie Stephen and Sidney Lee, eds. *Dictionary of National Biography,* 66 vols. (London: Smith, Elder, 1885–1901), 55:232–34; see also Philippa Hoskin, "Swinfield, Richard (d. 1317)," *Oxford Dictionary of National Biography* (Oxford: Oxford University Press, 2004): http://www.oxforddnb.com/view/article/26843, accessed February 26, 2009.

ford.[35] "Stay-at-home" indicates that his mobility had a local, or more precisely, a diocesan scale. In his disinclination to fare beyond his home region, this bishop differs from many of his own officials. Swinfield promoted Hereford interests by pressing for the canonization of his predecessor Thomas Cantilupe: died 1282, canonized 1320, translated 1349, and obscure ever since. The fortunes of Cantilupe's shrine need not be rehearsed here except in two essentials. First, pilgrim traffic to Hereford waxed and waned roughly in step with the region's advent and decline on the national political stage.[36] Second, Hereford officials spent long stretches lobbying at the Papal Curia and elsewhere. Swinfield was prime mover, but Cantilupe's canonization owed more to the influential Adam Orleton, who would parlay his position as leader of the English delegation into election as Swinfield's successor.

If Swinfield's sphere of activity was circumscribed, "there is no [such] lack of mobility discernable in Orleton's career," nor for those in his orbit.[37] A favorite of Pope John XXII (1316–34), Orleton made his mark at Avignon but became notorious during the baronial rebellions of the 1320s. Along with Queen Isabella and the Marcher lord, Roger Mortimer, he was a key player in the deposition of Edward II (1326/27). The tireless clerks who belonged to Bishop Adam's circle of intimates alternated between accompanying him on his domestic and foreign travels and operating on his behalf, whether as diplomatic proxies, administrative stewards, or (so the rumors went) nefarious political agents.[38]

[35] W. W. Capes, ed., *Registrum Ricardi de Swinfield, episcopi Herefordensis, AD 1283–1317* (London: Canterbury & York Soc., 1909); John Webb, ed., *A Roll of the Household Expenses of Richard de Swinfield, Bishop of Hereford, During Part of the Years 1289 and 1290*, 2 vols., nos. 59, 62 (London: Camden Society, 1854–55), esp. 1:68; 152–55 for minstrels.

[36] Overall, see Meryl Jancey, ed., *Saint Thomas Cantilupe, Bishop of Hereford: Essays in His Honour* (Hereford: Friends of Hereford Cathedral, 1982). For Swinfield's promotion of the cult, see Jancey, *St. Thomas of Hereford* (Newport, England: J. A. Dixon, 1978), 10–16. Ronald Finucane, *Miracles and Pilgrims: Popular Beliefs in Medieval England* (New York: St. Martin's, 1995), 173–88, provides demographic analysis.

[37] Roy Martin Haines, *The Church and Politics in Fourteenth-Century England: The Career of Adam Orleton, c. 1275–1345* (Cambridge: Cambridge University Press, 1978), 100; see also A. T. Bannister, ed., *Registrum Ade de Orleton, Episcopi Herefordensis, AD 1317–27* (Hereford: Wilson & Phillips, 1907).

[38] Haines, *Career*, esp. 81–96, 100, 206; also Haines, *The Administration of the Diocese of Worcester in the First Half of the Fourteenth Century* (London: SPCK, 1965), 90–98. For life-details of one such clerk, together with some gestures toward the larger project of which this essay is a part, see Daniel Birkholz, "Biography After Historicism: The Harley Lyrics, The Hereford Map, and the Life of Roger de Breynton," in *The Post-Historical Middle Ages*, ed. Elizabeth Scala and Sylvia Federico (New York: Palgrave Macmillan, 2009), 161–89.

This frenetic activity would in time be quelled. Yet the first half of the century presented Hereford and Worcester ecclesiastics, from notaries to canons, with unprecedented opportunity for travel, plus access to international literati. Meanwhile, these cathedral cities and their environs—village byways, urban centers, gentry manors, religious houses—saw a heightened flow of visitors and returned natives. Thus did a wide cross section of western clerks experience an enriched cultural traffic.

Hereford bishops enjoyed unusually good relations with their cathedral chapter during the early fourteenth century. Orleton's "group of faithful clerks" proved an "exceptionally stable *familia*"; many served with him under Swinfield and/or followed him to Worcester in 1327, but would return to Hereford positions upon their patron's 1333 move to Winchester.[39] My topic is "love," less in the carnal than in a familial sense; but beyond even their cohort loyalty and political instrumentality what is exceptional about the clerks under study is their degree of mobility, pronounced both for their day and by comparison with local officials earlier and later. "Frequent missions abroad" (to Avignon, then the French court) and perpetual administrative travel (on circuit with the consistory court or on visitation across the diocese) connected this species of clerk to cosmopolitan cultural centers, to a wide scattering of towns and courts, and, at home in the west country, to every level of household, from the highest lay magnate's to that of the most land-tied village priest.[40]

Any sketch of a region's standing over a stretch of decades must remain partial in its data and provisional in its claims. Still, the altered cultural geographics that post-plague conditions represent—compared with the years of thronged pilgrims at Hereford and the canonization push at Avignon (1280s–1320), followed by prominence for the region and diplomatic trips by Orleton protégés (1320s–1330s)—can only be described as dramatic. First, the disproportionate influence of western interests on national affairs waned; then came demographic collapse. In the wake of the Black Death, Orleton's nephew John Trillek (Bishop of

---

[39] Haines, *Career*, 97–100, 205–6; such was the trajectory of Roger Breynton (see previous note). Cf. Bannister: "Few indeed were the dioceses in which the bishop was not looked upon as an intruder in his own cathedral"; *Registrum Ade de Orleton*, xix.

[40] Haines, *Career*, 206, 100; see also Haines, *Administration*, 46–62. Senior administrative positions included oversight of priests across the diocese. For the papal curia as "a great meeting place of men and a clearinghouse of ideas," see W. A. Pantin, *The English Church in the Fourteenth Century* (Notre Dame, Ind.: University of Notre Dame Press, 1962), 120.

Hereford, 1344–60) instituted strict new policies designed to refocus the attention of Hereford's (surviving) priests on pastoral care. Leaves for study became far less common, dispensations for nonresidence were curtailed, and close involvement in international affairs came to an end.[41] Hereford returned to backwater status.

To account for love in its pre-Chaucerian, west-of-England lyric inflection, we must pay attention to travel. During the first half of the fourteenth century, Hereford-bred clerics experienced a marked spike in mobility. The usual temptation with anonymous work is to press on "authorship" and/or "original context," but to link the phenomenon of the Harley Lyrics to the mobility of Hereford clerics foregrounds more tractable issues: transmission, for example; reception; implied audience. Whatever textual dynamics and material conditions may be in play, these poems resonate with such a group's biographical experience.

When they talk about love, the lyrics of Harley 2253 engage with geography, in its various narrative and metaphorical incarnations. "Longyng," "suffering" [þolien], and other tribulations conventionally associated with "derne loue" [secret affairs] supply their chief themes, but woven into their projects of praise, lament, and sexual-devotional adventuring are topographical subthemes.[42] Most of these lyric articulations of space amount to variations on the experience of erotic dislocation: a vernacular lover's departure or removal, his suffering in exile or anticipated coital homecoming. Contemporary literary-historicist undertakings promise, and soon, to ground the Harley Manuscript once and for all, cordoning it off, as at an archaeological dig, upon the static site of this or that Marcher household.[43] But desire as the Harley Lyrics express it is anything but excavatable. Rather, these poems present a love that is mobile. The main Harley scribe may himself spend three dozen years

[41] William J. Dohar, *The Black Death and Pastoral Leadership in the Diocese of Hereford in the Fourteenth Century* (Philadelphia: University of Pennsylvania Press, 1995), 71–72; 58, 64, 79. See Bannister, *Registrum Ade de Orleton*, 390–92, for the high incidence of leaves previously.

[42] E.g., #4.35: "Betere is þolien whyle sore / þen mournen euermore" [It is better to suffer grievously for a while than to mourn forever]; cf. #24.30. For "derne" in a moralizing context (#2.89, #32.2), see Brook, *HL*, 11–12; see Fein ("A Saint 'Geynest under Gore,'" 351–52) for lyrics more enthusiastic about "derne" erotics (#3.36, #9.43).

[43] Beyond Revard, consider John Hines, "A Household Book and a Fourteenth-Century Literary Household: Archaeological Evidence and Harley 2253," paper presented to the Early Book Society (Durham, England, 2003); cf. Hines, *Voices in the Past: English Literature and Archaeology* (Cambridge: Brewer, 2004), 71–104.

in a single, provincial lay milieu,[44] but his lyric poems and their cultured narrators—not to mention their transmitting agents, generic affiliates, and embedded audiences—range considerably further afield.

In documenting Adam Orleton's career, R. M. Haines returns repeatedly to this embattled bishop's *familia*, which institution he treats as his subject's executive arm and basic social unit.[45] By the thirteenth century the episcopal *familia* was common across England and had analogues in other aristocratic and bureaucratic groupings. Hereford's version distinguished itself in its vanguard position with respect to the burgeoning documentary practices that were beginning to transform vernacular literary culture.[46] If imaginative literature is a by-product of expanding literate proficiency in a functional bureaucratic sense, then the Diocese of Hereford's progressive documentary practice during the century prior to the Black Death—especially when coupled with Hereford Cathedral's reputation as a scholarly center[47]—predicts a climate unusually conducive to vernacular poetic development.

Social-institutional structures and their unique quotidian pressures help determine what form new literary expression takes. In characterizing the relationship between Orleton and *familia*, Haines gravitates toward terms that are restrained and professional, yet certain documentary moments attest to "an intense personal attachment" between this

[44] Revard proposes a degree of mobility for the Harley scribe, based on potential affiliation with various patrons, but his "documentary discoveries" themselves ("Scribe and Provenance," 26–28) carry this working scrivener no further than a few miles from Ludlow, during a career spanning thirty-six years and forty-one charters.

[45] Haines, *Administration*, 92–97; *Career*, 81–100, 205–6. For "structural characteristics" of episcopal groupings, whose key "social bonds" include "identification with the group, predefined leadership, precedence of members, communication and solidarity," cf. Jacek A. Maciejewski, "The Episcopate as a Social Group in Late Medieval Poland," paper presented to the International Medieval Congress (Leeds, 2006).

[46] D. M. Smith, *Guide to Bishops' Registers of England and Wales* (London: Royal Historical Society, 1981), 95–104; cf. Smith, "Thomas Cantilupe's Register: The Administration of the Diocese of Hereford 1275–82," in Jancey, *Essays*, 83–101. See M. T. Clanchy, *From Memory to Written Record: England 1066–1307*, 2nd ed. (Oxford: Blackwell, 1993), 16–17, for Hereford as one of literacy's "[frontier] growing points," where innovation occurs because "cross-fertilization makes adaptation more necessary."

[47] Julia Barrow, "Aethelstan to Aigueblanche, 1056–1268," in *Hereford Cathedral: A History*, ed. Gerald Aylmer and John Tiller (London: Hambledon Press, 2000), 21–47 (42–43); Nicholas Orme, "The Cathedral School Before the Reformation," in *Hereford Cathedral,* ed. Aylmer and Tiller, 565–78 (565–67). The leadership of the cathedrals declined with the rise of the universities, but in the early fourteenth century these were viable scholarly centers; Pantin, *English Church*, 110, 177; Kathleen Edwards, *The English Secular Cathedrals in the Middle Ages*, 2nd ed. (Manchester: Manchester University Press, 1967), 187–208.

bishop-patron and his household clerks. Orleton had, indeed continues to have, copious detractors, but he displayed a "kindly concern for his clerks' welfare—a sentiment which they reciprocated."[48] Durable bonds also developed between familial clerks themselves.[49] Medieval amorous poems often contain homoerotic undercurrents, but such desires remain latent in Harley 2253. Whether despite this or because of it, these "familial love" lyrics have unmistakable homo*social* tendencies.[50] As other period documents and they themselves show, the Harley Lyrics are performative products, keyed to a male-coterie milieu. It is not historically incidental, I think, that this is an interpretive community from which they have yet to emerge.

What We Talk About When We Talk About Love

During the Swinfield and Orleton years, Hereford and Worcester appear to have been known nationally for their production of vernacular love poetry. As we shall see, the Harley Lyrics themselves help produce such an identity, but independent evidence for this reputation is found in an early fourteenth-century Anglo-Norman survey poem known as *The List of 108 English Towns*. This text's conceit is as simple as its syntax: insular place-names are enrolled with their signature product or attribute: "Escole [School] de Oxenford" (9), "Vend' de q'ts [Wine sellers] de Bristowe" (88), "Bayn [Waters] de Baa[th]" (28), "Furur [Furriers] de Cestre" (59), "Seyntuarie de Canterburg" (3), and so on.[51] Most entries are economic, institutional, or topographical; some reprise local sayings or reputations. One attribute is explicitly literary: the "Verse-makers"

[48] Haines, *Career*, 102–16 ("Orleton and the Chroniclers"); 205–6, 97–100; *Administration*, 92–97.

[49] For an example of such attachment, see *Calendar of Patent Rolls, Edward III, vol. 3, 1334–38* (London: Public Record Office, 1895), 247, in which Bishop's Treasurer Roger Breynton arranges masses for his deceased mentor, Nicholas Reigate (on whom, see Webb, *Roll of Expenses*, 1:33, 161–62).

[50] My use of the term "homosocial" derives from Eve Kosofsky Sedgwick, *Between Men: English Literature and Male Homosocial Desire* (New York: Columbia University Press, 1985).

[51] H. Rothwell, ed., *English Historical Documents, 1189–1327* (Oxford: Oxford University Press, 1975), 881–84. *The List of Towns* appears in an AN legal/administrative compendium (Statutes of the Realm; Walter of Henley's *Husbandry*; Bishop Robert Grosseteste's household-management *Rules*), whose likeliest users were royal clerks; see Daniel Birkholz, *The King's Two Maps: Cartography and Culture in Thirteenth-Century England* (New York: Routledge, 2004), 125–29.

or "Rhymers of Worcester" [Rhymeour de Wyrcestre] (58).[52] Others
may be implicitly so, such as the "Boues [Longbows] de Notyngham"
(53), made famous through the Robin Hood ballads.[53] Another of this
sort may be the "Maidens [Demayseles] of Hereford" (89).[54] Critics envision Harley verses blossoming suddenly, then rotting in sweet obscu-
rity. But these allusions suggest the *non*-parochialism of lyrics like ours.
The fame of "Worcester's Poets" and "Hereford's Damsels" speaks to
the regional modality of such poems, but also to their wider currency.

A disproportionate amount of early Middle English survives from the
southwest Midlands.[55] There have come to be competing perspectives
on the relationship between this material and late-century literary material in the northwestern dialect exemplified in the "regional" romance
Sir Gawain and the Green Knight,[56] but it is clear that vernacular poetry,
especially of the alliterative variety, had special currency along England's
western fringe. Old English, as Seth Lerer has argued, had a vibrant
"afterlife as a literary language" in the region—especially at Worces-

[52] Presumably for this reason, Worcester's is the only entry mentioned by *A Manual
of the Writings in Middle English, 1050–1500,* vol. 7, ed. Albert E. Hartung (New Haven:
Yale University Press, 1986), 2238.

[53] The earliest extant ballads are later, but Robin Hood tales appear to have circulated in some form from the thirteenth century. For a review of dating arguments, with
focus on the iconic place of the longbow, see Kelly DeVries, "Longbow Archery and the
Earliest Robin Hood Legends," in *Robin Hood in Popular Culture: Violence, Transgression,
and Justice,* ed. Thomas Hahn (Cambridge: D. S. Brewer, 2000), 41–60.

[54] The AN "interlude" *Gilote et Johane,* a pastourelle/fabliau hybrid that survives
uniquely amid Harley 2253's most famous ME lyrics (fols. 67v–68v), introduces its
protagonists with precisely this descriptor. Here the conventional French lyric term
"damoyseles" (5) works, like the "ieune chiualer" [young knight] who "one morning in
May went out to have a good time in a thick, green wood" [En may par vne matyne
s'en ala iuer / en vn vert bois ramé] (1–2), to communicate an initial set of generic
coordinates, although pastourelle conventions are soon riotously abandoned. See Daniel
Birkholz, "A Crack in the Bedroom Map: Gender, Genre, and the Reception of Medieval Cartography" (in preparation).

[55] Ralph Hanna III, "Alliterative Poetry," in *The Cambridge History of Medieval English
Literature,* ed. David Wallace (Cambridge: Cambridge University Press, 1999), 488–
512 (509). For manuscripts from the region, see N. R. Ker, *Medieval Libraries of Great
Britain: A List of Surviving Books,* 2nd ed. (London: Royal Historical Society, 1964),
96–100, 205–15. The recently launched University of Birmingham Web site "Manuscripts of the West Midlands," directed by Wendy Scase, features a searchable database
catalogue of vernacular manuscript books from the West Midlands, c. 1300–1475:
http://www.mwm.bham.ac.uk/.

[56] Hanna summarizes, but for a metrical perspective, see also Thomas Cable, *The
English Alliterative Tradition* (Philadelphia: University of Pennsylvania Press, 1991): "ME
poetry does not show the continuity of tradition that standard authorities . . . assert"
(3). For the "regional concerns" of *Sir Gawain and the Green Knight,* see Rhonda Knight,
"All Dressed Up with Someplace to Go: Regional Identity in *Sir Gawain and the Green
Knight,*" *SAC* 25 (2003): 259–84, esp. 278.

ter.[57] Elizabeth Salter, meanwhile, emphasizes the "decisively international" character of pre-plague English culture, and proposes an analogue for the production of sophisticated west-country lyric in the "complex European affiliations of Hereford art during the [previous] century."[58] Whatever the genealogical details,[59] it is in the wake of such combined factors that insular lyric begins to develop. Numerous early lyrics link to Worcester or Hereford, and, though the phenomenon is not exclusively regional, the extant material has a western inclination.[60]

In England, the earliest shards of vernacular lyric survive either as sermon tags or in the margins and flyleaves of ecclesiastical codices.[61] Extant manuscripts, Julia Boffey has observed, provide our most reliable "means of access" into lyric audiences and production milieux.[62] Later manuscripts have aristocratic contexts, but in its years of coalescence vernacular lyric is affiliated with the institution of the church. Relevant in this vein is a snatch of early Middle English prose that appears in Worcester Cathedral Library MS F.61, a fourteenth-century manuscript otherwise devoted to Latin grammatical texts. In the bottom margins of folios 283 and 285v, a contemporary Anglicana hand has spelled out a set of conjugations for the verb "loue" [love] in English, providing grammatical case in Latin:

[57] Seth Lerer, "Old English and Its Afterlife," in *Cambridge History of Medieval English Literature*, ed. Wallace, 7–34, esp. 24–25, 31–32. On Worcester Cathedral as "a great centre of native English culture," see Hilton, *A Medieval Society*, 25–26.

[58] Elizabeth Salter, *English and International: Studies in the Literature, Art, and Patronage of Medieval England*, ed. Derek Pearsall and Nicolette Zeeman (Cambridge: Cambridge University Press, 1988), 5–8, 67–71, 83. It would be "helpful," Salter muses, "if we could suppose that more than French architectural styles took root" under the Savoyard Pierre de Aigueblanche, Bishop of Hereford, 1240–68. Aigueblanche's Provençal ties lend credence to the speculation, but his cursory, "contentious" relationship to Hereford suggests a likely insulation from western vernacular literary culture; see Barrow, "Aethelstan to Aigueblanche," 21, 43–47.

[59] For a technical formal argument that uses Harley Lyrics to help dismantle the metrical binary of "foreign" and "native," see Thomas Cable, "Foreign Influence, Native Continuation, and Metrical Typology in Alliterative Lyrics," in *Approaches to the Metres of Alliterative Verse*, ed. Judith Jefferson and Ad Putter, Leeds Texts and Monographs, n.s. 17 (Leeds: Leeds Studies in English, 2009), 219–34.

[60] Siegfried Wenzel, *Verses in Sermons: Fasciculus Morum and Its Middle English Poems* (Cambridge, Mass.: Medieval Academy Publications, 1978), 40–41; Carleton Brown, *English Lyrics of the XIIIth Century* (Oxford: Clarendon Press, 1932), xii. Cf. Lerer, "Afterlife," 29–30. The Welsh Marches were also "unusually fertile areas for Anglo-Norman literature"; Barrow, "Aethelstan to Aigueblanche," 42–43.

[61] For a sampling, browse R. M. Thomson and Michael Gullick, *A Descriptive Catalogue of the Medieval Manuscripts in Worcester Cathedral Library* (Cambridge: Brewer, 2001); cf. Wenzel, *Verses in Sermons*.

[62] Boffey, *Manuscripts of English Courtly Love Lyrics*, 61.

indicatius modus amo i loue i louede ich haue iloued ich hadde iloued i schal loue imperatiuus loue þu loue þu or he optatiuuus modus ich wolde loue or scholde loue ich hadde loue or scholde ha loued at mi wille loue i coniuctiuus modus whenne i loue whenne i louede whenne ich haue iloued . . . [fol. 285v] me loueit me louede me hat ilouet me wol loueme louit me alleluya.[63]

This Middle English conjugation of "love" reinforces the Latinate context within which early insular love poetry is produced and received. This point is important not because a link between "secular" lyric and clerical figures comes as a surprise, but because this Worcester pedagogue's grammatical invocation—*amo, amas, amat*—conjures up that most foundational of communal masculine experiences, the ecclesiastical schoolroom.

Having delivered his breathless declination of vernacular "love," our western grammarian concludes with a spiritual ejaculation: "alleluya." Such a chaste exclamation point upon love's grammar helps characterize this incidental bit of prose as a "derne" act of love: "hidden" in the sense of being obscured from general view (Brook #3.25). The (holy?) fervency of this (erotic?) performance, moreover, encapsulates the difficulty of determining where the lines are to be drawn between structures of religion and regimes of sexual desire: where spiritual begins and carnal ends. Similarly troubled are any distinctions we might be inclined to make between modern notions of "individual" subjectivity, with its "private" sensibilities, and premodern experiences of an institutional (not to say "public") communal nature.[64] Does "alleluya" render harmless the egocentric dangers of this-worldly desire, "loue" that is "derne" ("hidden" in the sense of illicit; #2.8) and therefore damning? Can a bit of devotional punctuation ("God be praised") neuter the implicit eroticism of love in a vernacular idiom? Grafted onto that most basic of classroom practices, this is "love" as academic exercise, cribbed for translation and fully declined. The shared quality of these grammatical erotics defines vernacular desire as an experience that is recoverable for sacred communal ends.

[63] Valerie Edden, ed., *The Index of Middle English Prose: Handlist XV: Manuscripts in Midland Libraries* (Cambridge: D. S. Brewer, 2000), 59. See Ker, *Medieval Libraries*, 211, for WCL F.61's Worcester provenance.

[64] Georges Duby, ed., *A History of Private Life, Vol. II: Revelations of the Medieval World*, trans. Arthur Goldhammer (Cambridge, Mass.: Harvard University Press, 1988). Terms like "individual," "private," and "personal" have a vexed history with regard to early lyric; see Albright, *Lyricality*, 11–12, but esp. Boffey, *Manuscripts of English Courtly Love Lyrics*.

The most common path into the Hereford Bishop's *familia* ran through the Hereford Cathedral School. Here training in basic Latin literacy ("song") and in the bureaucratic practices necessary for an ecclesiastical career occurred simultaneously with students' inculcation with a professional clerical ethos.[65] Primary values included loyalty to cohort and devotion to home church.[66] Considering the Cantilupe canonization push (1287–1320), followed by Edward II's persecution of Orleton and despoiling of his diocese (1323–25), then the city's subsequent role as "insurgent headquarters" (1326–27),[67] such socialization programs may have taken on special intensity at Hereford. Most students were drawn from gentry households in the vicinity, or from artisan families attached to the cathedral's own estates; others, placed by prominent families, came from further afield but still chiefly from the region.[68] On top of their formative school bond and intertwined careers, the shared roots of those who comprised the episcopal *familia* under Swinfield and Orleton help explain the remarkable commitment of such men to the person of their bishop, to the diocesan enterprise, and—not least—to one another. Read in this institutional light, the lyrics of Harley 2253 attest to the continuing pressure exerted by local moorings, even (especially?) for men whose careers have carried them into realms of international consequence.

Lyric has grounding in collective identity formation. In reminding himself how English "loue" is conjugated, our Worcester grammarian reminds us that vernacular lyric is more rhetorical than "rustic," its eloquence more acquired than "natural," and its dynamics more communal than "personal"—whatever "hawthorn name[s]" the Harley Lyrics assign to their "Demayseles," as they plant them in verdant bowers across

[65] Attendance at a "song" school also "contribut[ed] to culture and literacy among"—and thus patronage by—"the laity"; Orme, "Cathedral School," 568–72.

[66] Edwards, *Secular Cathedrals*, 323–25. For an earlier configuration, in which cathedral schools "train[ed] talented young men in statesmanship," see C. Stephen Jaeger, *The Envy of Angels: Cathedral Schools and Social Ideals in Medieval Europe, 950–1200* (Philadelphia: University of Pennsylvania Press, 1994), 46–47.

[67] G. A. Usher, "The Career of a Political Bishop: Adam de Orleton (c. 1279–1345)," *Transactions of the Royal Historical Society*, 5th ser., 22 (1972): 33–47 (46).

[68] For geographical and social origins of Hereford students, see Orme, "Cathedral School," 568–69. Schoolmasters were "obscure men" but mostly "local" (573–76). For clerical backgrounds and career patterns, see Robert Swanson and David Lepine, "The Later Middle Ages, 1268–1535," in *Hereford Cathedral*, ed. Aylmer and Tiller, 48–86 (56–67); cf. Barrow, "Aethelstan and Aigueblanche," 38. Rates of canonical residence were high at Hereford c. 1270s–1330s.

the region.[69] "Ffrom Weye [s]he is wisist into Wyrhale" (Brook #3.27): if anyone can say who is "most desirable" from the River Wye (south along the Welsh border) to the Wirral Peninsula (in Cheshire),[70] it ought to be the Marcher clerics of Hereford Diocese, having been drawn from across the region themselves, into the Cathedral School and thence diocesan administration, with its duties of parish oversight and visitation. Yet despite citation of local geographical markers—"Weye," "Wyrhale"; the western streams "Lyne" and "Lone" (#3.33); a ride "by Rybbesdale" (#7.1)[71]—there is no dwelling at "home" in these poems, no inhabitation of a grounded locale, so much as perennial home*coming*. The Harley Lyrics present a veritable feedback loop of poignant departure and compulsively detailed bodily reunion. Still, they produce an alluringly landed sense of community. Contour lines are difficult to trace, but the Harley Manuscript's *vague* regionalism correlates well, paradoxically, with the distended, cross-jurisdictional geographical experience of area ecclesiastics.

Transformation in the Harley Lyrics is repeatedly figured through a nostalgic return to "lond," a proud but plaintive lover's journey back to the fecund bower of his local "leuedi," or lyric beloved, a fair maid who "woneþ by west" [dwells in the west]. In narrating such geographies, the Harley Lyrics partake of a growing regional boosterism during the fourteenth century, a "local patriotism" that Nigel Saul finds especially prevalent among the knights and esquires (or lesser gentry) of the southwest Midlands: a group with increasing social and political self-consciousness although "remarkably narrow horizons."[72] The Hereford clerics of my title were neither so neatly located nor so parochial as this provincial esquire class—from which, as promising youths, many of them had been drawn. Their hallmark travels brought them much and,

[69] See Brook, *HL*, 7, 21–22, 25, and Chambers, "Aspects," 274–79, for attribution to the Harley Lyrics of these and similar terms (e.g., "primal"; "homely"; "wholesome").

[70] Literally, "wisist" means "wisest, most intelligent," but considering context and alliteration, here it suggests "most discerning" (in her tastes) or "most discreet" (in conducting her affairs).

[71] Lyn (Devon) and Lune (Lancs.) are rivers; Brook, *HL*, 75. The dialect is northwestern, but both Herefordshire and Lancashire have rivers "Ribble"; no medieval documentation records the place-name "Rybbesdale."

[72] Nigel Saul, *Knights and Esquires: The Gloucestershire Gentry in the Fourteenth Century* (Oxford: Clarendon Press, 1981), 168, 255–57. Cf. Hilton, *A Medieval Society*, 59–61, who describes the lesser landowners of Worcester diocese as "extraordinarily localized in their movements": "the overwhelming impression . . . is of communities of gentry and freeholders with very local interests."

enriched by contact with Europe's cosmopolitan elite, they brought much back with them. But travel has its costs. With such profound itinerancy came ambivalence about their own placement. The lives that appear to us in the laconic, "seemingly unrevealing" sources of medieval ecclesiastical administration tend to have an evacuated feel.[73] But documentary lives, which furnish the shells of social experience, can be animated via creative application of cultural evidence—that embodied, say, in circulating poems. Any leap from antiquated literary form to localized social interpretation requires an intrepid scholarly spirit. Yet to judge by the extant documentary and literary data, these men had geographical "contradictions" to resolve.[74]

Love poetry provides a medium for this work of resolution. The Harley Lyrics invite projection, each auditor's placement within the husk of a narrating (or narrated) lyric persona.[75] Dislocation is a feature common to the medieval ecclesiastical career; the more successful the clerk, the more traveled—and so too the more socially distended, the more removed from local community. Due to an ever-expanding pilgrimage network's "localization of the holy in [scattered] sacred places," medieval Christian institutional geography came to have a complex pattern, one that "transcended while affirming local allegiances."[76] As a counterbalance to metropolitan distemper, there develops an eroticized longing for home, an attempt to recapture the authenticity of once having felt emplaced. The amorous lyrics preserved in Harley 2253 resolve their speakers' geographical and social contradictions through fetishism. In them we see a recurrent manipulation, in painstakingly crafted poetic form, of the "wel mad" body of the conjured beloved; its relentless division into "hendy" [gracious] parts; the blending of mundane and exotic qualities that allow the local body to outmatch the "wonder" of the world; and especially its insistent placement "in lond": the lyric maiden's confinement within a fecund "bour" of delight to which an itinerant

---

[73] Haines, *Career*, 97–98; also Smith, "Cantilupe's Register," 89–90.

[74] Anne McClintock describes the practice of "fetishism" as "the displacement onto an object (or person) of contradictions that the individual cannot resolve at a personal level"; "these contradictions may originate as social contradictions but are lived with profound intensity in the imagination and the flesh." *Imperial Leather: Race, Gender, and Sexuality in the Colonial Contest* (New York: Routledge, 1995), 183–85.

[75] See Albright, *Lyricality*, 12, 22, and Boffey, *Manuscripts of English Courtly Love Lyrics*, 62, for projection as a feature of the lyric mode.

[76] Eamon Duffy, *The Stripping of the Altars: Traditional Religion in England, c. 1400–c. 1580* (New Haven: Yale University Press, 1992), 191.

lover may return "by west," to spend a heavenly night as "hire gest."[77] Not all poems in the corpus participate equally in this narrative project. But in their intertwined semantics and complementary thematics, the Harley Lyrics, as a literary conglomerate, express the shared experience of being world-weary and down-home both.

Who Compiled the Harley Lyrics?

This is not the venue in which to marshal the circumstantial, codicological, and documentary evidence linking western episcopal clerks to the Harley Manuscript and its texts. In order to proceed, however, we need to rehearse certain essentials concerning my position on the book's compilation process. Provenance arguments can become pointillist in method, but the production picture this essay proposes can be distilled to a handful of points.

The first point is that the main scribe of Harley 2253, as noted above, has been traced to Ludlow, where from 1314 to 1349 he wrote charters for local tradesfolk and minor leaseholders (forty-one are extant), while probably also serving as chaplain or tutor for a gentle household. This firm localization of the Harley Manuscript, with precise dating for the copying of texts, is established through paleographical analysis. But the point is buttressed by vernacular contents (devotional material, ancestral romances, political complaints) that bespeak a secular household context for the book—apparently one with a strong female patron.[78]

The second point concerns the way in which, in commentary on the manuscript over the last few decades, the distinction between medieval author-functions has collapsed. Almost uniformly nowadays, scholars posit a Harley "scribe/compiler";[79] and where credentialed readers previously found miscellaneity in this scribe's handiwork, "a variety of texts

---

[77] For "wel mad," see Brook #7.74. The other terms proliferate.

[78] Revard, "Scribe and Provenance"; "From French Fabliau Manuscripts," n. 31.

[79] Ker, *Facsimile,* xxiii; Revard, "Scribe and Provenance," in Fein, *Studies,* Hathaway et al., eds., *Fouke le Fitz Waryn,* and Theo Stemmler, in "Miscellany or Anthology? The Structure of Medieval Manuscripts: MS Harley 2253, for Example," in Fein, *Studies,* 111–21, all agree on this point. Resisting such conflation are McSparran and Fein; see esp. Fein's "Compilation and Purpose in MS Harley 2253," in *Essays in Manuscript Geography: Vernacular Manuscripts of the English West Midlands from the Conquest to the Sixteenth Century,* ed. Wendy Scase (Turnhout: Brepols, 2007), 67–94. Although Fein sees "supreme scribal ability" in our copyist's textual layouts and frequent manipulation of opening lines "to achieve a desired [literary] effect," she offers salutary warnings about "when scribal agency becomes confused with authorship" (93–94).

in no order" with "no discernable relationship between them," recent critics find "principled" selection and arrangement, a placement of diverse texts in subtle, even "dialectical" counterpoint.[80] Arguments concerning the Harley scribe's ingenious thematic planning can become unwieldy, but I do not dissent from appreciative assessments of this manuscript's sophisticated literary *ordinatio*. Still, from the perspective of the book's lyrics, there is a problem in the emerging consensus that attributes to the copyist of Harley 2253 an authorial presence and compilatory agency so full and developed. Patronal connections such as Revard proposes may have carried the scribe beyond the area (about six miles in diameter) of his known activity. But so far as extant documentation goes, the Ludlow scribe's apparent immobility and modest social positioning limit his personal ability to procure texts, especially of such variety and cosmopolitan reach.

Point three: I suggest that the Ludlow legal scribe be conceded full and intelligent input concerning manuscript *ordinatio* (layout, arrangement, and selection of received texts), but that we assign the bulk of the procuring and transmission activity—the practicalities of *compilatio*—elsewhere.[81] Recent scholarly trends have inclined away from sharp divisions of labor, toward recognition of the overlap among the functions that together constitute medieval "authorship": *patron, auctor, compilator, redactor, scriptor*, annotating *lector*, and—not least—operative textual community. Such erosion in distinction between medieval authorial roles is worth keeping in mind, but it may be time, in the case of Harley 2253, to redivide "scribe" from "compiler."

An active commissioning or transmitting role may have been played by someone resident in the Harley scribe's sponsoring household, which "must have [included]" patrons of unusually "sophisticated" literary

---

[80] Ker, *Facsimile*, xx; Revard, "From French Fabliau Manuscripts." The extent to which this compilation should be regarded as haphazard or deliberately planned has become a driving question; see Fein, "Compilation and Purpose"; Stemmler, "Miscellany or Anthology?"; and Revard, esp. *"Gilote et Johane"* and "Oppositional Thematics and Metanarrative in MS Harley 2253, quires 1–6," in Scase, ed., *Manuscript Geography*, 95–112. At once microcosmically and more expansively, Seth Lerer sees Harley 2253's folio 76r as an especially apt manifestation of the "anthologistic impulse" characterizing medieval English literary culture. "Medieval English Literature and the Idea of the Anthology," *PMLA* 118, no. 5 (2003): 1251–67.

[81] M. B. Parkes, "The Influence of the Concepts of *Ordinatio* and *Compilatio* on the Development of the Book," in *Medieval Learning and Literature: Essays Presented to Richard William Hunt,* ed. J. J. G. Alexander and M. T. Gibson (Oxford: Clarendon Press, 1975), 115–41.

tastes (yet who also retained a fondness for popular burlesque, didactic *débat,* and factional doggerel).[82] "Patron-compiler," therefore, may be the more appropriate place for a collapse in distinction between Harley author-functions than "scribe-compiler." The earliest of the three codices assembled by our scribe, however, contains the model for another, to my mind more compelling picture of these books' composite production dynamics.

The fourth point in my compilation argument consists of a manuscript page. On folio 70r of MS Harley 273 (c. 1314–28)—chiefly consisting of Anglo-Norman devotional texts—there appears a multipart image-sequence, drawn in pen. In a first drawing (upper left), we see an aristocratic lady speaking with a mature priest, tonsured and amply robed; second (bottom left), we see this ecclesiastical protagonist convening with several fellow clerks; third (upper right), we see a younger clerk, slender and curly-haired, copying out a codex; and finally (bottom right), this scribe presents his finished volume to the lady of the first scene, with the more established, procuring clerk no longer present. All figures in this sequence deserve full attention with respect to the compilation dynamics they embody and the interpretive possibilities they raise. Others have adopted the Harley scribe as their protagonist, but my interest centers on the figure of the busy priestly go-between, who, integral to the initial panels but absent thereafter, acts as mobile intermediary between all other members of the production cast. Friend to ladies and clerks alike, this facilitator links the patroness of the first and last scenes to the junior scribal functionary of the third and fourth. He connects these high and low (local?) figures, moreover, to the second scene's nebulous crowd of clerkly associates—his several sources, presumably, for the textual matter copied in the third scene. The two scenes that begin the compilation process do not include the young copyist (whose dashing portrait, incidentally, is accorded frontispiece status by Fein's landmark *Studies in the Harley Manuscript*).[83] Yet whether initiative for the work resides ultimately with the lady-patron or with the senior clerk remains unclear. Literary authority appears shared, in this vision,

---

[82] Revard, "From French Fabliau Manuscripts," 261.

[83] Fein's book reproduces only the third drawing, captioned "A scribe at work." No mention is made of the other drawings. This decision to isolate the image of a solitary scribe has interpretive consequences, for to enshrine a scribe-portrait here (where a modern author-photo might lie!) lends iconic support to the notion of a Harley "scribe/compiler" of considerable independent agency and elides the contributions of other agents in the production process.

not simply among the three principals (each of whom figures in two scenes) but also, radiating outward, with a wider community of ecclesiastical contacts.

I do not suggest that these drawings in Harley 273, penned years prior to our scribe's mature work and by another hand, to accompany a popular courtly treatise,[84] should be understood as literally documenting the events surrounding Harley 2253's compilation. But even if imported, such a production picture has interpretive advantages. It reconciles Revard's documentary discoveries, which describe a local Ludlow scribe possessing basic legal and ecclesiastical training,[85] with other critics' suspicion that the book has important connections with Hereford Cathedral.[86] This, in essence, is point five. What I am *not* proposing is a Harley copyist attached to the retinue of one or another Hereford bishop.[87] Instead, my proposition is that Harley's lay owners or Revard's

[84] The drawings on folio 70r form a discrete preliminary set but also comprise part of a larger illustration sequence that extends throughout *trouvère*-poet and cathedral canon Richard de Fournival's *Bestiaire d'amour* (*c.* 1250–59), a bestiary adaptation, addressed to a lady, in which birds and animals represent aspects of love. The *Bestiaire*'s "fascinating blend of clerkly and lyric elements" comes to the fore in its prologue, "an important statement on the poetics of lyrical writing" to which, in subsequent manuscripts, various "programs of illumination" are keyed; Sylvia Huot, *From Song to Book: The Poetics of Writing in Old French Narrative, Lyrical, and Lyric Poetry* (Ithaca: Cornell University Press, 1987), 135–74. For our scribe's precise contributions to Harley 273, see Revard, "Scribe and Provenance," 67–69.

[85] I should point out that Revard and I (personal communication, December 2007) diverge on this question of the Harley scribe's degree of mobility, his position being that plausible patronal connections he has traced suggest a life involving considerable travel across the region, mine being that this scrivener's localizable manuscripts and autograph legal charters, upon which any biographical account must be grounded, do not place him anywhere but in Ludlow's immediate vicinity. My thanks to Professor Revard for his documentary generosity and intellectual affability. Cf. Fein's intermediate position: "We still have little sense of how [the Harley scribe] came across" the great variety of materials he copied into this book: "Whether he did it by travelling about or whether the manuscripts and single sheets were transported to [him] seems impossible to determine" ("Compilation and Purpose," 74–77).

[86] Most pre-1980s critics presume a Hereford link; see Isabel S. T. Aspin, *Anglo-Norman Political Songs* (Oxford: Blackwell, 1953), 25–26, and Revard's own early work: "The Lecher, the Legal Eagle, and the Papelard Priest: Middle English Confessional Satires in MS. Harley 2253 and Elsewhere," in *His Firm Estate: Essays for F. J. Eikenberry*, ed. D. E. Hayden (Tulsa: University of Tulsa Press, 1967), 54–71 (71). More recently, see David L. Jeffrey, "Authors, Anthologists, and Franciscan Spirituality," in Fein, *Studies*, 261–70 (268–69). McSparran posits "some kind of off-and-on relationship" between the Harley scribe and Hereford; "Language of the English Poems," 392–95, 411.

[87] Some have regarded him as "an entertainer in the household of Thomas Charlton [Bp. 1327–44]," others as "probably a canon of Hereford, and [categorically] a follower of Adam Orleton"; see Hogan, "Critical Study," i–v (cf. Jeffrey, "Franciscan Spirituality," 268–69; Aspin, *Anglo-Norman Political Songs*, 24–25) and Hathaway et al., eds., *Fouke le Fitz Waryn*, xxxvii, xli–xliii (cf. Ker, *Facsimile*, xxiii).

legal scrivener (perhaps both) had an abiding contact in Hereford's episcopal *familia* or cathedral administration, to both of which institutions Ludlow-area gentry families contributed younger sons. Full-scale biographical construction, documentary grounding, and literary animation of my proposed lyric transmitter lies beyond this essay's purview.[88] So too does examination of the Harley Manuscript in its vast codicological and textual complexity. The operative point is that we have two interpretive communities in play: the Ludlow-area lay household of the codex in which the Harley Lyrics are preserved; and, flickering behind this, a dynamic ecclesiastical household (and wider network of affiliates) within which these poems gestate and previously circulate. Sonorous poems like these flow easily across medieval social boundaries and geographical stretches, if less readily across wide gulfs of time and taste. But it is to an episcopal familial milieu—transmitting if not originary, and grounded "out west" though perpetually in motion—that the love lyrics of Harley most cogently speak.

"Men Have Anger With Me"

Despite their love-struck clerical narrators, less jarring to medieval than to modern audiences, the Harley Lyrics possess crossover secular appeal. But how do these poems demonstrate that their initial textual community is to be found in a mobile episcopal milieu, rather than in the more circumscribed lay-household context suggested by their Ludlow scribe and manuscript? The Harley Lyric known as *The Lover's Complaint* is representative of the corpus in terms of the audience it creates. The poem's opening lines (see epigraph) present a familiar conceit: "Wiþ longyng y am lad, / on molde y waxe mad" [with longing I am beset, on the earth/ground I go mad], for "a maide marreþ me" [a maiden injures or is aggrieving me] (Brook #5.1–3). Like other Harley narrators who "libbe [linger, dwell] in loue-longinge" (#4.5), our speaker yearns for "bote" [healing, remedy] (#5.9), a time when "[s]he may me blisse bringe" (#4.17). "Beloved," he pleads, "have pity on me!" [Leuedi, þou rewe me!]. Our conventional lover is "sad," "vnglad"; "y grede" [I lament], "y grone," for "resting" [peace] is impossible: "my reste is wiþ þe ro" [I'm skittish as a deer; or, I won't be at peace until I track down my quarry] (#5.4–7, 14, 17; cf. #10.50).

---

[88] For some practical and methodological issues involved, see Birkholz, "Biography After Historicism."

This lyric most resembles its companions in that the speaker's beloved deprives him of his rest ("[she] reueþ me mi rest," Brook #5.33), but another way *The Lover's Complaint* affiliates itself with other Harley poems is in its speaker's placement of his "leuedi" in emphatic geographical terms. He himself may dwell in an abstract state—one of delicious, borderless desire—but "þis wommon woneþ by west": she "dwells in the west-country" (#5.37). To be sure, the demands of Middle English rhyming provide semantic impetus here. It has been suggested that the Harley Lyrics' intermittent place-names and alliterative geographical sweeps—one "lemmon" [lover] ensconced "bituene Lyncolne ant Lyndeseye, Norhamptoun ant Lounde" (#25.17–19), another who spreads her healing "from Lyne to Lone" (#3.33)—provide clues as to compositional provenance or even authorial identity, after the manner of coterie masquerading conventions.[89] This speaker's location of his beloved "by west," however, works less by way of coy riddling— "out west" being about as helpful to identification as "from Irlond into Ynde" (#12.12)—than to correlate with his previous assertion of this lady's standing "[among] þe best" (#5.36–37). "West" and "best" pair recurrently in the Harley corpus (#15.45–47; #12.10–11).[90]

The poem begins as a complaint about (Brook #5.1–6), then becomes a complaint to (7–30), "a maide [that] marreþ me"; but by the final stanza (31–40), the speaker's project has evolved again, from supplication to boast, as if his lamentation itself produces the "bote" [remedy] (9) required. His "healing" would seem to be poetic, then, not sexual. Ultimately what drives the speaker is a need to establish the public value of his "leuedi." His initial request had been that his beloved should "les me out of bonde" [release me from my bondage] for "broht icham in wo" [I am driven into woe] (12–13)—sentiments conventional in a courtly context, but no less resonant of a Christian (specifically Marian) salvation economy. His confidence in eventual bodily favors being implicit, our speaker's early suffering gives way to the higher-priority issue of his beloved's standing in an imagined, maybe wholly imaginary market of local fair maids. Like others assembled body part by body part in the lyrics of

---

[89] Hogan, "Critical Study," 43; Brook, "The Original Dialects of the Harley Lyrics," *LeedsSE* 2 (1933): 38–61 (55–57). Dialect assignments tend to agree with provenances suggested by place-names.

[90] Cf. David Lawton on alliterative "ghosts": once certain words are established as semantic partners, the potential meanings of *all* are activated whenever *any* appears; "Alliterative Poetry," in *A Companion to "Piers Plowman,"* ed. John A. Alford (Berkeley and Los Angeles: University of California Press, 1988), 223–49 (239–41).

the Harley Manuscript, "þis wommon" is placed, as noted, vaguely "out west." One might think it more important that, among women "war ant wys" [discreet and discerning], "she bears away the prize" [hue bereþ þe pris] (34–38). Yet ours is a lover not unwilling to equivocate. Precisely speaking, his beloved is "burde *on of* þe best," a catch who is "*one of*" or "*among* the best" (36; emphasis added)—charming accommodation, I find, as to the equivalence of all our embowered "birds," as if to acknowledge that participation in weaving lines of "loue-longinge" (#4.5), being heard to lament over some "lef in lond" (#7.50), is more important than quibbling over precedence. There are prizes enough for everyone's "love in land," for all the "worly [splendid] wymmen" we can plant "by west" (#12.10). One latter-day reader—a cloistered *mid*-westerner, as it happens—admits to being "intrigued by the constant reference to beautiful women who live in the west."[91]

Critics have remarked upon the "good-natured" spirit of the Harley Lyrics. Such tonal observations fit well with what Boffey has described as late medieval lyric's "convivial purposes."[92] But more important to in-group conviviality than there being erotic laurels enough for all, surely, is that—in a perennially tight ecclesiastical job market—there be benefices enough for all. Critical admonitions that we not expect lyric narrative conditions to represent "actual personal relations" are salutary.[93] Yet few episcopal patrons provided for their clerks so effectively as did Adam Orleton—to the extent that charges of pluralism would catch up with some of them.[94] As in any retinue, a certain jockeying for position complicated familial affairs, but for Orleton's household (and Swinfield's), vitriolic internal competition appears to have been muted. It may be that questions of precedence were contested along a performative poetic axis, although with what mixture of collegial love and careerist animosity is impossible to say.

The Lover's Complaint indulges in a rash of first- and second-person pronouns. But though it is addressed to the poet's "leuedi" (Brook #5.7,

---

[91] Hogan, "Critical Study," 76, ii.

[92] Brook, *HL*, 22 (cf. Daniel J. Ransom, *Poets at Play: Irony and Parody in the Harley Lyrics* [Norman, Okla.: Pilgrim Books, 1985], 24); Boffey, *Manuscripts of English Courtly Love Lyrics,* 140; cf. 96.

[93] Brook, *HL*, 10, 20; cf. Boffey, *Manuscripts of English Courtly Love Lyrics,* 4–5, 61–63.

[94] Haines, *Career*, 91, 97. Episcopal clerks were "not expected to be resident in their benefices," but for a (posthumous) simony accusation against Orleton intimate Roger Breynton, see J. H. Parry, ed., *Registrum Johannis de Trillek, Episcopi Herefordensis, 1344–61* (London: Canterbury & York Society, 1912), 244–45.

11, 21) and claims as its subject "my loue," which "is on þe liht" [has alighted on you] (22), this poem is more concerned with two groups of men: first, the implied masculine audience with whom the speaker is pleased to share his "grede"-ing, "grone"-ing, and expectation of future sexual healing (a male-bonded cohort that includes most modern critics); and second, a group of "men," alluded to with offhand familiarity, that "to me han onde" [are angry with me, or, literally, have anger/enmity toward me] (18). Our speaker will not waver in his "loue": he will "ne lete for non of þo," will "not let up" in his loving "for any of them," whatever they say (19–20). And he is confident too of his reward: his "burde" is "brihtest vnder bys" [radiant when out of her clothing / beneath the covers] (38).[95] Scholars interested in tracing Harley derivations have observed that an openness about sex marks the northern French lyric tradition through which Provençal conventions are speculated to have traveled on their way to the English west country.[96] Still, the goal of this lover's rhetorical performance is not the "bote" to be received in "bour," his anticipated postcoital "reste," so much as his need to allay the "onde" or men's "anger" he has generated. He must prove himself equal in stubborn potency to the dour critique of such men.

Either way, the intercourse this lyric desires (and continues to facilitate) is not genital but social. More precisely, it is homosocial, meaning it has its base in relations of power, privilege, and affiliation between men, while yet being functionally concerned—not just ostensibly so— with matters of heterosexual coupling. As expounded by Eve Sedgwick, homosocial patriarchy's basic paradigm does not exclude the feminine but requires it: throughout English literary history, women's bodies serve as the vehicle through which men interact with one another.[97] It is the courtly affair's constituting paradox that it be constructed as "secret" [derne] only in order that it may, in poetic discourse, be revealed. The rhetoric may be boastful or self-deprecating, admonitory or philosophical, but whatever the mode, courtly poetics have their foundation

---

[95] This erotic radiance of the partially covered lyric body activates the Marian trope (Brook #6.19–22) in which the Virgin's womb is likened to a lantern containing the "light of all the world." See Fein, "A Saint 'Geynest under Gore,'" (351–76, esp. 358), who tracks the manifestations of this trope across the various texts of Quire 7—not just lyric and not only ME—to demonstrate Harley 2253's sophisticated local *ordinatio*.

[96] Brook, *HL*; Chambers, "Aspects," 274–76.

[97] Sedgwick, *Between Men*, 21–27. The Harley Lyrics confirm Sedgwick's argument that rather than there being some "separate male-homosocial literary canon," "the European canon as it exists is already such a canon," 17.

in a circulation, among the members of a competing or consoling masculine audience, of the joys and travails endemic to an amorous condition.[98] The temptation may be to declare the voyeuristic content in poems like these a red herring, mere cover for competitive professional erotics. But as a generation of work in the vein of Sedgwick insists, the sexual is an integral part of the social, into which it is perennially folded.

Why do men have "onde" [anger] with our speaker? At the poem's opening we found him going mad on the ground: "on molde y waxe mad" (Brook #5.2). If desire—even whipped-up fictional desire, a displacement of homosocial anxiety onto the body of a lyric maiden—be a species of madness, then what the angry men at the fringes of this lyric embody is a concern that "loue," excessive passion for some "burde in boure" (e.g., #14.5, #3.1), not interfere with masculine affairs. If misdirected, "love-longing" threatens to incapacitate a man, to have a negative impact on his performance of vocational—and affiliational—duty. A vernacular affair does preoccupy our speaker. Even so, the bawdy currency of the great body of his outland "burde" (recall her radiance "when undressed") underscores the extent to which the reproduction at issue here is public, masculine, and institutional, as opposed to hidden (provincially "derne") and embowered. In being surveyed and evaluated, compared and circulated, the body of the lyric beloved reveals the competitive heterosexual dynamics—and cosmopolitan homosocial circuitry—within which poems like these have their conception, as well as continuing erotic resonance.[99]

Love in Land, Men upon Molde

The theme of poetic competition, with its implications for male group bonding, sees elaboration in *The Poet's Repentance* or (as its first line runs) "Wepying haueþ myn wonges wet" (Brook #6.1). The "weeping" that has "wet" this narrator's "cheeks" [wonges] is not a result of the usual lover's complaint, but of his own "wikked werk ant wone of wyt"

[98] Tropes of a longed-for maiden's body and the geopolitical fantasies of male writers have been much discussed; see, for example, Margaret Brose, "Petrarch's Beloved Body: 'Italia Mia,'" in *Feminist Approaches to the Body in Medieval Literature*, ed. Linda Lomperis and Sarah Stanbury (Philadelphia: University of Pennsylvania Press, 1993), 1–20.

[99] For a complementary psychoanalytic argument, in which "the feminine body is ob*lite*rated ('written out')" during a "struggle for dialectal resolution or transcendence" in certain Harley Lyrics (not including Brook #5), see Margherita, *Romance of Origins*, 60–81.

[wicked work and lack of tact / want of wisdom] (2). Specifically, the poet repents of his antifeminist slander: "ofte in song y haue hem set, / þat is vnsemly þer hit syt" [often in songs I have placed {women} where it is unseemly that they appear] (7–8). He now declares "al wrong" what he has "seid in song" (10–12). In his defense, he has only stirred up wrong because of a certain "wyf"—not some fickle former love but rather she "þat made vs wo in world" (13–14). Talk of Eve begets talk of Mary. Fortunately, "there have been no wicked women since He was born [of her]" [wommen nes wicked non / seþþe he ybore was] (23–24). The overwrought nature of this assertion (an example of the Harley poems' "cheerful cynicism")[100] betrays itself in the poet's ensuing (and potentially mysterious) claim that "all [women] are as courteous as hawks in a chamber" [al {are} hende ase hauk in chete] (28). Whether we see irony here depends on what valence we assign to a conventional phrase: "hende ase hauk in chete" may signify women's inherent nobility (or grace), the appropriately "courteous" cast of female character.[101]

Our poet's repentance (he is "mot" [sorry]; Brook #6.29) feels disingenuous because his relationship with women is not his song's primary concern. This does not stop him from dramatic enactment of penance: "y falle to fete" [I fall at their feet], he declares twice in two lines (32–33). It requires a stretch of lines to illustrate this poem's concatenated quality, its suffusion with the techniques of alliteration and rhyme, syntactic inversion and semantic repetition:

Forþi on molde y waxe mot	*therefore*
þat y sawes haue seid vnsete,	*tales; unseemly*
my fykel fleish, mi falsly blod;	*fickle; most false*
on feld hem feole y falle to fete.	*on the ground before them*
To fet y falle hem feole	
for falslek fifti-folde,	*falsehoods*
of alle vntrewe on tele	*all of them*
wiþ tonge ase y her tolde.	*as I have here related*

(29–36)

---

[100] Brook, *HL*, 22. For the collection's tendency toward irony, see Ransom, *Poets at Play*, while for this particular text's "complex tone that cannot be entirely serious," see Fein, "A Saint 'Geynest under Gore,'" 358.

[101] This collocation also appears in *Pearl* (line 184). "Hende" as deployed in Harley (Brook #3.49; #4.9,39; #6.28; #7.42; #8.9; #14.57; #32.12) is not so double-edged as in Chaucer, even if the "derne loue" that animates certain lyrics "is deftly illustrated by" the *MilT*'s "hende Nicholas"; Fein, "A Saint 'Geynest under Gore,'" 353–54.

"Forþi on molde y waxe mot": "therefore [for my transgressions], upon the earth"—abject "on molde"—"I must wax repentant, must here waste away" (29). The word "molde" has powerful valence in the Harley Manuscript.[102] In our last poem (three folios prior), a lover "waxes mad," and does so, definitively as it were, on the earth or ground: "on *molde* y waxe mad" (#5.2; emphasis added). But far more affecting is the over-heard lamentation of "men vpo[n] mold," "men of the earth" in the sense of men who *work* the earth, encountered in a Middle English social complaint set between these two lyrics.[103] The downtrodden farmers of the *Song of the Husbandman* do not wax with love-longing "vpo[n] mold," but instead waste away on unplanted furrows—even their seed-corn has been sold to pay the king's tax (63–64). The combination of unforgiving weather, manorial graft, and feudal exploitation has driven them to star-vation—and worse, suicidal despair: "ase god i[s] swynden anon as so forte swynke" [it would be as good to die at once, as to labor so {i.e., in such hopelessness}] (72).

Another nearby political song—a caustic tale decrying outside au-thority's encroachment within a village community—is set into motion when its speaker happens to "[go] wiþ a mai" "on molde": that is, "has a go on the ground with a maiden" [ʒef ich on molde mote wiþ a mai . . .].[104] As in *Husbandman*, "molde" carries strong association with (and may literally denote) the furrow, characterizing this earthy sexual act—in its speaker's eyes at least—as an expression of agrarian connect-edness. To say that two kinds of plowing are going on captures my double meaning, but cheapens the poem's blending of "molde" as place of rural work and of vernacular passion alike. The usual modern title of this complaint is *A Satire on the Consistory Courts.*[105] It culminates with

---

[102] Fein argues that certain recurrent words link Harley's generically disparate con-tents along thematic lines; "molde" seems to be one such. "Compilation and Purpose," 78–88. Cf. Stemmler, "Miscellany or Anthology," 116.

[103] Robbins, *Historical Poems,* #2.1.

[104] Ibid., #6.4.

[105] Some use its incipit; see Thorlac Turville-Petre, "English Quaint and Strange in *Ne mai no lewed lued*," in *Individuality and Achievement in Middle English Poetry*, ed. O. S. Pickering (Cambridge: Cambridge University Press, 1997), 73–83. Turville-Petre en-dorses Revard's view ("From French Fabliau Manuscripts," n. 17) that this is a "self-satirizing dramatic monologue" better entitled "something like *A Sinner in the Archdea-con's Court.*" Still, the narrator's raillery against graft, pretension, and backbiting at the consistory court needn't mean that clerks accustomed to hearing "bisshopes plee" (79)—notaries in the employ of Archdeacon of Gloucester Roger Breynton, for exam-ple—would shrink from preserving such a piece, any more than nonpeasant status pro-hibits an interest in *Husbandman*.

the speaker, humiliated before an itinerant ecclesiastical court, declaring his refusal to fall at his judges' feet—"shal y to fote falle for mi fo?" [Shall I fall at the foot of my foe?] (67)—when ordered to take the "mai" he has impregnated (?)[106] officially to wife. Unsympathetic scholars have regarded the tale of this "rascal" as self-incriminating: "if he is such a nice guy, what is he doing in a satire?"[107] Yet however canonical the court's justice ("huere lay" [their teaching] or "lawe" [legal interpretation], 4, 65), this visiting body has disrupted village affairs. "Ne mai no lewed lued libben in londe" [Unlettered folk can hardly live in this country], the poem begins, "so lerede vs biledes" [because learned men jack us around so much] (1–3).[108] The speaker is driven to "fleo [flee from] my fere," in the doubled sense of "fere" as "companion/sexual partner" and as "community" or "set of companions" (16).[109] Outside inter-*fere*-ence has resulted in rupture to local community and of the lovers' bond (if it was a bond) alike. The terms used to convey a sense of community in *Satire* are precisely those used to describe "love-longing" in neighboring lyrics. Abjection, political or passionate, takes place "on molde"; social standing is expressed in falling "to fete"; and community, felt or fractured, lies embodied "in londe.

The manuscript proximity, stylistic similarity, and semantic borrow-

---

[106] After their copulation, she comes to court "bimodered ase a mor-hen" (58). Commentators have glossed this only literally, as "covered with mud." Middle English *bimodered* occurs here uniquely; since the *MED*'s only cross-reference is to Early Modern English "mother-scum", and considering our narrative circumstances, plus medieval hens' symbolic fertility (as in Chaucer's *NPT*), one suspects some association with the ubiquitous Middle English *moder* ("mother" or "woman" generally, but sometimes "a derogatory term for a young woman, wench"; "also used of animals and birds"). Thus, she is "dirty" in two senses, now that he has "made a woman out of her"—perhaps, literally made her into a mother—out on the furrow.

[107] Hogan, "Critical Study," 173; Revard, "The Lecher," 62. The intolerance of "lerede" [learned] modern critics for the poem's "lewed" [unlettered] speaker replicates, in its hierarchical flow of moral judgment, the action of the medieval narrative. Cf. Turville-Petre, "English Quaint and Strange," 79–83, and J. P. Oakden (1935), who dismisses *Satire* because it is "abusive in tone"; quoted in Robbins, *Historical Poems*, 258.

[108] Or less aggressively: "because learned men always give us the runaround." Robbins glosses "biledes" as "leads astray"; *Historical Poems*, 396. Whoever wrote the complaint was "lerede," of course, even if its protagonist is "lewed."

[109] See Bruce Mitchell and Fred C. Robinson, *A Guide to Old English*, 5th ed. (Oxford: Blackwell, 1992), 320, 194, for *(ge)fera* as "companion, comrade." The noun derives from *feran* [set out, proceed] but as seen in the cognates *(ge)ferscipe* [fellowship, community] and *gode geferan* [good companions], a sense of group comes to take precedence over the sense of travel. See Brook, *HL*, 97, for ME *fere* as "spouse" (#2.40, #9.30)—he refers to OE *(ge)fera*—but also #13.55–59 for companions less erotic (e.g., Pride, "my plowe-fere").

ing between Harley political songs and love lyrics indicates that overlap also existed between these texts' interpretive communities—if not at composition, then through subsequent circulation. Hereford and Worcester secular clergy knew and copied (if they did not also generate) both sets of texts, even if the primary audiences for each type were dissimilar in institutional placement and patronal loyalties. To be sure, there are differences in tone, genre, and social orientation: the anticlerical snarl of *Satire* and antiestablishment bitterness of *Husbandman* correlate imperfectly with the light and learned sophistication of the best lyrics. Scholars have found affiliation between Harley political complaints and provincial gentry landholders, whose interests these poems tend implicitly to promote (more than those of subaltern laborers, whose ventriloquized laments are put to partisan use).[110] Such social positioning fits better with the secular Marcher milieu tagged by Revard (and contextualized by Saul) than it does with the mobile ecclesiastics that form this essay's subject community. As with blended lay and clerical audiences, however, manuscripts harboring texts of mixed allegiance should not surprise, and need not invalidate a prior episcopal context— transmitting if not authorial—for the lyrics preserved in Harley 2253. It is precisely the burgeoning class activated by Harley's vernacular complaints, after all—rural gentry families whose allegiances came increasingly, during this period and for this region, to center upon provincial political institutions like the shire—from which the bulk of Hereford secular clergy were drawn.[111] The nostalgic, lyrical localism of these cosmopolitan clerks takes a different form from, but does not conflict with, the functional, jurisdictional localism that was taking root in their birth-families (with whom, as patronage and visitation patterns make clear, mature ecclesiastics remained interconnected). Harley political songs like *Husbandman* and *Satire* do more than just share a semantic terrain with lyrics such as *The Lover's Complaint* and *The Poet's Repentance*; they return us to lyric's tumultuous land of love-longing with an enriched sense of these genres' complementary yet distinct geographical thematics.

In place of a speaker who has spread evil tales about women around

[110] E.g., Aspin, *Anglo-Norman Political Songs*, xiv, 107.

[111] Saul, *Knights and Esquires*, 30, 82, 258; Swanson and Lepine, "Later Middle Ages," 56–62. The birth-families of many bishop's clerks fit this profile; see Birkholz, "Biography After Historicism," for property deals between cathedral clerk Roger Breynton (later, bishop's agent, proxy, and canon; executor to Swinfield and Orleton, etc.) and his brother Hugh de Topesleye, a minor landholder in suburban Hereford.

town ("told beon tales vntoun in toune"; Brook #6.37), and who is now, however disingenuously, languishing "on molde," *The Poet's Repentance* offers the admirable example of one "Richard" (60–61). "Rote of resoun ryht, / rykening of rym ant ron" (61–62), this Richard has been taken to be a "rival poet"[112]; he is "well-versed in right reasoning" and in "reckoning [estimation] of rhyme and rune"—that is, the clerical mystery of writing, with the added sense of invocational potency that "rune" conveys. The speaker's self-deprecation with regard to Richard has a different quality from his performance of abjection before the nameless women he has defamed. If any rivalry is present, it is of the affectionate variety. The tone bespeaks sardonic intimacy, compounded in that the poet's praise of Richard (straight compared with his apologia to "[al] wymmen," 53) amounts to an assertion of his right to grace by association. Women rightly prefer Richard to the speaker: he is "cunde comely ase a knyht" ["well-bred, shaped as nobly as a knight"], while at the same time "clerk ycud þat craftes con" [a clerk well-known for mastery of his craft] (65–66). No mention is made of any "song[s]" or "tales" by Richard—curious if he is a rival—but much is made of Richard's "rede": his "counsel" or kindly intervention (7, 37, 60).[113]

With his aristocratic breeding and clerical craft, his standing among noble women and sponsorship of an abject poet—plus, the praise of his metrical judgment—"Richard" comes across more like an episcopal mandarin than some fellow *clericus vagans* envied, as the implication tends to run, for his sexual prowess. An earlier reference to "kyng, cayser" [king, Kaiser] and "clerk wiþ croune" (Brook #6.43) is activated in the final stanza's apostrophe to Richard as "clerk most famous" [clerk ycud]: "in vch an hyrd þyn aþel ys hyht" [in every household, your nobility/worth is declared] (67).[114] The term "hyrd" [household] had appeared in the speaker's earlier promise: "From now on I will al-

---

[112] Brook, *HL*, 23; cf. Ransom, *Poets at Play*, 24. Margherita also finds "confrontation" with a "rival poet" here, though in a context of "explicitly homosocial and implicitly homoerotic exchange"; *Romance of Origins*, 71–75.

[113] Compare this supportive clerical "rede" to the oppressive "redes" [legal judgments] distributed by the pitiless black robes of *Satire* (Robbins, *Historical Poems*, #6.6).

[114] Richard's credentials as a networked aristocrat with patronal pull militate against the fabliau-style, "poor clerk on the make" readings that have become the norm for this poem (cf. Fein, "Lyrics of Harley 2253," 4177; Ransom, *Poets at Play*, 18, 22, 25–28; Brook, *HL*, 23; and, more generally, Chambers, "Aspects," 273–76). Following Brook (*HL*, 78), Bella Millet glosses "clerk wiþ croune" as "tonsured cleric," but this generic rendering obscures the line's emphasis on temporal rank ("king," "kaiser"); "Wessex Parallel Web-Texts," http://www.soton.ac.uk/~wpwt/.

ways praise women, and always *holde* with them [i.e., speak well of them] *in hyrd* [among the household]" (53–54). Gentle households like the one that owned Harley 2253 are home to just the sort of women among whom Richard's reputation shines; but Middle English "hyrd" retains remnants of its Anglo-Saxon sense as "warrior band," a lord's cadre of loyal retainers.[115] Through Richard's intercession a disgraced clerk has risen from contemplation of "cares colde" (52), a state of "wo" figured in terms of his disfavor with local women, into universal social investment: "nou wo in world ys went away / ant weole is come ase we wolde" [now suffering is gone from the world, and reward has come, as we wished] (49–50). The poet acknowledges that his elevation from "woe" into "weal" has been conferred by patronage: "þourh a mihti, meþful mai" [through a mighty, temperate/gracious maid] (51). Among earthly intercessors, however, credit for his transformation adheres not to Mary's lineage, that is, any of the "brudes bryht" [radiant birds] (39) he has defamed; it is just that I am finally listening to Richard: "soþ is þat y of hem ha wroht, as Richard erst con rede" [the truth is that I've begun treating them as Richard has always advised] (59–60). The poem announces its topic as "leuedis loue" [ladies' love/love of ladies] (5), but presses its praise on Richard. What women provide is occasion—and means. Richard has worldly "myht" [influence] specifically in consequence of his good standing among "gentle maidens" [of maidnes meke þou hast myth] (63). Thus invested, he effects a transformation upon poet—and audience. Secular "leuedis," female patrons of the sort who might commission manuscripts or control advowson (right of appointment) for some plump church benefice, may flutter in the wings;[116] but

---

[115] See Mitchell and Robinson, *Guide to Old English*, 330–33, for *hiredmann* as "retainer, warrior." The term's derivation from OE *hieran* [to obey], whose secondary meanings include "hearken to" and "hear," underlines the medieval association between poetic audiences and retaining, between listening and group-formation (cf. Brian Stock, *Listening for the Text: On the Uses of the Past* [Philadelphia: University of Pennsylvania Press, 1997]). See Brook, *HL*, 102, for ME *hyrd* as "household" or (in #8.34) "family." Brook glosses *hirmon*—which in #13.84–85 collocates with "hous" and "halle"—as "servant, retainer," citing OE *hiredmann*, although the increasingly domestic sense may indicate borrowing from OE *hyrde/hirde* [guardian, keeper, i.e., "herd"]; cf. #27.36, "hirdes" [shepherds]. *Hiredmen* appears in *Satire*, where it may denote either domestic retainers or agricultural workers: "hyrdmen hem hatieþ" [household-men {or herdsmen} hate them] (Robbins, *Historical Poems* #6.41). The quotations compiled by the *MED* describe *hyrd*, in its primary definition ("hired [n.], 1.[a]"), as a term specific to the ecclesiastical household.

[116] For advowson as a piece of real property that often triggered jurisdictional disputes, see Pantin, *English Church*, 86. Each collation to a benefice recorded in the Hereford registers names a patron or patroness, in addition to the clerk presented and reason for vacancy: Capes, *Registrum Ricardi de Swinfield*, 524–44; Bannister, *Registrum Ade de*

ultimately it is an institutional masculine relationship that *The Poet's Repentance* works to promote.

"Weole" [reward] has come, not as "I" but "as *all of us* wished" [as *we* wolde] (Brook #6.49–50; emphasis added). Commentators have found it surprising that early lyrics seldom address matters of real importance to their clerical authors, such as the "difficulty of finding preferment."[117] These may well be the worries that animate the Repentant Poet, his "cares colde," but what patterns of ecclesiastical promotion at Hereford and Worcester demonstrate, during the early fourteenth century, is the opposite of zero-sum competition. When the affairs of bishop and diocese thrive, Adam Orleton's household clerks are rewarded with additional or more lucrative benefices. Like the spoils of battle to Anglo-Saxon *hiredmenn* (ME *hyrdmen*), promotions to office do not come singly but are distributed to many at a time.[118] This reality of ecclesiastical life helps reinforce the collective nature of administrative undertaking, but a corollary is that such *esprit de corps* may characterize social and cultural undertakings as well. Well-recompensed pluralists, as Orleton's key clerks were to become, might be especially given to commemorating their advancement through poetic conviviality.

Combined with his deference to Richard, the perseverance of the poet's mischievous tone toward women—"I won't disagree with anything they tell me" [y ner nemnede þat heo nolde] (Brook #6.56)—suggests that what some Harley Lyrics are talking about, when they talk about "loue" (5), is their speakers' sense of gratitude to the (masculine) *familia* that sustains them, and especially to the "clerk wiþ croune," present, desired, or fondly remembered, at its head. An aristocratic Norman counterpart to the generic priestly "John" of a neighboring lyric (#3.50), "Richard" is probably a throwaway name, chosen to alliterate with "rede," "rykening," "rym ant ron" (#6.60–62).[119] Perceived to be "bearers of introspective insight," lyric poems are especially subject to

---

Orleton, 385–89. Lay patronage of ecclesiastical institutions was often negotiated through individual clerks on the basis of personal relations.

[117] Boffey, *Manuscripts of English Courtly Love Lyrics,* 4. Cf. Brook, *HL*, 10–11, and Albright, *Lyricality*, ix–x.

[118] Haines, *Career*, 96–97.

[119] Revard's intrepid researches have included a rundown of likely Richards and a roundup of Herefordshire Johns ("Richard Hurd," 199–200), but as Millet observes, the poem's addressee "has not been identified, and is unlikely to be"—"unless" (!) he is Richard de Grimhill, the "suggested compiler" of the late thirteenth-century miscellany Digby 86 (which many regard as Harley 2253's inspiration or prototype).

critical-biographical desire.[120] Considering, however, that there are intriguing visits and gift-exchanges plus patronal ties and family connections between Hereford episcopal clerks and various Ludlow households proposed as home to Harley 2253, we are obliged to consider that "Richard" could be allusion to a specific "clerk with crown" (or "mitre"). It can be dangerous to read too much into lyric narratives, let alone character names, since only rarely can they be shown to document historical relationships. But certainly, Richard Swinfield was fondly remembered by his *familia*.[121] Presumably, Bishop Richard was also beloved of the Mortimer-Talbot family of Richard's Castle (near Ludlow),[122] who had entertained him on visitation in May 1290; who later placed a son in the Hereford episcopal entourage; and whom Revard regards as leading candidates to have been Harley 2253's patrons.[123] Another Ludlow *domina* with ties to the manuscript, Katherine de Genville—an accounts-roll for her father Geoffrey's household served as its "wrapper"—also connects to Hereford's episcopal milieu and larger ecclesiastical net-

---

[120] Boffey, *Manuscripts of English Courtly Love Lyrics,* 61–86, esp. 62, 66. In later lyric manuscripts, "a record of authorship was felt to be necessary" (2), but "no two lyrics" in Harley "can with certainty [be] assign[ed] to the same poet" (Brook, *HL,* 26). It is not for lack of trying: see, in Fein, *Studies,* alone, groupings suggested by Revard, Stemmler, Fein, McSparran, Jeffrey, and more.

[121] I have here sprung the trap of biographical fallacy upon myself, but linkage between lyric characters and specific historical figures is in no way requisite to my argument. My point with the documentary details that precede and follow is not to enforce particular identities for Harley's copyists, patrons, or textual transmitters, so much as to note the traffic in these years between bishop's clerks and lay households near Ludlow.

[122] See Bannister, *Registrum Ade de Orleton,* 189–90, for a letter from Bishop Orleton to his official Nicholas de Ludlow ("our dear friend" [carus amicus noster]), absolving the latter's brother of blasphemy but requiring a public confession and apology, to be performed in Ludlow's parish church, for having spoken of Swinfield with "unseemly language" [verba inhonesta], if only "in thoughtlessness" [levitate] and without malice.

[123] Webb, *Roll of Expenses,* 2:ccix–ccx, 1:176. Revard regards a later Lady of Richard's Castle, Joan Mortimer Talbot (1291–1341), and her son John Talbot (1318–1355)—for whom our scribe drafts a letter patent in 1347—as among Harley's "most likely" patrons ("From French Fabliau Manuscripts," 278 n. 31, 41–42; see also "Scribe and Provenance," 22). Lady Joan's brother-in-law Thomas Talbot received his first benefice while still an acolyte in 1307 (Capes, *Registrum Ricardi de Swinfield,* 537); was made a Hereford Canon in 1320 (Bannister, *Registrum Ade de Orleton,* 386); and was a career-long associate of my protagonist Roger Breynton (though Thomas's earlier promotions underscore the Talbot family's influence with Swinfield and successors). In addition to being fellow Canons, Breynton and Talbot both appear in Orleton's *familia* at Avignon c. 1319; both appear thereafter in the company of the infamous Marcher lord, Roger Mortimer, as well as the obscure notary Richard Eastnor (*Registrum Ade de Orleton,* 92, 110; see Birkholz, "Biography After Historicism"); and they were together chosen, in 1346, to lay first stones for Flanesford Priory, founded by Thomas's nephew Richard Talbot (Parry, *Registrum Johannis de Trillek,* 88–89).

work: in 1287 Swinfield risked censure by collating her brother Nicho-las, then underage, to a valuable cathedral prebend, and years later (in 1317) his executors presented Katherine with a silver chalice, as a mark of friendship with the family.[124]

The Poet's Repentance reaches climax when it declares to Richard, "on molde y holde þe murgest mon" [I consider you the most pleasant/ bountiful man on earth] (Brook #6.64). In being "murgest" [most pleasing], Richard is the very thing that other Harley speakers declare their beloved ladies ("leuedis") to be (#14.43; cf.#7.37). Richard's de-scription as "murgest" man "on molde" [in the land / throughout the country], in addition to his fame "in vch an hyrd" [in every household] (#6.67) across the region, helps indicate what is at stake for the Harley Lyrics in imaginative geographical terms. The Repentant Poet's self-deprecation contains a healthy dose of antifeminist irony, even if the misogyny rides more lightly here than in the book's fabliaux and other "poems about love, women, and sex," some of them saccharine enco-mium, but the balance invective in the mode known as *blasmes des femmes*.[125] The political geography charted by the Harley Manuscript has a sharp regionalist slant, but its gender-ambiguous amatory landscaping begins to come into view when we place temperate, bountiful Richard beside a lyric opening appropriate almost anywhere in the collection. "In May hit murgeþ when hit dawes" [In May it is pleasing when it dawns] and "blosmes bredeþ on þe bowes" [blossoms breed on the boughs]; yet "y not non so freoli flour" [I know no flower as beautiful/

---

[124] For Harley 2253's Genville connection (and the presence of the name Talbot in the binding leaves), see Ker, *Facsimile*, ix, xxii–xxiii; cf. Revard, "Scribe and Prove-nance," 24. For Katherine's contact with Swinfield's executors (among them Orleton's friend Roger Breynton), see B. G. Charles and H. D. Emanuel, *A Calendar of the Earlier Hereford Cathedral Muniments* (typescript, 3 vols., 1955, 774 (#1046); cf. 61 (#478) for an earlier receipt from Katherine, dated at "Lodelawe," 1300: "in respect of two silver gilded cups . . . from the Dean and Chapter of Hereford." See also H. D. Emanuel, "The Will of Richard de Swinfield, Bishop of Hereford," *National Library of Wales Journal* 5, no. 4 (1948): i–v. For Nicholas de Genville, see Capes, *Registrum Ricardi de Swinfield*, 1–2, 14, 151–53, 526, 533. Folio 5 of the manuscript (Hereford Record Office, Register of Richard Swinfield [1283–1317] has a letter from Swinfield to Geoffrey unprinted by Capes. In 1283, Swinfield resisted conferring a benefice on Nicholas, then aged ten. See *Registrum Ricardi de Swinfield*, 195, for Swinfield's confirmation of Katherine's election as Prioress of Aconbury in 1288.

[125] For "the *propretés des femmes* (. . . 'what women are like') discourse," involving both "*blasme* [reproach] and praise," see Mary Dove, "Evading Textual Intimacy: The French Secular Verse," in Fein, *Studies*, 329–49. For texts, see Daniel Corbin Kennedy, "Anglo-Norman Poems About Love, Women, and Sex from BM MS. Harley 2253" (Ph.D. diss., Columbia University, 1973).

excellent] as the "splendid women who dwell out west" [so worly wym-men are by west] (#12.1–10).

Love of "lef" [beloved figure] and love of "lond" [land, the country-side] conjoin throughout the Harley corpus. But if, as critics often con-clude, the lyric "lady" is ultimately a fiction, are we then left with something so banal as hymns to a landscape, garden-variety praise of the "west country" as region? I don't believe so. "Lef in lond," "lusso-more in londe" (Brook #14.12), "leuedi of alle londe" (#5.11): the phrases alliterate, indeed proliferate, but they are not—as idiomatic translations tend to render them—interpretively empty.[126] There are figures in this landscape and topographies mapped onto these figures. The effect is that of still-life portraiture, yet the view is a sheltered one, as in the erotic dawn of the *aubade*, when lingering lovers lie encased by flowering boughs. Indeed this "agreeable" [mury, muriȝe], reclined perspective is so prevalent that the Harley lyric landscape (or "londe") consists of little in itself, exists mostly as "bour" or sequence of bowers. The final benediction of the praise-poem to Richard is that he "[be] sent / in londe of leuedis alle!" (#6.71–72): that he be received—how to parse this?—"into the land of all ladies"? "into the bowers [i.e., sex-ual graces] of all ladies in the land"? Does Richard inherit some kind of acoustic ladyland? "Murgest" [most pleasing] he becomes indeed, seems to be the poet's sly insinuation.

The expressions of *land*-"longyng" that appear in the Harley Lyrics amount not to district advocacy, but to nostalgia. We are met not with sacralized dwelling in the west, but with periodic return; a riding out, not inhabitation. "Mosti ryden by Rybbesdale, / wilde wymmen forte wale, / ant welde whuch ich wolde" [I'd like to ride out through Ribbl-esdale, to choose among the wanton women there, and possess the one I would . . .] (Brook #7.1–3): this is not the song of a resident, though it canonizes the figure of the "wilde," potentially "unruly" local beloved. Like *The Lover's Complaint* copied overleaf, *The Fair Maid of Ribblesdale* is the account of a traveler returning. The difference is that between occu-pation of a local chaplaincy or parish cure and the blur of diplomatic delegation and episcopal visitation.

---

[126] E.g., Brian Stone, *Medieval English Verse* (Baltimore: Penguin, 1964), whose six renderings of ME *lond* (Brook #5.10, #6.72, #12.19, #24.14, #7.8, #7.50) produce only one usage of Mod.E "land" or its cognates. Millet, "Wessex Webtexts," translates #7.50's "lef in lond" as "loved everywhere."

Playboys of the West of England

Harley lyric narrators tend to be men of "hyrd" who move "in world" and "in toune." They themselves are cosmopolitan, by and large— urbanely prone, as in the disingenuous *Advice to Women*, to a casual "tricherie" in matters of amorous "trouþe" (Brook #12.20–22). But as seen in our Ribblesdale Rider's preference for "wilde" [uncultivated] women, they require their vernacular maidens to be otherwise. At once predatory and paternalistic, the narrator of *Advice* embraces, as his ostensible rhetorical project, the need to warn hinterland women against the subtle likes of himself: "so wyde in world ys huere won [dwelling] / in vch a toune vntrewe is on / from Leycestre to Lounde" [unfaithful men are spread so wide across the world that you'll find one in every town, from {the city of} Leicester to {the village of} Lound] (28–30).[127] So impassioned is our speaker that some see him as "penitential"; credible or not, his admonitory performance acts as a hinge between the carnal sensibilities of preceding lyrics and the devotional mode of those that follow.[128] *Advice to Women* oscillates between an anxiety to preserve female bodily purity and its corollary: desire *for* bower penetration, for erotic access to that same salvific body. In line with neighboring lyrics, *Advice* clings to the prospect of a "heuene" to be "heuede here" (#7.84), where local transmutes unto universal, carnal unto spiritual.

Our speaker equivocates charismatically, but his ambivalence maps clearly. Outland bodies possess a redemptive innocence, while erotic "tricherie" is a symptom of worldliness. What "worly" western "wymmen" must "be on war" of (Brook #12.10, 34) is not the callow "wowyng" [lovemaking] of a narrator like *Alysoun*'s (#4.31), but clerkly urbanity: "when me ou woweþ, beþ war bifore / whuch is worldes ahte" [when someone like me woos you, beware of that which is the world's peril] (#12.41–42). "Worldes ahte" denotes both a naturalized sexual "peril that is in the world" and a more generalized "risk of being

---

[127] Brook judges it "possible" but unlikely that "Lounde" refers to "London"; he proposes "three places now called Lound in Lincs., Notts., and Suffolk," all "derived from ON *lundr* 'grove'"; *HL*, 81; cf. #25.17. Thus interpreted, the sweep extends from an urban center to the most obscure of village homes.

[128] Hogan finds a "teasing sense of ambiguity": the speaker displays "a gentle concern for deceived women," yet "seems somehow personally implicated"; "Critical Study," 76–78. *Advice* follows a run of nine amorous lyrics (#3–#11, 63r–71v; other texts are interspersed), while most of the rest are religious. #1 (59v), #29 (106r), #30 (114v), and #31–32 (128r–v) have less in common with the core lyrics of 62v–83r.

worldly." Only men—certain men—are equipped to navigate the complications of a cosmopolitan condition. For women so unfortunate as to miss this *Advice*, merely to fare out "in world" is to court bodily compromise,[129] hence social and spiritual disaster: in the groves and "dounes" [downs] of May-time "steuenyng" [meetings], when "lef is lyht on lynde" [love flits lightly on the bough], "ys fare is o to founde" [his behavior is always put to the test]. From the embrace of the "trichour," there is no return: "to late comeþ þe ȝeynchar" [too late comes any means of escape] (1–3, 27–35).

Smooth clerks are ubiquitous—scattered "wyde in world"—but "[vn]trouþe" resides especially "in toune" (Brook #12.22–28; cf. #24.9, #6.37).[130] That the collection's favored terms for "beloved" ("leuedy," "lef") are persistently collocated with "lond," whose associations include both "landscape" and "community," helps characterize male falseness as a plague upon the countryside. And when it comes to country matters, "Lut in londe are to leue" [few {men} in the land can be believed] (#12.19).[131] We have the finest women in the world "by west," and "one of hem ich herie [praise as] best"; but beware, good ladies, the ways of the world (10–11, 34).

The mobile terms of Harley love affairs—embowered vernacular "levedi," itinerant clerical lover—may be a consequence of genre (i.e., inherited from continental models). Still, movement away from and back to the local—the local "lef," the local "lond"—is endemic to this collection. One sophisticate languishes in the metropole, composing macaronic complaint "en mi de vile de Paris" [in the middle of the city of Paris] until, overcome with native longing, he drops Latin and French to conclude with English resignation: "ȝef hi deȝe for loue of hire, duel hit ys" [it would be a grievous thing if I died for love of her] (Brook #19.16–20). Another "clerc" promises that "þou art euer in my þoht in londe wher ich am" [you are always in my thoughts, no matter where

---

[129] Gale Sigal, "Courted in the Country: Woman's Precarious Place in the Troubadours' Lyric Landscape," in *Text and Territory: Geographical Imagination in the European Middle Ages,* ed. Sylvia Tomasch and Sealy Gilles (Philadelphia: University of Pennsylvania Press, 1998), 185–206.

[130] See Williams, *The Country and the City,* for this resilient literary trope.

[131] Recall the rutting "on molde" in *Satire,* whose abandoned "mai" comes to court "bimodered ase a mor-hen": dirt-covered and debauched, perhaps pregnant. The stern *Three Foes of Man* predicts hellfire for lovers "founden vnder felde" (Brook #2.39).

in the country I am],[132] but complains of suffering "fer from [hom]" [far from {home}] (#24.29, 14, 31).[133] In *Urbain le courtois*—a conduct-poem that follows debate pieces "in praise [or "dispraise"] of the fair Sex"[134]—a wise and worldly father ("vn sage honme") exhorts his "cher fitz" [dear son] to act responsibly "when you pass through the country" [quant vous passez par le païs].[135] This applies especially "if you become a cleric, as may be" [si clerc seiez com bien puet ester], in which case there follow two more directives on familial love: "avoid whores" [lessez puteynz] and "always love your master" [totdis amez vostre mestre] (286–88).[136]

Coterie obligations are standard for narrators of Harley 2253, but so too are careers of itinerancy. The passions and/or obligations of these men have taken them elsewhere. If a speaker is afflicted by love, as in the rollicking *Alysoun*, he must languish apart from the "blisse" of his "owen make" [mate, partner] (Brook #4.7,18). If he offends authority, he shall be expelled from the local community. Such was the future envisioned by *Satire*'s protagonist: bitter reward for one who "in hyrt" had proven "hauer of honde" [clever, handy].[137] This exilic condition comes full course in *Trailbaston*, an Anglo-Norman outlaw's song set between bourgeois *Urbain* and the outlying "village" lyric *The Man in the Moon* (Brook #30).[138] *Trailbaston* describes the dystopian conse-quences of itinerant justice: having fled false accusation "to the green-

---

[132] "Wher" he is, is "vnder þe wode-gore" [under the covering of the woods]; he flees to hide himself "from men," i.e., his "lemman"'s angry "kynne" (16–18, 31). In *The Meeting in the Wood*, a lover imagines he will "in vch an hyrd ben hated ant forhaht" [be hated and despised in every household] (#8.34).

[133] "Some word has clearly been omitted": Böddeker and Brook supply "hom"; Brown uses "bour" (*HL*, 85). Here are lines 29–32 in full: "whil y wes a clerc in scole, wel muchel y couþe of lore; / ych haue þoled for þy loue woundes fele sore, / fer from [. . .] ant eke from men vnder þe wode-gore. / Suete ledy, þou rewe of me; nou may y no more."

[134] *A Catalogue of the Harleian Manuscripts in the British Museum*, 4 vols. (London: Eyre and Strahan, 1802–12), vol. 2 (1808), 585–91 (590).

[135] Kennedy, "Anglo-Norman Poems About Love, Women, and Sex," #4, lines 1, 13, 179.

[136] *Urbain* survives in nine manuscripts (Cambridge UL Gg.i.1 has other Harley items), although only half include l.286 ("if you become a clerk . . ."); one replaces l.288's "puteynz" [whores] with "pucels" [girls].

[137] Robbins, *Historical Poems*, #6.2.

[138] *The Man in the Moon* (114v–115r) appears 31 folios after the core lyrics (#2–28, 62v–83r) and a dozen before the *contrafacta* that cap the collection, *The Way of Christ's Love* and *The Way of Woman's Love* (#31–32; 128rv). Like #1 (*Earth upon Earth*, 59v), *Moon* is neither devotional nor amorous.

wood" [al vert bois], the poem's speaker laments that "This is what the bad laws do to me . . . that I dare not come into peace among my kinsfolk"; "pray for me that I may go riding to my country," for as it stands, "I will not come within ten leagues or two of home."[139]

Virtually by definition, Harley speakers are away, "fer from" (or soon to depart) the places that matter to them.[140] Yet it is not an easy thing to establish where exactly "hom" lies, for Harley lyric protagonists; or, for that matter, where may lie the redolent "bours" dear to the erotic imaginations of these poems' initial, secondary, and ancillary audiences, down even to the present voyeuristic moment. One suspects that home for the Repentant Poet, while it may lie in a generalized way "by west," is most viscerally experienced "in hyrd": among fellow poet-administrators and in the memorialized presence of Richard, fount of "rede." So too the Complaining Lover, who worried what his friends might think. (Our Adviser to Women frets about what they're *doing*.) Even courteous *Urbain*, though neither lyric nor English, directs the young careerist not to take ("ne prenez") a woman "santz consail de vos amys" [against the advice of your friends].[141]

The Harley Lyrics' allusions to clerical "hyrd," western "lond," and familial "loue" will have struck a chord with, if they do not constitute a response to, the biographical experience of Hereford and Worcester secular clerks in these same years: their sojourning "fer from" home and bower; their "longyng" for coterie proximity; their profound dependence upon patronal "rede." The social conditions that animate such men have a material geographical base, in the reality of their perennial

[139] Aspin, *Anglo-Norman Political Songs,* 73–78; #7.54, 70–71, 91–94: "ce me fount les male leis par mout grant outrage, / qe n'os a la pes veynr entre mon lignage" (70–71); "pur moi vueillent prier / qe je pus a mon païs aler e chyvaucher" (93–94); "E le heyre n'aprocheroy de .x. lywes ou deus" (91). Aspin glosses "heyre" as "probably = aire < atrium, meaning 'threshing floor, yard', and by extension 'home.'"

[140] This is true of lyric and complaint alike: *Satire's* protagonist will suffer "er ich hom go" (Robbins, *Historical Poems*, #6.72), while *Husbandman's* laborers wait to depart the misery of this world. *Man in the Moon* begins with displacement—a peasant has fled the manor and taken refuge in the moon—then presents a jocular vernacular domesticity: ripe to be swindled, a manorial hayward is taken "hom to vr hous" where "oure dame douse [pleasant housewife] shal sitten hym by" until "he is dronke" (Brook #30.27–31).

[141] Kennedy, "Anglo-Norman Poems About Love, Women, and Sex," #4, lines 80–82. This sentiment derives from Cato's Distichs. For another passage relevant to a regional episcopal milieu, see lines 306–9; "pur vostre païs combatez / en tous lyws ou vous serrez / n'oiez de ly si bie noun / qe tu ne le defendez par resoun" [Fight for your country/homeland in every place where you might be. Don't hear anything about it that is not good without defending it with reason].

travel, on administrative circuit across and on diplomatic jags away from the diocese. Spatial displacement became a communal experience for ambitious western clerks in these years. In collision with the logic of incarnate geography, this professional experience produces a desire for vernacular grounding, for social and topographical integration. The figure of the vernacular maiden embodies geographical contradictions that the professional lives of these men have generated but that they cannot, it would seem, otherwise resolve. Through performative manipulation of a poetic fetish-object—the "lef in lond" who remains securely "in bour" (in her locality; in her place)—the Harley Lyrics dispel mobility's tensions. Formally speaking, these poems have their genesis in cross-vernacular literary exchange—as occurs at papal Avignon, for example, where in the years of the Hereford delegation there moved the likes of Dante and Petrarch,[142] and where a growing emphasis on "lyric genres [and] vernacular poetics" helped produce "a literary culture that extend[ed] across boundaries of dialect and idiom."[143] Avignon's clerical elite was differentiated by national origin, but integrated by Latinity and diplomatic professionalism. "In all its proverbial forms," "the city continues to be," as Vinay Dharwadker has said, "very much the archetypal geopolitical unit of cosmopolitanism." The obvious concourse at Avignon between matters spiritual and temporal emphasized the papal city's paradigmatic standing as a "site where power is concentrated and capital is accumulated and deployed"—patronal power and poetic capital not least.[144] Vernacular lyric's beginnings are urban and internationalist, but the end result of Harleian love-lament is the production of "bote," an erotic *local* balm that works as resolution to the profound *dis*location brought on by travel. The circulation, "by west," of Middle English poems that give voice to this experience helps bind together an ambitious, distinctive, and unusually mobile interpretive community: one whose underpinnings are ecclesiastical, whose contours are familial, and whose poetics are cosmopolitan, yet that finds its umbilicus in the radiant figure of the embowered regional beloved.

---

[142] Bannister, *Registrum Ade de Orleton*, vii.

[143] Edwards, " 'The Metropol and the Mayster-Toun,' " 39, 43. For the "little studied" topic of Avignon "as the context for [cultural] exchange," see *The Cultures of Papal Avignon, 1309–1378*, ed. Susan Noakes (Minneapolis: University of Minnesota Press, forthcoming).

[144] Dharwadker, "Cosmopolitanism," 10.

Medieval Allegiances, Cosmopolitan Dispositions

In 1999, Ralph Hanna endorsed the notion—promulgated by Brook in 1933—that despite being "recorded in Hereford," the lyrics preserved in Harley 2253 "represent [the] activities of many poets in diverse dialect regions."[145] The Harley Lyrics, I have argued, possess a regionalist and episcopal orientation that becomes heightened when their literary evidence is read against a biographical backdrop; but these poems were *not* all composed by West Midlands secular clergy. Hanna's mention comes during his reassessment of alliterative poetry's fraught place in English literary history.[146] He challenges the "triumph inherent in" the traditional narrative "whereby alliterative poetry was always conceived as the Other of Chaucerian verse and the assertion of a provincial baronial self-consciousness opposed to central hegemony." The terms Hanna contests are spatial ("provincial"; "central"; "anti-London"), so much so that his irritation with "the conventional history" seems a function of its propensity for "vague gestures towards the north and the west." Naive codicologically and geographically, such moves made a previous generation of medievalists "far too prone to construct originary arguments and to generalize these as totalizing narrative." Hanna's foregrounding of manuscript materiality and the story of "interregional penetration" it tells serves as empirical corrective to the easy oppositionality long prevailing in literary historiography: our habitual recourse, inherited along with canonical reading lists, to the shopworn binaries of center/periphery thinking.[147] If many Harley texts are "western" merely in scribal overlay while deep linguistic strata reveal an "original" regional identity for each, to plot Brook's findings—so many lyrics that "belong to" one or another dialect—is to map a demographic spread of

[145] Hanna, "Alliterative Poetry," 509. Expanding upon Böddeker (1878), Brook assigns the following regional identities: N (11), Mids. (5), N Mids. (2), NW Mids. (3), NE Mids. (3), W Mids. (2), E Mids. (1), S or SE Mids. (7). Six elude identification; "Original Dialects," 38–40, 55–57.

[146] The Harley Lyrics' place in Hanna's redrawn literary topography is modest, as in the 851-page *Cambridge History of Medieval English Literature* overall, which apart from its timeline makes five references: Hanna's two mentions and two notes, plus a half-sentence in Lerer, "Afterlife," 30. There are five mentions of other Harley texts or of the manuscript generally.

[147] Hanna, "Alliterative Poetry," 508–10; see 488–98 for a critique of the "Old Historicist" approach to ME alliterative poetry—specifically, its central concept of a "regional" alliterative "revival." For Hanna, this persistent literary formulation is best typified in J. R. Hulbert's "seminal" early essay, "A Hypothesis Concerning the Alliterative Revival," *MP* 28 (1931): 405–22.

Harley origins, against which the fact of their unique compilation "out west" discordantly grates.[148]

Many travelers to the past are finding it necessary, as Robert R. Edwards has said, "to revisit the literary and cultural geography that earlier medieval scholars could largely take for granted."[149] The Harley voices we have encountered indulge in just the sort of sloppy nostalgic mapping for which Hanna chastens his scholarly forbears: they make "vague gestures to" an "originary" "lond" "by west"—a space that is equal parts regional political community, sexual/textual fantasyland, and transubstantiated spiritual destination. Yet must the Harley Lyrics be therefore said to collude with those very Old Historicists whose reductive binaries have compromised them in the first place? Premature and provincial with respect to accepted English paradigms, the eruption of vernacular poetics represented by the Harley Lyrics has yet to be accounted for. But in being internationally sown and regionally grown, do these poems help produce their own marginality? Hanna reveals what may be at stake: "Just as Chaucerian verse emanated from London to inspire writers in far-removed provincial settings, so alliterative poetry—although with considerably less success—developed as one competing form of a national, not regional, literature."[150]

In a stocktaking essay that introduces the expansive *Cosmopolitan Geographies* (2001), Vinay Dharwadker describes modern geopolitical theory as preoccupied with the "multifarious interdependencies and tensions between nations and nationalism, on the one hand, and cosmopolitanism and internationalism, on the other." But cosmopolitanism "in its historically variable time and place," Dharwadker insists, "frequently differentiates itself from more than nationalism." Modern Indian cosmopolitanism, for example, "emerges from a dynamic rectangulation of empire, village, nation, and city" in which subjects might commit themselves to "[several] rather different objects of allegiance." These options for imagining community "were never mutually exclusive because they defined themselves in multiple, simultaneous relations of coordination and conflict. Thus, for instance, the Indian vil-

---

[148] That the Harley scribe's dialect is itself an uncertain amalgam of forms (Ludlow-based but Leominster- and Hereford-inflected?) illustrates the unreliability of dialectal features as firm evidence of compositional provenance; McSparran, "Language of the English Poems," 393.

[149] Edwards, "'The Metropol and the Mayster-Toun,'" 34.

[150] Hanna, "Alliterative Poetry," 509.

lage and the Indian city both opposed the empire, but they deployed distinct anti-metropolitan strategies and also opposed each other intransigently."[151] Our present case study lies some half a world and half a millennium away; germane to this territory, the forgotten "lond" of Harley Lyrics and Hereford clerics, is that just as modern Indian cosmopolitanism is a complex "not reducible to a simple nationalism-internationalism binary,"[152] so may medieval English social relations not be reduced to either a nationalism-internationalism or a nationalism-*regionalism* binary—not, at least, without literary-historical ramifications.

In line with long-standing disciplinary inclinations and recent theoretical trends, Harley scholarship has come to gather at the point where vernacular literary production meets the category, likewise incipient, of the territorially conceived English nation. In surveying this "political" terrain for Fein's *Studies in the Harley Manuscript*, John Scattergood concedes Thorlac Turville-Petre's 1996 argument that Harley 2253 "sets forth a generally nationalist set of ideas, a sense of England the nation." Yet many items, Scattergood notes, "express resistance to royal authority" and other "encroachments of centrality," such that the book may also be said to archive a "regionalism that cuts across the broader nationalist attitudes of the poems."[153] In an essay likely to frame future discussions of medieval cosmopolitanism, Edwards describes a situation even more crosshatched, where "in the fourteenth and fifteenth centuries, English literature stands at the intersection of cultural forces: cosmopolitan culture meets national and regional practices, and it exists simultaneously within and apart from a courtly social base." Edwards finds literary cosmopolitanism in medieval England to be "inseparable from the question of language and particularly the role of the vernacular," on which point he cites none other than Turville-Petre. In dovetailing arguments that lead ultimately back to Harley 2253, these scholars judge that "language, territory and people are the criteria for defining national identity."[154] This specialist medievalist claim helps generate a theoretical proposition with far-reaching implications for cosmopolitanism. As Dharwadker (who in turn deploys Edwards) asserts: "The vernacular is a nationalist creature."[155]

[151] Dharwadker, "Cosmopolitanism," 5–8.
[152] Ibid., 9.
[153] John Scattergood, "Authority and Resistance: The Political Verse," in Fein, *Studies*, 163–201 (168, 185).
[154] Edwards, "'The Metropol and the Mayster-Toun,'" 38.
[155] Dharwadker, "Cosmopolitanism," 5.

The Harley Lyrics are vernacular, but by no means are they nationalist creatures. They are cosmopolitan, but their cosmopolitanism does
not configure itself, as later, more consequential English texts do,
against the category of national identity so beloved of vernacular historiography. The Harley Lyrics are also regional; but their regionalism does
not depend upon a relationship of competitive opposition—literary or
otherwise—with respect to metropolitan, royal, or national interests. If
anything, Harley lyric-dialectics ignore these traditionally privileged
scales of aggregation.[156]

Edwards describes a "common political geography" that distinguishes
the literary cosmopolitanism of late medieval England from the curial
and vernacular cosmopolitanism that developed in Dante's wake (not
least at Avignon), as well as from "Augustine's geography," in which
worldly and heavenly cities "coexist and overlap," despite their "stark
dichotomy."[157] "From the standpoint of literary history," argues Edwards, the decisive element for "the English situation" is "the pervasive
yet disjunct presence of the English court," which as an interpretive
factor is "as important as the dialectic between cosmopolitanism and
national or regional claims."[158] Edwards is justified in emphasizing the
courtly here (better, though, to avoid blanket terms like "late medieval"
or "English"), just as Hanna is persuasive in characterizing late alliterative poetry as a "national, not regional" phenomenon. (So too are Turville-Petre's and Scattergood's readings of Harley political verse
reasonable in themselves, while Revard is not to be contravened on
scribal milieu, nor Fein on poetic *ordinatio*). And yet, as so often, the
best insights of literary history and critical philology either decline to
account for, or offer limited purchase upon, the unusual collectivity of
lyrics preserved in Harley 2253.[159]

[156] For the "pressing issue" of "aggregation," which "generates different kinds of
affiliations on different scales, opening up the question of what counts as an entity," see
Wai Chee Dimock, "Scales of Aggregation: Prenational, Subnational, Transnational,"
American Literary History 18, no. 2 (2006): 219–28. I foreground the institution of the
bishop's *familia*, but the answer to Dimock's driving question—"On what scale should
we study the transnational?"—can only be plural.

[157] Edwards, " 'The Metropol and the Mayster-Toun,' " 34–39.

[158] Edwards critiques the term "Ricardian" but deploys its canonized texts as paradigmatic nonetheless: "An international courtly culture remains our foundational explanation for high literary culture in the age"; Ibid., 42, 39.

[159] Love-lyric occupies a compromised position in arguments about Harley's geopolitical orientation. Scattergood makes one mention (noting the conflation of beloved and
overlord in Brook #14), while Turville-Petre renders the lyrics docile, first by denying
them national significance and then by finding them to confirm the spatial attitudes of
the political pieces. Even Revard, first drawn to Harley by its lyrics, has gravitated

Edwards's case studies are canonical, coeval, and thematically conver-gent: each turns upon an engagement with "the Troy story," a flexible myth of national translation that serves, "for the late Middle Ages," as "a paradigmatic cosmopolitan narrative." The alliterative *Saint Erken-wald*, for example—by joining "the Trojan origins of England to the Roman mission of Augustine of Canterbury"—establishes Britain's "founding culture" as one in which "national identity is already doubly cosmopolitan." Set "At London in Englond," yet written in a northwest-ern dialect, *Erkenwald* "balances regional and metropolitan interests" with configurations that are, by turns, "at once regional and cosmopoli-tan" and "at once cosmopolitan and national."[160] Such readings are pleasing, not least for their geographical plurality. Still, medieval En-glish literary culture as Edwards describes it remains oriented toward "political" community at the *regnal* level. By foregrounding "language, territory and people," Ricardian texts produce subjects whose "objects of allegiance" may be plural (courtly and ecclesiastical; metropolitan and regional; feudal and mercantile; genealogical and associational), yet whose "common" affiliations are always already "national" in inflection. Medieval allegiances are thus made to resemble our own.

In the worlds they sketch themselves, the Harley lyricists allude to a sacral western "lond," a "hom" that is emblematized in the figure of the vernacular beloved (whether ecclesiastical patron or linden maiden), whose favor the poet desires to secure (through "herian" [praise]) or displeasure to mitigate (via "mon" [complaint]), and with reference to whom an interpretive community's claims to allegiance are shaped and activated. My essay's attention to the institution of the bishop's house-hold or *familia episcopalis*, with its keen local clerks, its panoply of com-mitments, and its bodily focal point, has analogy in the dynamic mediating role assigned by Edwards to the English court, an institution whose epicenter lay in the peripatetic royal household or *familia regis*.[161] If the cosmopolitan (or universal) and the regional (or local) may be said to occupy poles along a spectrum of medieval geographical dispositions, and if Edwards finds his mediating factor in the body of that Richard

---

increasingly to the book's "political and historical pieces" since the lyrics "offer but little evidence as to its provenance"; "Scribe and Provenance," 73.

[160] Edwards, " 'The Metropol and the Mayster-Toun,' " 43–44, 47–51.

[161] Edwards describes the royal court as "a matrix for [literary] cosmopolitanism"; ibid., 43. Cf. Chris Given-Wilson, *The Royal Household and the King's Affinity: Service, Politics, and Finance in England, 1360–1413* (New Haven: Yale University Press, 1986).

who wears England's crown, my essay finds its fulcrum in that pleasant "clerk wiþ croune" of our own outland "hyrd": mitred, "murgest" Richard, so endowed of "crafte" and "rede." For the Harley Lyrics and the mobile clerks who knew them, what intervenes between cosmopolitan "world" and regional "hom" is not "England the nation," as for modern geopolitical theorists and current literary medievalists; it is not "the English court," however fluid a king's affinities (and Affinity) may be; and it is not "London in Englond," where "regional and metropolitan" are enfolded, where aspirations to national literary status are contested, and where journeys to distinction abroad or recuperation back home are channeled. The social entity and textual community that is the bishop's household is more narrow of parameter and flexible in application than these other bodies; but it is no less "essentially" geographical in nature (or for that matter, any less spatially multiple, considering its territorial jurisdiction, coterie mobility, and far-flung influence). To adapt Edwards, we might say that from the standpoint of *vernacular lyric* history, the pervasive yet disjunct presence of the *episcopal familia* is as important as the dialectic between cosmopolitanism (or universalism) and *diocesan* or regional claims.

Edwards's profoundest observation is that "in late medieval England, cosmopolitanism occupies a shifting rather than fixed geography."[162] How can we account for the Harley Lyrics? Only by bracketing, however temporarily, the calcified paradigms within which approaches to their interpretation have long been set—literary-critical *and* social-geographical. The Otherness of the Harley Lyrics with respect to mainstream English literary history is a result of the latter's overdeveloped allegiance to the concept of national vernacular development. Their provincial identity, though deriving partly from their own outland desires, is a consequence of historical-geographical valuations that become naturalized when we pay disproportionate attention to later (more metropolitan and "national") texts and milieus. If "the disposition of cosmopolitanism," as per Dharwadker, "is at once causal and structural, historical and geographical,"[163] this essay's contribution has been to present a literary-geographical case study that is distinctly *non*-national in its *pre*-dispositions. The archetypal geopolitical unit for this social and textual milieu is not, in fact, the city.[164] The professionalist ethics and

---

[162] Edwards, " 'The Metropol and the Mayster-Toun,' " 38.
[163] Dharwadker, "Cosmopolitanism," 10.
[164] This is not to deny the crucial role played by urban centers and their courtly and ecclesiastical conjuncts in the production of medieval cosmopolitan identities.

familial poetics, the ambivalent erotics and regional nostalgia we have encountered in one poet's Repentance, another's Complaint, a third's calculated Advice, and the wanton local Ride of a fourth, argue that Harley Lyric imaginations, while informed by an international urban experience, remain otherwise attuned. These speakers' amatory comforts and spiritual aspirations reside not "in toune," but "in bour," "in hyrd," somewhere vaguely "in londe." And whatever their origins, these lyrics congregate "by west."

"Leuedi, þou rewe me!": this plea from my epigraph may pertain, as it has been euphemized, to "the natural end of unsophisticated love,"[165] but it echoes nearby penitential lyrics ("Marie, reweþ þe," Brook #22.10; "Lord, merci, rewe me now," #29.31; cf. #20.19, 43; #24.13, 32). Against every swain keen for the restorative "hom" of a country "bour," there is arrayed another voice eager to censure erotic trysting. As *The Three Foes of Man* declares: "of sunful sauhting sone be sad / þat derne doþ þis derne dede" [he who secretly commits this secret deed will soon regret of his sinful covenant] (#2.7–8).[166] Just as do "worldly riches" [þis worldes won] (49), "carnal pleasures pass away" [þis wilde wille went awai] (16). Far from being the place of "blisse" that cohabiting lovers imagine (#3.19; #4.7; #9.26; #11.3; etc.), our "home here," warns *Three Foes*, "is a disastrous one, surpassed only by hell" [hom vnholdest her is on / wiþouten helle] (45–46). In such a cosmography, the local beloved is *not* the means to salvation; instead, "þat haþ to fere is meste fo" [the one you take as lover is your greatest foe] (40). Erotic consummation, however devoutly wished, does not commute humanity's sentence of exile; it intensifies bodily displacement.

The "delightful promise" of the Harley Lyrics is not that they document, for our aficionado prurience, a displaced mode of medieval longing; nor yet that they enact an immolation of desire. Instead, it is that they reconcile the realms of carnal and incarnate, providing a model for how to blend our competing desires for this-worldly and next-worldly "bours" of bliss. In their lyric "evasiveness of being," the Harley Lyrics communicate an ecstatic worldview: a quality of being sensually in this

---

[165] Chambers, "Aspects," 274.

[166] Since *Three Foes* is among the earliest Harley Lyrics in date (late thirteenth century) and placement (fol. 62v), its opening claim that "Middelerd for mon was mad" [This earthly life was made for lamentation] (1) sets terms for the lyric disputation to follow, in erotic point and religious counterpoint.

world ("y grone") while remaining oriented toward a next ("rewe me").[167] And if with a certain coy equivocation—one might say, a vernacular cosmopolitanism of the spirit—these poems flicker between ways of institutional being, this enables them to embrace loves both orthodox and transgressive.

The rhetorics of seduction, salvation, and literary canonization intertwine. To voice Harley 2253's erotic and devotional hymns, in the scholarly here and now, evokes a fabulist's landscape, an impossible "lond" of fond opposites. If the peripheral status that has been visited upon these poems by literary history is a function of their assigned geographical character, it may not be too much to say that the Harley Lyrics' future critical vitality depends on—their "lyf ys long on" (Brook #5.10)—our ability to relocate them. "Love," after all, is where you find it.

Appendix: Poems Discussed

Location, by folio number, in MS Harley 2253; editions referred to are: Brook, *Harley Lyrics;* Ker, *Facsimile;* Robbins, *Historical Poems;* Kennedy, "Anglo-Norman Poems About Love, Women, and Sex"; Aspin, *Anglo-Norman Political Songs*

Fol. 62v	*The Three Foes of Man* ("Middelerd for mon wes mad") Brook #2; Ker #27
Fol. 63	*Annot and John* ("Ichot a burde in a bour ase beryl so bryht") Brook #3; Ker #28
Fol. 63v	*Alysoun* ("Bytuene mersh ant aueril") Brook #4; Ker #29
Fol. 63v	*The Lover's Complaint* ("Wiþ longyng y am lad") Brook #5; Ker #30
Fol. 64	*Song of the Husbandman* ("Ich herde men upo mold") Robbins #2; Ker #31
Fol. 66	*The Poet's Repentance* ("Weping haueþ myn wonges wet") Brook #6; Ker #33
Fol. 66v	*The Fair Maid of Ribblesdale* ("Mosti ryden by rybbesdale") Brook #7; Ker #34
Fol. 66v	*The Meeting in the Wood* ("In a fryht as y con fare fremede") Brook #8; Ker #35

---

[167] Albright, *Lyricality*, viii. The propensity of their supporters to emphasize the light charm of the Harley Lyrics may contribute to their exclusion from the more consequential narratives of literary historiography.

Fol. 67v *Gilote et Johane* ("En may par vne matyne s'en ala iuer")
          Kennedy #10; Ker #37

Fol. 70v *A Satire on the Consistory Courts* ("Ne mai no lewed lued")
          Robbins #6; Ker #40

Fol. 71v *Spring* ("Lenten ys come wiþ loue to toune") Brook #11;
          Ker #43

Fol. 71v *Advice to Women* ("In may hit murgeþ when hit dawes")
          Brook #12; Ker #44

Fol. 72v *Blow, Northerne Wynd* ("Blow, northerne wynd") Brook
          #14; Ker #46

Fol. 76   *Dum ludis floribus* ("Dum ludis floribus velud lacinia")
          Brook #19; Ker #55

Fol. 80v *De Clerico et Puella* ("My deþ y loue my lyf ich hate") Brook
          #24; Ker #64

Fol. 83   *King Horn* ("Her begynneþ þe geste of Kyng Horn") Ker
          #70

Fol. 112 *Urbain le courtois* ("Vn sage honme de grant valour") Ken-
          nedy #4; Ker #79

Fol. 113v *Traillebaston* ("Talent me prent de rymer e de geste fere")
          Aspin #7; Ker #80

Fol. 114v *The Man in the Moon* ("Mon in þe mone stond ant strit")
          Brook #30; Ker #81

Fol. 128 *The Way of Christ's Love* ("Lvtel wot hit any mon") Brook
          #31; Ker #92

Fol. 128 *The Way of Woman's Love* ("Lutel wot hit any mon") Brook
          #32; Ker #93

Courtly Aesthetics and Courtly Ethics in *Sir Gawain and the Green Knight*

Jill Mann
Girton College, Cambridge
University of Notre Dame

LATE MEDIEVAL CHIVALRIC and courtly culture was characterized by display—or, to use Thorstein Veblen's term, "conspicuous consumption."[1] Splendid clothing, armor, jewels, lavish food and table
settings, ritual and spectacle of all kinds (tournaments, theatrical entertainments, pageants, processions, royal entries)—all these things were
means by which the courtly class defined itself and presented itself to
the world. Malcolm Vale has spoken of "the increasing sacralization of
the secular" in the courts of the period: "A more formal, ritualized element gradually invaded the domestic life of princely courts, receiving
its most marked—and often extravagant—expression at court feasts in
which vows were taken, elaborate interludes and *entremets* introduced,
and a more dramatic and theatrical dimension brought to the holding
of 'full' or 'solemn' courts."[2] The court of Richard II was notorious for

Early versions of this essay were delivered as papers to the aesthetics seminar at
Trinity College, Cambridge; to Mary Clemente Davlin's students at Dominican University, River Forest; and to the medieval graduate seminar at the University of Oxford. I
would like to thank the audiences on all these occasions for their enthusiastic interest
and comments. I would also like to thank Maura Nolan and Chris Cannon, who read
later drafts with special care and comments.

[1] Thorstein Veblen, *Theory of the Leisure Class: An Economic Study in the Evolution of
Institutions* (1899; repr. London: Unwin Books, 1970). In the first sentence of his introductory chapter, Veblen states that "the institution of a leisure class is found in its best
development at the highest stages of the barbarian culture; as, for instance, in feudal
Europe or feudal Japan." He discusses conspicuous consumption as a mark of the leisure
class in chapter 4.

[2] Malcolm Vale, *The Princely Court: Medieval Courts and Culture in North-West Europe,
1270–1380* (Oxford: Oxford University Press, 2001), 300.

this kind of extravagant display.[3] Nigel Saul calls him "an extravagant, luxury-loving prince. His tastes were expensive and he took a delight in beautiful objects. He owned a large and valuable collection of gold-smiths' work and plate. He was lavish in his spending on clothing, jewelry, tapestry and *objets d'art* generally: according to the Evesham chronicler, on one occasion he spent no less than £20,000 on a robe [decorated] with precious stones."[4] Already in the early years of his reign, there were complaints about the costs of Richard's household, although at this period, according to Chris Given-Wilson, they were not, comparatively speaking, excessive. There were cutbacks in the 1380s, but from 1393 onward domestic expenditure climbed dramatically, reaching more than £35,000 in each of the last three years of his reign.[5]

[3] The romanticized and enthusiastic account of courtly culture presented by Gervase Mathew in *The Court of Richard II* (London: John Murray, 1968) was followed by a more skeptical and cautious attitude in the essays included in *English Court Culture in the Later Middle Ages*, ed. V. J. Scattergood and J. W. Sherborne (London: Duckworth, 1983); see especially Sherborne, "Aspects of English Court Culture in the Later Fourteenth Century," 1–27; Scattergood, "Literary Culture at the Court of Richard II," 29–43; J. J. G. Alexander, "Painting and Manuscript Illumination for Royal Patrons in the Later Middle Ages," 141–62. Latterly, the pendulum has swung back again; see Michael J. Bennett, "The Court of Richard II and the Promotion of Literature," in *Chaucer's England: Literature in Historical Context*, ed. Barbara Hanawalt (Minneapolis: University of Minnesota Press, 1992), 3–20, esp. 7–10; Nigel Saul, *Richard II* (New Haven: Yale University Press, 1997), chap. 14, "The King and His Court," and John M. Bowers, *The Politics of "Pearl": Court Poetry in the Age of Richard II* (Cambridge: D. S. Brewer, 2001).

[4] Saul, *Richard II*, 354–55; I have substituted "decorated" for "lined" in Saul's text, as it seems more probable that the stones would appear on the outer side of the garment. For the Evesham chronicler's comment, see *Historia Vitae et Regni Ricardi Secundi*, ed. George B. Stow (Philadelphia: University of Pennsylvania Press, 1977), 156: "inter alias huius mundi diuicias, fecit sibi fieri unam tunicam, de perillis, et aliis lapidibus preciosis, et auro ex propria ordinacione factam, ad 30,000 marcarum in ualorem appreciatam." Despite the obviously exaggerated estimate of the monetary value of the garment, this comment gives a good idea of how Richard's magnificent clothing was perceived by contemporaries. See also Kay Staniland, "Extravagance or Regal Necessity? The Clothing of Richard II," in *The Regal Image of Richard II and the Wilton Diptych*, ed. Dillian Gordon, Lisa Monnas, and Caroline Elam (London: Harvey Miller, 1997), 85–93, and Marian Campbell, "'White Harts and Coronets': The Jewellery and Plate of Richard II," in ibid., 95–114.

[5] Chris Given-Wilson, *The Royal Household and the King's Affinity: Service, Politics, and Finance in England, 1360–1413* (New Haven: Yale University Press, 1986), 80–84 and 139–40; on parliamentary complaints about royal expenditure, see 113; for tables showing the relative costs of the royal household for the period 1360–1413, see 94 and 268–72. Truce with France in 1389 meant that more funds became available for luxury items: "Royal expenditure now shifted from armourers and bowyers to painters and goldsmiths." Caroline M. Barron, "Richard II and London," in *Richard II: The Art of*

Royal extravagance attracted criticism and controversy from some quarters. The alliterative poem known as *Richard the Redeless* (written around the time of Richard's deposition)[6] contains an indignant account of the extravagant attire favored by courtiers. Citing the text from Matthew's gospel (11:8), "They that are clothed in soft garments, are in the houses of kings," the author complains that the courtiers care for nothing other than "quentise of clothinge" (elegance of clothing) (III.176; cf. 120, 122). Their cloaks are wide and their sleeves are so long that they "slide on the erthe" (III.131, 152). They wear gold chains and ornament their belts and drinking-horns with silver (III.140). They run themselves into debt in order to buy expensive furs (III.148–51). Their garments are ornamented with "dagging," the edges cut into elaborate shapes, which costs ten times more for the stitching than for the cloth itself (III.162–69). These complaints are, as Patricia Eberle has put it, an indication that "the tradition of dress as a form of investment had become at the court of Richard II what we would now call investment dressing."[7] Toward the end of *Richard the Redeless*, the personified figure of Wisdom appears at court, clad in "the olde schappe," "in an holsum gyse" (III.212–13); predictably, he is rudely ejected by the well-dressed courtiers.

So much for the prosecution, but there was also a contemporary case for the defense. In the same article, Patricia Eberle also drew attention to the justification of courtly luxury found in a Latin treatise written by Roger Dymmok, a Dominican friar, in response to the twelve Lollard propositions contained in a document (purportedly) fixed to the door of Westminster Hall during the session of Parliament in 1395.[8] His trea-

---

Kingship, ed. Anthony Goodman and James Gillespie (Oxford: Clarendon Press, 1999), 129–54 (139–40).

[6] For an edition of the poem, see *The Piers Plowman Tradition*, ed. Helen Barr (London: J. M. Dent, 1993), 99–133. Citations included in my text refer to Passus and line numbers. Barr dates the poem shortly after Richard's deposition (Introduction, 14); David Carlson inclines to place it in late summer 1399, just before the deposition; "English Poetry, July–October 1399, and Lancastrian Crime," *SAC* 29 (2007): 375–418 (379–80). The poem survives in a single manuscript, Cambridge, University Library Ll.4.14, of the second quarter of the fifteenth century.

[7] Patricia Eberle, "The Politics of Courtly Style at the Court of Richard II," in *The Spirit of the Court: Selected Proceedings of the Fourth Congress of the International Courtly Literature Society (Toronto 1983)*, ed. Glyn S. Burgess and Robert A. Taylor (Cambridge: D. S. Brewer, 1985), 168–78 (171).

[8] *Rogeri Dymmok Liber Contra XII Errores et Hereses Lollardorum*, ed. H. S. Cronin (London: Kegan Paul, Trench, Trübner & Co., n.d.). The twelve Lollard propositions survive only in the writings of their opponents, viz.: *Fasciculi Zizaniorum*, ed. Walter Waddington Shirley, Rolls Series 5 (London: Longman, Brown, Green, Longmans, and Roberts, 1858), 360–69 (Latin), and Dymmok's refutation (Latin and English); for a separate

tise is dedicated to Richard II, and the manuscript now at Trinity Hall, Cambridge (MS 17) was evidently a presentation copy. Most of the Lollard propositions criticized the failings of the established Church, but the twelfth concerned secular life: it claimed that "þe multitude of craftis nout nedful" (such as goldsmiths and armorers) should be abolished, because they encourage "wast, curiosite and disgysing" (that is, elaborate display and fancy clothing).[9] In answer to this, Dymmok distinguished between two types of "necessity": first, there are those things needed simply to sustain life, but second, there are those things necessary to live decently ("conuenienter"). Drawing on Aristotle's discussion of "magnificence," or "the art of spending money lavishly," in the *Nicomachaean Ethics* (IV.ii.1–23), he argues that differences in social status need to be manifested in differences in food, clothing, and housing, and for this many crafts are necessary. As far as clothing is concerned, he explains that "princes and nobles" ("principes ac nobiles") should be distinguishable by their more elaborate dress, since it flies in the face of reason that the servant should be dressed like the master, a simple knight like a prince, or a monk like a layman. Furthermore, it is a way of striking fear into the lower orders and so it prevents them from rebelling against their betters ("ad incuciendum metum populis, ne nimis faciliter insurgant contra suos superiores").[10] Dymmok cites the advice given by Aristotle to Alexander in the *Secretum Secretorum* that he should never appear in public except in "fine and splendid dress," so that he should be held in greater reverence. Dymmok also cites the visit of the queen of Sheba to the court of King Solomon; having attempted to impress him with her own wealth, she was forced to recognize in the superior splendor of Solomon's court the superiority of his wisdom.[11] As Dymmok's defense suggests, the lavish display of Richard's court was not simply the result of a taste for soft living. It had a serious political purpose: it was designed to enhance the prestige of the monarch and to

---

edition of the English version of the propositions, see Anne Hudson, ed., *Selections from English Wycliffite Writings* (Cambridge: Cambridge University Press, 1978), 24–29, 150–55. For a recent discussion of Dymmok's treatise and its intended audience, see Fiona Somerset, *Clerical Discourse and Lay Audience in Late Medieval England* (Cambridge: Cambridge University Press, 1998), 103–34.

[9] *Dymmok*, ed. Cronin, XII, p. 292.

[10] On the role of clothing laws in reinforcing the social order in the fourteenth and fifteenth centuries, see Claire Sponsler, "Narrating the Social Order: Medieval Clothing Laws," *Clio* 21, no. 3 (1992): 265–83.

[11] *Dymmok*, ed. Cronin, XII.1, pp. 293–95.

induce an almost religious sense of awe in those who beheld him.[12] The most famous visual artifact of Richard's reign, the Wilton Diptych, illustrates Richard's sense of the religious dimensions of his kingship: on the left-hand panel, Richard is presented to the Christ Child not only by John the Baptist, to whom he was specially devoted, but also by his two sainted predecessors, King Edward the Confessor and King Edmund of Anglia, while on the right-hand side of the panel the heavenly angels accompanying the Virgin and Child all wear Richard's livery badge, the white hart.[13] The full-size (2.13 × 1.10 m) portrait of Richard, robed, crowned, and holding the scepter and orb, which was placed in Westminster Abbey, with its awe-inspiring "hieratic frontal pose," gave solemn authority to his kingship in a more public way.[14]

In this essay I propose to examine *Sir Gawain and the Green Knight* against the background of this conscious cultivation of royal and courtly display, and to argue that the poet is aiming to identify the raison d'être of courtly luxury in a far more sophisticated and interesting way than Dymmok. Instead of justifying courtly magnificence in terms of realpo-

---

[12] Saul (*Richard II*, 355–56) speaks of the "element of political calculation" in Richard's lavish expenditure; his aim "was to present a particular set of messages about himself." Display conveyed "the reality and effectiveness of his power," and also "bore visible witness to wisdom" (Saul quotes Dymmok's comparison with Solomon as evidence for the latter point). Richard Firth Green also points out "the propaganda value of a large and sumptuous household"; see *Poets and Princepleasers: Literature and the English Court in the Late Middle Ages* (Toronto: University of Toronto Press, 1980), 17–18. Staniland ("The Clothing of Richard II," 92), noting that Richard's "ostentatiously rich dressing" was "by no means a new departure and parallels can be found among his English and Continental peers," suggests that it could have provided "reassurance and [a] sense of authority . . . in the hostile environment of the English court." Lynn Staley emphasizes that Richard's attempts to create this awe-inspiring image of kingship belong to the last decade of his reign, and result from his desire to claw back the power wrested from him by the Appellants in 1388. *Languages of Power in the Age of Richard II* (University Park: Pennsylvania State University Press, 2005), 22, 75–76, 111–39.

[13] For detailed discussions of the techniques, functions, and iconography of the Diptych, see the essays in *The Regal Image of Richard II*, ed. Gordon et al. The Diptych was probably intended for private use, but it testifies to the image of kingship that Richard wished to associate with himself. Its date is uncertain, but internal indications have suggested a date in the late 1390s (1395–99); see Nigel Morgan, "The Signification of the Banner," in *The Regal Image of Richard II*, ed. Gordon et al., 179–88, esp. 187–88, and Maurice Keen, "The Wilton Diptych: The Case for a Crusading Context," in ibid., 189–96, esp. 189.

[14] See Jonathan J. G. Alexander, "The Portrait of Richard II in Westminster Abbey," in *The Regal Image of Richard II*, ed. Gordon et al., 197–206 (205). Cf. Paul Binski, *Westminster Abbey and the Plantagenets: Kingship and the Representation of Power, 1200–1400* (New Haven: Yale University Press, 1995), 206. As with the Diptych, the date of the portrait is uncertain, but it has been generally thought to belong to the 1390s (see Alexander, 201, 204; Binski, 205).

litik, as a means of intimidating the lower classes and maintaining social order by a visible display of wealth and power, the poet sees it as a natural expression of the inner splendor of courtly virtues (especially "trawþe" and "clannes") and a reflection of their special qualities. Outward display and inward virtues are mirror images of each other.[15] This fusion of material splendor and ethics is effected by significant strands in the vocabulary of the poem, and discussion of these strands will form the core of my argument. I shall, however, preface this discussion with a synthesis of recent work that points toward the Ricardian court, rather than the northwest of England, as the most probable context for this poem, and show how some features of the Cotton Nero poems become more readily comprehensible in this context. As a coda to the main discussion, I shall return to the political functions of the poem's fusion of courtly splendor and courtly virtues and make some suggestions as to why the particular ethical qualities celebrated in the poem are appropriate to the Ricardian context.

First, then, a brief consideration of the likely home of the poem. Not so long ago, it would have been thought self-evidently pointless to connect it with the royal court, since this poem and the three others that accompany it in the sole surviving manuscript (London, British Library Cotton Nero A.x) were confidently located, on the grounds of their dialect, in the northwest of England—even more precisely, in "a very small area either in SE Cheshire or just over the border in NE Staffordshire."[16]

---

[15] Cf. Elizabeth Keiser, *Courtly Desire and Medieval Homophobia* (New Haven: Yale University Press, 1997), 24: "The *Cleanness*-poet does not attempt to spiritualize and desecularize the class-specific behavior of his listeners. Rather, he incarnates the conception of the ethical and the divine in forms of life appealing to an aristocratic mentality." My argument does not depend on a claim that the *Gawain*-poet necessarily knew Dymmok's treatise (which would mean that *Gawain* was written after 1395), but, on the other hand, the possibility cannot be excluded. Cotton Nero A.x (which lies at least one remove from the author's holograph) is dated on paleographical grounds to the last quarter of the fourteenth century; its illustrations were added sometime later (c. 1400–1410). See Kathleen L. Scott, *Later Gothic Manuscripts, 1390–1490*, 2 vols. (London: Harvey Miller, 1996), 2:66–68, and A. S. G. Edwards, "The Manuscript: British Library MS Cotton Nero A.x," in *A Companion to the Gawain-Poet*, ed. Derek Brewer and Jonathan Gibson (Cambridge: D. S. Brewer, 1997), 197–219. Although it is not the main concern of this article to argue for a date of composition in the 1390s, it is worth noting that other indications (such as Richard's assembly of his Cheshire bodyguard) offer cumulative support for such a date; see also notes 5, 12, 19, 31, and 36.

[16] Angus McIntosh, "A New Approach to Middle English Dialectology," *ES* 44 (1963): 1–11 (5); see also *A Linguistic Atlas of Late Mediaeval English*, ed. Angus McIntosh, M. L. Samuels, and Michael Benskin, 4 vols. (Aberdeen: Aberdeen University Press, 1986), 3:37–38. On the basis of an analysis of the "disjunction between the poet's dialect and the scribe's," H. N. Duggan suggested that "if the *LALME* localization of the manuscript is correct and if the poems are not substantially earlier than the manu-

The poet's description of Gawain's journey through the Wirral, which demonstrates a knowledge of this part of the country, pleasingly harmonized with this indication of the poet's place of origin and served to confirm it.[17] The provincial court to which, it was supposed, the poet belonged, and for whose entertainment he wrote, was imagined as the counterpart of Bertilak's court in the poem, a baronial castle in the countryside.[18] This picture was first seriously troubled by the historian Michael Bennett, who, after a thorough study of Cheshire and Lancashire society in the later Middle Ages, concluded that it is "difficult to document any major centers of cultural life in the region" that would provide a plausible source of patronage and audience for the author of such a poem as this.[19] The major landholders in the region—such as

---

script," then the poet's dialect is more likely to derive from Staffordshire than from Cheshire, Lancashire, or Derbyshire; "Meter, Stanza, Vocabulary, Dialect," in *Companion to the Gawain-Poet*, ed. Brewer and Gibson, 221–42 (242). Duggan's proviso turns out to be important, since Ad Putter and Myra Stokes have recently conducted a thorough reexamination and critique of the *Linguistic Atlas*'s evidence for localizing the dialect of Cotton Nero A.x and have concluded that (at least until such time as further evidence is produced) Cheshire is more likely than Staffordshire. "The *Linguistic Atlas* and the Dialect of the *Gawain* Poems," *JEGP* 106 (2007): 468–91.

[17] For a recent attempt to read *Gawain* as a "border text," see Rhonda Knight, "All Dressed Up with Someplace to Go: Regional Identity in *Sir Gawain and the Green Knight*," *SAC* 25 (2003): 259–84.

[18] See James R. Hulbert, "A Hypothesis Concerning the Alliterative Revival," *MP* 28 (1931): 405–22, esp. 414 (though Hulbert acknowledged that he had found no castle in the northwest Midlands that could be identified with the Green Knight's abode [406 n. 1]).

[19] Michael J. Bennett, "Courtly Literature and Northwest England in the Later Middle Ages," in *Court and Poet: Selected Proceedings of the Third Congress of the International Courtly Literature Society (Liverpool 1980)*, ed. Glyn S. Burgess (Liverpool: Francis Cairns, 1981), 69–78 (70). See also Bennett, "The Court of Richard II and the Promotion of Literature"; "*Sir Gawain and the Green Knight* and the Literary Achievement of the North-West Midlands: The Historical Background," *Journal of Medieval History* 5 (1979): 63–88; *Community, Class, and Careerism: Cheshire and Lancashire Society in the Age of "Sir Gawain and the Green Knight"* (Cambridge: Cambridge University Press, 1983), 231–35; "The Historical Background," in *Companion to the Gawain-Poet*, ed. Brewer and Gibson, 71–90. Edward Wilson suggested that *Gawain* might have been composed for the Stanley family ("*Sir Gawain and the Green Knight* and the Stanley family of Stanley, Storeton, and Hooton," *RES* n.s. 30 [1979]: 308–16), but Ad Putter has pointed out that the most likely candidate for patron of the *Gawain*-poet is Sir John Stanley (d. 1414), who belonged to the Lathom branch of the family, and who "left his native area to pursue a career in the service of Richard II"; "he was appointed Deputy to the Lieutenant of Ireland, Robert de Vere, and soon afterward Lieutenant in his own right; in the 1390s [he] presided over Richard II's recruitment of his Cheshire bodyguard, becoming Controller of the Wardrobe in 1397"; *An Introduction to the Gawain-Poet* (London: Longman, 1996), 35. For further information on the Stanley family, see Bennett, *Community, Class, and Careerism*, 215–19; "'Good Lords' and King-Makers: The Stanleys of Lathom in English Politics, 1385–1485," *History Today* 31, no. 7 (July 1981): 12–17,

John of Gaunt or the earls of Arundel and Salisbury—had their main residences elsewhere. On the other hand, Bennett pointed out, Richard II, who was earl of Chester, had strong connections with the region. In the late 1380s and 1390s, he came to rely on the earldom of Chester as a power base from which he could draw loyal support.[20] In 1397, he raised Chester from a county palatinate to a principality (thus making himself prince of Chester). What is particularly relevant here is that at the same time he recruited a large retinue of men from Cheshire (estimated at around 750), from whose numbers was chosen the personal bodyguard of 311 archers, who accompanied him everywhere.[21] The king's partiality for his Cheshire men was widely resented and criticized (it was one of the articles offered in justification for his deposition).[22] Lately, scholars have been more and more willing to entertain the possibility that the *Gawain*-poet might have formed part of this major translocation of Cheshire men to London, and that his poems might have been addressed to a London audience—more precisely, the royal court.[23]

esp. 13; Barry Coward, *The Stanleys, Lords Stanley and Earls of Derby, 1385–1672* (Manchester: Chetham Society, 1983), 2–3.

[20] Richard spent some time in Cheshire and the northwest Midlands in July 1387; see Saul, *Richard II*, 172, 471.

[21] These figures are taken from R. R. Davies, "Richard II and the Principality of Chester 1397–9," in *The Reign of Richard II: Essays in Honour of May McKisack*, ed. F. R. H. Du Boulay and Caroline M. Barron (London: Athlone, 1971), 256–79 (268–69); for a more detailed discussion of the composition and numbers of the Cheshire retinue, see James L. Gillespie, "Richard II's Cheshire Archers," *Transactions of the Historic Society of Lancashire and Cheshire* 125 (1975): 1–39, esp. 11.

[22] See Gillespie, "Cheshire Archers," 23, 31–33; Saul, *Richard II*, 393–94.

[23] The poem *St. Erkenwald*, which is written in a dialect similar to that of the poems in Cotton Nero A.x, is "emphatically a London poem, written in praise of the capital's patron saint" (Malcolm Andrew, "Theories of Authorship," *Companion to the Gawain-Poet*, ed. Brewer and Gibson, 23–33 [26]). For evidence that other alliterative works were copied in the capital, see Putter, *Introduction to the Gawain-Poet*, 29–31, and A. I. Doyle, "The Manuscripts," in *Middle English Alliterative Poetry and Its Literary Background*, ed. David A. Lawton (Cambridge: D. S. Brewer, 1982), 88–100. Putter concludes: "Perhaps the group of royal household servants from the northwest would offer the sort of milieu most consistent with the characteristics of the *Gawain*-poet's work and his imagined audience: cosmopolitan, but not oblivious to regional identity; sophisticated and courtly, but no more socially exclusive than the circle of Cheshire courtiers at Richard II's court. To this tight network belonged not only knights like Sir John Stanley or Sir Richard Craddock, to whom Richard II entrusted his presentation copy of Jean Froissart's poems, but also clerics of the chancery and the privy seal like John Clitheroe and John Macclesfield, and the goldsmith Christopher Tildesley, clerk of the royal works" (36). Cf. Bennett, *Community, Class, and Careerism*, 233–34, and Bowers, *Politics of "Pearl*," 82 n. 26. Thorlac Turville-Petre has expressed resistance to "the attempt to make a Londoner out of the *Pearl*-poet," but this is not because he wishes to deny a connection with the Ricardian court; rather, he argues that *Gawain* "embraces a national audience and claims a status within the culture as central as the work of Chau-

In the context of the Ricardian court, a number of puzzling features of the *Gawain*-poet's works becomes more comprehensible. The poem *Cleanness*, for example, contains a passage of enthusiastic praise (voiced by God himself) for sex between a man and a woman, which is said to be a bliss exceeding that of Paradise itself. This unqualified praise of the sexual act, with no mention of the procreation of children (the usual sine qua non for an account of sinless sex), is without parallel or precedent in medieval literature. But Elizabeth Keiser has argued that it needs to be understood as the obverse of the poem's attack on male homosexuality.[24] Its context is the story of God's destruction of Sodom, as a punishment for the sexual perversions of the Sodomites. The two angels whom God sends to Sodom, and whom the Sodomites want to rape, are described as beardless youths of surpassing beauty (789–94), with skin like the briar-rose and radiant complexions. In contrast, the Sodomites are stout men, uncouth and rowdy. Keiser argues—persuasively, to my mind— that this scene makes sense if it is related to the style of elegant luxury adopted by the courtiers of Richard II, and exemplified in the angels of the Wilton Diptych, who are depicted (like Richard himself) as beardless youths, with long flowing hair and rosy complexions.[25] The message that *Cleanness* speaks on behalf of these elegant courtiers is: "We are feminized, but we are *not* effeminate." In other words, the poem deliberately differentiates the elegant courtier from the homosexual. Carolyn Dinshaw has argued that *Sir Gawain and the Green Knight* similarly— and probably for the same reason—raises the specter of homosexuality only to reject it.[26] The kisses exchanged between Gawain and the lord

---

cer, Gower, and Langland. . . . The implied audience for *Gawain* . . . is neither northern nor southern, but national." "The *Pearl*-Poet in his 'Fayre Regioun,' " in *Essays on Ricardian Literature in Honour of J. A. Burrow*, ed. A. J. Minnis, Charlotte C. Morse, and Thorlac Turville-Petre (Oxford: Clarendon Press, 1997), 276–94 (286, 287–88). Lynn Staley (*Languages of Power*, 196–263) has recently proposed that the *Gawain*-poet's works were produced under the patronage of John of Gaunt and his brother, Thomas of Woodstock (see also note 34 below), but her case is avowedly no more than speculative and to my mind the evidence for Richard's court is stronger.

[24] Keiser, *Courtly Desire*, 65–70, 149–59.

[25] Cf. the Green Knight's contemptuous reference to Arthur's courtiers as "berdlez chylder" (line 280).

[26] "A Kiss Is Just a Kiss: Heterosexuality and Its Consolations in *Sir Gawain and the Green Knight*," *Diacritics* 24 (1994): 205–26. Dinshaw cites Walsingham's accusation of homosexual relations between Richard II and Robert de Vere (222–23); as she says, even if the accusation was unfounded, there would be a point in Richard's supporters trying to deflect it. However, Dinshaw still sees the poem's "probable audience" as the regional society of Cheshire and Lancashire, and she does not make clear how she reconciles this with the link to the household of Richard II that she calls "very likely" (222).

of the castle—kisses that Gawain passes on as "comlyly," as "hendely," as "sauerly and sadly" as he can manage (1389, 1639, 1937)—far from suggesting the possibility of a homosexual relationship between them, are designed to make it unthinkable: as unthinkable as the possibility of Gawain's actually having sex with his host's wife and finding himself in the position of having to pass on this favor to her husband.[27] The poem establishes heterosexuality as normative, as "the only legitimacy, the only intelligibility";[28] only the courtly game, not personal predilections, can impel Gawain into simulated erotic behavior with another man.

The careful distancing of homosexual imputations assumes importance for the poem's context when we recall that Thomas Walsingham insinuated that Richard II had homosexual relations with his close friend Robert de Vere.[29] In this connection, it becomes startlingly significant

---

[27] Social kissing was of course conventional between men in this period; see *Piers Plowman* B.XVI.148–49 (I am grateful to Carl Schmidt for drawing my attention to this passage), and cf. *Gawain* line 2472 (at 596 and 1118, kisses of farewell seem to be exchanged with both lords and ladies). But Dinshaw's point is that the fact that the kisses were originally given by the lady, in a heavily charged erotic context, gives them a *potentially* erotic character when they are handed on to her husband. Edward Wilson has also drawn my attention to *The Vision of Edmund Leversedge,* ed. W. F. Nijenhuis (Nijmegen: Centrum voor Middeleeuwse Studies, Katholieke Universiteit Nijmegen, 1991], 122–23), written c. 1465–70, which testifies to the popularity of social kissing between men and women and its potentially erotic character; see Wilson's review of Nijenhuis's edition in *RES* n.s. 46 (1995): 255–57 (257), for further evidence of the prevalence of social kissing in England. See also J. A. Burrow, *Gestures and Looks in Medieval Narrative* (Cambridge: Cambridge University Press, 2002), 32–33, 50–57.

[28] "A Kiss Is Just a Kiss," 222.

[29] *The St Albans Chronicle: The Chronica maiora of Thomas Walsingham, I: 1376–1394,* ed. and trans. John Taylor, Wendy R. Childs, and Leslie Watkiss (Oxford: Clarendon Press, 2003), (anno 1386), 798: "[rex] tantum afficiebatur eidem, tantum coluit et amauit eundem, non sine nota, prout fertur, familiaritatis obscene" ["The king was very devoted to him, and greatly respected and loved him, but not without the ignominy, it is said, of an impure relationship"]. These words belong to the revisions that Walsingham seems to have made to his chronicle to make it more acceptable to the Lancastrians after their rise to power; see George B. Stow, "Richard II in Thomas Walsingham's Chronicles," *Speculum* 59 (1984): 68–102 (86), and John Taylor, *English Historical Literature in the Fourteenth Century* (Oxford: Clarendon Press, 1987; repr. 2000), 68, 74–76. But there is no reason to suppose that he was not belatedly putting on record gossip that had circulated much earlier and that (as Walsingham demonstrates) was remembered to the end of Richard's reign. Robert de Vere also had Cheshire connections: in the summer of 1387, he "ensconced himself in Chester Castle," where he "lived in some style, giving the region for a while the feeling of a real court. His fine furniture and tapestries at Chester were inventoried in 1388" (Bennett, "The Historical Background," 83). In September of the same year, Richard appointed him to the office of justice of Chester, and in December 1387 de Vere raised a force of Cheshire men who fought on the king's behalf at the battle of Radcot Bridge (Saul, *Richard II*, 172).

that the distinguishing feature of Robert de Vere's heraldic arms was a five-pointed star ("mullet"), blazoned on the upper-left-hand quarter of his shield (quarterly or and gules in the first quarter a mullet argent).[30] Although it lacks the crisscrossing internal lines of the pentangle, the "mullet" is otherwise identical with Gawain's own heraldic blazon, and it is hard to imagine that fourteenth-century readers would have failed to note the resemblance. I am not proposing that *Gawain* should be read as a roman à clef, with Gawain himself as a covert stand-in for de Vere, but simply that assigning him the pentangle as his heraldic blazon might have been a graceful way of associating Richard's beloved friend (or perhaps his memory) with the romance hero's virtues.[31]

The celebration of courtly magnificence that plays so large a role in three of the four Cotton Nero poems (*Sir Gawain and the Green Knight*, *Pearl*, *Cleanness*) fits easily into the context of the Ricardian court. For example, there seems to have been a fashion for pearls, perhaps stimulated by a spectacular crown brought to England by Anne of Bohemia;[32] at the end of Gower's *Confessio Amantis,* some of those in the assembly summoned by Cupid wear "grete Perles," according to "the newe guise

[30] These arms are recorded in several medieval armorial rolls, which are most conveniently accessed via the link "European Rolls of Arms of the Thirteenth Century" at http://www.medievalgenealogy.org.uk/links/herrefs.shtml#rolls. See The Falkirk Roll, H99; Glover's Roll, B11; The Camden Roll, D30; St. George's Roll, E15; The Heralds' Roll, HE 58; Charles's Roll, F17; Vermandois, VE 973. Derek Brewer mentions that the "mullet" is the shield device of the de Vere family, but he does not draw any further conclusions from this ("Armour II: The Arming Topos as Literature," *Companion to the Gawain-Poet*, ed. Brewer and Gibson, 175–79 [178]). Brewer points out that the most usual blazon for the French Gauvain in Arthurian romance was the two-headed eagle (177), which makes the choice of the pentangle for the English Gawain all the more striking. For the history of the pentangle figure and a discussion of its possible significance, see Richard Hamilton Green, "Gawain's Shield and the Quest for Perfection," *ELH* 29 (1962): 121–39 (esp. 129–35) (repr. in *Middle English Survey: Critical Essays*, ed. Edward Vasta (Notre Dame, Ind.: University of Notre Dame Press, 1965), 71–92 (83–88]), and Theodore Silverstein's edition of *Sir Gawain and the Green Knight* (Chicago: University of Chicago Press, 1974), note to lines 619ff. Silverstein's comment that no attempt so far has "succeeded in associating [the pentangle], or its supposed heraldic equivalent the mullet, with any contemporary circumstance or patron of the poet" obviously reflects scholarly concentration on the northwest as the poem's main context. Had the scope of scholarly inquiry been expanded to include the Ricardian court, the potential significance of de Vere's blazon might have been noticed earlier.

[31] De Vere was sent into exile in 1388 and died in 1392, but these dates do not necessarily provide a *terminus ante quem* for the poem; Richard's affection for him survived undiminished, and the pentangle might have been a tribute to his memory (perhaps at the time of his reburial at Earl's Colne in 1395).

[32] The crown is currently in Munich; for photographs, see Saul, *Richard II*, plate 16, and *The Regal Image of Richard II and the Wilton Diptych*, ed. Gordon et al., color plate 19.

of Beawme" (VIII.2469–70). The pearl is of course the central image in the poem that bears its name, and it also appears as a significant metaphor in *Gawain* (2364–65) and *Cleanness* (1117–32). More generally, John Bowers's book *The Politics of "Pearl"* has linked the Cotton Nero poems with the courtly display cultivated by Richard II. These poems not only describe such courtly display but can themselves be seen as courtly artifacts—highly wrought, intricate verbal constructions, decorated with vivid and colorful descriptions.[33] Bowers is, however, mainly concerned with *Pearl*,[34] and he pays almost no attention to *Sir Gawain and the Green Knight*, probably because he is hampered by an assumption that this poem is "a sophisticated satire on the Ricardian court."[35] In his eyes, it reflects and responds to a "crisis of chivalry" in Richard's court. The "unusual immaturity of King Arthur and his courtiers" reflects (he claims) "the adolescent profile as well as the headstrong adolescent attitudes that prevailed at Richard's own court during most of the 1380s."[36]

---

[33] Bowers, *Politics of "Pearl,"* 152 (he is speaking of *Pearl*, but the description applies equally well to the other poems). Cf. Felicity Riddy, "Jewels," in *Companion to the Gawain-Poet*, ed. Brewer and Gibson, 143–55: "As a jewel, the poem [*Pearl*] locates itself among other highly-wrought, prestigious art-objects, religious and secular, of the late fourteenth century: the elaborate reliquaries, caskets, crowns, brooches, and cups that were the products of the jeweller's craft. . . . The poem about jewels which is itself a jewel thus associates poetry in the English language for the first time with prestige art; *Pearl* associates itself with the international aristocratic luxury system—including fine food and wines, expensive horses, costly fabrics, tapestries and art works of various kinds—that is the matrix for one kind of high culture in the late Middle Ages" (147–48).

[34] Bowers makes some interesting suggestions (for example, he connects the procession of 144,000 virgins in the heavenly Jerusalem with the fraternity processions of late fourteenth-century London, and he sees the pearl emblems worn by these virgins as heavenly counterparts of the livery badges that were so popular at the time, the most notorious of course being Richard's badge of the white hart). But I am unable to accept his suggestion that the Pearl-maiden is a figure designed to fuse reminiscences of Richard's two queens, the dead Anne of Bohemia and the child bride Isabelle of France. Staley's suggestion (*Languages of Power*, 213–51) that *Pearl* was written for Thomas of Woodstock, and the Pearl-maiden is to be identified with his daughter Isabel, who did not die but was donated to a convent of Minoresses in infancy, seems equally implausible. In neither case would the discussion of the rights of "innocents" to salvation, which occupies the central space of the poem, have any point (since Anne was not an infant, and the two Isabel(le)s were not dead).

[35] *Politics of "Pearl,"* 172.

[36] *Politics of "Pearl,"* 17. It may well be the case that Arthur's youthfulness is meant to recall Richard's, but if so, it might plausibly be linked with Richard's impetuous bravery (recorded by Thomas Walsingham, Froissart, and others) in dealing with Wat Tyler and the rebels of 1381, when he was only fourteen years old (Saul, *Richard II*, 72). In that case, it would be a matter for admiration rather than criticism. An allusion to Richard's youthful bravery would not necessarily imply that *Gawain* was composed in the 1380s; the Wilton Diptych, which has been assigned to the late 1390s (see note 13

The dazzling array of rich details in *Gawain* matches the opulence of the royal court. . . . Even Fitt III's extended description of the hunting, killing, and dressing of game corresponds closely with Richard II's own well-attested enjoyment of the hunt. Indeed, the whole of Fitt III can be read as a wicked satire of Ricardian excesses, on the one hand devoting long passages to minute accounts of hunting as an aristocratic leisure pastime, on the other hand focusing on the unmanliness of Gawain's bedroom adventures—as if replying to Thomas Walsingham's famous contempt of Richard II's courtiers as "knights of Love rather than War, more capable in the bedchamber than on the battlefield."[37]

While I am entirely at one with Bowers in seeing Richard's court as an illuminating context for the Cotton Nero poems and as providing important clues for their understanding, I take a diametrically opposed view of the poet's attitude to courtly culture. My own analysis of *Gawain* starts from the conviction that the courtly splendor represented by Arthur and his knights is not being satirized but celebrated.

Courtly splendor takes many forms in *Sir Gawain and the Green Knight*, from feasting to architecture to the rituals of hunting, and, as already noted, the descriptions of these things adds to the sense of the poem itself as a carefully crafted *objet de luxe*. I shall, however, focus on the descriptions of the courtly dress and armor worn by Gawain and the Green Knight, because it is here that the poet's concept of the relation between outward appearance and inner qualities manifests itself most fully. I take my cue from a comment by Michel Stanesco on the late medieval chivalric class: "The aim of the gothic display is to indicate without mediation a qualitative and generalized truth. The splendid

---

above), still portrays him as a beardless youth, suggesting that youthfulness was a part of the image he cultivated.

[37] *Politics of "Pearl,"* 17–18. Cf. Bowers's comments on *Pearl:* "With even greater delicacy than was invested in the critique of chivalric ethics in *Gawain*, the poet adroitly manages to satirize Ricardian practices, whose public glitter scarcely concealed devious and self-serving motives, while he seems steadily to invoke heavenly models to validate and imbue with majesty these same social practices" (22). For Walsingham's comment, see *Chronica maiora* (anno 1387), 814: "Et hii nimirum milites plures erant Veneris quam Bellone, plus ualentes in thalamo quam in campo, plus lingua quam lancea premuniti, ad dicendum uigiles, ad faciendum acta marcia somnolenti." For a more sympathetic assessment of Richard's martial abilities, see James L. Gillespie, "Richard II: King of Battles?" in *The Age of Richard II*, ed. James L. Gillespie (Stroud: Sutton Publishing, 1997), 139–64. For an argument that "bedroom adventures," far from being unmanly, are designed as emblematic representations of the "passive heroism" characteristic of the medieval romance hero (as opposed to the battlefield adventures of the traditional warrior ethic), see Jill Mann, "Sir Gawain and the Romance Hero," in *Heroes and Heroines in Medieval English Literature*, ed. Leo Carruthers (Cambridge: D. S. Brewer, 1994), 105–17.

fashions of dress in the late Middle Ages, for example, are designed to reveal to the gaze the reality of the one who wears them."[38]

Splendid dress, that is, does not *cover up* or overlay an underlying reality; rather, it *manifests* an underlying reality and because of this it is not superfluous but essential. In 1986, I published "Price and Value in *Sir Gawain and the Green Knight*,"[39] in which I discussed the outer/inner connotations of the Middle English word "prys": it is applied both to the material value of gold, jewels, and rich cloth ("prys" as "price" or monetary value), and also to Gawain's inner worth ("prys" as moral worth), which is both matched and tested by his outward reputation ("prys" as "praise").[40] What I propose to do now is to extend that discussion into a consideration of other vocabulary-sets in the poem that identify outer with inner, material splendor with moral worth.

These vocabulary sets are most concentrated in the poet's description of the arming of Gawain at the beginning of Fitt 2.[41] This long passage establishes relations between exterior and interior by applying the same vocabulary to both (as with the word "prys").

He dowellez þer al þat day, and dressez on þe morn,		
Askez erly hys armez, and alle were þay broȝt.		
Fyrst a tulé tapit tyȝt ouer þe flet,		
And miche watz þe *gyld* gere þat *glent* þeralofte;	gilt	glinted
Þe stif mon steppez þeron, and þe stel hondelez,	570	
Dubbed in a dublet of a dere tars,		
And syþen a crafty capados, <u>closed</u> aloft,		fastened

---

[38] "Le but de la *monstration* [gothique] est d'indiquer sans médiation la qualité normative et vraie. La splendeur des modes vestimentaires, par exemple, à l'époque du Moyen Âge flamboyant doit révéler au regard la réalité de celui qui les porte." *Jeux d'errance du chevalier médiéval: Aspects ludiques de la fonction guerrière dans la littérature du moyen âge flamboyant* (Leiden: Brill, 1988), 222; my translation. Stanesco contrasts the splendid clothing of the French court in the baroque period, which aimed simply at effect at any cost, thus turning the royal court into "an immense opera" (ibid.).

[39] *EIC* 36 (1986): 294–318, repr. in *Medieval English Poetry*, ed. Stephanie Trigg (London: Longman, 1993), 119–37, and *Chaucer to Spenser: A Critical Reader*, ed. Derek Pearsall (Oxford: Blackwell, 1999), 187–205. At the conclusion of this article, I commented that the fusion of the knightly and the mercantile in the vocabulary of the poem suggested London as the most likely location for its audience (314–15).

[40] See *MED* senses 1 ("monetary value, price"), 4 ("non-monetary value, worth"), and 9 ("fame, renown; good reputation").

[41] The description of a hero arming is a *topos* in classical and medieval literature; see Derek Brewer, "The Arming of the Warrior in European Literature and Chaucer," in *Chaucerian Problems and Perspectives: Essays Presented to Paul E. Beichner C.S.C.*, ed. Edward Vasta and Zacharias P. Thundy (Notre Dame, Ind.: University of Notre Dame Press, 1979), 221–43, repr. in *Tradition and Innovation in Chaucer,* ed. Derek Brewer (London: Macmillan, 1982), 142–60, 170–73.

Þat wyth a *bryȝt* blaunner was <u>bounden</u> withinne.   shining adorned

Þenne set þay þe sabatounz vpon þe segge fotez,

His legez <u>lapped</u> in stel with luflych greuez,   575   wrapped

With polaynez <u>piched</u> þerto, *policed ful clene*,   attached very brightly polished

Aboute his knez <u>knaged</u> wyth <u>knotez</u> of *golde*;   fastened knots

Queme quyssewes þen, þat coyntlych <u>closed</u>   enclosed

His thik þrawen þyȝez, with þwonges to <u>tachched</u>   attached

And syþen þe brawden bryné of *bryȝt* stel ryngez   580

<u>Vmbeweued</u> þat wyȝ vpon wlonk stuffe,   enveloped

And wel *bornyst* brace vpon his boþe armes,   polished

With gode cowters and gay, and glouez of plate,

And alle þe godlych gere þat hym gayn schulde

  þat tyde;   585

  Wyth ryche cote-armure,

  His *gold* sporez <u>spend</u> with pryde,   fastened

  <u>Gurde</u> wyth a bront ful sure   girt

  With silk sayn vmbe his syde.

When he watz <u>hasped</u> in armes, his harnays watz ryche: 590 clasped

Þe lest <u>lachet</u> oþer <u>loupe</u> *lemed* of *golde*.   thong loop shone

So harnayst as he watz he herknez his masse,

Offred and honoured at þe heȝe auter.

Syþen he comez to þe kyng and to his cort-ferez,

Lachez lufly his leue at lordez and ladyez;   595

And þay hym kyst and conueyed, bikende hym to Kryst.

Bi þat watz Gryngolet grayth, and gurde with a sadel

Þat *glemed* ful gayly with mony *golde* frenges,

Ayquere naylet ful nwe, for þat note ryched;

Þe brydel barred aboute, with *bryȝt golde* <u>bounden</u>; 600 studded

Þe apparayl of þe payttrure and of þe proude skyrtez,

Þe cropore and þe couertor, acorded wyth þe arsounez;

And al watz rayled on red ryche *golde* naylez,

Þat al *glytered* and *glent* as *glem* of þe sunne.   glinted ray

Þenne hentes he þe helme, and hastily hit kysses, 605

Þat watz <u>stapled</u> stifly, and stoffed wythinne.

Hit watz hyȝe on his hede, <u>hasped</u> bihynde,   fastened

Wyth a *lyȝtly* vrysoun ouer þe auentayle,   gleaming

Enbrawden and <u>bounden</u> wyth þe best gemmez   studded

On brode sylkyn borde, and bryddez on semez, 610

As papiayez paynted peruyng bitwene,

Tortors and trulofez entayled so þyk
As mony burde þeraboute had ben seuen wynter
      in toune.
   Þe cercle watz more o prys   615
   Þat <u>vmbeclypped</u> hys croun,   encircled
   Of diamauntez a deuys
   Þat boþe were *bryȝt* and *broun*.[42]   shining

This description emphasizes two important aspects of the knight's appearance: brightness and enclosure. I have indicated brightness by italicizing words and enclosure by underlining them.[43] Brightness is emphasized in the words used for the shining metal of Gawain's armor: steel, gilded, polished, tied with golden thongs. His spurs are gold and his helmet is encircled with diamonds. Enclosure is evident in the frequent emphasis on the encasing of the body in armor, and the fastening of one piece of armor to another, clasped, knotted, tied. The image that this long passage presents is an image of the knight *enclosed* in his armor, protected by its impenetrable and glittering surface. The description of his horse forms part of the impression of brightness, its draperies glimmering and gleaming, its saddle studded with golden nails.

But this is by no means the end of the long description of Gawain's arming. It continues with a detailed account of the device on his shield, the pentangle that symbolizes his "trawþe." In this latter part of the description, enclosure and brightness take on an ethical character as they become linked with the pentangle virtues.

THEN þay schewed hym þe schelde, þat was of *schyr* goulez   bright
Wyth þe pentangel depaynt of *pure golde* hwez.   620
He braydez hit by þe bauderyk, aboute þe hals kestes,
Þat bisemed þe segge semlyly fayre.
And quy þe pentangel apendez to þat prynce noble
I am in tent yow to telle, þof tary hyt me schulde:
Hit is a syngne þat Salamon set sumquyle   625

---

[42] All quotations from *Sir Gawain and the Green Knight* are taken from the edition by J. R. R. Tolkien and E. V. Gordon, rev. Norman Davis (Oxford: Clarendon Press, 1967). I have added marginal glosses for the less-familiar words.

[43] I have included the word "bounden" in the "enclosure" group; its primary meanings are those of modern English "bind," but in *Sir Gawain and the Green Knight* it is also used to mean to "trim" or "embellish," and to "stud" with jewels or precious metal. It thus has links with both brightness and enclosure, but it seems to me that the primary meanings color the transferred sense and reinforce the vocabulary of enclosure.

In bytoknyng of trawþe, bi tytle þat hit habbez,		
For hit is a figure þat haldez fyue poyntez,		
And vche lyne <u>vmbelappez</u> and <u>loukez</u> in oþer,	overlaps	locks
And ayquere hit is endelez; and Englych hit callen		
Oueral, as I here, þe endeles <u>knot</u>. 630		
Forþy hit acordez to þis knyȝt and to his *cler* armez,		bright
For ay faythful in fyue and sere fyue syþez		
Gawan watz for gode knawen, and as *golde pured*,		purified
Voyded of vche vylany, wyth vertuez ennourned		
in mote; 635		
Forþy þe pentangel nwe		
He ber in schelde and cote,		
As tulk of tale most trwe		
And gentylest knyȝt of lote.		

. . . Þe fyft fyue þat I finde þat þe frek vsed		
Watz fraunchyse and felaȝschyp forbe al þyng,		
His *clannes* and his cortaysye croked were neuer,		
And pité, þat passez alle poyntez, þyse *pure* fyue		
Were harder <u>happed</u> on þat haþel þen on any oþer. 655		fastened
Now alle þese fyue syþez, for soþe, were <u>fetled</u> on þis knyȝt,		fixed
And vchone <u>halched</u> in oþer, þat non ende hade,		linked
And <u>fyched</u> vpon fyue poyntez, þat fayld neuer,		fixed
Ne samned neuer in no syde, ne sundred nouþer,		
Withouten ende at any noke I oquere fynde, 660		
Whereeuer þe gomen bygan, or glod to an ende.		
Þerfore on his *schene* schelde schapen watz þe <u>knot</u>		bright
Ryally wyth *red golde* vpon rede gowlez,		
Þat is þe *pure* pentaungel wyth þe peple called		
with lore. 665		

The pentangle first appears as a material image of brightness, with its "pure golde hwez" (620). It also embodies enclosure; it is a "knot" (630 and 662). Each of its lines "vmbelappes" (overlaps) and "loukez" (locks) into the others (628). The five virtues that are represented by the five lines of the pentangle are also described in the vocabulary of enclosure (see lines 655–62): the words "halched" (linked) and "fyched" (fixed) express the interlocking quality of these virtues (657–58), and the words "happed" (fastened) and "fetled" (fixed) indicate the tightness with which they are attached to Gawain's person—knotted to him, as it were. The interlocking quality of the five virtues makes up Gawain's truth (loyalty, fidelity, integrity); the virtues are, as it were, loyal to one another, linked in mutual bonds of relation. The loss of one is the loss of all, as critics have often noted.[44] The effect of this enclosure, I would suggest, is to create a clean central space, emptied of debasing elements: "Voyded of vche vylany" (634). The adverb "clene," used in line 576 of Gawain's brightly polished spurs, is here transformed into the noun "clannes," the moral purity that this cleared space represents. "Clene" is thus a word that represents both the cleansed center of enclosure and its glittering surface.[45] And since the adjective "clene" also means "complete, whole,"[46] it has the potential to evoke enclosure itself, as represented in the impenetrable intactness of the pentangle; this potential will be realized (in the adverbial form meaning "completely") later in the poem. The "pure golde hwez" of the pentangle are also transposed into moral terms: Gawain's virtue makes him "as golde pured" (633) (purified like gold). And finally, Gawain's moral character is "with vertues ennourned" (634) (adorned); his inner qualities share the splendor of his outer appearance.

The medieval French *Livre de l'ordre de chevalerie* contains a section on the significance of the knight's equipment and armor which provides an instructive contrast with this passage.[47] Like *Gawain*, it gives moral significance to the closure represented by the knight's armor: the hauberk is "clos & fermé" on all sides to signify that treachery, pride and disloyalty cannot gain entrance to the knight's "noble couraige." But its general procedure is to establish a set of metaphorical equivalents between the material and the moral, in a manner that reads like an inversion of St Paul's "armor of God" passage (Ephesians 6:11–18): for example, the knight's sword signifies the cross, and its two edges mean that a knight should maintain chivalry and justice. His lance signifies

---

[44] See, for example, J. A. Burrow, *A Reading of the Gawain-Poet* (London: Routledge and Kegan Paul, 1965), 49–50, and A. C. Spearing, *The Gawain-Poet: A Critical Study* (Cambridge: Cambridge University Press, 1970), 198.

[45] For a discussion of the resonances of the word "clene" in the *Gawain*-poet's works, and the other words with which he commonly links it, see Keiser, *Courtly Desire*, 23 and 265 n. 25.

[46] *MED* sense 6.

[47] See *Livre de l'ordre de chevalerie*, ed. Vincenzo Minervini, Biblioteca di filologia romanza 21 (Bari: Adriatica Editrice, 1972), chap. 6. This work is a late fourteenth-century French translation of Ramón Lull's *Libre del orde de cavalleria*. Caxton's translation of the French version was edited by A. T. P. Byles, *The Book of the Ordre of Chyualry*, EETS o.s. 168 (London: Oxford University Press, 1926).

truth, because truth is straight and upright. The helmet signifies his shamefulness and fear of reproof, for it obliges a knight to cast his eyes downward just as a shamefast person does. The spurs signify diligence and swiftness and the gorger signifies obedience.[48] The description of Gawain's arming does not work from exterior equipment to interior meaning through a set of one-to-one correspondences in this way. Instead, the ethical and the material merge into a single dazzling image of knightly excellence, embracing "clannes" in all its senses, and the connection between them appears to be not metaphorical, but intrinsic. Moreover, the movement is not only from outward adornment (the gold-embroidered pentangle) to inward virtue ("trawþe"), but also back again, as virtue is reconceived as adornment (Gawain is purified like gold and adorned with virtues).

The interlocking quality of Gawain's five virtues is not the only reason why the pentangle is a fitting symbol of his knightly worth. Another reason is that the language of enclosure is an indication of the self-sufficient nature of chivalric virtue. Gawain's task is not motivated or supported by any external considerations—there are no maidens to be rescued, no countries to be delivered from the oppressions of a giant or a dragon, no wrongs to be righted.[49] The only reason he has for keeping his promise is the promise itself. Although his immediate motivation in taking on the Green Knight's challenge is the need to rescue Arthur from the threat of decapitation,[50] Arthur himself has risen to the challenge in order to defend the "renoun" of the Round Table, which is itself a self-reflexive act. To uphold one's renown is to prove oneself to be what one asserts one is. Chivalric virtue is its own raison d'être; it is not supported by practical utility or even by divine command. Like the pentangle, it thus stands clear of external support, locked in itself; its driving aim is the maintenance of its own purity and integrity within an incomprehensible and threatening world, to which it offers a dazzling surface, brilliant in its perfection.

One last comment on Gawain's arming: the poet calls the pentangle a game ("gomen": 661), which is also what the Green Knight calls the challenge he offers to Arthur's court (273, 283). This word too can be

---

[48] *L'ordre de chevalerie*, ed. Minervini, 144–46.

[49] For further discussion of this point, see Mann, "Sir Gawain and the Romance Hero," 109.

[50] This immediate motive defers the question of why the challenge should be accepted, but the question recurs as Gawain leaves to search for the Green Knight, and the other courtiers criticize Arthur for letting their best knight go off on a frivolous and pointless mission (674–83).

linked to the language of closure, as Stanesco's account of the chivalric game makes clear: "Game is an activity which is localized, and above all closed. The preliminary to every game is the delimitation of a precise space or trajectory, which must be different from the rest of the world. It matters little whether the limits of this space are material or imaginary, the essential thing is that the player of the game finds himself in a protected space."[51] Yet this "protected space" is not designed to exclude danger or instability, but, on the contrary, to provide a place within which they can operate.

Insofar as it contains an unforeseen element, the tournament permits the player the liberty to envisage himself at the end of the game as different from what he was at its beginning. What determines the at times extremely complicated structure of a combat in a closed arena is precisely the sense of game: the possibility of becoming other, not by virtue of being masked, but in relation to what one was beforehand. The "principle of incertitude" creates the distance between what one is and what one can be; it is in this problematic interspace that the knight of the late Middle Ages installs himself.[52]

Stanesco's comments on the tournament help us to understand the relation between enclosure and incertitude in the "gomen" to which Gawain has committed himself; although it takes a unique form and leads him at first on unconfined wanderings, its rules nevertheless hold him within their bounds, creating by their very nature the principle of uncertainty that constitutes knightly adventure.[53]

However, the account of Gawain's arming is not the only, or even the first, description of courtly dress that we have encountered in the poem. That honor belongs to the description of the Green Knight at his entrance into Arthur's court. And in that description the same vocabu-

---

[51] *Jeux d'errance*, 134: "le jeu est une activité localisée et, surtout, fermée. Le geste préalable à tout jeu est la délimitation d'un endroit ou d'un trajet précis, qui doit être différent du reste du monde. Peu importe que les limites de cet espace soient matérielles ou imaginaires, l'essentiel est que le joueur se trouve dans un lieu protégé."

[52] *Jeux d'errance*, 122: "tant qu'il comprend une part d'imprévu, le tournoi permet au joueur la liberté de s'envisager à la fin du jeu comme différent de ce qu'il était au début. Ce qui détermine la structure parfois extrêmement compliquée d'un combat en champ clos, c'est justement le sens du jeu: la possibilité de devenir autre, non pas tant derrière un masque, mais par rapport à ce qu'on a été auparavant. Le 'principe d'incertitude' crée la distance entre ce qu'on est et ce qu'on peut être; c'est dans cet entre-deux problématique que s'installe le chevalier du Moyen Âge flamboyant."

[53] Cf. the poet's description of the knightly joust as a place where Fortune determines the outcome of events, at lines 96–99.

lary sets betokening brightness and enclosure appear, presenting the reader with a puzzle similar to the one he presents to Arthur's courtiers. Again I have italicized the words for brightness and underlined those indicating enclosure.

Ande al grayþed in grene þis gome and his wedes:

A strayte cote ful streȝt, þat stek on his sides,   *clung to*

A meré mantile abof, mensked withinne

With pelure pured apert, þe pane *ful clene*   *very splendid*

With blyþe blaunner ful *bryȝt*, and his hod boþe,   155

Þat watz laȝt fro his lokkez and layde on his schulderes;

Heme wel-haled hose of þat same,

Þat *spenet* on his sparlyr, and *clene* spures vnder   *clung*   *shining*

Of *bryȝt golde*, vpon silk bordes barred ful ryche,

And scholes vnder schankes þere þe schalk rides;   160

And alle his vesture uerayly watz *clene* verdure,   *pure*

Boþe þe barres of his belt and oþer blyþe stones,

Þat were richely rayled in his aray *clene*   *splendid/shining*

Aboutte hymself and his sadel, vpon silk werkez.

Þat were to tor for to telle of tryfles þe halue   165

Þat were enbrauded abof, wyth bryddes and flyȝes,

With gay gaudi of grene, þe *golde* ay inmyddes.

Þe pendauntes of his payttrure, þe proude cropure,

His molaynes, and alle þe metail anamayld was þenne,

Þe steropes þat he stod on stayned of þe same,   170

And his arsounz al after and his aþel skyrtes,

Þat euer *glemered* and *glent* al of grene stones;   *gleamed*   *glinted*

Þe fole þat he ferkkes on fyn of þat ilke,

    sertayn,

    A grene hors gret and þikke,   175

    A stede ful stif to strayne,

    In brawden brydel quik—

    To þe gome he watz ful gayn.

Wel gay watz þis gome gered in grene,

And þe here of his hed of his hors swete.   180

Fayre fannand fax vmbefoldes his schulderes   *enfolds*

A much berd as a busk ouer his brest henges,

Þat wyth his hiȝlich here þat of his hed reches

Watz euesed al vmbetorne abof his elbowes,

Þat half his armes þer-vnder were <u>halched</u> in þe wyse 185 enclosed
Of a kyngez capados þat <u>closes</u> his swyre encloses
Þe mane of þat mayn hors much to hit lyke,
Wel cresped and cemmed, wyth <u>knottes</u> ful mony
Folden in wyth *fildore* aboute þe fayre grene, gold thread
Ay a herle of þe here, an oþer of *golde*; 190
Þe tayl and his toppyng <u>twynnen</u> of a sute, twined/plaited
And <u>bounden</u> boþe wyth a bande of a *bryʒt* grene,
Dubbed wyth ful dere stonez, as þe dok lasted,
Syþen <u>þrawen</u> wyth a þwong a þwarle <u>knot</u> alofte, bound tight
Þer mony bellez ful *bryʒt* of *brende golde* rungen. 195
Such a fole vpon folde, ne freke þat hym rydes,
Watz neuer sene in þat sale wyth syʒt er þat tyme,
   with yʒe.
  He loked *as layt so lyʒt,* as bright as lightning
  So sayd al þat hym syʒe; 200
  Hit semed as no mon myʒt
  Vnder his dynttez dryʒe.

Wheþer hade he no helme ne hawbergh nauþer,
Ne no pysan ne no plate þat pented to armes,
Ne no schafte ne no schelde to schwue ne to smyte, 205
Bot in his on honde he hade a holyn bobbe,
Þat is grattest in grene when greuez ar bare,
And an ax in his oþer, a hoge and vnmete,
A spetos sparþe to expoun in spelle, quoso myʒt.
Þe lenkþe of an elnʒerde þe large hede hade, 210
Þe grayn al of grene stele and of *golde* hewen,
Þe bit *burnyst bryʒt*, with a brod egge brightly polished
As wel schapen to schere as scharp rasores,
Þe stele of a stif staf þe sturne hit bi grypte,
Þat watz <u>wounden</u> wyth yrn to þe wandez ende, 215 wound round
And al bigrauen with grene in gracios werkes;
A lace <u>lapped aboute</u>, þat <u>louked</u> at þe hede, wrapped fastened
And so after þe halme <u>halched</u> ful ofte, looped
Wyth tryed tasselez þerto <u>tacched</u> innoghe fastened
On botounz of þe *bryʒt* grene brayden ful ryche. 220

Although he is not wearing armor, the description of the Green
Knight's clothing emphasizes knotting, plaiting, encasing, enveloping,

on the one hand, and on the other, the surface brilliance of his array, glittering with gold, jewels, and gold embroidery. The ax that he carries is of brightly polished gold and steel, and the lace that is wound round it is described in the vocabulary of enclosure: "lapped, louked, halched, tacched." The word that is insistently repeated in this passage is the adjective "clene," used in several senses that relate to surface brilliance. The edging of the Green Knight's mantle is "ful clene" (*MED* sense 5(b): "splendid, elegant; shapely, comely, excellent"); he wears "clene spures" (*MED* sense 4(b): "bright, shining, gleaming, sparkling"); his clothing is all "clene verdure" (*MED* sense 1(a) "pure, unmixed, unalloyed, unadulterated, unpolluted"); his "aray" is "clene" (a mixture of "splendid" and "shining"?). The Green Knight's appearance has all the surface brilliance of courtly display. Nothing, it seems, is hidden; there is no shabby "underneath." The lining of his cloak is "apert," plainly visible (154), and it is no less splendid than the outside of his garment: it is "mensked," adorned, with "pelure pured" (153), trimmed fur.[54]

As with the words used to describe Gawain's arming, those used to describe the Green Knight are given moral senses elsewhere in the poem. "Pured" and "mensk" appear in close proximity again in Fitt 2, when the poet is describing the joy expressed in Bertilak's castle at Gawain's arrival; "mensk" is returned to its original meaning, "honor," while "pured" is used in a transferred sense of Gawain's "purified" virtues.

> And alle þe men in þat mote maden much joye
> To apere in his presense prestly þat tyme,
> Þat alle prys and prowes and *pured þewes*
> Apendes to hys persoun, and praysed is euer;
> Byfore alle men vpon molde his *mensk* is þe most.
>
> (910–14; my italics)

The adjective "clene" is used in a moral sense ("morally clean, pure, innocent, guileless") to describe the courtly conversation between Gawain and the lady of the castle at dinner on the night of his arrival, and significantly, it alliterates with "closed."

[54] Cf. the manuscript illumination of the wedding of Richard II and Anne of Bohemia in Oxford, Bodleian Library MS Lat. liturg. f. 3, fol. 65v, which shows Richard wearing an ermine-lined mantle, with its lining proudly visible (Staley, *Languages of Power*, fig. 4).

> Bot ȝet I wot þat Wawen and þe wale burde
> Such comfort of her compaynye caȝten togeder
> Þurȝ her dere dalyaunce of her derne wordez,
> Wyth *clene* cortays carp *closed* fro fylþe,
> Þat hor play watz passande vche prynce gomen,
>> in vayres.

(1010–15; my italics)

Like the pentangle, their talk is described as a "gomen," a game, and here too "vylany" ("fylthe") is kept outside its bounds. The journey through the wilderness of northwest England was only the apparent scene of Gawain's testing; the real test takes place, fittingly, within the enclosed space of the bedroom,[55] bounded by the rules of courtly game (the exchange of winnings as well as "cortays carp"). Enclosure excludes filth, maintaining the "voided" central space of cleanness. Excluding filth, enclosure also sets protective bounds around virtue, as we see when the lady refers to courtesy as "closed" within Gawain, again alliterating on "clene," here in its adverbial sense of "completely."

> "So god as Gawayn gaynly is halden,
> And cortaysye is *closed* so *clene* in hymseluen,   so completely enclosed
> Couth not lyȝtly haf lenged so long wyth a lady,
> Bot he had craued a cosse, bi his cortaysye,
> Bi sum towch of summe tryfle at sum talez ende."

(1296–1301; my italics)

The alliterating words suggest that enclosure creates wholeness, completeness, perfection. Unfortunately, for the lady's attempt to seduce Gawain, however, the completeness with which courtesy is enclosed in Gawain also makes him "clean" in the sense of "chaste," "morally clean."

It would be easy at this point to draw a contrast between the use of words such as "clene," "mensk," and "pured" in their material senses in the Green Knight's portrait and in their moral senses as used of Gawain.

---

[55] Stanesco, *Jeux d'errance*, 134: "L'espace dans lequel se meut le chevalier à la fin du Moyen Âge est essentiellement un espace clos: lice, château, chambre, lit, cour, jardin, prison. Il ignore ou méprise la nature, les étendues illimitées, les chevauchées sauvages, les routes qui s'allongent à perte de vue." *Gawain* does of course include nature, a long and wild journey, and "limitless spaces," but these are designed precisely as distractions, disguising the real knightly test, which takes place indoors.

Easy, but mistaken, as the description of Gawain's arming has already shown; there the language of moral worth emerges from, and is continuous with, the language of courtly splendor. What we might say is that the Green Knight represents a dazzling surface that it is Gawain's task to round out with moral content. The Green Knight presents Arthur's courtiers with an unsettling mirror image of themselves, rendered unfamiliar and alien by his green color, implicitly challenging the courtiers with the question of whether their brilliant surface *does* make visible an inner truth, whether their dazzling reputation ("los") is matched by reality.[56] The combination of his greenness with the most sophisticated luxury of courtly dress turns him into an enigmatic *spectacle*, one whose appearance is scrutinized in exhaustive detail over three long stanzas, as the courtiers (and the reader) try to decipher its meaning. He is at once totally open to inspection and totally opaque.[57]

The Green Knight's description associates courtly splendor with the idea of the public gaze.[58] Courtly display, that is to say, depends on an audience; it presents itself for visual consumption by beholders, in whom it finds its point and the realization of its meaning. Vance Smith has some perceptive remarks (made in discussion of *Sir Launfal*) about the social anxiety surrounding the notion of value (the outward manifestation of wealth), resulting from "the knowledge that one is being watched, and always being watched, interpellated as not only an economic subject but especially as a sumptuary subject."[59] So important is this public audience that in its absence the subject will mentally supply

[56] It will be clear that I disagree with the critical view represented by Larry D. Benson (among others) that the Green Knight "clearly champions a set of values completely opposite to those of the polished courtier," and that "he comes from another world altogether, from the world of nature"; *Art and Tradition in "Sir Gawain and the Green Knight"* (New Brunswick: Rutgers University Press, 1965), 81, 93. For a shrewd dismantling of the attempts to interpret the Green Knight as a version of the natural figure of the Green Man, see Bella Millett, "How Green Is the Green Knight?" *Nottingham Medieval Studies* 38 (1994): 138–51.

[57] As J. A. Burrow argues (*A Reading*, 13–17), the Green Knight's appearance is disturbing, not because it represents the polar opposite of the Arthurian courtly world, but because its combination of the civilized human (his fashionable dress and adornments) with hints of the supernatural (his greenness and his size) makes him *uncategorizable*; it is thus hard to see how he should be treated. In the event, Arthur's decision to treat him as a knight (cf. line 276: "Sir cortays knyȝt") turns out to be the right one.

[58] There is a brief anticipation of this in the early description of Guinevere (74–84), surrounded by canopies and hangings, offered up to the public gaze, so that she becomes part of the splendid spectacle of the feast.

[59] D. Vance Smith, *Arts of Possession: The Middle English Household Imaginary* (Minneapolis: University of Minnesota Press, 2003), 169.

it: to quote again from Smith, "Value brings with it an audience, the consciousness that its form is not just made visible in public, but that it *is* a kind of public, bearing with it its own logic of surveillance."[60]

These remarks will, I think, help us to understand how the theme of courtly display is extended into the account of Gawain's testing in Bertilak's castle, where it might seem to have disappeared entirely. For of course this testing is carried out when he is completely divested not only of his armor but also of his courtly clothing, as he lies naked in bed.[61] Yet the sense of *being watched*, of being subject to the "logic of surveillance" that is implied in courtly display, persists. This sense is very cleverly established on the first morning when Gawain is awakened by a little noise at his bedroom door and, peeping through the bed-curtains, sees the lady entering his room. When she nears the bed, he hastily lies down and pretends to be asleep; she sits on his bed and waits for him to wake up. Gawain's initial role as watcher is thus neatly inverted; he is now conscious of *being watched*, and I think that this sense of scrutiny persists throughout the encounters with the lady. Gawain watches himself constantly, sensitive to any suggestion that he may have failed to live up to his outward reputation. It is now his inner worth that is "on display," with enclosure and cleanness both manifested in his bodily intactness, his chastity, and in the completeness with which he maintains both his "trawþe" and his courtesy. The word "vnlouked," which is used of Gawain at last opening his eyes (1201), vividly conveys the idea of the unarmed body as itself an enclosure, making itself vulnerable but protected by its inner virtues. And this idea is also evident when Gawain meets the Green Knight's challenge, wearing his armor but renouncing its protection by removing his helmet and offering his naked neck to the ax blade. At this point, his only armor is the "trawþe" that the pentangle symbolizes, enclosing him within its locked boundaries.

The moment at which Gawain stops watching himself is of course the moment when he accepts the green girdle. He assumes that this action can be *hidden*, unaware that it is as available to the lord's gaze as his rejection of the lady's advances. In that sense he betrays the obliga-

---

[60] Ibid., 175. See also my earlier remarks about value being established only in terms of the valuation accorded by others; "Price and Value," 307–8.

[61] The poet does not make this explicit, but the illumination in Cotton Nero A.x (fol. 129), which shows the lady at Gawain's bedside while he pretends to sleep, depicts him as naked (*Companion to the Gawain-Poet*, ed. Brewer and Gibson, 215, fig. 10). It is true that the illuminations do not always represent the events of the poem with entire accuracy, but it seems that the illuminator thought it natural for people to sleep naked.

tion to be always on display, to make himself fully manifest. Yet of course he does unwittingly make his fault manifest by wearing the green girdle in open view of the Green Knight. He wraps it twice around his body, attempting to enclose himself in its protection rather than that of the "trawþe" which has the truly magic power that the girdle only fakes.[62] The Green Knight makes his fault manifest in a different way, in the tiny nick that he makes in Gawain's neck by way of punishment for this minor lapse (had he truly failed, he would of course have lost his head). For Gawain, of course, any breach of his knightly integrity destroys the perfect enclosure represented by the pentangle. His inner self no longer matches the brilliant perfection of his outer display. The ending of the poem is taken up with a series of moves designed to restore the intimate connection between interior and exterior. First, Gawain's immediate and uncompromising acceptance of his guilt both internalizes and displays for public inspection his new image of himself. Second, the Green Knight treats this confession as re-creating the continuity between his inner and outer selves. And the word used to describe this newly constituted self is "clene," used in its full richness of meaning:

> Thenn loȝe þat oþer leude and luflyly sayde:
> "I halde hit hardily hole, þe harme þat I hade.
> Þou art confessed so *clene*, beknowen of þy mysses,
> And hatz þe penaunce apert of þe poynt of myn egge,
> I halde þe *polysed* of þat plyȝt, and *pured as clene*
> As þou hadez neuer forfeted syþen þou watz fyrst borne.
>
> (2389–94; my italics)

Gawain's hidden fault becomes susceptible to healing precisely as it comes to the surface in the form of the nick that makes it visibly manifest—"apert," the word last used of the lining of the Green Knight's cloak. The word "clene" in line 2393 is most naturally taken to be an adverb meaning "completely," but it also suggests the sense "to a state of cleanness" (*MED* 1[a]). That is, the completeness of Gawain's confession has made him once more "clean," and not only in the sense of being freed from pollution but also in the sense of becoming "splendid, radiant." As in the scene of his arming, his virtues are conceived as

---

[62] See Mann, "Sir Gawain and the Romance Hero," 116–17.

courtly adornments: he is "pured" like gold and "polysed" like the shining steel of his armor. Gawain's confession has also restored his moral wholeness, his integrity, in the etymological sense of that word, making him "clene" in the sense of "complete." The Green Knight compares Gawain to a pearl, in comparison to other knights who are like white peas. The pearl, like the pentangle, offers an image of enclosure—an unbroken circle, an intact, inviolate sphere, which cannot be cut into without destroying its value, and which displays a smooth, shining surface to the world.[63]

By the time Gawain returns to Arthur's court, the nick in his neck has healed; it is "hole" as the Green Knight says his "harme" is. But Gawain insists on wearing the girdle as a permanent sign of his shame. Significantly, its vocabulary incorporates the twin elements of brightness (italicized) and enclosure (underlined):

> Þe hurt watz hole þat he hade hent in his nek,
> And þe *blykkande* belt he bere þeraboute   shining
> Abelef as a bauderyk bounden bi his syde,
> Loken vnder his lyfte arme, þe lace, with a knot,   fastened
> In tokenyng he watz tane in tech of a faute.
>
> (2484–88)

Recounting his adventures, Gawain once again confesses his fault, expressing his sense of enduring shame in the vocabulary of enclosure:

> "Þis is þe token of vntrawþe þat I am tan inne,
> And I mot nedez hit were wyle I may last;
> For mon may hyden his harme, bot vnhap ne may hit,   unfasten
> For þer hit onez is *tachched* twynne wil hit neuer." attached
>
> (2509–12)

Instead of the five virtues, disgrace is (in Gawain's eyes) "fastened" to him, like a shameful travesty of the fringes and tassels of courtly dress. But Arthur's courtiers agree with the Green Knight in emphasizing Gawain's major success rather than his minor failure. For them, to have

---

[63] See Jill Mann, "Satisfaction and Payment in Middle English Literature," *SAC* 5 (1983): 17–48 (26–27).

done as well as Gawain did would be no failure but an unimaginably high level of success.[64] They therefore determine that if Gawain wears the green girdle as a surface manifestation of the disgrace that is inwardly "attached" to him, they will wear it likewise, but as a token of honor.[65] They thus re-create the significance of the girdle by making it a courtly adornment, comparable to the knots and fringes and plaits that ornament courtly attire. This gesture gives the girdle an honorific status as part of the splendor of courtly display, one of the ways of making visible the inner qualities of Arthurian knighthood.[66] Enclosure is here realized not only in the form of the knotted girdle but also in the form of the unbroken circle of community that unites the members of the Round Table.

It should by now be clear how great a difference there is between the *Gawain*-poet's conceptualization of courtly display and Dymmok's notion of its role as political stratagem, a way of awing the lower classes into submission or surrounding the king with a mystique that will enhance his prestige and power. Instead, what we have in this poem is a truly imaginative spiritualization of courtly splendor, an attempt to read it as a material manifestation of the ethical qualities embodied in the courtly life and as itself constituting a challenge to be lived up to. The poem offers, in other words, a perfect example of Stanesco's definition of gothic display. Though its initial motivation was probably a celebration of the courtly magnificence cultivated by Richard II, it goes far beyond that aim, forging an ideal of knightly virtue as dazzling as the luxury of any court. This does not mean, however, that this particular

---

[64] At the risk of crudely simplifying the poet's subtle combination of perspectives, one might compare their reaction to Gawain's account of his failure with the likely reaction of an average student to a friend's lament that she had scored "only" 98 out of 100 in a recent test. Bertilak and the court focus on the 98 percent success, while Gawain focuses on the 2 percent failure, but this very fact recasts his performance as a perfect success. On acceptance of failure as a challenge that the romance hero must meet (exemplified in four of Chrétien's five romances), see Mann, "Sir Gawain and the Romance Hero," 114–15.

[65] Nicholas Perkins points out to me that the crown of thorns, referred to in the penultimate line of the poem (2529), is similarly a badge of shame that has been turned into a badge of honor (as it is in the Wilton Diptych, where the Christ Child's golden halo has the crown of thorns punched within it).

[66] Susan Crane discusses the pentangle and the girdle as outward signs of Gawain's inner identity (*The Performance of Self: Ritual, Clothing, and Identity During the Hundred Years War* [Philadelphia: University of Pennsylvania Press, 2002], 134–39), but she argues that "the difference between the meaning Gawain attributes to the girdle and the meanings urged by Bertilak and Arthur's courtiers marks the point where Gawain is, finally, estranged from his community" (136).

ideal of knightly virtue transcends political function altogether. It remains to ask, therefore, in what way the particular ethical qualities that the poet links with courtly display might serve the interests of the court of Richard II, and also of the poet himself. "Trawþe" is a traditional knightly (and kingly) virtue, but "clannes" may seem a rather more surprising choice as a courtly quality. There are several ways of accounting for it, some more speculative than others.[67] One might look for a reason in terms of the poet's own social status and ideology. If, as seems likely, he was a cleric,[68] the poem may be seen as part of a general reshaping of the knightly ideal in accordance with clerical values.[69] In the poem that goes by the name of *Cleanness*, a striking role is played by the prophet Daniel, who admonishes and counsels the erring king Belshazzar, interpreting the writing on the wall as the Chaldean clerks could not. The commanding figure of Daniel, whose "derne coninges" (1611) give him a moral ascendancy over his royal master, and who is rewarded with purple garments and gold adornment fit for a royal courtier, may be taken as a projection of the role the *Gawain*-poet aspired to play in Richard's court. The implication in this poem is that the holder of earthly power needs the cleric to guide his life. In inflecting courtly culture with clerical values, the poet is enhancing his own prestige and importance.

On the other hand, he can also be seen as enhancing the prestige of knighthood by associating it with the mystique of religious sanctity. The rejection of insistent amorous advances, the heroic virtue that provokes

---

[67] It may have appealed on an immediate and personal level to Richard himself, whose personal devotion to Edward the Confessor, and the fact that his marriage with Anne of Bohemia was affectionate but childless, have prompted modern speculations that he might have imitated the chaste marriage practiced by his royal predecessor. See C. M. Barron, "Richard II: Image and Reality," in *Making and Meaning: The Wilton Diptych*, ed. Dillian Gordon (London: National Gallery Publications, 1993), 13–19 (15), and John M. Bowers, "Chaste Marriage: Fashion and Texts at the Court of Richard II," *Pacific Coast Philology* 30 (1995): 15–26. Nigel Saul thinks that "the suggestion certainly makes sense in the context of the king's piety," but "what counts against it is Richard's need for a male heir" (*Richard II*, 457). The association of courtly culture with sexual restraint would also have served as a refutation of the contemporary gossip about homosexuality that I mentioned earlier.

[68] This is suggested by his probable range of reading (in Latin as well as French); see Putter, *Introduction to the Gawain-Poet*, 4–11, 14–17. Putter concludes that a cleric in minor orders, employed in an administrative capacity in a lay household, would best fit the evidence.

[69] Putter has given a thorough and convincing account of *Sir Gawain and the Green Knight* in these terms; see *"Sir Gawain and the Green Knight" and French Arthurian Romance* (Oxford: Clarendon Press, 1995), chap. 5.

such admiration from the Green Knight, is in origin a hagiographic motif. Stories are told of women forcing themselves on several saints, of whom Bernard of Clairvaux is the most notable. The *Vita prima*, written in Bernard's lifetime by his friend William of St Thierry, tells of two occasions in his youth when his striking good looks made him the object of aggressive female seduction. In the first case, a girl climbed naked into Bernard's bed as he lay sleeping; becoming aware of her presence, he turned away from her and went back to sleep. Even when she began to caress him, he made no response, so that eventually, confused and awed, she got up and left him. The second occasion more closely resembles Gawain's temptation by the lady of the castle: a married woman, in whose house Bernard was spending the night, three times in the course of the night crept into his bedroom. Each time, Bernard roused the household by shouting "Thieves! thieves!" and after the third failed attempt she gave up. (Bernard explained to his companions the next day that his cry was apt because she had been trying to steal the priceless treasure of his chastity.)[70] It seems to have been Chrétien de Troyes who first transposed this motif into a chivalric context, in the scene from *Le chevalier de la charete* in which Lancelot is obliged to go to bed with an amorous hostess, but lies stiffly far apart from her, proclaiming his unwillingness to touch her.[71] As in *Gawain*, the scene demonstrates that

---

[70] *Vita prima, Patrologia latina* 185. 230 D–231 B. For a translation, see *St Bernard of Clairvaux: The Story of his Life as recorded in the Vita Prima Bernardi by certain of his contemporaries, William of St. Thierry, Arnold of Bonnevaux, Geoffrey and Philip of Clairvaux, and Odo of Deuil*, trans. Geoffrey Webb and Adrian Walker (Westminster, Md.: Newman Press, 1960), 20–22. For a critique of the *Patrologia* edition, and a list of surviving manuscripts (more than 120) of the *Vita*, see Adriaan Hendrik Bredero, "Études sur la 'Vita prima' de Saint Bernard," *Analecta sacri ordinis cisterciensis* 17 (1961): 3–72. Similar stories are related of Bishop William of St. Brieuc (d. 1234), *Acta Sanctorum* Iul. VII, 122D–E, and the Spanish Dominican saint Peter Gonzales (d. 1246), *Acta Sanctorum* Apr. II, 393E–394E. For further examples, see Donald Weinstein and Rudolph M. Bell, *Saints and Society: Christendom, 1000–1700* (Chicago: University of Chicago Press, 1982), 81–83, 86–87. The motif is much older than the twelfth century; it occurs, for example, in Jerome's *Life of Paul of Thebes, Patrologia latina* 23, cols. 19–20, trans. Carolinne White, *Early Christian Lives* (Harmondsworth: Penguin, 1998), 76.

[71] *Le chevalier de la charrete*, ed. Mario Roques (Paris: Honoré Champion, 1968), lines 1192–280. Putter discusses this scene in relation to *Sir Gawain and the Green Knight*, as well as two other instances in which it is Gawain who is fending off sexual advances from ladies; see Putter, *"Sir Gawain and the Green Knight" and French Arthurian Romance*, 123–26 (Lancelot) and 101–2, 112–13 (Gawain). Other examples of romances in which "men turn down the advances of demanding women" are listed by Susan Crane, *Gender and Romance in Chaucer's "Canterbury Tales"* (Princeton: Princeton University Press, 1994), 40 n. 17. In contrast, some Anglo-Norman romances show women as active wooers whose advances are (sooner or later) welcome to the men concerned; see Judith Weiss, "The Wooing Woman in Anglo-Norman Romance," in *Romance in Medieval En-*

the courtly hero can control his desires as well as any saint.[72] And it also invests the courtly hero with the prestige that accrues to the saint, showing him as set apart from the common run of men. Gawain's chastity, however, is even more impressive than Lancelot's, since Lancelot is restrained by his single-minded devotion to Guinevere,[73] whereas Gawain's devotion is to his own inner "clannes" and his "trawþe" to his host. His allegiance is not to an earthly lady but to the Virgin Mary. And whereas Saint Bernard rejected his amorous hostess by setting the household in an uproar, Gawain's task is much harder: he has to reject Bertilak's wife so courteously that he is not noticeably doing so. Saintly chastity is inflected with courtly manners.

The fusion of clerical and chivalric values thus works to the benefit of both sides. If, on the one hand, clerical values find a lodging place in courtly life, on the other hand, religion itself is reconceived in aristocratic terms. The poet exploits the full semantic range of the word "clene," which provided a perfect opportunity to link the clerical and the courtly. "Clannes" embraces not only chastity but also the cleanliness, elegance, and dazzling beauty of courtly adornment. In a discussion of the *Gawain*-poet as "vernacular theologian," Nicholas Watson commented on the "specifically aristocratic articulation of the Christian life" that is contained in the four Cotton Nero poems, and identified the poet's project as "the displacement of the traditional categories of Christian heroism (embodied in virgins, martyrs and preachers) to make way for a new set, embodied in a figure closer to the aspirations and capacities of the poet's audience, Gawain himself."[74] In *Cleanness* and *Pearl*, heaven is conceived as a court, adorned by material luxury, organized along hierarchical lines, and presided over by a God whose autocratic power would be the envy of Richard II. In *Cleanness* as in *Gawain,* the word "clene" effects the linking of the material and the moral, the combination of courtly luxury and moral restraint.[75] In *Sir Gawain and the*

---

gland, ed. Maldwyn Mills, Jennifer Fellows, and Carol M. Meale (Cambridge: D. S. Brewer, 1991), 149–61.

[72] Chaucer parodies knightly chastity in *Sir Thopas*: "Ful many a maide bright in bour, / They moorne for him *par amour*, / Whan hem were bet to slepe. / But he was chaast and no lechour" (742–45).

[73] As Andreas Capellanus says, "love makes a man to be as it were adorned with the virtue of chastity" ("amor reddit hominem castitatis quasi virtute decoratum"). *On Love*, ed. P. G. Walsh (London: Duckworth, 1982) I.iv, p. 38.

[74] "The *Gawain*-Poet as a Vernacular Theologian," *Companion to the Gawain-Poet*, ed. Brewer and Gibson, 297, 311.

[75] A. C. Spearing has shown the importance of boundaries and order to the notion of cleanness in this poem; see "*Purity* and Danger," *EIC* 30 (1980): 293–310, repr. in

Green Knight, "clannes" likewise unites material and moral. Linked by alliteration with "cortaysye," it expresses the knight's freedom from "vylany," and is the quality that presides over courtly relations with women, which take the form of "clene cortays carp" rather than grossly physical relations. Here too it has important associations with the restraint that is symbolized in the knots and plaits of courtly attire, and with the maintenance of order and social decorum. So far from being an indication of extravagance and excess, the poet seems to be saying, courtly splendor incorporates self-discipline and self-control.

Finally, "clannes" in the form of chastity is important not only because it is a Christian virtue but because it can itself function as a metaphor, an image of bodily and spiritual intactness/integrity, of the knightly self-sufficiency represented by the hero encased in his armor, proof against the world. It represents the *mode* of virtue as much as its content, signalling an absoluteness of commitment to one's own "prys." It is in this respect that it resembles the virtue of "trawþe," which exhibits the same sort of self-sufficiency in the form of the pentangle, locked within itself. Although "trawþe" undoubtedly involves a sense of what is owed to others, and fidelity in one's relations with them, the source of this externally directed behavior is an inner integrity, a truth to oneself that is to be maintained as a primary duty. Gawain's disgust when he learns of his failure does not express itself as a consciousness of the way his behavior affects others (as indeed it hardly does), but as a consciousness that he has fallen short of his conception of himself.

> "For care of þy knokke cowardyse me taȝt
> To acorde me with couetyse, *my kynde to forsake,*
> Þat is larges and lewté þat longez to knyȝtez.
> Now am I fawty and falce, and ferde haf ben euer
> Of trecherye and vntrawþe . . ."
>
> (2379–82; my italics)

Knightly virtue in this poem is nonutilitarian; it involves being true to one's conception of what one is. It may be compared with the solemn self-display evident in the hieratic image of Richard's kingship in the Westminster portrait, which displays kingship not as function but as being: a king, it seems to say, is simply what Richard *is.*

Spearing, *Readings in Medieval Poetry* (Cambridge: Cambridge University Press, 1987), 173–94.

With all this, it should be added that the reshaped courtly ideal is probably as important for what it is *not* as much as for what it is. *Cleanness* offers a clue to this significance, in the contemptuous reference to the giants of the book of Genesis, fathered on the daughters of men by the "sons of God," who were characterized by a love of battle:

> Þose wern men meþelez and maȝty on vrþe,
> Þat for her lodlych laykez alosed þay were;
> He watz famed for fre that feȝt loued best,
> And ay the bigest in bale þe best watz halden.
>
> (273–76)[76]

What *Gawain* conspicuously rejects is the warrior ethic that defines heroism as fighting. In its place it sets the gentler and more sophisticated virtues that rule the civilized and courtly life, celebrated and articulated in courtly display. In the context of Richard's court, this would align the poet with the rejection of the war party represented (among others) by the Appellants, and with support for Richard's more conciliatory attitude to his "cousin" the king of France.[77] This conciliatory attitude persisted into the 1390s: the three-year truce with the French agreed at Leulingham in 1389 was renewed several times, and finally in 1396 a twenty-eight-year truce was agreed as a prelude to Richard's marriage with Isabelle, daughter of the French king.[78] *Sir Gawain and the Green Knight* harmonizes with this desire for peace by showing that heroism can take other forms than physical prowess or martial aggression, mani-

[76] I quote from the edition of *Cleanness* in *The Poems of the "Pearl" Manuscript*, ed. Malcolm Andrew and Ronald Waldron, 5th ed. (Exeter: University of Exeter Press, 2007).

[77] According to Henry Knighton, when under threat from parliament in October 1386, Richard horrified Thomas Woodstock, duke of Gloucester (later one of the five Lords Appellant), and Thomas Arundel, bishop of Ely, by saying that he could look for assistance from "cognatum nostrum regem Francie." *Knighton's Chronicle 1337–1396*, ed. and trans. G. H. Martin (Oxford: Clarendon Press, 1995), 352–61. On opposing attitudes to war with the French in Richard's reign, see Saul, *Richard II*, 140–42, 196–98, 204, 219, 312, 439. Richard of course engaged in military campaigns against the Scots and the Irish, but he seems to have regarded these as internal struggles that were different from continental warfare. Gillespie says he "used military force as a tool, not an end" ("Richard II: King of Battles?" 160).

[78] Saul, *Richard II*, 205–34 (the chapter title is "The Quest for Peace, 1389–98"). Saul comments that the truce of 1389 "inaugurated the longest break in hostilities since the resumption of the war in 1369" (205). Philippe de Mézières's *Letter to King Richard II* (ed. G. W. Coopland [Liverpool: Liverpool University Press, 1975]) is a passionate plea to Richard to put an end to the Anglo-French war and accept Isabelle as his bride.

festing itself in situations that demand even more physical courage than battle, but that also demand tact, diplomacy, humility, and self-restraint. With Richard's deposition and death, this attempt at promoting a different sort of heroism vanished like the wind, and hopes for peace with France were replaced by Lancastrian belligerence.[79]

[79] Thanking the people of London for their splendid reception of him in 1400, Henry IV reportedly swore that "neither my grandfather King Edward, nor my uncle the Prince of Wales, ever advanced so far in France as I shall do, if it please God and St George, or I shall die there in torment" ["vous jure et promech que monseigneur mon grant-pere le roy Edouard ne mon oncle le prince de Galles nallerent oncques sy avant en France comme je feray, sil plaist a Dieu et a monseigneur Saint George, ou je y morray en la paine"]. See *Recueil des croniques et anchiennes istories de la Grant Bretaigne, a present nomme Engleterre, par Jehan de Waurin, seigneur de Forestel . . . 1399–1422*, ed. William Hardy, Rolls Series 39, vol. 2 (London: Her Majesty's Stationery Office, 1868), 45. Although Henry was distracted by other concerns from mounting a full-scale campaign against the French, his son, Henry V, more than made up for the lack.

William Thorpe's Narrative Theology

Elizabeth Schirmer
New Mexico State University

T HE *TESTIMONY OF WILLIAM THORPE* is a first-person narrative account of its author's informal heresy trial at the hands of no less a personage than Thomas Arundel, Archbishop of Canterbury.[1] Thorpe dates the events he narrates to 1407:[2] six years after the 1401 statute *De heretico comburendo* officially provided for relapsed heretics to be turned over to the secular arm and burnt at the stake,[3] and two years before Arundel promulgated his anti-Lollard *Constitutions*, which seek to regulate academic speculation, preaching, and vernacular textuality.[4]

Earlier versions of this material were presented at three conferences: "The Culture of Books" (Berkeley, California, April 2002); The 37th International Congress on Medieval Studies (Kalamazoo, Michigan, May 2002); and "Narrative: An International Conference" (Berkeley, California, March 2003). The essay was completed with the support of a Mayers Fellowship from the Huntington Library, as well as a Faculty Research Award from the National Endowment for the Humanities.

[1] I cite Thorpe parenthetically throughout, by text and line number, from Anne Hudson, ed., *Two Wycliffite Texts*, EETS o.s. 301 (New York: Oxford University Press, 1993).

[2] For the latest evidence on the historicity of Thorpe's interrogation and his text, as well as a context for explaining its juridical anomalies, see Maureen Jurkowski, "The Arrest of William Thorpe in Shrewsbury and the Anti-Lollard Statute of 1406," *Historical Research* 75 (2002): 273–95. The *Testimony* survives in two versions, Latin and English (see Hudson, ed., *Two Wycliffite Texts*, xli–liii). With Hudson, I am inclined to support the primacy of the English version; with Rita Copeland, I am inclined to date the text itself shortly after the promulgation of Arundel's 1409 *Constitutions*. See her *Pedagogy, Intellectuals, and Dissent in the Later Middle Ages: Lollardy and Ideas of Learning* (Cambridge: Cambridge University Press, 2001), 191–218.

[3] See A. K. McHardy, "*De Heretico Comburendo*, 1401," in *Lollardy and the Gentry in the Later Middle Ages*, ed. Margaret Aston and Colin Richmond (Stroud: Sutton; New York: St. Martin's Press, 1997), 112–26.

[4] For the Latin text of the *Constitutions,* see David Wilkins, ed., *Concilia Magnae Britanniae et Hiberniae,* 4 vols. (London, 1737), 3:314–19. For two different perspectives on the impact of the *Constitutions,* see Nicholas Watson, "Censorship and Cultural Change in Late-Medieval England: Vernacular Theology, the Oxford Translation Debate, and Arundel's *Constitutions* of 1409," *Speculum* 70 (1995): 522–64; and Kathryn Kerby-Fulton, "Appendix A: Arundel's Constitutions of 1407–9 and Vernacular Literature," in her *Books Under Suspicion: Censorship and Tolerance of Revelatory Writing in Late Medieval England* (Notre Dame, Ind.: Notre Dame University Press, 2006), 397–401.

The *Testimony* is thus set between two landmarks of the anti-Lollard campaign waged by the archbishop and his colleagues under the aegis of the usurping Lancastrian regime.[5] Thorpe's text dramatizes the conflict between Lollardy and the ecclesiastical establishment—each embodied in one of its main characters, Wycliffite priest and Archbishop of Canterbury—at this key moment in the controversy. As an Oxford-trained priest with ties to the heresiarch, one of the few of that cohort to confront Arundel's campaign directly, Thorpe was uniquely positioned to confront the problem of how vernacular Wycliffism was to survive this new wave of persecution.[6]

The answer lay, for Thorpe, in discursive creativity. Thorpe's *Testimony*, I shall argue, sidesteps the textual strategies that had come to define both sides in the Lollard controversy, expanding the discursive territory of vernacular Wycliffism. In particular, Thorpe turns to narrative—a discursive mode shunned by the majority of his co-sectarians, and strongly associated with anti-Lollard textual programs—in order to enact his intertwined theological and political projects.[7] By the early fifteenth century, the Lollard controversy had calcified into a "textual struggle,"[8] with each side working to promulgate distinctive forms of vernacular textuality and lay religious experience. This "struggle" cen-

[5] See Jeremy Catto, "Religious Change under Henry V," in *Henry V: The Practice of Kingship*, ed. G. L. Harriss (Oxford: Oxford University Press, 1985), 97–115; see also Paul Strohm, "Counterfeiters, Lollards, and Lancastrian Unease," in *NML* 1 (1997): 31–58.

[6] See Copeland, *Pedagogy, Intellectuals, and Dissent*, 144, 191, 195.

[7] Critical interest in the *Testimony* (which has flourished since the publication of Anne Hudson's EETS edition in 1993) has focused on its vernacularizing of academic terms and techniques, on the one hand, and its affinities with the biblical drama—especially the tyrant's play—on the other. On the former see, e.g., Fiona Somerset, *Clerical Discourse and Lay Audience in Late Medieval England* (Cambridge: Cambridge University Press, 1998); Copeland, *Pedagogy, Intellectuals, and Dissent*, Part 2, "Violent Representation: Intellectuals and Prison Writing"; and Matti Peikola, "'Whom clepist þou trew pilgrimes?': Lollard Discourse on Pilgrimages in the *Testimony of William Thorpe*," in *Essays and Explorations: A "Freundschrift" for Lisa Dahl*, ed. Marita Gustafsson (Turku: University of Turku, 1996), 73–84. On the dramatic affinities of Thorpe's text, see Johanna Summers, *Late-Medieval Prison Writing and the Politics of Autobiography* (Oxford: Clarendon Press, 2004), 120 and passim; and Ritchie D. Kendall, *The Drama of Dissent: The Radical Poetics of Nonconformity, 1380–1590* (Chapel Hill: University of North Carolina Press, 1986), for whom Thorpe's *Testimony* is a paradigmatic instance of what he terms Lollard "displaced drama." The only discussion I know of Thorpe's text *as* narrative is in David Aers, *Sanctifying Signs: Making Christian Tradition in Late Medieval England* (Notre Dame, Ind.: University of Notre Dame Press, 2004), 83–97; as will become apparent, my reading differs significantly from his.

[8] Summers, *Prison Writing*, 137.

tered on the question of vernacular biblical transmission. It was initiated by early Wycliffite textual programs, which sought to flood the vernacular literary marketplace with highly standardized copies of the English Wycliffite Bible, the long Sermon Cycle, and related biblical texts.[9] Anti-Lollard efforts tended to mirror—that is, both to mimic and to reverse—Lollard textual programs. The *Festial* of John Mirk, perhaps intended as an orthodox alternative to the English Wycliffite cycle, goes so far as to do away with the biblical theme text, replacing the Lollard sermons' characteristic exposition *secundum ordinem textum* with "liturgical instructions" on the feasts of the church.[10] Mirk conducts these instructions, moreover, almost entirely through narrative: the exemplum, freed from subservience to biblical doctrine, merges with hagiography and takes over the content of the sermons. Mirk thus substitutes narrative for the biblical text and uses it to reify the gap between clerical and lay readers, resisting Lollard challenges to clerical authority.

For anti-Lollard writers like John Mirk, narrative, conceived of as inherently flesh-bound and affective, was the perfect discursive mode by which to define lay audiences as equally mired in the flesh and the world, dependent upon the discursive and sacramental mediation of the clergy and their church. Lancastrian anti-Lollard programs continue to

[9] The best description of Wycliffite scriptural manuscripts, and the best account of their distinctiveness, is still Anne Hudson's; see her "Introduction" to *English Wycliffite Sermons*, ed. Hudson and Pamela Gradon, 5 vols. (Oxford: Clarendon Press, 1983–1996), 1.189–202; see also her "A Lollard Sermon-Cycle and Its Implications," *MÆ* 40 (1971): 142–56, and "Some Aspects of Lollard Book Production," in *Lollards and Their Books* (London: Hambledon, 1985), 181–91. Hudson concludes from her detailed study of the manuscripts that the English Wycliffite Sermons (EWS) were produced "under tight control in a limited period of time and within a small number of centers," and "may have had some official standing in the movement"; she even proposes the hypothesis that they were produced in a single scriptorium, probably under the patronage of the Lollard knights. Ralph Hanna's study of the manuscript record finds that Wycliffite biblical texts "progressively infiltrate earlier, orthodox biblical versions, perhaps as a form of camouflaged circulation," until they "became a full substitute and drove out, destroyed the circulation of, competing biblical versions"; see Ralph Hanna, *London Literature: 1300–1380* (Cambridge: Cambridge University Press, 2005), 310; see also 305–13.

[10] Siegfried Wenzel, *Latin Sermon Collections from Late Medieval England: Orthodox Preaching in the Age of Wyclif* (Cambridge: Cambridge University Press, 2005), 60. I cite here from *Mirk's Festial*, ed. Theodor Erbe, EETS. e.s. 96 (London: Kegan Paul, Trench, Trübner, 1905). For Mirk's relationship to Lollardy, see, inter alia, Alan J. Fletcher, "John Mirk and the Lollards," *MÆ* 56 (1987): 217–22. While the manuscripts of Mirk's orthodox *Festial* vary more than those of the Wycliffite cycle, its textual tradition is still remarkably uniform for its genre; see Susan Powell, "Prolegomena to a New Edition of the *Festial*," *Manuscripta* 41 (1997): 171–84.

use narrative to construct lay audiences as affective and devotional, rather than intellective or contemplative. The classic articulation of this project is Nicholas Love's assertion that his "symple" readers, like children, need to be "fedde with mylke of ly3te doctrine & not with sadde mete of grete clargye & of hye contemplacioun." [11] Love's *Mirror of the Blessed Life of Jesus Christ* was famously authorized by Arundel himself on the heels of the 1409 legislation, implicitly as substitute for the Wycliffite bible translations banned by the new legislation.[12] Love's text offers its "symple" readers moral and doctrinal commentary on episodes from the life of Christ, inviting imaginative, affective engagement with biblical narratives in place of intellective or contemplative engagement with the biblical text.[13] Authorizing Love's stories of the life of Christ at nearly the same moment that he legislates against biblical translation, Arundel reinforces an implicit dichotomy between biblical narrative and biblical text, reserving the latter to clerical, Latinate readers.[14]

Citing Wyclif and confronting Arundel, Thorpe locates himself at the center of the Lollard controversy. Rather than call for biblical translation, however, Thorpe tells a paradigmatic story of confrontation between Lollardy and the ecclesiastical establishment. Thorpe participates in the Lollard controversy, in other words, precisely by representing it.[15] Narrative is central to Thorpe's representational strategies. For Thorpe, narrative is an experiential and exemplary, rather than an affective or devotional, mode. As such, it becomes the perfect vehicle for a Wycliffite theology conceived not as a set of propositions to be adhered to or debated, but as life lived in imitation of the Word. Doing Wycliffite theology in and through narrative, Thorpe reconfigures implicit dichot-

---

[11] Nicholas Love, *The Mirror of the Blessed Life of Jesus Christ: A Full Critical Edition*, ed. Michael G. Sargent (Exeter: University of Exeter Press, 2005), 10.

[12] A "Memorandum" giving the text Arundel's imprimatur and publicly commending it *ad fidelium edificationem, & hereticorum siue lollardorum confutationem*, in language that echoes Love's own in a key anti-Lollard addition to his source text, survives in seventeen extant manuscripts of the *Mirror*. See Sargent, ed. *Mirror*, Introduction, pp. 66, 148–49.

[13] For a more detailed articulation of this argument, see Elizabeth Schirmer, "Reading Lessons at Syon Abbey: *The Myroure of Oure Ladye* and the Mandates of Vernacular Theology," in *Voices in Dialogue: Reading Women in the Middle Ages*, ed. Linda Olson and Kathryn Kerby-Fulton (Notre Dame, Ind.: University of Notre Dame Press, 2005), 345–76.

[14] I build here on Nicholas Watson's reading of Love in "Conceptions of the Word: The Mother Tongue and the Incarnation of God," in *NML* 1 (1997): 85–124.

[15] I am indebted to Copeland's discussion of Thorpe's representational strategies, in *Pedagogy, Intellectuals, and Dissent*, chap. 4, "William Thorpe and the Historical Record."

omies between Word and narrative, affect and theology, equally central to the textual programs of both sides in the Lollard controversy.

In what follows, I begin by establishing the basic principles and strategies of Thorpe's narrative theology through an analysis of the paradigmatic story of the sacring bell. I then turn for comparison to a brief consideration of the role of narrative in Lollard polemic. In conclusion I offer a more detailed analysis of Thorpe's intertwined theological and political projects as they emerge from the narrative logic of the *Testimony* as a whole.

William Thorpe's *Testimony* is clearly a highly crafted, if not largely fictional, account of whatever may have transpired between Thorpe and Arundel. To see this, we need only compare it to the Latin *Gesta* of Richard Wyche, the only other first-person Lollard account of persecution to survive.[16] Wyche's *Gesta* span several days' worth of examinations over a period of months, making no pretense to record everything said on any given occasion. Thorpe's *Testimony*, by contrast, is so tightly structured as to obey the classical unities of time and place, and it is replete with the kind of verbal and thematic patterning that rewards formalist literary analysis. Every time Wyche notes that there were "many more words, but that was the essence of this day,"[17] he throws into sharp relief the unity and coherence of Thorpe's narrative, its evident investment in its own formal structure.

Wyche's letter is addressed to a specific Lollard community of which he is a member, a community that includes laypeople (indeed entire families), is organized around books, and practices a careful secrecy.[18] Wyche writes in part to request that books be sent to him through an undercover intermediary. Thorpe writes "for þe edificacioun of al holy chirche," addressing himself to "alle men and wymmen" and hoping to both comfort his friends and convert his enemies (27). To accomplish this goal, rather than calling for books, Thorpe turns to exemplary narrative genres.

[16] F. D. Matthew, ed., "The Trial of Richard Wyche," *EHR* 5 (1890): 530–44

[17] . . . *et multa alia verba. Sed hic quodammodo efectus* [sic] *illius diei* (Matthew, "Trial," 533). I am indebted to Steven Justice's unpublished translation.

[18] The community is evoked in vivid detail in the final pages of the *Gesta* (ibid., 541–44), where we learn, for example, the name of a young woman to whom Wyche counsels chastity, as well as the method by which illicit books are transmitted between members.

Thorpe deploys narrative on two diegetic levels of the *Testimony*.[19] On each level, he adopts and transforms a popular exemplary genre generally foreign to Wycliffite prose. On the diegetic (or intradiegetic) level, which narrates the encounter between Thorpe and Arundel, the text reads as a kind of auto-hagiography, a "substitute" (as Hudson puts it) for the saints' lives of which the Lollards "generally thoroughly disapproved."[20] On the metadiegetic level, Thorpe characteristically responds to Arundel's doctrinal charges by telling stories, using narrative to recast the discussion in Wycliffite terms. These metadiegetic stories are reminiscent in turn of sermon exempla, the genre most thoroughly excoriated in Lollard polemic. Wyche, too, engages in evasive discursive maneuvers, but his are almost exclusively procedural, culminating in his ill-fated consent to swear an oath "limited in his heart."[21] By the end of his *Gesta*, Wyche is reduced to claiming—and to his sympathetic audience, not merely to his interrogators—that this oath was invalid because it referred to Richard Wyche *of the diocese of Worcester*, "and I am not that man, for I am not of that diocese."[22] Instead of searching for legal loopholes, Thorpe enacts theological principles through narrative. Stripping both exemplary genres—hagiography and exemplum—of the miraculous and fictional elements most offensive to Lollard sensibilities, he transforms them into vehicles of a Wycliffite vernacular theology grounded in the principle of exemplarity.

To this narrative theology, Thorpe juxtaposes the text-bound discourses of the institutional church. "Arundel" (as Thorpe represents him) attempts to structure his interrogation of "Thorpe" around five

---

[19] I use here the concept of diegetic levels as developed by Gérard Genette in *Narrative Discourse*, trans. Jane E. Lewin (Ithaca: Cornell University Press, 1983), 227–43. Most basically, *"any event a narrative recounts is at a diegetic level immediately higher than the level at which the narrative act producing this narrative is placed"* (italics in original, 228). The level that the "fictional author" or narrator shares with the reader is called extradiegetic; this would include, for example, Thorpe's direct address to the reader in the Prologue. Thorpe's encounter with Arundel takes place on the diegetic, or intradiegetic, level (Genette uses the terms interchangeably). The stories that Thorpe tells Arundel, in turn, are metadiegetic. Thorpe at least once embeds a further narrative level within the metadiegetic; I refer to this simply as a doubly embedded story.

[20] Hudson, ed., *Two Wycliffite Texts*, lvi.

[21] *. . . in corde {suo} limitatum* (Matthew, "Trial," 534). When that fails him, Wyche resorts to due process, arguing that "if anyone must appear before a judge, and appears, and no one is sitting in judgment or issuing a continuance, he is not bound without a new process" (*. . . haberet idem et locum et sibi compareat nullo iudicio sedente nec continuante, ipse non tenetur comparere sine novo processu*, ibid., 537).

[22] *et ego non sum talis, quia non sum illius diocesis, ergo etc.* (ibid., 541).

heretical tenets that Thorpe was supposed to have preached during a particular sermon at Shrewsbury. These tenets are recorded on a "rolle" or "certificat" to which Arundel frequently refers (42.618, 42.624, and passim). The first charge on the certificate accuses Thorpe of having preached, during the Shrewsbury sermon, that "þe sacrament of þe auter was materiel breed after þe consecracioun" (52.932–33). This was, of course, the classic litmus test for Lollardy: it was his denial of the doctrine of transubstantiation that triggered Wyclif's condemnation, and the nature of the consecrated elements continued to be a central item of contention throughout the controversy, with each side accusing the other of denying the true presence.[23] Wyche defines the Eucharist as the "true body of Christ in the form of bread"; dodges a direct question regarding whether bread remains after consecration (scripture does not call it "material bread"); and concludes provocatively that the whole people, following the doctrine of the Church, is outside the true faith.[24] Rather than engage in such polemical sparring, Thorpe tells a story about an event that transpired during the preaching of his Shrewsbury sermon, transforming the occasion of the certificate of charges into an occasion for narrative theologizing.

The story Thorpe tells is worth citing in full:

> And I seide "Ser, I tell ȝou truli, I touchide no þing þere of þe sacrament of þe auter, no but in þis wise as I wol wiþ Goddis grace schewe here to ȝou. As I stood þere in þe pulpitte, bisiinge me to teche þe heestis of God, oon knyllide a sacringe belle, and herfor myche peple turned awei fersli and wiþ greet noyse runnen frowardis me. And I, seynge þis, seide to hem þus 'Goode men, ȝou were better to stoonden here stille and to heere Goddis word! For, certis, þe vertu and þe mede of þe moost holi sacrament of þe auter stondiþ myche moore in þe bileue þereof þat ȝe owen to haue in ȝoure soulis þan it doiþ in þe outward siȝt þerof. And þerfore ȝou were better to stonde stille quyetefulli and to heeren Goddis worde, siþ þoruȝ heeringe þerof men comen to veri bileue.' And oþer wise, ser, I am certeyne I spak not þere of þe worschipful sacrament of þe auter."

(52.934–46)

---

[23] For a recent discussion of the role of eucharistic theology in the Lollard controversy, see Aers, *Sanctifying Signs*, esp. chap. 3, "John Wyclif: *De Eucharista (Tractatus Maior)*," and chap. 4, "Early Wycliffite Theology of the Sacrament of the Altar: Walter Brut and William Thorpe."

[24] *Credo quod illa hostia est verum corpus Christi in forma panis . . . Scriptura sacra, dixi, non vocat illam hostiam panem materialem, quapropter nolo idem credere ut articulum fidei* (Matthew, "Trial," 532).

Thorpe refuses point-blank to address the certificate charge on its own terms, never touching on the nature of the consecrated elements—an omission he highlights twice, once at the beginning of the passage ("I touchide no þing þere of þe sacrament of þe auter, no but in þis wise") and again and its close ("And oþer wise, ser, I am certeyne I spak not þere of þe worschipful sacrament of þe auter"). No arcane formulation involving accidents and subjects, Thorpe's eucharistic theology grows out of the day-to-day exigencies of preaching the gospel and recalling those led astray by those who should properly be their teachers. To do theology, the story of the sacring bell suggests, is not to assert or debate propositional claims but to shape experience through narrative.

The story of the sacring bell reconfigures traditional relationships between preaching, narrative, and theology. Set during a sermon, this is the most exemplum-like story Thorpe tells: like a traditional sermon exemplum, it contains a narrative element—Thorpe's audience abandons his sermon wholesale at the sound of the sacring bell—followed by a propositional statement of moral or doctrine: the value of the Eucharist lies in inward belief, grounded in the Word, and not in outward sight of the consecrated elements. However, this story is *about* a sermon (and one Thorpe actually preached) rather than forming *part of* a sermon. Addressing the Archbishop of Canterbury in a genre associated with theologically illiterate audiences, Thorpe associates his own text with sermon discourse (he is a preacher telling an exemplary story). At the same time, by framing preaching within narrative (rather than the other way around), Thorpe suggests that narrative is the best means of transmitting the Word.

Thorpe is careful to distinguish his exemplary narrative from the miraculous or fictional tales associated with preaching of the friars, sticking to real-life events drawn from his own experience. It is thus difficult to separate Thorpe himself from the story he tells as the object of exemplary reading—a point to which I shall return. At the same time, Thorpe's exemplum modifies and complicates the relationship between narrative element and moral statement, privileging the former as theological discourse. The only propositional moral statement Thorpe makes is articulated on the same diegetic level as the narrative element: it consists of Thorpe's admonishment of the Shrewsbury deserters in the narrative past, *within* the story he tells Arundel in the narrative present of the interrogation. Narrative element and moral statement thus occupy the same diegetic level. Together, they constitute a "higher-level" exemplary narrative whose moral might be articulated, in turn, as follows: the doctrine of transubstantiation and the cult of the Eucharist have overmystified the host and drawn the people away from the Word; the job of a true preacher is to call them back to the gospel. This is, in fact, the moral enacted by the narrated episode as a whole: the people listening to Thorpe's sermon are literally lured away from it by the sound of the sacring bell, becoming almost animal-like in the process (they "turned awei fersli and wiþ greet noyse runnen frowardis me"). However, this "higher-level" moral is never articulated propositionally in the text. Thorpe does not, in other words, offer Arundel or his readers a moralizing statement that stands outside the narrative framework of the story he tells. True theology consists for Thorpe in narratable, imitable actions, not in the kinds of doctrinal statements that can be adduced for or against a suspect in a heresy trial. Nor do we know if Thorpe was successful in recalling his Shrewsbury audience; his job as a preacher is ongoing, carried over into his interactions with Arundel and the writing and reading of his text. The entire episode thus collapses into one exemplary whole, not only narrator and tale, but preaching and narrative, narrative and theology.

The narrative of the *Testimony* as it unfolds on the diegetic level, at least during the section of the interrogation governed by the certificate of charges, typically moves from doctrinal accusation through storytelling to academic debate. Through this structure Thorpe interrogates and explores the relationship between doctrine, narrative, and theology. In this instance, having substituted an exemplary story for a propositional articulation of eucharistic doctrine, Thorpe goes on, somewhat paradoxically, to engage the archbishop in theological debate about the nature of the consecrated elements. The story of the sacring bell has reframed the discussion as theological rather than inquisitorial; what is at stake now is the nature of the Eucharist rather than Thorpe's conformity (or lack thereof) to official church doctrine. Thorpe's exemplary narrative has, moreover, made the choice of discursive mode a matter of theological import. Doctrinal statements made in response to a charge of heresy do not, for Thorpe, rise to the level of theology, and so he refuses to make them.

Thorpe's attitude toward academic theology is, as we might expect for a University man, more complicated. He rejects the "curious and so sotil sofestrie" of scholastic eucharistic theology (55.1033); but he himself provides the Latin originals (*accidentem sine subiecto*) and corrects the archbishop's English terminology ("soget" rather than "substance," 55.1029). Thorpe here engages one of the besetting paradoxes of vernacular Lollardy: a people of the book who dismiss the physical text of the gospel as mere "creature," the Lollards vernacularize academic discourses while denigrating "scole-matere" (55.1030). Deploying this paradox rhetorically, Thorpe manages at once to suggest that he is a better academic theologian than the Archbishop of Canterbury, and to dismiss such academic skills as empty at best, leading literally to error: overcurious clerks "waden and wandren so in hem fro argument into argument wiþ *pro* and *contra* to þe time þat þei witen not ofte where þei ben neiþer vndirstonden not clerli hemself" (55.1034–36). By the end of this episode in Thorpe's *Testimony*, the text-based discourses of the institutional church, whether inquisitorial or academic, have failed to transmit the truth of the Word. New ways of doing theology are needed, grounded in lived experience and imitable action. Exemplary narrative, extracted from its established role in the "textual struggle" of the Lollard controversy, provides Thorpe with a discursive vehicle for this theological project.

Thorpe's language of wandering clerics, used in the *Testimony* to condemn scholastic theology, echoes a prominent strain of Lollard polemic that condemns the preaching of glosses and fables as adulterations of the Word. Wycliffite preachers and polemicists were deeply suspicious of anything that might seem to come between the people and the scriptural text. Sermon exempla, strongly associated with the preaching of the friars, are often singled out as especially pernicious; narrative per se tends to suffer by association and rarely puts in an appearance in Lollard prose. According to the author of the *Lanterne of Liȝt*, a long polemical treatise roughly contemporary with Thorpe's *Testimony*, storytelling is one of the things that identifies a preacher as a member of the fiend's church:

Þei prechen cronyclis wiþ poysis and dremyngis & many oþir helplis talis þat riȝt nouȝt availen. Þei coulten falsehed to þe trouþe wiþ mich vngroundid mater, tarying þe peple from trewe beleue þat þey may not knowe it. And þise prechours waueren aboute in many fleischeli lustis.[25]

[25] Lillian N. Swinburn, ed., *The Lanterne of Liȝt*, EETS o.s. 151 (London: K. Paul, Trench, Trübner & Co., 1917), 55. For the dating of the text, see Swinburn's Introduction.

Like the genre of the exemplum itself, this passage tends to efface distinctions among different narrative genres, condemning them all as "vngroundid."[26] The reference to "poysis and dremyngis" evokes, and rejects, Macrobian recuperations of classical narratives and mythology;[27] true histories or "croniclys" are equally "helples." To introduce such ungrounded matter into a sermon, whose purpose is to transmit the gospel, is unnaturally to couple falsehood to truth. A preacher's narrative wanderings from the Word, moreover, both signal and enable other kinds of clerical wandering, a "waver[ing] aboute in many fleischeli lustis." Unnatural discursive coupling slides metonymically into unnatural sexual coupling, reinforcing an association between narrative and the flesh. Such slippages between textual and sexual fidelity are common to Lollard antifraternal polemic in particular. "Weddid to signes" rather than to the gospel, the friars preach flesh-bound "talis" and "fablis" that threaten to divorce the people from the Word.[28] Through a densely allusive rhetoric built around key terms and catchphrases, such passages taint narrative with gospel charges of materialism and hypocrisy.

As we saw above, the sense of narrative as an affective, flesh-bound mode that emerges from Wycliffite antifraternal polemic was shared by the Lollards' opponents, although they of course deployed such associations very differently. Using narrative to reinforce boundaries between clerical and lay interpretive communities, Mirk and Love are redeploying discursive dichotomies developed by the Lollards themselves.[29] The

[26] Much excellent recent work has taught us to appreciate the narrative dynamics of the exemplum; see, e.g., Larry Scanlon, *Narrative, Authority, and Power: The Medieval Exemplum and the Chaucerian Tradition* (Cambridge: Cambridge University Press, 1994); Elizabeth Allen, *False Fables and Exemplary Truth in Later Middle English Literature* (New York: Palgrave Macmillan, 2005); and Claire Walters, "Talking the Talk: Access to the Vernacular in Medieval Preaching," in Fiona Somerset and Nicholas Watson, eds., *The Vulgar Tongue: Medieval and Postmedieval Vernacularity* (University Park: Pennsylvania State University Press, 2003), 31–42.

[27] For a helpful overview of Macrobian hermeneutics as they developed in the twelfth century, see Peter Dronke, *Fabula: Explorations into the Uses of Myth in Medieval Platonism* (Leiden: E. J. Brill, 1974). For a more recent discussion of medieval academic definitions of *poetria* and their relevance to vernacular writers and readers, see Nicolette Zeeman, "The Schools Give a License to Poets," in Rita Copeland, ed., *Criticism and Dissent in the Middle Ages* (Cambridge: Cambridge University Press, 1996), 151–80.

[28] Examples of such rhetoric are numerous and a thorough exploration is beyond the scope of this essay; but see, for example, the tract published by Matthew as "De officio pastorali," in *The English Works of Wyclif, hitherto unprinted*, EETS o.s. 74 (London: Trübner, 1880), 405–57.

[29] A full study of the role of narrative in the Lollard controversy is of course beyond the scope of this essay; what I offer here is intended as a brief sketch of the territory, as it is relevant to Thorpe's project.

English Wycliffite Sermons (EWS), produced in the 1380s and 1390s in the heyday of organized vernacular Lollardy, are particularly invested in an opposition between narrative and the Word. Dedicated to scriptural translation and exposition, the EWS address the entire lection (rather than excerpting from it a theme-text), eschew the divisions and subdivisions of the University sermon, and rigorously avoid anything that looks like storytelling. In this they follow the structure of Wyclif's Latin *Sermones*, on which they are based. In the EWS, however, Wyclif's objection to *fabulae poetarum et philosophie* evolves into a suspicion of narrative per se, which is cast repeatedly in opposition to the Word. The EWS use Middle English "fable" and its cousin "tale" to cover a multitude of Latin sins, using them to translate a variety of keywords in the *Sermones*: *{verba} apocrifa, prophana,* and *venenosa; ludicria;* and a range of terms referring to pagan or secular literature (*tragediis siue comediis, gesta gentilium, fabulas poetarum, gesta seculi*).[30] "Fable" thus becomes the primary keyword for nonscriptural discourse in the EWS.

At the same time, the Wycliffite sermons (along with many Lollard prose tracts) narrow and shape the discursive fields of "fable" and other Middle English narrative terms, so as to reinforce a distinction between storytelling and scripture.[31] The semantic fields of late Middle English narrative terms—notably "tale," "fable," "stori," and "proces"—are

---

[30] I cite here Iohannis Wyclif, *Sermones,* ed. Iohann Loserth, 4 vols. (London: Trübner for the Wyclif Society, 1890; repr. New York: Johnson Reprint Corporation, 1966). Latin words and phrases used to decry nonscriptural discourse in the *Sermones* include *fabulas mundanas; fabulas et apocrypha; fabulas, mendacia, detracciones et verba similia venenosa; prophana fabula; fabulatur traditiones hominum; verba venenosa; verba falsa; mendacia, ludicria, prophana* (the previous three terms often travel together); *heresis et alia verba mendacii venenosa; detracciones; dyaboli confabulacio; iocacionem; minstralli {et} ioculatores; gesta gentilium; fabulas poetarum; tragediis et fabulas poetarum; gesta seculi apocrifica; adinvenciones adulterinas modernas; falsum semen et mendacia; ludicria; doctrinas et mandatas hominum* (vs. *Domini*); and *semen illusionis antichristi.* These are opposed to *evangelizacio* (most commonly), *verbum Dei* (also very common), *solam scripturam sacre; lex Christi; historiam* or *sentenciam evangelicam; formam Christi; Christi evangelium; and quamlibet paginam vite Christi.* The EWS speak most commonly of "Godis lawe" and "holy wryt," and also of the "lore of ensaumples" in the Old and New Testaments, as well as of "prech[ing] the gospel" or "Christis gospel [freeli wiþouten fablis]," and "preching of Goddis word." Opposed to these are, tellingly, "fablis and lesyngus and lawis of men"; "worldi wordis, fablis, and gabbyngis on God"; "fablis or flaterynge"; "fables and heresies"; "fables and her begginge"; fablis and newe reules"; [take þe gospel and leeve] fablis"; "worldli songis and talis of iapis"; "fablus and falshedus"; "talis biside holy wryt"; and matter "gilded wiþ fablis."

[31] There is no late Middle English term whose meanings (as reflected in the *MED*) overlap exactly with those of Modern English "narrative"; "narracioun" and "narratif" come closest, but both are late (first cited c. 1450) and relatively rare.

broad and complex, and by no means are confined to narrative discourse: they encompass not only storytelling but explanation, argument, even speech or language; they can refer to oral or written discourse, to the literal text or to its meaning, *sentence*, or purpose. In the EWS, however, "tale" and "fable" nearly always refer pejoratively to storytelling, while "stori" is reserved for the literal or historical sense of scripture. Through patterns of collocation and repetition, "tale" and "fable" are placed at the center of corrupt clerical discourses and institutions, associating narrative generally with "faleshedus" and "sclaundres,"[32] "dremes" and "gabbyngis,"[33] "rymes or oþer fals witt,"[34] "worldly songis and talis of iapis,"[35] "feynode wondris,"[36] "veyne storyes,"[37] and "gabbyngis on God."[38]

The desire to enforce a categorical opposition between narrative and Word reveals itself most tellingly in the English Wycliffite sermonizers' attempts to downplay, gloss over, or explain away the ubiquitous narrative elements of the gospels. Parables are defined simply as figural language, a "word of stori" (not even the whole "stori"!) "þat by þat

---

[32] "And þis o defauȝte þat men han in heryng, þat þei wolon gladly here fablus and falshedus, and sclaundres of þer neyȝeborus, al ȝif þei knowon hem false" (Gradon, ed., *English Wycliffite Sermons*, 2:120).

[33] Christ "bad hem þanne go and preche þe gospel frely to alle maner men. And wo be to hem þat letten þis for iurisdiccion or oþer cause!—as wo is to hem þat leeuen þis and prechen dremes, fablis and gabbyngis" (Hudson, ed., *English Wycliffite Sermons*, 3:229).

[34] Ibid., 318.

[35] "Preyer of lippis bigiliþ many, and specialy whanne lippis ben pollut; for siche preyours of prestis don harm many gatis . . . as worldly songis and talis of iapis" (ibid., 313).

[36] "And mo feynode wondris of dremys and of false talis herde neuere man sown þan freris tellon here" (Gradon, ed., *English Wycliffite Sermons*, 2:340; "Of Mynystris in þe Chirche").

[37] "Þe secownde maner of vndirstondyng is of hooly wryt, þat þei entren not to vndirstondyng þerof, ne þei suffren oþre men to vndurstonden hit wel. Somme prechen fables and somme veyne storyes, somme dockon hooly wryt and somme feynon lesyngus; and so lore of Godis lawe is al put obac. And þus þe laddur þat men schulden come to heuene by, oþur wantuþ rongus, or ellys hit is not rerut" (ibid., 366–67; "Vae Octuplex").

[38] "But þis swerd failiþ now in prechynge of Goddis lawe, for prelatis han scaberkis wiþoute swerdis, and oþere haue swerdis of leed, bi whiche þei tellen worldli wordis wiþ fablis and gabbyngis on God. And so no wondir ȝif þis swerd assayle not enemyes as it dide" (Hudson, ed., *English Wycliffite Sermons* 1:689). A similar pattern is at work in the English Wycliffite Bible's renderings of Latin narrative terms. Whereas *narratio, historia,* and *fictio* are rendered consistently as "telling," "stori," and "feynyng," respectively, *fabulae* is rendered variously as "fables," "iangelynges," and "(vnwise) talys" in passages that oppose *fabulae* to God's law.

hyudyth a spiritual witt."[39] Nonparabolic elements prove harder to accommodate, as the sermon for Easter Monday delightfully attests. The lection for the day relates two disciples' postresurrection encounter with Jesus on the road to Emmaus. Interestingly, it contains the only use in the Vulgate gospels of *fabula*, here in verbal form: *Et factum est, dum fabularentur, et secum quaererunt: et ipse Jesus appropinquans ibat cum illas* (Luke 24:15). The problem this posed to the early Wycliffites should by now be clear: How could the disciples' discussion of Jesus, in the gospels themselves, be described as "fables"? The Later Version of the Wycliffite Bible dodges the question by rendering *fabularentur* here, uniquely, as the neutral "while they talkiden."[40] Both Wyclif's Latin *Sermones* and the EWS, however, confront the problem head on, with mixed results.

The Latin sermon proceeds by a confusing mixture of condemnation, rationalization, and allegory. The disciples, it begins, "*in fide ambigui musitarunt, et ideo propter loquelam eorum instabilem dicitur quod ad invicem erant fabulati,*"[41] and we are reminded that Peter and Paul's blasphemy does not license ours. However, we are not to think that these disciples

---

[39] Hudson, ed., *English Wycliffite Sermons*, 1:222. In some surviving configurations, this sermon's definition of parables opens the cycle—as it does in Thomas Arnold's earlier edition of the cycle, *Select English Works of John Wyclif*, 2 vols. (Oxford: Clarendon Press, 1869–71).

[40] This seems to be the approach also taken by the Wycliffite sermons preserved in Oxford, Bodleian Library, MS Laud misc. 200, recently discussed by Wenzel (*Latin Sermon Collections*, 91–93) and identified as Lollard by Christina von Nolcken ("An Unremarked Group of Wycliffite Sermons in Latin," *MP* 83 (1986): 233–49, quoted in Wenzel, 91). Here the two disciples, identified as Luke and Cleophas, are allegorized as the body and the soul walking toward the faith of Christians.

For the English Wycliffite Bible, I cite from Conrad Lindberg's editions of key manuscripts of the Early and Later Versions (EV and LV, respectively): for EV, *MS. Bodley 959: Genesis-Baruch 3:20 in the Earlier Version of the Wycliffite Bible,* Stockholm Studies in English 6, 8, 10, 13, 20 (Stockholm: Almqvist and Wiksell, 1959–68), and *The Earlier Version of the Wycliffite Bible . . . Edited from MS Christ Church 145,* Stockholm Studies in English 29, 81, 87 (Stockholm: Almqvist & Wiksell, 1973–95); and for LV, *King Henry's Bible: MS Bodley 277, The Revised Version of the Wyclif Bible,* Stockholm Studies in English 89, 94, 98, 100 (Stockholm: Almqvist and Wiksell, 1999–2004).

[41] My emphasis; the sermon is found in Wyclif, *Sermones*, ed. Loserth, 4:66–74. The relevant passage runs as follows: *Isti autem duo discipuli in fide ambigui musitarunt, et ideo propter loquelam eorum instabilem dicitur quod ad invicem erant fabulati. Sed ex hoc non sequitur quod in sermonibus vel aliis communicacionibus fabulis est utendum, sicut non sequitur quid isti duo discipuli hic intedebant fabulis, sic non sequitur: si discipuli ut Petrus vel Paulus in Dominum blasphemebant, ergo licet nobis ad imitacionem eorum taliter blasphemare. Non autem docetur quod isti duo discipuli in fide ambigui in suis locucionibus peccaverunt quod videtur figurari per suum exitum a Jerusalem in Emaus, cum illi qui a contemplativa visione pacis (signata per Jerusalem) ad Emaus (quod interpretatur desiderium consilii) signans illos qui instabiliter desiderant secundum prudenciorum viam Domino militare. Illi (inquam) sunt instabiles in sermone non servantes istam Petri regulam si quis loquitur, quasi sermones Dei* (4:67).

sinned, for figuratively they were leaving the contemplative vision of peace (Jerusalem) and entering the desire for counsel (Emmaus). Nevertheless, they are *instabiles in sermones*, and so do not follow the rule of Peter, *si quis loquitur, quasi sermones Dei*. The reasoning in the EWS, which tend to avoid mystical readings, is even more strained. The English sermon begins by worrying that some will take this passage as license to tell tales: "foolis arguen comunely þat it is leueful to telle fablis, for þus diden þes two disciplis aftir þat Crist was risyn to lyf"; but even the apostles sinned, and in this instance the disciples "fabliden as þei schulden not do."[42] The English sermon, too, is reluctant to condemn the disciples' stories completely, perhaps because of their impeccable subject matter. In place of the Latin's figurative reading, the EWS sermonizer offers an unprecedented *distinctio*:

But summe men seyen þat fablyng is taken on two maners: first for speche of mannus dede þat is vnknowen to oþere men, þat summe graunten and summe denyen for vncerteynte of þe dede; or fable is to speke fablis ydily, as many don, and þis is algatis yuel.[43]

This *distinctio*—unique, I believe, in the cycle—weakens any absolute opposition between narrative and true speech, shifting condemnation from "fablis" themselves to the manner in which they are spoken ("ydily"). The EWS sermonizers, however, do not stop even here. In a further step away from their customary categorical opposition, they identify one of the disciples as Peter and excuse his "fabling" on the grounds that having denied Christ, he "hadde moost nede to be counfortid by talis of Christ."[44] I find no other instance of the phrase, "talis of Christ," in the EWS. Storytelling has gone, over the course of this remarkable passage, from a sign of the disciples' sinfulness to a remedy for it, with stories of Christ's life offering comfort to sinners in a manner that would not be foreign to readers of Nicholas Love. The EWS sermonizers, committed in principle to an untenable opposition between narrative and Word, have fallen down a slippery slope of their own creation.

Not all Lollard prose texts are as rigorously antinarrative as the EWS. But these early Wycliffite programs proved enormously influential, es-

---

[42] Hudson, ed., *English Wycliffite Sermons*, 3:190.
[43] Ibid.
[44] Ibid., 192.

tablishing expectations and associations that shaped the textual strategies of both sides in the controversy. When Lollard polemicists and
preachers do tell stories, they tend to do so briefly—Kendall describes
these miniature narratives as "embryonic . . . allegories" or "abortive
tropes"—and they are careful to avoid the specific genres favored by
anti-Lollard writers like Mirk and Love.[45] They characteristically turn
instead for their narrative models to the satiric alliterative verse of the
Piers Plowman tradition, which proved conducive to Lollard (and Lollard-
like) reformist polemic.[46] The "bodily ensaumples" periodically indulged
in by the "Lollard Sermons" edited under that title by Gloria Cigman,
for example, range from catalogues of brief similes to more extensive
narrative analogies drawn from life. Sermon 9 in this cycle develops its
exposition of the parable of the seed with a miniature personification
allegory, in which the rich man who hears the Word is distracted by "þe
Bisynessse of þis World," by "Couetise of Catel," and finally by "Muk":

comeþ his Muk into his muynde and marreþ hym amydde, and seiþ:
"Leef þi labour for a litil tyme,
and go redresse þat is mysrulid or þou maist rue foreuere,
and do þi deuer anoþer dai and double it þerfore."[47]

Like other "embryonic allegories" in these sermons, this passage betrays
its influences by falling into a recognizable pattern of alliterative long
lines.[48] The rest of the sermon develops an extended *Piers*-like analogy
between plowing a field and preparing to hear the Word. There is nothing here of the biting anticlerical satire of the *Piers* tradition and other
Wycliffite/reformist verse—the interest of this text is overwhelmingly
pastoral and moral—but the verse tradition seems to have provided the
sermonizer with an alternative to the miracle tales and saints' lives
pressed into anti-Lollard service by Mirk.

[45] Kendall, *The Drama of Dissent*, 38–41.
[46] See James Simpson, "Saving Satire After Arundel's *Constitutions*: John Audelay's
'Marcol and Solomon,'" in *Text and Controversy from Wyclif to Bale: Essays in Honour
of Anne Hudson*, ed. Helen Barr and Ann M. Hutchison (Turnhout: Brepols, 2005),
387–404.
[47] Gloria Cigman, ed., *Lollard Sermons*, EETS 294 (Oxford: Oxford University Press,
1989), 96–98, line breaks added.
[48] I am indebted for my analysis of these sermons' use of alliteration (and for the
insight that many passages can be broken down into alliterative long lines) to Shannon
Gayk's paper, "Preaching the *Libri laicorum*: Lollard Sermons and the Image Debates,"
presented at the Lollard Society's panel on "Lollard Genres" at the 40th International
Congress on Medieval Studies, Kalamazoo, May 2005.

Even more interesting, for our purposes, is a brief narrative sequence in the *Lanterne of Liȝt*, the early fifteenth-century treatise whose antifabular rhetoric I cited earlier. Despite its classic articulation of Lollard antinarrative bias in the passage cited above, the *Lanterne* does tell the occasional story. The penultimate section of the *Lanterne* takes the form of a treatise on the Ten Commandments, an established Lollard genre that tropes on the orthodox genre of the penitential manual.[49] Like sermons, penitential manuals were classic sites of exemplary narrative. Robert Mannyng of Brunne's *Handlyng Synne* (c. 1330), the preeminent Middle English exemplar of the genre, is no fonder of secular "poysis" than the *Lanterne*; but rather than jettisoning narrative completely (as do the EWS), Mannyng sets out to convert the popular taste for romances by telling religious stories in octosyllabic verse.[50] As Mark Miller has brilliantly shown, Mannyng uses narrative to enact the slipperiness and pervasiveness of individual sin, rendering it accessible to his readers' grasp.[51] In the *Lanterne of Liȝt*, institutional corruption is similarly ubiquitous, and similarly impossible to pin down propositionally. Shifting easily from one venue to another, cropping up everywhere the same but clothed in different circumstances, the fiend's church is everywhere apparent but deceptively difficult to grasp—at once "open" (as the Lollards would put it) and "feyned."

The Ten Commandments section of the *Lanterne* is dotted with several brief narrative scenarios, but the two most striking are the (impeccably scriptural) story of Susannah, told under the eighth commandment, and a longer quasi-allegorical story of a "fool" seeking divorce (drawing on the rhetoric of the *Piers* tradition) told under the ninth. Susannah was popular with the Lollards as a scriptural exemplar of virtue persecuted.[52] Thorpe invokes her early in the *Testimony*, laicizing and feminizing himself as an object of clerical persecution (35). In the *Lanterne,* her story, told at moderate length and without pretense of direct scriptural quotation (both very unusual in this text), is prefaced by that

---

[49] Anne Hudson, *The Premature Reformation* (Oxford: Oxford University Press, 1988, repr. 2002), 34–35, 167.

[50] See Robert Mannyng of Brunne, *Handlyng Synne*, ed. Idelle Sullens (Binghamton, N.Y.: Medieval and Renaissance Texts and Studies, 1983), esp. lines 43–52.

[51] Mark Miller, "Displaced Souls, Idle Talk, Spectacular Scenes: *Handlyng Synne* and the Perspective of Agency," *Speculum* 71 (1996): 606–32.

[52] See David Lyle Jeffrey, "False Witness and the Just Use of Evidence in the Wycliffite *Pistel of Swete Susan*," in *The Judgment of Susannah: Authority and Witness*, ed. Ellen Spolsky (Atlanta: Scholars, 1996), 57–71.

of Jezebel's letter bearing false witness against an innocent man called Naboth, leading to his death. Together these paired stories of scriptural women form a kind of occluded romance narrative, with Jezebel the evil witch who causes the death of an innocent knight, Susannah (a positive exemplum to her negative one) the innocent maiden falsely accused by corrupt priests, and Daniel the young hero who rises up against clerical corruption to save his people. The immediate target of this Wycliffite moralized romance (the poet of *Mum and the Sothsegger* might call it a "romans[e] . . . of misse-reule")[53] is legal corruption—the passage ends with an appeal to " ӡe jourours" not to accept bribes—but by moving from Jezebel to Susannah it implicates ecclesiastical corruption as well, linking the two.

The common element of this ubiquitous corruption is a turning away from the Word to the world; its common figure is divorce, the breaking of the sacramental bond that connects not only husband and wife but human and divine. Once again, as in the antifabular passage cited above, sexual and spiritual relationships are mapped onto each other. Here, however, their relationship finds expression in quasi-allegorical narrative. The ninth commandment, we recall, forbids the coveting of one's neighbor's wife. In the *Lanterne's* exposition, the devil's primary "cautel" against this commandment is "discorde in hertis of hem þat ben weddid": he attacks the marriage between the individual and God, enabled by the Word, by undermining the "accord" between the hearts of married people. This is illustrated by the story of a "fool" who, ignoring biblical teaching, bribes a series of civil and ecclesiastical officials in order to obtain a divorce, culminating in the judge "Syr Symound's" dissolution of the marriage. The divorce that leads both the fool and wife into "hoordam; fro þat day forward" (in a parody of the language of the marriage ceremony) is parallel to and enabled by the divorce simony effects between the institutional church and the Word.[54] Their ultimate result is the divorce of the will from the Word, and the individual soul from God.

In these two stories, narrative enables the *Lanterne* author to capture on the level of discourse the insidious nature of the fiend's infiltration into every aspect of institutional life, dissolving distinctions between different kinds of relationship and revealing the master narrative (so to

[53] Helen Barr, ed., *The Piers Plowman Tradition* (London: J. M. Dent; Rutland, Vt.: Charles E. Tuttle, 1993), 12.

[54] Swinburn, ed., *Lanterne*, 124.

speak) behind them. This is a Thorpe-like (as well as a Mannyng-like) move. But the *Lanterne*, as we have seen, retains the antifabular rhetoric of the EWS, and its brief foray into storytelling does not present a systematic challenge to the narrative/Word opposition developed by the EWS. Thorpe, I think, does present such a challenge. His text is at once more self-consciously narrative and more explicitly Wycliffite than either Cigman's sermons or the *Lanterne of Li3t* (a text whose Lollardy has recently come into question).[55] This combination suggests a deliberate effort on Thorpe's part to step outside the limiting discursive parameters of the Lollard controversy as a whole, exploring the potential of narrative for Lollard projects.

Narrative allows Thorpe to construct true theology as lived and imitable rather than propositional and debatable, read in people more productively than in texts. Emergent rather than propositional, Thorpe's theology develops rhetorically over the course of the *Testimony*'s diegesis. Following this development, I divide the analysis that follows into three sections: the first considers the segment of the interrogation that precedes the introduction of the certificate of charges; the second, Thorpe's responses to those charges (we have already seen the first of these, in the story of the sacring bell); and the third, the disintegration of the proceedings after the certificate's material has been exhausted. Thematically, the three sections I delineate here treat loosely of exemplary reading and the church (pre-certificate), exemplary narrative and the Word (certificate), and Lollard hagiography and/as sermon discourse (post-certificate). By the end of the text, Thorpe has created a new, flexible mode of Wycliffite vernacular theology, one associated with pulpit discourse and shaped by the dramatic agon of persecution, but not ultimately bound by the discursive constraints of either.

Thorpe's opening salvo is a narrativized Creed. Wresting control of the proceedings away from Arundel from the start, and delaying the introduction of the certificate of charges, Thorpe (as he represents it) persuades the archbishop to let him articulate his faith if he is to be condemned for it. Arundel unwisely agrees. The creedal statement Thorpe produces is the first metadiegetic narrative of the *Testimony*. The Christian Creeds become less propositional and more narrative when

[55] Nicholas Watson, "Vernacular Apocalyptic: On the *Lanterne of Li3t*," *Revista Canaria de Estudios Ingleses* 47 (2003): 115–27.

discussing the second person of the Trinity; to profess the Incarnation, the direct intervention of the divine in human history, is perforce to name names and recount events. Thorpe expands considerably upon the skeletal narrative framework of incarnation, passion, resurrection, and judgment provided by the official creeds, adding several events from the gospel stories of Christ's life. Such narrative expansion invites comparison with the popular devotional passion narratives appropriated by Nicholas Love for the anti-Lollard campaign. But whereas Love's *Mirror* draws overtly on nonbiblical material—including the "dyuerse ymaginaciouns" of the reader herself[56]—the events Thorpe adds to the creed are all scripturally grounded: circumcision, naming, baptism, temptation, preaching, and last supper (30–32). Thorpe's emphasis, furthermore, is on Christ's "myndefulnesse," patience, and "wilful" suffering, rather than on the details of that suffering itself, inviting not affective engagement on Love's model but rather an answering mindfulness, a desire to learn Christ's "heestes" and above all to imitate his virtue. Rather than a suffering body inspiring penitential devotion and obedience to the church, as in Love, Christ here is portrayed as an exemplary life.[57]

This Wycliffite version of *imitatio Christi* grounds Thorpe's model of true priesthood, which is likewise developed through narrative. With the gospel conceived of less as a text to be read than a model to be followed, priesthood becomes an exemplary function in turn, enacted and authorized by imitable actions. The second metadiegetic story Thorpe tells is autobiographical, recounting his own reluctant journey to the priesthood. Unmoved by the urgings of friends and family— which are motivated mostly by considerations of status—Thorpe is finally persuaded to take orders by the example of Wyclif himself. The texts and teachings of Thorpe's Wyclif gain authority from his gospel living; his "open" "accord" with the scriptures inspires others in turn to "conferme her lyuyng like hereto þis lore of Ioon Wyclif" (41.569). Bringing his life and teaching into accord with the gospel, Wyclif becomes, like Christ, an object of exemplary reading.

Reading in the *Testimony* is less a matter of interpretation or medita-

---

[56] Love, *Mirror*, 11.

[57] Cf. David Aers and Lynn Staley, *The Powers of the Holy: Religion, Politics, and Gender in Late Medieval English Culture* (University Park: Pennsylvania State University Press, 1996), 42–58.

tion (as in the two classic Latinate modes of biblical reading, hermeneutics and *lectio divina*) than of discernment and imitation. Its most productive objects are less often texts than people. In a paradigmatic moment during a debate on the question of images, Thorpe argues "holi lyuyng, and trewe and busy techynge of preestes" should be "sufficient bokis and kalenders to knowe God bi and his sentis" (58.1135–37). Rather than call for biblical translation, Thorpe emphasizes the role of priests as objects of (implicitly lay) reading. Thorpe here gestures toward the much-cited Gregorian maxim that images are the books of the laity. But in Thorpe's unusual formulation, books and images alike are subordinated to the living and teaching of priests. This is a departure from Lollard rhetoric on the topic of images. Lollard positions on imagery range from cautious acknowledgment that they may be worshiped "in sum manere, as signes or tokones . . . as clerkis don her bokis,"[58] a position more commonly found among highly educated Lollards like Thorpe himself, to outright iconoclasm, such as Hawisia Moone's assertion that "no worship ne reuerence oweth to be do to ony ymages . . . for alle suche ymages be but idols." Moone argues that "worship and reuerence shuld to be do to þe ymage of God, whiche is oonly man,"[59] echoing the famous moment in Margery Baxter's trial when she stretches out her arms asserting (in the trial records' translation) "hic est vera crux Cristi."[60] The more moderate position takes textual reading as a model for engaging with images; Moone's and Baxter's more radical position would replace human-made images with human beings made in the image of God. Like Baxter and Moone, Thorpe would replace images with people. But for Thorpe, people and their actions provide not an object of reverence but an object of reading. Priests themselves are for Thorpe the books of the laity.

This may seem an unusually clericalist position for a Lollard to take, especially for those who would cast the Lollards as "democratizers" on the grounds that their translation and literacy programs "enfranchise"

---

[58] "Sixteen Points on which the Bishops Accuse Lollards," in Anne Hudson, ed., *Selections from English Wycliffite Writings* (Cambridge: Cambridge University Press, 1978, repr. 1997), 23.

[59] "Confession of Hawisia Moone of Loddon, 1430," ibid., 36.

[60] *"Vide, et tunc extendebat brachia sua in longum, dicens isti iurate, 'hic est vera crux Christi, et estam crucem tu debes et potes videre et adorare omni die hic in domo tua propria,"* Norman P. Tanner, ed., *Heresy Trials in the Diocese of Norwich, 1428–31,* Camden Fourth Series, no. 20 (London: Royal Historical Society, 1977), 44.

the laity both hermeneutically and politically.[61] But for Thorpe and many of his fellow Wycliffites, true enfranchisement of the laity is a matter of access not merely to the material text of the gospel, but, crucially, to the immaterial truth that text transmits. This is not to discount the importance of Wycliffite efforts to render the text of the Bible directly legible to vernacular readers—indeed, as I have suggested, these projects had a significant impact on the textual and religious cultures of late Middle English. Rather, I seek to emphasize that such projects were for their Lollard authors means to a less purely text-bound end—an end that Thorpe approaches from a different, "supra-textual" angle.[62] For Thorpe, textuality itself has become tainted (as for the EWS sermonizers narrative was tainted) with the corruption endemic to the institutional church. His turn to exemplary models of reading is meant to redress that corruption by refocusing attention on immaterial truths. Thorpe rejects the need for "bischopis letters" or preaching licenses, for example, on the grounds that Christ himself "wol be oure sufficient witnesse, if we be ensaumple of his holy lyuynge and techynge speciali bisien vs feiþfulli to do oure office iustli." Furthermore, "þe peple to whom we prechen, be þei feiþful eiþer vnfeiþful, schulde be oure lettris þat is oure witnesse-berers; for truþe whanne it is sowen may not be vnwitnessed" (47.772–76). Texts are here reduced to the instruments by which corrupt bishops strive to curtail the free preaching of the Word. It is people who are the true objects of salvific reading, which takes place here between the individual priest and those he teaches, and ultimately in the eschaton, where the saved and the

---

[61] Ralph Hanna uses the term "democratizing" to describe the Lollards' translation projects in " 'Vae Octuplex,' Lollard Socio-Textual Ideology, and Ricardian-Lancastrian Prose Translation," in *Criticism and Dissent in the Middle Ages*, ed. Rita Copeland (Cambridge: Cambridge University Press, 1996), 244–63. For Copeland, to offer laypeople the text of the Bible, while locating its fullest meaning in the literal sense, was (she contends) to enfranchise them as political and hermeneutic subjects (*Pedagogy, Intellectuals, and Dissent,* 53, 140). Other critics have begun to emphasize the "conservative" or "fundamentalist" impulses of the movement; see, e.g., Kerby-Fulton, *Censorship*, 209, 391. For an astute critique of this framework of analysis itself, see Katherine Zieman, *Singing the New Song: Literacy and Liturgy in Late Medieval England* (Philadelphia: University of Pennsylvania Press, 2008), chap. 4, "Extragrammatical Literacies: The Latinity of the Laity," esp. 119–20.

[62] The apt phrase is Kantik Ghosh's; see *The Wycliffite Heresy: Authority and the Interpretation of Texts* (Cambridge: Cambridge University Press, 2002), chap. 1, "John Wyclif and the Truth of Sacred Scripture." Ghosh identifies a tension in Wyclif's own exegetical theory and practice between a sciential model of reading grounded in academic exegesis and a sapiential model grounded in a combination of readerly virtue and divine grace— approaches that treat the Bible as, respectively, "text" and "supra-text."

damned among his audiences bear the preacher ultimate witness. It is in these immaterial spaces that Thorpe's true church, the *congregatio predestinatorum*, emerges.

Thorpe's model of exemplarity does, however, raise a crucial hermeneutic question: In a fallen world/material church rife with hypocrisy and misrepresentation, how is the reader to know whom to take as a positive exemplar and whom as a negative one? Thorpe seems to taunt Arundel, and the reader, with this question early in the *Testimony*. When the archbishop demands that Thorpe submit unequivocally to the authority of the Church, Thorpe, in keeping with his Wycliffite understanding of the true church as the congregation of the elect, counters that "I wole submitte me oonli to the rule and the gouernaunce of hem aftir my knowynge whom, bi þe hauynge and vsynge of þe foreseide vertues, *I perceuyve* to ben membris of holi chirche" (33.296–99; my emphasis). Shortly thereafter, adding insult to injury, Thorpe confidently excludes Arundel from their number. When Arundel threatens to have Thorpe burned at the stake ("bi seint Tomas þou schalt be schauen and sue þi fellow into Smeþefelde!" [36.408–09]), Thorpe is *"moued* in alle my wittis for to holde þe Archebischop neiþer prelat ne preest of God" (36.421–22; my emphasis). How, exactly, does he know? What hermeneutic principle—what precise combination of active "perception" and passive mental "movement"—guides Thorpe's reading of people outside the privileged realm of the gospel?

Thorpe takes this question seriously enough that he uses it to frame the diegetic level of narration, taking recanted heretics as a test case. Arundel and his clerks raise the issue of recanted heretics twice, once at the beginning of the interrogation (42) and again at its close (89–90). If Thorpe recognized Repingdon's exemplary authority when he was a Lollard, they ask, why not follow his example now and recant with him? The hermeneutic Thorpe articulates in response is unabashedly preemptive, involving a kind of quasi-Augustinian punt. If Repingdon et al. "hadden forsaken beneficies of temperel profit and worldly worschip," and "hadden taken hem to symple lyuynge and wilful pouerte," then they would have continued to serve as positive exemplars. But since they have "schamefulli and sclaundrousli done contrarie," they must be completely forsaken (89.2106–10). By seeking worldly advancement in the institutional church, these men have rendered themselves legible as negative exemplars.

This kind of "hermeneutic confidence" (as David Aers terms it) gets

Thorpe into trouble, both with his interrogators and with his modern critics. Aers identifies it as one of the "problems of Thorpe's theology that have escaped his attention": Thorpe claims the ability to determine who is authoritative, but agrees that he cannot know who is predestined.[63] "Arundel" raises this version of the question, too: challenging Thorpe's contention that tithes should be withheld from an openly sinful priest, he asks, "woldist þou herefore deme þis prest dampnable? And I seie to þee þat in þe turning aboute of an honde such a synner mai be very repentaunt" (76.1603–4). True, Thorpe acknowledges; but because priests "schulde be ensaumple to alle oþer, for to hate and flee synne," the open sin of a priest is indeed "dampnable," and he should only be deemed "verrili repentaunt" if that repentance is equally open and legible to all (73.1610–12). Because it is his particular job to be exemplary—because he will be read as an exemplar—what matters in a priest is neither his secret interiority nor his place in the eschaton, but his legible actions. Paradoxically, a priest's vocational status as an object of exemplary reading in this life can make his ultimate fate easier to read, because it is a damnable sin for a priest to be an exemplar of mortal sin. To be a priest—and, by extension, to be a Christian (for without asserting the priesthood of all believers Thorpe does seem to locate clerical and lay status along a continuum)—is to become, as it were, fully exteriorized as an object of reading, to have your relevant "text" be entirely the literal sense of your words and actions.[64]

Thorpe thus develops a literalism that governs the reading not of the biblical text but of the lives of priests. His scriptural hermeneutics, in turn, leans heavily toward the sapiential end of the spectrum.[65] From the earliest moments in the interrogation, Thorpe refuses repeatedly to swear an oath of obedience on a gospel book on the grounds that "a book is no þing ellis, no but a þing compilid togidere of diuerse creat-

---

[63] Aers, *Sanctifying Signs*, 93.

[64] My goal here is not to defend the viability of Thorpe's theology. Rather, I am interested in his negotiation of Wycliffite theology and its paradoxes through the discursive medium of narrative. This distinguishes my approach somewhat from that of Aers, who judges Thorpe and his master against the standards of Augustine's theology of sin and grace and finds them wanting; see Aers's critique of Thorpe's "Pelagianizing confidence in the will, wit, and judgment of the Wycliffite Christian," in "The *Testimony* of William Thorpe: Reflections on Self, Sin, and Salvation," in *Studies in Late Medieval and Early Renaissance Texts in Honour of John Scattergood: "The key of all good remembrance,"* ed. Anne Marie d'Arcy and Alan J. Fletcher (Portland, Ore.: Four Courts Press, 2005), 21–34.

[65] See note 62 above.

uris, and so to swere bi a book is to swere bi dyuerse craturis; and to swere bi ony creature boþe Goddis lawe and mannes lawe is þeraȝen" (34.336–39). Thorpe's insistent distinction between the physical text of scripture and the immaterial Word it transmits derives from Wyclif's distinctive brand of literalism, which locates the literal sense of the scripture not (somewhat paradoxically) in the *littera* on the page but in the mind of God. The Word, like the church, is for Thorpe fundamentally immaterial; its meaning, like the meaning of recanted heretics, is made accessible not through hermeneutic prowess but rather through gospel imitation and exemplification.

The interrogation proper, which is governed by the certificate of charges, takes up a range of sacramental and theological questions common to heresy trial records of the period. These issues—the Eucharist, images, pilgrimages, tithes, and oaths—are by the narrative logic of the *Testimony* at once subordinated to, and predicated upon, Thorpe's intertwined models of true church and right reading, as they are established in the text's opening sequences. This second segment of the *Testimony*, which opens with the episode of the sacring bell, culminates in a lengthy treatment of the question of book-oaths: the representation of the interrogation thus moves from narrative theology to scriptural hermeneutics, and from the nature of the Eucharist to the nature of the Word. In response to the final charge on the certificate, which accuses Thorpe of having preached that " 'it is not leueful to swere in ony case' " (74.1629–31), Thorpe continues to counterpose his own storytelling to the archbishop's texts. In the process, he represents true theology as emerging outside, and increasingly in opposition to, the structures and processes of the institutional church.

Thorpe begins, again, with a story. In this case, however, he is not its protagonist: he recounts instead a conversation he overheard in a gentleman's house, between two clerks, a lawyer, and a master of divinity. This story retains the framework of first-person narration while relocating theological debate to the house of a layman. The conclusion of this debate echoes Thorpe's earlier language: "euery book is noþing ellis, no but dyuerse creaturis of whiche it is made" (76.1684–85; cf. 34.336–39). Used to excuse Thorpe's refusal to swear an oath of obedience to Arundel, this claim had functioned on the diegetic level of the *Testimony* as an evasive maneuver not unlike those deployed by Wyche. Reframed through Thorpe's metadiegetic narrative, it is "not myn opynyoun, but þe opynyoun of oure sauyoure and of seynt Iame and Crissostom and of oþere dyuerse seyntis and doctouris" (76.1694–96). From extramural theological debate between clerics and educated laymen, retold as narrative in the face of persecution, emerges the authentic doctrine of the true church.

In the face of Thorpe's dazzling theological performance, Arundel has recourse to a text. Picking up on Thorpe's reference to Chrysostom, Arundel triumphantly produces a "rolle" containing a homily of Chrysostom, and demands that Thorpe expound it. This physical text, like Thorpe's objection to book-oaths, has a history on the diegetic level of the *Testimony*. It was, Arundel tells Thorpe, confiscated from a Lollard colleague of Thorpe's at Canterbury—along with Thorpe's own Psalter, which Arundel had referred to earlier in the *Testimony*:

"And herfore, losel, it is þat þou coueitist to haue aʒen þe Sauter þat I made to be taken fro þee at Cauntirbirie, forþi þat þou woldist gadere out þereof and recorde scharpe verses aʒens vs. But þou schalt neuere haue þat Sauter *neiþir ony oþer book*, til þat I wite þat þin hert and þi mouþ acorden fulli to be gouerned bi holi chirche."

(51.891–95, my emphasis)

By rendering Thorpe bookless, Arundel had hoped to cripple him theologically, restoring him to dependence on the institutional church. Thorpe's theology, however, does not depend on the kind of reading Arundel has in mind. Even when he had access to the text of Chrysostom's homily, he "hadde not bisyed me to stodie aboute þe witt þeroff" (76.1706–7). What saves him in the face of persecution is not textual facility of the sort Arundel demands, but rather a turn to gospel *imitatio*. "But, liftynge vp my mynde to God, I preied him of grace," Thorpe narrates; "And anoon I þouʒte how Crist seide to his disciplis 'Whanne for my name ʒe schulen be brouʒt before iugis, I schal ʒeue to ʒou mouþ and wisedom, þat alle ʒoure aduersaries schulen not aʒenseie" (76.1707.11). Taking the gospel as exemplar and invoking divine assistance, Thorpe produces an interpretation of the archbishop's text that supports not only Thorpe's own relatively limited objection to book-oaths, but the broader objections to swearing per se articulated in the certificate of charges.[66] In an extremely rare moment—Thorpe's Arun-

---

[66] "'For it is yuel don and gret synne for to swere truþe, whan in ony manere a man may excuse him wiþouten ooþ" (77.1729–30); cf. the certificate charge, "'Lo, it is here certefied aʒens þee þat þou prechedist at Schrouesbirie openly þat it is not leueful to swere in ony case'" (74.1629–31).

del is often bested in debate but rarely admits to being wrong—"þe Archebischop seide to me þat Crissostom myȝte be þus vndirstonde" (77.1731–32). Sapiential reading grounded in gospel exemplarity here scores its clearest rhetorical victory over sciential reading grounded in the academic exposition of texts. This victory opens the door to a return to textuality in the form of the writing of the *Testimony* itself—a point to which I shall return.

Thorpe has so far in response to the fifth certificate charge provided two narrative representations of the production of true theological knowledge outside or against the institutional church: dialogue in lay contexts (the metadiegetic story of the debate in the gentleman's house) and *spiritus intellectus* in the face of persecution (the story of the homily of Chrysostom, on the diegetic level). Only now, as if condescending to their level, is he willing to engage the archbishop and his clerks in academic debate. Having developed his ecclesiology, hermeneutics, and sacramental theology through narrative, locating all three outside the institutional and textual structures of Arundel's church, Thorpe now draws on the full resources of his University training, performing his own theological virtuosity to an unprecedented degree. Whereas in the earlier eucharistic debate Thorpe had ridiculed the academic terminology of *accidentum* and *subiectum*, here his own use of technical terms (e.g., "equypolent," "vnperfit speche") and citation of patristic authorities (e.g., Jerome's distinction between the "roote of resoun" and the "marwȝ of sentence") leave his clerical opponents befuddled and suspicious: "'Þou woldist make us alle madden wiþ þee! Seyn we not þat the gospels of Crist ben writen in þe masse book?'" one expostulates, while another calls Thorpe's intricate arguments "ful derk mater and vnsauery" (79.1785–86, 1804). Previously, on the topic of the eucharistic elements, Thorpe's target was over-"curious" scholastic discourse; here his point would seem to be that with the power to craft and enforce doctrine concentrated in the hands of a self-serving ecclesiastical hierarchy, the true academic theology of the ancient church, whether enacted through narrative or articulated by the church fathers or couched in the subtlest of scholastic terms, is rejected as madness and sorcery. Arundel's church has lost sight of the fundamental immateriality of the gospel; in so doing, it has become a purely material church, incapable even of comprehending apostolic and patristic theology. The true church remains, but its members are forced to operate increasingly outside Arundel's institution, and so are ultimately persecuted by it.

Appropriately, then, the final metadiegetic story Thorpe tells is set in prison, foreshadowing his incarceration at the end of the interrogation.[67] With the certificate of charges exhausted, the topic turns to confession, another contentious issue in the Lollard controversy, and the topic (apart from the Eucharist) mostly like to appear in orthodox sermons of the period.[68] In the *Testimony*, the topic emerges narratively, from the revelation of a betrayal. A man who had come to Thorpe in prison, ostensibly seeking his guidance regarding shrift, is revealed to have been "a man of my lordis" reporting back to Arundel. Thorpe is moved by "þis treeson" to recount the conversation at length (80–84). In this moment, the diegetic and metadiegetic levels of the *Testimony* come closest to collapsing into each other, as a narrative element on the diegetic level (Thorpe learns he has been betrayed) provides the impetus for its own metadiegetic framing (Thorpe's account of the conversation he had with the man in prison). The story Thorpe tells, moreover, is the longest and most involved of the *Testimony*, containing within it the doubly embedded story of a sermon preached at Canterbury—the site, we recall, of the confiscation of Thorpe's Psalter and his colleague's homily—by a monk of Feversham called Meredoun (83). No longer constrained by the textual framework of the certificate of charges, Thorpe's narrative strategies become more complex, and they ultimately lead him back through prison to the pulpit.

Thorpe's discourse on confession in this final prison narrative is itself akin to confessional discourse: an invention of truth—in the Latin rhetorical sense of *inventio*, at once a discovery and a creation—through self-narration. It thus constitutes yet another appropriation on Thorpe's part of a narrative genre viewed with suspicion by most Wycliffite polemicists. Promising to recount his prison conversation with the archbishop's spy exactly as it occurred, Thorpe begins by acknowledging his refusal to "assoil" the man on the (standard Wycliffite) grounds that only God can forgive sins (81–82). When the man objects that surely

---

[67] Earlier, when confronted with the fourth certificate charge regarding tithes, Thorpe had recounted another prison visit (66–69), though without the framework of betrayal. The sections of the *Testimony* devoted to the second and third charges, on images and pilgrimage, do not contain narrative material: Thorpe's argument about images is grounded in his claim (cited above) that *priests* should be a "kalendar to lewde men" (56.1073–74); in response to the charge on pilgrimage, Thorpe produces a Wycliffite version of Pecham's syllabus material with hagiographical overtones (62–63), describing the virtuous abstinence of "Crist and his sueris bi ensaumple" (62.1267).

[68] Wenzel, *Latin Sermon Collections*, 377–92.

the "lewid" have need to confess formally to priests (83.1915), Thorpe sweeps away two centuries of anxious post-Lateran penitential diagnostics with a single derisory sentence:

"But, certis, þat man or womman is ouer-lewid and to beestly which cunne not brynge her owne synnes into her mynde, bisiynge hem nyȝt and dai for to haten and forsaken alle her synnes, doyng aseeþ for hem aftir her cunnyng and her power."

(83.1922–25)

The sinning and penitent self is not the recalcitrant object of constant hermeneutic vigilance. Sin does not, as Robert Mannyng would have it, require perpetual "handlyng." Like the priestly self, the penitent self is legible in all the ways that really matter for living in accordance with the gospel. Assertions to the contrary are, like the worst scholastic theology, mere clerical obfuscation.

Thorpe's account of his prison conversation redefines the nature and purpose of confessional narrative. Asserting the legibility of the self, it shifts the purpose of autobiographical narration from self-discovery in the context of oral confession to self-assertion in the face of persecution. Rather than subjecting the self to institutional scrutiny and correction, self-narration as deployed by Thorpe in the *Testimony* subjects the institutional church to damning scrutiny, confronting it with gospel truth.

In the doubly embedded story of Meredoun's sermon, which is offered in support of Thorpe's position on shrift, Thorpe returns to preaching as the site of theological production. Like the story of the book-oath debate, this story cites the words of another in the context of a narrative flashback. Here, however, the scene has shifted from gentlemen's houses and prison cells to the pulpit, the origin both of the certificate of charges and of Thorpe's narrative theology in the story of the sacring bell. This final, double-embedded story of the monk's sermon echoes and supplants Arundel's inquisitional use of the Shrewsbury sermon preached by Thorpe. Preaching thus becomes the site of a discursive contest between Arundel and Thorpe over the nature of true theology. Developing this representation of preaching as battleground, one of Arundel's clerks condemns Thorpe for his role in a famous preaching contest: Thomas Alkerton had preached a sermon at Paul's Cross rebutting a Lollard sermon preached at Oxford; Thorpe had publicly reproved Alkerton's orthodox sermon.[69] This, we might say, is preaching as agon: a discursive contest out of which true theology can emerge.[70] That contest is replicated, moreover, in the argument that ensues between Arundel and Thorpe on the diegetic level of the *Testimony:* troping on Thorpe's Wycliffite language of openness, Arundel condemns the Oxford preacher and his sermon as "fals," which "he schewiþ opinly siþ he dare not stonde forþ and defende his preaching þat he prechid þan þere" (85.1978–80). Thorpe counters that the Lollard clerk's sermon—like the *Testimony* itself—"is *writun boþe in Latyn and Engelische,* and many men haue it and þei setten greet priys þerbi" (85.1984–85; my emphasis). Preaching-as-agon thus provides Thorpe with a model for the proper use of textuality: to assert and transmit the truth of a sermon. The written record of the Lollard clerk's sermon stands as an exemplum for Thorpe's textual project, which transforms persecution into exemplary theology and self-narration into Wycliffite discourse.

For Arundel and his clerks, things deteriorate from here. When Thorpe turns the tables on his interrogators and begins to catechize the archbishop (see, for example, 66–67), Arundel is rendered inarticulate by anger: "smytyng wiþ his fist fersli vpon a copbord," he storms off to the window and leaves his clerks to play good-cop/bad-cop with the victorious Thorpe (88.2070–71). As Thorpe takes discursive control of the proceedings, Arundel descends precipitously into a debilitating excess of affect—the very faculty that, according to Nicholas Love, defines the laity, rendering them incapable of digesting the "sadde mete of grete clargye & of hye contemplacioun."[71] The remainder of Arundel's discourse consists of personal threats, heightening the atmosphere of persecution and raising the specter of martyrdom.[72] In the most telling moment of this interchange, Arundel rages, "'I schal make þee as sikir as ony þeef þat is in Kent!'" (88.2073–74). I suspect the archbishop intends to allude darkly here to the Rising of 1381 (strongly associated with Kent), the event that precipitated the association in orthodox cir-

---

[69] Jurkowski, "Arrest," gives an overview of these events.

[70] Persecution is for many Lollards the quasi-sacramental generator of true discourse, the dramatic agon in which Lollard truths are represented as coming to light (Kendall, *Drama of Dissent,* 42, 59–60, 75, and passim).

[71] Love, *Mirror,* 10.

[72] "'I schal assaie if I can make þee þere as sorewful as it was told to me þat þou were glad of my laste goynge out of Yngelond'" (91.2169–71); "'Bi God, I schal sette vpon þi schynes a peire of pillers þat þou schalt be gladde to chaunge þy vois!'" (91.2191–92).

cles between Lollardy and sedition. Without intending to, however, Arundel also evokes the image of the good thief crucified with Christ, contributing to Thorpe's self-representation as a Christian martyr. Thus "rebukid and scorned and manassid on ech side" (92.2224), Thorpe, like Christ before Pilate, remains silent until he is returned to prison. This final sequence completes Thorpe's categorical reconfiguration of the discursive dichotomies of the Lollard controversy. Arundel, hampered by his knee-jerk reliance on the texts and doctrines of the institutional church, is reduced to pure affect, incapable of anything but the crudest tool of inquisitional discourse, the threat. Thorpe, in turn, has succeeded in creating a Wycliffite version of hagiography in which true theology emerges narratively out of the agon of interrogation.

In the *Testimony of William Thorpe*, we can see a member of Wyclif's original Oxford cohort responding creatively to the new constraints of the Lancastrian anti-Lollard campaign. Thorpe almost certainly knew the producers of the English Wycliffite Sermon cycle; he may very well have participated himself in early Lollard textual programs. Thorpe's *Testimony* does not participate directly in the discursive competition embodied most fully in the English Wycliffite Sermons and Mirk's *Festial*, a "textual struggle" in which the form of a sermon announces and enacts its polemical agenda. But he does engage that struggle at, so to speak, one representational remove. The interrogation itself is, in part, a discursive contest over the significance of Thorpe's Shrewsbury sermon, which is for Arundel the source of the certificate of charges and for Thorpe a resource for narrative theologizing, particularly in the story of the sacring bell. With the certificate of charges exhausted, preaching becomes increasingly the subject of Thorpe's narration, on both the intradiegetic and the diegetic levels (Meredoun's sermon; Thorpe's argument with Arundel and his clerks about the preaching contest between the Oxford Lollard and Alkerton). It is through this developing representation of preaching-as-agon that Thorpe represents the development of his own Wycliffite theology, grounded in gospel imitation and lived experience, shaped as narrative, and finally preserved and communicated in textual form in the *Testimony* itself.

Whereas many Lollards developed strategies to evade persecution—we might think here also of such texts as the "Sixteen Points on Which Bishops Accuse Lollards"—Thorpe, at least in the *Testimony*, embraced its theological (and polemical) potential.[73] Persecution becomes for Thorpe a site for rethinking the nature of true theological discourse. In prison at the end of the text, Thorpe images the interrogation he has just undergone as a discursive crucifixion: "as a tree leyde vpon anoþer tree ouerthwert on crosse wyse, so weren þe Archebischop and his þree clerkis alwei contrarie to me and I to hem" (93.2245–47).[74] This image, the culmination of Thorpe's Wycliffite hagiography, casts the persecuted Lollard priest in the role of the persecuted and crucified Christ, overlaying the narrative of Christ's life on Thorpe's own. We might turn again for comparison to the *Gesta* of Richard Wyche. After noting its protagonist's mundane personal suffering (constipation, hemorrhoids) in prison, Wyche's letter closes with the expectation of physical martyrdom ("Some say that they will make a solemn day").[75] Thorpe's martyrdom, like his *imitatio Christi*, is not physical—despite the very real threat of the fires of Smithfield that hangs ominously over the text—but rather discursive; it consists not of bodily suffering but (as Rita Copeland has noted) of intellectual labor.[76] Thorpe's closing image, moreover, figures him not only as persecuted martyr but also as an equal participant in a discursive contest, with each side likened to one of the trees that make up the cross. True theology emerges from this discursive agon.

Thorpe's *Testimony* has interested me here both as a rearticulation of Wycliffite theology in the face of persecution and as a creative evasion of the competing textual programs that had come to define the Lollard controversy. Both sides in the controversy proper, especially as it came to be articulated at key moments such as the development of competing sermon cycles in the 1380s and 1390s and the promulgation of the 1409 *Constitutions*, worked to promote monolithic modes of vernacular biblical discourse, foreclosing on the proliferation of textual modes and readerly strategies in English. The *Testimony* seems to me wary of such totalizing discursive programs. Thorpe's narrative theology finds its closest analogue not in the *Gesta* of Richard Wyche but in the *Book* of

---

[73] Hudson, *Selections from English Wycliffite Writings*, 19–24.

[74] Lollard and Lollard-associated texts image the crucifix in a variety of creative ways; see Margaret Aston, "Lollards and the Cross," in *Lollards and Their Influence in Late Medieval England*, ed. Fiona Somerset, Jill C. Havens, and Derrick G. Pitard (Woodbridge: Boydell, 2003), 99–113. This is, however, the only instance I know of a Lollard discursive crucifixion.

[75] *Aliqui dicunt quod facient diem sollempnem. Amen et cetera.* (Matthew, "Trial," 544).

[76] See Copeland, *Pedagogy, Intellectuals, and Dissent*, chap. 7.

Margery Kempe (though I doubt Thorpe himself would appreciate the comparison). Just as Lynn Staley has taught us to distinguish Margery the character from Kempe the author,[77] so Thorpe's *Testimony* asks us to consider the double agency of Thorpe as author and character, recognizing the theological significance of his discursive choices on both diegetic levels. Both Margery's *Book* and Thorpe's *Testimony*, moreover, expose and reject the limiting polarities that had come to define the "textual struggle" of the Lollard controversy. Kempe, like Thorpe, strategically represents her own persecution in order to foreground the failed logic of the anti-Lollard campaign.[78] Thorpe, like Kempe, represents the transformation of his own lived experiences into theological discourse through the discursive medium of narrative. Both suggest that far from "sealing . . . up . . . the canon" of Middle English religious writing,[79] the Lollard controversy—despite the best efforts of its most influential participants—created the opportunity, even the necessity, for discursive creativity in the development of vernacular theologies.

---

[77] Lynn Staley, *Margery Kempe's Dissenting Fictions* (University Park: Pennsylvania State University Press, 1994).

[78] See Elizabeth Schirmer, "Orthodoxy, Textuality, and the 'Tretys' of Margery Kempe," *Journal x* 1 (Fall 1996): 31–56.

[79] Watson, "Censorship and Cultural Change in Late-Medieval England," 835.

REVIEWS

STEPHEN A. BARNEY. *The Penn Commentary on "Piers Plowman. Vol. 5: C Passus 20–22; B Passus 18–20*. Philadelphia: University of Pennsylvania Press, 2006. Pp. xvi, 309. $65.00.

ANDREW GALLOWAY. *The Penn Commentary on "Piers Plowman." Vol. 1: C Prologue–Passus 4; B Prologue–Passus 4; A Prologue–Passus 4*. Philadelphia: University of Pennsylvania Press, 2006. Pp. xiv, 491. $95.00.

The foundations for these first two volumes of the *Penn Commentary on "Piers Plowman"* were laid over the last three decades: the Athlone editions (including Joseph Wittig's *Concordance*), the annotated editions of Derek Pearsall and A. V. C. Schmidt, and John Alford's heroic efforts to identify the poem's quotations and legal vocabulary. And looking back over this recent history, the *Penn Commentary* seems a natural outgrowth of the scholarly industry built up around the poem, which has tended to concentrate on the poem's textual cruxes and historical contexts, and whose work has most often taken the form of focused readings of particular episodes, rather than expansive, monograph-length readings of the entire texts.

From this perspective, the first two volumes of the *Penn Commentary* appear merely as further steps toward a more comprehensive apparatus. Like so much *Piers Plowman* scholarship, this project would seem to confirm that a text crafted out of pieces—exegesis, quotation, homiletic tropes, etc.—is best read in pieces. Or in Barney's words, the *Commentary* follows a "conviction that *Piers Plowman*, more than most poems, yields its riches to close examination of its individual passages and lines, and correspondingly less in its larger movements" and thus pays closest attention "to the detail of the poem" (xiii). Reading the poem as "sequential lemmas" in this way has a very long history.

Yet this familiar approach produces genuinely novel results when applied with the remarkable thoroughness of these *Penn Commentary* volumes: they are triumphant examples of close reading, not just learning. Barney declares that the aim is "to perform literary criticism," and both authors show keen attention to repetition, figurative language, and the evolution of verbal tropes (xiii). This has tangible rewards. For example, in the head note to Passus 4, Galloway notes that the shift from the controversy surrounding Meed's marriage to the trial of Meed and Wrong seems abrupt, but that the theme of trials as a means of inquiry "has been present explicitly from Holy Church's speech" in Passus 1: "When alle tresores ben tried, treuthe is the beste" (372). In his note on the distribution of graces in Passus 21, Barney points out the carefully controlled grammar and the scene's willingness to complete a catalogue of social categories that had been left unfinished elsewhere in the text (139). Previous scholarship has of course tracked some of the poem's verbal formulas—for example, "kynde knowing" or "love and leaute"— but Galloway's and Barney's notes take this kind of reading further.

Another example, Galloway's discussion of lines 230–34 of the Prologue (the cooks crying "Hote pyes, hote!"), is a masterpiece of scholarship and close reading (143–46). This extended note looks into the contemporary controversies surrounding cooks before diving deep into the history of vendors' street cries. Galloway then considers the satire possibly intended here, before stepping back and appreciating the way the Prologue begins with sight and ends with noise. Barney shows similar sensitivity to the end of Passus 20, pointing out the way Peace's piping and Truth's trumpet blend into Will's waking recognition of the bells ringing on Easter morning. These kinds of readings remind us that *Piers Plowman* is poetry, not merely an intersection of various contexts. The authors never make the mistake of reducing the text to its sources or analogues; instead, a careful review of the sources behind Holy Church's intriguing description of love as "the plant of peace" leads to an elegant recognition of the poem's originality (208).

The volumes base their entries on the Kane-Russell C-Text, though readings from the A- and B-Texts, as well as important manuscript variants, receive appropriate attention. Although the "Note to Readers" makes it clear that the *Commentary* is not intended as a variorum, the entries offer a fairly comprehensive review of criticism from Skeat onward.

Each volume shares "similar assumptions and formats, but presents an individual scholar's attention to . . . the poem," and there are recognizable differences between these two volumes (Galloway, xi). Galloway's notes tend to be longer, and offer many new readings. He demonstrates consistent interest in comparing *Piers Plowman* to the French allegorical tradition, including the *Roman de la Rose,* Nicholas

Bozon's *Char d'Orgeuil*, the works of Deguileville, *Le Roman de Fauvel*, and Huon de Méri's *Torneiment Anticrist*. Galloway also does an admirably thorough job of grounding *Piers Plowman* in the English alliterative tradition; *William of Palerne* merits as many mentions as the works of Augustine and Isidore of Seville combined. This represents a valuable shift in emphasis and opens up considerable room for further scholarship.

Barney's volume more closely resembles the (disclaimed) variorum model, reviewing scholarship rather than charting new territory, but he does not hesitate to weigh in on controversial questions, such as the validity of Need's arguments in Passus 22 or the influences behind *Piers Plowman*'s apocalypticism. Barney displays the sound judgment readers will recognize from his earlier work on the poem, as well as a knack for pithy conclusions. For example, summing up Kind's response to the problem of Need, Barney declares that "the solution is not taking, but giving"—a beautifully concise analysis (195).

Other differences between the two volumes simply reflect the variety of approaches to the poem's difficulties. Barney, unlike Galloway, is willing to invoke Langland as an author-figure. Barney shows slightly more interest in philological, metrical, and textual cruxes, while Galloway shows slightly more interest in the wider field of vernacular literature, including later satire, religious polemic, and allegory possibly indebted to *Piers Plowman* (such as Spenser's *Faerie Queene*). But both authors cast their nets widely. On rare occasions, this thoroughness may invent difficulties where few readers will find them, as in the examination of I.104–5 (a use of "cherubyn and seraphyn," which seems to be singular rather than plural), but these are forgivable consequences of reading the text so closely (193–94).

Inevitably for such an ambitious work, there are a few minor flaws. Galloway's index needs more consistency: Guillaume de Machaut is listed under "M," Huon de Méri under "D," and "Raoul de Houdenc" under "R" (Barney's seems to have fewer problems of this variety). The "nested structure" of the notes explained in the "Note to the Reader" provided in both volumes, whereby each passus, larger textual unit, and notable line receives its own commentary, may cause some difficulty for readers seeking quick answers. The enormous treasure of knowledge the authors want to share sometimes places pressure on this organizing scheme, as in the commentary on II.39–42 (241–45). Here the same four lines are treated under three separate headings, to slightly confusing effect. But most readers will want to peruse the commentary with some leisure, and the volumes are otherwise easily navigated. The cross-referencing within each volume is excellent, and ideally will be repro-duced for the entire series once complete. All readers will hope that the *Commentary* eventually appears in some incarnation online, where it might be updated by a larger team of editors and its immense value preserved.

These first two volumes are landmarks of scholarship and a salutary example of collaborative work combined with individual insight. When complete, the *Penn Commentary* will be invaluable for teaching *Piers Plowman*, perhaps less because it brings so much contextual reference to bear (since such context can distract or overwhelm first-time readers) than because of its demonstration that the poem can be enjoyed for its details. If the generation of readers who can approach this demanding poem as a whole, rather than in pieces, finally arrives, the *Penn Commentary* will have served its laudable purpose. In the meantime, it makes the delightful confusion that comes from reading *Piers Plowman* a little less confusing and even more delightful.

GEORGE SHUFFELTON
Carleton College

JESSICA BRANTLEY. *Reading in the Wilderness: Private Devotion and Public Performance in Late Medieval England*. Chicago: University of Chicago Press, 2007. Pp. xviii, 463. $45.00.

This book is the first detailed study of London, British Library MS Additional 37049, a densely illustrated mid- to late fifteenth-century compendium of Middle English texts with, most probably, Carthusian origins. That such an important manuscript has had to wait so long for in-depth analysis is a mark of its verbal and visual complexity, the preponderance of short and noncanonical texts among its 101 items, and the relatively unfashionable status of Carthusian studies. *Reading in the Wilderness* is an attractive headline for such a volume—an indication of the eremitical content and perhaps of the critic's labors—though the ambitiously phrased subtitle suggests a range and depth that the study of a single codex can hardly hope to achieve.

The pictorial and diagrammatic elements of MS Additional 37049 are well known, largely as a result of James Hogg's 1981 edition of the images. The subject of Brantley's sustained and at times compelling exploration is the scope and significance of the interplay of its verbal and visual representation. Her central argument, laid out in considerable detail in the opening two chapters, is that the manuscript embodies and shapes Carthusian meditative practice in a process of sustained reading and looking that is essentially the enactment of scripture and liturgy, a kind of devotional drama. The semantics of such terms as *play* and *pageant* are turned over in the exploration of this almost ritualized response, but the key notion is that the worship generated by this *lectio divina, visio divina* has a performative quality. To describe this indivisibility of picture and word, Brantley eschews standard hierarchical descriptions of such complexes (label, caption, illustration, picture) in favor of the term "imagetext," drawn from the work of visual theorist W. J. T. Mitchell.

Key to understanding Brantley's notion of performative devotion is her discussion of the *Desert of Religion* (chapter 3) and the large number of lyrics spread throughout the manuscript (chapter 4). The *Desert of Religion*, it is argued, stands at the heart of the reading experience of the whole volume with the reader's performance emerging through personal identification with images of adoring or meditating Carthusians. This work is the only Middle English text to have been invariably illustrated (85) and here "attests to its creator's interest in a fully composite art: the joining of picture and word to create a new, independent medium" (79); "it is not really separable from the manuscript's concerns, the physical structure, or the textual history of the rest of the manuscript" (118). Through close reading of the poem, comparative analysis with lavishly illustrated versions in British Library, MS Cotton Faustina B.vi (Pt II) and British Library, MS Stowe 39, and extended reference to Richard Rolle, Brantley contends that this poem's landscapes "introduce an eremetic community into the mystic's solitary devotional practice and model visionary experience in the desert" (97). The manuscript's interest in the short poems explores the "visual inheritance" of the meditative lyric (125) and allows the reader to position himself as the subject of the first-person texts. In these ways the reader acts out these meditative lyrics as they take up "performative modes of both authorial and readerly kinds" (123).

The notion of the reader as performer generates considerable interpretive possibilities, though occasionally the force of the argument diminishes in the face of such inquiry and some of the more obvious points of connection are only briefly addressed. Thus, speculation as to the identity of the non-Carthusian figures in the illustrations is collapsed into the possibility that "the monks seem so tantalizingly to represent the readers who were using it" (156). So, too, the workings of the meditative lyric beyond the immediate monastic context are largely passed over. Further, the appearance of numerous "imagetext" complexes in parish churches are referenced through standard examples such as the *Pricke of Conscience* window at All Saints, York. The desire to focus on the manuscript is understandable, yet to raise but not pursue references to the practice of visualizing or "beholding" (148) texts and image as central to the practice of lay worship represents a missed opportunity to locate the "imagetext" phenomenon in a much broader context of late medieval devotional activity and affective piety.

The strengths and weaknesses of Brantley's approach are replayed in the concluding chapters, which focus on the idea that, while not a liturgical codex, the book "reproduces through the mechanisms of private reading the character and meaning of liturgical events, reflecting the central position of the liturgy as an all consuming dimension of medieval life" (167). This is played out in the iconographic and thematic reflections of the Carthusian liturgy in the texts and images in the manuscript, and there is a rewarding discussion of the Cult of the Holy Name, which links back to Rolle, with and through whom it was linked and augmented (187).

The absence of a more nuanced assessment of the potential for these Carthusian habits of thought to be understood in other contexts is in some ways an inverse measure of Brantley's successful reading of the interplay of word and image. But it does reveal the limits of her investigation. Heavily visual and literary in character, the argument skirts around significant features of the manuscript. It is a particular shortcoming that there is no description of the book as an object, no formal record of its physical composition, and no discussion of either the hands or the corrections and annotations that are clearly identifiable in the reproduced images (and are a feature of Carthusian readerly activity and spiritual guidance). If the materiality of the manuscript is underplayed, so too are the implications of performative meditation for other Carthusian manuscripts, especially for those without any illustrative context. It is surprising that, for instance, only the briefest allusion is made to the early fifteenth-century manuscript known to have been at the Carthusian monastery at Beauvale (Oxford, Bodleian Library, MS Douce 114). This collection opens with Middle English lives of three continental women, all of which are structured around the same visual imaginings and liturgical reenactments revealed in MS Additional 37049, and could have formed an important point of comparison.

Author and publisher are to be congratulated on producing such a visually attractive volume. There are eight color plates depicting single- and double-page spreads from Additional 37049 and a generous one hundred halftone figures from this codex, related manuscripts, and analogues in other media. The apparatus is also helpful and confirms the study's undoubted scholarship. As well as a useful appendix that lists the manuscripts contents and provides critical references, there are nearly seventy pages of notes and a further sixty pages of bibliography. All in all, this is a welcome and significant contribution to scholarship on the English Carthusians and to manuscript studies more generally. Students of this and related manuscripts will want to address Brantley's idea of readerly play and performance, and it will become a useful companion volume to Marleen Cré's *Vernacular Mysticism in the Charterhouse* (2006), an equally detailed reading of the texts in British Library, MS Additional 37790. One can only hope, too, that it will have the desired effect of generating a much-needed critical edition of the entire manuscript.

DAVID GRIFFITH
University of Birmingham

JENNIFER BRYAN. *Looking Inward: Devotional Reading and the Private Self in Late Medieval England.* Philadelphia: University of Pennsylvania Press, 2008. Pp. 280. $49.95.

How did medieval men and women understand their inner lives? In what ways did vernacular religious writings help them see themselves? A number of recent books have taken up these questions, but Jennifer Bryan's *Looking Inward* will further enrich our understanding of the complex associations between late medieval vernacular reading, the tropes of seeing and mirroring, and interiority. While other studies have explored questions of interiority in relation to confessional discourses and meditative visual images, Bryan importantly directs our attention back to an understudied set of texts: vernacular devotional writings. Spanning two centuries and ranging from studies of canonical figures and texts (including Julian of Norwich, *The Cloud of Unknowing*, Nicholas Love, and Thomas Hoccleve) to less-discussed works (including *The Chastising of God's Children*, *The Prickynge of Love*, and *A Talkynge of the Love of God*), Bryan's monograph considers the ways in which late medieval vernacular devotional literature helped lay readers negotiate public and private selves by learning to "see" themselves in the mirroring structures of devotional writings.

After a lengthy introduction that provides the basic cultural context for the study, focusing on the rise of literacy and devotional interest among lay people (and women in particular) and the growing literatures addressed to those living the mixed life, the first chapter explores what "inwardness" means to the late medieval reader. As Bryan shows, there was no one way that inwardness was represented in the period. Rather, there are multiple models of interiority just as there are multiple types of spiritual identities that might be assumed. The chapter surveys seven models of inwardness, beginning with Richard Rolle's solitary and highly affective interiority and ending with the Augustinian representation of self-knowledge as derived from the labor of reading and self-examination exemplified by such texts as Walter Hilton's *Scale of Perfection* and Julian of Norwich's *Shewings*. This last model will govern the remainder of the book. In the following chapter, Bryan addresses the Augustinian influence even more directly, focusing on the notion of the text as mirror and thinking at more length about the relationship between notions of inwardness, reading, and vision. To do so, she first traces the Augustinian roots of the mirror-trope, next explores the relationship between rhetorics of sight and interiority in monastic spirituality as exemplified by *The Myroure of Oure Ladye* (written for the nuns at Syon), and finally concludes by juxtaposing two religious tracts, *The Cloud of Unknowing* and *The Chastising of God's Children,* that offer divergent representations of the role of sight and self-knowledge in contemplation.

The third chapter, "Private Passions," turns to vernacular passion meditations, an extraordinarily popular genre of religious writing in late medieval England, famously exemplified by Nicholas Love's early fifteenth-century translation of the Pseudo-Bonaventuran *Meditationes*

Vitae Christi. When these texts helped their readers imagine the suffering of Christ, Bryan argues, they encouraged those readers "to transform narratives of frenzied emotion into the grounds of more routine self-awareness and practical imitation" (112)—a lesson that, she notes, Margery Kempe evidently failed to understand. The chapter opens with an analysis of John Lydgate's *Testament,* which Bryan reads (somewhat surprisingly) as the poet's deeply personal though still exemplary response to a passion image. But the heart of the chapter offers close readings of *The Talkynge of the Love of God* and *The Prickynge of Love,* which use passion imagery and the language of suffering, longing, and beholding to produce readerly response, affective identification, and, ultimately, self-examination.

The final two chapters are single-author studies and examine how discourses of vision, reading, and interiority influence the writings of Julian of Norwich and Thomas Hoccleve. Although Bryan's readings of anonymous and understudied religious writing in the opening chapters are excellent, this pair of author-studies shows her at her best; these fresh readings give us new ways of thinking about both authors. Julian and Hoccleve represent, for Bryan, two different examples of how the discourses of "inward sight" modeled in vernacular devotional writing affected the representation of the negotiation of the public and private self in the culture more generally. Bryan reads Julian as "an exemplary devotional reader" (147), but also one who turns her introspection and private experience to public use by drawing theological generalizations from her visions. The Hoccleve chapter offers a powerful reading of the ever-anxious poet as a religious writer (he is most often considered a disciple of Chaucer, bureaucrat, or political writer) and also explores the extent to which Hoccleve's autobiographical poetry and religious lyrics participate in a larger set of discourses about sight and interiority.

The merits of this book are many: most important, it recovers a set of texts that were extraordinarily popular in their day but have been understudied by modern scholarship. It offers a sustained exploration of the influence of Augustinian theologies on English religious culture and explores the translation of monastic spiritual practices into those appropriate for the devout lay person. And its consideration of the mirror-trope will certainly further our understanding of contemporary, nonreligious speculum texts, such as mirrors for princes. Moreover, the study's commitment to tracing a common theme in devotional writings across a two-hundred-year period may be intellectually fruitful insofar as it reminds us that residual and emergent cultures are always coterminous. Even though this sort of thematic study might be seen as a distinctive strength of the book, it might also be argued that in the process of drawing out thematic continuities, the book ultimately flattens temporal and cultural difference. Bryan, for example, does not explore what is at stake in juxtaposing the passion imagery of Lydgate's *Testament* (c. 1460) with that of *The Talkynge of the Love of God* (late 1300s) in chapter 3, or tracing these models of inwardness through to the later poetry of Donne, Herbert, and Hopkins. But one might wonder if this historical difference and the cultural and theological changes occurring within the temporal gaps would affect the understandings of the passion narrative or interiority.

Indeed, insofar as Bryan's depiction of late medieval piety focuses on the popular and mainstream and progresses thematically rather than historically, it tends to marginalize cultural change, dissent, and controversy. For instance, Lollard writings have little place in Bryan's consideration of late medieval discourses of interiority, or indeed of late medieval culture more generally. Certainly others have taken up the relationship between interiority and dissent (most recently, Katherine C. Little). Yet despite the growing scholarly attention to the issues studied in Bryan's book, it references very few studies published after 2002, and the recent studies noted often get a bibliographic nod in lieu of real engagement (James Simpson's monumental *Reform and Cultural Revolution* is a case in point). Conspicuously absent are recent studies of interiority, vision, and confession by Michelle Karnes, Suzannah Biernoff, and Little. Nevertheless, although Bryan's book would have been enriched by closer engagement with recent scholarship, its eloquent close readings are fresh and compelling. And the book as a whole, while not a self-conscious interlocutor in recent conversations on interiority and religious literature, will certainly become an important one, not only because it goes a long way toward recuperating an important, but understudied, archive, but also because in doing so it shows us that the late medieval commitment to reflecting on the self may be much more central to private piety, public forms of devotion, and even nonreligious literature than we had hitherto imagined.

SHANNON GAYK
Indiana University

J. A. Burrow. *The Poetry of Praise*. Cambridge: Cambridge University Press, 2008. Pp. vii, 196. £45.00; $90.00.

An episode in *Monty Python and the Holy Grail* (1975) exemplifies modern attitudes toward medieval praise poetry. The Thopas-like Sir Robin sets out on a quest, listening with increasing unease while an irritating minstrel lauds his bravery in the face of future horrors. When challenged by a huge three-headed knight, "brave Sir Robin" scarpers; his minstrel now sings cheerily, "When danger reared its ugly head / he bravely turned his tail and fled." The medieval rhetoric of praise almost inevitably seems to us formulaic, insincere, and ripe for comic irony or bathos.

The key argument of John Burrow's book is that rhetorics of praise and blame are integral to premodern poetics. With characteristic clarity, and drawing on his extensive engagement with medieval English literature, Burrow suggests that praise should be read in ways more serious, less ironic, than modern readers are wont to, if we are fully to appreciate its tone and texture. Since praise "is no longer a prime function of poetic activity" (3), we search for undercurrents, if not wholesale undermining, where genuine admiration or awe is a more historically appropriate reading.

Chapter 1 surveys classical understandings of *laus* (*epainos*) and *vituperatio* (*psogos*), classified by Aristotle in the third branch of rhetoric, the demonstrative or epideictic. Central to praise was *auxesis*, or *amplificatio*—augmentation both in the sense of lengthening and of gilding the description of a hero, object, or event. Burrow traces these categories in medieval rhetorical treatises such as those of Matthew of Vendôme, Geoffrey of Vinsauf, John of Garland, and Hermann the German, closing with Benvenuto da Imola's commentary on Dante, which cites Hermann's Averroistic *Poetics* as saying that "every poem and every poetic utterance is either praise or blame; for every action and every trait of character turns on nothing but either virtue or vice" (23). This dichotomous and morally active tradition, Burrow argues, forms a vital substratum of vernacular poetry.

Chapter 2, on "Old English, especially *Beowulf*," surveys laudatory verse to God (*Caedmon's Hymn*; the *Advent Lyrics*; *Daniel*), before turning to military heroes. *The Battle of Maldon*, for example, distinguishes between praise for the brave and blame for the cowardly sons of Odda. But then there is Byrhtnoth's *ofermod*, which Burrow briefly ponders, suggesting that reckless boldness may yet be praiseworthy in an epideictic mode. Similar complications are writ large in *Beowulf*, whose formulae of superlative praise Burrow wishes to recuperate as wholehearted. He argues against critics (John Leyerle, Andy Orchard) who see the apposition between Beowulf and Heremod as gloomily proleptic, or who read Wiglaf's later speeches as a critique of Beowulf's rashness. Burrow's reading may help to modify some more extreme accounts of *Beowulf* as an indictment of revenge culture, but much remains debatable. I'm skeptical, for instance, of his claim that the *scop*'s account of the Finn episode eventually "redounds to the glory of Denmark" (45) and so is neutralized as a monitory narrative for audiences within and outside the text. Here more space would be needed to investigate ways in which voice, audience, and temporal apposition work to complicate, and frequently darken, the tone of the poem. This chapter briefly notes Ruth Finnegan's influential work on African oral poetry and makes reference to Norse traditions, but more discussion of the varying sources and listening situations of praise poetry in Anglo-Saxon England would have been useful. Indeed, one of the most ambivalent instances of praise poetry in Norse narrative is sited in Viking York—the moment in *Egils saga* where Egil Skallagrimsson composes overnight a *drápa* in honor of his enemy Erik Bloodaxe in order to save his own head.

Chapter 3 discusses a variety of Middle English poems. Following Gregory Nagy, Burrow distinguishes between "historical" praise of the deeds of heroes and "here-and-now" praise, as, for example, of the Virgin Mary or the "Annot" of a Harley lyric. Burrow himself calls these sections "sketchy" (61), and there is rarely time to explore his examples fully. He does pause over the Alliterative *Morte Arthure* and *The Wars of Alexander*, cautioning against what he sees as anachronistic readings treating ideological contradiction as necessarily a mark of criticism or anti-imperialism. Burrow suggests that such contradictions can coexist without being resolved into a final statement of account, especially when differing traditions "are not unified by the overall conception of any single author. Their dossier on Alexander included many things to his credit, but also a few that were not. Interpretation, it seems, can go no further than that" (92). *Sir Gawain and the Green Knight* also involves coexisting incompatibilities of public celebration and private shame. Burrow triangulates these with the Green Knight's assessment of Gawain, and suggests that here "discrepant judgements relate meaningfully to each other and to the positions from which they are spoken" (100).

This interest in the voicing of praise is Burrow's bridge into the core of the book, a fifty-page chapter on Chaucer, which provides a useful conspectus of the range of praise found across Chaucer's work. Burrow counters readings of Chaucer that make irony and subversion the grounding response to praise. Instead he focuses attention on the roots of Chaucer's auxetic writing, citing Jill Mann's discussion of Chaucer's "romance style" as one context in which we might learn to love his *laus*. The chapter encompasses the dream poems, some Canterbury tales, and especially *Troilus and Criseyde*, noting that "Chaucer pays particular attention to the sources from which praise comes" (117). It highlights moments when "the poetry of praise speaks wholeheartedly and without reservation" (127), among which descriptions of female figures are prominent, including Alceste, Constance, Emily, Griselda, Nature, the Virgin Mary, and the Black Knight's "White." Burrow also cautions against a buildup of ironic layers in *Troilus and Criseyde* that might obscure appreciation of praise per se, in readings avowedly intended to rebalance the dominance of a "hermeneutic of suspicion" (149) in recent studies. While many will demur from some specific claims, be frustrated by some equivocal or undeveloped readings, or will resist his founding assumptions, Burrow nevertheless challenges us to clarify and justify our understandings of intentionality and historically contextualized reading. In this sense, *The Poetry of Praise* shares some ground with A. C. Spearing's *Textual Subjectivity* (footnoted briefly, 149), which also wants to de-ironize approaches to medieval narrative, freeing Chaucer from the interpretive bottlenecks created from the limited perspectives of particular pilgrims or narrator personae.

Two final chapters face the impossible task of tracking the postmedieval "decline of praise" (150) and drawing some threads together. The former inevitably leaves many avenues untrodden, galloping through Spenser, Milton, Wordsworth, Byron, and Tennyson to Christopher Logue at alarming speed, while noting the development of ambivalent rhetorics of heroism. Burrow's limpid writing carries the reader through, but this is the least memorable part of a short book that draws together useful material (especially on rhetorical theory), raises valuable questions, yet leaves much to debate and explore.

NICHOLAS PERKINS
St. Hugh's College, Oxford

313

JEFFREY JEROME COHEN. *Hybridity, Identity, and Monstrosity in Medieval Britain: On Difficult Middles*. New York: Palgrave Macmillan, 2006. Pp. viii, 256. $84.95.

Jeffrey Jerome Cohen has in many ways defined the field of study known, following his seminal publication of the same title, as "Monster Theory," an incipient area currently gaining traction in medieval studies. His works, including *Monster Theory: Reading Culture* (1996) and *Of Giants: Sex, Monsters, and the Middle Ages* (1999), laid much of the groundwork for the examination of the ways in which reading monsters allows us to understand the cultures in which they were created and consumed. His approach, deeply indebted to notions of abjection and disgust derived from psychoanalytical theory, has of late focused more explicitly on the postcolonial approaches pioneered by Edward Said and Homi Bhabha, as foregrounded in *The Postcolonial Middle Ages* (2000), a collection edited by Cohen. Both this collection and *Hybridity* appear in the New Middle Ages series, edited by Bonnie Wheeler, which has offered some of the most interesting and innovative contributions to medieval studies in recent years.

In *Hybridity*, Cohen focuses on collective identity, and on the ways that it is both shaped and shattered by cultural perceptions of "otherness." The neat distinctions sought by medievals were, he argues, generally fictitious, and in reality the medieval world (like our own) was largely composed of what he calls "difficult middles." These middle-ground individuals and communities were hybrid in nature, much like many of the monsters that obsessed them. Cohen is quite clear that by "hybrid" he does not mean a beautifully synthetic whole formed by the merging of disparate parts, "not some third term that synthesizes two warring elements and renders them placid" (145). Rather, it is like the cynocephalus, described in the *Wonders of the East* as a man having the head of a dog, the tusks of a boar, and the mane of a horse: a disunity formed by the incomplete incorporation of its constituent parts—a monster. As he writes, "Hybridity is a fusion *and* a disjunction, a conjoining of differences that cannot simply harmonize" (2).

One of the insights emphasized throughout the text is that hybridity is not exclusive to marginal groups and beings. While the term is often used to describe the distant monsters of Africa and Asia, or "others within," such as Jews, and, in Spain, Saracens, Cohen emphasizes its relevance for mainstream European Christian cultures. The hybrid, hyphenated names used to describe cultures point to their unresolved natures. As he writes, "Contemporary scholars faced with medieval hybridities typically rely upon hyphenated terms like 'Anglo-Scandinavian' and 'Anglo-Norman'"—as well, one might add, as "Anglo-Saxon," embedded in their initial term—"[y]et these composite names have no counterpart in medieval terminology" (79). The hybridity of these groups, glossed over by unifying terms, was nonetheless palpable.

In his first and most overtly theoretical chapter, "Acts of Separation: Shaping Communal Bodies," Cohen articulates the method by which he will analyze his texts throughout the rest of the volume. Essentially, he follows the notion of "dependent differentiation," as articulated by Gillian Overing and Clare Lees. That is, collective identity is formed through "acts of separation" through which groups wall themselves off from others. This process, he argues, allows even groups hostile to one another (such as the Anglo-Saxons and Normans) to coalesce into rough unities, real hybrids, not imagined monsters but actual people living in interstitial situations. As Cohen writes of circumcised Christians and baptized Jews, "Such figures were in their very bodies caught in a difficult middle" (29). This process, though, had terribly real results for those who were its foils, the groups against which societies chose to define themselves. Anti-Jewish violence in medieval England, Cohen argues, was as much about the Anglo-Normans trying to define themselves as it was about the Jews themselves. Here as elsewhere, Cohen's focus on the High Middle Ages demonstrates how "composite in fact, homogeneous in theory, the English of the twelfth century similarly began to demarcate themselves from these monstrous peoples that limned the margins of their kingdom" (35). Still, this process had begun well before there was anything that we might really call an English kingdom, and it helped, through the very processes Cohen describes, to bring about such an entity.

The second and third chapters, "Between Belongings: History's Middles" and "In the Borderlands: The Identities of Gerald of Wales," are perhaps the strongest in the volume. Each applies the method outlined in the first chapter to texts central to identity formation within English culture. Cohen stresses the messiness of history and of collective identity, too often glossed over in texts dealing with such hybrid groups as the Anglo-Saxons. The enduring nature of such artificial constructs stands as a testament to the effectiveness of the texts Cohen highlights, especially (of course) Bede's *Ecclesiastical History*, but also William of Malmesbury's *History of the English Kings* and Geoffrey of Monmouth's *History of the Kings of Britain*. Cohen picks through these weighty texts, drawing out of them the destabilizing notes that sound beneath the overarching, overtly stabilizing narratives. Bede "imagines a past that, despite ample evidence to the contrary, seems monolithic, pure" (47), thereby creating a more unified present and future. The Norman England of William—himself an English-Norman hybrid (as Gerald of Wales was a Welsh-Norman one)—was colonial in the literal sense. William writes to conjoin the two histories of the "English" and the Normans, a task that first necessitated artificially unifying all of pre-Norman Britain, forming an English nation by ejecting others to the fringes. Still, as monstrously figured by a half-dead pair of conjoined twins (59), the entity William constructs is neither healthy nor completely unified. Cohen's reference to the illuminations integral to William's and Gerald's texts in these chapters is perhaps somewhat brief and a more extended discussion of the images of both texts (as well as a few illustrations) would have been welcome.

The fourth chapter is a departure from the pattern of textual criticism established to this point. Here, Cohen turns his postcolonial gaze not toward a text but toward the city of Norwich in the late eleventh century and the early twelfth. This chapter is therefore something of an extended establishment of context for chapter 5, "The Flow of Blood in Norwich," which deals with the *Life and Miracles of St. William of Norwich* by Thomas of Monmouth, an account famous as "the first time in written history we encounter . . . a figure destined to become familiar through medieval Christendom, the Jew whose murderous hands provoke an unceasing flow of blood"—the first blood libel tale (112). As background for what follows, chapter 4 is less theorized or analytical, though it drives home a key point touched on throughout: hybridity manifests itself not only in fiction, in myths about dog-men and bearded women. Rather, in this deeply colonial city, with its massive new cathedral and castle dominating the cityscape, its reconfigured streets and altered patterns of life, it "harbored the kind of heterogeneity in tempestuous admixture that Gerald of Wales embodied in figures like the Ox Man of Wicklow, a body irremovably at war with itself" (138). Cohen writes that "a possible way to uncover some of the effects of Norman subjugation on the city's community might be to map its architecture and physical space both before and after the alteration in national governance" (114). This is a promising method to be pursued in future studies of this pivotal problem in the history of medieval Jewish-Christian relations, and it would lend clearer visual form to the verbal narration of the transformations wrought on the city.

While Cohen does convincingly construct Norwich as colonial and heterogenous, the preceding chapters suggest that pre-Conquest England was equally heterogeneous and hybrid. In a "nation" composed of Romans, Britons, Angles, Saxons, Jutes, Danes, Irish, Scots, Welsh, and Picts, did the addition of Normans and Jews make it substantially more hybrid than it already was? In essence, is the cynocephalus, with its dog, horse, boar, and human elements *more* hybrid than Gerald's Ox Man, who is only dual in nature? Perhaps it is, with each new conjoined but unassimilated element compounding its hybridity. And yet it seems that, once a being or group loses the sought-after "monolithic, pure" unity imagined by Bede, all is hybrid, and the extent to which degrees of hybridity are significant remains unclear.

Cohen seems more comfortable and more convincing when interpreting literature than when dealing with the cityscape and its history. The final chapter examines the ways in which a threat of violence was used to bind the English and Normans into a community (as well as to raise funds for the religious community, a subtle note raised briefly). With the fractured image of Norwich established in the preceding chapter, there is a need for "the imagining of a purified collective identity for Norwich's discordant and heterogeneous population," which was brought about through the common rejection of the Jews (140). The martyr Saint William's "sacred blood . . . brings about the necessary suture, conjoining temporarily the French-descended and indigenous English, bringing together the clerics and the laity, monks and priests, the celibate and the married, the privileged and the impoverished, the women and the men" (162). Cohen's most interesting insight here is the apparent reversal of scale: Christendom is reduced to the local identity of the community of Norwich, whereas the more localized Jewish community is elevated to an international conspiracy, an ignominious accusation that has not died out over the past eight hundred years. It may have taken a few decades for the false accusations raised in the *Life of St. William* of Jewish attacks on the Christian *corpus*—leading to blood that "kept flowing drop by drop" (153)—to instigate the spilling of real Jewish blood, but indeed, "it is not likely an exaggeration to say that this text and the cult it promulgated were to trigger many more such flows" (173).

317

While the book is fully and explicitly focused on the Middle Ages, most readers will certainly detect the undercurrent of relevance it has to the present, to our own persistent troubles with hybridity and our difficult middles. When Cohen writes of Cædwala and the Britons as the "catalyst" for the creation of a unified *totum genus Anglorum* through "the endangerment that brings the possibility of a pan-English union into being" (49) or that "England envisioned itself as under siege at its borders by bellicose Welsh and Scots, and at its center by homicidal Jews" (12), it is impossible to miss the echoes of this process today, when unity is generally defined in similarly crude terms counterposing "us" and "them." In an era of flag pins, seven-hundred-mile-border fences, and persistent jingoism, it seems that we have not yet come to grips with our own difficult middles. We still look outward for groups from which we can separate ourselves, and against which we can thereby define our society. Cohen's book, constructing images of communities that reconfigured themselves as "imperiled" through the invention of fictitious enemies (152), is therefore not only a useful lens through which we might view the distant past, but (a rare and vital quality) also one through which we might reconsider our own troubled present.

ASA SIMON MITTMAN
California State University, Chico

ANDREW COLE. *Literature and Heresy in the Age of Chaucer.* Cambridge: Cambridge University Press, 2008. Pp. xx, 297. £50.00; $99.00.

Andrew Cole's book is a welcome contribution to the recent nuancing of the study of the Wycliffite heresy and its literary and other affiliations in the later fourteenth and fifteenth centuries in England. The 2003 collection of essays to which Cole contributed, *Lollards and Their Influence in Late Medieval England* (edited by Fiona Somerset, Jill Havens, and Derrick Pittard), already raised important questions about the various, and variously debated and co-opted, meanings of "orthodoxy" and "heresy," "Wycliffism" and "Lollardy," a development that has since seen much illuminating scholarship (from Ian Forrest, Mishtooni Bose, Fiona Somerset, and Anne Hudson among others), and to which a recent Oxford conference ("Lollard Affiliations," 2008) was in part devoted. Cole's new book further refines and interrogates many of the crucial terms of the debates and their scope and implication. Beginning with a detailed study of the 1382 Blackfriars Council, Cole proceeds to consider a range of Middle English authors, both major and minor, including William Langland, John Clanvowe, Geoffrey Chaucer, John Trevisa, Thomas Hoccleve, John Lydgate, and Margery Kempe. Cole's major claim is that Wycliffism was "an ideologically diverse and aesthetically enabling feature of late medieval literary culture and politics," and thereby "one of the central forces that shaped English literary history" (xiii). This clear enunciation of his main thesis, with its notable emphasis on the aesthetic, is followed by chapters that attempt to tease out, with impressive, though not always wholly convincing subtlety, the details of this fruitful exchange between the radical, sometimes sensational ideas of John Wyclif and his various followers, opponents, interlocutors or observers.

The book importantly suggests that ecclesiastical censure and legislation could function not only as an inhibitor or dampener but also as an unintended spur to creative and innovative developments in literary and intellectual history. However, Cole's presentation of the English church at times risks portraying it as overly monolithic and endows it with an almost creative malignity. "For whatever multiplicity of theological and political ideas among Wyclif and his students, Courtenay and his bishops at the Blackfriars Council constructed Wycliffism as a cohesive body of heretical thought and practice in order to render religious dissent as publicly visible, legally troublesome, conceptually easy to understand, and equally easy to fear," says Cole in his chapter on the Council (19). Yes and no, surely. It could be argued that heresy has always to be "invented" (though, equally, one has always to ask why; cf. Monique Zerner, ed., *Inventer l'hérésie? Discours polémiques et pouvoirs avant l'inquisition*, 1998). But the brilliantly idiosyncratic philosophy and polemics of Wyclif (as increasingly underlined by, among others, Alessandro Conti, Maarten Hoenen, Laurent Cesalli, and Paul Bakker),which yet built upon much that was already present and problematic (anticlericalism, a growing unease with inherited rhetorics and hermeneutics, the spread of academic ideas outside university genres, conventions and procedures), had as much to do with the peculiar resonance and visibility of what the Church tried to counter as "heresy." It is worth recalling that the late medieval era was a time of increasing porosity of the boundaries between academic speculation and extramural religio-intellectual endeavor across a range of European cultures. Wyclif's explosive and intransigent presence in such a context could have unforeseen effects. In other words, the material that Cole sees as "the [suspect] story of 'lollards' and 'lollardy' filling up England almost overnight" (18) could be read rather differently.

Cole's approach is most rewarding when he suggests that one should think of " 'lollardy' as a typology evoking rather specific topics," a typology that opened up "a space within which to articulate alternative and newer models of lay piety that became prominent during the age of Wycliffism" (53, 159); though one would have been interested in knowing how Cole would have engaged with the evidence of widespread continental usage of the word "lollard," both before and during the spread of Wycliffite ideas, as presented by Robert Lerner and Dietrich Kurze, neither of whom is cited in the bibliography. This approach results in stimulating close readings of Hoccleve, Lydgate, and Kempe that bring out well their complex negotiations of religio-political identity, theological doctrine, and social norms and behaviors, and make us rethink our apparent familiarity with these authors. Of particular interest is Cole's analysis of the intersection of literary and doctrinal concerns. The discussion of "figural eucharists and literary theologies" (146ff.) is provocative: Lydgate's "sacramental poetry," with its subtle engagement with issues of "form" and "figure," is held to conflate sacramental and literary signs in new ways. Cole's reading of Hoccleve's poetry, and its complex (re)-shaping of models of orthodox behavior in line with aristocratic and chivalric virtues, through a minute negotiation of the language of official texts, is also of note. And his bracing account of Chaucer's "English Lesson" in Wycliffite translation theory, as evidenced in the Prologue to his *Treatise on the Astrolabe* (already well known to readers from an earlier version of the chapter in *Speculum*), benefits from being placed in the context of his larger argument.

In the final analysis, despite some unevenness of argumentation, and the author's occasionally evident predilection for setting up straw men to knock down, Cole's book constitutes a salutary reminder that "Wycliffism is less a 'context' or 'background' of affairs than part of the processes of cultural negotiation itself" (186). Alexander Patchovsky and other historians of medieval religion have pointed out in recent years that "heresy" is to be located at the basis, not the margins, of medieval society, and it is much to Cole's credit that he convincingly illuminates how "heresy" may also be equally fundamental to what we think of as medieval "literature."

KANTIK GHOSH
Trinity College, Oxford

EDWARD I. CONDREN. *Chaucer from Prentice to Poet: The Metaphors of Love in Dream Visions and "Troilus and Criseyde."* Gainesville: University Press of Florida, 2008. Pp. 239. $59.95.

The "Prentice" of Edward Condren's study is largely the Chaucer of *The Book of the Duchess*, but more radically than in the usual interpretation. For Condren, the Man in Black cannot be John of Gaunt, and nor was the deceased lady of the poem originally Blanche, Duchess of Lancaster. Condren's arguments aim to resolve the problem (usually dismissed by Chaucer editors, perhaps too lightly, as deriving from scribal confusion over Roman numerals) that the Man in Black is "Of the age of foure and twenty yer," whereas in the year of Blanche's death (1368), John of Gaunt (b. 1340) was twenty-eight. Arguing from Chaucer's description of himself—in his evidence at the Scrope-Grosvenor trial (1386)—as being "forty years of age and more," Condren proposes that it was more likely to be Chaucer who was twenty-four in 1368. Moreover, his argument claims, since it would be socially unrealistic for Chaucer to have represented John of Gaunt as so unflatteringly gauche and verbally inept as the Man of Black appears (in Condren's judgment), it is more likely that in the Man in Black Chaucer portrays an alter ego of the poet. And since Philippa of Hainault died in 1369, with whom (extant records suggest) Chaucer had a much closer association than with Blanche, the ur-text of Chaucer's early elegiac poem began as a eulogy of Queen Philippa, revised some eight years later in honor of Blanche (c. 1377), after the Black Prince had predeceased Edward III and the court looked forward to John of Gaunt's prospective influence during the anticipated minority of the future Richard II.

Although Condren's enquiry is triggered by the problem of the twenty-four-year-old Man in Black and attempts to contextualize the mysterious interval of an eight-year sickness (in a section of the poem absent from extant manuscripts and supplied from Thynne), his argument also seems driven by an anachronistically unsympathetic estimate of the French-style courtly idiolect of praise poetry in which Blanche is recollected. There seems some curious mismatch here between a proper historicist respect for dates and evidence and a markedly unhistorical disrespect for medieval courtly stylistics. For Condren, the Man in Black "is simply a very bad poet," and so, to rescue Chaucer from any imputation of being a bad poet himself, the Man in Black must be Chaucer's ventriloquizing of his earlier, less accomplished self as a poet, now contextualized within the dramatized interaction with a dreamer figure who is the creator of the present, polished poem. Thus to frame the Man in Black's speeches is a clever device, but one only made necessary by an unexamined tendency to judge a courtly poetic style by twenty-first-century notions of what is lively and fresh. How the praise of young Blanche, and memories of her graciousness to her suitor, might ever have formed part of a eulogy for plump and plain Queen Philippa (aged fifty-five at her death) is never addressed here, and nor is a sympathetic courtly understanding of such conventions as the references to Pythagoras (lines 667, 1167), which become the peg for the first of the numerological expositions of the four poems discussed in this book.

Apart from very specific instances where numbers are referenced within texts, the inferences of most numerological studies tend to divide readerships into those whose appreciation of poems is enhanced into a different dimension by an awareness of the congruence of poetic structures with particular mathematical laws, and those who may feel that a talent for certain proportionalities—which may coincidentally parallel mathematical laws—will be part of the aesthetic makeup of creative artists in most ages and cultures. Interpretations based on counting lines—in preprint cultures without line-numbered texts, and where some lines were always likely to be omitted through scribal error—may appear wishful thinking, while the counterargument that such numerological meanings represent secret readings encoded by the author usually seems scarcely less wishful. In any event, Condren's numerological analysis of the *Parliament of Fowls* does not add significantly to the numerological interpretation of the poem as a calendar in Victoria Rothschild's 1984 essay (which Condren handsomely acknowledges). So we hear that the three sections of what Condren defines as Part 2 "satisfy a harmonic proportion according to Porphyry's formulation: 16 exceeds 12 by one third of 12, as 24 exceeds 16 by one third of 24" and all this is "to recapture an ancient method of construction that emphasizes the coherence and harmony of the created universe." Yet the argument here for the poem's reflection of a calendar structure depends over-much on classifying as "a marriage poem" a text that, according to its mere literal sense, postpones even betrothal for one whole year.

Two chapters are devoted to *The House of Fame*, which argue, as many will concur, that Chaucer never planned anything for this poem beyond what is now extant, intentionally leaving it as it now is. With all its distinctive metaliterary focus, Condren wants to date the poem later than usual, apparently to allow Chaucer more time (which one may not think he needed) to sophisticate those metaliterary concerns. Most inventively, Condren wants to see the *House* both as postdating *Troilus* yet also as complete and finished in its guise (as he sees it) as the prologue to *Troilus*. He imagines that the man of great authority's first words would have been the first lines of *Troilus,* thus developing the Trojan matter attended to in *The House of Fame*. For Condren, the continuities between the dream poems and *Troilus* lie in common interests in such technical concerns of literary composition as numerology and the art of reporting. The arguments for numerological meaning in such matters as the *Troilus* book-lengths are derived from Thomas Elwood Hart's 1981 essay and seem no less eccentrically unpersuasive than they did then. But for the cognoscenti, Pandarus's joke about "dulcarnoun" and "flemyng of wrecches" makes certain a larger numerological encoding in the poem's form and meaning, so that in *Troilus* rational and irrational triangles "capture well" irreconcilable human circumstances (144–45). At one with the book's wider impatience with the idioms of courtesy is Condren's reading of Criseyde's supplication to Hector (a scene closely imitated from *Filostrato*) as an attempted seduction of her patron (apparently for no other reason than because she courteously thanks him "And ofter wolde, and it hadde ben his wille," 1.125). This leads to a curious reading of Criseyde's Book 2 interview with Pandarus in which she is to be understood as being gravely disappointed when he eventually reveals that her mysterious admirer is not Hector but the second best, Troilus. Equally remarkable readings of courtly behaviors mean that for Condren "the crampe of deth" around Troilus's heart (describing his oncoming swoon) signals "the tightening of the male organ prior to orgasm," while when "The felyng . . . of aught elles, fled was out of towne," this is a euphemism for premature ejaculation. Pandarus's urging Criseyde "wol ye pullen out the thorn / That stiketh in his herte?" signifies only "Will you uncover the phallus that is intended to penetrate his loved one?" (161). Many readers will find their understanding of the consummation scene somewhat challenged by such readings. These are part of Condren's broader view of the poem that—unable to accept the real force of Troilus's courtly concern for Criseyde's good name—finds unreal the courtly stratagems in which both courtly lovers feel they must acquiesce.

Nevertheless, the interpretations brought together in Condren's book may be seen to contest in useful ways received opinions about the chronology of Chaucer's works and their courtly values and styles.

BARRY WINDEATT
Emmanuel College, Cambridge

LISA H. COOPER AND ANDREA DENNY-BROWN, eds. *Lydgate Matters: Poetry and Material Culture in the Fifteenth Century*. New York and Basingstoke: Palgrave Macmillan, 2008. Pp. 223. $79.95.

Even ten years ago it would have been unusual to find the words "Lydgate" and "matters" occurring in close proximity, unless perhaps they were quickly followed by the words "very little." Much has changed in the last decade, and this collection of essays earns a distinguished place alongside the other recent studies that have changed our understanding of John Lydgate's importance to English literature: the work of James Simpson, Nigel Mortimer, and Maura Nolan and the essays collected by Simpson and Larry Scanlon. The value of this collection lies in its focus on material culture and materiality in a more abstract sense. In a lucid introduction, Lisa Cooper and Andrea Denny-Brown explore the range of meanings that "mater(e)" can have in Lydgate's poetry: subject matter, inner meaning, "but also the body that weighs us down and holds us back; the objects, both necessary and less so, with which we furnish our everyday lives; and the intellectual and spiritual illumination that we urgently seek to find and strain toward when it seems within our grasp" (3). This generous definition provides a framework for a collection of essays that differ in their interpretation of materiality, and consequently in the vision of John Lydgate that they offer. Instead of being a weakness, this diversity offers the reader a nuanced exploration of the contribution that attention to material culture can make to the study of medieval poetry. The essays in this volume offer new insights into Lydgate's poetry and confer new importance on texts that had previously seemed unpromising objects of analysis.

Three of the essays focus on the material form of Lydgate's poetry, or the material relationships out of which individual poems emerged. Collectively, they contribute to our understanding of Lydgate's relationship with London's elites, specifically the corporations and individuals for whom he executed commissions during the late 1420s and early 1430s. As Michelle R. Warren puts it, " 'material Lydgate' is essentially 'London Lydgate' " (114). Claire Sponsler offers an essential caveat to the developing view of Lydgate as a contributor to an emerging public culture. Responding to recent assertions of Lydgate's ability to project a civic voice that constructs an imaginary but representative public, Sponsler reminds us that the actual public for which Lydgate deployed his voice comprised a tiny elite. Lydgate's London poems participate in "civic-sponsored, top-down events expected by the crown . . . and private, coterie-audience entertainments" (19); the manuscripts such as Shirley's anthologies that preserve these poems achieved a limited circulation among the same elites. Sponsler's cogent essay portrays Lydgate's London poems as part of an official culture. While this culture can imagine itself as public and representative, the material contexts of its performance and circulation narrowly circumscribe the extent to which Lydgate's poetry can be understood to participate in an emerging public sphere. Michelle Warren also explores Lydgate's relations with his elite London patrons, and uncovers remarkable similarities between his London productions and the Arthurian translations of Henry Lovelich. While Lovelich's circle of patronage and readership was dominated by the Skinners' Guild, and was thus narrower than Lydgate's, both authors envision a public function for their writing that links civic interests to a vision of community, and cultivate comparable poetic styles that assert their literary quality through dilation. Warren offers an illuminating comparison of Lovelich's awareness of "the materiality of textual production and reception" (126) with that of John Shirley, who played such an important role in preserving Lydgate's London poems: both understand writing as a physical activity that produces material objects. Among the most spectacular objects linked to Lydgate's poetry is perhaps the "steyned halle" commissioned by the Armorers' Guild. Jennifer Floyd makes a convincing case that this "halle" was a series of large-format painted textiles on which Lydgate's *Legend of St. George* appeared in its entirety. These textiles may have decorated the Armorers' guild-hall, and may even have been loaned to other corporations on special occasions. Floyd shows how valuable artifacts combined with prestigious poetry could enable one of the lesser guilds to negotiate its position in London's competitive hierarchy, revealing an important context in which Lydgate's cultural impact should be judged.

A second group of essays explores the symbolic resonance of materiality as an idea within Lydgate's poetry. Denny-Brown argues that Lydgate's *Bycorne and Chychevache* is more than a misogynistic fable, offering a "subtle and complicated interrogation of how to understand appetite as a type of intersection between two worlds: myth and reality, visual and textual, and spiritual and material" (44). In a similar vein, Maura Nolan argues that Lydgate's seemingly irretrievably mundane "Tretise for Lauandres" challenges modern notions of literariness. Exploring the figurative associations of stains, purgation, and the figure of the laundress, Nolan shows how the poem's practical advice can be linked metaphorically with sin and forgiveness. More challenging, the poem's presence in British Library MS Harley 2251, amid a sequence of poems honoring the Blessed Virgin and asserting the power of prayer to triumph over death, obliges the reader to engage in a process of literary interpretation, constructing meaning for the interpretative riddle posed by scribal juxtaposition. Paul Strohm compares two episodes in Lydgate's *Troy Book*—the rebuilding of Troy with an elaborate sewer system and the preservation of Hector's corpse—to show that in both cases sovereign power deploys technology to purge noxious fluids, to the benefit both of individual bodies and the body politic: "Priam fulfills the sovereign imperative by asserting his sway over life and death and his right to continued rule—if not by conquering death at least by delimiting death's dominion" (66). Lisa Cooper explores the function of craft imagery in Lydgate's *Pilgrimage of the Life of Man*. Like his source, Lydgate finds in artisanal production a powerful source of spiritual metaphors, but his ambivalence to this activity must be understood in a post-Lollard context, in which artisans were associated with heresy. This ambivalence shows "just how flexible craft imagery could be in the later Middle Ages, and how impossible it must have seemed, for even the most determined of propagandists, to force it into a completely coherent signifying system" (104). These essays are all carefully argued, rewarding explorations of the complex array of significations that the material world bears in Lydgate's poetry.

The final two essays stray somewhat from the volume's focus on materiality. John M. Ganim argues that Lydgate's *Life of St. Edmund* and *Miracles of St. Edmund* implicate him in the defense mounted by Bury St. Edmunds of its privileges. The resulting "poetics of exemption," in which Lydgate cultivates "a rhetoric of negotiation among shared temporal, spiritual, and political claims," is readily transferable to secular contexts such as his civic commissions (166). These commissions, insists Ganim, become part of London's material culture, functioning like archival documents to commemorate events such as Henry VI's entry into London in 1432, conferring upon them a "timeless and ritual quality" (179). In an afterword, D. Vance Smith explores Lydgate's "open when," most notorious from Lydgate's imitation of Chaucer in the prologue to his *Siege of Thebes*, in which Lydgate compounds numerous "when" clauses without ever providing a "then." Lydgate's syntactic dilation is a resistance to *deixis*, a repudiation of the real time of experience that exposes the limits of human capacity to attain knowledge and aesthetic pleasure.

Some readers might hesitate over the different interpretations of materiality that underlie the essays in this volume: the material circumstances of the production and dissemination of texts in some cases, in others a condition of existence for poetry to explore, and in others still a wellspring of metaphors by which poetry can be connected to the physical world. Readers might also wonder whether such a short volume needs an overview of its contents both in the introduction and in an afterword. Nevertheless, each of these essays makes an important contribution to its subject. Taken as a whole, *Lydgate Matters* is a groundbreaking volume that will influence many reassessments of Lydgate's well-known poems and will open up lesser-known poems to discussion. The book is a landmark in Lydgate studies and makes an important contribution to our understanding of what public culture means in fifteenth-century England.

Scott-Morgan Straker
Queen's University

Isabel Davis. *Writing Masculinity in the Later Middle Ages*. Cambridge: Cambridge University Press, 2007. Pp. xiii, 222. £50.00; $96.00.

The frontispiece of Isabel Davis's excellent book shows an early fifteenth-century misericord, which itself depicts a carver producing a misericord. This astonishingly self-reflexive object is the artfully chosen material example of a phenomenon that Davis locates in late fourteenth- and early fifteenth-century writing. The volume explores "intersections between medieval masculine subjectivity and the ethics of labor and living, within a group of texts that are geographically proximate and that span the two generations between c. 1360 and c. 1430" (2). This complex but arresting book brings together work on five major writers of this period—Langland, Usk, Gower, Chaucer, and Hoccleve—and is focused on three central ideas: life-writing, the representation of labor, and masculinity. These three things, as Davis compellingly shows, were closely related. Her analysis of "how" and "why" marshals a great deal of material—theoretical, historical, literary-critical—into some important new perspectives on all of these writers, and perhaps on late medieval culture on a broader, and deeper, level.

Davis traces the "fixation" (9) on labor in these texts (and one thinks particularly of Langland's *Piers Plowman* here) to the demographic and social changes of the fourteenth century, particularly acute in London, where the language of labor statutes collided with the newness, the fluidity, of social and labor identities in an especially palpable way. Indeed, it is this tension between "official" or traditional figures of labor and masculinity and the "unstable cusp identity" (9) of many of these writers (semiclerical; bureaucratic) that, Davis argues, goes some way to producing the vast and intricate complexity, and the self-reflexiveness and anxiety, of something like *Piers Plowman*. In this burst of vernacular writing in the years 1360–1430, we might see "a representation of a new masculine modality: a kind of *urbanitas*, a pragmatic non-heroic identity that is an unsteady accommodation between the 'common good' and the interior, appetitive self" (11). This is ultimately the wider argument of the book, which works to bind together some very detailed discussions of individual texts.

This idea—the "unheroic," practical, even bourgeois image of masculinity in many late medieval texts—is evocative of parts of J. A. Burrow's wonderful book *Ricardian Poetry* (1971), but Davis's formulation of it is both more historically specific and more theoretically sophisticated. For Davis's study is less interested in the possibilities of canon formation and literary periodization, which were important parts of Burrow's book. Instead, Davis centers her analysis on London culture and London writing in a distinctive and compelling way. But Davis's point is not that all these texts worry away at the issue of masculine selfhood and social roles in the same way. Importantly, the broad thesis about the shifting nature of masculine self-representation and its relation to late medieval economic and social history is never allowed to overpower the complex textual analysis of the individual works.

Chapter 1 focuses on Langland's *Piers Plowman*. This is an excellent analysis of the poem, which relates some familiar contexts for the poem (fourteenth-century labor legislation) with aspects of it that are less frequently emphasized. In a sequence of astute and artful close readings of Langland's verse, Davis's analysis describes how the poem's preoccupation with the language of labor is connected to issues of sexuality and marriage. This is an excellent point, for Langland's poem is often seen (and certainly regularly taught) as a poem whose focus is largely sociopolitical and/or anticlerical. Davis's reading of the poem helps to show how economic and political discourses were closely integrated with discourses about domesticity, sexuality, and selfhood. Most strikingly, perhaps, Davis shows how Langland can be seen to be "negotiating a more privileged place for marriage and fatherhood within his theological poetics" (14), and that Langland's representation of marriage "always looks for loopholes in the Catholic case for the primacy of virginity" (24).

This complex, erudite discussion leads into a substantial and important analysis of Thomas Usk's work that again grounds the book in the locality of London culture, particularly in terms of the civic politics surrounding the dramatic mayoral elections of the 1380s. Here Davis shapes an argument about Usk's sentimental evocations of London as home that acts as a strong and sensible corrective to much scholarship on Usk, which tends to formulate a punitive image of Usk's texts as "fundamentally dishonest" (39). The reasons for these reactions—Usk's alleged betrayal of an idealistic, populist cause in the shape of Northampton's political career—are perhaps difficult to argue against, but Davis's discussion works to interrogate some of the historical bases for this view, and offers an arresting argument about the close intersection of the politics of the 1383 election with the representation of the urban domestic household and the emotive evocation of "home."

Chapter 3 is one of the best pieces of scholarship on Gower's *Confessio* for some time. The opening gambit of this chapter rests on the idea of a comparison between the poem's author sailing up the Thames in one of the *Confessio*'s prologues, about to produce his "foundational" vernacular text "for Englond's sake," and Brutus's own geographic movement across Europe toward his founding of Britain. The connection, as Davis writes, places Gower in a genealogical relationship with a rather "cut-price hero" and sets up an important theme of "flawed masculinity" (77) in the poem. Heroic, aristocratic masculinity, the values of the knight-errant, are replaced in Gower's text by a masculinity that is potentially rather more errant in a different sense, for it is "a kind of *urbanitas*, a city-based and middling masculinity" (93), which creates new ideas of masculinity even as it appropriated some of the courtly mode of aristocratic masculinity. This is a particularly arresting idea when applied to many of Gower's "heroes." Gower's ethics might, as Davis argues, have rather more to do with the dynamics of domesticity than we had previously thought.

The chapter on Chaucer's *Canon's Yeoman's Tale* is also very good. Davis focuses on how the tale acts rather like the autobiographical movements of both the Wife of Bath and Pardoner, as a site of Butlerian "gender trouble." But the focus is again on the historically and geographically specific site of urban apprenticeship—the London-based debates about the homosocial bonds of master and apprentice. *The Canon's Yeoman's Tale*, Davis shows, is wrought with the marks of contemporary discourse about apprenticeship and the dangers of unruly juvenile masculinity, but in a way that is far more complex, more interiorized, than that of *The Cook's Tale*, which more clearly stigmatizes such a figure.

Hoccleve's moving descriptions of the dislocations of selfhood—"Nat haue I wist / how in my skyn to tourne" (*My Complaint*, 303)—are used by Davis as the head of a chapter entitled "Autobiography and Skin," which artfully uses Hoccleve's work to return to the image of the King's Lynn misericord, with which the book opened. As Davis argues, both carving and text, words and wood, direct our attention toward a complex, self-reflexive representation of masculinity. In many ways, Hoccleve's poetry works as the archetypal example of Davis's argument. Coming at the end of a sequence of compelling chapters, Hoccleve's writing, in many cases the product not only of his own poetic but also scribal labors, emphasizes the way that "work defines the masculine self" (142) in the remarkable literature of this period.

MIKE RODMAN JONES
University of Cambridge

ELISABETH DUTTON. *Julian of Norwich: The Influence of Late-Medieval Devotional Compilations*. Cambridge: D. S. Brewer, 2008. Pp. 189. £50.00; $95.00.

There has been a surge of Julian scholarship recently: a new edition of her *Revelation of Divine Love* by Nicholas Watson and Jacqueline Jenkins (2006), and a number of book-length studies and collections of critical essays. This scholarship tends to fall into two general categories: theorized readings, focusing on issues such as gender and corporeality, and more historicized, codicological readings, excavating the ecclesiastical context of Julian's *Revelation* (is it to be dated pre- or post-Archbishop Arundel's *Constitutions* of 1409?) and interpreting the variations between the short and long texts, and between different manuscripts. Elisabeth Dutton's book falls clearly within the latter category of approach. Building on essays by Vincent Gillespie, and more recent studies by Marleen Cré and Annie Sutherland, among others, Dutton seeks to contextualize the *Revelation* within a late fourteenth- and early fifteenth-century culture of devotional compilation, examining the possible influence of these compilations on the form and structure of Julian's text, and on the way in which it mediates *auctoritas*.

The main devotional compilations selected for extended discussion in this study are *Lyf of Soule* (c. 1375–1400), *Book to a Mother* (c. 1370–80), *Speculum Christiani* (c. 1390–1425), *The Chastising of God's Children* (c. 1391–1408), and *Contemplations of the Dread and Love of God* (c. 1375–1425). Dutton offers a useful overview of these somewhat understudied texts, skillfully tracing the mechanisms by which they assemble and synthesize various sources in the process of reiterating the catechetical materials of Archbishop Pecham's pastoral "syllabus" of 1281.

Points of possible comparison are identified between these compilations and Julian's *Revelation*: in Chapter 1, Dutton examines the *ordinatio* (the arrangement of material) of the short and long texts of the *Revelation*, and views the table of contents and chapter headings of the latter in relation to similar organizational devices in *Chastising* and other early fifteenth-century compilations. She argues that these organizational devices (the table of contents probably authored by Julian in her judgment, the chapter headings far less certainly so) encourage the reader to adopt a *selective* and meditative approach to the text: to participate in a "bit" reading, in effect, whereas the absence of similar textual divisions in the Amherst manuscript of the short text suggests the expectation of a more extended, *consecutive* reading.

In addition to relating at the level of *ordinatio*, Dutton maintains that the *Revelation* also shows similarities to the devotional compilation in the textual markers that it uses to introduce and guide interpretation, and in the ways in which it presents source material. Adapting compilers' techniques of citation, Julian cites Christ's voice as though he were an *auctor* ("he seyth"), and the *Revelation* as though it were a source text, so that the *Revelation* "gives the appearance of compiling itself" (84).

An appraisal of the roles played by voices in compilation texts carries into chapters 3 and 4. Chapter 3 uses the dialogic structure of *Lyf of Soule*, in which catechetical lists are arranged around questions that "Sir" puts to "Friend," as a springboard for considering Julian's *Revelation* as a dialogic text. The ways in which this dialogue is formulated and the nature of the voices in play can be construed variously. Dutton identifies ongoing interlocutions between the teachings of the holy church and the divine voice, and between Julian at the time of her visions and twenty years on, while also making extensive use of Nicholas Watson's designation of the long text as an extended dialogue between the voices of "Julian-the-inspired-visionary" and "Julian-the-questing-believer." Dutton sensitively explores the way in which the more questioning of the two voices within the *Revelation* is made available to readers for their own use and appropriation. In addition, she shows how the *mise-en-page* of one of the Sloane manuscripts of the long text supports this dialogic understanding, displaying the respective voices of the *Revelation* by means of underlining and larger script.

Chapter 4 studies the use of voices *outside* dialogue to structure material in devotional compilations. Using *Book to a Mother* as the point of departure, Dutton describes a characteristic process whereby voices from varied textual sources "circle" around central images, returning time and time again to these images from a range of vantage points, in a complex and inclusive act of structuring and interpretation. In *Book to a Mother*, the central image in question is that of Christ the book. Dutton identifies a similar use of "circling" in Julian's *Revelation*, both at the level of the verbal repetition of phrases, creating "small textual circles," and at a broader figurative level. Celebrated images, such as the "crucified Christ," the "mother," the "hazelnut," and the "lord and servant," are reassessed as examples of compilational ring composition, generating a submerged structure of fluid spirals beneath the apparent linearity of the sixteen revelations.

Dutton admits that some of the codicological evidence underpinning this study must be treated with caution, given the very late dates of the manuscripts for Julian's long text. And it is true that, at times, the arguments for the relation between the *Revelation* and the early fifteenth-century devotional compilation can seem a little thin, based on slightly slender or speculative premises. Nonetheless, this should not be allowed to detract from an appreciation of the excellent scholarship and usefulness of this study. Dutton provides an admirably clear account of the current state of codicological research on Julian's *Revelation*, supplemented by her own careful manuscript observations. She navigates the complex waters of the late medieval devotional compilation with assurance and authority and offers an invaluable overview, drawing out common features of form and structure and identifying characteristic approaches to the mediation of source material, and to didactic engagement with the reader. Finally, she offers a series of nigh-on faultless close readings of passages from the *Revelation*, weighing its complexities of voice, form, and texture with a judiciousness and balance that combine to render this book an important contribution to current Julian studies.

CHRISTIANIA WHITEHEAD
University of Warwick

RACHEL FULTON AND BRUCE W. HOLSINGER, eds. *History in the Comic Mode: Medieval Communities and the Matter of Person*. New York: Columbia University Press, 2007. Pp. 408. $46.50.

In her 1991 collection, *Fragmentation and Redemption*, Caroline Walker Bynum challenged historians to consider a new mode of inquiry, one that embraced the many possibilities of the past, the richness and sometimes improbability of its stories, and the contradictions and inconsistencies inherent in the historical record. Arguing in favor of what she termed "history in the comic mode," Bynum defended the writing of history as necessarily provisional and contingent, its goal not the revelation of historical "truth" but rather the celebration of the fragmentary and the intractable: what she presented as the glorious potential of the stories of the past. *History in the Comic Mode*, a *Festschrift* dedicated simply to "our teacher," takes up Bynum's challenge, offering what its editors describe as a "pointillist" history designed to provoke wonder and amusement, to raise many questions and suggest some answers, but above all to pay grateful tribute to the intellectual breadth, curiosity, and generosity of Caroline Walker Bynum.

This is a collection inspired by the fun of doing history. The essays, each in its way a tribute to Bynum's teaching and intellectual influence, readily embrace the fragmentary and the improbable, weaving from such diverse sources as saints' lives, alchemical treatises, political texts, medical compilations, illuminated manuscripts, sermons, reliquaries, charters, and the discarded scraps of merchants' letters, stories of devotion, contagion, commerce, trauma, magic, belief, sanctity, and suffering. United neither by a single overarching question nor by a new theoretical approach, the essays share instead in a common attention to the particular and the partial. It is here, in the fractional and incomplete, that the fun can be found. History is a game, the editors aver, although its "play" does nothing to detract from the volume's scholarly rigor. History can be fun precisely because it requires careful attention to the sources as well as critical engagement with the past. Although hard and fast conclusions ultimately prove elusive, each contribution nevertheless engages the reader in an exciting dialogue that invites response and refinement.

History in the comic mode is a risky business, in part because it refuses the security of closure. Its practitioners recognize—indeed, they celebrate—the open-endedness of their contributions. "Ultimately, we are left to wonder," Catherine M. Mooney concludes in her own contribution concerning the textual tradition of Angela of Foligno, leaving questions concerning Angela's family, her relationships with her husband, mother, and children, and their influence on her spiritual journey unanswered (67). Mooney's essay, like others in the volume, confronts the fragmentary nature of the medieval sources, highlighting the ways in which historians, in the face of the partial and incomplete, have tended to fill in the blanks. In Angela's case, the silences of the textual record (itself complicated, as Mooney shows) have given rise to multiple interpretations, which—changing over time—reflect the changing interests of historians and their changing approaches to the past. Angela, pictured variously as an adulterous, virtuous, and abused wife and mother, emerges from the historical record less as a figure in her own right than as a reflection of shifting ideas (medieval and modern) concerning female sanctity and sexuality.

As Angela's case demonstrates, the writing of history is necessarily a process of "continuous rethinking" (280). This rethinking is essential and to be welcomed since each generation, inspired by its own questions, is automatically part of the "story": "the only real mistake," the editors comment, "is to imagine that . . . we can ever fully, if indeed at all, abstract ourselves from the fray" (286). Like Bynum, whose writing often assumes a narrative "we," the contributors admit their own stake in the questions they ask: Sharon Farmer writes, noting her mounting interest in relations between East and West since September 11, 2001, "As historians we turn to those fragments of the past that speak to our own experience and concerns" (205). The risk of writing history in the comic mode, then, is not simply the risk of being wrong, but the risk of admitting a personal stake in the past, and in the telling of that past. The past is not "other," as many historians might like to think, but is instead radically connected to the present and to present concerns, as the editors observe: "There is no past except insofar as we are alive to think about it" (288). Like Bynum, who led a generation of scholars to consider medieval asceticism on its own terms, the contributors refuse the false comfort of "rhetorical distance" (289), refusing, too, to "smirk at the past" (287) or—perhaps most important—to treat such subjects as religion with the irony so common within scholarly discourse.

This is a volume rich both in part and in whole. Its twenty-one essays, primarily the work of Bynum's students, but including friends and colleagues, too, range chronologically from the ninth century (Frederick S. Paxton's study of the failed cult of Hathumoda, first abbess of Gandersheim) to the sixteenth (John Jeffries Martin's examination of personal identity, bodily integrity, and the fragmented soul within Reformed theology). Although they eschew grand theories, they nevertheless evince a shared attention to themes signaled in the volume's subtitle: medieval communities and the matter of person. The individual—previously the subject of debate and deliberation—has here been replaced by attention to relationships between persons, groups, and ideas. Relations between entities are also explored: body and soul, image and text, elite and popular culture, religion and science, and the living and the dead serve as touchstones throughout the book.

Inspired by questions that illuminate the how and why of medieval culture, rather than those that demand concrete answers, the authors ask how suffering binds the living to the dead (Anna Harrison), what impact religiosity has on economic development (Richard Landes), how sin can be thought to "infect" a community (Susan R. Kramer), what merchant "talk" might have meant in an economy predicated on reciprocal services (Jessica Goldberg), how the separated soul can suffer physical pain (Manuele Gragnolati), and why educated men came, after centuries of skepticism, to believe that witches could fly (Steven P. Marrone). Several essays interrogate the relationship between experience or devotion and textual or artistic production. Anne L. Clark asks how Elisabeth of Schönau's experience of Benedictine monasticism shaped her visionary corpus, assessing the value and limitations of cognitive theory in illuminating the "mindedness" of her practice. Alison K. Frazier, in a provocative essay that challenges its readers to reconsider their own complicity in the reproduction of trauma, asks how Machiavelli's experience of torture influenced his writing of *The Prince*. Marlene Villalobos Hennessy examines the blood piety of a late medieval Carthusian manuscript, showing how body and spirit, image and text, could fuse through devotional reading. Jacqueline E. Jung explores the devotional significance of the Visitation Group from St. Katharinenthal, with their crystalline wombs glowing strangely high in their chests. What might these luminous womb-hearts have meant to the nuns who gazed on them?

Other essays challenge the modern tendency to define medieval groups in stark terms. As Anna Trumbore Jones writes, canons and monks could serve similar spiritual roles for donors from the ninth to the eleventh century. Raymond Clemens shows how a late thirteenth-century Dominican could turn to the Franciscans as his spiritual allies, viewing the adoption of Franciscan poverty as a requirement for ecclesiastical renewal. Thomas Head reexamines references to heretics in the eleventh century, showing what it meant to call someone an Arian, or a Manichee. Mark Silk explains how a twelfth-century schoolman could challenge Augustine's criticism of Roman civil theology, arguing that even fraudulent elements in non-Christian religions could serve a civic purpose. Mary Harvey Doyno shows how not only the friars but also the local clergy could promote lay sanctity in the Italian communes. By contrast, John Coakley explores how one medieval churchman, Thomas of Cantimpré, worked to shore up distinctions between holy women and their priests, depicting women's spiritual power as distinct from the authority of ordained men.

These essays, wide-ranging and challenging, are a fitting tribute to a teacher who has inspired not only her own students but also an entire generation of medievalists by her scholarship. Designed to bring pleasure, but also to provoke response, they mark the continuation of discussions that, in many cases, Bynum initiated. If, as she proposed, "historians, like the fishes of the sea, regurgitate fragments" (281), then it stands to reason that the fragments presented here will be regurgitated by subsequent generations, who will fashion from them new, and different, stories.

FIONA GRIFFITHS
New York University

MATTHEW GIANCARLO. *Parliament and Literature in Late Medieval England.* Cambridge: Cambridge University Press, 2007. Pp. xiv, 289. £50.00; $95.00.

In *Parliament and Literature in Late Medieval England,* Matthew Giancarlo enters what is an increasingly complex conversation among literary historians regarding the degree to which we might understand literature in relation to developing political and social forms and modes. In tackling the topic of parliament and literature, Giancarlo indicates his willingness to think at once broadly and in depth. His courage is matched by his sense of discretion and order, for he handles a subject that could easily get out of hand, or grow turgid, with intelligence, dexterity, and learning. The plan he announces in his Preface serves him well as a rhetorical frame. Rather than slogging through text after text pointing out references to parliament, he describes the development of parliament as a place for "discussion" and "deliberation" (ix), arguing that late medieval England offered a "cultural moment" mutually expressed through both imaginative literature and parliamentary politics. Both can be described as frequently standing at the junctures constituting the very fabric of community—those competing interests of status, both economic and social, that were reformulated in the contemporary understanding of justice, of representation, of the limits (or powers) of the secular sphere, and of the constitution of that sphere. Giancarlo's interest in voice, or in the voicing that emerges from this "locus of public discourses" (15), owes much, as he acknowledges, to the seminal essay by Anne Middleton, "The Idea of Public Poetry in the Reign of Richard II." In choosing to focus on parliament as the site and idea of representation as it influenced or impinged on literary consciousness, he traces ways in which authors exploited topical resonances and institutional forms, such as petitions and bills, in a literature whose expansiveness paralleled that of parliament at the same time.

The book's six chapters suggest at once the scope and the underlying discipline of his argument. The first two are primarily historical, outlining the nature of parliament's representation, the gradual expansiveness of that representation, parliament's importance as a court of complaint, and its self-construction as a representative and a univocal body. Giancarlo begins this chapter by focusing on images of parliament to be found in late medieval and early modern books that provide pictures of the community of the realm, from the earlier baronial bodies to the later representations of both nobility and commons. If parliament is the "public," then how parliament is depicted says much about who that public is thought to be. Giancarlo goes on to consider Peter Langtoft and Robert Mannyng and their use of Arthurian "history" to comment on Edward I's relationship with his parliament and *Havelok the Dane*'s conceptualization of the *vox publica* as linked to a spiritual ideal of deliberative assembly, which, in turn, legitimates royal marriage and decisions. While such works provided pictures of ideal monarchs, they also provided pictures of communal unanimity, which were attached both negatively and positively to parliamentary Commons. Giancarlo follows historians in seeing the deposition of Edward II as crucial for the development of the identity of Commons as the voice of the commons and offers some fine critical readings of the language of the Parliament Rolls. Parliament's role and representation grew during the period, but it also became a focus for complaint and critique, as the second chapter demonstrates with its reading of the role of the Good Parliament of 1376, of the "Mercers Petition" of 1388, and of the *Modus Tenendi Parliamentum* and its discussion of critiques by both Thomas Brinton and John Bromyard, which take up the univocality of parliament as prompting silence in the face of injustice, fraud, and violence.

With the next three chapters, Giancarlo explores more obviously literary texts: Gower's *Mirour de l'Omme* and *Cronica Tripertita*; Chaucer's parliaments, particularly those in the *Parliament of Fowls*, the *Melibee*, and *Troilus and Criseyde*; and Langland's *Piers Plowman* and its sixteenth-century progeny. In the sixth and final chapter, which deals with poems like *Richard the Redeless* and *Mum and the Sothsegger*, Giancarlo argues that the topicality of later poems signals "the waning of parliament and *parlement* as a resource for the formal arrangement of narrative art." The increasing power of the king's parliament during the Lancastrian reign made it a topic, rather than a structuring idea (209). Giancarlo argues that the energy previously devoted to the idea of parliamentary representation as self-consciously mediatory passed to instances of civic culture and thus to new forms, such as mummings, drama, the triumph, and the lyric. Such literary transformations paralleled the growing emphasis on ideals of strong kingship during the political instabilities of the fifteenth century. Giancarlo's remarks here are speculative and need the attention of another such sustained study.

Parallel to some finely honed readings of major literary texts are some equally astute readings of parliamentary texts. Giancarlo spends time with the Septvauns affair of 1365–66, in which Gower unfortunately figures as part of a group of men who were held up as public examples by a parliament apparently less interested in the rights of heirs than in the fiscal interests of Crown and nation. He discusses the connection between parliament, property, and marriage, especially noble marriage, in his account of Elizabeth de Burgh, whose status and wealth made her the object of the Despensers' greed during the reign of Edward II and of petitionary restitution during the reign of Edward III, just as her marriages were matters of political (and thus parliamentary) import when they were arranged.

This is a rich book and a learned one. Giancarlo writes clearly and simply, offering real historical information about the history of parliament, parliamentary Commons, and parliamentary procedure. His account of parliament cannot be new—there is much important historical work cited in his notes—but his perspective on it and its cultural implications are noteworthy. His critical and cultural arguments emerge from his familiarity with texts in England's three languages, which he cannily employs in an argument for a common voice. He also offers some trenchant remarks about petitionary narrative, about gender—both historically and imaginatively represented—and about the development of literary forms in relation to historic events. In moving easily from the thirteenth to the early sixteenth century, he makes an implicit argument for grounding our understanding of the early modern period in an understanding of medieval forms and institutions. I can see much good work emerging from a study as filled with attentive readings, sound scholarship, and cultural awareness as this one.

LYNN STALEY
Colgate University

DOUGLAS GRAY. *Later Medieval English Literature*. Oxford: Oxford University Press, 2008. Pp. xiii, 712. £65.00; $130.00.

This comprehensive and engaging survey grows from Douglas Gray's long scholarly commitment to the literature of a period which he has done so much to rehabilitate—suitably dignified in the title of a 1997 Festschrift in his honor as "the long fifteenth century." Offered modestly as "a kind of guidebook for the curious traveller," the book maps the literary contours of the years from around 1400 to 1530 in generously descriptive detail. The texts covered are organized conventionally enough into sections on "prose," "poetry," "Scottish writing" and "drama," but each section contains its own multitudes, and one would be hard pressed to think of a work or a genre that does not get a mention. Schoolboy *vulgaria*, medical receipts and charms, "merry tales," ballads, and anonymous lyrics are all here alongside longer works by the likes of Lydgate and Pecok and More and Malory. Gray is avowedly keen to avoid arguing for particular "messages," whether those of individual texts or of larger cultural tendencies, but he provides in the first part of the book three chapters that explore the private, public, and technical aspects of late medieval human existence with compelling illustrative detail. Some gestures are made in these chapters (and intermittently in the rest of the book) to identifying "Dionysian" and "Apollonian" strands in late medieval culture, but such generalization is mostly avoided, and the introductory chapters concentrate rather on textual evidence relating to contemporary views on travel, exploration, nationhood, and geography; to court and popular culture; to bodily and mental health; to education, literacy, and language; and (in some especially absorbing pages) to the functioning of words and images in late medieval piety.

340

Within the succeeding sections of the book, individual chapters map roughly onto the divisions in Gray's *Oxford Book of Late Medieval Verse and Prose* (first published in 1985): the anthology's collection of "Nifles, Trifles, and Merry Jests," for example, is complemented in the new volume by a chapter on "Tales, Jests, and Novelle in Prose"; the anthology's section of "Chaucerian poems" by a chapter here with the same title. The method within individual chapters, after a paragraph or so of introductory discussion, is fairly straightforwardly descriptive. This has a number of virtues. The book is an enormously useful compendium of summaries, and enables readers efficiently to find out about and contextualize individual texts or genres (a short opening chronology and an unfussy index are further aids, although the amount of bibliography offered is strictly limited to editions and secondary works cited in discussion; one slightly irksome feature is that quotations are not referenced in any way). The summaries themselves are deft and illuminating, often witty, and full of well-chosen quotation—enough of this at times to give a spurious sense of close acquaintance with a work one has never read, and likely to be dangerously seductive for the student pressed for time. In the parts of the book occupied by summary, the writing is strikingly fluid, accommodating asides and parentheses alongside the many quotations in ways that give the flavor of an agreeable talk rather than of formal written discourse. Only when the end of a summary coincides with the end of a chapter does this strike an odd note, leaving one slightly high and dry as if suddenly deserted by an acquaintance in the middle of a conversation.

Gray's previous publications have included substantial studies of Henryson (*Robert Henryson*, 1979) and of Middle English religious lyrics (*Themes and Images in the Medieval Religious Lyric*, 1972), and he has done much to draw attention to Henryson's brilliance of style and to the imaginative power of a number of Middle English short poems. His perspicacity in noting features and effects of style and of narrative structure, and in exploring "the traditional imaginary museum which was well stocked with images and themes often derived from the liturgy or the Bible" (372), is in evidence throughout *Later Medieval English Literature*. The sections in this book on lyrics and on Henryson and other Scottish writing are among its highlights. Less predictably perhaps, the parts of the book devoted to Malory and to the mystery cycles offer richly detailed readings and much food for further thought. The discussion of the plays is prefaced by an introductory chapter on performance that takes in Brecht and non-naturalistic traditions of Southeast Asian drama as well as mummings and processions and pageants. Other especially effective passages of discussion are those dealing with letters and other forms of "practical" prose and with the "Romances and Tales," which include poems on Robin Hood. Notable throughout the whole volume is the ease with which Gray moves both within his chosen period and outside it. His understanding of late medieval literature is buttressed by knowledge of its antecedents and of what grew from it. The benefits of this are obvious, for example, in his pages on late medieval Wycliffite writings, where information about the fourteenth- and sixteenth-century transmission of such texts helps to clarify what was distinctive about their circulation in the fifteenth century. Elsewhere there are some suggestive forward references to Spenser (in connection with Hawes and other forms of verse allegory) and to Shakespeare (in connection with drama).

One of the sections of *The Oxford Book of Late Medieval Verse and Prose* is subtitled "Many More Diversities of Many Wonderful Things" (words quoted from Mandeville), and it may be that this less-mainstream material has always most caught Gray's interest and continues to do so in *Later Medieval English Literature*. From some points of view the book perhaps does more justice to "diversities" than it does to authors like Lydgate and Hoccleve, whose comparatively short chapter has a slightly weary air. But Gray is surely right to stress that the long late medieval period contains many things, and that among its textual richness even an oeuvre as abundant as Lydgate's needs to be put in perspective. Literary history, as offered in this volume, is precisely what it says it is: taking in all forms of writing, and reading them in the light of what can be constructed of the culture in which they were produced. Among the strengths of this book are Gray's hugely detailed knowledge of both texts and history, and the light touch with which readers are invited to share it.

JULIA BOFFEY
Queen Mary, University of London

D. H. GREEN. *Women Readers in the Middle Ages*. Cambridge: Cambridge University Press, 2007. Pp. 296. $95.00; £50.00.

On its dust jacket, D. H. Green's magisterial *Women Readers* sports Roger van der Weyden's famous image of the Magdalene reading (dated before 1438), one of the few surviving fragments of what must have been a magnificent altarpiece. It tells a now-familiar story about medieval women and their books. By the end of the Middle Ages, high-status women (as the sumptuously outfitted Magdalene surely is) were routinely taught to read as an aide to domestic devotion. The currency of images like this is a testament to the pioneering work of scholars in the 1980s and early 1990s (dating back, at least, to Susan Groag Bell's 1982 article in *Signs*), which put women's devotional literacy on the critical agenda and, of course, to the considerable scholarship that has been produced since. But, paradoxically, it does little justice to Green's volume.

The image of a solitary, reformed prostitute engrossed in a holy book works to confirm, rather than dispel, our preconceptions about the apparent limits of women's literacy, preconceptions that often converge with the prejudices of Latinate clerics and anxious moralists. The fifteenth-century Austin Fishmonger, for instance, imagined reading as part of a punishing routine designed to discipline women: "It syttyt fwyll wele a woman to be newere idyl, but eyþer workyng, prayyng, redyng, spynnynge, sewyng or wepyng or morning for synne"; he would have approved of the bookish Magdalene. The achievement of *Women Readers* is its author's insistence that we rephrase our questions: about women, about their reading practices, and about the rich body of evidence that survives.

The compass is broad: from Abbess Hilda of Whitby in the seventh century to Margaret Beaufort at the start of the sixteenth (with a particular focus on that perennial watershed, the twelfth century), in three countries (Germany, France, and England), and in no fewer than four languages. The examples Green uses are necessarily selective and he is palpably more at home in medieval Germany (of which he is a specialist) than England or, to a lesser extent, France, where his reliance on the accumulated insights of other scholars is most evident. This is not a criticism. One of the strengths of *Women Readers* is that Green readily acknowledges his perch on the shoulders of the proverbial giants. This is the first monograph to offer a comprehensive overview of a relatively new field of inquiry and, simultaneously, to try to think beyond the limits of individual case studies, many of which—like Roberta Krueger on women readers and Old French romance, Jeffrey Hamburger on the devotional images produced by the nuns of St. Walburg, Felicity Riddy on women "talking about the things of God"—are ground-breaking in their own right.

The volume is divided into two parts. The first, "Reading in the Middle Ages," offers a detailed discussion of what it meant to read, as well as to be literate, in the Middle Ages, for both women and men. Green exposes the clerical definition of literacy (as coincident with Latinity) for what it is—a blatant ploy to monopolize the power attributed to textual culture for itself—and instead seeks to valorize not only vernacular literacy but a much wider spectrum of often indirect reading practices, including most importantly the common medieval equation of reading with listening (the widely attested practice of reading with the ears). Here the disjunction between Van der Weyden's very modern solitary reader and the ones Green primarily charts is at its starkest.

It is in the second part, "Women and Reading in the Middle Ages," that Green's work is most exciting. The first of two chapters opens with a summary of recent scholarship on women's education, highlighting the significance of the domestication of literacy in the High Middle Ages, before turning to a catalogue-like analysis of the different types of women readers: laywomen, nuns, recluses, semireligious, and heretics. The chapter is, quite literally, stuffed (Green is no stylist) with evidence—documentary, visual, monumental, implied—and its greatest strength is methodological. No longer restricted to women who read with their eyes (although he finds more than enough of those), Green is able to recover a much richer, more nuanced, and more populated picture of women's reading activities than we have seen before. Indeed, it is through his foregrounding of a range of more fluid models of reading than we are accustomed to thinking about that Green is able to offer, in his final chapter, a radical reassessment of women's contribution to medieval literary culture.

What Green demonstrates, so provocatively, is that once we do away with our postromantic preoccupation with the "creative author" as the origin of literature (a preoccupation that is at odds with almost everything we know about medieval literary practice), we discover something really rather extraordinary. Medieval women—as the sponsors, the intended recipients, and sometimes the producers—were at the forefront of almost every major literary innovation of the Middle Ages, often in contrast to the conservative impulses of their fathers, husbands, or monastic brothers. To cite only a few examples: Abbess Hilda of Whitby encouraged the earliest Christian poetry in Anglo-Saxon; Hrosvitha of Gandersheim is the first named Christian dramatist; the first chronicles in French were initiated by women, Constance Fitzgilbert and Adeliza of Louvain; Marie de France introduced the *matière de Bretagne* into European literature; and Arthur entered the vernacular for Eleanor of Aquitaine, to whom Wace presented his *Roman de Brut*; to Mechthild of Magdeburg, we owe the first autobiographically structured work in German, while Margery Kempe and Julian of Norwich introduced a similar innovation in English; the nuns of both Syon and Barking took leading roles in the development of "vernacular theology" in England. And the list goes on.

With *Women Readers*, the medieval woman reader has come of age, but it is not a moment to sit back and celebrate. Green ends on a challenge: "Much remains to be done." Following Dennis Green's death in December 2008, it is now even more incumbent on us to take up the baton.

NICOLA MCDONALD
University of York

AMANDA HOLTON. *The Sources of Chaucer's Poetics*. Aldershot: Ashgate, 2008. Pp. x, 168. £55; $99.95.

Amanda Holton does not intend to explore (as her title might suggest) where Chaucer got his ideas about what poetry is and what it might do; rather, she compares the employment of a substantial list of specific narratological, rhetorical, and poetic techniques in a selection of Chaucerian narratives and their source texts, asking whether Chaucer follows the poetic techniques of those sources or reformulates them according to his own predilections (1). Those narratives—several legends of good women, some tragedies from *The Monk's Tale*, and the *Tales* of the Knight, Man of Law, Physician, and Manciple—are chosen because, being neither literal translations (like the *Melibee*) nor of mixed or uncertain derivation (*The Franklin's Tale*), they give the clearest evidence about the direction of Chaucer's changes.

Since analysis, not argument, structures Holton's inquiries, striking conclusions mingle with more familiar ones, definitive tendencies with what might be random practice. Thus a complete summary is hardly possible, and her central findings may be appropriately presented in a list:

- Chaucer consistently tells the same story as his source, varying from its plot only to exclude events deemed "inessential" (15–18) or to realign it chronologically (21–22).
- Descriptions of setting and character are kept or increased (27–28), and usually moved toward the beginning, regardless of their position in the source (25). This is further evidence of Chaucer's interest in clarity.
- As he narrates, Chaucer frequently pauses to judge the action, generalize from it, and (especially) provide metafictional commentary (33). Such commentary frequently conflicts with plot details, creating narrative friction for the reader, as in *The Physician's Tale* (38).
- Regardless of its deployment in the source, character speech occupies one-sixth to one-third of the Chaucerian narrative, which concentrates it in long speeches by major characters (49). In these passages, too, judgments are passed and narratological friction is generated, as in the "misplaced investment in a single god or power" (60) of Theseus's "First Mover" speech.
- Chaucer, more than his sources, shapes character speech into complaint about fortune: Virgil and Ovid give Dido and Philomena passionate, angry words that react meaningfully to their plights, but Chaucer's female characters more often bemoan (indeed perform) a lack of agency (50–52).
- Self-referential comments on narrative structure, quite pervasive, are *ipso facto* unlikely to be strategies for characterizing specific pilgrim-narrator characters (75–76).
  One important function of *occultatio* is to preserve (if only in a shortened form) the action narrated by respected sources like Ovid; other sources are cut silently (79–80).
- Chaucer uses the inexpressibility topos far more often in translating relatively uninteresting source texts—Holton cites Trevet—than highly articulate ones—Ovid. Insufficiency is located in the material Chaucer has to work with, not his own language (83–84).
- The predominant function of rhetorical figures is to generate emotion, especially "negative" emotions like reproach and distress (89).
- Chaucer uses metaphor and simile rather sparingly, in highly conventional forms (119). His similes are short and typically clustered in the text, making a single point in a variety of ways (123–30).

In her conclusion, Holton (appropriately abandoning the search for a single, consistent response) discusses *seriatim* Chaucer's varied responses to his source authors, tracing the different ways in which he finds each of them congenial (or not), and the different stimuli he is likely to follow (or not) in each (143–50).

My list highlights both strengths and weaknesses in Holton's analysis. If her structuralism seems somewhat dated, it nevertheless generates information we are not likely to discover through any other form of inquiry: poststructuralist narratology ignores the questions she wants to ask, questions that arise out of the nature of medieval texts in which, however intertextual the milieu, some antecedent texts are inescapably more significant than others. The breadth of Holton's analysis finesses the problems inherent in what Paul Strohm called "the straight-line transmission presumed by traditional source study" (*SAC* 17 [1995]: 26). She generates a large amount of meaningful data and almost always sifts through it carefully, consistently, and with some precision. Thus, a central negative conclusion—Chaucer neither uses nor responds to his sources in a uniform fashion—sits amid many positive, substantiated, and potentially generalizable findings: Chaucer's habit of setting narrative commentary or character speech against the grain of the action (consider *Troilus*), the emphasis placed on description and character speech (*Merchant's Tale*), the tendency of speech to suppress female agency (*Franklin's Tale*). Several of her conclusions are directly relevant to ongoing issues in Chaucerian interpretation, like debate about the degree to which Chaucer's narrators are characterized. The recognition that a couplet absent from the Hengwrt and Ellesmere manuscripts but included in the standard text of *The Knight's Tale* is a generalizing comment typical enough in Chaucer but atypical of that poem models another kind of usefulness (37).

But the problematics of source study have not been wholly eliminated. Holton notices a doubleness in that word—its ability to refer either to the series of events or the particular verbal texture Chaucer found in his source (79)—but never fully resolves the issues such doubleness creates. The degree to which Chaucer re-creates either structure varies considerably in the narratives Holton analyzes. Those interests coincide a great deal more when Ovid is the source, but John Fyler and Michael Calabrese have already taught us about that (as Holton, well read in secondary materials, reminds us). And supplying explanations for the phenomena it charted was never structuralism's strength: if "the fact that the story was exceptionally well-known" explains the paucity of descriptive "existents" in the *Legend of Dido* (26), might the usual abundance of such descriptions arise, not from a deeply ingrained narrative protocol, but from Chaucer's intellectual interest in telling unfamiliar tales? Classic structuralist studies—the sources of Holton's methodology—compare texts we would call analogues; structuralism, like other familiar narratological models, still stumbles over typical elements of medieval narration like the more complex source relationship.

Nor does Holton address the stretch required in accepting the narratives she discusses as definitive of Chaucer's practice. Among the texts she studies, only *The Knight's Tale* has generated much interest for its narratological qualities; many of them have consistently been disparaged as (specifically narratological) failures. Other examples, whose sources lie (for various reasons) outside Holton's purview, suggest limits to her conclusions: the *Tales* of the Clerk, Miller, Wife, and Nun's Priest all exceed Holton's upper limit on character speech: it makes up more than half of the latter two. Would anyone reading the Miller's description of Alison agree that "a wariness of the vagaries of figurative language" (141) is characteristic of Chaucer's narratology? Could a poet characterized by "a reluctance to disturb the surface of the text" (142) have written the epic similes in *The Nun's Priest's Tale*? Some of Holton's findings, especially about narrative structure (the tendency to substantial and front-loaded description), are confirmed in those narratives. But they also underscore the limits to what her study can tell us.

Thomas J. Farrell
Stetson University

William Kuskin. *Symbolic Caxton: Literary Culture and Print Capitalism.* Notre Dame, Ind.: University of Notre Dame Press, 2008. Pp. xxvi, 390. $40.00.

Most research into the works of William Caxton takes the form of bibliographical analyses and catalogues, which are the basis of all further research, or of biographical history, telling us of Caxton's personal achievement. What William Kuskin's monograph, *Symbolic Caxton,* offers instead is an analysis of Caxton's works through literary criticism. Influenced by the historicism of the 1980s and 1990s, this book also offers ideas about the role of Caxton's works in wider cultural history, such as the formation of the Chaucerian canon, the politics of Lancas-trian England (and, Kuskin wisely adds, Yorkist England), and the sup-posed divisions between "medieval" and "early modern." On the way, there are often unexpected critical readings of some neglected works, such as the book of hunting and arms printed at St. Albans in 1486 (56–67), Woodville's works (163–72), and of *Godfrey of Boloyne, Charles the Grete,* and Malory's *Morte d'Arthur* (216–32, in a chapter that first appeared in 1999). Other recent books, by Seth Lerer and Alexandra Gillespie, for example, have also blended the history of the book and literary criticism to good effect in considering Caxton's place in some of these stories, but Kuskin's book is distinctive in focusing solely on Caxton.

Kuskin's main conclusion is the sound reminder that print is not solely an innovative force but responds to, and reproduces, prior tradi-tions (3–5), something that scholars of Chaucerian and humanist print-ing have also suggested. He supports that point by noting how often fifteenth-century literature is itself interested in ideas of "reproduction" (18–20, 109). Then, most important, he extends the point to the argu-ment that Caxton and other early printers, by reproducing this earlier literature, prove that there is no divide between "medieval" and "early modern." In my view, we cannot dismantle this divide often enough. The Epilogue, one of the best bits of the book, reminds us how often fifteenth-century literature and Caxton's editions were reproduced in the sixteenth century (286–87) and how much fifteenth-century litera-ture is connected to phenomena that one might consider "modern." For example, *Everyman* survives as a printed book and is a play about the proliferation of commodities—and thus challenges what we think of as "medieval" drama (288–97).

Central to Kuskin's argument about Caxton's place in wider literary history are two phenomena of so-called early modernity: capitalism and humanism. The Introduction and chapters 1 and 2 discuss printing in relation to capitalism and finance, and they are interesting; indeed, chapter 2 was published in *New Medieval Literatures* in 1999 as a prize-winning essay. Kuskin offers "capital" as an alternative answer to the question whether it was patronage or commerce that dominated Cax-ton's career (81), although I suppose "capital" could be part of com-merce. Economic ideas shape some of the best bits of this book, about how "volume" affected what printers did (17) or how Caxton uses his printer's mark as a badge of commodity (50–73). In fact, I would have liked more discussion of the economic ideas, for the Introduction is fairly brief and allusive about the theoretical affiliations of the book (26). This book suggests how others might research further the impact of trade, finance, and consumerism in the late fifteenth century.

Chapter 6 offers an interesting discussion of Caxton's humanist interest in antiquity. The chapter confirms an argument by Seth Lerer and the present reviewer for likenesses between humanism and early English printing, although Kuskin uses different materials, notably a good interpretation of Caxton's *Eneydos* and *Ovyde* and the fears of classical paganism therein (243–57). The account of humanism threatens to find humanist study in cahoots with monarchy and aristocracy, as do many critics (279), but ends with a pleasingly complex—if overly complexly phrased—sense of the ambivalence in offering elite scholarship to the wider readerships of print (282–83).

Such views of the bigger picture and of the complexity in simple things are the successes of this monograph. Kuskin begins to imagine some intellectual frameworks for "the history of the book," even if he does not write in the mode of "the history of the book" itself.

There are just a very few comments that suggest uncertainty in describing early printed books; for example, an edition of Chartier's *Curyal* is described as having "one folio," rather than six folios in one quire (156). And although Kuskin conscientiously quotes from microfilms of original incunables, and not from modern editions, there are mistranscriptions—even when transcribing text shown in facsimile on adjacent pages (94/fig. 2.6, 140–42/fig. 3.2). The slips, though small, should be watched for: see, for example, "essugured" for "effugured," "almonelrye" for "almonesrye," "pyse" for "pyes," and "worldey" for "worldely" (65, 104, 293). There are also a few errors in titles and names in foreign languages (75, 187, 237, 302) and an edition of Pseudo-Phalaris is described as "unlisted by *STC*" but is in fact *STC* 19827 (75).

Finally, although this book *is* innovative in being a solely interpretive account of Caxton's work, it offers its ideas with too much portentousness. Of course there are the abstractions that obscure bright ideas in academic cliché ("a logic of," "the cultural economy," 8, 10), which we all sheeplikely use. But most annoying is the frequent use of the gravid phrase "I term this X" to introduce some term that everybody uses: Kuskin says of the influence of Chaucer, "I term this system the *Chaucerian inheritance*" and of humanism in the vernacular "I term this . . . *vernacular humanism*" (19, 21, 117, 236; see also 258, 298), although such terms are obvious and common. Kuskin even renames the literary work as "a specific object, call it a *text of art*, for future consumption" (6) or the process of reading and interpretation: "I term the study of the printed page *symbolic bibliography*" (74).

These minor criticisms must not hide the real achievement: thoughtful interpretation is not as common or as ambitious as it should be in studies of the history of the book or of Caxton's work, and so Kuskin has done something useful and enjoyable. I enjoyed being made to think about capital and being made to think about the big picture in relation to Caxton. And I hope that this book inspires others to research and think in this vein.

DANIEL WAKELIN
University of Cambridge

TIM WILLIAM MACHAN. *Chaucer's Boece: A Critical Edition Based on Cambridge University Library MS Ii.3.21, ff. 9r–180v.* Heidelberg: Universitätsverlag Winter. Pp. xli, 193. 58; $79.95. Paper.

Tim William Machan's edition of Chaucer's *Boece* makes an unusual addition to the Middle English Text Series, which until now has focused on the publication of works that have not previously been edited. In contrast, the *Boece* is conveniently and affordably available in the *Riverside Chaucer,* complete with explanatory and textual notes and glossary. As a forum for unpublished Middle English texts, this series is clearly aimed at the graduate student and scholarly market, while Machan's edition is evidently directed toward a wider audience, resulting in some rather uneasy compromises. For instance, Middle English Text Series editions generally present texts in their original spelling, whereas Machan's edition regularizes certain features of orthography and replaces medieval characters such as thorn and yogh in line with modern practice, presumably as an aid to the general reader. But despite this concession for a less-advanced reader, the edition does not include a glossary. There is a commentary that glosses some of the harder readings, but it is by no means an exhaustive glossary, and much of it is devoted to the noting of marginal glosses and their manuscript attestation. Readers who are interested in the historical and literary allusions of Chaucer's

351

work are advised to consult the "full and extremely valuable notes of Hannah [sic] and Lawler (1987)." It is not clear, then, which audience this edition is intended for, while the widespread availability of the *Riverside* edition among scholars and students alike suggests that its market will be limited.

The most radical difference between Machan's edition and the text of *Boece* as presented in the *Riverside Chaucer* concerns the choice of base text. Where the *Riverside* editors adopted Cambridge University Library MS Ii.1.38 (C1) as the base text for their edition, Machan elects to base his text on Cambridge University Library MS Ii.3.21 (C2), the manuscript used by Skeat as the basis for his Clarendon Press edition of 1894. C2 comprises a Boethian anthology in which Chaucer's text alternates with the corresponding Latin source and is accompanied by glosses taken from Nicholas Trevet's commentary. In the notes to the *Riverside Chaucer,* Hanna and Lawler express some doubts about the reliability of this manuscript, suggesting that previous editors who had used it as their base text were misled by the apparatus into overestimating its textual authority. Machan takes issue with this view and with previous editors' support for the "smoother readings" of C1, arguing that such readings are representative of "subsequent 'unauthoritative' refinements of what Chaucer actually wrote" (xxxii). Despite this choice of a different base text, Machan's edition does not present a text of the *Boece* that differs much from that of the *Riverside* edition. A sample collation of the first meter and prose sections reveals that both texts are substantially very similar, apart from a handful of differences where C2 is demonstrably inferior and has to be corrected by Machan by comparison with C1.

The most important contribution of this edition to the study of Chaucer's text is the admirably exhaustive textual apparatus, which comprises a complete corpus of variant readings found in all witnesses. In addition to allowing readers access to the full data upon which the present text was established, this corpus of variants will be of considerable value in allowing readers access to unoriginal readings. Scribal readings, and so-called bad texts, are of particular interest to scholars working on Chaucerian transmission and reception. In supplying a complete apparatus, on a scale simply not possible for the *Riverside* editors, Machan has provided scholars with an invaluable resource for research of this kind. Given the comprehensive recording of manuscript variation, it is disappointing that the descriptions of the manuscripts and early printed authorities are so brief, offering little more than a list of contents with references to the much fuller descriptions by Ralph Hanna in M. C. Seymour's *Catalogue of Chaucer Manuscripts*. The evidence for fifteenth-century ownership of the *Boece* manuscripts is unusually rich and it is surprising that Machan is so dismissive of the possibility of reconstructing the work's early readership (xii).

While this edition seems unlikely to become a replacement for the *Riverside* edition of Chaucer's *Boece*, it does make a valuable contribution to scholarly study of Chaucer's work. Read as a companion to Machan's earlier volume, *Sources of the "Boece,"* this edition will undoubtedly further our understanding of Chaucer's methods of translation and the reception and transmission of his work.

SIMON HOROBIN
Magdalen College, Oxford

ALASTAIR MINNIS. *Fallible Authors: Chaucer's Pardoner and Wife of Bath*. Philadelphia: University of Pennsylvania Press, 2008. Pp. xvi, 510. $69.95.

Alastair Minnis has few competitors among intellectual historians treating late medieval England, and none in the fields of literary scholarship. That does not mean that he has devoted more or deeper attention to medieval English literature itself than anyone around him. Instead, he has long focused on the concerns of "medieval literary criticism." That is, he has examined either what medieval academic or other learned commentary has to offer on topics of narrative form and purpose, authority, and authorship, especially in the Bible or ancient literature (in the charting of which Minnis made his name in the 1980s and 1990s), or the explicit use of such ideas by vernacular writers. A commitment to literature's thematic effects in themselves and its contextual meanings more generally defined—not to mention the modern critical debates that have sprung up around it—seems to come second. In *Fallible Authors*, though, Chaucer's two most famous figures are the capstone or portal of a magnificent edifice that will serve to orient a wide range of studies of other medieval writers and thinkers.

In this, his most magisterial study so far, Minnis traces the complex topic of how "authority" possessed two "bodies" in medieval culture (with a fittingly appreciative nod to Ernst Kantorowicz's 1957 study *The King's Two Bodies*, which "retains much of its original challenge" [10]): that of the transcendent moral utility of doctrine (or the salvific power of the sacraments), and that of the frail human vehicle of such higher forces. The broad terms of such a history—to offer an overly simplified capsule of Minnis's discussion—are that an earlier Augustinian insistence on the supreme force of the sacraments, no matter how sinful the human priest purveying them, encountered powerful resistance from resurgent Aristotelian traditions in the thirteenth century. Aristotelianism put far more weight on the human origins of authority, and began to treat artifice, verbal and other, as a separate thing from moral utility, with its own intrinsic (if therefore amoral) value. The focus on the human agent of sacramentality in turn helped create extreme Lollard positions in Chaucer's period that resembled the views of the early Donatists (Augustine's own antagonists), who claimed that the power of sacramentality or of a sermon was only as good as the moral worth of the human agent. Minnis traces the paradoxes of the treatments of these issues in the later Middle Ages in two domains: sinful clerics' moral sermons could still be spiritually efficacious, thanks to the transformative authority of priestly ordination itself; yet there remained a residual problem in the taint of scandal, which was managed in various awkward ways by orthodox commentary. At the same time, bodily gender still trumped moral discourse: even the highest doctrine offered by an old woman—conceived as the lowest creature of all, according to Minnis—could not achieve real authority.

Chaucer's two most famous figures, of course, epitomize and offer the opportunity for exploring the limit-cases of these questions, whose contemporary importance was at crisis point during the challenges of Lollardy in the 1390s, when Chaucer was writing. But intellectual history itself is the real star of this study. The two issues are woven and developed into an invaluable survey of what must be seen as the central paradoxes of late medieval ecclesiology and the grounds for the violent resolutions of the Reformation. And throughout the demonstration appears the question of how two such contradictory views of doctrinal authority's supremacy and a bodily, gendered barrier might coexist. That contradiction finds its clearest but not necessarily its most literarily supportive resolution in Lollardy, at whose intellectual strands Minnis's study offers the mostly finely grained look in recent years. *Fallible Authors* also offers at least glimpses of other key topics, as much cultural as literary or intellectual. The topic of "scandal," for example, here receives one of its best cameo histories I know of. For in spite of the orthodox Augustinian view that a sinful man could preach a moral sermon, the regular laity (and many of the religious) put great importance on the need to avoid scandal; this, in turn, led to an insistence that the preacher's sin be kept hidden. Another golden strand in Minnis's presentation is the nature of "professionalism" as a severing of "the office from the man" (related to the Aristotelian severing of artifice from morality). The effects of this are not explicitly developed in *Fallible Authors,* but they hardly need to be, at least for those already involved with the question of professional expertise in Chaucer's satiric portraits in *The General Prologue* and elsewhere.

In spite of the obvious value of laying such broad foundations, doing literary history within *longue-durée* intellectual history has always had known limitations and carried certain risks. One is that of being too narrowly confined to the explicit terms of the original materials—and original academic terms at that (surely never a perfect guide to poetry, even of its own periods). In previous books, Minnis has been unapologetic about resisting uses of "modern, not medieval, literary theory," which he there considered as "a tacit admission of defeat" (*Medieval Theory of Authorship* [1984], 1). In *Fallible Authors,* Minnis retains this Quentin Skinneresque agenda, but he picks up at least briefly Judith Butler and Michel de Certeau with some interest (especially the latter), and he points from the outset to the postmedieval Protestant world up to his own childhood that crudely collapsed the paradoxes of authority whose history he treats here. Another risk is that of treating intellectual history too much like a narrow syllogism: by focusing on a specific thread of discussion in intellectual history, one may miss how other kinds of charged topics of a period, and other encroaching pressures from context, are involved with that one. This risk Minnis more fully answers here, emphasizing that "medieval *auctor*-theory did not occupy some sort of autonomous, specially privileged site of its own . . . but rather partook of discourses which feature crucially in accounts of the formation of the king, the pope, the priest, the preacher" (10). If it is difficult to imagine the Minnis of *Medieval Theory of Authorship* writing a sentence like that—so tacitly informed by modern theory—we can only welcome the breadth of connections that he thereby opens to us in the rest of *Fallible Authors.*

In all these ways, the study is immensely valuable and finely nuanced, immaculately well presented and documented (I found only one typo or misreading, in a Latin quotation: *pertet* for, presumably, *pertinent* {137}). One might, though, still complain that not many surprises lie in Minnis's readings of Chaucer's works themselves. Minnis focuses with massive learnedness and stimulating lucidity on the very complex intellectual history behind what are finally the most obvious aspects of the Wife of Bath's and the Pardoner's narratives. He ends up reading both narratives rather flatly. The central contradiction between personal immorality and a moral tale is for Minnis the main and almost the only thing to track in *The Pardoner's Tale*. Other elements appear important to us only because of our own preoccupations. The Pardoner's sexual "deviancy" is not, for Minnis, a key to anything other than his general status as "extremely sinful": in contradiction to a long tradition of modern critics, carefully lined up, this may mean, Minnis avers, that he is simply lecherous or at least just generally socially "deviant" (146–61). But since the long discussion of the "impediment of gender" occasioned by the Wife of Bath has shown how bodily and social status can trump authority after all (170–245), is there not room here to consider more specifically how, against the tradition of debate about the limitations of women's gender for their authority, being "a geldying or a mare" might chip away at precisely the status of "maleness" that subtends the opposite configuration of authority? If we find (as clearly some of us do) that the Pardoner shows that masculinity as such is not so utterly stable, how well can the intellectual tradition about male ordination really address the issue of authority's stability, based on an essentialist presumption about gender? Other aspects of Chaucer's texts might have been used to elaborate further the issues that Minnis's fascinating survey offers. If only the male body was suited to "marks of ordination" that might allow even sinful instances of such bodies to carry sacramental, public authority (10), can we not consider the Wife's many kinds of permanent bodily "markings"—from the astrological "Martes mark" on her face and "another privee place," to the permanent deafness and marks on her "ribbes al by rewe" from Jankyn's blows, to the deeper marks of a lifetime of physically coerced listening to books and sermons—a kind of competing ordination? So too, with unabashed idealism, Minnis reads the conclusion of *The Wife of Bath's Tale*, where the knight grants dominion to the old Wyf, as that knight's final recognition of "beauty of soul" (330). But since the rapist knight has no choice but to offer to her the power to choose, is it not also possible to see him there—less idealistically—as having simply learned the Wife's own strategy of seeking subversive power through submission?

Minnis throughout avoids opening doors into "subjectivity," social valence, immediate political pressures in courtly cultures, views of the "metaphysics" of gender, and of course much else that modern criticism has posited in treating these two figures. But if his key terms and paradoxes are limited to those that medieval academics used and pondered (and that clearly find some at least indirect echo in Chaucer's figures), he is careful to display his materials fully, with an eye to their use for other pursuits and conclusions. His own conclusions are always carefully substantiated, but his more tentative suggestions are worth at least as much consideration. One of the major fruits of Aristotelian traditions in the later Middle Ages, for instance, the severing of "artifice" from "morality," allows Minnis to suggest, with fine tact more than once, that Chaucer's musing on this topic may spring from his long thought on the nature of the exquisitely fictive (e.g., 4–5, 134–35). Amid everything else so usefully surveyed and carefully demonstrated here, literary and cultural historians of all stripes should particularly welcome Minnis's deft suggestion of how the question of "the literary" might be at the center of all the other threads taken up in this major and foundational study.

ANDREW GALLOWAY
Cornell University

JENNI NUTTALL. *The Creation of Lancastrian Kingship: Literature, Language, and Politics in Late Medieval England*. Cambridge: Cambridge University Press, 2007. Pp. x, 187. £50.00; $90.00.

The title and subtitle of this book succinctly express its interdisciplinary ambitions. These ambitions, of course, are not at all unusual for scholars of Lancastrian literature, who have now for over two decades pursued them, earning various degrees of appreciation from political historians. Jenni Nuttall's book, however, achieves an unusually thorough and sustained level of interdisciplinarity. She manages this in part through broad and careful use of documentary evidence. In the study's most rewarding analyses, she applies close reading techniques across a range of text types, literary and documentary, to achieve the sort of mutual illumination that characterizes the best of historicist literary criticism. But more central in this regard are the book's two interanimating arguments. First is the claim, which Nuttall puts forward in the book's introduction, that the specific language legitimating the deposition of Richard II supplies the foundational terms of the succeeding government and thus also the language of the responsibilities to which it is held accountable—sometimes, ironically, at some cost to the credibility of that government. The second claim, also present in the introduction but articulated with most force in the book's conclusion, is that Lancastrian literature is infused with this political language, but makes creative rather than merely reflexive use of it. This language denotes political values to accomplish literary purposes that are neither simply propagandistic nor simply satirical, but instead are complexly meditative, critical, and exhortative. Each of these arguments plainly depends on the informing power of the other, and yet the most basic object of each resides comfortably within one disciplinary boundary. Early on, Nuttall asserts, "Political and literary cultures are inseparable, demanding simultaneous study and analysis" (4), and her subsequent approach to a diverse array of texts bears out this belief; but as this statement also implies, much of the book's hermeneutic power arises from simultaneously blurring and respecting disciplinary distinctions.

The common term of the book's two arguments is, obviously, *political language,* a phenomenon well served by Nuttall's approach because of its complex, varying degrees of sameness and difference across different illocutionary domains. This linguistic motility Nuttall examines with the help of historian J. G. A. Pocock, whose ideas about political speech acts are proximate enough to the traditional philological emphasis of medieval literary study that they seamlessly extend the book's interdisciplinarity to the level of theory (a happy marriage evident also in Paul Strohm's use of Pocock in his recent *Politique: Languages of Statecraft Between Chaucer and Shakespeare* [2005]). Nevertheless, neither this theory nor the book's two arguments will, I suspect, strike most students of Lancastrian literature as especially ground-breaking. First, while Pocock provides a convenient and flexible vocabulary for analyzing the shaping power and transformation of political language, it is not clear to me how fundamentally different Nuttall's approach is from that of some of the work on this period that examines political language without the benefit of Pocock—for example, Strohm's earlier *England's Empty Throne:*

Usurpation and the Language of Legitimation (1998), or, for the slightly earlier period, Lynn Staley's *Languages of Power in the Age of Richard II* (2005). Second, the book's historical argument—to phrase it in its most general sense, that the terms of the charges of political failure become the terms of political accountability—seems somewhat self-evident, as it describes an illocutionary dynamic that we may easily recognize today when, say, one politician's accusation against an opponent's tax plan entails a scrutiny of her own. While it is surely worth recognizing that the labile nature of political speech acts is not only a modern phenomenon (as Nuttall herself suggests in the penultimate sentence of the book), it is also surely not surprising. Finally, the book's literary argument—that Lancastrian literature is neither "rebellious criticism" nor "cowed propaganda" but rather offers "political engagements both pragmatic and innovative" (120)—while still perhaps a matter of debate, does not differ in basic emphasis from the argument about fifteenth-century poetry put forward long ago by David Lawton and much developed since. Not every monograph, however, need be groundbreaking; there is an important role to be played by studies, like this one, that intelligently and persuasively consolidate, deepen, and extend prior work. Moreover, what this study may lack in innovation it regains, in large part, by the sheer clarity and concision with which it articulates, organizes, and defends its arguments.

Following the introduction, the book divides into two sections, corresponding to "two languages or specialized idioms arising from the *demerita notoria* [an official list of "notorious faults"] which legitimized the deposition [of Richard II]" (3). These languages consist of, first, "household narratives," or the linguistic paradigms "of Richard and his household as simultaneously youthful and tyrannous, prone to luxury and self-indulgence, and dismissive of the advice of truthtellers and wise counselors"; and, second, the language of financial practices and their implications for governance, or the linguistic paradigms of "ideal reciprocal exchanges of love and credit" and, contrastingly, "fraudulent or contradictory exchanges" (3–4). The first chapter identifies and elucidates the first set of linguistic paradigms as they originate in the *demerita notoria*, while the second chapter traces their dissemination in *post hoc* chronicle accounts of the deposition and, more briefly, in the poem *Richard the Redeless*. Chapter 3 examines the relations between "pre-existing languages," or, more specifically, literary topoi in circulation prior to the deposition, and the same topoi, now "temporarily politicized and partisan" (17), with Passus III of *Richard the Redeless* receiving especial attention. Chapter 4 builds on this basis to pursue the book's argument that the linguistic "paradigms prioritized by the deposition schedule altered the nature of political debate in unforeseen ways, encumbering the Lancastrian Crown with consequences which it had not fully envisaged" (41). Receiving particular attention here is *Mum and the Sothsegger*, a poem most likely by the same author as *Richard the Redeless* and representing his later reappraisal of Henry IV and his government. The fifth chapter extends this exploration of "household narrative" paradigms to the work of Gower, Scogan, and, especially, Hoccleve. The next three chapters form Part Two of the book, which focuses on the language of finance and governance, or "credit and love," in Lancastrian discourse. Chapter 6 provides historical background on the legends and actualities of Ricardian and Lancastrian finances, and begins an examination of the complex ways Hoccleve's poetry engages "credit and love," an examination that continues throughout the second part and culminates in the extensive treatment given Hoccleve's *Regiment of Princes* in chapter 8. Among the several texts discussed in chapter 7 are, in addition to those by Hoccleve, Chaucer's *Legend of Good Women* and the anonymous *Crowned King*. The book's conclusion, as mentioned above, crystallizes the study's literary argument.

This summary has not been able to account for the many valuable details of argumentation and readings of texts. Some of the latter, especially in later chapters (such as chapter 8's reading of the John of Canace exemplum in Hoccleve's *Regiment*), demonstrate how hermeneutically productive closely contextualized readings of fifteenth-century English poetry can be. Ideally, these readings would also have engaged, somewhat more extensively than they do, the recent critical work done on this poetry, such as Ethan Knapp's important monograph, *The Bureaucratic Muse: Thomas Hoccleve and the Literature of Late Medieval England* (2001). Moreover, I wonder whether Richard's deposition schedule can so confidently be credited with originating or, as chapter 3 describes, temporarily politicizing the linguistic paradigms under study, which were not only in circulation prior to the deposition but may also have been already so politicized. That is, I wonder how we can be sure that *post hoc* chronicle accounts, parliamentary statutes, poems, and the many other Lancastrian writings Nuttall examines so well were in fact influenced specifically by the language of the deposition rather than by the same preexisting, already politicized language of royal critique and reform that the deposition schedule itself drew upon. (For example, Staley calls attention to the way the language of the deposition echoes that of the charges brought much earlier against Richard in the Merciless Parliament.) This is, admittedly, a kind of chicken-and-egg quibble, and, ultimately, the uncertainty of whether or not the deposition schedule possessed the full discursive agency Nuttall ascribes to it does not much affect the study's most valuable contribution: its uncommonly lucid analysis of the multifarious operations of linguistic paradigms across a broad array of Lancastrian writing, and especially their particularly fluid, complex, and ambivalent presence in the poetry of Hoccleve. For both literary scholars and historians working on this period, this book is essential reading.

ROBERT J. MEYER-LEE
Indiana University, South Bend

TISON PUGH. *Sexuality and Its Queer Discontents in Middle English Literature*. New York: Palgrave Macmillan, 2008. Pp. xii, 200. $74.95.

A more accurate title for this book might be *Masculinity and Its Queer Discontents in Middle English Literature*, for it is predominantly concerned with deployments of gender inversion as a means of disciplining male agents. Sexuality, if it is at issue at all, mainly enters the frame in the guise of heterosexual normalcy: it is queer gender that gets conscripted in the service of constructing this "heteronormative" masculine identity, and—allusions to the queerness of friendship and sword brotherhood aside—eroticism generally assumes a much less prominent role. Pugh's argument is that the exploitation of gender queerness in the service of normativity fulfills the needs of the prevailing ideological order; but this process also generates discontented subjects, since those who forswear the pleasures of queerness are engaged in an exclusionary process, which constructs a version of masculine selfhood that "may not be what the man desired in the first place" (12). This hypothesis is tested with reference to a series of close readings of male protagonists in Middle English texts: the Dreamer in *Pearl*, Harry Bailly, Chaucer's Clerk, and the eponymous heroes of *Amis and Amiloun* and *Eger and Grime*. The book concludes with an intriguing discussion of the genders and gendered

361

desires of medievalists themselves, mediated as they are by contemporary regimes of normativity.

Pugh's analysis is at its most compelling when he discusses the role of subjection and feminization in medieval Christian formations of selfhood. Examining the erotic bonds that link the Dreamer, the Pearl Maiden, and God in *Pearl*, Pugh makes the point that when God assumes a role within this triangulated scenario, the Dreamer's desires can only be directed one way—toward God himself—and that this requires the Dreamer to sacrifice his identity as a courtly lover. The consequences of this loss of self are queer because gender categories no longer follow their earthly trajectory: whereas the Pearl Maiden is "queerly described in male terms" (46), the Dreamer himself inhabits "an eroticised yet paradoxical position as his rival's bride" (26). Less successful are the analyses of Chaucerian masculinities that follow, where Pugh's "queering" describes a process that might, from a contemporary vantage point, look more like versions of misogyny and/or homophobia. Harry Bailly may well believe that his successive attempts to emasculate his fellow travelers (first the Cook, then the Clerk, then the Pardoner) reinforce his position as the "aller cok"—or, as Pugh has it, "alpha cock" (55)—of the Canterbury pilgrimage. But Pugh's point is that this gender-baiting vocabulary ultimately queers Harry himself: when the Knight compels him to bestow a kiss upon the Pardoner, he is forced into a secondary masculinity in which he henceforth plays "Robin to the Knight's Batman" (67). Still, what Pugh interprets as "queer chinks" in the Host's normative armor sometimes smack more of gender containment than gender subversion: Harry's "murye" intervention at the conclusion of *The Clerk's Tale*, to the effect that he wishes his wife back home would follow Griselda's example, evokes a desire for female submission within marriage that sits uneasily with the more expansive vision of gender performativity usually associated with queer readings. The complaint reveals the discontentment Harry experiences in his own Griselda-like attachment to marriage, for sure—but the misogyny is impossible to ignore all the same.

Pugh's point about *The Clerk's Tale* itself is that, by representing Walter and Griselda's "queer fidelity" to the tropes of male tyranny and female submission, the fictionality of gender binaries is exposed and ultimately transformed. As he puts it, "it takes balls—queer balls—to be such a faithful wife" (90), and it is precisely Griselda and Walter's sacrificial commitments to their respective roles that turn them into hermaphroditic figures. Yet this queering of category constitutes a necessary precursor to the tale's conclusion, which illustrates the "normative bliss of a reunited family" (92). The Clerk himself, taking up the feminized position accorded him by the Host in the tale's prologue ("Sire Clerk . . . Ye ryde as coy and stille as dooth a mayde"), manages to expose the Host's hypermasculinity as a lie while continuing to remain faithful to the rules of the tale-telling competition.

Formations of romance masculinity are brought into focus in the penultimate chapters on *Amis and Amiloun* and *Eger and Grime*. The first of these texts resolves the possibility of queerness through hagiography: Amis and Amiloun become saintlike figures in death, and the grave, for Pugh, is "the ultimate emasculator" (120) because it frees fraternity from any homoerotic aspersions. This relies on the assumption that eroticism and spirituality are necessarily opposed, whereas in the context of *Pearl,* Pugh had been prepared to countenance the possibility of queerly erotic relations within a spiritual setting. The argument does not fully engage with Alan Bray's analysis of idealized friendship as an embodied practice: death, for Bray, is precisely the point at which affective and spiritual meanings coalesce, and the materiality of friendship beyond the grave does at least hold out the potential for erotic meanings in certain settings. In *Eger and Grime*, comedy rather than death is the key to evacuating queerness: Eger's loss of a little finger taints him with phallic weakness, but through Grime's help he manages to find his way back to normative manhood. As if to confirm the restoration of masculine privilege, the narrative ends with Eger producing more progeny than his fraternal counterpart, so that "any hint of his queered and castrated identity appears finally to be forgotten" (143). Whereas Amis and Amiloun lie sexless in their hagiographic graves, a resolution that ignores the fact that they were "never really queer" (121) in the first place, Eger's missing finger does at least linger in the reader's mind as a queerly absent presence, "the spectral image of the impossibility of ever completely becoming a normal man" (144).

Pugh's attention to questions of genre and narrative structure in the book is consistently engaging, but the insistency with which he deploys the category of heteronormativity can be somewhat grating, not least in view of the influential critiques of the concept that have emerged in recent years. The slippage from sexuality to gender—a fault line that deserves to be interrogated theoretically as well as historically—is not subjected to as much analytic scrutiny as one might expect, despite the fact that gender norms are the book's overriding concern. In his Introduction, Pugh is happy to quote Karma Lochrie and James Schultz on the difficulties of applying concepts of normativity and heterosexuality to the Middle Ages, but, not wishing to "throw out the baby of a queer critical lexicon with the bathwater of anachronism" (8), he then continues to use the concept of heteronormativity uncritically—with little real effort to define what a medieval machinery of normalization might look like—in a manner that suggests, once the relevant voices of dissent have been cited, scholars can just get back to queer business as usual. I'm not sure it is simply the lexicon or the potential for anachronism that is at issue for critics of the concepts; it's also the guiding assumptions that motivate the terms' usage in contemporary settings.

ROBERT MILLS
King's College London

TISON PUGH and MARCIA SMITH MARZEC, eds. *Men and Masculinities in Chaucer's "Troilus and Criseyde."* Cambridge: D. S. Brewer, 2008. Pp. 216. £50.00; $95.00.

Over the last two decades, masculinity studies has developed into a discipline valid in its own right—albeit one that will forever be beholden to feminist studies for its inception—and several key medieval texts have been examined through its lens. Since Criseyde's centrality provides a continual reminder that the majority of characters in the poem, and all with any power, are men, it is perhaps surprising that this is the first full collection to be devoted to *Troilus and Criseyde*, whose context is, after all, the unassailably masculine setting of the Trojan War.

Several of the essays in *Men and Masculinities in Chaucer's "Troilus and Criseyde"* blend masculinity theory with other theoretical frameworks to good effect. Molly A. Martin reads the poem against medieval optical theory to challenge the tendency of visual studies scholars to equate viewer with active/male and viewed with passive/female, offering a convincing denial that Troilus's gaze ever empowers him. The ethics of power is considered by Holly A. Crocker and Tison Pugh, who argue that Troilus's "radical passivity" (90) in fact makes him superior to males with agency, all of whom lose power, while Troilus, ultimately, is elevated. Medieval optics recurs as a backdrop to Richard E. Zeikowitz's explanation of how the cinematic technique of "suturing" might be applied to the private conversation of Pandarus and Troilus in Book 1. Zeikowitz proposes that this visual conjecturing of the characters' responses to each other's words can increase understanding without betraying the text, although some of the potential homoerotic undercurrents that he identifies in his demonstration are already evident from a noncinematic reading. Robert S. Sturges applies Giorgio Agamben's concept of states of exception to posit that Criseyde is in "precisely the position described by Agamben, that of the one who may be killed with impunity" (33). Skillfully using Agamben's concepts and terms, Sturges explores the lack of clear sovereignty and the breakdown of juridical order in Troy, the "deactivation" of the distinction between public and private, and the transference of "sovereign masculinity," most particularly in relation to Criseyde's vulnerability, her "bare life," her "purely biological" existence (29).

There are some stimulating comparative readings. Michael Calabrese, proposing that both Chaucer and William Langland offer moral critiques of London, provides a fascinating examination of how Troilus's and Will's "male bodies" express, through the public enactment of manhood or the failure of its performance, "the nature of Christian civic and personal life" (162). In "Masculinity and Its Hydraulic Semiotics in *Troilus and Criseyde*," James J. Paxson draws on biblical allegory in suggesting that Troilus's abrupt arrival at Criseyde's bedside and Pandarus's description of Troilus appearing in his room via a "goter" together evoke David's entry to Jebus via a similar orifice, thus "valoriz[ing Troilus] as a hypermasculine figural type" (75). Similarly, the arrangement of the sleeping chambers in Pandarus's house parallels the layout of Solomon's First Temple. These hypotheses are well constructed, but the metaphorical significance of "hydraulic," presented first without and then with quotation marks in the first few pages, is initially unclear, and might usefully have been explained earlier than footnote 10. John M. Bowers suggests that Chaucer's *Miller's Tale* and *Legend of Good Women*, and Richard Maidstone's *Concordia* with its reference to Troilus and Absolon, encode criticism of Richard II's failure to procreate. This is a detailed, entertaining, and generally plausible proposition, if sometimes lacking in logical structure and occasionally undermined by omissions, notably the failure to consider Calchas's treachery when contending that there is no bar to Troilus publicly acknowledging Criseyde as concubine.

R. Allen Shoaf compares Chaucer's Troilus with Shakespeare's in an essay that offers thought-provoking ideas, interpretations, and etymologies. He alone confronts the volume's opening questions "What is a man? What groups together approximately half of the humans on this planet, in contrast to the other half?" (1) by offering a surprisingly profound analogy between Shakespeare's play and the romantic comedy *When Harry Met Sally*, both of which demonstrate that, post-coitus, women want to stay in bed, connected, while men seek separation from the partner in favor of a return into the world. However, the essay's psychoanalytic postmodernist construction feels somehow dated and out of place here, perhaps in part because Shoaf is markedly more interested in Shakespeare than Chaucer. Ultimately the subjective standpoint means that the concluding proposition, that Shakespeare was hurt by separation and "could never . . . leave the (m)other alone" (194), seems a projection rather than a critical evaluation.

The volume's greatest attention, as one might expect, is reserved for Troilus, although Diomede often features in terms of comparison, as does Hector, who is usefully contrasted with Troilus by Marcia Smith Marzec. Even Criseyde's masculinity is addressed, by Angela Jane Weisl, while Kate Koppelman considers how her femininity informs the reader's interpretation of Troilus and (his) maleness. It is thus both puzzling and disappointing that none of the essays attempts an extensive analysis of Pandarus within the framework of "men and masculinities," although Weisl suggests his ambiguity (117, 126).

That many of the contributors discuss Troilus's swoon and his general passivity rather highlights a lack of unity across the collection, especially when read chronologically. In the third essay, Gretchen Mieszkowski rebuts the frequent interpretation of the swoon as unmanly, demonstrating that modern audiences are misguided in correlating fainting in medieval romance with femininity (a postmedieval correspondence). Citing several examples, which might easily be augmented, she robustly establishes that passivity and fainting are entirely appropriate to the medieval male lover, serving to demonstrate the authenticity of his emotion. In the essay that follows, Marzec, who as co-editor must have had access to Mieszkowski's contribution, ignores it altogether when arguing that the "decidedly unconventional" faint (68) "renders Troilus . . . less manly" (68 n. 37). Later, Weisl declares that "anyone with a 'mannes herte' does not faint in bed"; she refers to Mieszkowski's reading, but dismisses it rather than engaging with it and, to support her own stance, offers a simple inversion of Alcuin Blamires's observation that "the female sexual drive was generally characterized as passive" as irrefutable evidence for "a reading of passive sexuality as feminine" (116). The failure to address such blatant contradictions explicitly, especially when eminently soluble, undermines the collection's coherence, and the various cross-references and brief commentaries that do occur between other essays tend to underline the lack of synergy here.

This volume will enlighten and entertain established scholars, and many of the essays may be useful to students. The text is generally well presented, although a few odd typographical errors have been overlooked, as well as some unfortunate inconsistencies, notably the references in one essay to "rime-royal" and "rhyme royal," and the appearance of both "Calchas" and "Calkas" in another. Martin uses the spelling "extramission" and Zeikowitz, "extromission"; this inconsistency is confusing to readers unfamiliar with medieval optics—are they the same term?—and might usefully have been harmonized. Some part lines in inset quotations are neither indented nor marked with ellipses and, on page 126, the combination of square brackets around "Criseyde" and the content of the associated footnote suggest that inverted commas have been omitted from quoted material. There are some infelicities of syntax, notably the wince-inducing "to make them 'biddeth'" and "she has never (and may never) meet," and, given the small place of dreams in Koppelman's essay, the unattributed quotation in the first part of its title ("The Dreams in Which I'm Dying") seems spurious.

AMANDA HOPKINS
University of Warwick

WENDY SCASE. *Literature and Complaint in England, 1272–1553.* Oxford: Oxford University Press, 2007. Pp. xii, 215. 18 b/w illus. £53.00; $95.00.

In this erudite and rigorous study, Wendy Scase sets out to expand our sense of the importance of what she calls an English "literature of clamour" in the later medieval and early modern periods. Scase works through a close examination of the nature of both legal and literary complaint. Whereas complaint has often been recognized as a sort of subgenre in English literature of the period, one particularly vital to the composition of love lyric and political satire, Scase works to ground this notion of literary complaint in the legal history of judicial plaints. Taking as her starting point the controversies over the legal admissibility of peasant complaints in the reign of Edward I, she then moves forward to demonstrate the ways in which the juridical issues of admissibility, evidential standing, and remedy continue to shape the complaints produced in both juridical and extrajuridical contexts in the succeeding centuries. The result is a fascinating study that provides an extremely valuable contribution to the ongoing study of the relations between a developing English literature and the political and bureaucratic institutions that provided, as Scase names it, the "force-field" in which its categories were theorized and through which its texts were disseminated (2).

The opening two chapters of this book are concerned largely to establish the conventions through which complaints were treated in judicial contexts, and they do so by introducing a welter of "subliterary" materials (3). The first chapter focuses on the question of admissibility: as legal reform under Edward I created precedent for the use of written complaint as a way to initiate legal action, the question arose as to whether petitions presented on the behalf of the common people of a community might be admitted for such purposes. As Scase shows through the analysis of such texts as the *Poem on Disputed Villein Services*, it was in the attempt to argue for their admissibility that the peasant complaint took on many of the rhetorical markers (the category of common interest, the reference to the interests of the crown, and the shaping of remedy as the restoration of traditional rights) that would characterize such complaints from this moment on through to their later incarnation in such works as Robert Crowley's *An informacioun and peticion agaynst the oppressours of the pore commons of this Realme* (1548). Chapter 2 takes this story into the fourteenth century, arguing that the initiation of a trial through a private, individual bill opens the way for *clamour*, for the notion that such action might be initiated through complaint that was widespread, diffuse, and derived from a general consensus of the people. The emphasis here is on procedure, on the processes by which cases were brought to court. And this emphasis allows Scase to offer a compelling sense of the way in which documents such as the Mercers' petition against Nicholas Brembre were organized by the category of a literature of clamour. In a fine piece of materialist analysis, she is able to show that the surviving petitions against Brembre were a coordinated effort, with the texts produced, circulated, and displayed not just to be presented at court but to create the grounds for action at court, to create *clamour* itself.

The third and fourth chapters of *Literature and Complaint in England* follow *clamour* out of the court and into a more literary, or cultural, set of documents. The third chapter treats first the petitions, libels, and bills stemming from the Lollard movement and then the texts associated with the Cade rebellion of the 1450s. Here the texts are rather better known than many of those in the earlier chapters, and here the invocation of a "literature of *clamour*" produces, I think, two chief benefits. First, Scase's determined attention to the way that the knowledge of legal procedures might have spread beyond the narrow bounds of those professionally engaged with lawsuits pays great dividends in creating a concrete sense of the projected audience for such materials. For example, her analysis of the very knowing way in which the framers of the *Twelve Conclusions of the Lollards* style themselves as the "*procuratores*" of God is exceedingly suggestive as to the spread of such procedural terms beyond the courts (90). In addition to this, the context of *clamour* specifies a powerful new sort of historical intertexuality at work in these texts. Particularly, perhaps, in the analysis of Cade's revolt and the Yorkist controversies treated in chapter 4, Scase is able to use *clamour* as a way to emphasize the noisy and public nature of these texts, the fact that these texts were created to make noise, to shout out their claims and to shout each other down. This is an intertextuality of a particularly raucous sort, a tone important to the materials and one often lost in other modes of analysis.

The final chapter turns to a set of more canonical literary texts to look at the way in which the judicial plaint had a dictamenal influence on vernacular literature of the later medieval period. The analyses of individual authors and works in this section are brief, and the chapter feels a bit like a coda to the work, but it does demonstrate the extent to which the terminology and conventions, and even the theory, of judicial plaint entered into the works of poets such as Chaucer, Gower, and Hoccleve, particularly when they wrote or translated letters (Hoccleve's translation of *L'epistre au Dieu d'Amours*) or embedded letters into larger works (Chaucer's *Troilus*).

In addition to the local analyses of these individual works and historical controversies, Scase's study raises a number of very valuable recurring motifs across this broad historical sweep. First, and most fundamentally, the study performs a very valuable service in establishing a much more precise lexical register than is often used in discussion of the complaint, a lexicon that refers us back repeatedly to the juridical nexus in which these materials were first formed. Second, this work provides a marvelous sense of the peculiar motility of the complaint, the capacity of the language and tropes of the peasant complaining of specific economic and legal oppressions to appear in a ventriloquized voice uttered by clerical authors, by baronial agents, and by lovers of all degrees. Such moments have certainly drawn attention in the analysis of individual texts, but by stringing them together and placing them into a historical context as part of the broadening out of complaint in the later Middle Ages, Scase is able to demonstrate their use as a topical rhetorical tactic in which those in power are able to project an imaginary loss of such power, an imaginary reversion into the legal nonpersonhood of the villein.

If this book has a shortcoming, it may be that it is relatively self-enclosed. The analyses made and the history sketched out are persuasive and sure to inspire further thought and work. But there are also moments at which it would be useful to hear how these theses on complaint and *clamour* might be related to other work on the relation between medieval institutions and a nascent vernacular literature. This is, of course, only to wish for yet more from what is a remarkable book and one that is sure to become required reading for all those interested in the material history of late medieval literature.

ETHAN KNAPP
Ohio State University

JAMES SIMPSON. *Burning to Read: English Fundamentalism and Its Reformation Opponents*. Cambridge, Mass.: Harvard University Press, 2007. Pp. 368. $27.95.

A reviewer knows he is reviewing an important book when, a year or so after its publication—in the normal course of things—he finds himself turning to the task with the belated sense that half the intellectual world has already digested its contents, and the field itself already seems shaped by it. James Simpson's *Burning to Read* is a polemical book with a powerful, urgent message. It argues that fundamentalism is rooted paradoxically in the very event seen by traditional historiography as one of the origins of Liberalism, the Protestant Reformation. A concept almost synonymous with "progressive" in Whig historiography, "reformation" in Simpson's view had a far more complex role. "Contrary to the liberal tradition's often complacent assumption that fundamentalism is reactionary and 'conservative,'" Simpson maintains, "fundamentalism is a distinctly modern phenomenon, the inevitable product of newly impersonal and imperious forms of textuality, and of the application of ever fewer textual instruments to ever larger jurisdictions" (3). Participating in a rethinking of the Reformation that has been undertaken by such scholars as Eamon Duffy and Christopher Haigh, Simpson retraces Reformation history in terms of the changing nature of reading itself, and in particular the "imperious forms of textuality" that informed emergent systems of belief.

With this larger argument about the origins of fundamentalism as its framework, the book focuses its analysis on the uneasy birth of Protestantism in England. The detailed analysis spans chronologically from William Tyndale's efforts to introduce the vernacular Bible in the 1520s to the death of Henry VIII in 1547. But before turning to this close analysis, the first chapter, entitled "Two Hundred Years of Biblical Violence," draws a broad history that, Simpson suggests, partially produced—and reinforced—the rigorous forms of textualism inherent to the new evangelical program. (Simpson prefers the historically accurate term "evangelical" to "Protestant," which was not yet in active use by reformers at this stage; "fundamentalism," though an acknowledged anachronism, nonetheless suits the book's larger claim that the early modern practice of biblical literalism cannot only be identified in familiar contemporary terms, but is also connected historically to contemporary practices.) In an effort to capture the violent consequences of the reform movement, this first chapter begins where Simpson's detailed analysis ends, at the scripturally informed installation of Henry's son Edward VI—the first English king to be anointed in the new church. Edward was seen as a second Josiah, a biblical child king whose high priest, like Archbishop Cranmer, had discovered the sacred text (the vernacular English Bible). Josiah provides a biblical exemplar of kingship at a turning point of religious history with the book at the center of transformation. But his story also provides scriptural examples of violent, exclusionist practices against other religions, as when Josiah destroys the altars of the worshipers of Baal and sacrifices the priests themselves (2 Kings 23). Christian violence was not only authorized by strict evangelical use of scripture, but it also reinforced the rigorousness with which scripture was read.

The next several chapters explore paradoxes in the evangelical program of reading, some related to this history of violence. The first of these chapters, "Good Biblical News," records the extraordinary efforts of Tyndale in producing a vernacular New Testament, which he did from exile in Worms in 1526. By the early 1530s, he had also translated much of the Hebrew Bible, which he labored over in prison before being convicted of heresy in 1536, when he was then strangled prior to being burned. It is a painful and well-rehearsed historical irony that this occurred only a few years prior to Henry VIII's issuance of a patent for printers to provide "in our own maternal English tongue" (39) a Bible profoundly indebted, as was the English evangelical movement itself, to Tyndale's efforts. In accord with the Protestant biases that still dominate our conception of this story—biases perhaps out of place in rigorous historical analysis—it can hardly be denied that Tyndale's efforts were admirable, and the fundamental cause, the liberation of a text, just. Yet to understand the evangelical program of reading merely in terms of liberation is to omit a large part of the story. The real significance of this history has been distorted, Simpson argues, by a misconception of the new cultures of reading that emerged, not only in the original work of reformers such as Luther but also from hotly charged religious tensions and debates. These tensions were shaped by the threat of physical violence associated with heresy, which shut down debate and reinforced a defensively rigid interpretive position. But the debates themselves—those between More and Tyndale, or Erasmus and Luther—also revealingly indicate the ways in which truer forms of textual liberty were peremptorily foreclosed at defining moments.

The third chapter, "Salvation, Reading, and Textual Hatred," investigates the prologues to early English Bibles, which, inflected by Lutheran self-loathing, often invited readers paradoxically into a dark ineluctable maze. Such a predicament is evident in passages in which Tyndale, "in the first welcome to the first printed English vernacular text" (96), writes with wonderful admonition: "the more thou readest it, the blinder thou art, and the more contrariety thou findest in it, and the more tangled art thou herein, and canst nowhere through" (95). Tyndale and Luther relied for their translations on Erasmus's immense philological project in recovering, retranslating, and explaining the Greek original; they were also energized by his *Paraclesis* (1516), which urged a broad vernacular readership. Yet the differences between these seemingly similar efforts were profound. Erasmus's rethinking of the Vulgate's translation of Matthew 3:2, "Poenitentiam agite," "Do Penance," had serious implications for Protestant theology, yet Erasmus approached this rethinking in an "irenic mode, the choice of one translation often as good as another" (77). In 1525, Erasmus broke publicly (though civilly) with Luther after an "uneasy stand off" (99) that ended with the publication of *De Libero Arbitrio*, which initiated a hermeneutically significant debate between the two. Taking a literalist perspective against Erasmus's "miserable refuge in tropes," Luther insists that what "God says must be taken quite simply at face value" (101).

As Simpson argues forcefully throughout the book, this literalist conception of the face value of scripture produced what were often deeply conflicted, narrow, and opaque readings. "Any reading culture that proposes that the meaning of the words is wholly contained in the words themselves, unaided by the interpretive, unwritten assumptions of the interpretive community, will end up with authoritarian versions of interpretive authority" (107). He turns in the next chapter to consider "The Literal Sense and Predestination," showing how the "insistence on the literal sense alone leads in fact directly to an intensely institutional account of textual meaning, via predestination" (127). The fifth chapter, "Bible Reading, Persecution, and Paranoia," considers the degrees to which *scriptura sola* has not merely a paradoxical relationship with Protestantism's other central doctrine, "faith alone," but also leaves the reader "isolated" and potentially part of a factionalized social body (143). These described social conditions contribute to rich contextualist readings of the Ecclesiastes and Psalm paraphrases of Surrey and Wyatt.

Simpson's final chapters deal with the "opponents" to scriptural fundamentalism, what he calls "a civilized, meditated, and partially plausible alternative modernity" (3). The main source for this alternative derives here from the character who emerges as the real protagonist of this history: More. Not against vernacular scripture in principle, More recognized that there was no truly pure *scriptura sola* if the Bibles were translated in certain ways and packaged with instructions and theologies that insist on a particular reading. The question, he wrote in *The Confutation of Tyndale's Answer* (1532–33), rests "not upon the scripture itself, but upon the construction thereof" (233). In a brilliant reading of

More's layering of oral, manuscript, and print communication in *The Dialogue Concerning Heresies* (1529), Simpson illustrates More's point that "the full meaning of texts is not available in their literal sense, or on the page; that meaning is dependent instead on layers of necessarily unwritten trust" (242).

Burning to Read challenges readers with a deeply provocative scholarly experiment. The book's biggest provocation lies in its engagement with the same kind of moral judgment, though in this case negative, of historical players that has long characterized the history of the Reformation. But it does so with the recognition that disinterested scholarship could never in this case turn the tide, or set the story straight.

THOMAS FULTON
Rutgers University

SEBASTIAN I. SOBECKI. *The Sea and Medieval English Literature.* Cambridge: D. S. Brewer, 2008. Pp. xii, 205. £42.75; $90.00.

The Sea and Medieval English Literature provides what its book jacket calls "the first cultural history of the sea in medieval literature." To this end, Sebastian Sobecki's book displays a radical generic expansiveness (taking a consciously "liberal view of the term 'literature' and view[ing] it as synonymous with 'writing' in the broadest sense" [22]). It adopts a broadly comparative approach (as the book jacket promises, we encounter an unusually "wide range of insular and continental writings"). And in the vein of much recent work, it exerts an altogether daunting diachronic reach (from prehistory's "ocean-birth[s]" and "foundation myths" [7–9] to recent developments in maritime law [140ff.]). Notwithstanding such extravagant parameters, the book is launched by a disarmingly elemental question: "What is the sea?" Sobecki's answer is banal but surprisingly productive: "The sea is not land" (5). This simple distinction becomes paradigmatic for *The Sea and Medieval English Literature* insofar as, Sobecki avers, "this antithesis of land and sea permeates our civilization, ranging from the basic, elemental dichotomy to more sophisticated literary contexts" (9–10). In its early going, *The Sea and Medieval English Literature* thus insists on the sea's universal importance "as a source of myths" (9), even "synonymous with myth" (7). A "central objective" of the undertaking, correspondingly, is "to study the changing role of the sea as a mythopoeic agent" (10).

Yet if, as Sobecki declares, "it is the development of this cultural life of the sea, as mediated by literature, that I wish to chart" (24), the book also proposes to intervene in critical conversations more acutely focused. Drawing on the wartime rhetoric of Winston Churchill, Sobecki finds in Britain's "island identity" "a synecdoche for Britishness: Britain may be more than the Island but the Island is culturally in and of Britain" (2, 10). In Sobecki's view, this distinctive geographic, political, and imaginative condition helps produce, over the course of a long, apparently protonational premodernity, "narratives of Englishness that are inseparable from the sea" (10). In a set of readings that push the bounds of the terms "medieval" and "English" (as well as of "literature," as we have seen), Sobecki underscores the shared tendency of diverse texts to "call on maritime motifs"—topoi themselves "remarkably mobile across genres"—in order "to define England geographically and culturally against the presence of the sea" (3, 24). What is specially constitutive of medieval English collective identity, then, is the realm's basic maritime embeddedness—practically speaking, its insularity. In this way, "the literary history of the sea in English literature becomes a part of the vernacular discourse of Englishness" (4). To the extent that, for Sobecki, "the liminal positioning of Britain and, therefore, of England" compounds the medieval realm's operative "island identity" (10), this book's geo-critical orientation is reminiscent of Kathy Lavezzo's (duly cited) *Angels on the Edge of the World: Geography, Literature, and English Community, 1000–1534* (2006). What distinguishes the present study is its taxonomic foregrounding of evolving maritime attitudes and nautical topoi themselves.

Despite a center of gravity in post-Conquest Britain, *The Sea and Medieval English Literature* cheerfully spans the centuries and the nations. In "Traditions" (chapter 1) we move from the Church Fathers, their Bible, and some "classical readings of the sea" (25) preceding them—groping back even to the Babylonian epic *Gilgamesh*—all the way forward to Anglo-Saxon England (dispatched, more or less, in "A Note on English Writings Before the Conquest," 41–47). By the Epilogue we will have reached Shakespeare's *The Tempest*, a sketched reading of which—since this is a play "steeped in the rich insular traditions of the sea"—Sobecki offers "as a commentary on the chapters of this book," which is to say, on the preceding centuries' incremental "absorption and appropriation of the sea" (165–66). Lying between prehistory and Shakespeare are five chapters—each cut into uncannily proportional halves—which together offer a pleasing array of infrequently met texts. "Deserts and Forests in the Ocean" (chapter 2) begins with the Irish *immram* ("rowing about") or *peregrinatio pro amore Dei* tradition, tracking how this "maritime voyage-tale" genre (49) is transformed in Benedeit's Anglo-Norman *Voyage de Saint Brandan* (c. 1118). This chapter's second half ("Tristan's Bitter Sea of Romance") proceeds according to Sobecki's other structural preference, comparing sea crossings in increasingly elusive redactions and fragments of the tale. Latin, Irish, French, German, Norse: the fact that typically translations are Sobecki's own (e.g., 57 n. 32, 59 n. 36, 62 n. 42) helps illustrate the study's substantial philological range.

"Almost Beyond the World" (chapter 3) surveys the sea attitudes and geographic (also cartographic) practices of Anglo-Latin chroniclers from the likes of Gildas (sixth century) and Bede (eighth century) to Geoffrey of Monmouth (early twelfth century) and Matthew Paris (mid-thirteenth century). "Realms in Abeyance" (chapter 4) examines Thomas of England's Anglo-Norman *Romance d'Horn* (twelfth century), along its way to John Gower's Tale of Apollonius in the *Confessio Amantis* (late fourteenth century), while "Between the Devil and the Deep Blue Sea" (chapter 5) reads *Patience* (late fourteenth century), with its primeval "centrality of the sea" (131)—unfortunately for him, "Jonah's God is a land-dwelling God" (121)—followed by Margery Kempe's brief but devotionally freighted Book II sea voyage to Dansk. Finally, "A Thousand Furlongs of Sea" (chapter 6) dusts off famous scenes in medieval maritime jurisprudence (such as natural law justifications of sovereign "claims to the sea" by Bologna's twelfth-century Glossators [142–45]), before culminating in a point-by-point explication of *The Libelle of Englyshe Polycye* (1436/37), an impassioned plea for England to defend its surrounding seas, which Sobecki rates among "the most important early political poems written in English" (145). If *The Sea and Medieval English Literature*'s beginnings lie in the primordial surf of comparative mythography, by voyage's end we have crossed over into a discursive realm that, despite predictably epochal "epistemological shifts" (159), is similarly murky, and just as persistently dichotomous, on the essential relation between land and sea. No less than does international law itself, Sobecki displays an abiding fascination for the paradoxical concept of "territorial waters"—in effect, sea that *is* land (water that is *terre*-strial), or at least acts like it. It didn't always—for example, when Xerxes lashed the disobedient Hellespont, in a sign of his overweening irrationality (xii, 7). We have, it seems, been moving throughout this diachronic history toward certain "[newly emergent] discourses of the fifteenth century" in which there develops a "gradual measuring and quantification of the sea" (159). These practices result finally in an outright and apparently irreversible "legal understanding of the *sea as territory*" (my emphasis), although as Sobecki demonstrates, this development "represents only the last stage of stripping the sea of its mythical, unpredictable qualities" (159).

That it has been Sobecki's central goal "[to show] how profoundly the perception of the sea has evolved in those spheres of human activity that can be traced in literature" (159) is not something, to my mind, that should require apology. It is an unsettling feature of *The Sea and Medieval English Literature*, however, that even as it presents a straightforward account of its source material (and of itself), against this tide there pulls a certain recurrent protestation—a kind of rhetorical undertow—as to the methodological underpinnings and organizational logic of the project. When Sobecki asserts, for example, that "although this book discusses the development of literary representations of the sea, the chapters do not form a strictly chronological sequence to avoid running the risk of creating an illusion of comprehensiveness" (23), this seems a rhetorical gambit designed to preempt critical objection: that is, to assure all concerned that the book's historiographical credentials are in proper order, which is to say, in line with prevailing academic orthodoxies. Surely the reasonable reader can agree that "the sheer volume of texts that refer to the sea during the 1000 years that separate Gildas from Shakespeare is overwhelming" (23). But to flee therefore from the possible charge of old-style survey naïveté is to undercut the project's own implicit (and by no means indefensible) disciplinary rationale. As a declared "cultural history" whose first instinct is duly to tally "significant work" so far as "[previous] comprehensive or diachronic studies of the sea in medieval English literature are concerned" (19), *The Sea and Medieval English Literature* wants to have its teleology and disavow it, too. It needn't. If the book is weirdly medieval itself, in its irrepressible delight for the compilation of authoritative maritime *florilegia* down the ages (the average page-opening takes footnote side trips to three or four distinctive eras and linguistic traditions), these encyclopedicist tendencies constitute not a quaint impediment to the modern academic endeavor—some kind of embarrassing, fusty limitation—but rather a substantial, increasingly rare technical strength. I smiled to read Sobecki's tactful critique of a previous plower of the field that is the literary sea, for her 1920s commitment to "[maintaining] the breadth of a survey," in which "none of the texts is analysed save in passing," the point rather lying in the "frequency and quantity of references to the sea" (19). For—times do change—I found myself similarly apprecia-tive of Sobecki's "formidable range" (19) but also wishing, in turn, that each of his ten-page, set-piece readings would extend its insights further into their respective textual and contextual worlds (taking account, for example, not just of Margery Kempe's "attitude to the sea in Book II" in its own right, but also, to at least some extent, of the messy, multifari-ous balance of the *Book*, with its richly contested shipboard scenes and other maritime motifs). Ultimately, of course, such complaints inhabit the realm of critical taste and its prerogatives, communicating more about reader than about book. To be clear, this is medieval English literature "off the beaten path," and its author may himself float the notion (self-defeating) that his eclectic textual choices are "not necessar-ily themselves representative of the understanding of the sea in a given period of time" (23). Yet it is precisely the audacious temporal sweep and comparative-linguistic ambit of the project, together with its philo-logical dexterity and synthetic breadth of learning, that constitute *The Sea and Medieval English Literature*'s signal contribution to the field.

DANIEL BIRKHOLZ
University of Texas at Austin

SARAH STANBURY. *The Visual Object of Desire in Late Medieval England.* Philadelphia: University of Pennsylvania Press, 2008. Pp. 320. $65.00.

During the late fourteenth century and well into the fifteenth, the pro-liferation of devotional images fueled debate over their uses and abuses. Sarah Stanbury's richly illustrated and provocative monograph explores the ramifications of the "image explosion" that transformed church inte-riors, altered the relations between lay sponsors and clerical users of images, and linked "the parish and public in vital new alliances and conflicts" (17). She analyzes the ethical stakes and economic underpinnings of the image debate and reflects on how that debate worked to "redefine the terms of orthodoxy and dissent" (17). The reformist opposition to devotional images, Stanbury argues, construed them as what anthropologists would later term "fetishes"—objects of a desire that is excessive, sensual, perverse, illicit, and insatiable. Underlying this construction of the image as fetish is a host of anxieties about social control and, above all, the economics of spirituality. "Devotional images trouble reformers," Stanbury contends, "not only because they threaten a material intrusion in the devotional sphere but also because they signify the very market-based operations of the spiritual system itself" (14).

Stanbury summons an eclectic assortment of textual witnesses to and participants in the image debate—saints' lives and mystical writings, Knighton's *Chronicle,* the so-called Despenser Retable in Norwich Cathedral, the hagiographies and pseudo-hagiographies of Chaucer, Love's *Mirror of the Blessed Life of Jesus Christ*, and *The Book of Margery Kempe.* Some of these are, or are explicitly about, images—including relics, church architecture and statuary, heraldic emblems, ritual accessories, and devotional icons—while others are inflected by their authors' experience of devotional imagery. In either case, Stanbury's analysis productively puts images in conversation with their written counterparts in ways that illuminate the devotional culture of late medieval England. Her exploration relies upon an abundance of visual evidence, and one of the book's many strengths is its wealth of reproductions.

Stanbury divides her study into three major sections. Part One, "Fetish, Idol, Icon," begins by contrasting three authors' uses of "feminized devotional images" to address issues surrounding the "display and potency of devotional objects" (37). In her first example, the chronicler Henry Knighton recounts a notorious act of iconoclasm—Lollards William Smith and Richard Waytestathe using a wooden statue of Saint Katherine to cook cabbage stew—as a virgin martyr legend, with the Lollards in the roles of pagan persecutors and the statue cast as the saint, to illustrate the "horrors of Lollardy" (63). Writing at roughly the same time as Knighton, Walter Hilton "adopts language nuanced by contemporary reformist discourse for use in a devotional romance" (36–37). In creating the "merk ymage" of his *Scale of Perfection,* Hilton "invests an image with even greater horror" than the Lollards do (58), echoing "the materialist critique of images to underwrite an ascetic spirituality" (63). For her third example, Stanbury returns to Saint Katherine as she was represented by John Capgrave, circa 1445. Where Knighton construes a statue as a saint, Capgrave transforms the saint into "an embodied devotional image in a struggle against idolatry, with her famous wheel as both fetish item and idol" (14–15). "By unsettling subject positions in the image debate," she argues, "Capgrave's text gives both sides of the question brilliant play" (66) and "offers a metacommentary on the troubling similarity between images and idols" (64).

Stanbury next turns to the Despenser Retable of Norwich Cathedral, hypothesized to be a gift of thanks from prominent local families (whose coats of arms are blazoned into the frame of the retable) to Bishop Despenser in recognition of his role in suppressing the rebellion of 1381. She reads the retable convincingly and eloquently as a "framed narrative about social disruption and the restoration of order" that is "as much about orthodoxy, community, and class in late fourteenth-century Norwich as it is about the Passion" (93).

Stanbury's second section, "Chaucer's Sacramental Poetic," uses the image debate as a backdrop for discussing Chaucer's "construction of textual bodies" and his "arts of describing the human form" (100). Writing at the height of the image controversy, Chaucer developed "a critical aesthetic that . . . engages directly if ironically with the debate" (111). The Pardoner's relics, "grotesquely inert," suggest Chaucer's sympathy with a reformist stance on "devotional paraphernalia" (117). However, his *Knight's Tale* and *Legend of Good Women* show images that seduce their beholders and marvelously come to life; they evince Chaucer's own appreciation of the "dynamic hold" icons have on "the psychic and imaginative life" (116). "As an ethicist and cultural critic," Chaucer may assert the deadness of images, but as a writer he "kneels before them and lets them do what they will" (121). In his *Clerk's Tale* and *Prioress's Tale,* Chaucer "stages a kind of sacramental theater" to "dramatize the theatrics of faith" (127): both tales locate a sacrificial subject at the center, surrounded by those who believe and those who doubt.

In her third section, "Moving Pictures," Stanbury looks at Love's *Mirror* and Kempe's *Book.* In both texts, she argues, "Christ operates as a dynamic image, a figure articulated within reformist discourse on devotional icons and animated by a carefully orchestrated devotional gaze" (15–16). Although Love does not have much to say directly about devotional images, he enters into the image debate by virtue of his pervasive attention to visualizing the events of Christ's life. By inviting readers to imagine the kinds of scenes they might have seen in their parish churches and cathedrals, he orchestrates a "drama of communal witnessing" (182). Stanbury reads the *Book of Margery Kempe* as "a quixotic and highly localized fifteenth-century benefactor list" (193), where contributions are registered in souls rather than cash. Kempe constructs a "public self" that is "deeply indebted . . . to contemporary donor images," also powerful expressions of selfhood at the time (193).

As the above synopsis suggests, *The Visual Object of Desire* is less a unified examination of the debate over devotional imagery in late medieval England than an occasion for Stanbury to reflect, usually persuasively and always inventively, on the image—broadly construed to encompass the body, the imagined object of an imagined gaze, and so on—as it occurs in various texts. It is not an easy read; too often Stanbury's prose slips into critical patois at the expense of clarity and precision. Nor are its arguments always satisfying; some of Stanbury's most ambitious claims—for example, that Chaucer "sacralizes vernacular poetry" (151) via Griselda's marriage vow—rely more on metaphor and association of ideas than on specific textual evidence and clear argumentation. I began the chapter on *The Book of Margery Kempe* intrigued by Stanbury's idea that it could be read as a donor list, and I ended it still intrigued but also unpersuaded, indeed unsure whether I was supposed to find the idea persuasive or merely novel. Yet even if Stanbury does not always convince, her bold readings and unusual juxtaposition of texts challenge us to think in new ways about the late medieval image debate.

KAREN WINSTEAD
Ohio State University

PAUL STROHM, ed. *Middle English.* Oxford Twenty-First Century Approaches to Literature. Oxford: Oxford University Press, 2007. Pp. 521. £93.00; $199.00. Paper, 2009. $55.00.

This excellent collection of essays largely fulfills its ambitious promise to "enter the zone of the not-yet known," resisting the traditional aim of the companion volume: that is, to offer an assessment of a field or subfield, accounting for information and methodologies veteran scholars have come to agree upon. Instead, *Middle English* seeks to avoid consensus, provoke debate, and suggest where the field might go in the next several years.

The book is unevenly organized across four sections: "Conditions and Contexts," "Vantage Points," "Textual Kinds and Categories," and "Writing and the World." Without short introductions to these sections, I found it difficult to discern the coagulating agent of each segment or to see how they speak to one another. Indeed, even as I outline these sections in the description of many of the volume's essays below, I illustrate some connections between the essays in different sections to demonstrate the volume's generative richness.

This is not to say, however, that the essays that make up each part do not work well together. For example, the first section includes several articles that attempt to understand Middle English culture as "multilingual," demonstrating, as Robert M. Stein does convincingly, that "the polyglot reality of medieval life" is also a literary phenomenon in the Middle Ages (28). Christopher Baswell's essay, "Multilingualism on the Page," shows how material text studies can inform our understanding of multilingualism, particularly with respect to the interdependence of Latin and the vernacular. Michelle Warren's contribution on "Translation" proposes a reconceptualization of the status of translated texts. According to Warren, translation enabled vernacular texts gradually to emerge as self-sufficient authorities, acting outside the putatively originary tongue, Latin. These essays all demonstrate how multilingualism builds on and stretches medieval studies' long-standing interest in vernacularity. Likewise, in a different section, Vincent Gillespie reevaluates "vernacular theology," a phrase developed by Ian Doyle and Bernard McGinn and influentially discussed by Nicholas Watson, to show that devotional texts written in English depict "intralingual ambition" (402). He thus crucially reframes our sometimes monolithic account of vernacular theology as "multiple, interlocking, and overlapping vernacular theologies" (406).

The second and largest section, "Vantage Points," reveals (among other topics) a rigorous theoretical investment in form, anchored by Christopher Cannon's argument that Middle English texts often obfuscate their own formal properties, with the result that our task is to explore texts' ostensible oddities via larger structural principles. Elizabeth Allen pursues such exploration in "Episodes," in which she posits "narrative incoherence" as a crucial formal principle of Middle English romance. Such an aesthetic, she argues, articulates these texts' concern with dynastic incoherence and familial disruption. (In the next section, Matthew Giancarlo makes a similar argument: for him, romance's investment in foundational kinship ties reveals its affiliations with historiography and chronicles.) For Maura Nolan, thinking about form allows her to postulate broad questions about beauty, aesthetic pleasure, and artifice; as she persuasively argues with respect to *The Miller's Tale*, beauty mediates between idealization and particularity, between universal aesthetics and individual reader response.

If one of the second section's concerns is form, the third section, "Textual Kinds and Categories," moves to genre. Yet the first essay of this section, Alfred Hiatt's "Genre Without System," dismantles genre as a stable analytic category, pursuing "ungenre" as a potential avenue of analysis. He suggests we pay attention to moments of textual disorientation or inexplicability in the service of recognizing the kind of "boundary disturbances" (291) fundamental to Middle English literature. Similarly, Bruce Holsinger's essay on liturgy suggests that we "detheologize" English liturgical writing to register "the space between professed belief and material practice" (298). Karen Winstead's focus on saints' lives deconstructs the force of "exemplarity" by illustrating how medieval hagiography invites divergent interpretations and responses. In this section, "genre" is rendered flexible and dynamic, with new takes on old genres and the formulation of heretofore unrecognized generic frameworks.

The final section, "Writing and the World," turns to extra- and paraliterary texts to think about the relationship between textual production and other kinds of production. This relationship is rigorously and fascinatingly pursued in Lisa H. Cooper's "Poetics of Practicality," which reads "how-to" manuals like Alexander Nequam's *De nominibus utensilium* and a fifteenth-century recipe book to explore the overlaps between the "literary" and the "artisanal." A similar exploration drives Kellie Robertson's "Authorial Work," which interrogates the problem of labor with respect to poetic production. These essays revise how we might understand the relationship between the symbolic order of language and modes of behavior. In this vein, Stephanie Trigg uses conduct manuals as material for thinking about how the Middle Ages might have understood performance, particularly vis-à-vis gendered behavior; in an earlier section, Sheila Lindenbaum provocatively suggests we can extract medieval drama from a theoretical investment in performance to read it as text and, in doing so, use medieval drama to understand "more primary cultural activities rather than a special ludic occasion" (388).

This description is by no means comprehensive, and it is clear that readers will formulate their own connections between these essays. In the spirit of the volume's design to provoke "future-oriented discussions" (3), I want to end by suggesting two topics of inquiry that might have been more prominently included in this volume. The first is "medievalism," a subject that has received much attention lately. Carol Symes's "Manuscript Matrix, Modern Canon," the first essay in the volume, describes how the editing and "taming" of *Beowulf* exposes the ways in which medieval literature depends on modern trends of preservation and recognition; I would have liked to have seen more exploration of how the "Middle Ages" was produced as an object of study. Another topic might have been "secularity," along the lines of Andrew Cole's beautifully written "Heresy and Humanism." Here, Cole posits a fifteenth-century "mirror for bishops" tradition that deploys techniques drawn from mirrors for princes to imagine an *ecclesia* invested in classical models of identity and virtue. Troubling the boundary between the "secular" and the "sacred" is the unstated consequence of several essays in the collection, but a more explicit discussion would certainly have fitted the volume's aims. Finally, while the volume's title announces its investment in Middle English textual production (and while many essays mention or even use Anglo-Saxon texts), I think medieval studies would benefit from a self-critical accounting of the relationship between Old and Middle English, both in our research and in our classrooms.

In sum, this is a rich, generative volume of essays, and it manages to speak to both seasoned scholars and newcomers to the field. It will be indispensable for research and teaching (many of the essays discuss how Middle English literature is presented in the classroom), and illustrates an excitingly diverse set of methodologies and interests.

JAMIE TAYLOR
Bryn Mawr College

JENNIFER SUMMIT. *Memory's Library: Medieval Books in Early Modern England*. Chicago: University of Chicago Press, 2008. Pp. 336. $35.00.

At the end of her learned and lucid new book, Jennifer Summit draws readers' attention to a 1993 article from *Wired* magazine in which the dark age of the library is fast receding. "Books once hoarded in subterranean stacks will be scanned . . . and made available to anyone." "Instead of fortresses of knowledge," there will be "information"; instead of "guardians of tradition," there will be "change" (234). The vision, Summit argues, is a medievalized one: our digital future has the imaginative shape of our bookish past. The idea of library as fortress, as a too-well-guarded cave, hoarding knowledge from the light of understanding is, in the case of England, as old as the institutionalized library itself. In the fifteenth century, English monasteries and university colleges began to set aside special spaces for collections of books previously held in choirs, cloisters, and refectories, and these new rooms quickly became witness to a vigorous contest for the control and use of texts. Bury St. Edmunds consolidated its collection in the early 1400s in the wake of fourteenth-century attacks on the monastery by townsfolk, to whose ire over the foundation's privileged control of the town old records and books fell victim. And Duke Humfrey and John Lydgate together made the duke's library a place where learned tomes and clerkly reading of them guarded against the "comounte" (40), notably Wycliffites, who—like digital futurists—saw the libraries of their day as "closed" places, where books "waxe rotyn" (from "How Religious men should keep certain Articles," 18).

These particular histories of English libraries are the subject of the first chapter of Summit's study, but they suggest the contours of her project. Summit does not set out to correct an impression of libraries as fortresses for rotting books. By writing of English libraries over two centuries—amid changes wrought by humanism, printing, dissolution, reformation, and the rise of experimental science—she argues instead for the dynamic historicity of this and every way of conceiving of the library. In this book, libraries are not static spaces for reading but "readable space" (5)—generative of the multiple meanings of the texts they contain and of the reading practices associated with those texts. It is in this sense that Summit is writing of *Memory's Library*. Cognitive science teaches us that memory involves not the passive collection, but the active and creative selection and so invention of experience. By such processes, which are akin to those that occur as libraries are formed and used, cultural identities are forged.

Such is the book's broad approach; Summit's specific line of argument is that in the famous libraries she describes—including those of Duke Humfrey, Thomas More, Henry VIII, Matthew Parker, Thomas

Bodley, and Robert Cotton—medieval books and bookish practices were appropriated to serve competing ideological concerns. Summit's history of the early English library thus seems a history of irreconcilable differences: of new uses found for *compilatio, lectio divina, allegoresis*, and manuscripts themselves that invent and then police divisions—between past and present, between people of different faith or social status, between science and the humanities, and even between an individual's own impulses. Thus Lydgate's clerkly envoys in his *Fall of Princes* give his book a semblance of his patron Humfrey's library not only in their deference to monastic and humanist learning, but in their effort to guard against the opinions of the rebellious commons. Thus the libraries that More describes (Pico's collection or the cargo of that purveyor of nonsense to Utopia, Hythloday) and those he inhabited—the Carthusian cell in the London Charterhouse that inspired his New Building and ironically anticipated his prison cell—cast doubt on his capacity to "reconcile humanism's active virtues with the aims of the Christian life" (63). In the 1560s–80s, men associated with the Parker library turned Augustinian *allegoresis* into a "*lectio* of suspicion" (121). In their writings, the metaphor of "chaff" is extended, from the coverings of truth in pagan tales to whole categories of books that needed to be shucked off and cast away. Stephen Batman and John Bale deplore the loss of books occasioned by dissolution and iconoclasm—but only the loss of some books, or some part of them. Part of the literature of the Middle Ages *should* be torn out as weeds, or "nailede up vpon postes in all common howses of easment" (89)—as were, one of Cromwell's agents reported, Oxford copies of Duns Scotus in 1535. In Robert Cotton's library, books were disbound and reassembled as miniature libraries of historical evidence. This was, Summit argues, one logical development of the medieval practice of *compilatio*—as in Ranulf Higden's history writing, for instance. Higden's *Polychronicon*, in Cotton Nero D. viii, was "one of the founding works of the Cotton Library" (145). But where Higden accommodated the saints' legends in his account of the past, Cotton "desanctified" holy books, stripped them, like saints' shrines, of their devotional significance.

In her final chapter, Summit observes that Francis Bacon was one of those who—by describing Reformation libraries like the one Cotton would assemble as "shrines," but shrines "without delusion or imposture" (from the *Advancement of Learning,* 197)—contributed the contradictory language "of destruction and preservation, redemption and transformation that had come to define the post-Reformation Library" (198). She goes on to write of another uneasy pairing. Bacon, as a scientific writer, was hostile to library learning. The books collected in libraries seem to him to reveal "the scantiness of the matters which have taken over and tenanted the minds of men" (206). To maintain the distinction between a stagnant intellectual past and the bright future he wants for learning, Bacon has to overwrite another history, in which the library is itself learning's future. He ignores, for instance, the work of his contemporary, Bodley's librarian, Thomas James. As James finds that "the best remedie for a diseased book" is "4. or 5. Old Manuscripts, compounded together, and the best of them distilled through the Limbeck of a good Diuines braine" (200), he imagines the library as Bacon's "Inginary" (198), a space in which analytic work on medieval books yields the knowledge of a new age.

With James, Summit's stories of "destruction and preservation," contest and discord, likewise yield to something more productive. Summit reminds us that such stories are about what is lost, found, but also *produced* as the past becomes past—a matter of memory. The Middle Ages are partly the invention, she shows, of fragments collected in the early modern period. But the early modern period is equally a confection of the ideas and artifacts it took from a newly defined "medieval" moment. Summit's project "stakes a claim for a distinctly literary perspective on the events and institutions it considers" (6). It is appropriate, then, that I find Spenser's Arthur to be Summit's most powerful figure for the work of *Memory's Library*. In chapter 3, Summit describes Arthur's "wonder," his "secret pleasure" (*Faerie Queene* 2.10.68; p. 126) as he comes to the end of his own doubtful history, made more doubtful by early modernity's wanton destruction of medieval records. But of course, all the books in the world would not allow for perfect recall. With lack and loss, in gaps in the archive, during debates over the meaning of the past, memory begins. And it is there that Summit has found the basis for this elegant, compelling, and important account of the making of medieval, early modern—and our own—culture between the walls of England's early libraries.

ALEXANDRA GILLESPIE
University of Toronto

DANIEL WAKELIN. *Humanism, Reading, and English Literature, 1430–1530.* Oxford: Oxford University Press, 2007. Pp. xii, 254. £56.00; $110.00.

Daniel Wakelin defines humanism as "a self-conscious commitment to return to the classics." The work of several decades has charted "a small but fertile field of humanist activity in England during the fifteenth century" (4). It is, however, generally thought that humanism in Latin, whether of England or of Italy, had little impact on English literature of the century. Wakelin's purpose is to identify English literature of the fifteenth century that "studies or imitates classical literature in this self-conscious way" (8). The chapters are arranged chronologically, but over-all Wakelin's aim is to disrupt old narratives rather than to offer a new one. Instead of offering a summary, map, or itinerary to guide readers and shape their expectations, he offers a metaphor. His monograph will mix anew the materials of literary history and the history of humanism with the history of reading. In the six chapters that follow, we are invited to observe Wakelin in his literary laboratory, assembling large amounts of original data and reading them closely. The result "blends an unpredictable compound"; received histories will "dissolve" and "we must begin concocting them afresh" (22).

An introductory chapter discusses humanism as a practice of reading, focusing on readings of Boethius. The translations of *De consolatione philosophiae* by Chaucer and John Walton, and a translation of Vegetius's *Epitoma rei militaris* possibly also by Walton, are analyzed in relation to evidence for humanist readings of these texts. Marginal comments and glosses and parallel texts (English alongside Latin) suggest that later readers have "intruded their classical passions into the English transla tions" (14). Wakelin handles the evidence with exemplary care and imagination. It reveals a "process," though not its full extents or purposes (as Wakelin observes with his characteristically dry wit, "thoughts which fit into margins are small ones" [17]).

Chapter 2 focuses on the role of Humfrey, Duke of Gloucester (1390–1447), in promoting humanism and its impact on vernacular literature. Duke Humfrey's historical role as patron of Italian authors and scholars and collector and donor of humanist books is less the focus here than his representation as a reader—which, Wakelin points out, strongly shapes our knowledge of his historical role. The focal texts in this chapter are Lydgate's *Fall of Princes* (commissioned by Humfrey), the anonymous *On Husbondrie* (1441–43), and various letters. In these sources, Humfrey's reading is represented as essential to the prince and statesman. The very page design of *On Husbondrie* (helpfully described in detail, though an illustration would have been useful) implies that the text is intended for a reader trained in the reading of Latin taught in school and university. Humfrey, as an "imaginary humanist reader" (49), serves as a model for real readers to emulate. One example of emulation is *Knyghthode and Bataile* (1460), another translation of Vegetius, whose form and page design in all three copies imitate those of *On Husbondrie*.

Wakelin returns to *Knyghthode and Bataile* in chapter 3, considering this translation of Vegetius alongside a translation, ascribed to Osbern Bokenham, of *De consulatu Stilichonis*, a fourth-century poem by Claudian in praise of general Stilicho. This translation was made for Richard, Duke of York, in 1445 and survives in only one manuscript. This copy provides the Latin original in parallel with the English translation. Wakelin carries out a close comparison of source and (mis-) translation to substantiate his point that "in trying not to say much a poem one thousand years out-of-date proves ideal" (77). The message is in the process itself: "The activities of translation and allusion . . . themselves suggest the greatness of the present just by recovering antiquity" (80). So with *Knyghthode and Bataile*. Ancient practical instruction in warfare is unimportant (hardly surprisingly); "what matters instead is the humanist process of recovering of the past" (81), though this text also demonstrably responds to contemporary politics.

Chapter 4 focuses on the reading and writing of William Worcester (1415–c. 1483), probably best known as secretary to Sir John Fastolf. Worcester's literary activities have bequeathed to us an extensive corpus of material—six notebooks, twenty-three annotated manuscripts, and two authored works: *The Boke of Noblesse* (1461–75), a book of political exempla based on classical sources, and a translation of *De senectute* by Cicero. Wakelin suggests that for Worcester humanist reading and thinking are essential to public service. Members of the political community must engage in "careful interpretation" (122) of examples from the past, using their reading to inform their own acts of service. Perhaps drawing on ideas in Cicero's *De amicitia*, Worcester's own works draw "the reader into an imaginary readership of people familiar with certain literary and historical materials," suggesting a community that shares "certain forms of literary and historical culture, certain rhetorical forms"

(124). As always, Wakelin triangulates internal evidence with material evidence. *The Boke of Noblesse* survives only in one manuscript. On this evidence, this "commonweal of readers" was wholly imaginary (125).

Wakelin does not, however, give up on the idea of a commonweal of readers. He applies it in the next chapter in an investigation of vernacular humanism and print. This chapter focuses on how humanist reading practices and ideals could be reproduced. As always, committed to disturbing received literary histories, Wakelin rejects the obvious argument that print reproduced humanism, offering instead the more interesting and productive suggestion that humanism, and the idea of the "commonweal of readers," "drives how Caxton imagines uses for the technology" (157). It is true that print can speed the replication of the means and materials for instruction in the classics. However, "the printer will not create but, instead, meet a market" (156). In a final twist, though, Wakelin triangulates his deductions from Caxton's own prefaces with evidence for what actual readers were doing. In part, the evidence suggests that they did "imagine their humanist community for themselves," but these readers are also "inconsistent, independent, and unpredictable in this response" (159).

Chapter 6 examines fifteenth-century debate poems that are modeled on classical dialogues and forms, such as the *declamatio* or exercise in arguing for and against a proposition. Thomas Chaundler's *Libellus de laudibus duarum civitatum*, presented to Thomas Bekynton, bishop of Bath and Wells, before 1464, is a Latin example in which two speakers debate the qualities of the cities of Bath and Wells. Wakelin shows that form, not content, is really at issue, for the text lifts large portions from a pair of texts that debate the relative merits of Florence and Milan. The point of the debate is to show that eloquence unifies society. This model informs Wakelin's illuminating analysis of the *Somnium Vigilantis*. This intriguing multilingual text supports the attainder of the Yorkist rebels in 1459, representing an eloquent debate between an orator for the king and a speaker for the rebels. Wakelin interestingly identifies a classical source for this work: a debate in the senate about whether rebels should be treated with leniency or harshness at the end of Sallust's *Catilina*. Despite treating a contemporary political issue in the form of the classical eloquent debate, however, the author of the *Somnium Vigilantis* defends an absolutist position that prevents real exchange and inquiry. Responses by Sir John Tiptoft (1427–70) and Henry Medwall to the

Declamatio de vera nobilitate (1420s) by the Florentine Buonaccorso da Montemagno are very different. Tiptoft's *The Declamacion of Noblesse* is "an exercise . . . in intelligent and independent reading" (173). Medwall's *Fulgens and Lucrece* draws on classical ideas of the importance of human reason.

The final chapter considers efforts to "limit and define" (196) humanist reading in the opening decades of the sixteenth century as evidenced in textbooks and university and school curricula by John Colet, William Lily, Richard Fox and others, considering alongside them the more liberal regimes of Thomas Lupset's *An Exhortation to yonge men* and *The boke named the Gouernour* by Sir Thomas Elyot. Both authors trust in the humanist ideal of the reader's own judgment in the face of authoritarianism, heresy, and censorship. Paradoxically, though, like their predecessors, these authors "sought to tell their readers—though they did not always succeed—how to study and imitate antiquity in a manner that was very directed, not very free at all" (210).

In keeping perhaps with the humanist ideals that he has described, Wakelin provides no conclusion. Many readers, especially those who are short of time and/or looking for quotable "soundbites" will perhaps wish for more direction, more of an overview, more explicit statement of thesis and argument, at least a chapter at the end that brings everything together. I surmise that Wakelin has made a positive decision not to conform to these conventions of the monograph. Instead, he provides a huge amount of little-known material and a model for reading it. His book requires that its readers follow every step of the way, reviewing the evidence, analyzing it and reasoning about it, and then that they draw their own conclusions. This sometimes arduous process is leavened with the author's laconic wit and his unfailing attention to all the possibilities for reading the evidence. The sense of being taken on a mystery tour is frequently rewarded with genuinely striking new perspectives on reading and its histories. Nor are the book's interests only historical; they are ethical and pedagogic also. This original, hard-working, and imaginative volume prompts reflection on the relationships between our own varied reading practices (the close reading distinctive of the Cambridge English Tripos in Wakelin's case) and the traditions of the past.

WENDY SCASE
University of Birmingham

KATHERINE ZIEMAN. *Singing the New Song: Literacy and Literature in Late Medieval England.* Philadelphia: University of Pennsylvania Press, 2008. Pp. xviii, 294. $59.95.

"Go, litel boke"—as Katherine Zieman acknowledges via the closing lines of *Troilus and Criseyde,* writing can find its way into the hands of readers with interests quite different from those of an imagined or intended audience. As a specialist in early medieval music and director of music at a collegiate institution, my claims to authority in reviewing this book are at best partial. What follows is accordingly less an attempt at comprehensive evaluation than a weaving together of at times unexpectedly shared concerns.

Zieman's central proposal is that, from the late thirteenth century through the early fifteenth, ritual practices of "reading and singing" became unmoored from their deployment within choral communities. Such practices expanded beyond the confines of clerical literacy, mutating into portable skills that served to transform a variety of modes of public discourse, thereby complicating notions that the late medieval period was one in which writing supplanted forms of oral communication. Particularly attractive is the claim that this period witnessed a passage from repertory-based knowledge to an era in which ritual reading and singing were fundamental to civic representation and the formation of an English vernacular voice.

While making occasional appeal to musicality, it is mainly changes in verbal practice that Zieman examines through select readings. The first chapter opens with the unnamed felawe's confession in *The Prioress's Tale* that "I lerne song; I kan but small grammeere," which is taken as a starting point for unpicking the idea that grammatical instruction was foundational to medieval education. Emphasis is placed rather on vocational knowledge, with liturgical practices of "reading and singing" considered an outcome of clerical membership rather than a precondition for learning. Earlier medieval practice is summed up in two sentences taken from an early ninth-century letter by Archbishop Leidrad of Lyon detailing his establishment of schools for cantors and readers, while Zieman argues that it is only with new forms of benefaction in the thirteenth century that boys were required to undertake such tasks as specialist choristers, these stipulations in turn serving as an incentive for their wider learning. Ongoing research into the liturgical roles assigned to young people in the earlier Middle Ages by, among others,

Susan Boynton and Christopher Page would suggest that the historical divide is not quite as neat as Zieman implies, yet the general point that specialized song schools for choristers were a later medieval invention and focused educational attention on preparation for liturgical celebration appears well founded.

Chapter 2 focuses on the terms *clericus* and *litteratus*, tracing a fragmentation of the former through specialization and a lowering of basic requirements, while the latter is held to shift from an identification of status to a skill. Two examples are discussed in some detail: William of Wykeham's dispute in 1370 with masters of St. Cross Hospital over the extent of their duties, and the misbehavior of one William Elys of Salisbury. The former case turns on whether St. Cross was a hospital with responsibility to the infirm and poor or a choral institution, the latter on the level of literacy expected of vicars choral. With boundaries between an increasingly literate laity and an expanding body of clerics becoming ever more porous, such questions of definition serve to chart changing expectations of literacy itself. The ways found to discipline those whose claims to clerical status rested increasingly on a minimum of literate skills might again not seem unusual to an earlier medievalist, the Benedictine intention *mens concordet voci* appearing to overlap considerably with the requirement *psallite sapienter*.

A similar emphasis on interior understanding and discipline as a basis for legitimation in the face of a migration of ritual reading and singing beyond the confines of choral communities is traced in the third chapter, this time woven through extracts from *The Simonie* and John Gower's *Mirour de l'Omme*. Chapter 4 loosens the opposition between the external authority of Latin and the seeming potential for democratization and interiority associated with the vernacular, pointing to a newfound sense of agency underpinning both the rise of vernacular theology and the development of books of hours and other technologies of Latin prayer. Specific examples stress the attention required of the laity and the way in which public ceremonies sought to claim the language of sacrality. Finally, chapters 5 and 6 turn to liturgical and devotional practice as models for vernacular poetics in, respectively, Langland's *Piers Plowman* and Chaucer's *Prioress's* and *Second Nun's Tale*. At this point, Zieman is particularly concerned with the associations of specific textual practices and literacies that serve to bestow a sense of authority and a defined place within public discourse to the vernacular subject.

Summed up in this way, Zieman's work appears to make a contribution within ongoing debates about definitions of literacy, its practice and performance, and attempts to reconceive the dividé between Latin and the vernacular in late medieval England. Yet this would be to miss a distinctive feature of her writing, which is the way a toolkit of broadly postmodern critical concerns (e.g., interpellation, repetition, writing as absence, symbolic capital, and many others) is used to open up new ways of thinking about premodern literacy. This approach relies heavily on force of argument to present alternative explanations of often-familiar historical details, yet while there is an instinctive "rightness" about many of the claims made, especially to someone trained in and around choral institutions that have retained much of their medieval doctrine, there is also an occasional sense of being overwhelmed by interpretation. With this said, there is much to be explored in this richly reflexive book, and insofar as it had me reaching for books on shelves left undisturbed for several years, it has already motivated one singer to begin thinking about newer songs in new ways.

SAM BARRETT
University of Cambridge

Books Received

Andrew, Malcolm, and Ronald Waldron, eds. *The Poems of the Pearl Manuscript: "Pearl," "Cleanness," "Patience," "Sir Gawain and the Green Knight."* Fifth edition, revised. Exeter: University of Exeter Press, 2007. Pp. x, 373, CD-ROM. £16.99, $35.00 paper, £60.00, $100.00 cloth.

Ashe, Laura. *Fiction and History in England, 1066–1200.* Cambridge: Cambridge University Press, 2007. Pp. 260. £50.00; $95.00.

Beadle, Richard, and Alan J. Fletcher, eds. *The Cambridge Companion to Medieval Theatre.* Second edition. Cambridge: Cambridge University Press. Pp. xxi, 398. £45.00, $90.00 cloth; £17.99, $29.99 paper.

Bliss, Jane. *Naming and Namelessness in Medieval Romance.* Cambridge: D. S. Brewer, 2008. Pp. 266. £50.00; $95.00.

Boenig, Robert, and Andrew Taylor, eds. *The Canterbury Tales.* Buffalo, N.Y.: Broadview Press, 2008. Pp. 502. $26.95 paper.

Brown-Grant, Rosalind. *French Romance of the Later Middle Ages: Gender, Morality, and Desire.* Oxford: Oxford University Press, 2008. Pp. xi, 254. £55.00; $110.00.

Carruthers, Mary. *The Book of Memory: A Study of Memory in Medieval Culture.* Second edition. Cambridge: Cambridge University Press, 2008. Pp. xvi, 519. $90.00 cloth; $29.99 paper.

Cartlidge, Neil, ed. *Boundaries in Medieval Romance.* Cambridge: D. S. Brewer, 2008. Pp. 208. £50.00; $95.00.

Cohen, Jeffrey Jerome, ed. *Cultural Diversity in the British Middle Ages: Archipelago, Island, England.* New York: Palgrave Macmillan, 2008. Pp. 252. $79.95.

Davlin, Mary Clemente, O.P. *A Journey into Love: Meditating with Piers Plowman*. Los Angeles: Marymount Institute Press, 2008. Pp. x, 170. $14.95 paper.

Dove, Mary. *The First English Bible: The Text and Context of the Wycliffite Versions*. Cambridge: Cambridge University Press, 2007. Pp. 332. £55.00; $99.00.

Field, P. J. C., ed. *"Le Morte Darthur": The Seventh and Eighth Tales*. Revised edition. Indianapolis: Hackett, 2008. Pp. 304. $14.95 paper.

Haywood, Louise M. *Sex, Scandal, and Sermon in Fourteenth-Century Spain: Juan Ruiz's "Libro de Buen Amor."* New York: Palgrave Macmillan, 2008. Pp. 224. $74.95.

Hill, T. E. *"She, This in Blak": Vision, Truth, and Will in Geoffrey Chaucer's "Troilus and Criseyde."* London: Routledge, 2008. Pp. 140. £65.00; $115.00 cloth. £20.00; $35.95 paper.

Hudson, Anne. *Studies in the Transmission of Wyclif's Writings*. Aldershot: Ashgate Variorum, 2008. Pp. xiv, 376. £75.00; $144.95.

Joyce, Jane Wilson, trans. Statius, *Thebaid: A Song of Thebes*. Ithaca: Cornell University Press, 2008. Pp. 544. $65.00 cloth; $27.95 paper.

Kelen, Sarah A. *Langland's Early Modern Identities*. New York: Palgrave Macmillan, 2007. Pp. xiii, 225. $79.95.

Keller, Wolfram R. *Selves and Nations: The Troy Story from Sicily to England in the Middle Ages*. Heidelberg: Universitätsverlag Winter, 2008. Pp. xiv, 644. €68.00; $132.75.

Knapp, Peggy A. *Chaucerian Aesthetics*. New York: Palgrave Macmillan, 2008. Pp. x, 242. $79.95.

Martin, Joanna. *Kingship and Love in Scottish Poetry, 1424–1540*. Aldershot: Ashgate, 2008. Pp. x, 200. £50; $99.95.

Meier, Nicole, ed. *The Poems of Walter Kennedy*. Woodbridge: Boydell & Brewer, 2008. Pp. cxvii, 449. £35.00; $70.00.

Patterson, Lee, ed. *Geoffrey Chaucer's "The Canterbury Tales": A Casebook.* Oxford: Oxford University Press, 2007. Pp. x, 241. £21.99; $40.00.

Pearsall, Derek, ed. *"Piers Plowman" by William Langland: A New Annotated Edition of the C-Text.* Exeter: University of Exeter Press, 2008. Pp. 432. £50.00; $95.00 cloth. £10.99; $20.00 paper.

Phillips, Helen, ed. *Bandit Territories: British Outlaws and Their Traditions.* Cardiff: University of Wales Press, 2008. Pp. xvii, 350. £75.00; $85.00.

Quinn, Esther Casier. *Geoffrey Chaucer and the Poetics of Disguise*. Lanham, Md.: University Press of America, 2008. Pp. xii, 251. $37.00 paper.

Rayner, Samantha J. *Images of Kingship in Chaucer and His Ricardian Contemporaries.* Cambridge: D. S. Brewer, 2008. pp. x, 180. £45.00; $90.00.

Sylvester, Louise M. *Medieval Romance and the Construction of Heterosexuality.* New York: Palgrave Macmillan, 2008. Pp. xii, 202. $74.95.

Waters, Claire M., ed. *Virgins and Scholars: A Fifteenth-Century Compilation of the Lives of John the Baptist, John the Evangelist, Jerome, and Katherine of Alexandria.* Turnhout: Brepols, 2008. Pp. xii, 494. €90.00; $131.00.

Wetherbee, Winthrop. *The Ancient Flame: Dante and the Poets*. Notre Dame, Ind.: University of Notre Dame Press, 2008. Pp. xii, 304. $35.00 paper.

An Annotated Chaucer Bibliography 2007

Compiled and edited by Mark Allen and Bege K. Bowers

Regular contributors:

Bruce W. Hozeski, *Ball State University* (Indiana)
George Nicholas, *Benedictine College* (Kansas)
Debra Best, *California State University at Dominguez Hills*
Gregory M. Sadlek, *Cleveland State University* (Ohio)
David Sprunger, *Concordia College* (Minnesota)
Winthrop Wetherbee, *Cornell University* (New York)
Elizabeth Dobbs, *Grinnell College* (Iowa)
Andrew James Johnston, *Humboldt-Universität zu Berlin*
Teresa P. Reed, *Jacksonville State University* (Alabama)
William Snell, *Keio University* (Japan)
Denise Stodola, *Kettering University* (Michigan)
Brian A. Shaw, *London, Ontario*
William Schipper, *Memorial University* (Newfoundland, Canada)
Martha Rust, *New York University*
Warren S. Moore, III, *Newberry College* (South Carolina)
Amy Goodwin, *Randolph-Macon College* (Virginia)
Cindy L. Vitto, *Rowan College of New Jersey*
Richard H. Osberg, *Santa Clara University* (California)
Brother Anthony (Sonjae An), *Sogang University* (South Korea)
Anne Thornton, *Tufts University* (Massachusetts)
Martine Yvernault, *Université de Limoges*
R. D. Eaton, *Universiteit van Amsterdam* (The Netherlands)
Elaine Whitaker, *Georgia College & State University*
Stefania D'Agata D'Ottavi, *University of Macerata* (Italy)
Cynthia Ho, *University of North Carolina, Asheville*
Margaret Connolly, *University of St. Andrews* (Scotland)
Rebecca Beal, *University of Scranton* (Pennsylvania)
Mark Allen and R. L. Smith, *University of Texas at San Antonio*

John M. Crafton, *West Georgia College*
Bege K. Bowers, *Youngstown State University* (Ohio)

Ad hoc contributions were made by Thies Bornemann (Freie Universität Berlin), Edwin D. Craun (Washington and Lee University, Virginia), Sven Duncan Durie (Freie Universität Berlin), Philipp Hinz (Freie Universität Berlin), Elisabeth Kempf (Freie Universität Berlin), Laszlo Nagypal (Budapest), Claudia Ortega (University of Texas at San Antonio), and Susan Presley (Georgia College & State University). The bibliographers acknowledge with gratitude the MLA typesimulation provided by the Center for Bibliographical Services of the Modern Language Association; postage from the University of Texas at San Antonio Department of English; and assistance from the library staff, especially Susan McCray, at the University of Texas at San Antonio.

This bibliography continues the bibliographies published since 1975 in previous volumes of *Studies in the Age of Chaucer*. Bibliographic information up to 1975 can be found in Eleanor P. Hammond, *Chaucer: A Bibliographic Manual* (1908; reprint, New York: Peter Smith, 1933); D. D. Griffith, *Bibliography of Chaucer, 1908–1953* (Seattle: University of Washington Press, 1955); William R. Crawford, *Bibliography of Chaucer, 1954–63* (Seattle: University of Washington Press, 1967); and Lorrayne Y. Baird, *Bibliography of Chaucer, 1964–1973* (Boston: G. K. Hall, 1977). See also Lorrayne Y. Baird-Lange and Hildegard Schnuttgen, *Bibliography of Chaucer, 1974–1985* (Hamden, Conn.: Shoe String Press, 1988); and Bege K. Bowers and Mark Allen, eds., *Annotated Chaucer Bibliography, 1986–1996* (Notre Dame, Ind.: University of Notre Dame, 2002).

Additions and corrections to this bibliography should be sent to Mark Allen, Bibliographic Division, The New Chaucer Society, Department of English, University of Texas at San Antonio 78249-0643 (fax: 210-458-5366; e-mail: mark.allen@utsa.edu). An electronic version of this bibliography (1975–2006) is available via The New Chaucer Society Web page at http://artsci.wustl.edu/~chaucer/ or directly at http://uchaucer.utsa.edu. Authors are urged to send annotations for articles, reviews, and books that have been or might be overlooked.

Classifications

Abbreviations of Chaucer's Works

ABC	*An ABC*
Adam	*Adam Scriveyn*
Anel	*Anelida and Arcite*
Astr	*A Treatise on the Astrolabe*
Bal Compl	*A Balade of Complaint*
BD	*The Book of the Duchess*
Bo	*Boece*
Buk	*The Envoy to Bukton*
CkT, CkP, Rv–CkL	*The Cook's Tale, The Cook's Prologue, Reeve–Cook Link*
ClT, ClP, Cl–MerL	*The Clerk's Tale, The Clerk's Prologue, Clerk–Merchant Link*
Compl d'Am	*Complaynt d'Amours*
CT	*The Canterbury Tales*
CYT, CYP	*The Canon's Yeoman's Tale, The Canon's Yeoman's Prologue*
Equat	*The Equatorie of the Planetis*
For	*Fortune*
Form Age	*The Former Age*
FranT, FranP	*The Franklin's Tale, The Franklin's Prologue*
FrT, FrP, Fr–SumL	*The Friar's Tale, The Friar's Prologue, Friar–Summoner Link*
Gent	*Gentilesse*
GP	*The General Prologue*
HF	*The House of Fame*
KnT, Kn–MilL	*The Knight's Tale, Knight–Miller Link*
Lady	*A Complaint to His Lady*
LGW, LGWP	*The Legend of Good Women, The Legend of Good Women Prologue*
ManT, ManP	*The Manciple's Tale, The Manciple's Prologue*
Mars	*The Complaint of Mars*
Mel, Mel–MkL	*The Tale of Melibee, Melibee–Monk Link*
MercB	*Merciles Beaute*

MerT, MerE–SqH	*The Merchant's Tale, Merchant Endlink–Squire Headlink*
MilT, MilP, Mil–RvL	*The Miller's Tale, The Miller's Prologue, Miller–Reeve Link*
MkT, MkP, Mk–NPL	*The Monk's Tale, The Monk's Prologue, Monk–Nun's Priest Link*
MLT, MLH, MLP, MLE	*The Man of Law's Tale, Man of Law Headlink, The Man of Law's Prologue, Man of Law Endlink*
NPT, NPP, NPE	*The Nun's Priest's Tale, The Nun's Priest's Prologue, Nun's Priest's Endlink*
PardT, PardP	*The Pardoner's Tale, The Pardoner's Prologue*
ParsT, ParsP	*The Parson's Tale, The Parson's Prologue*
PF	*The Parliament of Fowls*
PhyT, Phy–PardL	*The Physician's Tale, Physician–Pardoner Link*
Pity	*The Complaint unto Pity*
Prov	*Proverbs*
PrT, PrP, Pr–ThL	*The Prioress's Tale, The Prioress's Prologue, Prioress–Thopas Link*
Purse	*The Complaint of Chaucer to His Purse*
Ret	*Chaucer's Retraction {Retractation}*
Rom	*The Romaunt of the Rose*
Ros	*To Rosemounde*
RvT, RvP	*The Reeve's Tale, The Reeve's Prologue*
Scog	*The Envoy to Scogan*
ShT, Sh–PrL	*The Shipman's Tale, Shipman–Prioress Link*
SNT, SNP, SN–CYL	*The Second Nun's Tale, The Second Nun's Prologue, Second Nun–Canon's Yeoman Link*
SqT, SqH, Sq–FranL	*The Squire's Tale, Squire Headlink, Squire–Franklin Link*
Sted	*Lak of Stedfastnesse*
SumT, SumP	*The Summoner's Tale, The Summoner's Prologue*
TC	*Troilus and Criseyde*
Th,Th–MelL	*The Tale of Sir Thopas, Sir Thopas–Melibee Link*

Truth	*Truth*
Ven	*The Complaint of Venus*
WBT, WBP, WB–FrL	*The Wife of Bath's Tale, The Wife of Bath's Prologue, Wife of Bath–Friar Link*
Wom Nob	*Womanly Noblesse*
Wom Unc	*Against Women Unconstant*

Periodical Abbreviations

AdI	*Annali d'Italianistica*
Anglia	*Anglia: Zeitschrift für Englische Philologie*
Anglistik	*Anglistik: Mitteilungen des Verbandes deutscher Anglisten*
AnLM	*Anuario de Letras Modernas*
ANQ	*ANQ: A Quarterly Journal of Short Articles, Notes, and Reviews*
Archiv	*Archiv für das Studium der Neueren Sprachen und Literaturen*
Arthuriana	*Arthuriana*
Atlantis	*Atlantis: Revista de la Asociacion Española de Estudios Anglo-Norteamericanos*
AUMLA	*AUMLA: Journal of the Australasian Universities Language and Literature Association*
BAM	*Bulletin des Anglicistes Médiévistes*
BJRL	*Bulletin of the John Rylands University Library of Manchester*
C&L	*Christianity and Literature*
CarmP	*Carmina Philosophiae: Journal of the International Boethius Society*
CE	*College English*
ChauR	*Chaucer Review*
CL	*Comparative Literature* (Eugene, Ore.)
Clio	*CLIO: A Journal of Literature, History, and the Philosophy of History*
CLS	*Comparative Literature Studies*
CML	*Classical and Modern Literature: A Quarterly* (Columbia, Mo.)
CollL	*College Literature*
Comitatus	*Comitatus: A Journal of Medieval and Renaissance Studies*
CRCL	*Canadian Review of Comparative Literature/Revue Canadienne de Littérature Comparée*
DAI	*Dissertation Abstracts International*

DR	*Dalhousie Review*
ÉA	*Études Anglaises: Grand-Bretagne, États-Unis*
EHR	*English Historical Review*
EIC	*Essays in Criticism: A Quarterly Journal of Literary Criticism*
EJ	*English Journal*
ELH	*ELH: English Literary History*
ELN	*English Language Notes*
ELR	*English Literary Renaissance*
EMS	*English Manuscript Studies, 1100–1700*
EMSt	*Essays in Medieval Studies*
Encomia	*Encomia: Bibliographical Bulletin of the International Courtly Literature Society*
English	*English: The Journal of the English Association*
Envoi	*Envoi: A Review Journal of Medieval Literature*
ES	*English Studies*
ESC	*English Studies in Canada*
Exemplaria	*Exemplaria: A Journal of Theory in Medieval and Renaissance Studies*
Expl	*Explicator*
Fabula	*Fabula: Zeitschrift für Erzählforschung/Journal of Folktale Studies*
FCS	*Fifteenth-Century Studies*
Florilegium	*Florilegium: Carleton University Papers on Late Antiquity and the Middle Ages*
FMLS	*Forum for Modern Language Studies*
Genre	*Genre: Forms of Discourse and Culture*
HLQ	*Huntington Library Quarterly: Studies in English and American History and Literature* (San Marino, Calif.)
Hortulus	*Hortulus: The Online Graduate Journal of Medieval Studies* http://www.hortulus.net
IJES	*International Journal of English Studies*
JAIS	*Journal of Anglo-Italian Studies*
JEBS	*Journal of the Early Book Society*
JEGP	*Journal of English and Germanic Philology*
JELL	*Journal of English Language and Literature* (Korea)
JEngL	*Journal of English Linguistics*
JGN	*John Gower Newsletter*

JHiP	*Journal of Historical Pragmatics*
JMEMSt	*Journal of Medieval and Early Modern Studies*
JMH	*Journal of Medieval History*
JML	*Journal of Modern Literature*
JNT	*Journal of Narrative Theory*
JRMMRA	*Quidditas: Journal of the Rocky Mountain Medieval and Renaissance Association*
L&LC	*Literary and Linguistic Computing: Journal of the Association for Literary and Linguistic Computing*
L&P	*Literature and Psychology*
L&T	*Literature and Theology: An International Journal of Religion, Theory, and Culture*
Lang&Lit	*Language and Literature: Journal of the Poetics and Linguistics Association*
Lang&S	*Language and Style: An International Journal*
LeedsSE	*Leeds Studies in English*
Library	*The Library: The Transactions of the Bibliographical Society*
MA	*Le Moyen Age: Revue d'Histoire et de Philologie* (Brussels)
MÆ	*Medium Ævum*
M&H	*Medievalia et Humanistica: Studies in Medieval and Renaissance Culture*
Manuscripta	*Manuscripta* (Saint Louis, Mo.)
Marginalia	*Marginalia: The Journal of the Medieval Reading Group at the University of Cambridge* http://www.marginalia.co.uk/journal/
Mediaevalia	*Mediaevalia: An Interdisciplinary Journal of Medieval Studies Worldwide*
MedievalF	*Medieval Forum* http://www.sfsu.edu/~medieval/index.html
MedPers	*Medieval Perspectives*
MES	*Medieval and Early Modern English Studies*
MFF	*Medieval Feminist Forum*
MichA	*Michigan Academician* (Ann Arbor)
MLQ	*Modern Language Quarterly: A Journal of Literary History*
MLR	*The Modern Language Review*
MP	*Modern Philology: A Journal Devoted to Research in Medieval and Modern Literature*

N&Q	*Notes and Queries*
Neophil	*Neophilologus* (Dordrecht, Netherlands)
NLH	*New Literary History: A Journal of Theory and Interpretation*
NM	*Neuphilologische Mitteilungen: Bulletin of the Modern Language Society*
NML	*New Medieval Literatures*
NMS	*Nottingham Medieval Studies*
NOWELE	*NOWELE: North-Western European Language Evolution*
Parergon	*Parergon: Bulletin of the Australian and New Zealand Association for Medieval and Early Modern Studies*
PBA	*Proceedings of the British Academy*
PBSA	*Papers of the Bibliographical Society of America*
PLL	*Papers on Language and Literature: A Journal for Scholars and Critics of Language and Literature*
PMAM	*Publications of the Medieval Association of the Midwest*
PMLA	*Publications of the Modern Language Association of America*
PoeticaT	*Poetica: An International Journal of Linguistic Literary Studies*
PQ	*Philological Quarterly*
RCEI	*Revista Canaria de Estudios Ingleses*
RenD	*Renaissance Drama*
RenQ	*Renaissance Quarterly*
RES	*Review of English Studies*
RMRev	*Reading Medieval Reviews* www.rdg.ac.uk/AcaDepts/In/Medieval/rmr.htm
SAC	*Studies in the Age of Chaucer*
SAP	*Studia Anglica Posnaniensia: An International Review of English*
SAQ	*South Atlantic Quarterly*
SB	*Studies in Bibliography: Papers of the Bibliographical Society of the University of Virginia*
SCJ	*The Sixteenth Century Journal: Journal of Early Modern Studies* (Kirksville, Mo.)
SEL	*SEL: Studies in English Literature, 1500–1900*
SELIM	*SELIM: Journal of the Spanish Society for Medieval English Language and Literature*

ShakS	*Shakespeare Studies*
SIcon	*Studies in Iconography*
SiM	*Studies in Medievalism*
SIMELL	*Studies in Medieval English Language and Literature*
SMART	*Studies in Medieval and Renaissance Teaching*
SN	*Studia Neophilologica: A Journal of Germanic and Romance Languages and Literatures*
SoAR	*South Atlantic Review*
SP	*Studies in Philology*
Speculum	*Speculum: A Journal of Medieval Studies*
SSF	*Studies in Short Fiction*
SSt	*Spenser Studies: A Renaissance Poetry Annual*
TCBS	*Transactions of the Cambridge Bibliographical Society*
Text	*Text: Transactions of the Society for Textual Scholarship*
TLS	*Times Literary Supplement* (London)
TMR	*The Medieval Review* http://www.hti.umich.edu/t/tmr/
Tr&Lit	*Translation and Literature*
TSLL	*Texas Studies in Literature and Language*
UTQ	*University of Toronto Quarterly: A Canadian Journal of the Humanities* (Toronto)
Viator	*Viator: Medieval and Renaissance Studies*
WS	*Women's Studies: An Interdisciplinary Journal*
YES	*Yearbook of English Studies*
YWES	*Year's Work in English Studies*
YLS	*The Yearbook of Langland Studies*

Bibliographical Citations and Annotations

Bibliographies, Reports, and Reference

1. Allen, Mark, and Bege K. Bowers. "An Annotated Chaucer Bibliography, 2005." *SAC* 29 (2007): 565–660. Continuation of *SAC* annual annotated bibliography (since 1975); based on contributions from an international bibliographic team, independent research, and *MLA Bibliography* listings. 333 items, plus listing of reviews for 85 books. Includes an author index.

2. Allen, Valerie, and Margaret Connolly. "Middle English: Chaucer." *YWES* 86 (2007): 279–309. A discursive bibliography of Chaucer studies for 2005, divided into four subcategories: general, *CT*, *TC*, and other works.

3. Brown, Peter, ed. *A Companion to Medieval English Literature and Culture, c. 1350–c. 1500.* Blackwell Companions to Literature and Culture, no. 42. Malden, Mass.: Blackwell, 2007. xvii, 668 pp. 12 b&w illus. Thirty-eight essays by various authors, arranged in seven subheadings: "Overviews"; "The Production and Reception of Texts"; "Language and Literature"; "Encounters with Other Cultures"; "Special Themes"; "Genres"; "Readings." Each essay includes suggestions for further reading, and the volume is indexed. Includes recurrent references to Chaucer, with one essay dedicated to him; see no. 162.

4. Rogers, Shannon L. *All Things Chaucer: An Encyclopedia of Chaucer's World.* 2 vols.: A–J; K–Z. Westfield, Conn.: Greenwood Press, 2007. xxxvi, 507 pp. Map; b&w illus. Nearly 200 encyclopedia entries on wide-ranging topics, allusions, and sociohistorical contexts, many with illustrations and all with suggestions for further reading. Does not include entries for individual works by Chaucer but surveys them in the biographical introduction, which is printed in each volume. The second volume includes appendices: genealogy of Edward III, map of the route from London to Canterbury, bibliography, and comprehensive index.

5. Rossignol, Rosalyn. *Critical Companion to Chaucer: A Literary Reference to His Life and Work.* New York: Facts on File, 2007. viii, 648 pp. Map; b&w illus. Revised, expanded version of the author's *Chaucer A to Z. The Essential Reference to His Life and Works* (1999; *SAC* 23 [2001], no. 5), with a more extensive biographical introduction to Chaucer, critical

summaries of each of his works, and a more comprehensive survey of encyclopedic entries on Chaucerian topics. Appendices include a dateline, a list of works, a map of the Canterbury route, a brief bibliography, and an index to the volume.

Recordings and Films

6. Blandeau, Agnès. "Perception du Moyen Âge au cinéma: Mises en scène des *Canterbury Tales* de Chaucer." In Sandra Gorgievski and Xavier Leroux, eds. *Le Moyen Âge mis en scène: Perspectives contemporaines.* Babel, no. 15. [Toulon]: Université du Sud Toulon-Var, Faculté des Lettres et Sciences Humaines, 2007, pp. 17–31. Blandeau explores how three films capture the spirit if not the letter of *CT.*

7. Brewer, Derek, prod., with notes by Derek Brewer. *The Pardoners Tale, The Frankeleyns Tale, The Nonne Preestes Tale.* Franklin, Tenn.: Naxos AudioBooks, 2007. 2 CD-ROMs; 8-page booklet. 2 hrs., 38 min., 52 sec. Middle English reading of *PardPT* (6.327–966), *FranPT* (complete), and *NPT* (complete), with introductory notes in accompanying booklet. Read by Richard Bebb; edited by Sarah Butcher. Recorded at Motivation Sound Studios, London.

8. Crocker, Holly A. "Chaucer's Man Show: Anachronistic Authority in Brian Helgeland's *A Knight's Tale.*" In Lynn T. Ramey and Tison Pugh, eds. *Race, Class, and Gender in "Medieval" Cinema.* New York: Palgrave Macmillan, 2007, pp. 183–97. The characterization of Chaucer in Helgeland's film reinforces the film's concerns with authority and masculinity, ultimately revealing that "canonical authority" is "anachronistic."

9. Harty, Kevin J. "Chaucer for a New Millennium: *The BBC Canterbury Tales.*" In David W. Marshall, ed. *Mass Market Medieval: Essays on the Middle Ages in Popular Culture.* Jefferson, N.C.: McFarland, 2007, pp. 13–27. Compares the six tales of *The BBC Canterbury Tales* (*MilT, WBP, KnT, ShT, PardT,* and *MLT*) with their Chaucerian originals. Emphasizes plot parallels, modern themes, and the lack of interconnection among the "six stand-alone telefilms."

10. Larrington, Carolyne. "*The Canterbury Tales,* Parts One and Two—Geoffrey Chaucer, Adapted by Mike Poulton (Swan Theatre, Stratford-upon-Avon)." *TLS,* January 20, 2006, p. 16. Summary and review of the stage production of Poulton's adaptation of *CT.*

See also nos. 50, 52, 180, 195.

Chaucer's Life

11. Gil Ortega, María Auxiliadora, trans. *Chaucer*. Madrid: Ediciones Luis Revenga, 2007. 210 pp. Spanish translation of G. K. Chesterton's biography of Chaucer and his times.

12. Mead, Jenna. "Chaucer and the Subject of Bureaucracy." *Exemplaria* 19 (2007): 39–66. Scholars such as Sheila Delany, Derek Pearsall, and Thomas Frederick Tout have used bureaucratic records of Chaucer—and records of Chaucer as bureaucrat—to construct subjective portraits of the poet. Mead explores the processes of "reading" bureaucracy that produce partial, provisional, and subjective visions of a historical Chaucer.

13. Milowicki, Edward J. "Chaucer, Astronomy, and Astrology: A Courtly Connection." In Keith Busby and Christopher Kleinhenz, eds. *Courtly Arts and the Art of Courtliness: Selected Papers from the Eleventh Triennial Congress of the International Courtly Literature Society. University of Wisconsin–Madison, 29 July–4 August 2004*. Cambridge, D. S. Brewer, 2006, pp. 477–88. Milowicki advances several "speculations" about Chaucer's "French connections," particularly his possible introduction at the French court to the "study of the stars" and to the controversy of the relationship between astronomy and astrology reflected in *FranT*. Chaucer's son Lewis, cited in *Astr*, may have been named after Louis, son of Charles V of France. See also no. 339.

14. Sanna, Ellyn. "Biography of Geoffrey Chaucer." In Harold Bloom, ed. *Geoffrey Chaucer* (*SAC* 31 [2009], no. 85), pp. 5–36. Provides details about Chaucer's life and works.

15. Yeager, R. F. "Chaucer Translates the Matter of Spain." In María Bullón-Fernández, ed. *England and Iberia in the Middle Ages, 12th–15th Century: Cultural, Literary, and Political Exchanges*. The New Middle Ages. New York: Palgrave Macmillan, 2007, pp. 189–214. Considers the importance of Spain in Chaucer's life, in the politics of his age, and in his literary allusions, arguing that Chaucer could read Spanish and that his familiarity with the tale collections of Petrus Alfonsi and Don Juan Manuel "would have increased his receptivity" to Boccaccio's works later in his career.

See also nos. 25, 58, 158, 244.

Facsimiles, Editions, and Translations

16. Aita, Shuichi. "A Diplomatic Edition of Chaucer's *Parson's Tale* (Bodleian MS Arch. Selden B.14, fol. 269ʳ, l.104–fol. 275ᵛ, l. 290): A Supplement to Furnivall's *A Six-Text Print of Chaucer's Canterbury Tales* (Series 1, No. 49) in the Chaucer Society." *Language and Culture* (Osaka Prefecture University) 3 (2004): 1–16. Furnivall's *Six-Text Print* transcribes *ParsT* from Selden B.17, except for lines 104–290, which come from Lansdowne 851.

17. Bishop, Laura M. "Father Chaucer and the Vivification of Print." *JEGP* 106 (2007): 336–63. Bishop assesses how the apparatus ("peritext") in Speght's edition of Chaucer's *Works* evokes Chaucer as a living presence and situates his poetry in the midst of Tudor politics. Although Speght derives much of his peritext from Thynne and Stow, his additions intensify Chaucer's role as father and as living voice.

18. Bowden, Betsy. "A Note on the Urry-Edition Pilgrim Portraits." *ChauR* 41 (2007): 455–56. Contrary to Stephen R. Reimer's crediting them to George Vertue (in *ChauR* 41 [2006]), the drawings for the Urry portraits were executed by J. Chalmer and printed thereafter from engravings by Vertue.

19. Dempsey, James, trans. *The Court Poetry of Chaucer: A Facing-Page Translation in Modern English.* Lewiston, N.Y.: Mellen, 2007. ii, 192 pp. Modernizations of Chaucer's short poems, maintaining original rhyme schemes and metrical patterns, with facing-page texts from *The Riverside Chaucer* and Walter Skeat's edition. Includes, in the following order, *ABC, Pity, Lady, Mars, Ros, Wom Nob, Adam, Sted, Form Age, For, Truth, Gent, Ven, Scog, Buk, Purse, Wom Unc, Compl d'Am, MercB, Bal Compl, Prov,* and *Anel.* The introduction (pp. 1 12) comments on the practice and history of modernizing Chaucer.

20. Haydock, Nickolas. "False and Sooth Compounded in Caxton's Ending of Chaucer's *House of Fame*." *Atenea* (University of Puerto Rico) 26 (2006): 107–29. Haydock reads Caxton's spurious ending and epilogue to *HF* in the 1483 *Book of Fame* as a "canny as well as sympathetic reaction to the poem's ubiquitous concern with the transmission of literature."

21. Hilmo, Maidie. "The Clerk's 'Unscholarly Bow'": Seeing and Reading Chaucer's Clerk from the Ellesmere MS to Caxton." *JEBS* 10 (2007): 71–105. Hilmo encourages the view that woodcuts enhance text through visual rhetoric; specifically, Caxton's addition of a bow to

Chaucer's Clerk in his edition of *CT* represents the Clerk as a moral satirist.

22. LaPorte, Charles. "Morris's Compromises: On Victorian Editorial Theory and the Kelmscott *Chaucer*." 6 b&w illus. In David Latham, ed. *Writing on the Image: Reading William Morris*. Toronto: University of Toronto Press, 2007, pp. 209–19. Morris's decision to present Chaucer's works in "clear-text" format (without editorial apparatus) conflicts with Victorian theories of editing. Yet his presentations of *Ret* and the envoy to *TC* belie his efforts to imitate medieval traditions.

23. Lee, Dongill, and Dong-Ch'un Lee, trans. *Geoffrey Chaucer: The Canterbury Tales*. Seoul, South Korea: Hangook University of Foreign Studies Press, 2007. 672 pp. Korean translation of the complete *CT*, with poetry translated as poetry and prose as prose.

24. Lynch, Kathryn L., ed. *Dream Visions and Other Poems: Authoritative Texts, Contexts, Criticism*. Norton Critical Editions. New York: Norton, 2007. xx, 396 pp. Includes *BD, HF, PF, LGW, Anel, ABC, Adam, MercB, Ros, Truth, Gent, Sted, Scog, Buk*, and *Purse*, with a general preface, an introduction for each of the longer works, selected background works and critical assessments (focusing on the dream visions), a chronology, an introduction to Chaucer's Middle English, and a brief bibliography. Texts include marginal glosses and explanatory notes at the bottom of each page.

25. Matthews, David. "Public Ambition, Private Desire, and the Last Tudor Chaucer." In Gordon McMullan and David Matthews, eds. *Reading the Medieval in Early Modern England* (*SAC* 31 [2009], no. 56), pp. 74–88. Matthews focuses on Thomas Speght's 1598 and 1602 editions of Chaucer and their role in reimagining Chaucer as an early modern rather than a medieval author. The prefatory poem, "The Reader to Geffrey Chaucer," suggests that early editions had approached Chaucer philologically, whereas Speght will treat him personally. Speght's editions build up seventeenth-century belief in Chaucer's connections to the Lancastrians, Wycliff, and Cambridge University.

26. Mosser, Daniel W. "The Manuscript Glosses of the *Canterbury Tales* and the University of London's Copy of Pynson's [1492] Edition: Witness to a Lost Exemplar." *ChauR* 41 (2007): 360–92. Scribal glosses in a copy of this third incunabular edition of *CT* (STC 5084) provide further evidence of manuscript W, a hypothesized manuscript affiliated with Trinity College, Cambridge, MS R.3.15, and Wynkyn de Worde's

edition of *CT*. They also evince the intermingling of scribal and print modes of production at the close of the fifteenth century.

27. Partridge, Stephen. "Wynkyn de Worde's Manuscript Source for the *Canterbury Tales*: Evidence from the Glosses." *ChauR* 41 (2007): 325–59. The glosses to *Mel* and *ParsT* in Wynkyn de Worde's *CT* (1498, STC 5085) are closely related to those in Trinity College, Cambridge, MS R.3.15, suggesting that they shared a common exemplar, W. That hypothetical exemplar clarifies aspects of the history of the text at the beginning of the fifteenth century, almost a century before the production of de Worde's version.

28. Tuttle, Peter, trans. *The Canterbury Tales*. New York: Barnes & Noble, 2006. xl, 356 pp. Facing-page translation of selections from *CT*: *GP*, *KnT*, *MilT*, *RvT*, *WBPT*, *ClT*, *FranT*, *PardPT*, and *NPT*. Includes a chronology, brief notes (pp. 503–18), a survey of commentary on Chaucer through the ages, four discussion questions, suggestions for further reading, and an introduction by Robert W. Hanning that includes a brief biography and comments on sources, critical issues, and Chaucer's literary achievement.

See also nos. 128, 169, 184, 187, 205, 214, 281, 296.

Manuscripts and Textual Studies

29. Da Rold, Orietta. "The Significance of Scribal Corrections in Cambridge, University Library MS Dd.4.24 of Chaucer's *Canterbury Tales*." *ChauR* 41 (2007): 393–438. Systematic analysis of corrections disproves the notion that the Dd scribe was either careless or meddling, suggesting instead that his corrections were executed in the course of checking his copying against his exemplar. The remaining corrections were made in response to at most one other authoritative exemplar.

30. Fletcher, Alan J. "The Criteria for Scribal Attribution: Dublin, Trinity College, MS 244, Some Early Copies of the Works of Geoffrey Chaucer, and the Canon of Adam Pynkhurst Manuscripts." *RES* 58 (2007): 597–632. Evidence suggests that Chaucer's careless scribe in *Adam* is Adam Pynkhurst. The Trinity College manuscript, containing prose tracts evincing Wyclif's influence, may be in Pynkhurst's hand. Chaucer's connection with this scribe could account for Wycliffite themes in Chaucer's works.

31. Horobin, Simon. "Teaching the Language of Chaucer Manu-

scripts." In Gail Ashton and Louise Sylvester, eds. *Teaching Chaucer* (*SAC* 31 [2009], no. 82), pp. 96–104. Argues that analyzing Chaucerian manuscripts and comparing them with edited versions can help students discover important principles of variation and evidence.

32. Mosser, Daniel W. "Dating the Manuscripts of the 'Hammond Scribe': What the Paper Evidence Tells Us." *JEBS* 10 (2007): 31–70. Mosser uses paper stock to sequence the Hammond Scribe's work. The article includes photographs of watermarks.

33. Perkins, Nicholas. "John Bale, Thomas Hoccleve, and a Lost Chaucer Manuscript." *N&Q* 54 (2007): 128–31. A heretofore unrecognized reference to *KnT* in the *Index Britanniae Scriptorum*, compiled by sixteenth-century antiquarian John Bale, provides evidence of a lost manuscript containing Hoccleve's *Regiment of Princes* plus at least Chaucer's *KnT* and possibly the entire *CT*.

34. Rust, Martha Dana. *Imaginary Worlds in Medieval Books: Exploring the Manuscript Matrix*. New Middle Ages. New York and Basingstoke: Palgrave Macmillan, 2007. xii, 290 pp. 35 b&w illus. Explores relationships between texts and their paratexts in English and Scottish books produced between 1400 and 1490, considering a "variety of pre- and extralinguistic modes of interacting with and thinking through books." Examines letter-forms, "doodles," illuminations, and other graphic features, exploring how a "perceptual dimension" comes into being as books are used. Comments recurrently on Chaucerian texts, including *ABC*, *BD*, and *TC* at some length.

35. Stubbs, Estelle. "'Here's One I Prepared Earlier': The Work of Scribe D on Oxford, Corpus Christi College, MS 198." *RES* 58 (2007): 133–53. Codicological analyses of the structure and details of Corpus Christi 198 support early suggestions by Carleton Brown, Charles Owen, and John Fisher about Chaucer's ongoing revision of *CT*, especially when considered in light of other early manuscripts. Includes tabular analysis of the construction of Corpus Christi 198.

See also nos. 26, 27, 128, 148, 303, 304, 320.

Sources, Analogues, and Literary Relations

36. Boitani, Piero. "Chaucer and the Italians." In Giuseppe Galigani, ed. *Italomania(s): Italy and the English Speaking World from Chaucer to Seamus Heaney. Proceedings of the Georgetown and Kent State University Confer-*

ence Held in Florence in [sic] *June 20–21, 2005*. Florence: Mauro Pagliai, 2007, pp. 15–25. Boitani surveys Chaucer's "ongoing dialogue" with Dante, Petrarch, and Boccaccio, discussing how Chaucer's borrowings reflect his "prodigious memory and striking associative and intertextual skill." Draws examples from *PF*, *TC*, *KnT*, and *ClT* and comments on fifteenth- and sixteenth-century legacies of Italian influence on English literature.

37. Bowers, John M. *Chaucer and Langland: The Antagonistic Tradition*. Notre Dame, Ind.: University of Notre Dame Press, 2007. xii, 405 pp. Chaucer's preeminence over Langland is an effect of historical and social forces and must be revised, because tradition is a conflicted notion that helps construct understanding of past, present, and future. Chaucer was a medium of this process, "the literary 'first mover' meant to generate succession and guarantee cultural continuity." Topics include destabilization of Chaucer as origin of the tradition; naming as a source of his authority; appropriation of Langland by various forces in history as opposed to a "coherent, self-conscious" attempt by Hoccleve and Lydgate to establish Chaucer as "father" so that they might inherit the tradition; and the role of print culture in establishing reputations of each author. Bowers focuses on *CT* generally, with some attention to *CkT*, the Host, *MkT*, *ParsT*, and *TC*. See also no. 337.

38. Cook, Alexandra Kollontai. "Risking Desire: Chaucerian Representations of Erotic Love and the Pagan Past." *DAI* A67.10 (2007): n.p. Like many of his predecessors, Chaucer explores risks in dealing with pagan sources, but he renders such risks pleasurable as a means to "destabilize Christian constructs of safety."

39. Fehrman, Craig T. "Did Chaucer Read the Wycliffite Bible?" *ChauR* 42 (2007): 111–38. Studying *CT* alongside early and late versions of the Wycliffite Bible reveals examples of Chaucer's nearly direct quotations from LV and of his sympathy with developments in translation theory from EV to LV, which favored more idiomatic renderings of the original Latin.

40. Galloway, Andrew. "Gower's Quarrel with Chaucer, and the Origins of Bourgeois Didacticism in Fourteenth-Century London Poetry." In Annette Harder, Alasdair A. MacDonald, and Gerrit J. Reinink, eds. *Calliope's Classroom: Studies in Didactic Poetry from Antiquity to the Renaissance*. Dudley, Mass.: Peeters, 2007, pp. 245–67. Chaucer and Gower compete in seeking to articulate political and moral ideals. Whereas Gower endorses "communal governance of the ideology of self-interest,"

Chaucer explores a less certain "ideal union" among political, moral, and personal forms of absolutism. Galloway examines *PhyT*, the tale of Lucrece (*LGW*), and *ManT* in relation to their analogues in Gower's *Confessio Amantis* and discusses these medieval outlooks as adumbrations of theories of John Locke and Thomas Hobbes.

41. Gould, Mica Dawn. "Reading the Reader: Metafictional Romance in Ricardian London." *DAI* A68.02 (2007): n.p. Chaucer and Gower distance themselves from French influence in the 1380s and 1390s as a way to criticize Richard's "predilection for French literature" and to train their readers to read and interpret.

42. Hasan, Masoodul. *Sufism and English Literature: Chaucer to the Present Age—Echoes and Images.* New Delhi: Adam, 2007. xi, 331 pp. Surveys British literary responses to "some aspects of the Muslim spiritual system," identifying instances in which British literature was influenced by Sufi mysticism or reflects awareness of it. Includes summary (pp. 37–39) of parallels between Middle Eastern narratives and Chaucer's *CT* and *PF*; also mentions his "general awareness of Muslim people and their faith" in *MLT* and *SqT*.

43. Jeffrey, David Lyle. "Dante and Chaucer." In Jeffrey P. Greenman, Timothy Larsen, and Stephen R. Spencer, eds. *The Sermon on the Mount Through the Centuries.* Grand Rapids, Mich.: Brazos, 2007), pp. 81–107. Jeffrey explores Chaucer's allusions to the Sermon on the Mount (Matthew 5–7), arguing that they reflect Chaucer's distrust of glossing and that the Sermon underpins theological themes of *CT* most evident in *Mel* and *ParsT*: peacemaking and obedience.

44. Kamath, Stephanie Anne Viereck Gibbs. "Unveiling the 'I': Allegory and Authorship in the Franco-English Tradition, 1270–1450." *DAI* A67.08 (2007): n.p. Kamath traces "the impact of the innovative form of the *Roman de la Rose* in French and English history," considering the use of "vernacular first-person allegory" by writers such as Deguileville, Chaucer, Lydgate, and Hoccleve.

45. Kirkpatrick, Robin. *English and Italian Literature from Dante to Shakespeare: A Study of Source, Analogue, and Divergence.* New York: Longman, 1995. ix, 328 pp. Surveys the sustained influence of Italian culture in England from Chaucer through Wyatt, Sidney, Spenser, Gascoigne, Marston, Fletcher, and Shakespeare. Summarizes the development of Italian city-states and explores topics such as Italian influence on English education, humanism, and literary genres and modes: epic, comedy, novella, and pastoral. Individual chapters examine Italian influence

421

on Chaucer and on Shakespeare, including the influence of Dante, Petrarch, and Boccaccio on *HF*, *CT*, and *TC*.

46. Ramdass, Harold Nigel. "Miswriting Tragedy: Genealogy, History, and Orthography in the *Canterbury Tales*, Fragment One." *DAI* A68.05 (2007): n.p. Fragment 1 of *CT* (*KnT*, *MilT*, and *RvT*) "posit[s] contra-factual histories" for Chaucer's source texts while employing imagery of "sodomy, rape and monstrous hybrids" as refutations of those histories' threats to the structure of a salvation comedy.

47. Taylor, Karla. "Chaucer's Volumes: Toward a New Model of Literary History in the *Canterbury Tales*." *SAC* 29 (2007): 43–85. Using the image of a volume of collected leaves, Chaucer explores the "twin problems of rivalry and rehearsal" in his sequence of *MilP* (the narrator's apology), *MLP* (the Man of Law's comments on Chaucer's writings), and *WBPT* (the tearing of Jankyn's book and the Midas exemplum). Responding in subtle ways to Dante, Virgil, and Ovid, Chaucer is concerned with poetic tradition and with shaping audience response as a way to make tradition. His adaptations reveal his awareness that English literature, written in an unrelated vernacular, depends on classical literature in ways that differ from Italian literary dependence on the classics.

See also nos. 15, 89, 101, 158, 166, 179, 185, 186, 190, 198, 201, 203, 204, 208, 209, 219–21, 226, 229, 231, 236, 241, 243, 245, 246, 254, 257, 260, 269, 274, 285–87, 302, 307, 308, 312, 314, 316, 319.

Chaucer's Influence and Later Allusion

48. Alexander, Michael. *Medievalism: The Middle Ages in Modern England*. New Haven: Yale University Press, 2007. xxvii, 306 pp. 106 b& w and color illus. Alexander traces the "set of ideals" underlying English medievalism, commenting on art, architecture, politics, and religion but focusing on literature. The study contains recurrent references to Chaucer's influence, including investigation of Walter Scott's uses of Chaucer.

49. Arnell, Carla. "Chaucer's Wife of Bath and John Fowles's Quaker Maid: Tale-Telling and the Trial of Personal Experience and Written Authority." *MLR* 102 (2007): 933–46. John Fowles's novel *A Maggot*, set in eighteenth-century England, is similar to *CT* in several ways, from its opening premise to its general structure as a series of "tales" (reconstructions of mysterious events surrounding a death) told by various characters first introduced through detailed portrait-like de-

scriptions. The female protagonist, the "Quaker Maid" Rebecca Lee, revisits the debate that appears in *WBT* about personal experience versus written authority as a legitimate source of knowledge.

50. Barrington, Candace. *American Chaucers.* The New Middle Ages. New York: Palgrave Macmillan, 2007. xiv, 224 pp. Barrington studies examples of "Chaucer's appearances in American popular culture over the past two hundred years": Percy MacKaye's play, pageant, and opera; James Norman Hall's World War I memoir *Flying with Chaucer* (1930); Anne Maurey's pageant *May Day in Canterbury* (1926); Katherine Gordon Brinley's performance piece *Chaucer Lives* (1921); and Brian Helgeland's movie *A Knight's Tale* (2000). She comments briefly on a wide variety of related texts that reflect reception of Chaucer in the United States.

51. Finke, Laurie A. "The Politics of the Canon: Christine de Pizan and the Fifteenth-Century Chaucerians." *Exemplaria* 19 (2007): 16–38. In the fifteenth century, Chaucer was admired chiefly as the founder of English eloquence, betraying English anxiety about French influences. The patronage networks that promoted Chaucer as a literary icon also promoted translations of the works of Pizan. Appropriation of her work through literary circles, centered on men such as Thomas Hoccleve, John of Bedford, Sir John Fastolf, Stephen Scrope, Anthony Woodville, and William Caxton, serves "as a metonymy for what was specifically English about English literature."

52. Freer, Scott. "The Mythical Method: Eliot's 'The Waste Land' and *A Canterbury Tale* (1944)." *Historical Journal of Film, Radio, and Television* 27 (2007): 357–70. Freer examines modernist uses of the past in Eliot's *The Waste Land* and the English movie *A Canterbury Tale*, directed by Michael Powell and Emeric Pressburger. Explores several allusions to Chaucer.

53. Heffernan, Carol F[alvo]. "Heliodorus's *Æthiopica* and Sidney's *Arcadia*: A Reconsideration." *ELN* 42.1 (2004): 12–20. Suggests that *SqT* may have influenced the narrative techniques of Philip Sidney's *Arcadia*, specifically its "interlocking structure."

54. Kim, Uirak. "The Medieval Poetics of Pilgrimage and Multiple Voices." *MES* 15 (2007): 289–305. Kim gauges T. S. Eliot's debt to *CT* in *The Waste Land*, examining Eliot's poem as a pilgrimage that modifies a number of Chaucer's techniques and devices: the opening *reverdie*, multiple voices and tales, use of sources, focus on marriage, and more.

55. Knutson, Karla. "Constructing Chaucer in the Fifteenth Cen-

tury: The Inherent Anti-Feminism of the Paternal Paradigm." In Bruce
E. Brandt and Michael S. Nagy, eds. *Proceedings of the 14th Northern
Plains Conference on Earlier British Literature, April 7–8, 2006* (*SAC* 31
[2009], no. 88), pp. 95–106. Knutson argues that fifteenth-century im-
itators of Chaucer identified themselves as descendants of Chaucer,
whom they constructed as father, to promote a conservative agenda,
simultaneously antifeminist, hierarchical, and heteronormative.

56. McMullan, Gordon, and David Matthews, eds. *Reading the
Medieval in Early Modern England*. Cambridge: Cambridge University
Press, 2007. xiv, 287 pp. Twelve essays by individual authors, with an
introduction by the editors that discusses early modern England's ambivalent fascination with the Middle Ages, including, briefly, Shakespeare and Fletcher's *Two Noble Kinsmen*—an adaptation of Chaucer's
KnT. Other topics range widely, addressing drama, reading, editorial
practice, religious reform, and ideas of nationhood. For two essays that
pertain to Chaucer, see nos. 25 and 60.

57. Meyer-Lee, Robert J. *Poets and Power from Chaucer to Wyatt*. Cambridge and New York: Cambridge University Press, 2007. xii, 297 pp.
Fifteenth-century English poets "responded" to an evolving "climate of
patronage by inventing a new tradition of public and elite poetry" that
included the role of poet laureate (although the office was not official
until John Dryden's appointment in 1668). Poets who proclaimed
themselves Chaucer's disciples, particularly John Lydgate, retroactively
fashioned Chaucer as England's first poet laureate, even though Chaucer
himself was suspicious of the concept. Many causes contributed to the
change in climate, particularly Bolingbroke's seizure of the throne from
Richard II in 1399 and the concomitant changes in relationships between princes and poets, between poets and audiences, and between
audiences and the English language. Makes passing references to *BD,
ClT, FranT, KnT, MLT, Ret, Th, HF, LGW*, and *TC*. See also no. 372.

58. O'Connor, Garry. *Chaucer's Triumph: Including the Case of Cecilia
Chaumpaigne, the Seduction of Katherine Swynford, the Murder of Her Husband, the Interment of John of Gaunt and Other Offices of the Flesh in the Year
1399*. London: Petrak, 2007. viii, 294 pp. Historical novel told in a
pastiche of first-person flashbacks, narrated by Chaucer, Adam Scriveyn,
Philippa Chaucer, Katherine Swynford, and John of Gaunt.

59. Reverand, Cedric D. "Dryden's 'To the Duchess of Ormond':
Identifying Her Plantagenet Predecessor." *N&Q* 54 (2007): 57–60. In
the opening poem of *Fables Ancient and Modern*, Dryden draws a parallel

between himself and Chaucer. The "fairest Nymph" in that parallel should be identified as the Duchess of Lancaster, as proposed by Walter Scott in 1808, rather than Joan of Kent, "the standard gloss" that George C. Craik put forward in 1897.

60. Simpson, James. "Diachronic History and the Shortcomings of Medieval Studies." In Gordon McMullan and David Matthews, eds. *Reading the Medieval in Early Modern England* (*SAC* 31 [2009], no. 56), pp. 17–30. Whereas fifteenth-century writers such as Hoccleve, Lydgate, and Skelton wrote texts that engaged in "a kind of conversation" with Chaucer, sixteenth-century writers treated Chaucer as a distant topic of philological study. Simpson argues that this contrast is emblematic of English literary history as practiced today.

61. Wallace, David. "New Chaucer Topographies." *SAC* 29 (2007): 3–19. The Presidential Address, The New Chaucer Society, Fifteenth International Congress, 27–31 July 2006, Fordham University. Comments on twenty-first-century adaptations of *CT* on stage and screen, in rap performance, and in imitative fiction, e.g., Peter Ackroyd's *Clerkenwell Tales*, Baba Brinkman's *Rap Canterbury Tales*, RSC and BBC productions, David Dabydeen's *The Intended*, and Marilyn Nelson's *The Cachoeira Tales*. These and other renditions reflect the adaptability of *CT* to new, global places and spaces. Nelson's version, in particular, successfully reimagines Chaucer's idea of cultural fellowship.

62. Weber, Lindsay. "James Norman Hall: *Flying with Chaucer*—A World War I Memoir." In Jon Alexander, ed. *American POW Memoirs from the Revolutionary War Through the Vietnam War: The Autobiography Seminar, Providence College, Spring Semester 2006.* Eugene, Ore.: Wipf & Stock, 2007, pp. 71–78. Describes the context and content of Hall's 1930 publication, *Flying with Chaucer*, focusing on his quotations from *CT* and their role in his memoir.

See also nos. 8, 25, 37, 96, 128, 278, 296, 322.

Style and Versification

63. Bourgne, Florence. "Chaucer's New Ekphrasis." *BAM* 71 (2007): 7–20. Bourgne studies Chaucer's description of architecture in literary compositions ("his new ekphrasis").

64. ———. "Poésie et architecture en angleterre à la fin du Moyen Âge." In Martine Yvernault and Sophie Cassagnes-Brouquet, eds. *Poètes*

et artistes: La figure du créateur en europe au Moyen Âge et à la Renaissance. Limoges: Presses Universitaires de Limoges, 2007, pp. 185–204. Drawing on *BD*, *TC*, and the Gawain poet, Bourgne studies the influence of architecture on poetry.

65. Lawton, David. "Donaldson and Irony." *ChauR* 41 (2007): 231–39. "Working within and yet exploding New Critical terminology," E. Talbot Donaldson's studies of Chaucer's irony—exemplified in his writing on Criseyde—are grounded in his deep understanding of rhetoric. They anticipate Linda Hutcheon's theory of irony, in which "the said and the unsaid simultaneously make up the ironic meaning."

66. Putter, Ad. "Chaucer's Verse and Alliterative Poetry: Grammar, Metre, and Some Secrets of the Syllable Count." *PoeticaT* 67 (2007): 19–35. Putter compares Chaucer's techniques to the "close control" of syllable counting by alliterative poets. Although the metrical goals of these poets differ from those of Chaucer, the means whereby alliterative poets achieve control are similar to Chaucer's—e.g., using verbs that allow various forms (*lien* and *shinen*) and capitalizing on flexible morphology, especially final *-e*.

See also nos. 175, 185, 235, 268, 274, 305.

Language and Word Studies

67. Bergeson, Anita K. "Chaucer's Questioning Impulse: Reading the Dream Visions and *Troilus and Criseyde*." *DAI* A67.10 (2007): n.p. Bergeson explores the semantic and dramatic range of Middle English *reden*—advise, counsel, read, interpret—as it is used and enacted in *BD*, *HF*, *PF*, and *TC*.

68. Cox, Bonita M. "Geoffrey Chaucer: '[T]he firste fyndere of our faire langage.'" In Harold Bloom, ed. *Geoffrey Chaucer* (*SAC* 31 [2009], no. 85), pp. 37–68. Surveys Chaucer's works, commenting on their relationships with late medieval linguistic and political conditions.

69. Horobin, Simon. *Chaucer's Language*. New York: Palgrave Macmillan, 2007. x, 198 pp. Discursive description of Middle English, focusing on Chaucer's dialect and usage, divided into eight chapters: (1) Why Study Chaucer's Language? (2) Writing in English; (3) What Was Middle English? (4) Spelling and Pronunciation; (5) Vocabulary; (6) Grammar (includes parts of speech and syntax); (7) Language and Style (includes prose style); and (8) Discourse and Pragmatics (includes forms

of address, politeness, swearing, discourse markers, and styles of speech). Each section offers recommendations for further reading. The volume includes an appendix of sample texts, a glossary of linguistic terms, a bibliography, and a brief index.

70. Ingham, Richard. "Negative Concord and the Loss of the Negative Particle *ne* in Late Middle English." *SAP* 42 (2006): 77–97. Includes several examples from Chaucer's prose writings.

71. Jucker, Andreas H. " 'Thou art so loothly and so oold also': The Use of *Ye* and *Thou* in Chaucer's *Canterbury Tales*." *Anglistik* 17.2 (2006): 57–72. The choices between *ye* and *thou* in *CT* are governed by the "interactional status of the characters," a set of principles differing "considerably from modern address systems." Jucker surveys previous criticism on the topic and assesses exchanges and their conditions in *WBT*, *SNT*, *FrT*, and *NPT*.

72. Knappe, Gabriele, and Michael Schümann. "*Thou* and *Ye*: A Collocational-Phraseological Approach to Pronoun Change in Chaucer's *Canterbury Tales*." *SAP* 42 (2006): 213–38. Chaucer's use of *thou* and *ye* usually follows the standard pattern of his day. Some pronoun switching does appear, sometimes because of rhyme or textual variants but often because Chaucer uses a common formula, quotation, or other habitual lexical combination.

73. Lerer, Seth. "Lord of This Langage: Chaucer's English." In Seth Lerer. *Inventing English: A Portable History of the Language*. New York: Columbia University Press, 2007, pp. 70–84. Characterizes the language of Chaucer's day and emphasizes his range and synthesis of styles, exemplifying features of Middle English and Chaucer's dexterous uses of it in poetry and prose. Comments at length on the opening of *GP*, on *Astr*, on uses of second-person pronouns, on vocabulary, and on range in linguistic register.

74. Nakao, Yoshiyuki. "Chaucer's *Gentil* with a Focus on Its Modal Implication." In Jacek Fisiak and Hye-Kyung Kang, eds. *Recent Trends in Medieval English Language and Literature in Honour of Young-Bae Park* (*SAC* 31 [2009], no. 98), vol. 1, pp. 321–45. Nakao examines uses of *gentil* in *TC*, *MerT*, and *FranT*, gauging the level of subjectivity involved on the part of the character, the narrator, and/or the author, modified by the audience's subjective understanding. Poses a "double-prism" structure through which such evaluative terms gain valence.

75. Peters, Robert A. *Chaucer's Language. Journal of English Linguistics* Occasional Monographs, no. 1. Bellingham, Wash.: Western Washing-

ton University, 1980. vii, 125 pp. After briefly placing Chaucer's language in the history of the development of English, Peters describes Chaucer's vocabulary, phonology, morphology, and syntax. The study is presented as a "one-text description of Chaucer's language for the student of Chaucer's literature."

76. Shackleton, Robert G., Jr. "Phonetic Variation in the Traditional English Dialects: A Computational Analysis." *JEngL* 35 (2007): 30–102. Employing the "standard" ME dialect of the Home Counties of southeastern England as a baseline, Shackleton applies a number of quantitative variational measures—clustering, distance regressions, variant-area regressions, barrier analysis, and principal-components analysis—to 57 ME-derived long vowels, short vowels, and diphthongs. Shackleton comments on the success of each approach and concludes that the techniques complement one another as means of delineating modern dialect localities.

77. Sylvester, Louise. "Teaching the Language of Chaucer." In Gail Ashton and Louise Sylvester, eds. *Teaching Chaucer* (*SAC* 31 [2009], no. 82), pp. 81–95. Explores an apparent disconnect between pedagogical goals of classes that study Chaucer's literature and those that study the history of the English language, suggesting that sociolinguistic approaches can help bridge the gap.

78. Twomey, Michael W. "Chaucer's Latinity." In Hans Sauer and Renate Bauer, eds. *"Beowulf" and Beyond*. Studies in English Medieval Language and Literature, no. 18. Frankfurt am Main: Peter Lang, 2007, pp. 205–11. Scrutinizes Chaucer's use of Latin, demonstrating that his intratextual and extratextual Latin terms, phrases, and sentences are "formulas" and "quotations," not his own inventions. Twomey briefly surveys the development of Anglo-Latin and its pronunciation in relation to English.

See also nos. 66, 117, 121, 149, 167, 189, 232, 256, 274.

Background and General Criticism

79. Akahori, Naoko. "On Chaucer's Shorter Poems: Geoffrey Chaucer and King Richard 2." *Research Reports of the Nagaoka Technical College* 32.1 (1996): 3–10. In *Sted* and *Mel*, Chaucer either could not or did not make his attitude about the political and religious problems of his day

clear. Akahori examines why he gave his hearty, moral advice to Richard II and what he really intended to say.

80. Anderson, Judith H. "Commenting on Donaldson's Commentaries." *ChauR* 41 (2007): 271–78. E. Talbot Donaldson's commentary on *FranT* in *Chaucer's Poetry* exemplifies his criticism "at its best": "[c]onstructive provocation, rather than dogmatic mastery."

81. Ashton, Gail. "Creating Learning Communities in Chaucer Studies: Process and Product." In Gail Ashton and Louise Sylvester, eds. *Teaching Chaucer* (*SAC* 31 [2009], no. 82), pp. 105–19. Suggests and discusses the value of several group projects for teaching a large class of Chaucer students (200 plus).

82. ———, and Louise Sylvester, eds. *Teaching Chaucer*. Teaching the New English. New York and Basingstoke: Palgrave Macmillan, 2007. xi, 167 pp. Nine essays on pedagogical topics by various authors, with Web resources, suggestions for further reading, and index. The introduction (by Ashton) emphasizes the need for teachers to facilitate active learning. For individual essays, see nos. 31, 77, 81, 94, 99, 129, 156, 157, and 300.

83. Beidler, Peter G., and Sierra Gitlin. "Chaucer and the (He)art of Teaching: A Professor and Student in Dialogue." In John Cartafalsa and Lynne Anderson, eds. *The Joy of Teaching: A Chorus of Voices*. Lanham, Md.: University Press of America, 2007, pp. 3–17. An epistolary exchange between teacher and student on the intellectual and emotional challenges of reading Chaucer in a twenty-first-century undergraduate classroom.

84. Bleeth, Kenneth. "Chaucerian Gardens and the Spirit of Play." In Laura L. Howes, ed. *Place, Space, and Landscape in Medieval Narrative* (*SAC* 31 [2009], no. 112), pp. 107–17. Bleeth examines the ways that gardens in *TC*, *KnT*, *MerT*, and *FranT* reveal Chaucer's discomfort with the aristocratic fantasy of "pure play," idealized in the *Roman de la Rose* and separated from the world.

85. Bloom, Harold, ed. *Geoffrey Chaucer*. Bloom's Biocritiques. Philadelphia: Chelsea House, 2003. xiii, 159 pp. Five essays by various authors, a brief introduction by the editor, a chronology, and selective bibliographies on Chaucer's work, primary and secondary. Three essays are reprints (George L. Kittredge's on the marriage group; Larry D. Benson's on Chaucer's English style; and John H. Fisher's on Lancastrian language policy). For two newly published essays, see nos. 14 and 68.

86. ———. *Geoffrey Chaucer: Updated Edition*. Bloom's Modern Critical Views. New York: Bloom's Literary Criticism, 2007. vii, 259 pp. Ten previously printed or excerpted essays by various authors, with an introduction by the editor, a Chaucer chronology, and a bibliography. Topics include the ending of *TC* (E. Talbot Donaldson); *LGWP* (Robert Worth Frank Jr.); interplay between *KnT* and *MilT* (Richard Neuse); sovereignty in *WBT* (Manuel Aguirre); Ovidianism and the Wife of Bath (Michael A. Calabrese); *SNT* and apocalyptic imagination (Eileen Jankowski); Oedipal fantasies in *ClT*, *MLT*, and *PrT* (Barrie Ruth Strauss); *ShT* as fabliau (John Finlayson); time as topos in Chaucer's poetry (Martin Camargo); and joy in *TC* (John M. Hill).

87. Borroff, Marie. "Donaldson and the Romantic Poets." *ChauR* 41 (2007): 225–30. Revisiting E. Talbot Donaldson's scholarship provokes nostalgia as well as the recognition that, for Donaldson, "poems of the order of Chaucer's arouse feelings as well as thoughts, feelings based on the critic's own experience."

88. Brandt, Bruce E., and Michael S. Nagy, eds. *Proceedings of the 14th Northern Plains Conference on Earlier British Literature, April 7–8, 2006*. Brookings, S.D.: English Department, South Dakota State University, 2006. 220 pp. Thirteen papers on topics ranging from Old English to eighteenth-century British literature. For three papers that pertain to Chaucer, see nos. 55, 206, and 302.

89. Brown, Peter. *Chaucer and the Making of Optical Space*. Oxford and New York: Peter Lang, 2007. 377 pp. Brown traces classical and medieval study of optics in various kinds of writing, arguing that in the late Middle Ages the science of *perspectiva* became part of intellectual consciousness, influencing Chaucer and several of his models (Jean de Meun, Dante, and Boccaccio). Chaucer draws on his knowledge of *perspectiva* to varying degrees, superficially using the discourse of optics in *SqT* and drawing on discussions of defective vision in *RvT* and *MerT*. In *HF*, having absorbed optical principles from Dante's *Commedia*, Chaucer deploys these principles innovatively to link visual activity to spatial phenomena and identity. Brown treats the characters' visual activities and manipulations of material and symbolic spaces in *BD*, *KnT*, *MilT*, and *TC* and examines Chaucer's use of space to extend treatment of social, political, and ethical issues.

90. Cartwright, John [H]. "Medieval Cosmology and European Literature: Dante and Chaucer." In John H. Cartwright and Brian Baker, eds. *Literature and Science: Social Impact and Interaction*. Science and Soci-

ety: Impact and Interaction. Santa Barbara, Calif.: ABC-CLIO, 2005, pp. 1–29. Summarizes "Aristotelian cosmology" and describes its role as a structural and thematic device in Dante's *Paradiso*. Describes the roles of astrology, the humours, and alchemy in Chaucer's *CT*, especially in the description of the Physician and in *CYPT*. Includes a brief bibliographical essay on science in the works of the two poets.

91. Cawsey, Kathy, and Jason Harris, eds. *Transmission and Transformation in the Middle Ages: Texts and Contexts*. Dublin: Four Courts Press, 2007. 212 pp. Ten essays by various authors, with an introduction by the editors and a comprehensive index. Topics range from Jerome's theory of translation to Julian of Norwich to Protestant reception of medieval literature. For three essays that pertain to Chaucer, see nos. 251, 272, and 325.

92. Coleman, Joyce. "Aurality." In Paul Strohm, ed. *Middle English* (*SAC* 31 [2009], no. 133), pp. 68–85. Coleman clarifies differences between "aurality" and "orality," assessing references to reading aloud and speaking aloud in Middle English texts, especially Chaucer's works, and citing depictions of such practice in manuscript illustrations, including two depictions from Chaucer: the *Troilus* frontispiece (Cambridge, Corpus Christi College 61) and an initial in Lansdowne 851 (British Library).

93. Collette, Carolyn P. *Performing Polity: Women and Agency in the Anglo-French Tradition, 1385–1620*. Medieval Women: Texts and Contexts, no. 15. Turnhout, Belgium: Brepols, 2006. 218 pp. Collette surveys literary and historical evidence that women in the Anglo-French tradition played the role of mediator, i.e., someone who "negotiates, bridges, and unites differences"—evidence of the "ideology and practice of women's agency" in the late Middle Ages and early modern period. Discusses works by Christine de Pizan, Philippe de Mézières, Nicolas Oresme, Lydgate, and Chaucer, plus several cycle plays, Griselda narratives, treatises on the Virgin, and accounts of Henry VIII's attempts to divorce Catherine of Aragon. Considers at length *ClT*, *PrT*, and *SNT*. See also no. 343.

94. Coote, Lesley. "Chaucer and the Visual Image: Learning, Teaching, Assessing." In Gail Ashton and Louise Sylvester, eds. *Teaching Chaucer* (*SAC* 31 [2009], no. 82), pp. 139–52. Describes and promotes the use of image-rich material and virtual learning environments for teaching Chaucer. Includes cautions and recommendations.

95. Crocker, Holly A. *Chaucer's Visions of Manhood*. The New Middle

Ages. New York: Palgrave Macmillan, 2007. xiii, 250 pp. Crocker investigates how the visibility and invisibility of gender in Chaucer are linked to performativity and cultural privilege, especially for men. Discusses the figurative tradition of engendering sight as background to how Prudence in *Mel* is the "visibly unseen" part of her husband's visible masculinity. In *PhyT* and accounts of a court scandal concerning Elizabeth of Lancaster, women who are visibly associated with passivity consolidate men's claims to authority. *BD* attempts to resolve the scandal of gender's visibility through its relational construction of a memorial poetics. Crocker also includes expanded versions of previously published discussions of female invisibility in *ShT* and *WBT* (*SAC* 29 [2007], no. 234) and gender concerns in the Chaucerian proverbs of Harley MS 7333 (*SAC* 29 [2007], no. 54).

96. Dor, Juliette. "Caroline Spurgeon and Her Relationship to Chaucer. The Text of Her *Viva* Presentation at the Sorbonne." In Thea Summerfield and Keith Busby, eds. *People and Texts: Relationships in Medieval Literature. Studies Presented to Erik Kooper* (*SAC* 31 [2009], no. 134), pp. 87–98. Comments on archival records of Chaucer scholar Caroline Spurgeon, seeking information about Spurgeon's reasons for studying the reception of Chaucer in France and England. Dor transcribes and translates into English the French text of Spurgeon's *viva* (defense) for her doctorate at the University of Paris.

97. Fender, Janelle Diane. "Remembering and Forgetting in Late Medieval and Early Reformation English Literature: A Study of Remnants." *DAI* A67.09 (2007): n.p. Interdependence of parts and wholes in Chaucer's works anticipates a sustained concern with fragments and remnants in later literature, especially among Reformation bibliophiles who were struggling to "re-member" the past as a form of nascent nationalism.

98. Fisiak, Jacek, and Hye-Kyung Kang, eds. *Recent Trends in Medieval English Language and Literature in Honour of Young-Bae Park*. Vol. 1. Seoul, South Korea: Thaehaksa, 2005. viii, 480 pp. Twenty essays by various authors on topics in theoretical linguistics and in Old and Middle English linguistics and literature, including three that pertain to Chaucer; see nos. 74, 172, and 223.

99. Fitzgibbons, Moira. " 'Cross-Voiced' Assignments and the Critical 'I.' " In Gail Ashton and Louise Sylvester, eds. *Teaching Chaucer* (*SAC* 31 [2009], no. 82), pp. 65–80. Explores the pedagogical value of en-

couraging students to combine analysis and creativity in performing (aloud and in writing) from the points of view of individual Chaucerian characters. Suggests using Chaucer's characters to critique those of Christine de Pizan and vice versa.

100. Fujiki, Takayoshi. "Chaucer's Proverbs About Hoods (in Memory of the Late Professor Emeritus Hideshi Kishi)." *Sapientia* 41 (2007): 231–45 (in Japanese). Looks at Chaucer's use of proverbs associated with hoods for satiric and comic purposes.

101. Fyler, John M. *Language and the Declining World in Chaucer, Dante, and Jean de Meun.* Cambridge Studies in Medieval Literature, no. 63. New York: Cambridge University Press, 2007. xii, 306 pp. Following an exposition of received biblical history and medieval commentaries in which the Fall and Babel represent declensions from unity and clarity, Fyler addresses Jean's *Roman*, Dante's *Commedia, HF, SNT,* and *CYT* intertextually and in the context of those traditions. Dante envisions linguistic redemption; Jean de Meun suggests the imposition of alienating categories on prelapsarian plenitude; and Chaucer stages a reenactment of the Fall between *SNT* and *CYT*.

102. Galloway, Andrew. *Medieval Literature and Culture.* Introductions to British Literature and Culture Series. London and New York: Continuum, 2006. 154 pp. A guide to Old and Middle English literature, its contexts, and its reception. Separate sections address political and social contexts; literary genres and the communities that produced them; reception from the Renaissance to current debates; and several "resources for independent study": datelines, glossary, royal genealogy, suggestions for further reading, and an index. Refers to Chaucer recurrently.

103. Giancarlo, Matthew. *Parliament and Literature in Late Medieval England.* Cambridge Studies in Medieval Literature, no. 64. New York: Cambridge University Press, 2007. xiii, 289 pp. 8 b&w illus. Studies the intersection between the "growth of parliament" and the "development of poetry" from c. 1376 to 1414, focusing on depictions of parliaments in literature. Poets such as Langland, Gower, and Chaucer had "extensive parliamentary connections," and their works represent "anxieties about voice, representation, and the vision of a cohesive community in a fractured world." Giancarlo examines parliamentary records and commentaries, complaint literature, Gower's *Mirour de l'Omme* and *Cronica Tripertita*, Langland's *Piers Plowman*, and works by Chaucer. *PF* is a "unique representation of parliamentary practice," *GP* and *Mel* re-

flect the language and technique of parliaments, and *CT* is structured in accord with the "mediational dynamics" of parliamentarism.

104. Green, D. H. *Women Readers in the Middle Ages.* Cambridge Studies in Medieval Literature, no. 65. Cambridge: Cambridge University Press, 2007. xi, 296 pp. Studies the literary climate of women readers, real and fictional, who inform Chaucer's world, with commentary on the depiction of women reading in *TC*.

105. Gust, Geoffrey W. "Revaluating 'Chaucer the Pilgrim' and Donaldson's Enduring Persona." *ChauR* 41 (2007): 311–23. Despite his tendency to view Chaucer's narrative persona in *CT* autobiographically, E. Talbot Donaldson's exploration of this persona paved the way "for the proliferation of studies that have taken account of Chaucer's narrators," studies in which narrator and author are viewed as "largely sundered and separate."

106. Gust, Geoffrey William. "Constructing Chaucer(s): Author and Persona in the Critical Tradition." *DAI* C67.02 (2006): 496. Examines the "many ways in which the I-speaker has been deployed by both Chaucer and Chaucerians," considering concepts of the persona, influences from Chaucer's biographies, and representations of the poet in his short poems and *CT*.

107. Gutiérrez Arranz, José María, "Notas a tres personajes mitológicos en Chaucer: Ascálafo, Cánace y Midas." *Anglogermanica online: Revista electrónica periódica de filología alemana e inglesa* http://www.uv.es/anglogermanica/ 5 (2007): 39–49. Classifies approximately 220 mythological characters that appear in Chaucer's works: supernatural creatures, human beings, and other classical references. Describes and analyzes the presence of Ascalafo, Canace, and Midas in Chaucer, focusing especially on Midas.

108. Hanna, Ralph. "Donaldson and Robertson: An Obligatory Conjunction." *ChauR* 41 (2007): 240–49. In juxtaposition to D. W. Robertson's comprehensive historicist method, E. Talbot Donaldson's "fundamentally rhetorical mode of analysis" also constituted a historicist approach, but one that moved from philological detail "toward some larger whole," the opposite of Robertson's approach from "grand theory" to individual case.

109. Hanning, Robert W. "No [One] Way to Treat a Text: Donaldson and the Criticism of Engagement." *ChauR* 41 (2007): 261–70. In opposition to Robertson's "patristic exegesis," Donaldson models a practice of engaging the autonomy of medieval texts. In the process, he

adopts a critical persona that, feminist critiques notwithstanding, "is a decorous fiction which *may* or *may not* correspond to its creator's patriarchal attitude toward women and texts."

110. Hopkins, Amanda, and Cory James Rushton, eds. *The Erotic in the Literature of Medieval Britain*. Rochester, N.Y.; and Cambridge: D. S. Brewer, 2007. [xi], 182 pp. Thirteen essays by various authors, most focusing on depictions or deferrals of the erotic in Middle English romances, with other topics such as a branch of the *Mabinogi*, female Jewish libido, fifteenth-century letters, and more. The editors' introduction surveys the critical context of the topics and comments on Chaucer as the only major Middle English writer who is "routinely allowed some genuine erotic feeling," perhaps because he acknowledges tacitly and otherwise the inherent violence of sex. For three essays that pertain to Chaucer, see nos. 217, 224, and 311.

111. Hordis, Sandra M., and Paul Hardwick, eds. *Medieval English Comedy*. Profane Arts of the Middle Ages. Turnhout, Belgium: Brepols, 2007. 230 pp. Ten essays by various authors discuss comedy in Old English literature and in several Middle English media: drama, narrative poetry, stained glass, illuminations, and misericords. Three of the essays pertain to Chaucer; see nos. 185, 255, and 262.

112. Howes, Laura L., ed. *Place, Space, and Landscape in Medieval Narrative*. Tennessee Studies in Literature, no. 43. Knoxville: University of Tennessee Press, 2007. xxix, 208 pp. Eleven essays by various authors, with an introduction by the editor and a survey of spatial theory and medieval literature by John M. Ganim. For four essays that pertain to Chaucer, see nos. 84, 197, 310, and 324.

113. Hubbard-Brown, Janet. *Chaucer: Celebrated Poet and Author*. Makers of the Middle Ages and Renaissance. Philadelphia: Chelsea House, 2006. 138 pp. 19 b&w illus. An introduction to Chaucer for elementary and junior high school students, with nine chapters arranged biographically from boyhood to "final years." Each chapter includes a quiz. The apparatus includes a chronology and time line, a bibliography, and an index.

114. Joy, Eileen A., Myra J. Seaman, Kimberly K. Bell, and Mary K. Ramsey, eds. *Cultural Studies of the Modern Middle Ages*. The New Middle Ages. New York: Palgrave Macmillan, 2007. xiii, 305 pp. Ten essays by various authors, along with a foreword, an introduction, an "otherword," and an afterword. Topics range from high to low culture and explore relationships between reality and performance, including

comparisons of medieval literature to contemporary reality television; analyses of truth claims in fiction, history, and medieval studies; and examinations of modern politics through medieval history and literature. For two essays that pertain to Chaucer, see nos. 261 and 293.

115. Kinzer, Craig Robert. "Prayer in Middle English Literature: Theology, Form, Genre." *DAI* A68.06 (2007): n.p. Discusses prayer in various contexts. Chaucer depicts prayer as a means to explore "thorny issues of theology" and often places his prayers in "pagan contexts."

116. Kirk, Elizabeth D. "Donaldson Teaching and Learning." *ChauR* 41 (2007): 279–88. A review of four semesters' course work with E. Talbot Donaldson suggests the organic connection for him between teaching and scholarship.

117. Krygier, Marcin, and Liliana Sikorska, eds. *To Make His Englissh Sweete upon His Tonge*. Medieval English Mirror, no. 3. New York: Peter Lang, 2007. 133 pp. Includes three essays on Middle English language (fricative spellings, *before* as a temporal conjunction, and multiple negation) and four on Middle English literature (an East Anglian miracle play, Malory's *Morte Darthur*, *TC*, and Sheela-na-gig figures and literature). For two that pertain to Chaucer, see nos. 200 and 312.

118. Lightsey, Scott. *Manmade Marvels in Medieval Culture and Literature*. The New Middle Ages. New York: Palgrave Macmillan, 2007. xv, 212 pp. 9 b&w illus. Considers classical and medieval attitudes toward automata and *mirabilia* as context for analyzing their presence and depictions in late medieval English culture, especially in works by Langland, Chaucer, Gower, and Mandeville. Chapter 2, "Chaucer and the Culture of Commodified *Mirabilia*," is a revised version of an earlier essay on *SqT* and *FranT* (see *SAC* 25 [2003], no. 218). Chapter 3, "Chaucer's Body: The Subject of Technology," discusses how *NPT* and *CYT* examine the "spiritual effects of manmade marvels on the human subject," also reflected in *Form Age*.

119. Lochrie, Karma. *Heterosyncrasies: Female Sexuality When Normal Wasn't*. Minneapolis: University of Minnesota Press, 2005. xviii, 178 pp. Lochrie theorizes what sexualities, particularly female sexuality, might "have looked like before heterosexuality and the normal" were constructed in the nineteenth and twentieth centuries by statistical practices, exploring various medieval texts, Latin and vernacular, to disclose "preheteronormative" sexuality. Examines the "Virginity Group" of *CT* (*KnT*, *ClT*, *PhyT*, *PrT*, and *SNT*) in the context of "Lollard anxieties" about female chastity and orthodox critiques of affective female spiritu-

ality, also considering the Prioress in this light. Considers the close attention to female clitoral desire in *WBPT* and argues for thematic connections among the Wife, the Pardoner, and *SNT*. Like other medieval representations of Amazons, Hippolyta and Emily of *KnT* link violence, chastity, and female masculinity, which are also linked in *MilT* and elsewhere in *CT*. See also no. 366.

120. Lynch, Kathryn L. "Dating Chaucer." *ChauR* 42 (2007): 1–22. Objective evaluation reveals the "elusive" and contradictory "evidence" on which chronologies of Chaucer's works—and, most notably, constructions of his artistic maturation—are based. These constructions are essentially interpretive activities; Chaucer critics too often "entertain unproven theories about date as if they were fact."

121. Masciandaro, Nicola. *The Voice of the Hammer: The Meaning of Work in Middle English Literature*. Notre Dame, Ind.: University of Notre Dame Press, 2007. xii, 209 pp. Masciandaro investigates the vocabulary of work (*travail, labour, swink, werk, craft*) and its cultural significance in late medieval England, exploring depictions of the history of work in Middle English literature (including Gower, a treatise on masonry in the Cooke MS, and Chaucer's *Form Age*, a "critique of contemporary primitivism"). Also compares depictions of work as a "subjective necessity" in Langland and Chaucer (particularly in part 8 of *CT*). In *SNT* and *CYT*, Chaucer presents work as "an intrinsic requirement of the human person." See also no. 368.

122. Pearsall, Derek. "How English Is Chaucer?" *TLS*, January 12, 2007, pp. 12–13. Examines attempts to associate Chaucer's works with qualities (assumed or inferred) that constitute "Englishness" and argues that such associations were products of nineteenth- and twentieth-century xenophobia (usually anti-French). Chaucer's works are better regarded as efforts to achieve international European status than as expressions of English spirit or nationalism.

123. Phillips, Susan E. *Transforming Talk: The Problem with Gossip in Late Medieval England*. University Park: Pennsylvania State University Press, 2007. x, 238 pp. Phillips investigates "the intersection between unofficial speech, pastoral practice, and literary production in late medieval England," focusing on pastoral and penitential injunctions against gossip, "idle talk," and "janglyng" and on literary depictions of gossip, kinship relationships (godsibs), and female speech groups. Works discussed include William Dunbar's *Tretis of Twa Mariit Wemen*, Robert

Mannyng's *Handlyng Synne*, John Mirk's *Festial* and *Instructions*, the *Gospelles of Dystaues*, *Fyftene Joyes of Maryage*, various exempla and carols, and works by Chaucer, especially *HF*, *WBPT*, *SumT*, *ShT*, *PhyT*, and *ManT*. See also no. 379.

124. Pugh, Tison, and Angela Jane Weisl, eds. *Approaches to Teaching Chaucer's "Troilus and Criseyde" and the Shorter Poems*. New York: Modern Language Association, 2007. xiii, 217 pp. Thirty brief essays on teaching *TC*, *BD*, *HF*, *PF*, *LGW*, and the lyrics, divided into four groups and an appendix: (1) materials (survey of editions and teaching aids by the editors); (2) backgrounds (lyrics, William A. Quinn; French tradition, Karla Taylor; Italian tradition, Warren Ginsberg; Boethius, Dante, and tragedy, Noel Harold Kaylor Jr.; vernacular writing, Susannah Mary Chewning; paleography and codicology, Julia Boffey; paganism and Christianity, Scott Lightsey; contemporary politics and the New Troy, Alison A. Baker; women and female agency, Lynn Arner; masculinities and Brian Helgeland's *A Knight's Tale*, Holly A. Crocker); (3) approaches (performance, William A. Quinn; critical tradition, Glenn A. Steinberg; three lyrics, Carolynn Van Dyke; postmodern dream visions, Myra Seaman; *LGW*, Michael Calabrese; *TC* as dialogic, Clare R. Kinney; words, antiquity, and the narrator in *TC*, Peggy A. Knapp; gender theory, the editors; Chaucer, Henryson, and Shakespeare, Roger Apfelbaum; deconstruction, historicism, and psychoanalysis, James J. Paxson; grammar and *An ABC*, Martha Rust; prosody in *Rom* and *PF*, Alan T. Gaylord; reading Middle English, Barbara Stevenson; visual approaches, Glenn Davis; Grandson and Chaucer, Jean-François Kosta-Théfaine); (4) course contexts (notes from first-time teaching, Jenifer Sutherland; using journals and debates, Marcia Smith Marzec; teaching nonmajors, Adam Brooke Davis; teaching graduate students, Lorraine Kochanske Stock); (5) appendix on reading aloud, Alan T. Gaylord.

125. Raybin, David. "Chaucer as a London Poet: A Review Essay." *EMSt* 24 (2007): 21–29. Reviews scholarship on Chaucer and London and briefly examines the impact of the Black Death, noting that "the threat of death is everywhere in Chaucer's work." An appendix lists "Recent Studies Treating Chaucer and London."

126. Robertson, Elizabeth. "Medieval Feminism in Middle English Studies: A Retrospective." *Tulsa Studies in Women's Literature* 26 (2007): 67–79. Includes recurrent attention to Chaucer studies, while exploring the history of feminism in medieval studies and the need for a "dialec-

tical questioning" between concerns of particular historical women and their more general contexts.

127. Scase, Wendy. *Literature and Complaint in England: 1272–1553.* New York: Oxford University Press, 2007. xii, 215 pp. 18 b&w illus. Studies the "impact of judicial complaint on the formation of literary practice" in late medieval England, describing the "emergence and development" of the "literature of clamour" and exploring the influence of this literature on the rise of English vernacular writing. Especially in its development within the *ars dictaminis* tradition, complaint literature created a "force-field" that helped shape works by Langland, Gower, Chaucer, Usk, Hoccleve, and others. Considers among Chaucer's works *Anel, Buk, For, Sted, Mars, Pity, Purse, Scogan,* and *Venus.*

128. Schoff, Rebecca L. *Reformations: Three Medieval Authors in Manuscript and Movable Type.* Texts and Transitions: Studies in the History of Manuscripts and Printed Books, no. 4. Turnhout, Belgium: Brepols, 2007. xv, 230 pp. Circumstances of transmission affect not only how authors are received but also how they write. This effect was particularly strong in late medieval culture, when authors such as Chaucer, William Langland, and Margery Kempe were aware that readers used and reworked their texts. Schoff considers themes of reception, group dynamics, and the flexibility of sources in *WBP* and *FrT,* comparing them with concerns of textual stability in *ClT, PardT,* and *MLT.* Also examines how apocryphal additions to *CT* manuscripts (including endings to *CkT*) reveal readers' reactions to Chaucer's textual dynamics, concluding with analysis of how early editors used and adjusted the manuscripts.

129. Semper, Philippa. " 'The wondres that they myghte seen or heere': Designing and Using Web-based Resources to Teach Medieval Literature." In Gail Ashton and Louise Sylvester, eds. *Teaching Chaucer* (*SAC* 31 [2009], no. 82), pp. 120–38. Describes efforts at the University of Birmingham (between 2000 and 2005) to incorporate Web-based materials (computer-mediated materials and virtual learning environments) into teaching Chaucer and Middle English. Also considers methods of assessing such efforts.

130. Shields, J. Scott. "The Art of Imitation." *EJ* 96.6 (2007): 56–60. Suggests that efforts to create "verse-narratives" in the manner of Dante and Chaucer might be useful tools in the teaching of writing.

131. Shippey, Tom. "Geoffrey Chaucer." In Joseph Epstein, ed. *Literary Genius: 25 Classic Writers Who Define English & American Literature.* Philadelphia, Pa.: Paul Dry Books, 2007, pp. 8–15. Commentary on

Chaucer's life and works, focused on his narrative timing, depth of characterization, and linguistic subtlety as means to express sympathy for human weakness. Includes three glossed passages from *CT* and two wood engravings by Barry Moser (portrait of Chaucer and the Tabard Inn).

132. Solopova, Elizabeth, and Stuart D. Lee. *Key Concepts in Medieval Literature*. Palgrave Key Concepts. New York and Basingstoke: Palgrave Macmillan, 2007. xiii, 338 pp. Describes "key themes, texts, terminologies and methods" related to medieval English literature, divided into four sections: (1) Introductory Key Concepts; (2) Old English; (3) Middle English; and (4) Approaches, Theory and Practice. Recurrent references to Chaucer, with a brief section (pp. 192–204) emphasizing his literary self-consciousness and summarizing his life and works.

133. Strohm, Paul, ed. *Middle English*. Oxford Twenty-First Century Approaches to Literature. Oxford: Oxford University Press, 2007. xii, 521 pp. 8 b&w figs. Twenty-nine essays by various authors, each essay with suggestions for further reading. The volume has three indices: Medieval Authors and Titles; Names; and Subject. It seeks "to avoid settled consensus in favour of unresolved debate, to prefer the emergent, the unfinalized, the yet-to-be done." Topics range widely, arranged in four groups: (1) Conditions and Contexts (manuscripts, audience, language); (2) Vantage Points (intellectual, theoretical, and emotional frames); (3) Textual Kinds and Categories (genres, liturgy, theology, humanism); and (4) Writing and the World (authorship, work, gossip). Chaucer is referred to throughout. For eleven essays that treat Chaucer in a sustained way, see nos. 92, 139, 142, 174, 188, 267, 273, 284, 290, 306, and 323.

134. Summerfield, Thea, and Keith Busby, eds. *People and Texts: Relationships in Medieval Literature. Studies Presented to Erik Kooper*. Costerus, n.s., no. 166. Amsterdam and New York: Rodopi, 2007. xi, 205 pp. Fourteen essays by various writers and a bibliography of works published by Erik Kooper, presented to Kooper on the occasion of his sixty-fifth birthday. Topics range widely in English and French medieval traditions, with recurrent focus on romance. For two essays that pertain to Chaucer, see nos. 96 and 326.

135. Swanson, R. N., ed. *Promissory Notes on the Treasury of Merits: Indulgences in Late Medieval Europe*. Brill's Companions to the Christian Tradition, no. 5. Boston and Leiden: Brill, 2006. xii, 360 pp. Twelve essays by various authors and an introduction by the editor. General

commentary on the theology of indulgences and more focused studies of the history and literary depiction of indulgences in European nations/ institutions in the late Middle Ages and early Reformation: Italy, Spain, Czech lands, the Low Countries, England, pilgrimage, and crusading. For an essay that pertains to Chaucer, see no. 249.

136. Symons, Dana. "Long-Lasting Love: Teaming Chaucer with *The Trials and Joys of Marriage*." *SMART* 14.1 (2007): 133–46. Argues for exposing students to a greater range of medieval perspectives than is afforded by traditional single-author courses on Chaucer, explaining the pedagogy of teaching Chaucer in conjunction with the TEAMS Middle English Texts anthology *The Trials and Joys of Marriage* (2002, edited by Eve Salisbury).

137. Thomas, Alfred. *A Blessed Shore: England and Bohemia from Chaucer to Shakespeare*. Ithaca: Cornell University Press, 2007. xi, 239 pp. Studies artistic, religious, and political exchanges between England and Bohemia in the late Middle Ages and the Renaissance, including Anne of Bohemia's influence in England, Wyclif's influence in Bohemia, Shakespeare's formulation of Bohemia, and the history of English men and women in Prague. Among topics of cultural exchange, Thomas discusses concerns with Troy in the two countries (mentioning *TC*) and the ways that Anne of Bohemia influenced English artists and writers, including Chaucer, from her arrival until the Merciless Parliament in 1388. Comments on a number of Czech and English works, such as *PF*, *LGW*, *SNT*, *Pearl*, and *Sir Gawain and the Green Knight*.

138. Turner, Marion. *Chaucerian Conflict: Languages of Antagonism in Late Fourteenth-Century London*. Oxford English Monographs. Oxford: Clarendon Press, 2007. x, 213 pp. Explores how social division and civic dissent were articulated and addressed in late fourteenth-century literature. As evident in *HF*, *TC*, and *CT*, Chaucer was persistently interested in the slipperiness of truth and in the power of language. Figures such as Fame and the Host, who try to control and regulate discourse, expose the difficulties inherent in trying to limit what people can say. In the house of Rumour and on the Canterbury pilgrimage, discursive conflict can run riot, resisting authoritative meaning or peaceful resolution. *Mel* suggests that antagonism will always force its way to the surface and that reconciliation can at most be a temporary, politic state of affairs. See also no. 400.

139. ———. "Conflict." In Paul Strohm, ed. *Middle English* (*SAC* 31 [2009], no. 133), pp. 258–73. Turner asks whether "literary practice

and socio-political conflict" were "mutually dependent" in Ricardian England, arguing that writers and scribes—including Chaucer and Adam Pinkhurst—worked for "politically active and volatile guilds" and suggesting that at that time "discourse was everywhere foregrounded as a cause of contention."

140. Turville-Petre, Thorlac. *Reading Middle English Literature*. Blackwell Introductions to Literature, no. 15. Oxford: Blackwell, 2007. ix, 211 pp. 11 b&w illus. A survey of Middle English literature, designed to accompany the author's anthology *A Book of Middle English* (with J. A. Burrow; 3rd ed., 2005). Treats six topics: the English language; manuscripts, scribes, and audiences; literature and society, history and romance; piety; and love and marriage. Refers to Chaucer's works frequently and considers the following at greater length: *PrT* (with *Pearl*); *RvT* (and social tensions); *PF* (linguistic register and love); and *TC* (love and Criseyde's status).

141. Van Dyke, Carolynn. "Amorous Behavior: Sexism, Sin, and the Donaldson Persona." *ChauR* 41 (2007): 250–60. Exemplified by those of Carolyn Dinshaw and Elaine Tuttle Hansen, feminist critiques of E. Talbot Donaldson's scholarship are curiously similar to D. W. Robertson's critiques of that scholarship. These critiques find fault in its subjectivity and thus overlook Donaldson's authorial persona: a "fictional first person" who "models a way into the text for readers, who are, like him"—and like Chaucer—"both gendered roles and personal facts."

142. Warren, Michelle R. "Translation." In Paul Strohm, ed. *Middle English* (*SAC* 31 [2009], no. 133), pp. 51–67. Warren challenges the notion that translations are worth less than their "originals," arguing that each work is a particular cultural manifestation. She treats Chaucer as the "text-book case of an 'author-translator'" (in contrast with Henry Lovelich) and suggests that the diversity and rich cultural context of Middle English complicate the notion of monolingualism, citing *TC*, *LGW*, and *NPT*.

143. Wheeler, Bonnie. "The Legacy of New Criticism: Revisiting the Work of E. Talbot Donaldson." *ChauR* 41 (2007): 216–24. The essays in *ChauR* 41.3 explore Donaldson's accomplishments in "his guises as editor, philologist, and New Critic" and the continued relevance of that work in the early twenty-first century. See nos. 65, 80, 87, 105, 108, 109, 116, 141, 264, and 315.

144. Williams, David. *Language Redeemed: Chaucer's Mature Poetry*. Naples: Fla.: Sapientia Press of Ave Maria University, 2007. viii, 133

pp. Chaucer is a philosophical realist whose naive narrators, tale-within-a-tale structuring, and focus on irony and linguistic slippage enable him to assert Truth while exposing the limitations of individual human perspectives. Williams examines the five books of *TC* in separate chapters and then devotes individual chapters to *GP*, *WBP*, *WBT*, *PardP*, *PardT*, and *NPT*. Readings are based on translations in Modern English.

145. Worsfold, Brian J., ed. *Women Ageing Through Literature and Experience*. DEDAL-LIT, no. 4. Lleida and Catalunya, Spain: Department of English and Linguistics, University of Lleida, 2005. xxiii, 141 pp. Thirteen essays by various authors, with an introduction by the editor and a preface by Tavengwa M. Nhongo. Literary topics include Chaucer and modern fiction and poetry. For two essays that pertain to Chaucer, see nos. 202 and 218.

146. Zeeman, Nicolette. "The Gender of Song in Chaucer." *SAC* 29 (2007): 141–82. Male singers in Chaucer's works recurrently—perhaps inevitably—embody narcissism and receive "brutal," scatological punishment as a result of their deserved, comic victimhood. Psychoanalytic understanding of love as "affect" and of song as gender-bending underpins readings of *Ros*, *MilT* (both Nicholas and Absolon), *MerT*, the Pardoner, *PrT*, *Th*, *ManT*, *NPT*, and *TC*. Chaucer's depictions of male singing (and poetry?) may be phobic.

See also no. 309.

The Canterbury Tales—General

147. Ashton, Gail. *Chaucer's "The Canterbury Tales."* Continuum Reader's Guides. New York: Continuum, 2007. v, 121 pp. An introduction to *CT* designed for student use, with questions for discussion, research suggestions, and a review at the end of several topical sections: (1) biography and socioliterary setting; (2) language, style, and form; (3) reading *CT*; (4) survey of critical approaches; and (5) Chaucer's influence and adaptations. The volume includes suggestions for further reading and a brief index.

148. Bahr, Arthur William. "Convocational and Compilational Play in Medieval London Literary Culture." *DAI* A68.02 (2007): n.p. Bahr explores parallels between manuscripts as compilations and groups of people as affinities in late medieval London. Chaucer in *CT* and Gower

in *Confessio Amantis* differ in how they conceive of literary and social organization.

149. Blandeau, Agnès. "Les liens adelphiques dans quelques textes du Moyen Âge: 'Ce surgissement des violences au sein des alliances.'" In Martine Yvernault and Sophie Cassagnes-Brouquet, eds. *Frères et sœurs: Les liens adelphiques dans l'Occident antique et médiéval*. Histoires de famille; La parenté au Moyen Âge, no. 8. Turnhout, Belgium: Brepols, 2007, pp. 229–36. Blandeau examines meanings and connotations of the terms *brother*, *brotherly*, and *brotherhood* in *CT* and other medieval texts, from *Beowulf* to *Le Morte Darthur*. Brotherhood ranges widely and can extend to a universal fraternity in a world where the original brotherly conflict between God and Lucifer has left a lasting mark.

150. ———. "The Trader's Time and Narrative Time in Chaucer's *Canterbury Tales*." *BAM* 72 (2007): 21–29. Late fourteenth-century traders' time of profit-making synchronizes with narrative time in Chaucer's tales, enabling the poet to articulate the relationship between time as physically experienced and Christian time, both linear and cyclical.

151. Bloom, Harold, ed. *Geoffrey Chaucer*. Bloom's Major Poets. Broomall, Pa.: Chelsea House, 1999. 112 pp. Includes a brief biography, bibliography, and introduction to *CT*; summaries of *GP*, *KnT*, *WBPT*, and *PardPT*; and excerpts from critical studies of these sections of *CT*.

152. Bowen, Nancy E. "Chaucer and the Harp: Stringed Musical Instruments in *The Canterbury Tales*." *DAI* A68.01 (2007): n.p. Bowen considers the treatment of stringed instruments in Chaucer's Latin sources, their treatment as symbols of "celebration and peace" for characters in *CT*, and connections between the instruments and concepts of bodies. Stringed instruments "function as figurae" in Chaucer's work.

153. Dixon, Chris Jennings, ed. *Lesson Plans for Teaching Writing*. Urbana, Ill.: National Council of Teachers of English, 2007. xv, 249 pp. Seventy-five lesson plans for teaching writing to high school students, arranged in seven categories: Writing Process, Portfolios, Literature, Research, Grammar, Writing on Demand, and Media. Two of the plans for writing about literature focus on Chaucer: writing a parody based on descriptions in *GP* (by Elizabeth H. Beagle) and comparing audio versions of *CT* to rap music (by Dorothy K. Fletcher).

154. Dubs, Kathleen E. "Marking Time in the *Canterbury Tales*." In Tibor Fabiny, ed. *"What, Then, Is Time?": Responses in English and American Literature*. Pázmány Papers in English and American Studies, no.

1. Piliscsaba, Hungary: Pázmány Péter Catholic University, 2001, pp. 71–81. Dubs considers medieval notions of simultaneity; describes Boethius's concept of eternity; explores Chaucer's uses of the zodiac in *CT* (*FranT, MLT, GP, NPT*) and *Astr*; and considers spring as the natural and spiritual season of renewal connected with the pilgrimage of life in *GP, ParsP,* and *Truth.*

155. Greenwood, Maria. "Advice of Friends and Emergence of Right Judgement in Three of Chaucer's *Canterbury Tales: The Franklin's Tale, The Merchant's Tale,* and *The Tale of Melibee.*" In Colette Stévanovitch, ed. *L'articulation langue-littérature dans les textes médiévaux anglais, IV.* Actes des journées d'étude de juin 2005 et juin 2007 à l'Université de Nancy. Publications de l'Association des Médiévistes Anglicistes de l'Enseignement Supérieur. Collection GRENDEL, no. 9. Nancy: AMAES, 2007, pp. 125–34. Greenwood studies types of friendship, plus the positive and negative values attached to friendship, in *FranT, MerT,* and *Mel.*

156. Knapp, Peggy A. "Chaucer for Fun and Profit." In Gail Ashton and Louise Sylvester, eds. *Teaching Chaucer* (*SAC* 31 [2009], no. 82), pp. 17–29. Uses theoretical perspectives from Raymond Williams, Emmanuel Kant, and Hans-Georg Gadamer to explain and justify a pedagogical approach to *CT* based on student pursuit of individual "keywords" in the text and students' selection of a single pilgrim from whose perspective they will judge the Canterbury contest.

157. Kruger, Steven F. "A Series of Linked Assignments for the Undergraduate Course on Chaucer's *Canterbury Tales.*" In Gail Ashton and Louise Sylvester, eds. *Teaching Chaucer* (*SAC* 31 [2009], no. 82), pp. 30–45. Pedagogical approach to *CT* combining traditional "high-stakes" formal writing and "low-stakes" informal writing, incorporated in a broader portfolio of student responses and projects.

158. Lindeboom, B. W. *Venus' Owne Clerk: Chaucer's Debt to the "Confessio Amantis."* Costerus, n.s., no. 167. New York: Rodopi, 2007. vii, 477 pp. Chaucer reconceptualized *CT* in response to a challenge levied in Gower's *Confessio Amantis.* Shaping the Wife of Bath and the Pardoner to embody the Seven Deadly Sins, Chaucer responded to Gower's taxonomy in the *Confessio* and, in doing so, revamped his plan for the Canterbury fiction. We see in *MLPT* Chaucer's intention to pursue a "Gower-oriented direction"—writing a "testament of love"; and the shift from Sergeant of Law to Man of Law affirms Gower's influence. Under pressure of this influence, Chaucer reassigned tales to the Man of Law and

the Wife of Bath, developed the Pardoner to "outvoice" Gower's anticlerical criticism, and resolved to make the Parson "act as confessor" to the pilgrims. Responding to gibes in the *Confessio*, Chaucer wrote parts of *CT* "to put Gower in his place." The volume considers the relationship between the poets, the relative dates of their works (including *LGW* and parts of *CT*), and the thematic imprint of Gower on *CT*.

159. Lynch, Kathryn L. "From Tavern to Pie Shop: The Raw, the Cooked, and the Rotten in Fragment 1 of Chaucer's *Canterbury Tales*." *Exemplaria* 19 (2007): 117–38. Examines food imagery in *MilT, RvT, CkT*, and *GP*. These portions of *CT* threaten, but do not quite achieve, the collapse of Lévi-Strauss's "culinary triangle."

160. Lynch, Tom Liam. "Illuminating Chaucer Through Poetry, Manuscript Illuminations, and a Critical Rap Album." *EJ* 96.6 (2007): 43–49. Describes an approach to teaching *CT* involving the composition and recording of rap lyrics and the creation of illuminated manuscripts.

161. Mertens-Foncke, Paule. "The *Canterbury Tales* and the *Via Moderna*." *PoeticaT* 67 (2007): 37–51. The "structural features" of *GP* reflect "the medieval philosophical debate over universals" and the epistemology of the *via moderna*. Chaucer's number and arrangement of pilgrims suggest the "inadequacy of categories," whereas the balanced opposition of the Prioress and the Wife of Bath echoes the genre of Clerk-Knight debates and obliquely engages the "nominalist concept of divine omnipotence." Other balancings in *CT* (and in the *GP* description of the Monk) reflect debate structure and the opposition between universality and particularity.

162. Miller, Mark. "Subjectivity and Ideology in the *Canterbury Tales*." In Peter Brown, ed. *A Companion to Medieval English Literature and Culture, c. 1350–c. 1500* (*SAC* 31 [2009], no. 3), pp. 554–69. Miller presents *CT* as a series of case studies on how social and ideological formulations shape subjectivities. He focuses on "aristocratic formalism" in *KnT*, sexuality and commodification in *WBP*, and notions of ethical perfection and moral purity in *PardP* and *ParsT*.

163. Mueller, Crystal L. "Technologies of the Late Medieval Self: Ineffability, Distance, and Subjectivity in the 'Book of Margery Kempe.'" *DAI* A68.05 (2007): n.p. Discusses *CT*, especially *WBP*, in a study of the construction of the "self" in the late medieval and early modern periods. Focuses on how a complex sense of the self is constructed in *The Book of Margery Kempe* and developed into the seventeenth century.

164. Patterson, Lee, ed. *Geoffrey Chaucer's "The Canterbury Tales": A Casebook*. Casebooks in Criticism. New York: Oxford University Press, 2007. x, 241 pp. Ten previously published essays or excerpts from longer works by various authors, with an introduction and a brief bibliography of suggested readings. Topics include *GP* and estates literature (Jill Mann); design and chaos in *KnT* (Robert W. Hanning); religion and cycle drama in *MilT* (V. A. Kolve); public and private feminism in *WBT* (H. Marshall Leicester Jr.); structure and imagery in *MerT* (Karl Wentersdorf); pleasure and responsibility in *FranT* (Harry Berger Jr.); the Pardoner's sexuality (Lee Patterson); love and intolerance in *PrT* (Stephen Spector); and *NPT* and mockery (Derek Pearsall) and theological discourse (Jim Rhodes).

165. Sadlek, Gregory M. "Chaucer in the Dock: Literature, Women, and Medieval Antifeminism." *SMART* 14.1 (2007): 117–31. Describes a pedagogical experiment featuring a mock trial of Chaucer—asking students to prosecute and defend Chaucer on the charge of perpetrating medieval antifeminism through his characterization of women in *CT* and *TC*.

166. Sandidge, Marilyn. "Forty Years of Plague: Attitudes Toward Old Age in the Tales of Boccaccio and Chaucer." In Albrecht Classen, ed. *Old Age in the Middle Ages and the Renaissance: Interdisciplinary Approaches to a Neglected Topic*. Fundamentals of Medieval and Early Modern Culture, no. 2. New York: Walter de Gruyter, 2007, pp. 357–73. Youthful attitudes toward old age in the works of Boccaccio and Chaucer differ strikingly, perhaps because of demographic changes caused by the Black Plague. In Boccaccio, youth respects the wisdom of age, whereas in Chaucer young people resent the advice, authority, wealth, and existence of elders. *KnT* introduces the conflict between the generations, a motif throughout *CT*.

167. Sova, Dawn B. *Literature Suppressed on Social Grounds*. Rev. ed. Banned Books. New York: Facts on File, 2006. xx, 380 pp. Sova surveys 115 books threatened with censorship in the United States because of objections to their social (rather than political, religious, or sexual) depictions. Arranged alphabetically by title of the work, each entry includes a plot summary, a censorship history, and suggestions for further reading. *CT* is included in the listing, with comments on expurgations and legal proceedings that cite the diction and characterizations in CT as objectionable.

168. Watson, Nicholas. "Langland and Chaucer." In Andrew Hass,

David Jasper, and Elisabeth Jay, eds. *The Oxford Handbook of English Literature and Theology*. Oxford Handbooks in Religion and Theology. Oxford and New York: Oxford University Press, 2007, pp. 363–81. Watson summarizes the theocentrism of the late Middle Ages, examines Langland's critique of formal theology in *Piers Plowman*, and discusses how *CT* disclaims theological authority in exploring truth and moral utility. Argues that *Mel* may be the "theological center" of *CT*.

169. Williams, Marcia. *Here Bygynneth Chaucer's "Canterbury Tales," Retold and Illustrated by Marcia Williams*. Cambridge, Mass.: Candlewick Press, 2007. 45 pp. *GP, KnT, MilT, RvT, WBT, SumT, ClT, FranT, PardT*, and *NPT* in comic-book style, with watercolor-and-ink drawings and synoptic modern English text. Middle English phrases included in illustrations. Designed for young readers (grades 3–7).

170. Xiao, Minghan. "Plurality and Polyphony in *The Canterbury Tales*." *Foreign Literature Studies* (*Wai Guo Wen Xue Yan Jiu*) 28.4 (2006): 74–83 (in Chinese, with English summary). Emphasizes the dialogic openness of *CT*, commenting on competing and unresolved characters, social classes, and themes.

171. Yager, Susan. "Howard's *Idea* and the Idea of Hypertext." *MedievalF* 6 (2007): n.p. Explores the "kinship" between hypertext theory and the mode of analysis in Donald Howard's *The Idea of the "Canterbury Tales"* (1976), commenting on memory and associative thinking, nonlinearity and closure, and the technology of the book. Also comments on the implications of this kinship in pedagogy and criticism.

See also nos. 9, 10, 23, 26–28, 35, 37, 39, 42, 45, 49, 62, 104, 106, 119, 131, 135, 138, 276.

CT—The General Prologue

172. An, Sonjae (Brother Anthony). "'Unacknowledged Legislators': Prophetic Poets from Chaucer to Today." In Jacek Fisiak and Hye-Kyung Kang, eds. *Recent Trends in Medieval English Language and Literature in Honour of Young-Bae Park* (*SAC* 31 [2009], no. 98), vol. 1, pp. 283–308. The compassion for human failure and potential failure in Chaucer's *GP* reflects Christian awareness of sin and grace. Like later poets Christopher Hill, Seamus Heaney, and Ko Un (Korea), Chaucer is a "prophet-poet," whose recognition of human suffering and error is modified by awareness of beauty.

173. Daróczy, Anikó. "Word and Image in the *General Prologue* to the *Canterbury Tales*." *AnaChronisT: Journal of English and American Studies* 1 (1995): 1–27. Daróczy outlines the Latin rhetorical tradition as background to Chaucer's techniques of characterization in *GP*: groupings of pilgrims, omitted details, the order and juxtaposition of the portraits, epithets, and summarizing lines. Emphasizes musical devices and parallels from fine arts.

174. Robertson, Kellie. "Authorial Work." In Paul Strohm, ed. *Middle English* (*SAC* 31 [2009], no. 133), pp. 441–58. Robertson explores effects of the English labor laws of 1349 on attitudes toward writing, surveying reactions by various writers and using Chaucer's *GP* "as a lens through which to view the critical stakes in thinking about" work—particularly the tension between labor and leisure.

See also nos. 73, 103, 151, 159, 161, 264, 265.

CT—The Knight and His Tale

175. Epstein, Robert. "'With many a floryn he the hewes boghte': Ekphrasis and Symbolic Violence in the *Knight's Tale*." *PQ* 85 (2006): 49–68. Chaucer employs ekphrasis ("verbal representation of a visual representation") in the temples in *KnT* to comment on the social contexts and cultural production of art. The paintings and sculptures aesthetically justify Theseus's own authority, but their negativity indicates a power grounded in violence. The phrase "many a floryn" calls attention to the patron's ability to afford expensive pigment and to the artist's complicity in glorifying that wealth and concomitant power.

176. Haruta, Setsuko. "'What with his wysdom and his chivalrie': Political Theseus in Chaucer's *Knight's Tale*." *SIMELL* 22 (2007): 55–63. Examines Theseus as political hero in light of the literary history of *KnT*. The character combines wisdom and chivalry and reflects the *Tale*'s narrator, including his attitude toward women.

177. Jardillier, Claire. "Architecture and Nature in *The Knight's Tale*: Action Overt and Covert." *BAM* 71 (2007): 35–41. Explores connections between text and places (landscapes, architecture, textual architecture) in *KnT*, focusing on Theseus's efforts to organize space and events and on the narrative's introduction of original motifs and discrepancies.

178. Kowalik, Barbara. "Genre and Gender in Chaucer's *Knight's Tale*." In Maria Edelson, ed. *Studies in Literature and Culture in Honour*

of Professor Irena Janicka-Świderska. Łódz: Wydawnictwo Uniwersytetu Łódzkiego, 2002, pp. 100–110. Increased concern with female characters in *KnT* distinguishes it from traditional epics, and its presentation of women and gender relationships embodies "evolutionary changes" in the romance genre. Nonetheless, Emily is imprisoned at the end "in yet another impoverished pattern of femininity designed for her by men."

179. Mitchell-Smith, Ilan. "'As Olde Stories Tellen Us': Chivalry, Violence, and Geoffrey Chaucer's Critical Perspective in *The Knight's Tale*." *FCS* 32 (2007): 83–99. Violence and all excess reveal the uncontrollable nature of the world Theseus tries to order. Chaucer makes his story less chivalric than Boccaccio's to emphasize that humans, completely at the whim of Fortune, are incapable of maintaining any control.

180. Paxson, James J. "The Anachronism of Imagining Film in the Middle Ages: Wegener's *Der Golem* and Chaucer's *Knight's Tale*." *Exemplaria* 19 (2007): 290–309. Medieval allegory "prefigures cinematic consciousness." In Wegener's film *Der Golem*, "Judaeo-Christian figural allegory, coupled with the narratology and the phenomenology of film," shifts "the deep past into the present in centrifugal, shocking, and transformative ways." In *KnT*, Chaucer describes murals that contain "an implicit and illusory *movement*," like film, moving the viewer "from one perspective to another in mobile fashion." *KnT* "bespeak[s] a proto-cinematic consciousness."

181. Rudd, Gillian. *Greenery: Ecocritical Readings of Late Medieval English Literature*. Manchester Medieval Literature. New York: Manchester University Press, 2007. 221 pp. Explores relationships between humankind and natural landscapes through critical readings that combine ecological emphases with literary analysis. In a chapter titled "Trees," Rudd suggests that the eventual fate of the forest in *KnT* illuminates the anxieties of "humanity's relation to the non-human world."

182. Sancery, Arlette. "Frères de sang, frères de pacte: Les liens adelphiques en literature moyen-anglaise." In Martine Yvernault and Sophie Cassagnes-Brouquet, eds. *Frères et sœurs: Les liens adelphiques dans l'Occident antique et médiéval*. Histoires de famille; La parenté au Moyen Âge, no. 8. Turnhout, Belgium: Brepols, 2007, pp. 221–28. Focuses on the meaning of brotherhood in *Ipomadon*, *Octavian*, and Chaucer's *KnT*.

183. Sutton, John William. *Death and Violence in Old and Middle English Literature*. Lewiston, N.Y.: Mellen, 2007. v, 229 pp. Gauges the degree of "heroism" in death scenes in a variety of narratives, consider-

ing in individual chapters *The Battle of Maldon*, *Beowulf* and *Judith*, Layamon's *Brut*, the *Alliterative Morte Authure*, the death of Arcite in *KnT*, the "near-death experience" in *Sir Gawain and the Green Knight*, and several death scenes in Malory's *Le Morte Darthur*. The later works question the heroic ethos and reflect a particular horror of death. Foreword by Sarah L. Higley.

See also nos. 33, 46, 56, 84, 89, 119, 151, 162, 166, 305.

CT—The Miller and His Tale

184. Allen, Valerie, ed. *The Miller's Prologue and Tale*. Cambridge School Chaucer. New York: Cambridge University Press, 2007. 96 pp. A school-text Middle English edition of *MilPT* and the *GP* description of the Miller, with notes, a running narrative summary, and facing-page glosses. Accompanied by commentary on several topics (Chaucer's language, town versus gown in Oxford, pilgrimage, astronomy and astrology, comparisons with *KnT*), discussion questions, and several line drawings and photographs.

185. Beidler, Peter G. "From Snickers to Laughter: Believable Comedy in Chaucer's *Miller's Tale*." In Sandra M. Hordis and Paul Hardwick, eds. *Medieval English Comedy* (*SAC* 31 [2009], no. 111), pp. 195–208. Beidler compares and contrasts *MilT* with its likely source, the Middle Dutch *Hiele van Beersele*. Of the two, *MilT* provokes greater laughter because it is more plausible, a result of more carefully deployed details.

186. Blamires, Alcuin. "Philosophical Sleaze? The 'Strok of Thoght' in the *Miller's Tale* and Chaucerian Fabliau." *MLR* 102 (2007): 621–40. Chaucer's special contribution to the fabliau genre is the design whereby apparently disconnected, often spontaneous plot incidents are suddenly "knit up"—that is, perceived by readers as belonging to a providential master plan. Although *MilT* is the prime example, all of Chaucer's fabliaux are informed by Boethian philosophy. Chaucer as author assumes the role of Maker, bringing his audience to a moment of epiphany in which what appeared to be chance is perceived as part of a larger design.

187. Mack, Peter, and Chris Walton, eds. *The Miller's Tale*, by Geoffrey Chaucer. 2nd ed. Oxford Student Texts. Oxford and New York: Oxford University Press, 2007. x, 198 pp. Revised, expanded version of the 1995 publication; see *SAC* 22 (2000), no. 202.

188. Nolan, Maura. "Beauty." In Paul Strohm, ed. *Middle English*

(*SAC* 31 [2009], no. 133), pp. 207–21. Nolan argues that the description of Alison in *MilT* is Chaucer's means to "stage an investigation or exploration of the relationship of beauty to individual perspectives . . . and the idea of a universal aesthetic." The passage also confronts the "problem" of the usefulness of beauty.

189. Shibata, Takeo. "*Pryvetee* in Chaucer's *Miller's Tale*." *Review of Kobe Shinwa Women's University* 40 (2007): 39–50 (in Japanese). Examines *pryvetee* as a key word and its association with the two love triangles in *MilT*.

See also nos. 46, 47, 89, 119, 146, 159, 262.

CT—The Reeve and His Tale

190. Crocker, Holly A. "Affective Politics in Chaucer's *Reeve's Tale*: 'Cherl' Masculinity After 1381." *SAC* 29 (2007): 225–58. By "acknowledging and exploiting the affections of [its] female characters," *RvT* "fashions a masculine collective." By excluding Symkyn from this collective, the *Tale* demonstrates that "cherl" identity after the uprising of 1381 was ethically and politically "limited." *RvT* "issues a call to confront the ethical consequences of affective appeals *within* their social contexts." Crocker considers gender relations of *RvT* in light of medieval conduct literature and encourages attention to "affect" in literary criticism.

See also nos. 46, 89, 140, 159.

CT—The Cook and His Tale

191. Benson, C. David. "Some Poets' Tours of Medieval London: Varieties of Literary Urban Experience." *EMSt* 24 (2007): 1–20. Benson describes the very different views of London produced by Chaucer, Gower, Hoccleve, and Lydgate, as well as the depictions in William FitzStephen's *Description of London* (1174) and *London Lickpenny* (fifteenth-century). These representations suggest that there is "no single medieval view" and that London stimulated poets in various powerful ways, including Chaucer's depiction of a lower level of society in *CkT*.

192. Crawford, Donna. "Revel and Youth in *The Cook's Tale* and *The Tale of Gamelyn*." *Archiv* 243 (2006): 32–43. Crawford discusses the un-

finished *CkT* in relation to the *Tale of Gamelyn*; their thematic associations; connections to the Peasants' Revolt of 1381; who added the *Tale of Gamelyn* to *CT*; and why it was inserted right after *CkT*.

193. Forkin, Thomas Carney. " 'Oure Citee': Illegality and Criminality in Fourteenth-Century London." *EMSt* 24 (2007): 31–41. Close reading of *CkT,* of descriptions of Roger the Cook in *CT,* and of relevant late fourteenth-century laws and statutes reveals that Chaucer's powers of observation extend to the lower levels of society and the workings of London's "underworld."

See also nos. 37, 159, 271.

CT—The Man of Law and His Tale

194. Goldstein, R. James. "Future Perfect: The Augustinian Theology of Perfection and the *Canterbury Tales*." *SAC* 29 (2007): 87–140. Goldstein considers Custance of *MLT* and Alisoun of *WBP* in relation to the Augustinian theology of perfection, particularly in light of late fourteenth-century adaptations of Augustine, both orthodox and heterodox. *MLT* exemplifies the deterministic operation of grace, while the Wife of Bath's autobiography comically explores a "mediocritist" outlook. Goldstein posits a "perfection group" (on the model of the "marriage group") that anatomizes Augustinian ideals of perfection: i.e., *MLT, WBP, ClT, SumT, MerT, SNT, CYT,* and *ParsT*.

195. Heinzelman, Susan Sage. "Chaucer's Lawyers and Priests." In Susan Sage Heinzelman. *Representing Justice: Stories of Law and Literature, Parts 1 and 2*. The Great Courses. Chantilly, Va.: Teaching Company, 2006, part 1, disc 3, lecture 6; 30 min. Audio recording (on CD) of a lecture about the "inextricability" of religious and secular law in Chaucer's age as reflected in *PardT, ParsT,* and especially *MLT*. Heinzelman contrasts material and spiritual wealth in *PardT* and *ParsT* and explores the possibility that human law and divine law are synonymous in *MLT*.

196. Landers, Samara Pauline. "The Construction of Identity in Middle English Romance." *DAI* A67.09 (2007): n.p. Uses *MLT,* among other works, to show that in Middle English romance, with its limited expression of characters' inner lives, identity is expressed and revealed through "external signs," outward behavior, and immutable "key characteristics."

197. Warner, Lawrence. "Adventurous Custance: St. Thomas of

Acre and Chaucer's *Man of Law's Tale*." In Laura L. Howes, ed. *Place, Space, and Landscape in Medieval Narrative* (*SAC* 31 [2009], no. 112), pp. 43–59. Warner examines affiliations of the London Church of St. Thomas of Acre with mercantile interests that, in turn, help to clarify features of *MLT*, including its concerns with merchants, with the Crusades, and with legal discourse. *MLT* also explores modes of adventuring.

See also nos. 42, 47, 128, 158.

CT—The Wife of Bath and Her Tale

198. Biebel-Stanley, Elizabeth M. "Sovereignty Through the Lady: 'The Wife of Bath's Tale' and the Queenship of Anne of Bohemia." In S. Elizabeth Passmore and Susan Carter, eds. *The English "Loathly Lady" Tales: Boundaries, Traditions, Motifs* (*SAC* 31 [2009], no. 219), pp. 73–82. Rooted in Irish analogues, the sovereignty theme is anchored in the queen figure in *WBT*. The theme reflects "women's integral role in governance," a "wishful vision of a movement toward more egalitarian society," and Anne of Bohemia's role in the court of Richard II.

199. Bobac, Andrea Delia. "Justice on Trial: Judicial Abuse and Acculturation in Late Medieval English Literature, 1381–1481." *DAI* A67.07 (2007): 2570. Bobac examines the "social life of medieval justice as discursively constituted," considering *WBT* as an example of a text that explores the "theory and purpose of the punishments for rape."

200. Borysławski, Rafał. "Sirith-na-Gig? *Dame Sirith* and the Fabliau Hags as Textual Analogues to the Sheela-figures." In Marcin Krygier and Liliana Sikorska, eds. *To Make His Englissh Sweete upon His Tonge* (*SAC* 31 [2009], no. 117), pp. 121–33. Discusses how sheela-na-gig carvings share appearance and function with loathly lady figures in Middle English literature, including the one found in *WBT*.

201. Caldwell, Ellen M. "Brains or Beauty. Limited Sovereignty in the Loathly Lady Tales: 'The Wife of Bath's Tale,' 'Thomas of Erceldoune,' and 'The Wedding of Sir Gawain and Dame Ragnelle.'" In S. Elizabeth Passmore and Susan Carter, eds. *The English "Loathly Lady" Tales: Boundaries, Traditions, Motifs* (*SAC* 31 [2009], no. 219), pp. 235–56. Loathly lady tales "reveal the consequences" for women of "ungendered" transgressive behavior: the lady "enjoys more power" when she performs roles counter to her biological gender, and she loses the power

when she subsides into feminine roles. When the lady in *WBT* abandons her ugliness, she gives up her challenges to male sovereignty in marriage and to "aristocratic women's superiority."

202. Carrillo Linares, María José. "What Thing Is It That People Most (Un)desire? A View on Chaucer's Portrayal of the Process of Aging." In Brian J. Worsfold, ed. *Women Ageing Through Literature and Experience* (*SAC* 31 [2009], no. 145), pp. 21–30. Depictions of female and male aging in *WBT* and *MerT* reflect the reality that human beings wish to remain desirable "in spite of advanced aging."

203. Carter, Susan. "A Hymenation of Hags." In S. Elizabeth Passmore and Susan Carter, eds. *The English "Loathly Lady" Tales: Boundaries, Traditions, Motifs* (*SAC* 31 [2009], no. 219), pp. 83–99. Because the loathly lady in *WBT* is not enchanted but is a shape-shifter under her own power, she likely is not virginal. Carter explores the implications of this likelihood, as well as parallel concerns in *WBT* and several analogues.

204. Craun, Edwin D. "'Allas, allas! That evere love was synne': Excuses for Sin and the Wife of Bath's Stars." In Edwin D. Craun, ed. *The Hands of the Tongue: Essays on Deviant Speech.* Kalamazoo, Mich.: Medieval Institute Publications, 2007, pp. 33–60. Reads the Wife's comments on her constellation (*WBP* 3.609–23) in light of late medieval pastoral commentary on astral determinism as an excuse for sin. The Wife mocks male-authored confessional speech but embraces male-authored astrological discourse uncritically, indicating that her agency is limited.

205. Croft, Steven, ed. *The Wife of Bath*, by Geoffrey Chaucer. Oxford Student Texts. Oxford and New York: Oxford University Press, 2007. vi, 170 pp. A school-text Middle English edition of *WBPT* and the *GP* description of the Wife, with notes and glosses after the text, along with comments on critical approaches and contexts and on Chaucer's language and pronunciation; pedagogical activities and essay topics; a chronology; a glossary; and suggestions for further reading. Includes several black-and-white illustrations.

206. Dennis, Erin N. "Social Consciousness and Religious Authority in 'The Wife of Bath's Prologue' and 'Tale.'" In Bruce E. Brandt and Michael S. Nagy, eds. *Proceedings of the 14th Northern Plains Conference on Earlier British Literature, April 7–8, 2006* (*SAC* 31 [2009], no. 88), pp. 107–23. Dennis explores how *WBP* and *WBT* affirm and challenge the patriarchal assumptions of medieval literary and social traditions.

207. Edwards, Suzanne M. "Beyond Raptus: Pedagogies and Fantasies of Sexual Violence in Late-Medieval England." *DAI* A 67.11 (2007): n.p. Surveys representations of sexual violence as both gender oppression and means to self-awareness between the thirteenth and fifteenth centuries in England, discussing *WBPT* and *Mel*, among other texts.

208. Fumo, Jamie C. "Argus' Eyes, Midas' Ears, and the Wife of Bath as Storyteller." In Alison Keith and Stephen Rupp, eds. *Metamorphosis: The Changing Face of Ovid in Medieval and Early Modern Europe*. Toronto: Centre for Reformation and Renaissance Studies, 2007, pp. 129–50. The Wife of Bath's "manipulations of the Argus and Midas myths" reflect her Ovid-like "delight in sensuality and embeddedness of narrative" and her recognition of the power of story to "control and deceive." The myths help unify *WBPT*; through them, Chaucer explores the techniques and motivations of story-telling.

209. Gaffney, Paul. "Controlling the Loathly Lady, or What Really Frees Dame Ragnelle." In S. Elizabeth Passmore and Susan Carter, eds. *The English "Loathly Lady" Tales: Boundaries, Traditions, Motifs* (*SAC* 31 [2009], no. 219), pp. 146–62. As an example of popular folk narrative, "The Wedding of Sir Gawain and Dame Ragnelle" is flexibly open to multiple interpretations. Addressed to an elite audience, Gower's "Tale of Florent" and *WBT* lay claim to authority and function as exempla.

210. Hall, Kathryn A. "Teaching Margery Kempe in Tandem with the Wife of Bath: Lollardy, Mysticism, and 'Wandrynge by the Weye.' " *SoAR* 72.4 (2007): 59–71. Encourages pairing Margery Kempe and *WBT* in British literature surveys, noting that Kempe was "a good deal more vulnerable than the fictitious Wife of Bath."

211. Haruta, Setsuko. "The Wife of Bath and Her Arthurian Fantasy." In Josef Fürnkäs, Masato Izumi, and Ralf Schnell, eds. *Zwischenzeiten—Zwischenwelten: Festschrift für Kozo Hirao*. Frankfurt am Main: Peter Lang, 2001, pp. 259–65. Introduction to *WBT* and its primary motifs, focusing on the raped maiden, the loathly lady, and Arthur's queen. Suggests that the Wife of Bath's "feminism is essentially phallocentricism [*sic*] in reverse."

212. Hill-Vásquez, Heather. "Chaucer's Wife of Bath, Hoccleve's Arguing Women, and Lydgate's Hertford Wives: Lay Interpretation and the Figure of the Spinning Woman in Late Medieval England." *Florilegium* 23 (2006): 169–95. In later medieval thought, spinning women represent two often contradictory ideas: rebellion against hierarchical order and, paradoxically, Marian obedience. Citing scripture,

Chaucer's Wife fuses both viewpoints in *WBP*. When Lancastrian mores prevailed, the spinning woman came to epitomize Lollard threats to the status quo. Lydgate's and Hoccleve's spinners lack Chaucer's toleration.

213. Hopper, Sarah. *Mothers, Mystics, and Merrymakers: Medieval Women Pilgrims*. Thrupp, Gloucestershire: Sutton, 2006. xvii, 206 pp. 2 maps; 31 b&w and color illus. Surveys "some of the many roles played and influences exerted by women in the practice of medieval pilgrimage," considering literary texts and cultural contexts from the fall of Rome until Margery Kempe and the Paston women in the fifteenth century. References to Canterbury and to Chaucer recur throughout, with one chapter dedicated to discussion of the "wayward, over-experienced" Wife of Bath and the "corrupted innocence" of the Prioress as examples of Chaucer's efforts to expose contemporary corruption.

214. Kumar, Jyotika, trans. *The Wife of Bath's Tale: Chaucer*. Delhi: Academic Excellence, 2007. 211 pp. Interlinear Modern English translation of *WBPT*, with accompanying introduction and commentary presented as a pastiche of observations and reactions.

215. Masi, Michael. "Boethius, the Wife of Bath, and the Dialectic of Paradox." In Noel Harold Kaylor Jr. and Philip Edward Phillips, eds. *New Directions in Boethian Studies*. Studies in Medieval Culture, no. 45. Kalamazoo, Mich.: Medieval Institute Publications, 2007, pp. 143–54. Traces the logic of paradox from its roots in Zeno through Boethius's *Consolation* to its uses in *WBPT*. Notes examples from Alain de Lille and Jean de Meun and discusses the Wife of Bath's uses of synthesis beyond contradiction and paradox.

216. Moon, Hi Kyung. "Authorship, Authority, and the Polemics of Rachel Speght and the Wife of Bath." *MES* 14 (2006): 431–46. Compares and contrasts the strategies and outspoken polemics of *WBP* with those of Speght's *A Mouzell for Melastomus* (1617). Speght exposes antagonist Joseph Swetnam in ways similar to those used by Chaucer to expose the Wife.

217. Niebrzydowski, Sue. " 'So wel koude he me glose': The Wife of Bath and the Eroticism of Touch." In Amanda Hopkins and Cory James Rushton, eds. *The Erotic in the Literature of Medieval Britain* (*SAC* 31 [2009], no. 110), pp. 18–26. Surveys medieval commentary on women's enjoyment of sex, noting that sexual pleasure distinguishes Alisoun's marriage to Jankyn in *WBP*—a result of Jankyn's ability to read his wife's body like a text. Niebrzydowski contrasts Alisoun's sexual pleasure with that of May in *MerT*.

218. O'Neill, Maria. "Gender, Economics, and Morality: Sexuality and Ageing as Depicted in Geoffrey Chaucer's *The Canterbury Tales*." In Brian J. Worsfold, ed. *Women Ageing Through Literature and Experience* (*SAC* 31 [2009], no. 145), pp. 73–81. O'Neill surveys Chaucer's attitudes toward age and gender in *CT*, with particular focus on *WBPT*. In *CT*, the "medieval, ageing Englishwoman as a sexual being emerges with . . . dignity and vitality."

219. Passmore, S. Elizabeth, and Susan Carter, eds. *The English "Loathly Lady" Tales: Boundaries, Traditions, Motifs*. Studies in Medieval Culture, no. 48. Kalamazoo, Mich.: Medieval Institute Publications, 2007. xix, 272 pp. Eleven essays by various authors and an introduction by the editors. Each of the essays touches on *WBT* and its relationship with Irish and/or English analogues, and seven of them consider *WBT* at length. The volume includes an index. See nos. 198, 201, 203, 209, 220, 221, and 226.

220. Passmore, S. Elizabeth. "Through the Counsel of a Lady: The Irish and English Loathly Lady Tales and the 'Mirrors for Princes' Genre." In S. Elizabeth Passmore and Susan Carter, eds. *The English "Loathly Lady" Tales: Boundaries, Traditions, Motifs* (*SAC* 31 [2009], no. 219), pp. 3–41. Female counsel is a consistent theme in Irish and English versions of the loathly lady story, in which women offer advice or prophesy to aristocrats. This theme reinforces connections among the analogous tales, paralleling the visual motif of female ugliness. *WBT* counsels true gentility.

221. Peck, Russell A. "Folklore and Powerful Women in Gower's 'Tale of Florent.'" In S. Elizabeth Passmore and Susan Carter, eds. *The English "Loathly Lady" Tales: Boundaries, Traditions, Motifs* (*SAC* 31 [2009], no. 219), pp. 100–145. Gower's "Tale of Florent" was composed before its English analogues, including *WBT*, and is here anatomized as a series of folktale motifs. Peck also explores how the narrative is "put in a new dress" and made appropriate to its new functions by Chaucer and others who follow Gower.

222. Pugh, Tison. "Squire Jankyn's Legs and Feet: Physiognomy, Social Class, and Fantasy in *The Wife of Bath's Prologue and Tale*." *M&H*, n.s., 32 (2007): 83–101. Alison constructs Jankyn as a liminal figure combining both courtly and clerical ideals so that she can celebrate "her triumph over a representative figure of both arenas" (95).

223. Salisbury, Eve. "Chaucer's 'Wife,' the Law, and the Middle English Breton Lays." In Jacek Fisiak and Hye-Kyung Kang, eds. *Recent*

Trends in Medieval English Language and Literature in Honour of Young-Bae Park (*SAC* 31 [2009], no. 98), vol. 1, pp. 347–75. Assesses how *WBT*, *FranT*, and other Breton lays in Middle English "underwrite and reinforce the laws of the land"—laws that allowed for domestic violence and left ambiguous the relations between rape and marriage.

224. Saunders, Corinne. "Erotic Magic: The Enchantress in Middle English Romance." In Amanda Hopkins and Cory James Rushton, eds. *The Erotic in the Literature of Medieval Britain* (*SAC* 31 [2009], no. 110), pp. 38–52. Through otherworldly female characters, a number of Middle English romances and their French ancestors "interweave" heterosexual, romantic desire with magic and the supernatural. *WBT*, however, "subverts" this convention by reproving the violence of rape.

225. Scheitzeneder, Franziska. "'For myn entente nys but for to pleye': On the Playground with the Wife of Bath, the Clerk of Oxford, and Jacques Derrida." In Winfried Rudolf, Thomas Honegger, and Andrew James Johnston, eds. *Clerks, Wives, and Historians: Essays on Medieval Language and Literature.* Variations, no. 8. New York: Peter Lang, 2007, pp. 47–68. Derridean analysis of the opposition between the Wife of Bath and the Clerk as a "negotiation of the contrary emotional reactions that arise from and that shape textual creation and interpretation." Both pilgrims affirm and attack literary authority. See also *SAC* 30 (2008), no. 207.

226. Wollstadt, Lynn M. "Repainting the Lion: 'The Wife of Bath's Tale' and a Traditional British Ballad." In S. Elizabeth Passmore and Susan Carter, eds. *The English "Loathly Lady" Tales: Boundaries, Traditions, Motifs* (*SAC* 31 [2009], no. 219), pp. 199–212. Wollstadt explores similarities between *WBT* and the ballad "The Knight and the Shepherd's Daughter," considering the rape motif, concern with "authority and victimization," the possibility that the ballad was transmitted by female oral singers, and the conflation in the ballad of the raped maiden and the wife.

See also nos. 47, 49, 71, 95, 119, 123, 128, 144, 151, 158, 161–63, 194, 298, 305, 311.

CT—The Friar and His Tale

227. Bryant, Brantley L. "'By Extorcions I Lyve': Chaucer's *Friar's Tale* and Corrupt Officials." *ChauR* 42 (2007): 180–95. Numerous four-

teenth-century documents that address the practice of extortion by institutional "middlemen" point to systemic problems rather than to individual turpitude. *FrT* reflects this contemporary explanation, albeit without exonerating the Summoner's viciousness.

See also nos. 71, 128.

CT—The Summoner and His Tale

228. Finlayson, John. "Chaucer's *Summoner's Tale*: Flatulence, Blasphemy, and the Emperor's Clothes." *SP* 104 (2007): 455–70. *SumT* is not a hidden allegory, but a narrative that exploits characteristics of the fabliau to explore larger issues of morality and ethics. By focusing almost solely on the distribution of the "gift," critics have ignored most of the story and missed Chaucer's concern with the foundations of ecclesiastical claims of "authority."

229. Pitard, Derrick G. "Greed and Anti-Fraternalism in Chaucer's 'Summoner's Tale.'" In Richard Newhauser, ed. *The Seven Deadly Sins: From Communities to Individuals*. Studies in Medieval and Reformation Traditions: History, Culture, Religion, Ideas, no. 123. Boston and Leiden: Brill, 2007, pp. 207–27. Pitard comments on William of St. Amour's *Tractatus brevis* and assesses *SumT* as a vernacularized adaptation of it—one in which fraternal pretenses are satirized for their Latinate elitism. The satire occurs because "it is hilarious that the friar is *not* insulted by the fart."

See also nos. 123, 227.

CT—The Clerk and His Tale

230. Johnston, Andrew James. "Walter's Two Bodies: Sovereignty and Individuality in Chaucer's *Clerk's Tale*." In Lilo Moessner and Christa M. Schmidt, eds. *Anglistentag 2004 Aachen*. Proceedings of the Conference of the German Association of University Teachers of English, no. 16. Trier: Wissenschaftlicher Verlag Trier, 2005, pp. 19–29. Highlights political aspects of *ClT*, interpreting the cruelty Walter inflicts on Griselda as a projection of his inner conflict between a hereditary ruler's "body politic" and his "body natural"—a conflict prompted by the pressure to provide an heir to the throne exerted by his subjects.

231. Luttecke, Francisco. "The Oxford Scholar's Tale: La versión disidente de Chaucer." In Carmen Rabell, ed. *Ficciones legales: Ensayos sobre ley, retórica y narración*. San Juan, P.R.: Maitén III, 2007, pp. 125–39. Compares *ClT* with Boccaccio's tale of Griselda and the version by Juan de Timoneda, showing that Chaucer makes more extensive, more explicit, and more radical the class politics of the narrative, critiquing traditional assumptions about marriage and feudal order.

See also nos. 21, 93, 119, 128.

CT—The Merchant and His Tale

232. Akahori, Naoko. "Is May in the *Merchant's Tale* Beautiful as 'May'?" *Bulletin of the Institute of Women's Culture* (Showa Women's University) 34 (2007): 29–38. Akahori analyzes characteristics of May in *MerT*, focusing on her presence in January's garden and nuances of the adjective *fressh*. Exploring instances of the word throughout *CT*, the author shows that its use in *MerT* is sarcastic.

233. Lopez, Alan. "Corpses and Cogitos and the Sympathetic Self: Exhuming Sovereignty and Its Sympathetic Subjects." *DAI* A68.05 (2007): n.p. In a larger investigation of the philosophical concept of sympathy, Lopez discusses the lack of sympathy, both personal and spatiotemporal, between May and January in *MerT*.

See also nos. 74, 84, 89, 146, 155, 202, 217, 305.

CT—The Squire and His Tale

234. Crane, Susan. "For the Birds." *SAC* 29 (2007): 23–41. The Biennial Chaucer Lecture, The New Chaucer Society, Fifteenth International Congress, 27–31 July 2006, Fordham University. The two portions of *SqT* align the cultural differences between the Mamluk emissary and the Mogul court with the species differences between the falcon and Canacee. Capitalizing on symbolic, metonymic connections between animals and humans and reflecting the Middle English dual meaning of *kynde* (denoting both species and compassionate), the bird section diminishes the orientalism of the court scene and poses possibilities for interspecies compassion.

235. Jones, Lindsey M. "Chaucer's Anxiety of Poetic Craft: The

Squire's Tale." Style 41 (2007): 300–318. *SqT* illustrates how "a poet may come to poetic and prosodic mastery." Chaucer's conscious creation of an inept teller who overuses or misuses rhyme, enjambment, and caesura illustrates the difficult process of maturing as a poet.

See also nos. 42, 53, 89.

CT—The Franklin and His Tale

236. Calabrese, Michael. "Chaucer's Dorigen and Boccaccio's Female Voices." *SAC* 29 (2007): 259–92. Hard and soft analogues to Dorigen's conversations with Aurelius in *FranT* indicate that she is less a victim than someone playfully complicit in "flirtation." Offering "positive rhetorical models," Boccaccio and Christine de Pizan depict women who effectively use language to "rout the advances of unwanted suitors," while Dorigen's words evoke the "inflammation of anxious desire in herself, her neighbor, and her husband."

237. Conrad-O'Briain, Helen. "Chaucer, Technology, and the Rise of Science Fiction in English." In Philip Coleman, ed. *On Literature and Science: Essays, Reflections, Provocation.* Dublin: Four Courts Press, 2007, pp. 27–42. Considers *FranT* rather than *CYT* Chaucer's clearest contribution to science fiction, a genre here presented with an ancient legacy. In *FranT*, Chaucer uses the "tension at the heart of science fiction—between the possible and the not necessarily impossible—to intensify the misdirection of human desires and strivings."

238. Haas, Kurtis B. "'The Franklin's Tale' and the Medieval Trivium: A Call for Critical Thinking." *JEGP* 106 (2007): 45–63. Dorigen and Arveragus of *FranT* "demonstrate . . . deficiency in the cognitive skills inculcated by the medieval *trivium*," making them "vulnerable to the Orleans clerk's corruptions of the *quadrivium*." Weak critical thinking undermines their ability to behave ethically, and *FranT* exposes a society in which "elementary reasoning skills have been lost to pseudoscience and thickheaded versions of chivalric honor."

239. Lee, Dongchoon. "*The Franklin's Tale*: A Moral Tale or a Fiction?" *MES* 14 (2006): 265–300 (in Korean, with English abstract). Reads *FranT* as Chaucer's satiric portrayal of the narrator, focusing on the character of the Franklin, contradictions within his narrative, his characters' concern with public show, and legal aspects of Arveragus and Dorigen's clandestine marriage.

240. Lipton, Emma. *Affections of the Mind: The Politics of Sacramental Marriage in Late Medieval English Literature.* Notre Dame, Ind.: University of Notre Dame Press, 2007. x, 246 pp. Depictions of marriage in a range of late Middle English texts engage concerns with lay and ecclesiastical authority and promote interests of "the lay middle strata." The book opens with a reading of how *FranT* expresses in its "discourse of mutuality" a "vocabulary for promoting civic values" appropriate to the Franklin's social position. Subsequent chapters consider Gower's *Traitié pour Essampler les Amantz Marietz*, the N-Town Mary plays, and *The Book of Margery Kempe.*

See also nos. 7, 13, 74, 80, 84, 155, 223.

CT—The Physician and His Tale

241. Crafton, John Micheal. "'The cause of everiche maladye': A New Source of the *Physician's Tale.*" *PQ* 84 (2005): 259–85. As a treatise on continence, the last chapter of the *Summa virtutem remediis anime* provides significant analogues to *PhyT*. Virginia represents true virginity and in her martyrdom appears saintly. Virginius represents foolish virginity, especially given his sacrifice of his daughter, a sacrifice made unnecessary and cruel in light of the source text, which locates virginity in the spirit—not the flesh.

242. ———. "'The Physician's Tale' and Jephtha's Daughter." *ANQ* 20.1 (2007): 8–13. Middle English sermons and manuals of vices and virtues indicate that Chaucer's audience would have understood Jephtha's daughter as a figure of a loose woman. Through allusion to her, Chaucer creates a painfully ironic moment that characterizes Virginius as a false or foolish judge and Virginia as a victim of lust, corruption, and stupidity.

243. Giaccherini, Enrico. "Tradition as Collaboration: The Public and the Private in the *Physician's Tale.*" In Silvia Bigliazzi and Sharon Wood, eds. *Collaboration in the Arts from the Middle Ages to the Present.* Studies in European Cultural Transition, no. 35. Burlington, Vt.: Ashgate, 2006, pp. 7–15. Giaccherini reads *PhyT* as an experiment in "collaboration"—Chaucer's adaptation of the plot from Livy and the *Roman de la Rose*—that develops a concern for the private realm while downplaying the public.

244. Kline, Daniel T. "Wardship and *Raptus* in the *Physician's Tale.*"

In Joel T. Rosenthal, ed. *Essays on Medieval Childhood: Responses to Recent Debates*. Donington, Lincolnshire: Shaun Tyas, 2007, pp. 108–23. Chaucer's additions to his sources in *PhyT* emphasize the "domestic contours" of the story. *PhyT* is a critique of the "social efficacy of the patriarchal family." Virginius first fails to protect his daughter and then murders her; he is "no better a governor of his family than Apius is of the region." The court case in *PhyT* reflects Chaucer's own experiences with court proceedings that involve *raptus*.

See also nos. 40, 90, 95, 119, 123.

CT—The Pardoner and His Tale

245. Friedman, John Block. "Chaucer's Pardoner, Rutebeuf's 'Dit de l'Herberie,' the 'Dit du Mercier,' and Cultural History." *Viator* 38.1 (2007): 289–319. Friedman argues that French comic "trade" literature is source material for *PardP*, identifying parallels in details and in the hucksterish rhetoric of the works. He suggests that the Pardoner's sexuality may have been influenced by discussion of the spice "garingaut" in the anonymous "Dit du Mercier" and identifies a number of medieval works—French and English—in the broad tradition of sales-pitch literature. Includes modern English translations of the "Dit du Mercier" and Rutebeuf's "Dit de l'Herberie."

246. Heffernan, Carol Falvo. "Boccaccio's *Decameron* 6.10 and Chaucer's *Canterbury Tales* VI.287–968: Thinking on Your Feet and the Set-Piece." *Florilegium* 22 (2005): 105–20. Cipolla's tale concludes a set of stories focusing on wit, and *PardT* ends a fragment that precedes one centered on poetic language. The tales of both speakers coincide in "genre, character, theme, and placement," even though Cipolla improvises his story and the Pardoner relies on a set text.

247. Klassen, Norman. "Two Possible Sources for Chaucer's Description of the Pardoner." *N&Q* 54 (2007): 233–36. Sallust's association of avarice with effeminacy in *The War with Catiline* and Aulus Gellius's subsequent reiteration of the link in his *Attic Nights* are two possible sources for the combination of avarice with effeminacy in Chaucer's Pardoner.

248. Legassie, Shayne Aaron. "Chaucer's Pardoner and Host—On the Road, in the Alehouse." *SAC* 29 (2007): 183–223. Combines psychoanalysis, ethnography, and "queer theory" to examine pilgrimage,

travel, and specific locations as narrative devices that undermine and assert masculinities in *CT*, especially those of the Pardoner, the Host, and the Knight in the "alehouse scene" of Part 6. Female gender performance is not similarly destabilized by travel and location in Chaucer's poem. Legassie draws comparisons and contrasts from various pilgrimage accounts and from the Guild Hall memorandum concerning the John/Eleanor Rykener trial; also challenges notions of the "liminality" of travel.

249. Minnis, Alastair. "The Construction of Chaucer's Pardoner." In R. N. Swanson, ed. *Promissory Notes on the Treasury of Merits: Indulgences in Late Medieval Europe* (*SAC* 31 [2009], no. 135), pp. 169–95. There is a paucity of writing on indulgences in medieval vernacular literatures. Minnis explores depictions of pardoners and indulgences in *PardP*, Langland's *Piers Plowman*, and John Heywood's *The Foure PP* and *The Pardoner and the Frere*. Chaucer's Pardoner is best understood as "an aberrant *quaestor*," a lay usurper of the powers granted only to members of the ecclesiastical major orders.

250. ———. "Purchasing Pardon: Material and Spiritual Economies on the Canterbury Pilgrimage." In Lawrence Besserman, ed. *Sacred and Secular in Medieval and Early Modern Cultures: New Essays*. New York: Palgrave Macmillan, 2006, pp. 63–82. Minnis explores medieval attempts to "explain the difficult and dangerous relationship" between "material and spiritual economies" underlying pardons or indulgences, commenting on the explanations of Albert the Great, Aquinas, and Bonaventure and examining late medieval English defense (perhaps by canon lawyer Richard Godmersham) of the plenary status of the indulgence for a pilgrimage to Canterbury. In this light, Chaucer's Pardoner is an example of "rapacious greed" who ignores the principles of indulgence.

251. Pattwell, Niamh. " 'The venym of symony': The Debate on the Eucharist in the Late Fourteenth Century and *The Pardoner's Prologue and Tale*." In Kathy Cawsey and Jason Harris, eds. *Transmission and Transformation in the Middle Ages: Texts and Contexts* (*SAC* 31 [2009], no. 91), pp. 115–30. Patwell explores how the Pardoner "transgresses the boundaries between lay man and cleric and between lollardy and orthodoxy," focusing on how in *PardPT* Chaucer exposes extreme views about the Eucharist and how he targets what is being condemned without condemning any particular doctrinal system.

252. Tolmie, Sarah. "The Professional: Thomas Hoccleve." *SAC* 29

(2007): 341–73. Assesses Hoccleve's use of an "enfeebled persona" as a means to compete seriously with the "tasteful silences" of Chaucer and the "guilty fulminations" of Langland on the topic of vernacular poetic identity. Compares Hoccleve's *Male Regle* with *PardPT* and with the Seven Deadly Sins section of the B-text of *Piers Plowman*, treating them as variations of an exemplum against sin, situated in a food-and-drink setting. Whereas Langland struggles to represent poetic personhood directly, Chaucer uses the ironic device of an unreliable narrator. Hoccleve, "by dint of his chronically complaining persona," focuses attention on the poet as the "logical spokesperson for the disenchanted world."

253. Yvernault, Martine. "Le corps comme relique(s), reste(s), fragment(s) dans le *Conte du vendeur d'indulgences* de Chaucer." In Eduardo Ramos-Izquierdo, ed. *Seminaria 1—Les Espaces du Corps 1: Littérature.* Mexico and Paris: RILMA2/ADEHL (Association pour le Développement des Études Hispaniques en Limousin), 2007, pp. 9–26. Focuses on the rich meanings and implications of *fragment* in *PardPT*.

See also nos. 7, 119, 128, 144, 146, 151, 158, 162, 195.

CT—The Shipman and His Tale

254. Beidler, Peter G. "Chaucer's French Accent: Gardens and Sex-Talk in the *Shipman's Tale*." In Holly A. Crocker, ed. *Comic Provocations: Exposing the Corpus of Old French Fabliaux.* Studies in Arthurian and Courtly Cultures. New York: Palgrave Macmillan, 2006, pp. 149–61. When Chaucer used Boccaccio's *Decameron* 8.1 as his source for *ShT*, he was also influenced by French fabliaux, particularly a garden scene in the thirteenth-century *Aloul* and, more generally, the animal euphemisms typical of the genre in French tradition.

255. Sheridan, Christian. "Funny Money: Puns and Currency in the *Shipman's Tale*." In Sandra M. Hordis and Paul Hardwick, eds. *Medieval English Comedy* (*SAC* 31 [2009], no. 111), pp. 111–23. Sheridan assesses the "common logic" of puns and money in *ShT*. Both pose the threat of vacuity—meaninglessness or lack of value—while simultaneously offering pleasure.

See also nos. 95, 123.

CT—The Prioress and Her Tale

256. Farrell, Thomas J. "The Prioress's Fair Forehead." *ChauR* 42 (2007): 211–21. Looking beyond the *OED's* definition of "span"—a length of roughly nine inches—to a range of medieval senses of the word suggests that the width of the Prioress's forehead "offers no meaningful foothold for objecting to her."

257. Kelly, Henry Ansgar. "'The Prioress's Tale' in Context: Good and Bad Reports of Non-Christians in Fourteenth-Century England." *Studies in Medieval and Renaissance History*, 3rd ser., 3 (2007): 71–129. Kelly surveys depictions of non-Christians in Chaucer's works and in works familiar to Chaucer: *Speculum historiale* by Vincent of Beauvais, *Legenda aurea* by Jacob of Voragine, English legendaries, miracles of the Virgin, pictorial tradition, and works by John Bromyard, Bishop Brinton, and William Langland. Attitudes toward non-Christians, including Jews, vary in these works (including Chaucer's), depending on "mood and circumstance."

258. Orth, William. "The Problem of Performance in Chaucer's Prioress Sequence." *ChauR* 42 (2007): 196–210. Whereas the *GP* portrait of the Prioress raises questions about the operation of performances in general, we see in *PrPT* the efficacy of performative utterances in particular. Details of the boy's murder and postmortem singing demonstrate that the success of such an utterance rests on a speaker's understanding of its "perlocutionary object."

259. Rudat, Wolfgang E. H. "'Infernus et os vulvae': A Second Look at Proverbs and Chaucer's Prioress." *CEA Critic* 58.2 (1996): 35–47. Allusive echoes among the *GP* description of the Prioress, *WBP*, and the biblical Proverbs suggest that Chaucer subtly condemns the Prioress for sexual excess.

260. Williams Boyarin, Adrienne Suzanne. "Miracles of the Virgin in England: Origins, Development, Contexts." *DAI* A67.08 (2007): n.p. Discusses *PrT* and other versions of Marian miracles.

See also nos. 93, 119, 140, 146, 161, 213.

CT—The Tale of Sir Thopas

261. Bell, Kimberly K. "Models of (Im)Perfection: Parodic Refunctioning in Spike TV's *The Joe Schmo Show* and Geoffrey Chaucer's 'Tale

of Sir Thopas.'" In Eileen A. Joy, Myra J. Seaman, Kimberly K. Bell, and Mary K. Ramsey, eds. *Cultural Studies of the Modern Middle Ages* (*SAC* 31 [2009], no. 114), pp. 23–47. Bell argues that *The Joe Schmo Show* and *Th* "use metafictional parody to 'refunction' generic forms and critique stereotypes of masculinity."

262. Symons, Dana M. "Comic Pleasures: Chaucer and Popular Romance." In Sandra M. Hordis and Paul Hardwick, eds. *Medieval English Comedy* (*SAC* 31 [2009], no. 111), pp. 83–109. Symons compares and contrasts the comic inaction of *Th* with comic spectacle in *MilT* and in the popular romance *Sir Tristrem*. A "sophisticatedly 'bad' poem," *Th* depends for its success on expectations that differ from those of popular literature.

See also no. 146.

CT—The Tale of Melibee

263. Forhan, Kate L. "Poets and Politics: Just War in Geoffrey Chaucer and Christine de Pizan." In Henrik Syse and Gregory M. Reichberg, eds. *Ethics, Nationalism, and Just War: Medieval and Contemporary Perspectives*. Washington, D.C.: Catholic University Press, 2007, pp. 99–116. Forhan summarizes the "dynastic quarrel" of the Hundred Years' War and describes the pacifist recommendations as prudent in Chaucer's *Mel* and in several works by Christine de Pizan. Treats the two writers as "catalysts" in the late medieval "laicization and secularization of power." In *Mel*, prudential pacifism is a matter of self-interest.

See also nos. 43, 79, 95, 103, 138, 155, 168, 207.

CT—The Monk and His Tale

264. Farrell, Thomas J. "The Persistence of Donaldson's Memory." *ChauR* 41 (2007): 289–97. Despite their diverse emphases, critical responses to the Monk's portrait in *GP* evince the same "close reading instinct" that generated E. Talbot Donaldson's "Chaucer the Pilgrim" essay and that has persisted "in an almost universal unwillingness . . . to read the *Prologue* straight."

265. Fizzard, Allison D. "Shoes, Boots, Leggings, and Cloaks: The Augustinian Canons and Dress in Later Medieval England." *Journal of*

British Studies 46 (2007): 245–62. Fizzard considers Chaucer's *GP* description of the Monk among other satires and accounts of monastic dress, exploring in particular debates about standards of dress among Augustinian monks.

See also nos. 37, 161.

CT—The Nun's Priest and His Tale

266. Adamina, Maia. "The Priest and the Fox: Tricksters in Chaucer's *Nun's Priest's Tale*." *Trickster's Way* http://www.trinity.edu/org/tricksters/trixway 4.1 (2005): n.p. Adamina assesses the trickster qualities of the fox and of the Nun's Priest, including various kinds of linguistic slipperiness, doubleness, and flattery.

267. Brantley, Jessica. "Vision, Image, Text." In Paul Strohm, ed. *Middle English* (*SAC* 31 [2009], no. 133), pp. 315–34. Brantley describes "texts that record acts of looking" as a "distinct medieval literary genre and a distinctly medieval way of knowing," addressing dream visions (including *BD*, *PF*, *HF*, and *LGWP*), mystical visions, and the parody of a visionary experience in *NPT*.

268. Green, Eugene. "Civic Voices in English Fables: *The Owl and the Nightingale* and *The Nun's Priest's Tale*." *AUMLA* 108 (2007): 1–32. Compares *The Owl and the Nightingale* and *NPT* as the "best beast fables" in Middle English, examining how the diction of each poem helps to create "voice" and thereby engage an audience.

See also nos. 7, 71, 118, 142, 144, 146.

CT—The Second Nun and Her Tale

269. Treanor, Lucia. "The Cross as *te* in 'The Canticle of Creatures,' Dante's 'Virgin Mother,' and Chaucer's 'Invocation to Mary.'" In Santa Casciani, ed. *Dante and the Franciscans*. The Medieval Franciscans, no. 3. Boston and Leiden: Brill, 2006, pp. 229–88. Pope Innocent III explicitly recognized the Greek letter *tau* as representing the form of the cross and saw it as a sign of renewal in the church. Likewise the syllable *te* was interpreted as a sign of the cross. Treanor explores graphic figurations of the cross as the figure *te* in several works, including Chaucer's "Invoca-

tion to Mary" in *SNP*. Chaucer's poem follows the palindromic structures and patterns of its classical and medieval antecedents.

See also nos. 71, 93, 101, 119, 121, 137, 272, 298.

CT—The Canon's Yeoman and His Tale

270. Bishop, Louise M. *Words, Stones, and Herbs: The Healing Word in Medieval and Early Modern England*. Syracuse: Syracuse University Press, 2007. xiv, 276 pp. 4 b&w illus. Surveys medical metaphors and the rise of English vernacular writing to trace diminution of belief in the "intrinsic healing quality" of words. As the healing power "evaporates," we find the separation of material and immaterial things, healing and piety, physician and priest, body and soul. Bishop examines Lollard vernacular works, *Piers Plowman*, *CYT*, and other works for evidence of a growing separation of verbalization and material effect and traces the outgrowths of this separation in early modern literature. She argues that *CYT* asserts the dangers of translation and reading as well as alchemy.

271. Davis, Isabel. *Writing Masculinity in the Later Middle Ages*. Cambridge Studies in Medieval Literature, no. 62. New York: Cambridge University Press, 2007. xiii, 222 pp. Davis explores "intersections between medieval masculine subjectivity and the ethics of labour and living" in Langland's *Piers Plowman*, Usk's *The Testament of Love*, Gower's *Confessio Amantis*, the poetry of Hoccleve, and Chaucer's *CYPT*. Reads the Canon's Yeoman's performance as a "site of 'gender' trouble" similar to those of the Wife of Bath and of the Pardoner, more specifically a negotiation of "contemporary ideals about moderate, obedient, and industrious masculinity." Discusses various householders and the Cook. References to masculinity and labor in Chaucer's works occur throughout the volume.

272. O'Connell, Brendan. "'Ignotum per ignocius': Alchemy, Analogy, and Poetics in Fragment VIII of *The Canterbury Tales*." In Kathy Cawsey and Jason Harris, eds. *Transmission and Transformation in the Middle Ages: Texts and Contexts* (*SAC* 31 [2009], no. 91), pp. 131–56. Chaucer addresses the "late medieval attack on analogical thought through his discussion of the failure of alchemy." *SNT* presents analogical thinking through its clear, but bridgeable, contrasts of spirit and body, whereas *CYT* offers an uncertain relationship between the two.

Moreover, poetry—like alchemy—may suffer from uncertainty about the relationship between the universal and the particular.

273. Phillips, Susan E. "Gossip and (Un)official Writing." In Paul Strohm, ed. *Middle English* (*SAC* 31 [2009], no. 133), pp. 476–90. Gossip transgresses the servant-master relationship in *CYP*, and *CYT* indicates that gossip underpins the discourse of official culture as well. Gossip is also fundamental to the exemplarity of Robert Mannyng's *Handlyng Synne*.

See also nos. 90, 101, 118, 121, 237, 289.

CT—The Manciple and His Tale

See nos. 40, 123, 146.

CT—The Parson and His Tale

274. McCormack, Frances. *Chaucer and the Culture of Dissent: The Lollard Context and Subtext of the Parson's Tale*. Dublin: Four Courts Press, 2007. 252 pp. Investigates Lollard vocabulary, translation strategies, and rhetorical tropes, arguing that the Parson and *ParsT* cannot categorically be identified as Lollard. Nonetheless, unmistakable elements of Lollardy undercut the hermeneutic stability of what should be a stable penitential text.

275. Newhauser, Richard. *Sin: Essays on the Moral Tradition in the Western Middle Ages*. Variorum Collected Studies. Burlington, Vt.: Ashgate, 2007. xii, 290 pp. Reprints fifteen essays by Newhauser on sin, vice, and medieval moral theology, including "The *Parson's Tale* and Its Generic Affiliations" (*SAC* 24 [2002], no. 334).

See also nos. 16, 37, 43, 158, 162, 195.

CT—*Chaucer's Retraction*

276. Kelly, Stuart. "Geoffrey Chaucer." In Stuart Kelly. *The Book of Lost Books: An Incomplete History of All the Great Books You Will Never Read*. New York: Random House, 2005, pp. 105–9. Comments on im-

plications of the lists of works in Chaucer's *Ret* and their relationship to the fragmentary nature of *CT*.

See also nos. 22, 280, 290.

Anelida and Arcite

See no. 24.

A Treatise on the Astrolabe

277. Basquin, Edmond A. "The First Technical Writer in English: Geoffrey Chaucer." *Technical Communication* 28 (1981): 22–24. Summary description of *Astr* that describes Chaucer's "admirable textbook method" and comments on his "rules of good technical writing," including simple diction and syntax, awareness of audience, repetition for emphasis, and copious illustrations.

278. Eagleton, Catherine. "'Chaucer's own astrolabe': Text, Image, and Object." *Studies in History and Philosophy of Science* 38 (2007): 303–26. Evidence from diagrams in the manuscripts of *Astr* suggests that the diagrams may have influenced construction of later extant medieval astrolabes, perhaps encouraged by Chaucer's "posthumous fame." Includes black-and-white and color illustrations.

279. Laird, Edgar. "Chaucer and Friends: The Audience for the *Treatise on the Astrolabe*." *ChauR* 41 (2007): 439–44. Given its resonance with references to duties of friendship that preface many astrolabe treatises, Chaucer's reference to his young son Lewis as his "frend" may accede to the wishes of adult friends who also wished for "a companionable guide to astronomy."

See also nos. 13, 73, 154.

Boece

280. Johnson, Ian. "The Ascending Soul and the Virtue of Hope: The Spiritual Temper of Chaucer's *Boece* and *Retracciouns*." *ES* 88 (2007): 245–61. Johnson examines Chaucer's attitudes about and representations of the "workings of the soul in stirring itself towards God," com-

paring *Bo* to its Boethian original in light of late fourteenth-century pastoral instruction and tracing similar sentiments in *Ret*.

The Book of the Duchess

281. Richmond, E. B., trans. *The Book of the Duchess*, by Geoffrey Chaucer. London: Hesperus, 2007. xviii, 94 pp. Facing-page translation of *BD*, based on the *Riverside* edition and rendered in modern octosyllabic couplets. Includes brief notes, a biographical note about Chaucer, an introduction by the translator, and a foreword by Bernard O'Donoghue.

282. Templeton, Willis Lee, II. "Unmanned Countenances: Representations of Masculine Grief in Middle English Literature." *DAI* A67.07 (2007): n.p. Compares the "displays of masculine grief" in *BD*, the *Alliterative Morte Arthure*, and *Sir Orfeo* with "norms of chivalric masculinity," investigating them in light of theories of Judith Butler and Jacques Derrida.

283. Yvernault, Martine. "'I have lost more than thow wenest': Past, Present, and (Re)presentation in Chaucer's *Book of the Duchess*." *BAM* 72 (2007): 31–45. Examines the interweaving of tenses and time sequences in the boxed-in structure of the narrative in *BD*.

284. Zeeman, Nicolette. "Imaginative Theory." In Paul Strohm, ed. *Middle English* (*SAC* 31 [2009], no. 133), pp. 222–40. Zeeman treats the "*chanson d'aventure*" as an imaginative (rather than expository) articulation of literary theory, focusing on use of the device in *BD*, *LGWP*, the opening of *Piers Plowman*, and other works.

See also nos. 24, 34, 64, 67, 89, 95, 124, 267.

The Equatorie of the Planetis

[No entries]

The House of Fame

285. Flannery, Mary C. "Brunhilde on Trial: *Fama* and Lydgatean Poetics." *ChauR* 42 (2007): 139–60. Lydgate's poetic trial of Brunhilde indicates a conviction that poets have a central role in shaping and trans-

mitting *fama*. In sharp contrast, Chaucer depicts *fama* as a function of "aventure" in *HF*.

286. Fumo, Jamie C. "Chaucer as *Vates?* Reading Ovid Through Dante in the *House of Fame*, Book 3." In Janet Levarie Smarr, ed. *Writers Reading Writers: Intertextual Studies in Medieval and Early Modern Literature in Honor of Robert Hollander*. Newark: University of Delaware Press, 2007, pp. 89–108. Fumo compares and contrasts Chaucer's invocation of Apollo in *HF* to its source in Dante's *Paradiso*, arguing that Chaucer shares with Dante a "fundamental interest in defining the poet's role" as a "vessel of prophetic truth." Both poets are concerned with the potential disconnect between the "transcendent experience of inspiration" and the "reality of failure." Christian truth serves to bridge that disconnect for Dante, whereas Chaucer is "more interested in the problem than the solution" and thereby more faithful to classical tradition.

287. Kang, Jisoo. "The Story of Aeneas and Dido on the Tablet of Memory: The *House of Fame* and the Reader." *MES* 14 (2006): 33–56 (in Korean, with English abstract). Medieval texts interact with their sources as memory operates, according to classical tradition, in individual cognition. Chaucer's depiction in *HF* of Virgil's story of Dido and Aeneas exemplifies this interaction and lets readers determine what is true and false.

288. Silec, Tatjana. "Allégorie et grotesque dans *The House of Fame*." *BAM* 71 (2007): 21–33. Explores the architectural features of *HF*, particularly in relation to memory, allegory, and the function of the grotesque.

289. St. John, Michael. "Alchemy and the Metamorphosis of History in Chaucer's *House of Fame*." In Carla Dente, George Ferzoco, Miriam Gill, and Marina Spunta, eds. *Proteus: The Language of Metamorphosis*. Studies in European Cultural Transition, no. 26. Burlington, Vt.: Ashgate, 2005, pp. 83–92. Argues that an "individual's knowledge of history" is presented in *HF* in a way that is metaphorically linked to alchemical transformation—with "tydynges" either substantially transformed or flying into uncontrollable energy. *CYT* shows Chaucer's knowledge of alchemy.

290. Warren, Nancy Bradley. "Incarnational (Auto)biography." In Paul Strohm, ed. *Middle English* (*SAC* 31 [2009], no. 133), pp. 369–85. The "transubstantiation" of the word being made flesh underlies the autobiographical impulse in Julian of Norwich's *Showings*, Langland's

Piers Plowman, and Chaucer's *HF*. Warren also comments on Chaucer's *Ret* as autobiography.

See also nos. 20, 24, 45, 67, 89, 101, 123, 138, 267.

The Legend of Good Women

291. Coleman, Joyce. "'A bok for king Richardes sake': Royal Patronage, the *Confessio*, and the *Legend of Good Women*." In R. F. Yeager, ed. *On John Gower: Essays at the Millennium*. Studies in Medieval Culture, no. 46. Kalamazoo, Mich.: Medieval Institute Publications, 2007, pp. 104–23. Coleman considers the first recension of Gower's *Confessio Amantis* and the F version of *LGWP* for evidence of royal patronage, arguing that both were inspired by Anne of Bohemia and by the popularity of the "Flower and Leaf" conventions that Anne introduced to Richard's court.

292. Getty, Laura J. "'Other Smale Ymaad Before': Chaucer as Historiographer in the *Legend of Good Women*." *ChauR* 42 (2007): 48–75. Each of the legends makes use of "the metonymic possibilities of objects and bodies" to represent the difficulty of discerning truth from fable in written sources available to the historiographer.

293. McCormick, Betsy. "Back to the Future: Living the Liminal Life in the Manor House and the Medieval Dream." In Eileen A. Joy, Myra J. Seaman, Kimberly K. Bell, and Mary K. Ramsey, eds. *Cultural Studies of the Modern Middle Ages* (*SAC* 31 [2009], no. 114), pp. 91–117. McCormick compares *LGW* and Christine de Pisan's *Le livre de la cité des dames* with the reality TV show *Manor House*, exploring how each poses a "liminal space" from which to "contemplate societal stereotypes and strictures by revisiting the past."

294. McCormick, Elizabeth. "It's How You Play the Game: Chaucer and Christine Debate 'Woman.'" *DAI* A67.07 (2007): n.p. McCormick uses game theory and the debate genre to investigate the structure of *LGW* and of Pizan's *Le livre de la cité des dames*. The former is "a ludic puzzle"; the latter, "an architectural mnemonic."

295. Meyer, Cathryn Marie. "Producing the Middle English Corpus: Confession and Medieval Bodies." *DAI* A68.05 (2007): n.p. Meyer examines confessional discourse in John Gower's *Confessio Amantis*, Chaucer's *LGW, The Book of Margery Kempe*, and Robert Henryson's *Testament*

of Cresseid, assessing how this discourse "produc[es] truth" and conveys "textualized bodies."

296. Phillips, Helen. "Nature, Masculinity, and Suffering Women: The Remaking of the *Flower and the Leaf* and Chaucer's *Legend of Good Women* in the Nineteenth Century." In Marios Costambeys, Andrew Hamer, and Martin Heale, eds. *The Making of the Middle Ages: Liverpool Essays*. Liverpool: Liverpool University Press, 2007, pp. 71–92. Phillips gauges Romantic responses to *LGW* and the *Flower and the Leaf* (attributed to Chaucer in the Romantic age), indicating that Keats, Tennyson, William Morris, the Pre-Raphaelite artists, and others admired the poems for their depictions of nature and for their views of gender, particularly their depictions of feminine suffering.

297. Reis, Huriye. "The 'Trial' of the Narrator in Chaucer's Prologue to the *Legend of Good Women*." *Edebiyat Fakültesi Dergisi* (Hacettepe University) 20.1 (2003): 140–49. Reads *LGWP* as an indication of Chaucer's theory that writing is based largely on the reading of others. Chaucer's narrator is confronted with the implications of this theory.

298. Sanok, Catherine. *Her Life Historical: Exemplarity and Female Saints' Lives in Late Medieval England*. Philadelphia: University of Pennsylvania Press, 2007. xvii, 256 pp. Discusses the creation of female audiences, examining *LGW* and other works (including *WBT*) to explore how saints' lives shaped literary history, thus making women "visible participants" in vernacular literary culture. Alceste is a metonym for a broader audience and a "distinctively 'feminine' response." *SNT* offers new perspectives on the limits and meaning of hagiographic exemplarity through the public performance of an imitation of a virgin martyr.

299. Sayers, William. "Chaucer's Description of the Battle of Actium in the *Legend of Cleopatra* and the Medieval Tradition of Vegetius's *De Re Militari*." *ChauR* 42 (2007): 76–90. Chaucer's depiction of the legendary battle of Actium likely reflects both his understanding of contemporary naval warfare technology and his awareness of military treatises by Vegetius and Giles of Rome.

300. Tolhurst, Fiona. "Why We Should Teach—and Our Students Perform—*The Legend of Good Women*." In Gail Ashton and Louise Sylvester, eds. *Teaching Chaucer* (*SAC* 31 [2009], no. 82), pp. 46–64. Describes procedures for incorporating student performances of portions of *LGW* into classroom activities and using these performances to help students evaluate other Chaucerian texts.

See also nos. 40, 124, 137, 142, 158, 267, 284, 305.

The Parliament of Fowls

301. Johnston, Andrew James. "Literary Politics in Debate: Chaucer's *Parliament of Fowls* and Clanvowe's *Book of Cupid*." In Sabine Volk-Birke and Julia Lippert, eds. *Anglistentag 2006 Halle*. Proceedings of the Conference of the German Association of University Teachers of English, no. 28. Trier: Wissenschaftlicher Verlag Trier, 2007, pp. 147–57. Johnston discusses the treatment of political concerns in *PF* and Clanvowe's *Book of Cupid*. *PF* defuses the political conflicts it conjures up through a conscious policy of aesthetic deferral, whereas the *Book of Cupid* openly shows the violence inherent in aristocratic courtly love.

302. Kerr, John. "Consumption and Memory in Chaucer's *Parliament of Fowls*." In Bruce E. Brandt and Michael S. Nagy, eds. *Proceedings of the 14th Northern Plains Conference on Earlier British Literature, April 7–8, 2006* (*SAC* 31 [2009], no. 88), pp. 77–93. Kerr argues that the sixth canto of Dante's *Inferno* was the model for Chaucer's use of gluttony and alimentary metaphors in *PF*, particularly the latter's concern with literary transmission and the birds' debate.

303. Kinch, Ashby. "'To thenke what was in hir wille': A Female Reading Context for the Findern Anthology." *Neophil* 91 (2007): 729–44. Female involvement in construction of the Findern anthology (Cambridge University Library MS Ff 1.6) resulted in "subtle interventions" in thematic concerns of several works included in the anthology: for example, "female eloquence" (in Gower's story of Peronelle and in Richard Roos's translation of Alain Chartier's *La Belle Dame Sans Mercy*) and the "tension between female choice and social compulsion" (in *PF*).

304. Preston, Todd. "A Place Among the Leaves: The Manuscript Contexts of Chaucer's *Parliament of Fowls*." *Comitatus* 38 (2007): 69–86. Using the fourteen extant manuscripts of *PF* as points of reference, Preston questions reductive thematic approaches to compilations and argues that other factors—authorial attribution and class, for instance—are equally plausible as explanations for compilation.

See also nos. 24, 42, 67, 103, 124, 137, 140, 267.

Troilus and Criseyde

305. Archibald, Elizabeth. "Chaucer's Lovers in Metaphorical Heaven." In Carolyn Muessig and Ad Putter, eds. *Envisaging Heaven in*

the Middle Ages. Routledge Studies in Medieval Religion and Culture, no. 6. London and New York: Routledge, 2007, pp. 222–36. Archibald surveys Italian, French, and English literary instances of love compared to heaven, hell, paradise, or purgatory, commenting on Chaucer's uses in *CT* (*WBT*, *KnT*, and especially *MerT*) and *LGW* and exploring the more sustained use of this set of figures in *TC*.

306. Cannon, Christopher. "Form." In Paul Strohm, ed. *Middle English* (*SAC* 31 [2009], no. 133), pp. 177–90. Cannon summarizes medieval theories of literary form, including that of Geoffrey of Vinsauf, as adapted by Chaucer in *TC*. Applies the theories to various works in Middle English.

307. Chatterjee, M. "Rivalry, Rape, and Manhood: Gower and Chaucer." In M. Chatterjee. *Violence Against Women*. Jaipur: Aavishkar, 2006, pp. 103–17. Traces a connection between the aggression of rape and the construction of an aggressive competition between Chaucer and Gower, defining both as functions of a "structure of indifference" in Western thought. Explores Gower's tale of Philomela as a gloss on Criseyde's dream of the eagle in *TC*.

308. Edwards, Robert R. " 'The Metropol and the Mayster-Toun': Cosmopolitanism and Late Medieval Literature." In Vinay Dharwadker, ed. *Cosmopolitan Geographies: New Locations in Literature and Culture*. Essays from the English Institute. New York: Routledge, 2001, pp. 33–62. Crossing tendencies characterize the "cosmopolitanism" of the late Middle Ages, and the story of Troy is the "paradigmatic cosmopolitan narrative." Edwards comments on Lydgate's *Troy Book* and addresses the mysterious pagan judge of *Saint Erkenwald*. Troilus's laughter at the end of *TC* "interrogates" the cosmopolitanism of "medieval adaptations of classical literary conventions."

309. Federico, Sylvia. "Chaucer and the Masculinity of Historicism." *MFF* 43.1 (2007): 72–75. Discusses, on the one hand, psychoanalytic approaches to literature, femininity, and various aspects of Troilus and the narrator of *TC*; and, on the other hand, historicism, masculinity, and other features of Troilus and the narrator. Points out parallels between the approaches and advocates combining psychoanalytic and historicist approaches in medieval criticism.

310. ———. "The Place of Chivalry in the New Trojan Court: Gawain, Troilus, and Richard II." In Laura L. Howes, ed. *Place, Space, and Landscape in Medieval Narrative* (*SAC* 31 [2009], no. 112), pp. 171–79. Federico explores how "Ricardian court culture haunts the chivalric

spaces inhabited and visited by" Chaucer's Troilus and by Gawain in *Sir Gawain and the Green Knight*. Parallels between the "moral lapses" of Richard II and those of the two protagonists are cast into relief by the ideal of Troy.

311. Hopkins, Amanda. "'[W]ordy vnthur wede': Clothing, Nakedness, and the Erotic in Some Romances of Medieval Britain." In Amanda Hopkins and Cory James Rushton, eds. *The Erotic in the Literature of Medieval Britain* (*SAC* 31 [2009], no. 110), pp. 53–70. Hopkins explores depictions of sexual *frisson*, or arousal, in a variety of Middle English romances, focusing on the presentation of clothing, nudity, and partial nudity. She surveys examples in which female ugliness is represented almost as often as beauty, works in which partial beauty "can be more erotic than complete nakedness," and depictions of male and female erotic potential. In *TC*, Chaucer focuses on male pleasure. He explores female pleasure in *WBPT*.

312. Kaylor, Harold. "Chaucer's *Troilus and Criseyde* and Boethius's *Consolation of Philosophy*." In Marcin Krygier and Liliana Sikorska, eds. *To Make His Englissh Sweete upon His Tonge* (*SAC* 31 [2009], no. 117), pp. 11–19. Following a four-part epistemological scheme posed in Boethius's *Consolatio*, Chaucer develops Troilus's love in *TC* from senses through images and reason to intelligence. As a figure of emotion, subject to tragedy, Troilus serves as a contrast to Criseyde, who is impervious to tragedy because she is led by reason—a Boethian opposition.

313. Koster, Josephine A. "*Privitee, Habitus*, and Proximity: Conduct and Domestic Space in Chaucer's *Troilus and Criseyde*." *EMSt* 24 (2007): 79–91. Examination of social spaces and residential settings that Criseyde inhabits reveals that she is not isolated (as generally argued) until she enters the Greek camp. She conforms to the social expectations, the *habitus,* of her social sphere, even as her behavior seems "unforgivable."

314. Lee, Jenny. "'Of Your Herte Up Casteth the Visage': Turning Troilo/Troilus's Eyes to God." *Hortulus* 3.1 (2007): n. p. Although he derives it from Boccaccio, Chaucer alters the topos of the lover's gaze at the end of *TC*, transforming it into a Boethian, Christian vision of God. The article includes a coda on Criseyde's prudential "third eye."

315. Mieszkowski, Gretchen. "'The Least Innocent of All Innocent-Sounding Lines': The Legacy of Donaldson's *Troilus* Criticism." *ChauR* 41 (2007): 299–310. In his analyses of the *TC* narrator as a character in his own right—most notably in "The Ending of Chaucer's *Troilus*" and "Criseide and Her Narrator"—E. Talbot Donaldson "created the

most clear-cut paradigm shift in twentieth-century readings of the poem," one that continues to enable new insights into the poem.

316. Mitchell, J. Allan. "Boethius and Pandarus: A Source in Maximian's *Elegies*." *N&Q* 50.4 (2003): 377–80. Argues that Maximian's *Third Elegy* inspired the figure of Pandarus in *TC*. In Maximian, Boethius is a character who is "astonishingly iconoclastic" and "richly ironic," anticipating Pandarus in several ways.

317. Morey, James H. "Chaucer, the 'Corones Tweyne,' and the Eve of Saint Agnes." *Traditio* 62 (2007): 119–33. Pandarus's reference to two crowns (*TC* 2.1735), when speaking to Criseyde before she visits Troilus in Deiphebus's house, alludes to Saint Agnes, sets the date of this meeting as Saint Agnes's Eve (January 20), and thus establishes a chronology for the poem. Invoking Agnes may also link Chaucer's complex attitude toward Criseyde to that toward his mother, Agnes de Copton, and other women in his family.

318. Noh, Kyung Lee. "Acedia as a Motive in Troilus' Tragedy." *MES* 15 (2007): 271–87 (in Korean, with English abstract). Inactivity is Troilus's "tragic flaw," but it is also what makes his love noble and "ideal." His inactivity is contrasted by the "practical" and ignoble activity of both Pandarus and Diomedes.

319. Oka, Saburo. "Chaucer's *Troilus* in a New Comparative Context." In Hans Sauer and Renate Bauer, eds. *"Beowulf" and Beyond*. Studies in English Medieval Language and Literature, no. 18. Frankfurt am Main: Peter Lang, 2007, pp. 223–34. Oka compares various classical and medieval descriptions of Troilus and then offers *The Book of Troilus* or simply *Troilus* as a more appropriate title for Chaucer's *Troilus and Criseyde*. Also traces the personal development of Troilus from a "fierse and proude knyght" to a person "maturing" through "his love experience," thus suggesting a vertical structure in the narrative, supported by Troilus's ascent to heaven.

320. Pérez Fernández, Tamara, and Ana Sáez Hidalgo. "'A man textueel': Scribal Readings and Interpretations of *Troilus and Criseyde* Through the Glosses in Manuscript British Library Harley 2392." *SELIM* 14 (2007): 197–220. Analyzes the unique marginal annotations in the Harley 2392 version of *TC*, exploring the role played by the scribe of the manuscript. The marginalia seem to hint at something beyond the task of a copyist, since they entail interpretation of what Chaucer wrote.

321. Smyth, Karen Elaine. "Reassessing Chaucer's Cosmological

Discourse at the End of *Troilus and Criseyde* (c.1385)." *FCS* 32 (2007): 150–63. Troilus ultimately travels to the ninth—not the eighth—sphere at the end of *TC*, a place ripe with "symbolic valence," reinforcing Chaucer's narrative focus on constant change and the ambiguity that comes with it.

322. Utz, Richard. "Writing Alternative Worlds: Rituals of Authorship and Authority in Late Medieval Theological and Literary Discourse." In Sven Rune Havsteen, Nils Holger Petersen, Heinrich W. Schwab, and Eyolf Østrem, eds. *Creations: Medieval Rituals, the Arts, and the Concept of Creation*. Ritus et Artes, no. 2. Turnhout, Belgium: Brepols, 2007, pp. 121–38. The nominalist concept of absolute divine power may underpin Chaucer's experiments "with a variety of authorship roles." In *TC*, both Pandarus and the narrator complicate the author's pose as a mere compiler or translator. Robert Henryson's *Testament of Cresseid* and John Metham's *Amoryus and Cleopes* indicate and imitate Chaucer's "playful experiment with authorial omniscience."

See also nos. 22, 34, 37, 45, 64, 67, 74, 84, 89, 104, 124, 137, 138, 140, 142, 144, 146, 165.

Lyrics and Short Poems

See nos. 19, 24, 106, 124, 127.

An ABC

See no. 34.

Adam Scriveyn

323. Gillespie, Alexandra. "Books." In Paul Strohm, ed. *Middle English* (*SAC* 31 [2009], no. 133), pp. 86–103. Focusing on perspectives evident in Chaucer's *Adam* (and the career of Adam Pinkhurst) and *Mum and the Sothsegger*, Gillespie explores the importance of "the book" as a technology that spans the oral-print divide.

See also no. 30.

The Complaint of Mars

324. Askins, William R. "A Camp Wedding: The Cultural Context of Chaucer's *Brooch of Thebes*." In Laura L. Howes, ed. *Place, Space, and Landscape in Medieval Narrative* (*SAC* 31 [2009], no. 112), pp. 27–41. Askins treats *Mars* and *Ven* as two halves of a single poem, reading them together as the "first epithalamium" in English, a celebration of the marriage that took place in spring 1386 between Elizabeth of Lancaster (daughter of Gaunt) and John Holland. Askins argues that Philippa Chaucer died soon after the wedding, while accompanying the Lancastrian retinue to Spain; Chaucer and Oton de Grandson also attended the ceremony.

The Complaint of Venus

See no. 324.

The Former Age

See nos. 118, 121.

Lak of Stedfastnesse

See no. 79.

Proverbs

See no. 95.

To Rosemounde

See no. 146.

Truth

See no. 154.

Chaucerian Apocrypha

325. Cawsey, Kathy. "'I Playne Piers' and the Protestant Plowman Prints: The Transformation of a Medieval Figure." In Kathy Cawsey

and Jason Harris, eds. *Transmission and Transformation in the Middle Ages: Texts and Contexts* (*SAC* 31 [2009], no. 91), pp. 189–206. Cawsey surveys the legacy of the plowman figure in England from the late Middle Ages into the Renaissance, focusing on the composite work "I Playne Piers." *The Plowman's Tale* was used and reused in multiple ways, presented variously by editors and compilers.

326. Iersel, Geert van. "The Twenty-Five Ploughs of Sir John: *The Tale of Gamelyn* and the Implications of Acreage." In Thea Summerfield and Keith Busby, eds. *People and Texts: Relationships in Medieval Literature. Studies Presented to Erik Kooper* (*SAC* 31 [2009], no. 134), pp. 111–22. Examines concern with land ownership in the *Tale of Gamelyn* in light of contemporary land values and incomes. The audience of the poem may have considered Sir John's division of his property in the poem both legal and morally justified.

See also nos. 128, 192, 296.

Book Reviews

327. Adams, Jenny. *Power Play: The Literature and Politics of Chess in the Late Middle Ages* (*SAC* 30 [2008], no. 100). Rev. Hans Petschar, *TMR* 07.10.22, n.p.

328. Allen, Elizabeth. *False Fables and Exemplary Truth in Later Middle English Literature* (*SAC* 29 [2007], no. 86). Rev. Judith Ferster, *Speculum* 82 (2007): 950–52; Alison Ganze, *TMR* 07.09.06, n.p.

329. Altmann, Barbara K., and R. Barton Palmer, trans. and eds. *An Anthology of Medieval Love Debate Poetry* (*SAC* 30 [2008], no. 15). Rev. Daisy Delogu, *TMR* 07.05.09, n.p.; Norris J. Lacy, *Encomia* 28 (2006): 21–22.

330. Amodio, Mark C. *New Directions in Oral Theory: Essays on Ancient and Medieval Literatures* (*SAC* 29 [2007], no. 301). Rev. Slavica Rankovic, *TMR* 07.02.10, n.p.

331. ———. *Oral Poetics in Middle English Poetry* (*SAC* 18 [1996], no. 71). Rev. Norbert A. Wethington, *SCJ* 37 (2006): 1217–18.

332. Bardsley, Sandy. *Venomous Tongues: Speech and Gender in Late Medieval England* (*SAC* 30 [2008], no. 196). Rev. Michael Kuczynski, *TMR* 07.12.05, n.p.; Jennifer A. Smith, *Comitatus* 38 (2007): 181–83.

333. Barolini, Teodolinda, ed. *Medieval Constructions in Gender and*

Identity: Essays in Honor of Joan M. Ferrante (*SAC* 29 [2007], no. 171). Rev. Thomas O'Donnell, *Comitatus* 38 (2007): 260–62.

334. Bernau, Anke, Ruth Evans, and Sarah Salih, eds. *Medieval Virginities* (*SAC* 27 [2005], no. 197). Rev. Wendy R. Larson, *SCJ* 37 (2006): 930–31.

335. Blamires, Alcuin. *Chaucer, Ethics, and Gender* (*SAC* 30 [2008], no. 105). Rev. Carolyn P. Collette, *Speculum* 82 (2007): 965–67; Ann Dobyns, *TMR* 07.12.02, n.p.; Cate Gunn, *EIC* 57 (2007): 59–65; Norman Klassen, *MÆ* 76.1 (2007): 135–37; Angela Jane Weisl, *SAC* 29 (2007): 467–70.

336. Boitani, Piero, and Jill Mann, eds. *The Cambridge Companion to Chaucer.* 2nd ed. (*SAC* 27 [2005], no. 92). Rev. Robert Boenig, *M&H* 32 (2007): 137–38; Lilo Moessner, *Anglistik* 18 (2007): 205–9.

337. Bowers, John M. *Chaucer and Langland: The Antagonistic Tradition* (*SAC* 31 [2009], no. 37). Rev. C. David Benson, *The Weekly Standard*, August 20–27, 2007, pp. 35–37; Carolyn P. Collette, *Arthuriana* 17.4 (2007): 119.

338. Burger, Glenn. *Chaucer's Queer Nation* (*SAC* 27 [2005], no. 143). Rev. Robert Mills, *JEGP* 106 (2007): 536–39; Diane Watt, *MÆ* 76.1 (2007): 135–37.

339. Busby, Keith, and Christopher Kleinhenz, eds. *Courtly Arts and the Art of Courtliness: Selected Papers from the Eleventh Triennial Congress of the International Courtly Literature Society. University of Wisconsin–Madison, 29 July–4 August 2004* (*SAC* 31 [2009], no. 13). Rev. Carleton W. Carroll, *Encomia* 28 (2006): 32–35.

340. Butterfield, Ardis, ed. *Chaucer and the City* (*SAC* 30 [2008], no. 108). Rev. Robert Costomiris, *TMR* 07.07.05, n.p.; Sylvia Federico, *SAC* 29 (2007): 470–73; Kathy Lavezzo, *Speculum* 82 (2007): 686–88; David Raybin, *EMSt* 24 (2007): 21–29.

341. Cannon, Christopher. *The Grounds of English Literature* (*SAC* 29 [2007], no. 99). Rev. Linda Georgianna, *MLQ* 68 (2007): 437–40.

342. Chewning, Susannah Mary, ed. *Intersections of Sexuality and the Divine in Medieval Culture: The Word Made Flesh* (*SAC* 29 [2007], no. 222). Rev. Robin Norris, *N&Q* 54 (2007): 187–88.

343. Collette, Carolyn P. *Performing Polity: Women and Agency in the Anglo-French Tradition, 1385–1620* (*SAC* 31 [2009], no. 93). Rev. Glenn Burger, *SAC* 29 (2007): 473–75; Sally Parkin, *Parergon* 24.2 (2007): 180–82.

344. Cooney, Helen, ed. *Writings on Love in the English Middle Ages*

(*SAC* 30 [2008], no. 111). Rev. Kathleen M. Blumreich, *Encomia* 28 (2006): 35–36.

345. Correale, Robert M., and Mary Hamel, eds. *Sources and Analogues of the "Canterbury Tales."* Vol. 2 (*SAC* 29 [2007], no. 46). Rev. Peter Brown, *MÆ* 76.1 (2007): 132–33; Warren Ginsberg, *SAC* 29 (2007): 476–79; Linne R. Mooney, *JEBS* 19 (2007): 244–45.

346. Cox, Catherine S. *The Judaic Other in Dante, the "Gawain" Poet, and Chaucer* (*SAC* 29 [2007], no. 231). Rev. Anthony Bale, *MÆ* 76.1 (2007): 129–30; Lisa Lampert-Weissig, *MLR* 102 (2007): 194–95; Andrew Rabin, *MP* 104 (2007): 566–70; Sylvia Tomasch, *SAC* 29 (2007): 479–82.

347. Desmond, Marilynn. *Ovid's Art and the Wife of Bath: The Ethics of Erotic Violence* (*SAC* 30 [2008], no. 199). Rev. Michael Calabrese, *SAC* 29 (2007): 482–85; Edna Edith Sayers, *TMR* 07.10.15, n.p.

348. Ellis, Steve, ed. *Chaucer: An Oxford Guide* (*SAC* 29 [2007], no. 108). Rev. Matthew Boyd Goldie, *SAC* 29 (2007): 485–89.

349. Evans, Ruth, Helen Fulton, and David Matthews, eds. *Medieval Cultural Studies: Essays in Honour of Stephen Knight* (*SAC* 30 [2008], no. 115). Rev. Margaret Connolly, *JEBS* 10 (2007): 248–50.

350. Farber, Lianna. *An Anatomy of Trade in Medieval Writing: Value, Consent, and Community* (*SAC* 30 [2008], no. 117). Rev. Andrew Fogleman, *Comitatus* 38 (2007): 220–22; Kathy Lavezzo, *SAC* 29 (2007): 489–92.

351. Forni, Kathleen, ed. *The Chaucerian Apocrypha: A Counterfeit Canon* (*SAC* 25 [2003], no. 292). Rev. John M. Bowers, *SAC* 29 (2007): 495–99.

352. Gillespie, Alexandra. *Print Culture and the Medieval Author: Chaucer, Lydgate, and Their Books, 1473–1557* (*SAC* 30 [2008], no. 23). Rev. Isabel Davis, *TLS* May 18, 2007, p. 12; Martha W. Driver, *RenQ* 60 (2007): 1021–23.

353. Grady, Frank. *Representing Righteous Heathens in Late Medieval England* (*SAC* 30 [2008], no. 280). Rev. Christine Chism, *Speculum* 82 (2007): 992–94.

354. Grigsby, Byron Lee. *Pestilence in Medieval and Early Modern Britain* (*SAC* 28 [2006], no. 151). Rev. William H. Spates, *SCJ* 38 (2007): 260–61.

355. Hanna, Ralph. *London Literature, 1300–1380* (*SAC* 29 [2007], no. 116). Rev. Simon Horobin, *JEBS* 9 (2006): 183–85; Ben Parsons,

Sixteenth Century Literature 38 (2007): 191–92; Míceál F. Vaughan, *Speculum* 82 (2007): 446–47.

356. Hirsh, John C. *Chaucer and the "Canterbury Tales": A Short Introduction* (*SAC* 27 [2005], no. 151). Rev. Marion Turner, *MÆ* 76.2 (2007): 323–24.

357. Hodges, Laura. *Chaucer and Clothing: Clerical and Academic Costume in the General Prologue to "The Canterbury Tales"* (*SAC* 29 [2007], no. 170). Rev. Gerald Morgan, *MLR* 102 (2007): 834–35.

358. Johnston, Andrew James. *Clerks and Courtiers: Chaucer, Late Middle English Literature, and the State Formation Process* (*SAC* 25 [2003], no. 111). Rev. Joerg O. Fichte, *Zeitschrift für Anglistik und Amerikanistik* 51 (2003): 317–19.

359. Jones, Terry, Robert Yeager, Terry Dolan, Alan Fletcher, and Juliette Dor. *Who Murdered Chaucer? A Medieval Mystery* (*SAC* 27 [2005], no. 14). Rev. Isamu Saito, *SIMELL* 22 (2007): 147–55; Barry Windeatt, *MÆ* 76.1 (2007): 130–32.

360. Kerby-Fulton, Kathryn. *Books Under Suspicion: Censorship and Tolerance of Revelatory Writing in Late Medieval England* (*SAC* 30 [2008], no. 125). Rev. Ruth Mazo Karras, John H. Arnold, Dyan Elliott, Anne Hudson, and Scott Lucas, *Journal of British Studies* 46 (2007): 764–73; Henrietta Leyser, *TMR* 07.06.22, n.p.; Martha Dana Rust, *JEBS* 10 (2007): 260–63.

361. Kuskin, William, ed. *Caxton's Trace: Studies in the History of English Printing* (*SAC* 30 [2008], no. 25). Rev. Julia Boffey, *SAC* 29 (2007): 505–8; Lauren Shohet, *Journal of British Studies* 46 (2007): 149–51.

362. Lampert, Lisa. *Gender and Jewish Difference from Paul to Shakespeare* (*SAC* 28 [2006], no. 157). Rev. Heide Estes, *TMR* 07.01.12, n.p.; Marianne Krummel, *Envoi* 11.2 (2007): 169–76.

363. Lavezzo, Kathy. *Angels on the Edge of the World: Geography, Literature, and English Community, 1000–1534* (*SAC* 30 [2008], no. 192). Rev. Robert Barrett, *MFF* 43.1 (2007): 126–28; Daniel Birkholz, *SAC* 29 (2007): 508–11; Karolyn Kinane, *Journal of British Studies* 46 (2007): 909–10; Richard Raiswell, *TMR* 07.04.16, n.p.

364. Lerer, Seth, ed. *The Yale Companion to Chaucer* (*SAC* 30 [2008], no. 131). Rev. Mark Miller, *SAC* 29 (2007): 511–14.

365. Little, Katherine C. *Confession and Resistance: Defining the Self in Late Medieval England* (*SAC* 30 [2008], no. 245). Rev. Shannon Gayk, *TMR* 07.05.05, n.p.; Robert J. Meyer-Lee, *SAC* 29 (2007): 514–17;

Emily Runde, *Comitatus* 38 (2007): 251–53; Wendy Scase, *Speculum* 82 (2007): 725–27.

366. Lochrie, Karma. *Heterosyncracies: Female Sexuality When Normal Wasn't* (*SAC* 31 [2009], no. 119). Rev. Aranye Fradenburg, *SAC* 29 (2007): 517–20.

367. Machan, Tim William, ed., with the assistance of A. J. Minnis. *Sources of the Boece* (*SAC* 29 [2007], no. 271). Rev. Jennifer Arch, *SAC* 29 (2007): 520–23; Andrew Breeze, *MLR* 102 (2007): 478–79.

368. Masciandaro, Nicola. *The Voice of the Hammer: The Meaning of Work in Middle English Literature* (*SAC* 31 [2009], no. 121). Rev. Isabel Davis, *TMR* 07.06.09, n.p.; Kevin Teo, *Comitatus* 38 (2007): 257–59.

369. McCarthy, Conor, ed. *Love, Sex, and Marriage in the Middle Ages: A Sourcebook* (*SAC* 28 [2006], no. 79). Rev. April Harper, *TMR* 07.04.12, n.p.

370. McSheffrey, Shannon. *Marriage, Sex, and Civic Culture in Late Medieval London* (*SAC* 30 [2008], no. 133). Rev. Philip Daileader, *TMR* 07.06.16, n.p.; Vanessa Harding, *Journal of British Studies* 46 (2007): 650–52.

371. McTurk, Rory. *Chaucer and the Norse and Celtic Worlds* (*SAC* 29 [2007], no. 48). Rev. Siân Grønlie, *MÆ* 76.2 (2007): 325–26.

372. Meyer-Lee, Robert J. *Poets and Power from Chaucer to Wyatt* (*SAC* 31 [2009], no. 57). Rev. George Shuffelton, *TMR* 07.09.03, n.p.

373. Meyerson, Mark D., Daniel Thiery, and Oren Falk, eds. *"A Great Effusion of Blood"? Interpreting Medieval Violence* (*SAC* 28 [2006], no. 138). Rev. Eileen A. Joy, *SCJ* 37 (2006): 927–29.

374. Mieszkowski, Gretchen. *Medieval Go-Betweens and Chaucer's Pandarus* (*SAC* 30 [2008], no. 285). Rev. Tison Pugh, *SAC* 29 (2007): 526–28; Shannon K. Valenzuela, *TMR* 07.06.21, n.p.

375. Miller, Mark. *Philosophical Chaucer: Love, Sex, and Agency in the "Canterbury Tales"* (*SAC* 29 [2007], no. 164). Rev. Karma Lochrie, *Speculum* 82 (2007): 216–17; Gerald Morgan, *MLR* 102 (2007): 477–78.

376. Mitchell, J. Allan. *Ethics and Exemplary Narrative in Chaucer and Gower* (*SAC* 28 [2006], no. 101). Rev. Elizabeth Allen, *SAC* 29 (2007): 528–31.

377. Morgan, Gerald. *The Tragic Argument of "Troilus and Criseyde"* (*SAC* 30 [2008], no. 286). Rev. A. V. C. Schmidt, *EIC* 57 (2007): 350–58.

378. Moulton, Ian Frederick, ed. *Reading and Literacy in the Middle*

Ages and Renaissance (*SAC* 29 [2007], no. 129). Rev. Helmut Puff, *SCJ* 37 (2006): 774–75.

379. Phillips, Susan E. *Transforming Talk: The Problem with Gossip in Late Medieval England* (*SAC* 31 [2009], no. 123). Rev. Wendy A. Matlock, *TMR* 07.11.24, n.p.

380. Prendergast, Thomas A. *Chaucer's Dead Body: From Corpse to Corpus* (*SAC* 28 [2006], no. 46). Rev. Andrew Lynch, *MÆ* 76.1 (2007): 134–35.

381. Pugh, Tison. *Queering Medieval Genres* (*SAC* 29 [2007], no. 132). Rev. Robert Mills, *JEGP* 106 (2007): 536–39; Michael O'Rourke, *SCJ* 38 (2007): 244–46.

382. Richmond, Velma Bourgeois. *Chaucer as Children's Literature: Retellings from the Victorian and Edwardian Eras* (*SAC* 29 [2007], no. 137). Rev. Candace Barrington, *Children's Literature* 35 (2007): 198–201.

383. Robertson, Kellie. *The Laborer's Two Bodies: Labor and the "Work" of the Text in Medieval Britain, 1350–1500* (*SAC* 30 [2008], no. 267). Rev. Kathleen Ashley, *SAC* 29 (2007): 539–42; Andrew Galloway, *Speculum* 82 (2007): 758–59; Verena Postel, *TMR* 07.04.15, n.p. [Note: The book is also titled *The Laborer's Two Bodies: Literary and Legal Productions in Britain, 1350–1500*.]

384. Rudd, Gillian. *The Complete Critical Guide to Chaucer* (*SAC* 25 [2003], no. 133). Rev. Linda R. Bates, *Marginalia* 6 (2007): n.p.

385. Saunders, Corinne. *Chaucer* (*SAC* 25 [2003], no. 136). Rev. Colin Wilcockson, *Anglistik* 15 (2004): 167–68.

386. ———, ed. *A Companion to Romance: From Classical to Contemporary* (*SAC* 29 [2007], no. 140). Rev. Robert Rouse, *TMR* 07.01.03, n.p.

387. ———, ed. *A Concise Companion to Chaucer* (*SAC* 30 [2008], no. 143). Rev. Robert W. Barrett Jr., *TMR* 07.04.13, n.p.

388. Scanlon, Larry, and James Simpson, eds. *John Lydgate: Poetry, Culture, and Lancastrian England* (*SAC* 30 [2008], no. 71). Rev. Lisa H. Cooper, *SAC* 29 (2007): 542–45.

389. Schaefer, Ursula, ed. *The Beginnings of Standardization: Language and Culture in Fourteenth-Century England* (*SAC* 30 [2008], no. 144). Rev. Richard Marsden, *TMR* 07.09.15, n.p.

390. Schibanoff, Susan. *Chaucer's Queer Poetics: Rereading the Dream Trio* (*SAC* 30 [2008], no. 145). Rev. Stephen Guy-Bray, *Canadian Literature* 194 (2007): 177–79; Karma Lochrie, *Encomia* 28 (2006): 71–72;

Robert Mills, *MÆ* 76.2 (2007): 321–22; Kevin Teo, *Comitatus* 38 (2007): 271–74; Diane Watt, *TMR* 07.05.10, n.p.

391. Schildgen, Brenda Deen. *Pagans, Tartars, Moslems, and Jews in Chaucer's "Canterbury Tales"* (*SAC* 25 [2003], no. 165). Rev. A. S. G. Edwards, *CRCL* 31 (2004): 91–96.

392. Shepard, Alan, and Stephen D. Powell, eds. *Fantasies of Troy: Classical Tales and the Social Imaginary in Medieval and Early Modern Europe* (*SAC* 29 [2007], no. 286). Rev. Audrey DeLong, *SCJ* 38 (2007): 512–13.

393. Simpson, James. *The Oxford English Literary History, Volume 2, 1350–1547: Reform and Cultural Revolution* (*SAC* 26 [2004], no. 152). Rev. Helen Cooper, *SAC* 29 (2007): 545–48.

394. Spearing, A. C. *Textual Subjectivity: The Encoding of Subjectivity in Medieval Narratives and Lyrics* (*SAC* 29 [2007], no. 143). Rev. Andrew Breeze, *MLR* 102 (2007): 835–36; Alfred David, *SAC* 29 (2007): 548–51; Bill Friesen, *N&Q* 54 (2007): 29–93.

395. Stein, Robert M., and Sandra Pierson Prior, eds. *Reading Medieval Culture: Essays in Honor of Robert W. Hanning* (*SAC* 29 [2007], no. 146). Rev. Lawrence M. Clopper, *Encomia* 28 (2006): 74–76.

396. Strohm, Paul. *Politique: Languages of Statecraft Between Chaucer and Shakespeare* (*SAC* 29 [2007], no. 257). Rev. Robert J. Meyer-Lee, *MP* 104 (2007): 570–74; Wendy Scase, *SAC* 29 (2007): 551–54.

397. Symons, Dana M., ed. *Chaucerian Dream Visions and Complaints* (*SAC* 28 [2006], no. 218). Rev. John M. Bowers, *SAC* 29 (2007): 495–99.

398. Thomas, Paul, ed., with Bárbara Bordalejo and Orietta Da Rold and contributions by Daniel W. Mosser and Peter Robinson. *"The Nun's Priest's Tale" on CD-ROM* (*SAC* 30 [2008], no. 30). Rev. Susan Yager, *MedievalF* 6 (2007): n.p.

399. Troyan, Scott D., ed. *Medieval Rhetoric: A Casebook* (*SAC* 28 [2006], no. 89). Rev. John O. Ward, *Parergon* 24.1 (2007): 227–33.

400. Turner, Marion. *Chaucerian Conflict: Languages of Antagonism in Late Fourteenth-Century London* (*SAC* 31 [2009], no. 138). Rev. K. P. Clarke, *RES* 58 (2007): 555–57.

401. Van Dyke, Carolynn. *Chaucer's Agents: Cause and Representation in Chaucerian Narrative* (*SAC* 29 [2007], no. 151). Rev. A. S. G. Edwards, *RES* 58 (2007): 399–400; Tara Williams, *SAC* 29 (2007): 554–57.

402. Walker, Greg. *Writing Under Tyranny: English Literature and the*

Henrician Reform (*SAC* 29 [2007], no. 33). Rev. Christopher Highley, *Journal of British Studies* 46 (2007): 155–57; Christine E. Hutchins, *SCJ* 38 (2007): 1175–76; Jason Powell, *N&Q* 54 (2007): 95–97; Lucy Wooding, *EHR* 122 (2007): 1396–99.

403. Walker, Simon; ed. Michael J. Braddick; introd. G. L. Harriss. *Political Culture in Later Medieval England*. New York and Manchester: Manchester University Press, 2006. Rev. Gwilym Dodd, *TMR* 07.05.07, n.p.

404. Wallace, David. *Chaucerian Polity: Absolute Lineages and Associational Forms in England and Italy* (*SAC* 21 [1999], no. 155). Rev. David Raybin, *EMSt* 24 (2007): 21–29.

405. ———. *Premodern Places: Calais to Surinam, Chaucer to Aphra Behn* (*SAC* 28 [2006], no. 92). Rev. Stephanie Trigg, *SAC* 29 (2007): 557–59.

406. Williams, Deanne. *The French Fetish from Chaucer to Shakespeare* (*SAC* 28 [2006], no. 94). Rev. Helen Cooper, *MLR* 102 (2007): 203–4; Larissa Tracey, *SCJ* 37 (2006): 1121–22; Jean-Sébastien Windle, *M&H* 32 (2007): 149–51.

Author Index—Bibliography

The New Chaucer Society
Sixteenth International Congress
July 17–22, 2008
Swansea University

THURSDAY, JULY 17

13:00–19:00: Registration

14:00–15:30: Graduate Workshops 1 and 2
Chair: Alexandra Gillespie, University of Toronto
- Daniel Wakelin, Christ's College, Cambridge
  "Introduction to MS Description"
- Orietta Da Rold, University of Leicester
  "MS Materials"

15:00–18:00: Trustees' meeting

15:45–16:30: Graduate Workshop 3
Chair: Alexandra Gillespie, University of Toronto
- Linne Mooney, University of York
  "Scribal Hands"

16:30–17:00: Afternoon Tea

17:00–18:30: Graduate Workshops 4 and 5
Chair: Alexandra Gillespie, University of Toronto
- Alison Wiggins, University of Glasgow
  "Scribal Dialect"
- Toshiyuki Takamiya, Keio University, Japan
  "The Use of Digital Technologies for Studying Manuscripts"

19:00–20:00: Dinner

FRIDAY, JULY 18

8:30–9:00: Registration

Concurrent Sessions (1–7)
9:00–10:30

Session 1: Romances and Their Readers: The Manuscript Context
Session Organizer: Andrew Taylor, University of Ottawa

Session chair: Alexandra Gillespie, University of Toronto
- " 'The meaning is in the use': The Irelands and Their Romances," Michael Johnston, University of North Texas
- "Reading Closely to Disclose and Disperse, or, Greatness Scattered," Myra Seaman, College of Charleston
- "The Variant Text and the Variant Reader," Michael Foster, University of Nottingham

Session 2: Medieval Pathologies
Session Organizer and Chair: Tom Prendergast, College of Wooster
- "Chaucer's Canon's Yeoman: A Study in Pathology," Frances Beer, York University, Toronto
- "Chaucerian Immunity and Inherited Pathologies," Sealy Gilles, Long Island University, Brooklyn
- "Court Ritual and the Pathologies of the Past," Stephanie Trigg, University of Melbourne

Session 3: Chaucer And The Crusades (1)
Session Organizer and Chair: John Bowers, University of Nevada–Las Vegas
- "Tale of Two Diplomats: Chaucer and Ibn Khaldun at the Court of Pedro the Cruel of Castile in the 1360s," Victoria L. Weiss, Oglethorpe University
- "Chaucer, Chivalric Nostalgia, and the Despenser Crusade," Patricia DeMarco, Ohio Wesleyan University
- "Traversing Somatic Limits: The Function of Violence in *The Siege of Jerusalem,*" Jamie Friedman, Cornell University
- " 'Of Mescreantz' in John Gower's *In Praise of Peace,*" David Watt University of Manitoba

Session 4: The Natural World: Animal and Plant Life in Late Medieval England
Session Organizer and Chair: Lisa Kiser, Ohio State University
- "Chaucer's Daisy," Gillian Rudd, University of Liverpool
- "Animals and the Animal Body in the Middle English *Dialogue of Solomon and Marcolf,*" Nancy Mason Bradbury, Smith College
- "Nature's Hierarchy in *The Parlement of Foules,*" Susan Crane, Columbia University
- "The 'Knight's Tale's Trees," Brenda Deen Schildgen, University of California, Davis

Session 5: Gower's Geography
Session Organizer and Chair: Lynn Arner, Brock University
- "Mapping the Trojan World in Gower's Poetry," Tamara F. O'Callaghan, Northern Kentucky University
- "London as a Widowed City in John Gower's *Vox Clamantis*," Yoshiko Kobayashi, University of Tokyo
- "Gower and the Matter of Spain," Jamie Taylor, Bryn Mawr College

Session 6: Reading Lucan's *Bellum Civile* in the Middle Ages
Session Organizer: Cathy Sanok, University of Michigan
Chair: Chris Baswell, Columbia University
- "'That Sonne That Roos as Red as Rose': Republican Poetics in the *Legend of Good Women*," Timothy D. Arner, Pennsylvania State University
- "Using Lucan to Undo Gower: The *Bellum Civile* and Chaucer's *Man of Law's Tale*," Steele Nowlin, Hampden-Sydney College, Virginia
- "The Late Medieval Reception of Lucan's Geography," Alfred Hiatt, University of Leeds

Session 7: Chaucer: Middle English Sources and Models
Session Organizer and Chair: John Hines, Cardiff University
- "Chaucer's Minstrel Disguise: 'The Tale of Sir Thopas' and the Romances of the Auchinleck Manuscript," Sarah Dawson, University of Notre Dame
- "A Comparison of Rhyme and Metre in Chaucer's and Gower's English," Gyöngyi Werthmüller, Eötvös Loránd University, Budapest
- "Custance and the Church Boys: Chaucer on Conversion, True or False," R. F. Yeager, University of West Florida

10:30–11:00: Morning Tea

Plenary Session
11:00–11:30: Session 8: Welcome and General Meeting

11:30–12:30: Session 9: Biennial Lecture
Chair: John Ganim, University of California, Riverside
Ardis Butterfield, Reader in English, University College London
"Chaucerian Vernaculars"

Conference Photograph
12.30–1.00:

13.00–14:00: Lunch

Concurrent Sessions (10–16)
14:00–15:30

Session 10: Writing Outside the Book
Session Organizer and Chair: Alfred Hiatt, University of Leeds
- "Clerks, Books, and Ephemera in the 1380s," Marion Turner, Jesus College, Oxford
- "Interrupting the Past: Yorkist Insertions in John Hardyng's *Chronicle*," Alyssa Meyers, Columbia University
- "Reading the Premodern Title: Materiality, Concept, Theory," Victoria Louise Gibbons, Cardiff University
- "Scribal Uncertainty: An Examination of the *Charters of Christ*," Sarah Noonan, Washington University, Saint Louis

Session 11: Devotional Aesthetics
Session Organizer and Chair: Tara Williams, Oregon State University
- "The Devotional Literary: Lydgate's *Life of Our Lady*," Robert Meyer-Lee, Goshen College
- "Chaucer Iscariot," Rosemary O'Neill, University of Pennsylvania
- "Vision and Revision in Julian of Norwich's *Showings*," Kathleen Smith, Columbia University

Session 12: Haunted Chaucer
Session Organizers and Chairs: George Edmondson, Dartmouth College, and Robert Stein, Purchase College
- "The Ghostly Hand of Fate: Spectral Futurity in Chaucer's 'Knight's Tale,'" Brooke Hunter, University of Texas at Austin
- "'I am but ded': Elegiac Chaucer / Elegizing Chaucer," Jamie C. Fumo, McGill University
- "Chaucer's Spectral Objects" [read by George Edmondson in Patricia Ingham's absence] Patricia Clare Ingham, Indiana University

Session 13: Appropriating Chaucer: Medievalisms
Session Organizer: NCS Program Committee

Chair: David Matthews, University of Manchester
- "Blake in/and/or/as Medievalism," Betsy Bowden, Rutgers Camden
- "Th' Apostel and the Wyf: Militant Poet-Thinkers and the Perils/ Potential of Medievalism," Mark Sherman, Rhode Island School of Design
- "The Naked Pitchman and the Desperate Housewife of Bath: Relocating Gender in Films of the Middle Ages," Arthur Lindley, University of Birmingham
- "Polishing Chaucer: Dryden, Pope, and the Danish translator Thomas Christopher Bruun," Ebbe Klitgård, Roskilde University

Session 14: Expanding the Syllabus
Session Organizer and Chair: Thomas Hahn, University of Rochester
- "Chaucer and Literary Pilgrimage," Eve Salisbury, Western Michigan University
- "Chaucer Lost in Translation—and Found," Alan Baragona, Virginia Military Institute
- "Myth, Modernism, and Medievalism," Rob Gossedge, Cardiff University

Session 15: In Praise of the Middle English Variant
Session Organizer: Andrew Taylor, University of Ottawa
Chair: Robert Hanning, Columbia University
- "The (Relative) Importance of Variants in *The Canterbury Tales*," Barbara Bordalejo, Institute for Textual Scholarship and Electronic Editing, University of Birmingham
- "Essence and Variance," Susan Yager, Iowa State University
- "Move over, *mouvance*," Derek Pearsall, Harvard; University of York

Session 16: *Interpretation of Dreams*, Dream Vision Poetics
Session Organizer and Chair: Erin Felicia Labbie, Bowling Green State University
- "Getting Started: Authorial Self-Fashioning in Chaucer's *The Book of the Duchess*," Douglas Brooks, Texas A&M University
- "Chaucer's Dream of Good Women: Oneiric Poetics and/as Oneiric Ontology," Gila Aloni, Lynn University
- "Iconophilia: Uncanny Responses to Tradition in Chaucer's and Freud's Dream-Visions and Visions of Dreams," Andrew Galloway, Cornell University

- "The Affective/Somatic Postures of Medieval Dream Poetry," Steven Kruger, CUNY
- "Condensation and Displacement in Chaucer's Dream Poems," Stefania D'Agata D'Ottavi, Università per Stranieri–Siena

15:30–16:00: Afternoon Tea

Plenary Session
16:00–17:30: Session 17: "Chaucer Beside Himself"
Chair: Helen Fulton, Swansea University
- Catherine Belsey, Research Professor in English at Swansea University
  "The Poverty of Historicism"
- Colin McCabe, Professor of English and Humanities, Birkbeck London
  "Dating English as a National Language"

18:00–19:00: Drinks Reception
Sponsored by the Society for the Study of Mediaeval Languages and Literature and *New Medieval Literatures*
Vice-Chancellor's Welcome: Professor Richard B. Davies

19:00–20:00: Dinner

20:00–21:00: Poetry Reading
Dafydd Johnston, Jessica Harkins, Nigel Jenkins, Cynthia Kraman, Carter Revard

SATURDAY, JULY 19

8:30–9:00: Registration

Concurrent Sessions (18–23)

9:00–10:30

Session 18: Form
Session Organizer and Chair: Christopher Cannon, Girton College, Cambridge
- "Authorial Recitation as an Informing Principle: Chaucer's *pronuntiatio* as *enarratio*," William Quinn, University of Arkansas

- "Antiformalism and Complaint," Mark Rasmussen, Centre College
- "Formalism and Narrative," Amanda Holton, St. Hilda's College, Oxford
- "Chaucer's Formal Fantasy: *The Legend of Good Women*," Ingrid Nelson, Harvard University
- "Nicholas of Lyra's Model of Close Reading," Judith Tschann, University of Redlands

Session 19: The Value of Medievalism

Session Organizer: Jenna Mead, University of Tasmania
Chair: David Lawton, Washington University, Saint Louis

- "The Middle Ages: Practical Applications," David Matthews, University of Manchester
- "What Do the Middle Ages Want?" Erin Labbie, Bowling Green State University
- "The Show That Never Ends: Chaucer's Invention of the Literary," Larry Scanlon, Rutgers University
- "A 'sharp tender shock': Medievalism and the Literary," Ruth Evans, University of Stirling

Session 20: Chaucer and the Crusades (2)

Session Organizer: John Bowers, University of Nevada–Las Vegas
Chair: Helen Cooper, Magdalene College, Cambridge

- "A Crusade Not Told: Knight, Squire, and the Family Drama of the Exotic," Andrew James Johnston, Freie Universität Berlin
- "Crusader 'Femenye': or, Why Does the Knight Tell 'The Knight's Tale'?" Jennifer Summit, Stanford University
- "Mixed Blood: Understanding Baptism by Blood in 'The Man of Law's Tale,'" Cord Whitaker, Duke University

Session 21: Age and Growing Old in Chaucer

Session Organizer and Chair: Sue Niebrzydowski, University of Wales, Bangor

- "The Old Man in 'The Pardoner's Tale,'" Matthias Galler, University of Münich
- "Masks of Old Age: The Pardoner, Morgan le Fay, and Sublime Decrepitude," Randy P. Schiff, SUNY Buffalo
- "'Old Men Losing Out': Chaucer's Representation of Old Age in *The Canterbury Tales*," Huriye Reis, Hacettepe University, Ankara

- "The Body and Time in 'The Wife of Bath's Prologue and Tale' and *The Book of the Duchess*," Michelle Wright, University of Glamorgan

Session 22: Non-English Books: Reading and Writing
Session Organizer and Chair: Helen Fulton, Swansea University
- "Glosses, Rubrics, and the Circulation of Authorship," Carolynn Van Dyke, Lafayette College
- "'. . . the grease of a black cat': Some Evidence for Late Medieval Reading Practices in Manuscripts from the National Library of Wales," Elisabeth Salter, University of Wales Aberystwyth
- "London Guilds and English/French Bilingualisms: A Literary Methodology?" Jonathan Hsy, George Washington University

Session 23: Gendered Spaces and Sexualized Spaces
Session Organizer: Michelle M. Sauer, University of North Dakota
Chair: Catherine Clarke, Swansea University
- "Time and Space in Chaucerian Fabliaux: The Miller's and Reeve's Tales," Jean E. Jost, Bradley University
- "Genealogical Space in 'The Merchant's Tale' and Elsewhere: Whose Trees?" Alcuin Blamires, Goldsmith's College London
- "The Chaucerian Garden as Place and Space," Robert Stretter, Providence College, Rhode Island
- "Heteronormatizing the Chaucerian Bedroom: Sexual Empowerment and Gendering Space," Michelle M. Sauer, University of North Dakota

10:30–11:00: Morning Tea

Concurrent Sessions (24–30)
11:00–12:30

Session 24: Technology
Session Organizer: D. Vance Smith, Princeton University
Chair: Ruth Evans, University of Stirling
- "'For myn entente is nat but for to wynne': The Technology of Money and the Pardoner's Intentions," Robert Epstein, Fairfield University
- "Facts and Fictions: Technologies of Rhetoric and Accounting in the

Production of Fact in 'The Manciple's Tale,' " Cara Hersh, University of Portland, Oregon
- "After Gower: Printing and the Biopolitics of Affect and Attachment," Nic D'Alessio, University of Texas at Austin

Session 25: Crossing Boundaries: The Dramatic Traditions of Medieval Britain
Session Organizer and Chair: John T. Sebastian, Loyola University, New Orleans
- "Subtle Subversion and the Benefits of Barriers: The Development of Cornish Drama in England," Gloria J. Betcher, Iowa State University
- "Playing the Crucifixion in Medieval Wales," David N. Klausner, Centre for Medieval Studies, University of Toronto
- " 'May we see þe same/Euen in oure pase puruayed': Tourism and Spectacle Along England's Western Border," Matthew Sergi, University of California–Berkeley
- "The Early Modern Origins of Medieval Drama," Theresa Coletti, University of Maryland, and Gail McMurray Gibson, Davidson College

Session 26: Borders, Landscapes, Regions, Nations (1)
Session Organizer: Patricia Ingham, Indiana University
Chair: Daniel Birkholz, University of Texas at Austin
- "London in Late Medieval Welsh Poetry," Morgan Davies, Colgate University
- " 'Fer in the North, I cannot tell where': Collapsing Spaces and the Extimate North in Chaucer's *Reeve's Tale*," Joseph Taylor, University of Texas at Austin
- "Negotiating Linguistic Domains: Register-Switching in Chaucer and Usk," Rebecca Fields, Exeter College, Oxford
- "Turning England Inside Out in Gower's *Vox Clamantis*, Book I," David W. Marshall, California State University, San Bernardino
- "Locating the Humor of 'Sir Thopas': Flanders, London, and Beyond," Arthur W. Bahr, MIT

Session 27: Gender in the Fifteenth Century
Session Organizer and Chair: Nicole Sidhu, East Carolina University
- " 'How-to' Masculinity in Hoccleve's *Series*," Holly Crocker, University of South Carolina

509

- "All in the Family: Comedy, Domesticity, and Royal Authority in John Lydgate's *Mumming at Hertford*," Nicole Nolan Sidhu, East Carolina University
- "The Marriages of Margery Kempe," Rebecca Perederin, University of Virginia
- "Managing Medea: Representations of a Troublesome Woman in Fifteenth-Century Literature," Katherine Heavey, University of Durham

Session 28: Religion and Affect (1)
Session Organizer: Fiona Somerset, Duke University
Chair: Sarah McNamer, Georgetown University
- "Timor Mortis," Amy Appleford, Harvard University
- "Terror, Pleasure, and Judaism: Affective Passions in Late Medieval English Culture," Anthony Bale, Birkbeck College London
- "Governing Affect: Textual, Legal, and Social Controls on Devotion in Late Medieval England," Christopher Bradley, Balliol College, Oxford
- "'Drede' and the Popular Intellect in *The Prick of Conscience*," Moira Fitzgibbons, Marist College

Session 29: Rethinking the Contexts and Sources of Chaucer's Poetry
Session Organizer: NCS Program Committee
Chair: Jerome Mandel, Tel Aviv University
- "Deliberative Chaucer: Aristotle in *The Canterbury Tales*," Amy W. Goodwin, Randolph-Macon College
- "Apuleius, Boccaccio, and Chaucer: Reconsidering the Gaps," Jessica Harkins, College of Saint Benedict–Saint John's University
- "Not as Glorious as It Seems: Authorial Self-Glossing by Italian and English Writers," Karen Gross, Lewis & Clark College
- "Visions of the Afterlife and 'The Summoner's Tale,'" J. Justin Brent, Presbyterian College
- "Chaucer and the Imprisoned Fish: Socio-Economic History and Critical Arguments," Helen Phillips, Cardiff University

Session 30: Scenes of Writing
Session Organizer and Chair: Nicholas Perkins, St. Hugh's College, Oxford
- "'Withyn a temple ymad of glas': Writing, Glazing, and Patronage in *The House of Fame*," David Coley, University of Maryland

- "A *'dooly sesoun'* for a *'cairfull dyte'*: Ambivalence, Anxiety, and Desire in Henryson's Scenes of Writing," Deborah Strickland, Indiana University
- "Embedding Literature," Margaret Bridges, University of Bern
- "Writing and Memory in John Metham's *Amoryus and Cleopes,*" Chloë Morgan, Centre for Medieval Studies, University of York

12:30–14:00: Lunch

Plenary Session
14:00–15:30: Session 31: "Before Chaucer"
Chair: David Lawton, Washington University, Saint Louis
- "Pearls of Literature," Valerie Allen, Professor of English, John Jay College of Criminal Justice, CUNY
- "Not Before Time: Anglo-Saxon Studies Before, After, and Beyond Chaucer," Clare Lees, Professor of Medieval Literature, King's College London
- "Before, During, and After Chaucer: The French of England," Jocelyn Wogan-Browne, Professor of English, Centre for Medieval Studies, University of York, UK
- "Before the Pardoner, Before the Cook: Eccentric Body Cultures Prior to Chaucer," Chris Baswell, Olin Chair of English at Barnard College and Professor of English at Columbia University

15:30–16:00: Afternoon Tea

Concurrent Sessions (32–38)
16:00–17:30

Session 32: (Roundtable): Teaching Chaucer (1)
Session Organizer: Thomas Hahn, University of Rochester
Chair: Helen Phillips, Cardiff University
- Peter Beidler, Lehigh University
- Ken Bleeth, Connecticut College
- Warren Ginsberg, University of Oregon
- Tom Hanks, Baylor University
- Teresa Harings, BASIS Tucson Upper School, Tucson
- Cynthia Kraman, College of New Rochelle
- Atilla Starcevic, Eötvös Loránd University, Budapest

Session 33: The Politics of Memory
Session Organizer and Chair: Ruth Evans, University of Stirling

- "Remembrance of Things Future: Memory and Contrition in 'The Parson's Tale,'" Krista Twu, University of Minnesota–Duluth
- "Fragments Shored Against Our Ruin: The *Habitus* of Memory in *The Legend of Good Women*," Betsy McCormick, Mt. San Antonio College
- "'They held hem paied of the fructes þat þey ete': Moral Choices and Memory in *Former Age*," John Plummer, Vanderbilt University
- "The Wife of Bath and the Politics of Memory," Ruth Summar McIntyre, Georgia State University
- "Forgotten Realms," Jeffrey Jerome Cohen, George Washington University
- "Bodies That Will Not Rest: Chaucer on Death," Roger Nicholson, University of Auckland

Session 34: New Work in Textual Scholarship
Session Organizer: NCS Program Committee
Chair: Satoko Tokunaga, Keio University

- "Does It Matter What Text of Chaucer We Read?" Peter Robinson, Institute for Textual Scholarship and Electronic Editing, University of Birmingham
- "Hg BD: An Experimental Restoration of Chaucer's Damaged Masterpiece," Murray McGillivray, University of Calgary
- "'Olde Books' and 'Drasty Rymyng': The Structuring of Early Vernacular *Compilatio*-Texts," Helen Marshall, Centre for Medieval Studies, Toronto
- "A Project for a Comprehensive Collation of the Two Manuscripts (Hengwrt and Ellesmere) and the Two Editions (Blake [1980] and Benson [1987]) of *The Canterbury Tales*," Yoshiyuki Nakao, Akiyuki Jimura, and Masatsugu Matsuo, Hiroshima University

Session 35: *Troilus and Criseyde*
Session Organizer: NCS Program Committee
Chair: Sarah Stanbury, College of the Holy Cross

- "Pandarus's 'Brother': Calkas as Rhetorician of Troy's End," Rebecca Beal, University of Scranton
- "'I am myn owene womman, wel at ese': Criseyde and the Wife of Bath," Setsuko Haruta, Shirayuri College, Tokyo

- "Rereading Criseyde: Cassandra as Prophetess and Patron," Amy N. Vines, University of North Carolina–Greensboro
- "In Thrall to History: A Reading of *Troilus and Criseyde*," Teresa P. Reed, Jacksonville State University, Alabama

Session 36: Wales and England
Session Organizer and Chair: Helen Fulton, Swansea University
- "Comparative Political Poetics: Iolo Goch and Geoffrey Chaucer," Jon Kenneth Williams, Columbia University
- "Making Chaucer Welsh: Early Modern Readings of Chaucer in Wales," Simon Meecham-Jones, University of Cambridge and Swansea University
- "Early Printed Copies of Chaucer in Welsh Collections," Geraint Evans, Swansea University

Session 37: New Feminist Approaches to Chaucer and His Contemporaries
Session Organizer and Chair: Liz Herbert McAvoy, Swansea University
- "Chaucer and the Irish Witch: Re-Reading the Wife of Bath," Susannah Chewning, Union County College
- "A Gelding or a Mare? Chaucer's Pardoner and Constructions of Gender in Middle English Literature," Jed Chandler, Swansea University
- "'. . . as it had been a thonder-dent': Speaking of the Unspeakable in *The Canterbury Tales*," Victoria Bludd, King's College, University of London

Session 38: In Praise of the Middle English Variant: Textual Integrity
Session Organizer: Andrew Taylor, University of Ottawa
Chair: Alexandra Gillespie, University of Toronto
- "Close Reading the Zero Text," Erick Kelemen, University of Kentucky
- "Scribal Correction and the Close Reading of Variants," Daniel Wakelin, Christ's College, Cambridge
- "Some Assembly Required: Following the *Instructions* for (Re)Constructing the Work of Peter Idley," Matthew Giancarlo, University of Kentucky

18:00–onward: Outing to Gower and Oxwich Bay Hotel (dinner included)

SUNDAY, JULY 20

8:30–9:00: Registration

Concurrent Sessions (39–45)
9:00–10:30

Session 39: Queer Times and Places
Session Organizer and Chair: Robert Mills, King's College London
- "Out of Sync: Feeling Time in the Body?" Carolyn Dinshaw, New York University
- "Queer Typology and St. Erkenwald," Kathy Lavezzo, University of Iowa
- "The Queer Itinerary of the Medieval Flâneuse: A Reading of Margery Kempe and the Wife of Bath," Ingrid Abreu-Scherer, Emmanuel College, Cambridge

Session 40: Chaucer's Manuscripts
Session Organizer and Chair: Estelle Stubbs, University of Sheffield
- "Middle English Scribes in the London Letter Books," Linne Mooney, Centre for Medieval Studies, University of York, and Estelle Stubbs, University of Sheffield
- "The Scribe of Bodley 619 and the Early Readership of Chaucer's *Treatise on the Astrolabe,*" Simon Horobin, Magdalen College, Oxford
- "The Beryn Scribe and Princeton MS 100 (the Helmingham MS) of *The Canterbury Tales,*" Dan Mosser, Virginia Tech
- "Teaching Textual *auctoritee* in the Christ Church *Canterbury Tales,*" Alexander Vaughan Ames, Georgia Institute of Technology

Session 41: Chaucerian "Sciences": Medicine, Optics and Music
Session Organizer: Nicolette Zeeman, University of Cambridge
Chair: Elizabeth Edwards, Dalhousie, Canada
- "An Introduction to Colour, Seeing, and Seeing Colour in Chaucer," Michael J. Huxtable, University of Durham
- "Chaucer's Medical Poetic," Katie Walter, University of Bochum

- "Chaucer's Bird Singers," Elizabeth Leach, Royal Holloway, University of London

Session 42: Religion and Affect (2)
Session Organizer: Fiona Somerset, Duke University
Chair: Anthony Bale, Birkbeck College London
- "Inordinate Affections and the Devotional Image in Fifteenth-Century Religious Writing," Shannon Gayk, Indiana University
- "You Comes Into the Picture: Passionate Speech and Liturgical Space in *Troilus and Criseyde*," Jim Knowles, Duke University
- "Beholding: Middle English Meets Affective Neuroscience," Sarah McNamer, Georgetown University
- "Affect, Group Identity, and Medieval Women's Spiritual Autobiography: Psychoanalytic Theory as Social Theory," John Pitcher, University College of the Fraser Valley, BC

Session 43: Adapting Chaucer for Differing Readerships
Session Organizer: Thomas Hahn, University of Rochester
Chair: Sylvia Tomasch, Hunter College/CUNY Honors College
- "The First Chaucer Elementary School Textbook: Mary Eliza Haweis," Mary Flowers Braswell, University of Alabama, Birmingham
- "Canterbury in the Cornfields," David Raybin, Eastern Illinois University
- "Close Reading, Middle English, and the Indifferent Student," Candace Barrington, Central Connecticut State University

Session 44: The Body and Embodiment
Session Organizer: NCS Program Committee
Chair: Liz Herbert McAvoy, Swansea University
- "Separating the Aesthetic in Chaucer's 'The Prioress's Tale,'" Sarah Breckenridge, Pennsylvania State University
- "Fifteenth-Century Manuscript Redactions of 'The Prioress's Tale' and the Horror of Antisemitism," Miriamne Ara Krummel, University of Dayton
- "Queer Time and the Body in 'The Prioress's Tale,'" Bettina Bildhauer, University of St. Andrews

Session 45: Late Medieval Readers and Reading
Session Organizer: NCS Program Committee

Chair: Lynn Staley, Colgate University
- "Chaucer and the *jeux-partis*," Neil Cartlidge, University of Durham
- "Amateur Readers and Devotional Performance," Katherine Zieman, University of Notre Dame
- "Reading and Seeing in Late Medieval England," Kathryn McKinley, Florida International University
- "The Newberry Library *Regiment of Princes* and Bibliographic Multi-vocality," Elon Lang, Washington University, Saint Louis
- "'Romynge to and fro': *The Knight's Tale* and Reading Narratives," Nicholas Perkins, St. Hugh's College, Oxford

10:30–11:00: Morning Tea

Plenary Session
11:00–12:30: Session 46: "Book History"
Chair: Alexandra Gillespie, University of Toronto
- "Reading in Space," Peter McDonald, Fellow of St. Hugh's College and Lecturer in English, University of Oxford
- "Making Like a Manuscript: Facsimiles, Auras, Impulses," Siân Echard, Professor of English, University of British Columbia

12:30–14:00: Lunch

13:15–onward: Free Afternoon and Optional Outings

West Wales—Kidwelly Castle; Laugharne, home of Dylan Thomas, OR Carreg Cennen, fortress of medieval Welsh marcher lords.

Caerphilly—Caerphilly Castle, medieval village and archaeological site at Cosmeston.

MONDAY, JULY 21

8:30–9:00: Registration

Concurrent Sessions (47–53)
9:00–10:30

Session 47: Aesthetics (1)

Session Organizer and Chair: Maura Nolan, University of California, Berkeley

- "Sensing the Sentence: Boethius, Boece, and the Aesthetics of Prose," Eleanor Johnson, University of California, Berkeley
- "Aesthetics and Things," James Knapp, University of Pittsburgh
- "Aesthetics and Genre," Peggy Knapp, Carnegie Mellon University

Session 48: The Religious Imagination, Gender and *Gentilesse* in Gower

Session Organizer: NCS Program Committee
Chair: Malte Urban, Queen's University, Belfast

- "Marian Meditations in the *Mirour de l'Omme*," Georgiana Donavin, Westminster College
- "Pagans Past and Pagans Present in Gower's *Confessio Amantis*," Lynn Shutters, Idaho State University
- "Profit and Repose: Gower's 'Alconomie' of Poetry," Matthew Irvin, Duke University

Session 49: Manuscripts Before Chaucer

Session Organizer and Chair: Elaine Treharne, Florida State University

- "Dismantling the Paradigms of Manuscript Production, 1200–1400," Orietta Da Rold, University of Leicester
- "Early Manuscripts of the *South English Legendary* and the Emergence of a Vernacular Literary Community," William Robins, University of Toronto
- "A General Prologue for the Ludlow Scribe's Chaucerian Book, MS Harley 2253 and Its 'Pilgrim' Audience," Carter Revard, Washington University, Saint Louis

Session 50: Textual Diasporas

Session Organizer and Chair: Jessica Brantley, Yale University

- "Monks, Mercers, and the Spiritual Life: HM 744 and the Long Arm of the Twelfth-Century Monastic Reform," Mary Agnes Edsall, Bowdoin College
- "Catherine of Siena: From the Charterhouse to Caxton," Jennifer N. Brown, University of Hartford
- "Walter Hilton's *Scale of Perfection*: Different Texts, Different Audiences," Michael G. Sargent, Queen's College, CUNY

Session 51: Nature and Magic
Session Organizer and Chair: Corinne Saunders, Durham University
- "Demonism and Intellect in the Summoner's Tale," Glending Olson, Cleveland State University
- "Chaucer's Use of *Incubus* in the Wife of Bath's Tale," Richard F. Green, Ohio State University
- "'A foul confusion': Alchemy and the Decay of Language in Dante and Chaucer," Brendan O'Connell, Trinity College, Dublin
- "'Wise wordes': The Vocabulary of Natural Philosophy and 'magyk naturel' in the Works of Chaucer," Shane Collins, Durham University

Session 52: Technique and Technology in the Classroom
Session Organizer: Thomas Hahn, University of Rochester
Chair: Theresa Coletti, University of Maryland
- "Filming Chaucer in the Classroom and Other Multimedia Approaches," Martha Driver, Pace University
- "'Quiting' Your Classmates: Digitizing Chaucerian Debate," Alex Mueller, SUNY Plattsburgh
- "Game Theory and the Teaching of *The Canterbury Tales*," Kurt Haas, Mesa State College

Session 53: Form and Close Reading: A Debate
Session Organizer and Chair: Christopher Cannon, Girton College, Cambridge
- "What's Wrong with Formalism?" James Simpson, Harvard University
- "The Inevitability of Form/The Inescapability of Form," Jill Mann, University of Notre Dame
Respondents: Christopher Cannon and Ethan Knapp

10:30–11:00: Morning Tea

Concurrent Sessions (54–59)
11:00–12:30

Session 54: Borders, Landscapes, Regions, Nations (2)
Session Organizer: Patricia Ingham, Indiana University
Chair: John Ganim, University of California, Riverside
- "Ye goon to . . . Hereford?: British Library MS Harley 2253, Regional

Devotion, and England's *Other* Saint Thomas," Daniel Birkholz, University of Texas at Austin

- "Mongols in the Marches: A Postcolonial / Archipelagic Reading of *Mum and the Sothsegger*," Robert W. Barrett Jr., University of Illinois at Urbana–Champaign
- "Communities Without Buildings in Medieval Romance," Elliot Kendall, University of Exeter

Session 55: Assimilation And Dissimulation
Session Organizer and Chair: Christine Chism, Rutgers University
- "Relics and Their Textual Re-Performances," Siobhain Bly Calkin, Carleton University
- "Relics and Texts in 'The Second Nun's Tale,'" Thomas O'Donnell, University of California, Los Angeles
- "Aquinas, Averroës, Augustine, and Archisynagogus," Sylvia Tomasch, Hunter College/CUNY Honors College

Session 56: Gower and Repose
Session Organizer: Elizabeth Allen, University of California, Irvine
Chair: Lynn Arner, Brock University
- "Ovid and Repose," Karla Taylor, University of Michigan
- "*Studiosus plurima scripsi:* Gower's Effortful Otium," Jeremy Dimmick, St. Catherine's College, Oxford
- "Sanctuary and Status in the *Miroir de L'Omme*," Elizabeth Allen, University of California, Irvine

Session 57: (Roundtable): Teaching Chaucer (2)
Session Organizer: Thomas Hahn, University of Rochester
Chair: Helen Cooper, Magdalene College, Cambridge
- Kara Crawford, The Bishop's School, La Jolla, California
- Tom Farrell, Stetson University
- Susanna Fein, Kent State University
- Sandy Feinstein, Pennsylvania State University, Berks
- Roger Ladd, University of North Carolina, Pembroke
- Jim Rhodes, Southern Connecticut State University
- David Wallace, University of Pennsylvania

Session 58: New Work on "The Prioress's Tale"
Session Organizers and Chairs: Kathy Lavezzo, University of Iowa, and Geraldine Heng, University of Texas at Austin

- "Reading the 'Prioress's Tale' and the 'Physician's Tale' Together," Daniel Kline, University of Alaska, Anchorage
- "Forensicphiles: 'The Prioress's Tale' and Medieval Murder Investigations," Shayne Aaron Legassie, Columbia University
- "English Historical Narratives of Mock-Crucifixion as Sources of 'The 'Prioress's Tale,'" Roger Dahood, University of Arizona

Response: Debra Higgs Strickland, Glasgow Centre for Medieval and Renaissance Studies

Session 59: Lydgate and the Poetry of War
Session Organizer and Chair: Cathy Sanok, University of Michigan
- "War Propaganda and Lancastrianism in the *Troy Book* and *Siege of Thebes*," William Sweet, Oxford University
- "Lydgate's Problematic Commission: *The Legend of St. Edmund* in a Time of War," Jennifer Sisk, Yale University
- "Manhood and Melancholy in Lydgate's War," Andrew Lynch, University of Western Australia

12:30–14:00: Lunch

Concurrent Sessions (60–66)
14:00–15:30

Session 60: Gender Versus Sexuality
Session Organizer and Chair: Karma Lochrie, Indiana University
- "Back to the Future, or, Temporal Drag," Robert Mills, King's College London
- "Temporal Virgins," Cathy Sanok, University of Michigan
- "Becoming Undone," Glenn Burger, CUNY
- "Queer Talking: Sex, Gender, and Collaboration," Diane Watt, Aberystwyth University and Clare Lees, King's College London
- "Gender, Sexuality, and the Medieval Family Portrait," Isabel Davis, University of London

Session 61: Periodization and the Archive
Session Organizer: Kathleen Davis, University of Rhode Island
Chair: Sarah Stanbury, College of the Holy Cross
- "Other Times, Other Archives: Strange Knowledge in Chaucer's *Treatise on the Astrolabe*," Christine Chism, Rutgers University

- "Reformation, Secularization, and the Survival of Medieval Vernacular Books," Sara S. Poor, Princeton University
- "Novelty, Fact, and the Recycled Archive: Visual Culture around 1500," Thomas Hahn, University of Rochester

Respondent: Jennifer Summit, Stanford University

Session 62: Aesthetics (2)

Session Organizer and Chair: Maura Nolan, University of California, Berkeley

- " 'What a poet I will flay myself into': Chaucer's Aesthetics of Negation," Carroll Balot, University of Toronto
- "Chaucer's Magical Aesthetics," Tara Williams, Oregon State University
- "Field of Power, Literary Field, Poetic Dispositions: The Relative Autonomy of Chaucerian Aesthetics," R. James Goldstein, Auburn University

Session 63: Hermeneutics and Difference

Session Organizer: Lisa Lampert-Weissig, University of California, San Diego
Chair: Simon Meecham-Jones, University of Cambridge and Swansea University

- "Feminized Hermeneutics in *The Legend of Good Women*," Leona Fisher, University of California, Riverside
- "The Language of the Law and the Rise of a Vernacular Hermeneutic of Englishness," Sebastian Sobecki, McGill University
- "The Queer Rose of Guillaume de Deguileville and Jean Molinet," Stephanie A.V.G. Kamath, University of Massachusetts–Boston

Session 64: Late Medieval Reading

Session Organizer and Chair: James Simpson, Harvard University

- "Revolutionary Reading: Reginald Pecock's Books," Kirsty Campbell, University of Toronto
- " 'The Redynge of Histories': Caxton's *Polychronicon*," Kathleen Tonry, University of Connecticut
- "Late Medieval Plays for Reading: *The Book of Brome*," Jessica Brantley, Yale University

Session 65: Chaucer's Pardoner

Session Organizer: NCS Program Committee
Chair: Lynn Staley, Colgate University

- "How (Not) to Preach: Thomas Waleys and Chaucer's Pardoner," Martin Camargo, University of Illinois
- "Chaucer, the Pardoner, and the Eucharist: The Influence of Vernacular Religious Writing of the Late Middle Ages on 'The Pardoner's Prologue' and 'Tale,'" Niamh Pattwell, University College, Dublin
- "The Pardoner's Relics and the Aesthetics of Denial," Robyn Malo, Purdue University
- "When a Kiss Is Not Just a Kiss: The Pardoner's Kiss and the Technics of Peace," José R. Nebres, University of Connecticut

Session 66: Allegory, Variants, Miscellanies, Neighbors, Portraits, and Last Things
Session Organizer: NCS Program Committee
Chair: Helen Fulton, Swansea University
- "The Aporetic Allegory: Chess and the Limits of Meaning in the *Esches Amoureux*, *Reson and Sensuallyte*, and *The Book of the Duchess*," Gregory Heyworth, University of Mississippi at Oxford
- "A Gothic Aesthetics of the Variant," Laura Kendrick, Université de Versailles
- "Mercantile Miscellanies and Fungible Couplets," Christina M. Fitzgerald, University of Toledo
- "Neighbors, Natural and Otherwise, in the Middle English Version of 'The Fox and the Wolf,'" George Edmondson, Dartmouth College
- "Fifteenth- and Sixteenth-Century Portraits of Chaucer as Social Mapping," Roberta Magnani, Cardiff University
- "'Nat for to knowe oure wyl': Writing, 'Execucion,' and Eschatology in 'The Clerk's Tale,'" Brandon Tilley, Harvard University

15:30–16:00: Afternoon Tea

Plenary Session
16:00–17:00: Session 67: Presidential Lecture
Chair: Richard Firth Green
John Ganim, University of California, Riverside
Panel Discussion:
- Bettina Bildhauer
- George Edmondson
- Marion Turner
- Cord Whitaker

17:00–17:30: Conference Close
David Lawton, Executive Director NCS
18:15–19:45:
Civic Reception at Brangwyn Hall
Special performance by the Morriston Orpheus Choir

INDEX